George!

A Guide to All Things Washington

A miniature of George Washington painted by Charles Willson Peale (Courtesy of Mount Vernon)

George!

A Guide to All Things Washington

Frank E. Grizzard, Jr.

MARINER
PUBLISHING

BUENA VISTA · CHARLOTTESVILLE, VIRGINIA

Library of Congress Control Number: 2005926791

ISBN 0-9768238-0-2 (pbk.)

09   08   07   06   05   10   9   8   7   6   5   4   3   2   1 (softcover)

Mariner Publishing
Mariner Companies, Inc.
Buena Vista • Charlottesville, Virginia
http://www.marinermedia.com

First published in the U.S. and United Kingdom as *George Washington: A Biographical Companion,* 2002.
First Mariner Edition, published with revisions and corrections, 2005.

Cataloging-in-Publication data for this book is available from the Library of Congress.

This book is printed on acid-free paper.

Manufactured in the United States of America

For My Mother and Father
Earlene Pearson and Frank E. Grizzard, Sr.

CONTENTS

George! A Guide to All Things Washington

Selected Writings, 361

ACKNOWLEDGMENTS

I would like to thank the editors at the Papers of George Washington at the University of Virginia, both present and former, without whom this volume would not have been possible: W. W. Abbot, Philander D. Chase, Robert F. Haggard, David R. Hoth, Beverly S. Kirsch, Edward G. Lengel, Mark A. Mastromarino, Beverly H. Runge, Dorothy Twohig, Christine S. Patrick, and Jack D. Warren, Jr.

Additionally, I am indebted to several people who read all or parts of the manuscript and offered comments, criticisms, and suggestions. David B. Mattern, associate editor of the Papers of James Madison, first introduced me to the ABC-CLIO Biographical Companion series, of which this work was originally a part of. In addition to being a good friend and respected colleague, David read the entire manuscript, parts of it several times, and his suggestions and encouragement were invaluable. Christine Patrick gave much of the manuscript a very close reading, and many of the entries bear the imprint of her finely honed editorial skills. Beverly Runge and Peter R. Henriques, associate professor of history at George Mason University, read many of the entries and caught errors of fact that only scholars as knowledgeable as they about the intricacies and minutiae of Washington's life could have discovered. Beverly also was particularly helpful with the material relating to the Washington family and genealogy. Edward G. Lengel drafted the entries on Brandywine, Germantown, and the Quasi-War. Henry Wiencek offered suggestions for the slavery entry, and Mary V. Thompson, research specialist at Mount Vernon, assisted with the Washington genealogy. In addition to the production team at ABC-CLIO that assisted with the original edition—Alicia Merritt, Martha Witt, Liz Kincaid, Will Reichard, and Gina Zondarak—I would like to thank the partners of Mariner Publishing, Andy Wolfe, Patricia F. Gibson, and Rick Britton, for having the vision and energy to see this work back into print. To all of these individuals I owe much.

Last, I thank my children, Jewel, Sarah, Noah, Hannah, Mary Katherine, and Margaret, for their love and sacrifice during this endeavor, and my wife, Pamela, who makes it all worthwhile.

INTRODUCTION

Few, if any, Americans have so completely dominated the historical stage of their era as did George Washington. Without doubt, Washington was the most important figure in eighteenth-century America. Even while alive he was a legend, a status only reinforced by his many biographers over the last 200 years. Countless interpretations of Washington by historians, novelists, political scientists, and others have appeared in print, as well as several editions of his writings. The sheer magnitude of Washington's correspondence, the complexity of events in which he was involved, and the many surviving artifacts from the material culture surrounding his life present an overwhelming and often confusing array of problems for those interested in him. It is hoped that this volume, the first encyclopedic work devoted exclusively to Washington, will assist in making Washington more accessible to modern researchers. The range of subjects discussed is not limited to the conventional inquiries into Washington's roles as military leader and first president, but includes much about his personal and family life, his landholdings and business dealings, and his many correspondents. The format is alphabetical, and most of the entries can be divided into three main categories: people, events, and interests. For the most part the entries are based on primary sources, incorporating where possible Washington's own words and those of his contemporaries. Following the alphabetical entries are appendices listing Washington's familial connections, Revolutionary War military family, the principal executive officers during his presidential administrations, and a selection of Washington's writings.

Washington often has been accused of being reserved, cold, aloof, unknown, and unknowable. Nothing could be further from the truth. His papers, among the most numerous of any individual in colonial America, reveal a man who was a very effective communicator. While it is true that as he became famous he increasingly chose to hide his feelings and to keep information close to his own breast, especially on matters related to public policy, his silence and reserve were conscious. To his friends and family he could be as candid as he was noncommittal to his foes. Anecdotes written by both those who knew him well and those who met him only in passing indicate that they found Washington to be extremely convivial by nature and "truly noble and majestic" in appearance. Silas Deane might have spoken for many when he wrote that, after knowing Washington for two days, "the more I am acquainted with, the more I esteem him."

The Washington who emerges from the historical record is neither of the ones we are most familiar with—the dignified but silent figure engraved on the dollar bill, or the noble and elegant-looking man portrayed on the common twenty-five-cent piece. The first, modeled on Gilbert Stuart's famous painting, is a drab, colorless, and ultimately stuffy-looking individual, apparently suffering from sore gums and probably a toothache, who is not only past his prime but also in his decline. The second image may better portray a leader among men carrying upon his shoulders the burdens of a cause more important than his own life, but the transference from stone to metal makes Washington seem even more inaccessible than in Houdon's original marble sculpture. But Washington, despite his protestations, which began near the end of the war with a declaration that he had grown gray and nearly blind in the service of his country, was neither feeble nor unapproachable. Almost to the very moment of his untimely death in 1799, Washington was a leader of men, the patriarch of a large extended family, and the manager of a grand estate. Although prone to serious illness, he was a man of boundless energy. Like his father, Augustine, Washington was ambitious and enterprising, always on the lookout for ways to improve his status in life. He did not have the benefit of an exemplary education, but he apparently was tutored adequately in reading, writing, and arithmetic, all of which served him well in the practical pursuit of wealth, both in his early career as a surveyor and later as a substantial planter and businessman. He took a genuine interest in learning throughout his life, but his interests ran more to the practical application of knowledge than abstract reasoning or speculative philosophy. In fact, he had very little time for contemplating religious or philosophic subjects, even if he had been so inclined, and by the surviving evidence, he was not much given to either.

Washington was usually optimistic, with some notable exceptions, and all his life he had a strong temper, which he learned early to control, even when greatly agitated. He could be stern and demanding when necessary, and (for most twentieth-century observers) overly moral, but his contemporaries praised his virtues and eagerly sought his companionship. Chief among those virtues was complete honesty. Washington, wrote James Madison, "was the last man in the world to whom any measure whatever of a deceptive tendency could be credibly attributed." Washington also had a great sense of humor, as the famous life portraits painted by Charles Willson Peale in 1772 and 1776 and the Peale miniature painted for Martha Washington between 1777 and 1779 show. It is evident in these portraits that Washington, then over age 40, still retained the vitality of his youth. The Washington of the miniature especially not only grins, but seems to enjoy doing so immensely, as though he is on the verge of chuckling at some story that Parson Weems or grandson George Washington Parke Custis would later tell about his childhood—one of the famous ones, of his barking the cherry tree, tossing the bar, or skipping rocks across the Rappahannock River at Ferry Farm, his childhood home.

Samuel Eliot Morison once quipped that Washington was the "last person you would ever suspect of having been a young man." The reason such a remark sounds so plausible is that so many of the traits and avocations associated with the mature Washington were developed while he was a very young man. Historians traditionally have conjectured that Washington's older half brother Lawrence exerted an early influence on Washington, and recently Don Higgonbotham has speculated that after Lawrence's death in 1752 the 20-year-old Washington never again looked to another individual as a role model. Be that as it may, Lawrence's military occupation apparently served as a model for his younger brother, and Lawrence's interest in western lands may have sparked Washington's own desire to become a great landholder. Washington's early surveying career and his French and Indian War service, both short in time, were formative experiences. Both familiarized him with the inefficiency of the colonial and British governmental apparatuses. And both introduced him to the west, revealing the vastness of the lands, the incursions of the French, and the omnipresence of the Indian, and whetted his appetite for land. With his marriage to Martha Dandridge Custis in 1759, Washington became the administrator of one of the wealthiest estates in the colony and began to settle into the comfortable life of the Virginia planter elite, with the myriad duties of plantation management and the predictable routines of the civic churchman, the vestryman, the Mason, and the businessman. By all accounts he had a happy home life with Martha and her children, marred only by the deaths of his beloved stepdaughter Patsy Custis in 1773 and her older brother Jacky eight years later, and other family members and in-laws, an inescapable part of eighteenth-century life. Despite such sorrows, he knew how to enjoy life. His days were filled with diversions like foxhunting and cockfighting or attending horse races, and his evenings consisted of dining and playing cards and visiting the theater. During the war such social events were replaced with the society of the officers' mess or the local tavern keeper, and punctuated by an occasional ball thrown for the officers and their wives at army headquarters. The pattern was in place, although it again altered during the presidential years, when his amusements became more dignified and refined, as befitted a world leader.

During the war and presidential years, keeping up with the endless number of letters flowing in from Congress, from the chief executives of the various states, and from army officers filled much of Washington's time. As commander in chief of the Continental army, Washington was, or became, a master administrator, as much involved with equipping troops and moving supplies as with the framing of strategy and the study of tactics, and his success was due as much to his effectiveness as an administrator as to his skill as a military strategist. The administrative skills acquired during his military service served him well as first president when the responsibilities of setting up the initial governmental apparatus fell to him, and much of his time was occupied with conferences with his cabinet, negotiating with Congress, conducting foreign policy, and establishing the Federal City. As Douglas Southall Freeman observed in his magnificent Pulitzer Prize-winning biography of Washington: "Burdensome was, in

heaviest reality, the word to apply to Washington's administrative duties around the clock and through every year."

Whether Washington's role in the winning of American independence and in the framing and executing of a new government was "indispensable" is a question for those who enjoy the mental gymnastics of contemplating the unresolvable "What might have beens?" of history. Many have said so, and it is certain that the course of the history of the United States would have taken a significantly different turn had not Washington been a prominent actor in the Revolution. Those who have taken the time to study him carefully have all been struck by the fact that Washington was primarily a man of deeds. Indeed, he was, but even a cursory reading of his wartime writings reveals that at every turn his actions were constrained by a profound respect for and deference to civil authority. During the war Washington was always extremely careful to operate within the boundaries set by the Continental Congress, even though this deference was all too often to his and the army's disadvantage. His insistence, too, on cooperating not only with the individual governments of the states and their chief executives but also with local committees of safety and other bodies kept him and his aides-de-camp up late many a night writing and copying an endless array of letters that eventually numbered in the tens of thousands. (In fact, two-thirds of the 135,000 letters and copies of letters that have been cataloged by the Papers of George Washington documentary editing project at the University of Virginia are from the Revolutionary War years.) Washington's sense of the primacy of civil authority was confirmed by his subsequent service to his country.

While Washington's subservience to civil authority has been celebrated justly as among the chief of his many virtues, it is important to note that the subservience arose in part from his accurate assessment of what was and was not practical in a society ostensibly governed by freeholders. Washington's pragmatism in facing the seemingly insurmountable challenges forced upon him by necessity sometimes goes unnoticed, whereas his respect for civil-military relations does not, but where you find one you usually find the other, and together they have led some astute observers to conclude that in Washington we have the consummate politician of American history. Washington was cautious, despite the fact that he sometimes risked his life with reckless abandon on the battlefield. If the vicissitudes of events during the French and Indian War had taught him anything, it was that the fortunes of war are fickle, a lesson reinforced many times during the War for Independence. It was better to contemplate the possible consequences of a deed before it was done than to regret later the lack of proper forethought and planning. The result was that he was slow to make up his mind. Jefferson confirmed this aspect of Washington's character in his accurate assessment more than a decade after Washington's death. "His mind was great and powerful," Jefferson wrote, "without being of the very first order; his penetration strong, though not so acute as that of a Newton, Bacon, or Locke; and as far as he saw, no judgment was ever sounder. It was slow in operation, being little aided by invention or imagination, but sure in conclusion. Hence the common remark of his officers, of the advantage he derived from councils of war, where hearing all suggestions, he selected whatever was best; and certainly no General ever planned his battles more judiciously."

Washington had a clear vision of what he wanted to see accomplished during the Revolution—a unified America—and, as former West Point superintendent Gen. David Palmer has so aptly observed, Washington set his goals with that vision in mind and never, ever strayed in his pursuit of that vision. It is what inspired him to command the Continental army without pay during the war. "To merit the approbation of good and virtuous Men," he wrote Jefferson in February 1783, "is the height of my ambition, and will be a full compensation for all my toils and Sufferings in the long and painful Contest we have been engaged." And it provided him with the stamina to withstand the darkest days of the war, the courage to risk his reputation by presiding over the Constitutional Convention, and the strength to see the American Revolution to completion by serving two terms as president.

A NOTE ABOUT PRIMARY SOURCES

The abbreviations *Col. Ser., Con. Ser., Pres. Ser., Ret. Ser.,* and *War Ser.* that appear in the Suggestions for Further Reading sections following the entries are from the *Colonial, Confederation, Presidential, Retirement,* and *Revolutionary War* series of *The Papers of George Washington,* edited by W. W. Abbot, Dorothy Twohig, Philander D. Chase, et al. (Charlottesville, VA, 1983–; 47 vols. to date). The sections also contain the following short titles for a number of documentary editions that are fully cited in the bibliography: *Diaries:* see Jackson, Donald; *Greene Papers:* see Showman, Richard K.; *Lafayette Papers:* see Idzerda, Stanley J.; *Letters of Delegates:* see Smith, Paul H.; *Hamilton Papers:* see Syrett, Harold C.; *Thornton Papers:* see Harris, C. M.; *Writings:* see Fitzpatrick, John C.

George!

A Guide to All Things Washington

Adams, John (1735–1826)

"The history of our Revolution," wrote Vice President John Adams to a correspondent in 1790, "will be one continued lie from one end to the other. The essence of the whole will be that Dr. Franklin's electrical rod smote the earth and out sprang General Washington; that Franklin electrified him with his rod—and thence forward these two conducted all the policy, negotiations, legislatures, and war." Historian Douglas Southall Freeman called Adams's remarks ungenerous, noting that Adams's "tongue and his pen were as acid as his mind was keen." Indeed, by 1790 Adams's acerbity regarding the veneration accorded Washington was long-standing, even though Adams had been the first to propose the appointment of "the modest and virtuous, the amiable, generous and brave George Washington" as commander in chief of the Continental army. In 1777, following the Battle of Saratoga, with everyone praising Maj. Gen. Horatio Gates, Adams succumbed to criticizing Washington: "we can allow a certain citizen to be wise, virtuous and good without thinking him a deity or a savior."

Abigail Adams, in contrast, was, as Freeman observed, Washington's advocate and champion. "You had prepared me to entertain a favorable opinion of General Washington," she wrote John after her first introduction to Washington, "but I thought the half was not told me. Dignity with ease and complacency, the gentleman and soldier, look agreeably blended in him. Modesty marks every line and feature of his face." Abigail's undiminishing esteem for Washington is evidenced, for example, in a letter written to her sister in September 1789: "I hope you will see our worthy President. He is much a favorite of mine, I do assure you." When Washington was gravely ill in 1790, she declared it "appears to me that union of the States, and consequently the permanency of the Government depend upon his life. . . . His death would, I fear, have had most disastrous consequences." According to Freeman, Abigail was not only an ardent supporter of Washington's administration but was also Martha's "loyal lieutenant" as well, although Abigail's real loyalty lay with the interest and welfare of her husband, for whom she was, to quote Freeman again, "chief informant, wise counsellor, defender."

Adams's acerbic criticism of his role as Washington's vice president is as well known as his comments about Franklin and Washington's roles in the Revolution: "My country has in its wisdom contrived for me the most insignificant office that ever the invention of man contrived or his imagination conceived." Yet Washington had endorsed Adams as vice president because New York governor George Clinton, who had a chance to win, although a friend of

Washington, was a fierce opponent of the Federal Constitution. Adams supported Washington's administration, but Adams "stood apart, a man without party, distrusted by Jefferson and Madison as a potential monarchist, and avoided by Hamilton as an unmanageable individualist." To Washington, Adams, who in his *Thoughts on Government* (1776) became an early advocate of the three-branch system of government, was a good choice. By 1789 Adams's assessment of Washington was beginning to change. "If we look over the catalogue of the first magistrates of nations . . . where shall we find one, whose commanding talents and virtues, whose overruling good fortune, have so completely united all hearts and voices in his favor?" It was the last months of Washington's second term before the two men entered into a political discussion so frank that Adams could inform his wife afterward, "I found his opinions and sentiments are more exactly like mine than I ever knew before." "His example is complete," Adams at last concluded near the end of his own presidency, "and it will teach wisdom and virtue to Magistrates, Citizens, and Men, not only in the present age, but in future generations."

Adams called Washington out of retirement to take command of the provisional army in the summer of 1798 when it appeared that a war with France loomed on the horizon. Washington hoped the preference might be "given to a man more in his prime," but his sense of duty would not allow him to refuse his former vice president. "I . . . go with as much reluctance from my present peaceful abode," he wrote, "as I should go to the tombs of my Ancestors." Fortunately, the crisis was averted before the army took the field.

Adams died on the same day as Thomas Jefferson, exactly fifty years to the day of the signing of the Declaration of Independence.

Related entries: Appointment as Commander in Chief; Presidency; Quasi-War

Suggestions for further reading:
"To John Adams," 25 September 1798 (*Ret. Ser.,* vol. 3).
Butterfield, L. H. et al., eds. 1961. 4 vols. *Diary and Autobiography of John Adams.* Cambridge, MA.
Hutson, J. H. 1980. *John Adams and the Diplomacy of the American Revolution.* Lexington, KY.

Aides-de-Camp

See Fitzgerald, John; Gibbs, Caleb; Grayson, William; Hamilton, Alexander; Humphreys, David; Laurens, John; McHenry, James; Mercer, George; Mifflin, Thomas; Reed, Joseph; Tilghman, Tench; Trumbull, John; Varick, Richard; Washington, George Augustine; Webb, Samuel Blachley.

Alexander, Robert (d. 1793)

Robert Alexander was Washington's neighbor and the brother-in-law of Washington's nephew, Fielding Lewis, Jr. (1751–1803). Alexander's earliest association with Washington seems to have taken place in 1759, when he began efforts to breed Washington's English stallion with his own stock. Washington sold the stallion to Alexander for £100 in 1761. Later, beginning in January 1768 and lasting until 1775, when Washington left home on the eve of the Revolutionary War, Alexander frequently visited Mount Vernon for foxhunting and overnight stays, and Washington occasionally went to Alexander's as well to hunt foxes or spend the night. On at least one occasion, in September 1768, Alexander and Washington attended a purse race together.

In June 1769 Alexander agreed to sell Washington a tract of land in Maryland belonging to his wife, Mariamne Stoddard Alexander, who was not of "Suffiteant age" to enter into the agreement, for £500

Maryland currency—land that Washington wanted to trade for nearly 500 acres adjacent to Mount Vernon owned by Thomas Hanson Marshall (1731–1801), who lived directly across the Potomac River from Mount Vernon at Marshall Hall in Charles County, Maryland. Alexander's wife later refused to consent to the sale, however, and the transaction lingered without settlement until 1779, when Washington's farm manager Lund Washington was able to buy Marshall's land outright for his employer. Washington did not receive reimbursement for the £500 that he had paid Alexander until 1789.

The land-swap deal was not the only misunderstanding between Alexander and Washington involving land. In 1778 Alexander sold Washington's stepson, Jacky Custis, a house and a 900-acre tract on the Potomac River, Abingdon, for £12 an acre, Custis agreeing to pay the principal and compound interest over twenty-four years. Disgusted at the agreement and at the general management of his stepson's large estate, Washington scolded Jacky by pointing out that £12,000 at compound rates would climb to over £48,000 during the period of the agreement. After Custis's death in 1781, the administrators of his estate sought to end the transaction by entering into a lawsuit with Alexander over the terms of the contract, forcing Washington to give court testimony in Alexandria several times in 1788. In 1792, after many years of wrangling, Alexander finally agreed to take the property back in exchange for the payment of a fair rent for the years that Custis and his administrators had held it. The dispute left David Stuart (1753–c.1814), the new husband of Custis's widow, thinking Alexander was the "most trifling, undecided character that ever I met with."

Although the land deals apparently soured the relationship between Washington and Alexander, Washington did call on Alexander once in February 1786 while chasing a fox across his land.

Related entry: Custis, John Parke

Suggestions for further reading:
Diaries, vols. 1–6.
"From Thomas Hanson Marshall," 18 June 1769 (*Col. Ser.,* vol. 8).
"Land Agreement," 22 June 1769 (*Col. Ser.,* vol. 8).
"From Thomas Hanson Marshall," 8, 12 March 1770 (*Col. Ser.,* vol. 8).
"To Thomas Hanson Marshall," 9, 16 March 1770 (*Col. Ser.,* vol. 8).
"From David Stuart," 11 March 1790 (*Pres. Ser.,* vol. 5).

Alexandria Academy

Sometimes called the first free school in Virginia, Alexandria Academy was established as an "ordinary elementary school" in 1785 by a group of Alexandria-area residents, chief of whom was Dr. William Brown (c.1752–c.1792), a physician trained at the University of Edinburgh who had been practicing medicine in the town since before the Revolutionary War. A new building, which in time came to be known as the Washington Building, was erected for the school during its first year of existence. (The modest structure was used well into the twentieth century for classroom instruction by the public school system of Alexandria.)

Washington heartily approved of the formation of Alexandria Academy, and it was from his connection with the institution that its "free" character emerged. He allowed his name to be enrolled among the academy's "Managers," noting that "nothing is of more importance than the education of youth" and promising to give the school his support "as far as it is in my power." Washington soon revealed that he wanted to render more than nominal support to the academy, however, when he invited the trustees of the institution to consider making the academy more than just an ordinary preparatory school for college. The education of orphans and children of indigent parents, especially children of former Revolutionary War soldiers, was an idea that Washington had been contemplating for quite some time, and he particularly hoped that something might be done for the needy in Alexandria. He thus pledged an endowment of £1,000 to Alexandria Academy, as he recorded in a diary entry, "to be applied towards the establishment of a charity School for the education of Orphan and other poor Children—which offer was accepted." In addition to the customary classical curriculum offered by eighteenth-century private schools, Washington hoped that with his endowment Alexandria Academy also could provide that "kind of education which would be most extensively useful to people of the lower class of citizens, viz.— reading, writing & arithmetic, so as to fit them for mechanical purposes." In lieu of giving the principal right away, however, which his pecuniary circumstances then prohibited, Washington promised £50 annually (an amount assumed equivalent to the principal's yearly interest) until some more convenient time, or until his death, when the money would be paid out of his estate. In his will Washington left the academy twenty shares of stock in the Bank of Alexandria, by then valued at $4,000, which more than fulfilled the promise.

As a result of Washington's endowment the charity school was incorporated as an integral part of Alexandria Academy and was governed by the same board of trustees. In 1786 there were twenty charity children attending the school, and that year Washington also agreed to permit up to one-fifth of the scholars who received assistance from his endowment to be "girls who may Fitly share the benefits of the institution" along with area boys. Washington sent two of his nephews, George Steptoe Washington (c.1773–1808) and Lawrence Augustine Washington (1775–1824), sons of his brother Samuel, to Alexandria Academy in the 1780s. William McWhir (1759–1851), a Presbyterian clergyman born in Ireland,

was in charge of the academy when Washington's nephews were in attendance.

Related entries: Education; National University

Suggestions for further reading:
Diaries, vol. 4.
"To William Brown," 24 November 1785 (*Con. Ser.,* vol. 3).
"To Trustees of the Alexandria Academy," 17 December 1785 (*Con. Ser.,* vol. 3).
"From William Brown," 17 December 1785 (*Con. Ser.,* vol. 3).
"Last Will and Testament," 9 July 1799 (*Ret. Ser.,* vol. 4).

Ancestry

Washington himself knew little about his ancestors. In 1792 he recalled that he often had heard older family members say that his father's family had lived long ago in a county in northern England, "but whether from Lancashire, Yorkshire or one still more northerly I do not precisely remember." It was a subject, he declared to Sir Isaac Heard, an English correspondent interested in tracing the Washington family ancestry, "to which I confess I have paid very little attention. My time has been so much occupied in the busy and active scenes of life from an early period of it that but a small portion of it could have been devoted to researches of this nature, even if my inclination or particular circumstances should have prompted the enquiry." Nevertheless, Washington at the same time freely offered what little assistance he could in providing information and expressed a desire to be informed of the result of Heard's inquiries, and of the "ancient pedigree of the family."

About seventy-five years before George Washington's birth, two brothers, John and Lawrence Washington (born about 1632 and 1635 respectively, and both died in 1677), had settled at Bridges Creek on the Potomac River in Westmoreland County, Virginia.

George descended from John and Anne Pope Washington (d. 1668) through their son, George's grandfather, also named Lawrence. (Lawrence was a favorite first name for males of the Washington family.) The line of the brothers' descent went back to another Lawrence Washington, a successful wool merchant born about 1500, who became mayor of the town of Northampton, England, in 1532. Gaps in the genealogical record make it impossible to discover Washington's ancestry before that time with complete certainty. During Lawrence's life branches of the family lived not only in Northamptonshire but Northumberland, Yorkshire, Lancashire, and Warwickshire. It is likely that Lawrence the wool merchant was a tenth-generation member of a family of de Wessyngton, which lived near the border of Lancashire and Westmoreland in the second half of the thirteenth century. The name apparently had been assumed by chevalier William de Hertburn, a member of the resident family of a parish in the county of Durham that had borne the name Wessyngton since the late twelfth century. In 1539, after Henry VIII's dissolution of the monasteries, Lawrence acquired one of the three estates of Sulgrave Manor, St. Andrew's Priory, which he and his wife, Anne, and then their eldest son, Robert, who was twice married, occupied until 1619. Robert Washington's grandson Lawrence (b. 1602), named after his own father, apparently became the first of the family to graduate from Oxford, taking degrees at Brasenose College in 1623 and 1626.

This Lawrence, the father of the Washington brothers who settled in Virginia, served as a lecturer and proctor at Oxford until his marriage to Amphillis Twigden in 1631 forced him to resign his fellowship. He then served as rector of All Saints, Purleigh Parish, Essex, until 1643, when he was removed on charges of being a "common frequenter of Ale-houses, not only himself sitting daily tippling there, but also encouraging others in that beastly vice." Although his parishioners acknowledged that Lawrence was "oft drunk," they helped him secure a position preaching at Little Braxted, Essex, where he remained until his death in 1652. His son John, who apparently had been taught something about seafaring, found his way to Virginia as a mate on Capt. Edward Prescott's ketch, the *Sea Horse of London,* in late 1656 or early 1657. In the early 1770s George did correspond briefly with a great-grandson of his great-grandfather John Washington's second wife, Anne Gerrard Broadhurst Brett Washington (d. c.1675).

Little is known about Washington's maternal ancestry. Joseph Ball, the father of Washington's mother, Mary Ball Washington, was born in England around 1649. Ball's grandfather, William Ball of Lincoln's Inn, was one of four attorneys for the office of pleas and exchequer. William Ball's son and namesake—Joseph's father—immigrated to Virginia, establishing himself as a planter and trader, in 1657. The younger William soon settled his family and servants at Millenbeck, a plantation he acquired near the mouth of Corotoman Creek in Lancaster County. By the time he died in 1680 William Ball had risen to local prominence, serving in the Virginia House of Burgesses and as major of the county militia. Of Joseph's mother, Hannah Atherold Ball, virtually nothing is known beyond the facts that she bore her husband at least four children and outlived him by fourteen years, dying in 1694.

As for Joseph Ball, he had already reared one family by the time he married Mary Johnson, a widow with two children, in 1707. Not much is known of Ball's first wife, Elizabeth Rogers (or Romney) Ball, except that she bore five daughters and a son and died around 1703. The early history of Mary Johnson Ball is as obscure as that of Ball's mother and first wife; not even the first name of her first husband has been discovered, nor her maiden name—although some have speculated that it may have been Bennett or Montague. That she was illiterate is proved by the fact that in witnessing a deed in 1703 she could only affix her mark. Posterity would not have remembered her name at all if it had not been for the daughter (the mother of George Washington) born to her and Joseph at Epping Forest in the winter of 1708–1709, whom they named Mary Ball, after her. Mary Johnson outlived three husbands, Johnson, Ball (who died in the summer of 1711), and Richard Hewes of Cherry Point in Northumberland County, Virginia, who died in early 1713 after only one year of marriage. When Mary Johnson Ball Hewes herself died in 1721, Washington's mother was left an orphan at the age of 12; she was placed under the "tutelage and government" of George Eskridge, a wealthy lawyer and prominent member of the House of Burgesses.

Related entries: Coat of Arms; Popes Creek; Washington, Augustine; Washington, Lawrence; Washington, Mary Ball

Suggestions for further reading:
"From Thomas Addenbrooke," 16 December 1771 (*Col. Ser.,* vol. 8).
"From Thomas Addenbrooke," 26 July 1773 (*Col. Ser.,* vol. 9).
"To Thomas Addenbrooke," May 1774 (*Col. Ser.,* vol. 8).
"To Isaac Heard," 2 May 1792 (*Writings,* vol. 32).
"To William Augustine Washington," 14 November 1796 (*Writings,* vol. 35).
"Washington's English Ancestors of the Direct Paternal Line" (vol. 1, appendix 4). Douglas Southall Freeman. 1948–1957. 7 vols. *George Washington: A Biography.* New York.
"The American Ancestry of Mary Ball" (vol. 1, appendix 5). Douglas Southall Freeman. 1948–1957. 7 vols. *George Washington: A Biography.* New York.
"Origin and Genealogy of the Washington Family" (vol. 1, appendix 1). Jared Sparks. 1834–1837. 12 vols. *The Writings of George Washington.* Boston.

The Two James Andersons

Besides having the same name, the only things shared by the two James Andersons were that both were Scotsmen with a knowledge of agriculture, and both entered Washington's life during the last decade of his life.

The first James Anderson (1739–1808) was the author and editor of numerous publications relating to agriculture and economics in the 1780s and 1790s, including the *Bee,* a weekly journal subscribed to by Washington that was published in Edinburgh from 1790 to 1794. Anderson wrote Washington in September 1791, enclosing a pamphlet on wool, six volumes of the *Bee,* and a pack of Swedish turnip seeds, opening a correspondence that lasted until Washington's death eight years later. Washington gratefully acknowledged Anderson's overture in a reply the following June, writing that "As I have spent [a] great part of my life (and that not the least pleasing) in rural affairs, I am always obliged by receiving such communications or novelties in that way, as may tend to promote the system of husbandry in this Country." Although his responsibilities as president greatly curtailed the time he could devote to reading about agriculture, Washington tried to keep abreast of experiments and developments in the field, and depended especially on people like Anderson to keep him informed. Hence he reiterated those sentiments from time to time, as when he told Anderson that "No pursuit is more congenial with my nature and gratifications, than that of agriculture; nor none I so much pant after as again to become a tiller of the Earth. Any books therefore on this subject giving the *principles* and combining practice with theory, will always be as pleasing as they must prove instructive to me; whose whole life in a manner having been little less, than a continued bustle, I must now benefit from the studies and experience of others, but a remnant of it being left to essay either myself."

Other subjects in the correspondence of Anderson and Washington range from personal matters like news about Anderson's children and the renting of Washington's farms to the making of cloth from goats' wool and the practicality of iron bridges over stone or wood, to religion and politics, including, in Washington's words, "the unjust, ambitious and intoxicated conduct of France towards these U. States." Anderson also sent Washington his pamphlets on cochineal insects, the cultivation of silk, and an inscribed copy of *A Practical Treatise on Draining Bogs and Swampy Grounds* (London, 1797). Washington thought very highly of Anderson and took pains to see that his name was put forward for membership in the American Philosophical Society at Philadelphia.

In 1797 Washington sought Anderson's assistance in procuring a gardener for Mount Vernon, choosing not to renew the contract with John Christian Ehlers, his German gardener since 1789. Anderson procured the services of a young Scot, William Spence, who arrived at Mount Vernon in October 1797. Washington was extremely pleased with Spence, he informed Anderson the next summer: "The Gardener you were so obliging as to send me continues to conduct himself extremely well. He is industrious sober and orderly—and understands his business—In short I never had a hired servant that pleased me better, and what adds to my satisfaction is that he is content himself, having declared that he never was happyer in his life."

After Washington's death Anderson published his *Selections from the Correspondence of George Washington and James Anderson, LL.D.* (Charlestown, Massachusetts, 1800).

"An honest, industrious and judicious Scotchman five years since from the County of Fife," is how Washington described his farm manager James Anderson (b. c.1745) in April 1797. Indeed, with a salary set at £140 per year, Washington had hired Anderson the previous October only after receiving Landon Carter, Jr.'s assurance that Anderson was "a man adapted to business" who might assist Washington in the profitable management of Washington's

farms. After his arrival at Mount Vernon, Anderson quickly implemented a system for running the farms, and by June he had established a "distillery, on a small scale" and, with Washington's approbation, had enlarged it by the end of the year to the point that it included a new stone house and "five Stills, Boilers—&ca."

In December 1797, Washington gave this appraisal to Anderson of his work during his first season: "as a Manager of my concerns . . . that they have been conducted with integrity—zeal—and ability; and, of course have met my approbation. There are some things however which I conceive may be improved, and candour, mixed with motives of friendship, have induced me to mention them to you." The criticisms that Washington enumerated included tardiness in executing planned work, "shifting suddenly from one kind of work to another . . . ordering people to come from the Farms to the Mansion (sometimes with Carts) and keeping them waiting more than half a day before you come to dispatch them—sending Carts frequently to Alexa[ndria] with, or for, trifles," resulting in making two trips to accomplish what one would answer for. These deficiencies, said Washington, arose from "a want of arrangement" and could be corrected if the "whole business of Farms" were "systematical directed—not from day to day—or week to week—but for as long a time as can well be foreseen and the persons who are immediately to have the conducting thereof to be informed accordingly."

Nevertheless, Washington was generally pleased with Anderson's management and was dismayed to hear in May 1798 that he was seeking other employment. Anderson misunderstood Washington's directions concerning improvements on the plantations at times, and confessed "myself Guilty in promising too freely" at other times, adding that "I think the things promised have generally been performed tho not always at the time, And I will say, that I never promised with an intent to deceive, and always have expected to perform as promised." Anderson did admit that Washington's observations about his management style "are well worth my attention." Realizing that Anderson's "attention is too much divided, & called to so many different objects, that notwithstanding your Zeal, and Industry, with wch I always have been, & still am perfectly satisfied," Washington determined to alleviate Anderson's dissatisfaction by reassigning his duties, but that only hurt the manager's feelings. As Washington related it, "although he expresses a wish to be governed in *all things*, you can find fault with *nothing* without hurting his feelings; but these do not show themselves in the least kind of indecency, or impertinance; on the contrary there is no man more obliging." Anderson later took sick, and Washington told him, "I was sorry to hear of your indisposition. I fear the charge with which you are entrusted, is too much for your health, and that to execute it properly, will rather increase than diminish your complaint." Washington at the end of his life was still trying to work things out with the farm manger, writing to Anderson on the day before his death, in fact.

One of the important duties delegated to Anderson by Washington was the making of detailed farm reports based on the reports of overseers of individual farms, and which include meteorological accounts of the weather at Mount Vernon.

In November 1797 Anderson devised a scheme for renting some of Washington's land on the Great Kanawha, but nothing came of it, although at the time of Washington's death Anderson was about to set out for the Ohio to inspect Washington's western lands, perhaps with an eye to settling there himself.

Related entries: Distillery; Mount Vernon

Suggestions for further reading:
"To James Anderson (of Scotland)," 20 June 1792 (*Writings,* vol. 32).

"Farm Reports," 2–8 April 1797 (*Ret. Ser.*, vol. 1).
"To James Anderson (of Scotland)," 7 April 1797 (*Ret. Ser.*, vol. 1).
"To James Anderson," 18 June 1797 (*Ret. Ser.,* vol. 1).
"From James Anderson (of Scotland)," 21 June 1797 (*Ret. Ser.,* vol. 1).
"To James Anderson," 16 September 1798 (*Ret. Ser.,* vol. 3).
"From James Anderson (of Scotland)," 15 April 1799 (*Ret. Ser.,* vol. 3).
"To James Anderson," 10, 16 September 1799 (*Ret. Ser.,* vol. 4).
"To James Anderson," 13 December 1799 (*Ret. Ser.,* vol. 4).

André, John (1751–1780)

*T*he fate of John André, a British army officer with a short but honorable career, was inextricably mixed with that of the Continental army officer whose name is synonymous with treachery in American lore, Benedict Arnold. The contrast could not be greater, as Washington's biographer Douglas Southall Freeman observed, for André "went to the gallows with perfect courage, as if he wished to show the ages how a man should die, and thereby he assured himself an immortality that to some seemed more to be desired than long life."

Educated in Geneva before his Swiss-merchant father settled in London, John André was commissioned a lieutenant in the British army in March 1771. He went to America with the Seventh British Regiment in 1774 and was taken prisoner when the garrison at St. Jean surrendered to its American besiegers in November 1775. He was paroled to Pennsylvania and exchanged about a year later, after which he was promoted to captain of the Twenty-sixth Regiment. He served as an aide-de-camp to Gen. Charles Grey during the British occupation of Philadelphia, and while in the city he organized stage performances for the occupying force. After the British evacuation of Philadelphia he served as an aide-de-camp to Gen. Henry Clinton in New

The capture of Maj. John André. Lithograph by Currier and Ives (Library of Congress)

York, where he was placed in charge of dealing with secret agents and informers. It was in this capacity that in May 1779 he began the sixteen-month correspondence with Benedict Arnold that ended in André's death. In the fall of 1779, André was promoted to major, and the following year he accompanied Clinton on the expedition to Charleston, South Carolina. By then he had taken on the duties of adjutant general for the British army, which he continued upon his return to New York.

The renewed communication between André and Arnold, which culminated in André's capture, trial, and execution, took place in the early-morning hours of 22 September 1780, when André, under an assumed name, quietly departed the safety of a British warship, the *Vulture,* for a clandestine meeting with Arnold in woods that lay firmly in American control. An unexpected attack on the *Vulture* prevented André from going back to the ship, however, and at Arnold's urging he attempted to return by land to the British lines. He was soon picked up by volunteers of the New York militia. André's false papers included instructions from Arnold that he be sent to Arnold in case he was picked up on the way to the American lines from New York City. Lt. Col. John Jameson, the Continental officer to whom André was carried after his capture, was perplexed that the prisoner had been taken behind the lines and unsure of what to do. His decision proved fateful for both André and Arnold: he sent the prisoner to Arnold but the captured papers to Washington. American intelligence officer Maj. Benjamin Tallmadge, learning of what had taken place, suspected treason on the part of Arnold and managed to prevent André from being delivered to Arnold. Meanwhile, the American general made his getaway.

Washington described the extent of André's involvement with Arnold in a letter to William Heath, the major general at Boston in command of the eastern department. "I cannot conclude without informing

You," he wrote Heath, "of an event which has happened here which will strike You with astonishment and indignation. Major General Arnold has gone to the Enemy. He had had an interview with Major André, Adjutant Genl. of the British Army, and had put into his possession a state of our Army; of the Garrison at this post; of the number of Men considered as necessary for the defence of it; a Return of the Ordnance, and the disposition of the Artillery Corps in case of an Alarm." It was only by "a most providential interposition," said Washington, that André had been discovered "with all these papers in General Arnold's hand writing, who hearing of the matter kept it secret, left his Quarters immediately under pretence of going over to West point . . . then pushed down the river in the barge . . . and got on board the Vulture Ship of War, which lay a few miles below." André also had in his possession two other documents in Arnold's writing, a copy of a recent American council of war and a written pass permitting André, in the name of John Anderson, to go by the American guards at White Plains or below on public business.

André's capture was announced in General Orders on 26 September, and the following day Washington instructed Maj. Gen. Nathanael Greene to prepare "*separate Houses in Camp*" for André and Joshua Hett Smith, "who has had a great hand in carrying on the business between him and Arnold." The men had not been permitted to see one another, and Washington wished for them to remain apart. A "strong Trusty Guards trebly officered" was assigned to the prisoners. "I would wish the room for Mr André to be a decent one," Washington concluded, "and that he may be treated with civility; but that he may be so guarded as to preclude a possibility of his escaping, which he will certainly attempt to effect if it shall seem practicable in the most distant degree. Smith must also be carefully secured and not treated with asperity." Both André and Smith were closely confined to a guard headed by Isaac Hubbell, an assistant to the deputy adjutant general, and allowed no visitors or pen, ink, or paper.

On 29 September Washington ordered the board of general officers to examine André, informing the board that André had crossed into the American lines at night for an interview with Arnold "in an assumed character" and when taken was in "a disguised habit, with a pass under a feigned name." The board was given the papers found concealed on André and orders to examine him carefully and "as speedily as possible, to report a precise state of his case, together with your opinion of the light, in which he ought to be considered, and the punishment, that ought to be inflicted." By the following day Washington could inform British general Henry Clinton that André had given a "free and voluntary confession" to the board in which he detailed his crossing the American lines to meet with Arnold in "a private and secret manner" and that he had changed his dress, feigned a name, and moved in a disguised habit past the American works at Stoney and Verplanks points before being captured at Tarrytown. André's own candor in confessing that it was "impossible for him to suppose he came on shore under the sanction of a Flag" left the board no alternative except to report to Washington that he "ought to be considered as a Spy from the Enemy, and that agreable to the Law and usage of Nations it is their opinion he ought to suffer death."

The board's determinations were made public in the General Orders of 1 October, with the commander in chief's direction that the execution of the sentence take place "in the usual way this afternoon at five o'-clock precisely." After Orders were issued later in the day delaying the execution for one day after Washington received a letter of the previous day from General Clinton requesting the American commander to receive a delegation that would "give you a true State of facts, and to declare to You my Sentiments and Resolutions." The meeting was held but failed to win clemency for André, and Evening Orders were issued resetting the time of execution at "twelve o'-clock precisely a Battalion of Eight files from each wing to attend the Execution."

In his report to Congress of André's execution, Washington noted that André had written him asking that he might be put to death by a firing squad rather than hanging, "but," as Washington informed the president of Congress, Joseph Reed, "the practice and usage of war, circumstanced as he was, were against the indulgence." Washington also requested that Congress reward the three Dutchess County militia soldiers who had captured André with "a handsome gratuity" from the public. The men had, he said, refused to release André "notwithstanding the most earnest importunities and assurances of a liberal reward on his part." Congress agreed and resolved to commend the three, John Paulding, David Williams, and Isaac Van Wart, for their "virtuous and patriotic conduct," awarding them each an annual pension for life of $200 in specie and a silver medal.

Although the Americans would have preferred to hang Arnold rather than André, there was no way to save the major's life. His execution could not be avoided, Washington wrote the count de Rochambeau, because the "circumstances he was taken in justified it and policy required a sacrifice; but as he was more unfortunate than criminal in the affair, and as there was much in his character to interest, while we yielded to the necessity of rigor, we could not but lament it." "André has met his fate," Washington wrote John Laurens, "and with that fortitude which was to be expected from an accomplished man, and gallant Officer."

The British army went into official mourning upon notification of André's death; his body was moved to Westminster in 1821, where a monument was erected to his memory.

Related entry: Arnold, Benedict

Suggestions for further reading:
"General Orders," 26 September 1780 (*Writings,* vol. 20).
"To William Heath," 26 September 1780 (*Writings,* vol. 20).
"To Nathanael Greene," 27 September 1780 (*Writings,* vol. 20).
"To Rochambeau," 10 October 1780 (*Writings,* vol. 20).
André, John. 1904. *Major André's Journal: Operations of the British Army . . . June, 1777, to November 1778. . . .* Tarrytown, NY.

Appointment as Commander in Chief

By the time the Continental Congress voted to adopt as Continental the provincial forces besieging the British army at Boston in June 1775, the eyes of thousands throughout the colonies already had rested upon Washington as in many respects the best qualified to be placed at the head of the army. There were other officers in the colonies, of course, who had served honorably in previous wars, and whose military reputations merited consideration by the delegates at Philadelphia. Charles Lee and Horatio Gates, for instance, were thought by many to have more experience and talent in military affairs than Washington, but their foreign births tempered their popularity among the delegates, who firmly held to a resolution to elevate none but a native-born American to such a lofty position of honor and authority. Support for Artemas Ward, older than Washington, also experienced and already in command of the rebel troops outside Boston, was voiced by his friends and advocates in Massachusetts. Citizens of other colonies undoubtedly were prejudiced in favor of their own favorite sons, too, like Israel Putnam of Connecticut, for example.

The selection of a competent commander in chief acceptable to all the colonies was a matter of great concern and difficulty as well as a potential embarrassment to Congress. Its members were acutely aware of the crucial role that the Continental army was expected to play in the ongoing struggle between the colonies and Great Britain. As the delegates weighed the momentous political implications of the appointment, it quickly became apparent that the interests of the whole continent might be advanced more by choosing an officer from a southern colony. Large and influential Virginia, which with Massachusetts had taken the lead in adopting bold and decided measures in the grievances against Great Britain, especially needed to be enlisted in the common cause. But while it was necessary that the appointment of the new commander secure the support of the southern colonies, it was also critical that the appointment not alienate the four New England provinces from which the troops had been wholly raised. Fortunately, personal attachments and local biases among the delegates gradually yielded to more noble and generous patriotic impulses, and enthusiastic support for Washington began to grow.

Advocates for consolidation and Continental support of the New England troops outside Boston and for Washington's appointment as their commander in chief was strong as early as 4 June 1775, when Elbridge Gerry, one of the leaders in the Massachusetts provincial congress meeting at Watertown, wrote to his colony's delegation in Congress: "I should heartily rejoice to see this way the beloved Colonel Washington, and do not doubt the New England generals would acquiesce in showing to our sister colony Virginia the respect, which she has before experienced from the continent, in making him generalissimo. This is a matter in which Dr. [Joseph] Warren agrees with me, and we had intended to write to you jointly on the affair." It was a member of the Massachusetts delegation, John Adams, who ten days later formally introduced the motion in Congress to adopt and support the New England army outside of Boston and appoint a general to command it. In making this motion Adams made it clear that it was his intention to propose for the office of commander in chief a member of their own body, a gentleman from Virginia. The appointment was postponed until the following day, when Washington was nominated, not by Adams, as often is erroneously stated, but by an old acquaintance of Washington, Thomas Johnson, then a delegate to Congress and later wartime governor of Maryland. The votes were cast and Washington was unanimously elected. Congress then adjourned until the next day, 16 June 1775, when it reconvened to officially notify Washington of the appointment and receive acceptance of it. After being informed by President John Hancock that the Congress had unanimously chosen him to be "General & Commander in Chief of the American Forces" and had requested that he accept the appointment, Washington, "standing in his place" before the members, expressed doubts about his abilities and military experience, while promising to support the "glorious Cause" with every power in his possession. Washington then briefly thanked Congress for the honor that it was bestowing upon him, stated once again that he did not think himself equal to the command, and declared his intentions not to accept any salary for his service. Two days afterward, Silas Deane wrote that Washington's acceptance was "modest and polite . . . [he] is said to be as fixed and resolute in having his orders on all occasions executed, as he is cool and deliberate in giving them."

Washington's refusal to accept any personal compensation for his service generally pleased the delegates, although at least one delegate feared that the expenses allowed for his military "family, Aide Camps, Secretary Servts &c, beside a Constant table for more or less of his officers, daily expresses, dispatches &c Must be very expensive."

Related entries: Adams, John; Washington Elm

Suggestions for further reading:
"Address to the Continental Congress," 16 June
1775 (*War Ser.*, vol. 1).
"Eliphalet Dyer to Joseph Trumbull," 17 June
1775 (*Letters of Delegates*, vol. 1).
"Commission from the Continental Congress,"
19 June 1775 (*War Ser.*, vol. 1).
"Washington's Appointment as Commander-in-
Chief of the American Army" (vol. 3,
appendix 1). Jared Sparks. 1834–1837. 12
vols. *The Writings of George Washington.*
Boston.

Arnold, Benedict (1741–1801)

Although the most notorious traitor of the Revolutionary War made important contributions to the American war effort and was both liked and heralded by Washington before defecting to the British army in 1780, Benedict Arnold's treachery and the resulting folktales and mythology surrounding his life have, until recently, all but overshadowed those contributions. His father's failure in the mercantile business in 1755 forced the youth to forsake his preparation for eventual matriculation at Yale College, and he was apprenticed from 1756 to 1760 to Daniel and Joshua Lathrop of Norwich, Connecticut, his mother's prosperous cousins, to learn the apothecary business. Arnold faithfully completed the terms of his apprenticeship contract, and in 1760 the Lathrops welcomed him as a junior partner and set him up in business in New Haven.

Arnold emerged over the next decade as one of New Haven's most prominent and wealthiest citizens. Direct access to the extensive trading network of his cousins allowed him to expand his financial pursuits beyond the confines of the apothecary-merchant shop into the wider world of commercial shipping. By 1765 "Captain" Arnold and Adam Babcock, a wealthy New Haven merchant with whom Arnold had entered into partnership a year or two before, were ferrying trade goods as far away as Canada and the West Indies on board three brigantines, *Fortune, Charming Sally,* and *Three Brothers.* While engaged in this new venture, Arnold and Babcock began smuggling prohibited goods to evade the British custom restrictions that had followed Parliament's passage of the Currency and Sugar acts in April 1764, and Arnold began to align himself with the anti-British faction in New Haven, becoming one of New Haven's most fiery defenders of American "liberties." In 1774 he played a leading role among the sixty-five citizens of the town who organized themselves into a militia company, and when the company was formally designated the Governor's Second Company of Guards in March 1775, Arnold was elected its captain. News

Undated portrait of Benedict Arnold (Library of Congress)

of the fighting at Lexington and Concord on 14 April 1775 reached New Haven one week later, and Arnold and his men departed for Massachusetts the following morning—after demanding (with threats) and receiving permission from the local selectmen an appropriation of weapons, ammunition, and other supplies from the town's magazine. Arnold's only previous military service had been limited to an abortive march with the Norwich militia during the French and Indian War when it mustered arms for the assistance of Fort William Henry on the southern shore of Lake George, besieged by French and Indian forces under the command of the French Canadian governor, Louis Joseph, marquis de Montcalm.

Three days after Arnold's arrival at Cambridge, the Massachusetts committee of safety appointed him colonel of a regiment authorized to seize the arms-rich garrison at Ticonderoga, New York. With the help of Col. Ethan Allen, the mission was accomplished on 10 May 1775, when the unsuspecting British were overtaken in less than ten minutes and forced to surrender the fort and its 201 pieces of artillery. Endless bickering with Allen and his Green Mountain Boys and disputes about command finally led to Arnold's resignation six weeks later, however, and he left for Albany, New York, where he won the friendship and patronage of Maj. Gen. Philip Schuyler, recently appointed commander of the Continental army's northern department. From Albany Arnold traveled back to Massachusetts to settle his accounts and to present himself to Washington, who during Arnold's absence had taken command of the American forces at Cambridge.

Exactly when Washington and Arnold met for the first time is not known with certainty, but it appears to have been by mid-August 1775. At that meeting Washington beheld in Arnold an energetic, powerfully built, well-dressed, and respectable-looking man of average height with impeccable manners, light blue eyes, black hair, and a dark complexion. All in all, Arnold had a commanding presence, and he exhibited none of the impatience that sometimes flowed from his restless, fiery nature and often led him to quarrel with fellow officers. Arnold undoubtedly recounted to Washington his own role in the capture of Ticonderoga as he summarized affairs in the northern department and discussed a possible invasion of Canada. Washington, optimistic of success, supported Arnold's bid to lead an expedition to Quebec, and the Continental Congress soon agreed, commissioning Arnold a colonel in the Continental army. After Arnold led a remarkable and difficult march through the northern wilderness in the fall of 1775, justly celebrated since as one of the unparalleled feats in American military history, Washington offered Arnold unqualified praise for his efforts: "It is not in the power of any man to command success, but you have done more—you have deserved it, & before this I hope, have met with the Laurels which are due to your Toils, in the possession of Quebec—My thanks are due, & sincerely offered to you, for your Enterprizing & perservering spirit—To your brave followers I likewise present them." The victory Washington hoped for was not to be, however, for when the assault finally was made on the fortifications at Quebec, it proved unsuccessful.

Arnold remained near Quebec through a long and bitter winter, and he took part in the American army's evacuation of Montreal in the spring of 1776. With Washington's approval he supervised the construction of the American fleet on Lake Champlain, a delaying action that gave the American army valuable time to strengthen its forces. The fleet was destroyed at Valcour Island, but not before Arnold had given a good account of himself, making a dramatic escape. He then distinguished himself once more in April 1777, valiantly defending the military stores at Danbury, Connecticut, against a British raiding party from New York City. The Continental Congress, which had snubbed Arnold earlier by ignoring Washington's recommendation to promote him to major general, now finally recognized his merit by giving him the promotion, although it did not restore the seniority that would have been his had Congress acted earlier. Even Washington's praise of Arnold was not enough to win Arnold favor with Congress: "It is needless to say anything of this gentleman's military character. It is universally known that he has always distinguished himself, as a judicious, brave officer, of great activity, enterprize and perseverance." Washington was able to persuade Arnold not to resign his commission, however, and at Washington's request Arnold went to the northern department to assist Major General Schuyler in preparing the region against British general John Burgoyne's encroaching forces.

After arriving in the northern department, Arnold defended Schuyler against charges of treason resulting from Fort Ticonderoga's fall back into the hands of the British. When the anti-Schuyler faction finally succeeded in having Schuyler replaced by Maj. Gen. Horatio Gates, it also was able to alienate Gates against Arnold, and Arnold's near defeat of the British at the Battle of Freeman's Farm in September 1777 did nothing to win favor with Gates, who had sat by idly with a 4,000-man force, refusing to send reinforcements. Arnold played a conspicuous leadership role at the Battle of Bemis Heights two weeks later, even though Gates had relieved him of his command; he led an assault on Breymann's Redoubt, during which he was hit with a musket ball in the same leg that had been wounded at Quebec. Arnold's efforts were vital in the Americans' success at the Battle of Saratoga, which resulted in the capture of Burgoyne's forces of more than 5,700 men, and triggered France's entrance into the war. It was Gates, however, who was credited with the victory and who received the appellation "the hero of Saratoga," while Arnold was sent to the Continental army's hospital in Albany to nurse his multiple-fractured leg for the next five months. Arnold's sacrifice did not go unnoticed by Washington, however, who honored Arnold the following May with a set of "epaulettes and sword-knots" that he had recently received from France, as a "testimony" of his "sincere regard and approbation" of Arnold's courage and conduct. Two weeks after receiving the emblems Arnold showed up at the Continental army headquarters at Valley Forge, Pennsylvania, and an astonished Washington appointed him commander of the Continental forces that moved into Philadelphia after the British evacuated the city a few weeks later.

Arnold's stay at Philadelphia during the ensuing months can be characterized as a period full of petty quarrels with delegates of the Continental Congress and with members of Pennsylvania's radical-minded revolutionaries. The latter accused Arnold of misusing his military authority for personal gain in 1779, and, to his great astonishment, a court-martial held at his own insistence found him guilty in January 1780, resulting in a mild reprimand by Washington at the direction of Congress. Arnold interpreted the verdict and sentence not only as blatant ingratitude for his military service but also as a rejection of all his former sacrifices for the American cause, and the exaggerated sense of disgrace that he felt led directly to his treason later in the same year. Washington attempted to soothe Arnold's wounded pride the following August by offering him one of two wing commands in the upcoming campaign, but Arnold, by that time in treasonous correspondence with British major John André, demurred, saying, as Washington later recalled, that he was "incapable of active Service; but could discharge the duties of a stationary command without much inconvenience or uneasiness to his Leg." Upon receiving that declaration, Washington appointed Arnold commander of West Point. The events that then rapidly unfolded have been delineated perhaps most succinctly by Washington himself in a letter to Virginia governor Thomas Jefferson written on 10 October 1780:

Your Excellency will have heard probably before this reaches You, of the perfidy of Major General Arnold. On the 25th of Septr he went to the Enemy. He had entered very deeply into a combination with them, as far as we can judge, for putting them in possession of the important post of West point, where he commanded and the command of which he had solicited. For this purpose he had contrived an interview with Major André Adjutant General to their Army, on the night of the 21st and delivered to him, A Copy of a State of matters I had laid before a Council of Genl Officers the 6th of Septr. An Estimate of the force at West point and its Dependencies; of Men to man the Works at West point. Remarks on those Works. A Return of Ordnance at West point and its Dependencies. Artillery orders for the disposition of the Corps in case of an alarm at West point. A permit to Major André, under the assumed name of John Anderson to pass our Guards. This Officer with all those papers in Arnold's hand writing, was taken by a most extraordinary and providential intervention of circumstances, under the assumed name of John Anderson and in a disguised habit, about Fifteen miles from the Enemy's Outpost at King's bridge [New York], by a small Militia patrol, who acted with great virtue upon the occasion, as he was returning to New York; having been all the night of the 21st and next day in the vicinity of our posts at Stony and Verplanks points [New York], and passed by them the night preceding his capture. Arnold got information of the event on the morning of the 25th before it was known to any of the Officers under his command or any in authority and pushed down the River in a barge to the Vulture [British] Sloop of War, which lay a few miles below Stony

Point. Major André was tried by a Board of General Officers, and on his free and voluntary confession and Letters, was sentenced to suffer death, agreeable to the practice and usage of Nations in like cases, which he has accordingly suffered. He acted with great candor after he avowed himself untill he was executed. Your Excellency will probably see the whole of the proceedings in his case published. We have no doubt now, whatever may be the future Objects and measures of the Enemy, that the primary and principal design of the embarkation they were making, was to take West point, which through the preconcerted arrangements between them and Mr Arnold, in all human probability, would have inevitably fallen into their hands and most likely in the course of a few days after the discovery. The Enemy have not laid aside from the accounts I continue to receive, their preparations for an expedition, and must now mean to make a push in some other more remote quarter. Hence Your Excellency will perceive that they leave nothing unessayed to carry their point; but I trust there are more than abundant virtue, as well as means in our hands, if these are properly directed, to withstand and baffle easily all their most vigorous and artful efforts.

Reaction to Arnold's treason was as swift and decisive as it was predictable. Its discovery was announced to the army in the General Orders of 26 September: "Treason of the blackest dye was yesterday discovered!" John André was executed within the week. The Continental Congress on 4 October resolved to direct the Board of War to "erase from the register of the names of the officers of the army of the United States, the name of Benedict Arnold." Courts of inquiries were ordered to look into the conduct of Arnold's aides-de-camp, Lt. Col. Richard Varick and Maj. David Solebury Franks, although both men were believed by Washington to be "perfectly innocent" and not implicated in the affair (the inquiries eventually cleared both officers with honor). Washington declared to the count de Rochambeau that Arnold had "sullied his former glory by the blackest treason" and said that Arnold's defection gave him "equal regret and mortification." Never again would Arnold be esteemed by Washington. "Arnold's conduct," wrote Washington to his old aide-de-camp Joseph Reed, now president of the Continental Congress, "is so villainously perfidious, that there are no terms that can describe the baseness of his heart. . . . The confidence, and folly which has marked the subsequent conduct of this man, are of a piece with his villainy; and all three are perfect in their kind." To John Laurens's suggestion that Arnold "must undergo a punishment incomparably more severe in the permanent increasing torment of a mental hell," Washington replied, "But I am mistaken if at *this time,* Arnold is undergoing the torments of a mental Hell. He wants feeling! From some traits of his character which have lately come to my knowledge, he seems to have been so hackneyed in villainy, and so lost to all sense of honor and shame that while his faculties will enable him to continue his sordid pursuits there will be not time for remorse." Washington, however, brushed aside suggestions that Arnold "had really intended to involve my fate with that of the Garrison."

As for Arnold, if he ever felt any remorse for his actions, he never showed it. He wrote Washington on the same day that he fled to the British, pleading that his wife, Peggy Shippen Arnold, who had passed letters between her husband and Major André, might be allowed to pass the American lines and join him on board the *Vulture.* "She is as good, and as Inocent as an Angel," Arnold wrote, "and is Incapeble of doing Wrong." The request was denied, however. A few weeks later Washington approved Maj. Henry Lee's plan to capture Arnold, leaving to Lee the "whole to the guidance of your own judgment, with this express stipulation, and pointed injunction, that he A——d is brought to me alive. No circumstance whatever shall obtain my consent to his being put to death. The idea which would accompany such an event would be that Ruffians had been hired to assassinate him. My aim is to make a public example of him." Arnold was not captured, however.

Arnold, following his defection, was commissioned a brigadier general in the British army, but he was never completely trusted by the men of his new allegiance, even after leading raids into Virginia and Connecticut. An additional motive for betraying West Point, an expected payment of £10,000 from the British, was only partially fulfilled, and that only after much wrangling. He took his family to London after the American victory at Yorktown; he later moved to St. Jean, New Brunswick, and entered the shipping business for a time before moving back to England. He then went into the West Indian trade, where he lost much of his fortune in investments in privateering.

"Brave, desperately brave, he certainly was," were the words one nineteenth-century historian used to describe America's most famous villain. That Arnold was often bold if not plain reckless, no one can deny. Like Washington, Arnold seemed to find exhilaration in danger, and the energetic and elegant speeches that he delivered to his troops before important actions usually motivated his men to accomplish their goals. Traits often associated with him— avarice, voluptuousness, insensibility, and selfishness—highlight his self-centeredness, of course. But his courage, once thought to be the solitary virtue of his character, can hardly be denied. Historians probably will continue to debate, as they have in the past, whether Arnold was a "finished scoundrel from early manhood to his grave," a "criminal," an "evil genius," or simply a "sane man" who somehow became possessed of the "spirit of evil." And his treachery will always call into question the motivations for his early attachment to the Patriot cause and obscure the valuable contributions, made at great personal sacrifice.

Related entry: André, John

Suggestions for further reading:
"Instructions to Benedict Arnold," 14 September 1775 (*War Ser.*, vol. 1).
"To Benedict Arnold," 5 December 1775 (*War Ser.*, vol. 2).
"To Rochambeau," 27 September 1780 (*Writings*, vol. 20).
"To Thomas Jefferson," 10 October 1780 (*Writings*, vol. 20).
Brandt, Clare. 1994. *The Man in the Mirror: A Life of Benedict Arnold.* New York.
Martin, James Kirby. 1997. *Benedict Arnold: Revolutionary Hero, An American Warrior Reconsidered.* New York.
Roberts, Kenneth, ed. 1947. *March to Quebec, Journals of the Members of Arnold's Expedition.* New York.
Van Doren, Carl. 1941. *Secret History of the American Revolution.* Garden City, NJ.
Wallace, Willard M. 1954. *Traitorous Hero: The Life and Fortunes of Benedict Arnold.* New York.

Asgill Affair

This unfortunate and embarrassing series of incidents began in April 1782 with the hanging of an American prisoner of war, New Jersey militia artillery captain Joshua Huddy, who had been released by the British into the custody of the Associated Loyalists for the purpose of being exchanged. The Loyalists, however, claiming that Huddy had killed one of their partisans, Philip White, made no effort to exchange him but instead hanged him to a tree with a placard pinned to his breast promising to revenge "man for man" their cohorts, and ending with the line, "Up Goes Huddy for Phillip White." Upon learning the details of Huddy's execution, Washington appealed to British general Henry Clinton for redress, and Clinton, after looking into the matter, ordered the court-martial of Capt. Richard Lippincott,

the commander of Huddy's escort. Lippincott, however, was acquitted on grounds that he had simply followed orders.

Dissatisfied that the "Perpetrators of that horrid deed" had not been punished, Washington ordered Brig. Gen. Moses Hazen to select by lot a British officer, an "unconditional Prisoner," to be executed in retaliation, directing also that "every possible tenderness, that is consistent with the Security of him, should be shewn to the person whose unfortunate Lot it may be to suffer." The lot fell upon a young captain in the First British Regiment of Foot, Charles Asgill (c.1762–1823), the son of Sir Charles Asgill, former lord mayor of London, and Theresa Pratviel Asgill, the daughter of a wealthy French Huguenot émigré. Asgill had been captured at Yorktown and thus was entitled to protection under the terms of the capitulation, a fact exceedingly distressing to Washington. "Congress by their resolve have unanimously approved of my determination to retaliate," wrote Washington. "The Army have advised it, and the Country look for it. But how far it is justifiable upon an officer under the faith of a capitulation, if none other can be had, is the question?" Hazen's sending Asgill on for the purpose made the matter even more distressing, "as the whole business will have the appearance of a farce, if some person is not sacrificed to the manes of poor Huddy, which will be the case, if an unconditional prisoner can not be found, and Asgill escapes."

Asgill was neither executed nor restored to his former status, and the affair lingered through the spring and summer into the fall of 1782, with Washington privately wishing for Asgill's release. Lady Asgill successfully pleaded the injustice of her son's predicament with Charles Gravier, comte de Vergennes (1717–1787), the French foreign minister, who presented her plea to the French court. The king directed Vergennes to intercede with the Americans on behalf of the young man, and his life was spared by a resolution passed by Congress in November 1782. Washington gladly released Asgill, granting him a pass to go to New York for passage to Europe, if he so desired.

Asgill's release did not close the matter, however, for the repercussions outlasted the event. Most immediately, the British commanders stripped the Associated Loyalists of all their powers, and actively sought to bring to justice Huddy's executioners. After the war the affair became the subject of Lebarbier the Younger's *Asgill, Drame, en Cinq Actes, en Prose; Dédié à Madame Asgill* (Paris, 1785), a "dramatic piece" set at Washington's headquarters that portrayed the commander in chief sympathetically as "one who is trapped by circumstances but in the end is magnanimous." About the same time, rumors circulated in Europe and in America to the effect that Asgill claimed to have been confined to a jail where, with a scaffold outside his window, he was treated cruelly and inundated with insults, "all of whch he believes were countenanced by General Washington who was well inclined to execute the Sentence on him but was restrained by the French General Rochambeau." Incensed at the rumors, Washington claimed that Asgill had been indulged with permission to ride about the countryside for miles around the area of his confinement, and that Asgill's situation had filled him with the "keenest anguish . . . & not the least, when viewing him as a man of humor & sentiment how unfortunate it was for him that a wretch who possesses neither, should be the means of causing in him a single pang, or a disagreeable sensation." He also denied ever having spoken to Rochambeau about the subject. Washington had his secretary Tobias Lear copy all the documents relating to Asgill's plight and send them to David Humphreys with directions to prepare them for publication. The documents, with an introductory essay by Humphreys, were published in November 1786.

Related entry: Rochambeau

Suggestions for further reading:
"To the Secretary at War," 5 June 1782 (*Writings*, vol. 24).
"To Charles Asgill," 13 November 1782 (*Writings*, vol. 25).
"From Lebarbier," 4 March 1785 (*Con. Ser.*, vol. 2).
"To James Tilghman," 5 June 1786 (*Con. Ser.*, vol. 4).
Mayo, Katherine. 1938. *General Washington's Dilemma*. New York.

SIC ITUR AD ASTRA

45ᵗʰ Afcention and the firſt
made in America January
9ᵗʰ 1793. at Philadelphia
39°56′ N. Latitude by
Mr. J. P. Blanchard.

45°. afcenfion et la premiere
faite en Amerique Le 9 Jan-
vier 1793 a Philadelphie 39°
56′ Latitude N. par.
Mr. J. P. Blanchard.

Frontispiece of Jean Pierre Blanchard's Journal of My Forty-Fifth Ascension, Philadelphia, 1793
(Library of Congress)

B

Balloons

When Washington first read the newspaper accounts of the balloon craze that began in France and swept across Europe in 1783, he was unsure of what credence to give them. He told a French correspondent in April 1784 that "the tales related of them are marvelous, & lead us to expect that our friends at Paris, in a little time, will come flying thro' the air, instead [of] ploughing the Ocean to get to America." Duportail, the French officer who served as commandant of engineers for the Continental army, had written Washington the month before that he had seen "for the first time a man in the Clouds," expressing his regret that Washington "Could not enjoy so extraordinary [a] view."

Experiments with balloons began in June 1783, when brothers Jacques-Etienne and Joseph-Michel Montgolfier released a hot-air balloon near Lyon, and a short time later when the physicist Jean-Alexandre-Césare Charles sent up a hydrogen balloon in Paris. These experiments, at first considered by many in France to be only the arcane efforts of misguided scientists or foolish enthusiasts, soon took on an appealing aura of national triumph when Jean Pilâtre and the marquis d'Arlandes went up in a hot-air balloon above Paris in November 1783 and Charles and M. N. Robert quickly followed suit in a hydrogen balloon.

Washington found the experiments of these Frenchmen intriguing, as evidenced by the jocular opening of a letter written from Maryland to the marquis de Lafayette in late December 1784, occasioned by the Virginia legislature unexpectedly asking Washington to travel to Annapolis to negotiate a plan with representatives of Maryland to extend the inland navigation of the Potomac River. "You would scarcely expect," Washington wrote his old comrade-in-arms, "to receive a letter from me at this place: a few hours before I set out for it, I as little expected to cross the Potomac again this winter, or even to be fifteen miles from home before the first of April, as I did to make you a visit in an air Balloon in France."

He was not insensitive to either the potential benefits or the immediate dangers of such flights, however. He scolded another foreign correspondent, Edward Newenham (1732–1814), a member of the Irish Parliament who had supported the Americans in their struggle with Great Britain, for going up in a balloon. "Had I been present & apprized of your intention of making an aerial voyage with Monsr Potain," Washington wrote Newenham in November 1785, "I should have joined my entreaties to those of Lady Newenham to have prevented it. As yet, I see no object to warrant a gentleman of fortune (happy in himself—happy in a family wch might be rendered miserable by a disaster, against which no human foresight can guard) running such a risk." On the other hand, Washington added, such experiments ought not be discouraged. "It may do for young men of science & spirit to explore the upper regions: the observations there made may serve to ascertain the utility of the first discovery, & how far it may be applied to valuable purposes. To such *alone* I think these voyages ought at present to be consigned—& to them handsome public encouragements should be offer'd for the risk they run in ascertaining its usefulness, or the inutility of the pursuit." Ironically, only two weeks after Washington wrote his letter scolding Newenham, a Monsieur Busselot raised a balloon at the Capitol Square in Richmond, which, after ascending to a great height, was carried away by a northeast wind; night had fallen before Busselot could set the balloon down ten miles away in neighboring Hanover County.

Washington was especially pleased when during his presidency another French aeronaut decided to fly a balloon in Philadelphia, offering him a chance to actually witness firsthand these amazing feats against gravity. The Frenchman, Jean Pierre Blanchard, appealed to Washington for a "passport" on the day of his flight, 9 January 1793, which Washington gladly provided:

To all to whom these presents shall come. The bearer hereof, Mr. Blanchard, a citizen of France, proposing to ascend in a balloon from the city of Philadelphia at 10 A.M. this day to pass in such direction and to descend in such place as circumstances may render most convenient.

These are there to recommend to all citizens of the United States and others that in his passage, descent, return, or journeying elsewhere, they oppose no hindrance or molestation to the said Mr. Blanchard: and that on the contrary, they receive and aid him with that humanity and good will which may render honor to their country and justice to an individual so distinguished by his efforts to establish and advance his art in order to make it useful to mankind in general.

According to accounts of the event that appeared in the Philadelphia newspapers the next day, Blanchard's balloon traveled about fifteen miles and descended near Woodbury in Gloucester County, New Jersey.

Related entry: Lafayette

Suggestions for further reading:
"From Duportail," 3 March 1784 (*Con. Ser.,* vol. 1).
"To Duportail," 4 April 1784 (*Con. Ser.,* vol. 1).
"To Lafayette," 23 December 1784 (*Con. Ser.,* vol. 2).
"To Edward Newenham," 25 November 1785 (*Con. Ser.,* vol. 3).
Virginia Journal. and Alexandria Advertiser, 8 December 1785.
American Daily Advertiser, 10 January 1793.
Philadelphia General Advertiser, 10 January 1793.

Barbados

Washington's only trip outside the continental United States took place during the winter of 1751–1752, when he accompanied his older half brother Lawrence to the Leeward Islands in search of restorative cures for the latter's failing health. An entry in Washington's fragmented diary account of the voyage indicates that he prepared for the trip by reading the Reverend Griffith Hughes's *Natural History of Barbados* (London, 1750), a folio volume "heavily laden with botanical lore." Lawrence and George apparently sailed to Barbados on board Capt. Jeremiah Cranston's forty-ton square-sterned merchant sloop, the *Success,* which was moving down the Potomac River about 28 September 1751 with a crew of eight men and a cargo of 31 barrels of herring, 984 bushels of corn, 4,480 barrel staves, and 7,627 feet of lumber. Washington's diary entries written during the voyage, kept in the form of a captain's log, concentrated on the sloop's progress and the severe weather caused by hurricanes in the area of Jamaica and a strong earthquake centered at Santo Domingo. Once at their destination the brothers sought out prominent island merchant and planter Gedney Clarke (1711–1764), a native of Salem, Massachusetts, who owned property in Virginia and whose sister Deborah was the wife of Lawrence Washington's father-in-law, William Fairfax. George mentioned by name about two dozen people in his diary, including physicians, ship masters, and friends and relations of the Clarkes.

Upon arriving at Bridgetown, on Carlisle Bay, on 2 November, the Washingtons found temporary lodging at the home of James Carter (d. 1753), a former member of the council and at that time chief justice of grand sessions, who introduced the brothers to other members of the island's political and commercial elite. Lawrence immediately sought medical advice for his pulmonary condition from Dr. William Hillary (1697–1763), a newly arrived physician who had been trained at Leyden. When Lawrence's health was declared, in George's words, "not so fixed but that a cure might be effectually made," he and his brother then rented a house overlooking the bay from a Captain Croftan (or Crofton) for £15 a month, a sum considered extravagant by the two Virginians. Despite the initial favorable prognosis, however, Lawrence's health continued to deteriorate rapidly, and he began to think that the climate of Bermuda might offer him a better chance for recovery. Meanwhile, George himself was struck with smallpox on 16 November, a relatively mild attack that lasted nearly a month. Dr. John Lanahan, a third-generation resident of the island, treated George during his illness. George's bout with smallpox while at Barbados had the valuable effect of protecting him from the disease for the rest of his life, the implications of which were especially significant when the disease was rampant during the Revolutionary War. It also was probably the reason that he became an early advocate of immunization.

Even sickness could not prevent the two brothers from enjoying their brief stay on the island, however. Long conversations with prominent islanders about shipping and trade, agriculture, and military affairs were punctuated by solitary morning rides, prescribed for Lawrence's health, and evenings of dancing and socializing. George's lifelong love of the theater may have gotten its start at Barbados, when he attended a performance of George Lillo's *The London Merchant, or the History of George Barnwell.*

On 19 December, with his elder half brother destined for Bermuda, Washington placed his clothes on board Capt. John Saunders's fifty-ton square-sterned brig, the *Industry,* which sailed away from Barbados three days later with seven men and a cargo that included 1,230 gallons of rum. A "brisk trade Wind and pretty large Swell" on the second day at sea "made the Ship rowl much and me very sick at 2 P:M:," wrote George, and on Christmas eve, "A Fresh gale for what in this part of the World is called a fiery Breize hurried us pass the Leeward Islands," forcing the captain to alter the vessel's course. Christmas day was calmer, "fine clear and pleasant with moderate Sea," and the voyagers celebrated the holiday by eating "Irish goose," which had been saved "for the purpose some Weeks" before, and drinking "a health to our absent friends." The *Industry,* after clearing the Virginia capes at sunrise on a day in late January 1752, sailed into the mouth of the York River around 11 P.M. that evening, where it was met by a pilot boat that guided it up the river. On his way home Washington stopped at Williamsburg, where he dined with Gov. Robert Dinwiddie, whose service as surveyor general of customs for the

Southern District of America had taken him to Gedney Clarke's home in Barbados as early as 1738.

Related entry: Washington, Lawrence

Suggestion for further reading:
Diaries, vol. 1.

Bassett, Burwell, Sr. (1734–1793)

George Washington must have had an extremely affectionate relationship with Burwell Bassett, the husband of Martha Washington's sister Anna Maria Dandridge Bassett (1739–1777), for an early letter to Bassett from Washington was written so lightly, said Douglas Southall Freeman, "almost facetiously, and in a tone and spirit wholly different" from that usually employed by Washington, that the historian regarded it as spurious. The original manuscript in Washington's own hand, written on 28 August 1762, since has come to light, however. After chiding Bassett in jest about penning a letter on Sunday morning "when you ought to have been at Church, praying as becomes every good Christian Man who has as much to answer for as you have," Washington accused him of sitting around "lost in admiration" of a newborn child to the neglect of "your Crops &c.—pray how will this be reconciled to that anxious care and vigilance, which is so escencially necessary at a time when our growing Property—meaning the Tobacco—is assailed by every villainous worm that has had an existence since the days of Noah (how unkind it was of Noah now I have mentioned his name to suffer such a brood of Vermin to get a birth in the Ark) but perhaps you may be as well of[f] as we are—that is, have no Tobacco for them to eat and there I think we nicked the Dogs, as I think to do you if you expect any more."

Bassett, who had been one of the four commissioners for the estate of Martha Washington's first husband, Daniel Parke Custis (1711–1757), lived with his family at Eltham, a plantation a few miles outside Williamsburg on the Pamunkey River in New Kent County. Washington usually stopped by Eltham when business dealings or the Virginia general assembly drew him to Williamsburg, and if Martha and the children were along, which frequently was the case, the family lodged with the Bassetts. While on these trips the Washingtons sometimes visited the Williamsburg home of Burwell's mother, Elizabeth Churchill Bassett Dawson (1709–1779), who had remarried after the death of Bassett's father, William Bassett III (d. 1752). Washington often relied on his brother-in-law to transact business for him in Williamsburg, and thus the correspondence between the two men is filled not only with the latest news and gossip and their views about the politics of the moment but also with discussions about personal finances, tobacco, agriculture, horses, and livestock breeding. Bassett also joined Washington and Fielding Lewis (husband of Washington's sister, Betty), and some few others in forming a company empowered by the Virginia general assembly to drain the Great Dismal Swamp of Virginia for the purpose of harvesting its timber and converting it into farmland, and in May 1763 he accompanied Washington on the latter's first trip to the swamp.

Bassett, like his more famous brother-in-law, had aligned himself with more radical-minded men during his tenure as a delegate to the Virginia House of Burgesses, 1762 to 1775, the very years during which the dispute between the colonies and the mother country began to heat up. He was an energetic representative of Patriot interests in the first four Virginia conventions, between 1774 and 1776, and an active member of the New Kent County committee of safety in 1775 and 1776. Over the years Bassett was more privy than most to Washington's private opinions on the impending crisis with Great Britain, and it was to Bassett that Washington's thoughts turned on the day he was commissioned commander in chief of the Continental army, 19 June 1776. "I am now Imbarkd on a tempestuous Ocean," Washington confided in a letter to Bassett from Philadelphia on that date, "from whence, perhaps, no friendly harbour is to be found. I have been called upon by the unanimous Voice of the Colonies to the Command of the Continental Army—It is an honour I by no means aspired to—It is an honour I wished to avoid, as well from an unwillingness to quit the peaceful enjoyment of my Family as from a thorough conviction of my own Incapacity & want of experience in the conduct of so momentous a concern—but the partiallity of the Congress added to some political motives, left me without a choice." Washington ended the missive by entreating Bassett and his wife to travel to Mount Vernon and relieve the "great uneasiness" he felt about Martha's "lonesome Situation" by taking her home with them to Eltham. Burwell and Anna Maria of course extended an open invitation to Martha and her son, Jacky, to come live at Eltham, an offer occasionally accepted on Martha's part more as an outlet for recreation than as a refuge sought by fears over personal safety. During the war Bassett also helped look after Washington's interest in his Ohio lands, of which Washington informed Bassett "in the worst event, they will serve for an Asylum." (The two had been forced to abandon a planned trip together to the Ohio in 1774 because of pressing business in the Virginia general assembly.)

Characteristic of the time in which they lived, the Bassett and Washington families endured together their share of sorrows. Burwell and Anna Maria, who had married in 1757, lost a daughter, named after her mother, in 1760. Tragedy struck both families in the spring of 1773, when they lost daughters about three months apart. Elizabeth ("Betcy") Bassett (1758–1773), whom Washington described as "so dutiful a Child," and "so promising a young Lady," died in March 1773, and Washington's stepdaughter, Martha Parke "Patsy" Custis, died suddenly three months later. The Bassetts lost another daughter the following July, 10-year-old Anna Maria ("Nancy"), and their eldest son, 14-year-old William ("Billy"), died in November 1774, his passing described by Washington as a "melancholy occasion." In early November 1781, only two weeks after Lord Cornwallis's surrender at Yorktown, Martha Washington's only surviving son, Jacky Custis, died at Eltham, where he had been moved after contracting a fever in the camp at Yorktown. Washington arrived at the Bassetts' home just in time to see his stepson "breathe his last," and stayed several days to attend to his burial.

After the war Washington continued on very cordial terms with Bassett, whose daughter Frances ("Fanny") married Washington's nephew George Augustine Washington in October 1785 to the delight of both families. Both Bassett and his son-in-law died at Eltham within a few weeks of each other in late 1792 and early 1793, the former from a stroke suffered while traveling to Mount Vernon, and the latter after a lingering pulmonary illness. Bassett's namesake and eldest surviving son, Burwell, Jr. (1764–1841), who served for many years in the Virginia general assembly and in the U.S. House of Representatives and was the heir of Eltham, was also a great favorite of his aunt and uncle.

Related entries: Humor; Washington, George Augustine; Washington, Martha Dandridge Custis

Suggestions for further reading:
Diaries, vols. 1–5.
"To Burwell Bassett," 28 August 1762 (*Col. Ser.*, vol. 7).
"To Burwell Bassett," 10 June 1775 (*War Ser.*, vol. 1).

"To Burwell Bassett," 30 October 1778 (*Writings,* vol. 13).

"To Burwell Bassett," 23 May 1785 (*Con. Ser.,* vol. 3).

Belvoir

On the southern shore of the Potomac River in Fairfax County, Virginia, not far below Mount Vernon, once lay the beautiful country seat of Col. William Fairfax, land agent for his distant cousin Thomas, Lord Fairfax, the sole owner of the Northern Neck Proprietary. Built around 1741, Belvoir, meaning in the French language "beautiful to see," was the nearest large estate on the river to Mount Vernon, just a brief carriage ride or even briefer boat trip away. With its handsome and commodious rooms adorned by luxurious carpets and rich furniture imported from England, Belvoir was one of the most richly furnished homes in the colony. Washington was first introduced to Belvoir's refined atmosphere and cultivated company, augmented by uniformed servants, while in his early teens, during stays at Mount Vernon with his half brother Lawrence, who was married to William and Deborah Clarke Fairfax's daughter Anne. The gay scenes provided at the house gave the youth his first exposure to Old World elegance and English excellence. At Belvoir, Washington established intimate and lasting friendships with the colonel's sons George William and Bryan; with George William's wife, Sarah Cary ("Sally") Fairfax; and with Lord Fairfax himself.

Belvoir was the home of George William and Sally Fairfax beginning in 1757. Before they sailed for England in July 1773, never to return, George William gave Washington power of attorney to manage his business affairs in America, which included the supervision of Belvoir, with the plantation's mansion house, slaves, gardens, fields, pasture, timber, fisheries, and livestock. Washington assumed the responsibility until the spring of 1775, when he left the colony to take command of the Continental army.

A newspaper advertisement designed to attract a lessee for the property in June 1774 gives a contemporary description of Belvoir at the time that it was under Washington's supervision:

> BELVOIR, the beautiful Seat of the Honourable *George William Fairfax,* Esq; lying upon *Potowmack* River in *Fairfax* County, about fourteen Miles below *Alexandria.* The Mansion House is of Brick, two Stories high, with four convenient Rooms and a large Passage on the lower Floor, five Rooms and a Passage on the second, and a Servants Hall and Cellars below, convenient Offices, Stables, and Coach House adjoining, as also a large and well furnished Garden, stored with a great Variety of valuable Fruits, in good Order. Appertaining to the Tract on which these Houses stand, and which contains near 2000 Acres (surrounded in a Manner by navigable Water) are several valuable Fisheries, and a good Deal of cleared Land in different Parts, which may be let altogether, or separately, as shall be found most convenient. The Terms may be known of Colonel *Washington,* who lives near the Premises, or of me in *Berkeley* County. FRANCIS WILLIS, Junior.

Accompanying the advertisement was a notice that the "HOUSEHOLD and KITCHEN furniture of every Kind" would be sold at public auction the following August. Washington was one of the larger purchasers at the sale, paying a total of £169.12.6 for a variety of items, including, in addition to a number of beds, carpets, and looking glasses, £12.10 for "1 Mahogy Chest & drawers in Mrs Ffs. Chamber" (still at Mount Vernon), £12.5 for "1 mahogy Side board," £31 for "12 Chairs & 3 window Curtains from the dining room," £1.6 for "2 Candlesticks & a bust of the Immortal shakespear," and £4 for "a mahogy Card Table." Washington's stepson, John Parke

Custis, also purchased some of the house's furnishings at the sale.

The house was destroyed by fire in 1783. A nineteenth-century visitor to the estate, William H. Snowden, said that the ruins at Belvoir indicated that the two-storied brick house, resting over a full basement, measured sixty by thirty-six feet. At least five brick outbuildings were constructed at the estate, including the land office, a coach house, and stables.

In a letter to George William Fairfax in 1785, Washington expressed an earnest wish to see Fairfax and his wife resettled at the old place, and even offered to open Mount Vernon's doors to them until they "could build with convenience." Washington allowed himself to reminisce, uncharacteristically:

But alas! Belvoir is no more! I took a ride there the other day to visit the ruins—& ruins indeed they are. The dwelling house & the two brick buildings in front, underwent the ravages of the fire; the walls of which are very much injured: the other Houses are sinking under the depredation of time & inattention, & I believe are now scarcely worth repairing. In a word, the whole are, or very soon will be a heap of ruin. When I viewed them—when I considered that the happiest moments of my life had been spent there—when I could not trace a room in the house (now all rubbish) that did not bring to my mind the recollection of pleasing scenes; I was obliged to fly from them; & came home with painful sensations, & sorrowing for the contrast.

Fairfax replied from England that he and Mrs. Fairfax were "extremely obliged, by your very friendly and polite Invitation to Mount Vernon, which it is impossible for us to think of accepting," at this late point of life. "Your pathetic discription of the Ruin of Belvoir House produced many tears & sighs from the former Mistress of it, tho' at the first hearing of the Fire, she felt no shock." In May 1798, a full half century after his first visits to the estate, Washington

wrote Sarah Fairfax: "And it is matter of sore regret, when I cast my eyes towards Belvoir, which I often do, to reflect that the former Inhabitants of it, with whom we lived in such harmony & friendship, no longer reside there; and that the ruins can only be viewed as the memento of former pleasures." Plans to rebuild Belvoir by a younger member of the family in the early 1790s never materialized, and in 1814 the remaining walls of the house were leveled by shells from British ships.

Related entry: Fairfax, William

Suggestions for further reading:
Diaries, vols. 1–4.
"From George William Fairfax," 10 January 1774 (*Col. Ser.*, vol. 9).
"To George William Fairfax," 27 February 1785 (*Con. Ser.*, vol. 2).
"To John Sinclair," 11 December 1796 (*Writings*, vol. 35).
"To Sarah Cary Fairfax," 16 May 1798 (*Ret. Ser.*, vol. 2).
Snowden, William H. 1894. *Some Old Historic Landmarks of Virginia and Maryland Described in a Hand-book for the Tourist . . .* Philadelphia.
Stegeman, John F. 1984. "Lady of Belvoir: This Matter of Sally Fairfax" (*Virginia Cavalcade*, vol. 34).
Waterman, Thomas Tileston. 1946. *The Mansions of Virginia, 1706–1776.* Chapel Hill, NC.

Biddle, Clement (1740–1814)

Philadelphia merchant Clement Biddle served as Washington's purchasing agent and seller of produce for Mount Vernon in the 1780s and 1790s. The two had become acquainted during the Revolutionary War, when, with the rank of colonel, Biddle served as deputy quartermaster general, commissary general of forage, and aide-de-camp to Maj. Gen. Nathanael Greene in the Continental army, and as quartermaster general for the Pennsylvania militia. Biddle became a judge in the Pennsylvania Court of Common Pleas in 1788, and in September 1789 Washington named him U.S. marshal for Pennsylvania. The correspondence between Biddle and Washington is full of mundane affairs related to purchases for Mount Vernon. Washington frequently requested Biddle to obtain a myriad of items for use at Mount Vernon, including coffee, wine, grass seed, livery lace, surveying chains, broadcloth, spinning wheels, blankets, Windsor chairs, candles, curtains, mattresses, brass-wired sieves, papier-mâché room decorations, glass, nails, and hinges. Biddle also negotiated bills of exchange for Washington and placed advertisements in Philadelphia newspapers respecting Washington's western lands, as well as obtaining more personal items for Washington, including boots, shoes, and books on agriculture. Biddle failed at business three separate times, forcing Washington to discreetly inquire about his ability to conduct business on occasion, but nevertheless Washington used him over the years to conduct "all my business in Philadelphia . . . to my satisfaction."

Related entries: Greene, Nathanael; Mount Vernon; Presidency

Suggestions for further reading:
Diaries, vols. 4–6.
"From Clement Biddle," 7 March 1785 (*Con. Ser.,* vol. 2).
"To Clement Biddle," 5 December 1786 (*Con. Ser.,* vol. 4).
"To Clement Biddle," 15 March 1789 (*Pres. Ser.,* vol. 1).
"To Oliver Wolcott, Jr.," 22 January 1798 (*Ret. Ser.,* vol. 2).

Birthday

"*G*eorge Washington Son to Augustine & Mary his Wife was born the 11th Day of February 1731/2 about 10 in the Morning & was baptised the 5th of April following Mr Beverley Whiting & Capt. Christopher Brooks Godfathers and Mrs Mildred Gregory Godmother." So reads the record of Washington's birth in the family Bible. The old-style calendar entry of 11 February 1731/32 became obsolete in 1752, when the British corrected their calendar by adding eleven days, making Washington's birth date under the new style 22 February 1732. Yet during Washington's lifetime there remained some confusion about when to celebrate his birthday.

Washington himself apparently took little, if any, notice of his birthday before the Revolutionary War. One of the earliest public celebrations took place at Valley Forge, Pennsylvania, on 22 February 1778, when musicians from Col. Thomas Proctor's Continental Artillery Regiment serenaded their commander in chief. The count de Rochambeau declared Monday, 12 February 1781, a holiday for the French army; the cessation from labor was accompanied by a parade and an artillery salute. Washington's diary entries for the years before 1788 for the days of both 11 and 22 February indicate that he was busy about his typical plantation routine—riding about the farms, fixing fences, mending a favorite horse's smashed leg, foxhunting, etc. However, the title of a pamphlet printed in Philadelphia in 1786, *Virginia: A Pastoral Drama, on the Birth-day of an Illustrious Personage and the Return of Peace, February 11th, 1784,* indicates that by 1784 at least some across the country were beginning to think of birthday celebrations as a fitting way to honor the victorious American general. But as Washington wrote to Rochambeau following the 1781 celebration, "The flattering distinction paid to the anniversary of my birthday is an honor for which I dare not attempt to express my gratitude. I confide in your Excellency's sensibility to interpret my feelings for this, and for the obliging manner in which you are pleased to announce it."

By 1788, however, Washington too was celebrating his birthday, for in that year he intended to celebrate his fifty-sixth birthday on 11 February, new style, with a party of visitors that included former French and

A composite illustration for Washington's birthday, from "Gleason's Pictorial," 1854 (Library of Congress)

British officers touring the United States, and some local friends from the neighborhood of Mount Vernon, but bad weather postponed the festivities until the afternoon of 13 February. After dinner the ladies left the room, recalled British officer John Enys, "but the Gentlemen continued for some time longer. There were no public toasts of any kind given, the General himself introducing a round of Ladies as soon as the Cloath was removed, by saying he had always a very great esteem for the Ladies, and therefore drank them in preference to any thing else."

Washington himself still seemed to harbor some ambivalence about the subject, however, as evidenced in his letter to Clement Biddle of 14 February 1790: "In reply to your wish to know the Presidents birthday it will be sufficient to observe that it is on the 11th of February *Old Style;* but the almanack makers have generally set it

down opposite to the 11th day of February of the present Style; how far that may go towards establishing it on that day I dont know; but I could never consider it any otherways than as stealing so many days from his valuable life as is the difference between the old and the new Style." Four days later the *New-York Journal, and Weekly Register* called attention to the fact that "the Birth-Day of the President of the United States was celebrated at Philadelphia the eleventh inst.," which of course was 11 February *new style*. In New York City, however, the Society of St. Tammany held an elaborate celebration on 22 February after resolving unanimously "That the 22d day of February (corresponding with the 11th Feb. old stile) be this day, and ever hereafter, commemorated by this Society as the BIRTH DAY of the illustrious GEORGE WASHINGTON." The president's birthday apparently was celebrated on the latter date in many other places as well, and Philadelphia followed suit the following year.

Other cities, including Baltimore and Boston, celebrated 11 February new style. Henry Jackson, a native of the latter city who had served as a colonel of one of Washington's Sixteen Additional Continental Regiments during the Revolutionary War, briefly described the happenings that took place in Boston in Washington's honor on 11 February 1791 in a letter to Henry Knox written two days later. "Friday we Celebrated the Presidents Birthday," Jackson informed Knox, then a member of Washington's cabinet, and "at day light 13 Cannon were discharged, and all the Vessels in the harbour display'd their Flags—upwards of Eighty gentlemen dined at Concert Hall, and after dinner, 13 Cannon were fire'd on giving the President as the first Toast . . . in the Eveng we adjourn'd to Feby 11. 1792—We had four Clergymen with us . . . we passed a joyous day which we closed with the greatest harmony and friendship—yesterday I paid for *82* Bottles of Maderia Wine we drank on the Occasion." Washington, however, as his secretary Tobias Lear informed Thomas Jefferson on 11 February 1792, already had begun considering the "22d day of this month as his birth day—having been born on the 11th old Style[.] T. Lear further adds, that the President does not expect to see any Company today on the above occasion." That birthday, Washington's sixtieth, was celebrated ceremoniously, with the Senate and House of Representatives adjourning to pay Washington a visit in a body, and with numerous balls thrown across Philadelphia. In 1793, coming on the heels of the count of the electoral vote, the celebration was "as hearty and affectionate as ever." Freneau printed a twenty-eight-line ode to Washington on his birthday in the latter year in the 23 February issue of the *Gazette of the United States*.

Washington alluded to some of the other birthday celebrations held in his honor in his diary entries. For instance, on 22 February 1797 Washington went to an "elegant entertainmt. given on my birth night," at Ricketts's Amphitheatre in Philadelphia, followed by, according to *Claypoole's Advertiser,* a ball "which for Splendour, Taste and Elegance, was, perhaps, never excelled by any similar Entertainment in the United States." The following year, however, Washington celebrated his birthday with his family by attending a ball given in his honor by the citizens of Alexandria, Virginia, on the evening of Monday, 12 February. Washington's granddaughter Nelly Custis's old Philadelphia music master was performing with the band that evening. "His clarinet sounds as sweetly as ever," wrote Nelly, and the ballroom was "crouded, there were twenty five or thirty couples in the first two setts . . . we danced until two o'clock." Washington celebrated his last birthday in similar fashion, on 11 February 1799: "Went up to Alexandria to the celebration of my birth day. Many Manæuvres were performed by the Uniform Corps and an elegant Ball & Supper at Night." Following Washington's death annual observances of his birthday quickly became the nearest thing to a national holiday.

Related entries: Ancestry; Lewis, Eleanor Parke Custis; Popes Creek; Rochambeau

Suggestions for further reading:
Diaries, vols. 5–6.
"To Rochambeau," 24 February 1781 (*Writings,* vol. 21).
"To Clement Biddle," 14 February 1790 (*Writings,* vol. 31).
"Tobias Lear to Thomas Jefferson," 11 February 1792 (*Pres. Ser.,* vol. 9).
"Tobias Lear to David Humphreys," 8 April 1792 (*Pres. Ser.,* vol. 9).
"Fisher Ames to Christopher Gore," 25 February 1798 (*Works of Fisher Ames,* vol. 2).
New-York Journal, and Weekly Register, 18 February 1790.
Gazette of the United States (Philadelphia), 23 February 1791.
Claypoole's Advertiser (Philadelphia), 23 February 1797.

Boston, Siege of

hen Washington arrived at Cambridge, Massachusetts, in July 1775, the British were already confined to Boston across the Charles River. The American troops lay sprawled about the outskirts of Boston. It was an army short of uniforms and equipment, weapons and ammunition, steady rations and decent barracks, and, most important, training and discipline. Washington's first course of action was to ascertain American strength by demanding exact returns of troops and supplies. The returns from the army's thirty-six regiments filtered in slowly, showing a total of 16,770 troops, consisting of 1,598 sick, 1,429 absent, and 13,743 present and fit for duty. Washington reorganized the army into three divisions of two brigades each, with six regiments in each brigade. The three divisions were encamped at Prospect Hill, Cambridge, and Roxbury, commanded by Charles Lee, Israel Putnam, and Artemas Ward, respectively. As weeks passed without any major military action, both sides settled into demoralizing inactivity. Over time, however, the fortunes of the poorly supplied British troops declined daily, while those of the Americans grew as the various states sent food and supplies to their troops. In August proposals for blockading Boston Harbor were entertained, with no success, but later in the month Plowed Hill on the Mystic River was occupied, to the consternation of the British, although the Americans could not take advantage of their success owing to a lack of powder. In September, Washington polled his general officers as to the feasibility of attacking the British so as to bring "a speedy finish of the dispute," but a council of war unanimously agreed it was "not expedient to make the Attempt at present at least." In October committees from the Continental Congress and the New England governments converged on Washington's headquarters to discuss the state of the army. The question

George Washington (on horseback) and American troops look out toward ships in the harbor as the British evacuate Boston (Library of Congress)

of whether to attack Boston was revisited and again dismissed. As winter approached, the main concern on the American side was the preparation of winter quarters and the scheduled year-end expiration of enlistments, and the possibility that a large number of soldiers would return to their homes and farms. As the weather began to turn cold, Washington sent Henry Knox to bring cannon from Ticonderoga and Crown Point. Upon Knox's return some of the cannon were deposited at the existing American works at Lechmere Point, Cobble Hill, and Roxbury. In March the Americans' overnight fortification of Dorchester Heights so completely surprised the British that one officer exclaimed the works had been "raised with an expedition to equal to that of the Genii belonging to Aladdin's Wonderful Lamp." Unprepared, the British put up only token resistance for a few days before making a hasty and confused evacuation of Boston, completed on 17 March 1776.

Related entries: Gage, Thomas; Lee, Charles; Putnam, Israel; Ward, Artemas; Washington Elm

Suggestions for further reading:
"Council of War," 11 September 1775 (*War Ser.,* vol. 1).
"Council of War," 8, 18 October 1775 (*War Ser.,* vol. 2).
"Proceedings of the Committee of Conference," 18–24 October 1775 (*War Ser.,* vol. 2).

Boucher, Jonathan (1738–1804)

Jonathan Boucher came to Virginia from Cumberland, England, in 1759 as a tutor in a gentleman's family at Port Royal in King George County. In 1764, after taking orders in the Episcopal ministry, he became rector of St. Mary's Parish in Caroline County, about six miles from Fredericksburg, where, with his unmarried sister Jane ("Jenny"), he opened a popular boarding school for boys. Washington placed Martha's son, Jacky Custis, with Boucher in 1768, when Jacky was fourteen. For the next five years Boucher and Washington frequently exchanged letters regarding Jacky's progress, or lack of it. Boucher initially thought his amiable charge was an "exceedingly mild & meek" tempered boy with a "peculiar Innocence & *Sanctity of Manners.*" Jacky was, it was true, "far fm being a brilliant Genius," said Boucher, but he held out a fair promise of growing into "a good & a useful Man." Later Boucher came to believe Jacky nearly incorrigible and told Washington so: "I must confess to you I never did in my life know a youth so exceedingly indolent or so surprisingly voluptuous: one would suppose Nature had intended him for some Asiatic Prince."

Boucher considered young Custis the most important of his pupils, which at times numbered more than thirty, and he treated him accordingly. He accompanied Jacky to Mount Vernon for holidays and other festivities, and Washington sometimes lodged with Boucher at Annapolis, Maryland, after Boucher moved his school to the city in 1770. At Washington's insistence, but without letting the boy's mother know, Boucher took Jacky to Baltimore, where they successfully underwent inoculation against smallpox. He attempted to persuade the boy's parents that a proper gentleman's education could be provided Jacky only in Europe, with himself as guide and mentor, but Martha eventually decided a sea voyage was too risky and convinced Washington that it would be a pecuniary waste given Jacky's unpreparedness to benefit from such a trip. In the end Boucher taught the boy little, and he reflected that his attention to Jacky was not "so close nor so rigid, as I wish'd, or, as it ought to have been . . . I have hitherto, I thank God, conducted Him with tolerable Safety, thro' some pretty trying & perilous Scenes; &, remiss as I am, or may seem to be, I doubt not, in due Time, to deliver Him up to You a *good* Man, if not a very *learned* one." When Washington finally decided that Jacky was old enough to go to college, Boucher steered Washington into sending him to King's College in New York, rather than the College of William and Mary in Williamsburg or the College of New Jersey at Princeton.

Boucher remained loyal to the Crown during the Revolutionary War even though he earlier had been a vigorous supporter of the nonimportation association formed by the colonies as a result of their opposition to British policy. In August 1775 Boucher wrote a long letter to Washington, who was by then commander in chief of the Continental army at Cambridge, Massachusetts, complaining about Washington's inattention to Boucher's treatment by local Whigs, who had expelled him from his parish. He was writing not to reiterate "the great points so long and so fruitlessly debated between us," said Boucher, but rather to raise the ground where "I complain of you and those with whom you side." Although he did not directly accuse Washington of being the cause of his own misfortune, Boucher nevertheless told his former employer that "it is not a little that you have to answer for with respect to myself." Charging Washington with standing "at least as an unconcerned spectator, if not an abettor" to his sufferings, he concluded: "You are no longer worthy of my friendship: a man of honour can no longer without dishonour be connected with you. With your cause I renounce you." About a month later Boucher sailed to England aboard the British ship *Choptank Frigate,* never to return to America. Boucher served as vicar of Epsom from 1785 to his death.

In the spring of 1784 Boucher attempted to renew a correspondence with Washington, writing not "to trouble You with any Reflections of mine," he said, "on the many great Events that have taken Place within the last Eight or nine years," or to discuss how the two had differed in their opinions, but to request Washington to "do something for the Religious Interests" of the new American nation, similar to what he had accomplished for its "Civil Concerns." His own motives were pure, Boucher insisted, arising only from "Zeal for the Church & the best Interests of Mankind." The "Thing should be attended to, & soon, & that You are particularly concerned to attend it, because no other Man can do it with such Advantage." Washington typically did not occupy himself with religious concerns, and no reply to Boucher's letter has been identified. Boucher wrote Washington a final time in November 1797 to convey a volume of political tracts that he dedicated to Washington, which the latter acknowledged with his thanks the following year.

Related entries: Custis, John Parke; Education

Suggestions for further reading:
Diaries, vols. 2, 3.
"From Jonathan Boucher," 2 August 1768 (*Col. Ser.*, vol. 8).
"From Jonathan Boucher," 19 November 1771 (*Col. Ser.*, vol. 8).
"From Jonathan Boucher," 6 August 1775 (*War Ser.*, vol. 1).
"From Jonathan Boucher," 25 May 1784 (*Con. Ser.*, vol. 1).
"From Jonathan Boucher," 8 November 1797 (*Ret. Ser.*, vol. 1).
Boucher, Jonathan. 1797. *A View of the Causes and Consequences of the American Revolution in Thirteen Discourses. Preached in North America between the Years 1763 and 1775.* London.

Bouquet, Henry (1719–1765)

See Forbes Campaign.

Braddock's Defeat

"We have been most scandalously beaten by a trifling body of men," was Washington's immediate assessment of the disastrous culmination on 9 July 1755 of Braddock's expedition against

The burial of General Braddock (Library of Congress)

the French at Fort Duquesne. "When we came there, we were attackd by a body of French and Indns whose number (I am certain) did not exceed 300 Men; our's consisted of abt 1,300 well armed Troops; *chiefly* of the English Soldiers, who were struck with such a panick, that they behavd with more cowardice than it is possible to conceive."

Following Washington's capitulation of Fort Necessity in July 1754, the British ministry decided to send two regiments of British regulars to America under the command of Maj. Gen. Edward Braddock (c.1695–1755). By this time Braddock, who was born in Ireland but not of Irish descent, had been in active service for nearly forty-five years, much of it in the Coldstream Guards. He landed at Hampton Roads, Virginia, in February 1755, and was followed soon by about a thousand Irish troops. Alexandria was designated as the initial rendezvous point for the troops, provisions, and artillery needed for the expedition. Convoys set off for Wills Creek in

April, converging in the area in late May. Braddock planned to remove the French from Fort Duquesne, construct and garrison a strong British fort on the Ohio, and drive the French from British-claimed territory on the Great Lakes, on Lake Champlain, and in Nova Scotia.

Washington initially declined to serve in the campaign because of the "disagreeableness" he thought would arise over the regulation of command between regular and provincial officers. Braddock extended an invitation for him to join his military family, "by which all inconveniences of that kind will be obviated." Washington accepted the offer "agreeably enough, as I am thereby freed from all command but his, and give Order's to all, which must be implicitly obey'd. I have now a good oppertunity, and shall not neglect it, of forming an acquaintance which may be serviceable hereafter, if I can find it worth while to push my Fortune in the Military way." In serving, Washington declared, he wished for "nothing more earnestly, than to attain a small degree of knowledge in the Military Art." He communicated with Braddock through Robert Orme (d. 1790), Braddock's principal aide-de-camp, with whom he became good friends during the course of the campaign.

By early June Braddock's force consisted of 1,760 troops, including a thousand men from the Forty-fourth and Forty-eighth British regiments, a detachment of royal artillery, three independent companies, 463 provincials, companies from North Carolina and Maryland, and thirty British sailors. Between Wills Creek and the Great Crossing of the Youghiogheny River, the troops were harassed by small parties of French and Indians. Washington fell ill on 14 June with "Fevers and Pains" and five days later had to remain behind while the army moved forward. He was carried to the front in a covered wagon on 8 July and witnessed the disastrous defeat the following day.

Washington gave an account of the battle in his 1787 "Remarks" for David Humphreys' biography of him. About midmorning on 9 July, after the vanguard had crossed the Monongahela River, about seven miles from the French fort, "and the rear yet in the River the front was attacked; and by the unusual Hallooing and whooping of the enemy, whom they could not see, were so disconcerted and confused as soon to fall into irretrievable disorder." The rear came forward to support the vanguard, "but seeing no enemy, and themselves falling every moment from the fire, a general panic took place among the Troops from which no exertions of the Officers could recover them. . . . before it was *too late,* & the confusion became general an offer was made by G. W. to head the Provincials, & engage the enemy in their own way; but the propriety of it was not seen into until it was too late for execution." During the two-hour battle, Braddock received his fatal wound, "but previous to it, had several horses killed &

disabled under him." Washington placed the general in a "small covered Cart, which carried some of his most essential equipage, and in the best order he could," transported him back across the Monongahela. Of Braddock, Washington wrote, "thus died a man, whose good & bad qualities were intimtely blended. He was brave even to a fault and in regular Service would have done honor to his profession—His attachments were warm—his enmities were strong—and having no disguise about him, both appeared in full force. He was generous & disinterested—but plain and blunt in his manner even to rudeness." Braddock was buried "in two Blankits in the high Road that was cut for the Wagons, that all the Wagons might March Over him and the Army to hinder" any Indians from taking him up and scalping him.

Braddock's officers suffered heavy casualties as well; of ninety-six, twenty-six were killed and thirty-six wounded. His aides-de-camp were all wounded, too, except for Washington, who "remained his sole aid through the day," although Washington too had "one horse killed, and two wounded under him—A ball through his hat—and several through his clothes, but escaped unhurt." "The shocking Scenes which presented themselves in this Nights March are not to be described—The dead—the dying—the groans—lamentation—and crys along the Road of the wounded for help . . . were enough to pierce a heart of adamant. the gloom & horror of which was not a little encreased by the impervious darkness occasioned by the close shade of thick woods." Fortunately for the retreating wounded, the enemy was more interested in scrambling for the baggage than pursuing the troops. The troops went to Great Meadows to regroup before continuing their retreat to Fort Cumberland.

Washington was appointed colonel of the Virginia Regiment in the wake of Braddock's defeat, and the so-called Indian Prophecy that Washington would not die in battle had its origin in Washington's emergence unscathed from Braddock's defeat.

Related entries: Carlyle, John; Gage, Thomas; The Indian Prophecy

Suggestions for further reading:
"The Letter Book for the Braddock Campaign," 2 March–14 August 1755 (*Col. Ser.*, vol. 1).
"From Edward Braddock," 15 May 1755 (*Col. Ser.*, vol. 1).
"To Mary Ball Washington," 18 July 1755 (*Col. Ser.*, vol. 1).
"To Robert Dinwiddie," 18 July 1755 (*Col. Ser.*, vol. 1).
"Appointment as Colonel of the Virginia Regiment," 14 August 1755 (*Col. Ser.*, vol. 2).
"Braddock's Defeat" (vol. 2, appendix 4). Jared Sparks. 1834–1837. 12 vols. *The Writings of George Washington.* Boston.
Hamilton, Charles, ed. 1959. *Braddock's Defeat.* Norman, OK.
Zagarri, Rosemarie. 1991. *David Humphreys' "Life of General Washington" with George Washington's "Remarks."* Athens, GA.

Brandywine, Battle of

The Battle of Brandywine on 11 September 1777 was a bitter defeat for Washington and the American army. Combined with British general William Howe's subsequent outmaneuvering of Washington and entry into Philadelphia on 26 September, it resulted in a blow to American prestige that would be redeemed only partially by Maj. Gen. Horatio Gates's victory at Saratoga. Although contemporary observers rarely ventured to criticize Washington's conduct, preferring to vent their anger on subordinates like Maj. Gen. John Sullivan, the Battle of Brandywine marked one of the poorest performances by an army under Washington's command.

The Philadelphia campaign began on 25 August with the landing of British troops under Howe at Turkey Point, eight miles below Head of Elk, Maryland. The British landing surprised Washington, who had expected the enemy fleet that left Sandy Hook, New Jersey, in July to land somewhere near Charleston, South Carolina. Even so, Washington's army, numbering roughly 16,000 men, was in a good position to defeat or at least contain Howe's advance. Washington had set his troops into motion immediately after British ships were sighted in the Chesapeake Bay, reaching Wilmington, Delaware, just as the British began to land.

While Howe rested his seasick soldiers in the following days, Washington led reconnaissance parties near the British lines. On the night of 26 August, a storm forced him to spend a night with Nathanael Greene and Lafayette in a farmhouse quite close to enemy positions. The British moved forward on 3 September in two divisions, converging at what is now Glasgow, Delaware, where they brushed aside an advance guard of American light infantry at Cooch's Bridge.

Washington ordered the main army to encamp behind Red Clay Creek just west of Newport, Delaware, on the direct route to Philadelphia. Howe threw his army into motion again on 8 September, sending a small force to demonstrate against the American front while the main army marched around Washington's right. By early the next day, Washington had seen through Howe's plan and ordered a redeployment to Chadds Ford on the Brandywine. Howe, meanwhile, proceeded to Kennett Square, reaching it on 10 September. Chadds Ford, where the American army now took up positions, was the last natural line of defense before the Schuylkill River, which could be forded at so many points that it was practically indefensible. The Brandywine, a shallow (knee- to waist-high) but fast-flowing creek, was fordable at comparatively few places and so, it seemed, could be defended fairly easily.

The most vulnerable point of the American position, as Washington and his generals were aware, was on the right. Washington therefore ordered Sullivan, whose division stood on the American right flank,

The Battle of Brandywine, Chadds Ford, Pennsylvania (Library of Congress)

to provide adequate cover at all the known fords in that area. Sullivan, however, delegated responsibility for a part of the flank to the ineffective light horse under the command of Col. Theodorick Bland. Neither Bland nor any of the locals, however, informed Washington or Sullivan of the existence of two fords further north on the Brandywine, known as Jeffries's and Trimble's, which provided an entirely unguarded route around the American right flank. Unfortunately for the Americans, Howe was better acquainted with the local geography.

Early in the morning of 11 September, Howe sent one column of his army under the Hessian lieutenant general Baron Wilhelm von Knyphausen directly toward Chadds Ford; meanwhile Howe marched with 8,200 men northeast from Kennett Square up the Great Valley Road, intending to turn east across the Brandywine at Trimble's and Jeffries's fords, and then around the American right flank. A dense fog cover initially shielded Howe's march, and locals kept him well informed of his route.

In the course of the battle that followed, Washington grappled with poor and often contradictory intelligence reports. Initial reports indicated that Howe had split his forces, but although Knyphausen's forces were in view, it was not clear what had happened to the main column under Howe and Cornwallis. At one point Washington ordered a general attack on Knyphausen's force, which appeared isolated at Chadds Ford, but he canceled the assault after learning that the British forces might not have divided after all. Sullivan was also uncertain about British intentions, but at no point did he request, or Washington offer, any extra precautions for the protection of the right flank. At least one scout, a Pennsylvania militia major, told them that there were no British troops marching in that direction.

Howe's column marched seventeen miles in sweltering heat, crossing the west branch of the Brandywine at Trimble's Ford about 11 o'clock and crossing the east branch at Jeffries's Ford about three hours later. It was not until after one o'clock that Bland sent Washington intelligence of the British movement, but by then it was impossible for Washington to make the proper dispositions to defend against the enemy force now in the rear of his right flank. Three American divisions attempted to hold off the British troops at Birmingham Hill, and fought bravely for a time, but after their defeat there was no choice but to withdraw the army to Chester as quickly as possible.

Washington had presciently positioned Greene's division as a rear guard after the loss of Birmingham Hill, and he personally supervised the preparation of their positions, which would have to hold while the rest of the army left the battlefield. The rear guard's success in fending off the enemy made it possible for the main body of the army to reach Chester that evening without many additional casualties. The official British casualty figure for the day was 89 killed and 488 wounded; the American losses have never been conclusively ascertained, but they were roughly 1,100, consisting of 200 killed, 500 wounded, and 400 captured.

On the whole the American troops had performed well on the battlefield, and Washington himself had shown admirable presence of mind when the tide of battle began to turn in favor of the British. A less-able commander might not have been able to prevent a total rout. The poor American battlefield dispositions, though in large part the result of faulty intelligence (the limitations of which Washington was aware of), were nevertheless ultimately attributable to Washington and his staff. Though in theory defending home territory, Washington's familiarity with the ground over which he would have to fight was in every way inferior to that of Howe. The result for the American army was very nearly disastrous.

The Brandywine Battlefield Park in present-day Delaware County, Pennsylvania, now includes about 50 acres of rolling ground overlooking Chadds Ford and the main battle area. In addition to the park's museum, Lafayette's restored quarters at the Gideon Gilpin House and Washington's reconstructed headquarters at the Benjamin Ring House are open to the public.

Related entry: Germantown, Battle of

Suggestions for further reading:
"Battle of Brandywine," 11 September 1777 (*War Ser.*, vol. 11).
"To John Hancock," 11 September 1777 (*War Ser.*, vol. 11).
Smith, Samuel S. 1976. *The Battle of Brandywine.* Monmouth Beach, NJ.

Bridges Creek

See Popes Creek; Washington, Augustine.

Bullskin Lands (Mountain Quarter)

Bullskin Run empties into the Shenandoah River a few miles northeast of Winchester, Virginia, and a few miles south of Charles Town in present-day Jefferson County, West Virginia. Washington surveyed a number of tracts along the creek beginning in the fall of 1750, including ones for Lord Fairfax and for Richard Stephenson, the stepfather of Washington's close friends William and Valentine Crawford. By March 1752 Washington had acquired for himself by grant or purchase four tracts along the Bullskin, totaling 1,861 acres. He eventually secured several additional, but smaller, tracts on the Bullskin, including one that came into his possession after the death of his half brother Lawrence. Washington's first land purchase in the lower Shenandoah Valley, a 453-acre tract near the head of Evitts Run, also was nearby, as was a 500-acre tract granted to his half brother Augustine in 1750.

The plantations established on the Bullskin lands were used for raising tobacco as early as 1754, and wheat, oats, and corn in the years following. In April 1755 Washington turned over management of the plantations, along with those of Ferry Farm and Mount Vernon, to his brother John Augustine, who looked after them for the next three years. By 1758, when a severe drought struck the area, the operations at Bullskin included a resident overseer, Christopher Hardwick, who served from 1756 to 1762; wagon driver John Adams; about a dozen slaves; a few oxen, cattle, and pigs; and "Horses Enough to do any Business we have to do." Washington was not altogether pleased with the reports he received of the management of the plantations by "my Rascally Overseer Hardwick," however, who was accused of sometimes beating the wagoner. In May 1760 outbreaks of both measles and smallpox ran through the area, prompting Washington to visit the lands, where he found Hardwick laid up with a broken leg and "every thing in the utmost confusion, disorder & backwardness." Hardwick left the Bullskin in 1762, when he agreed to take over Washington's 240-acre tract in Hampshire County, but neither his replacement, Edward Violet, previously the overseer at Washington's Muddy Hole farm at Mount Vernon, nor a succession of other overseers and tenants ever altered Washington's 1760 assessment.

In December 1771 Washington sold 180 acres of his Bullskin land to Philip Pendleton, who in turn sold it the following year to Washington's brother Samuel. Since Pendleton had not yet paid for his purchase, Samuel Washington assumed its responsibility. Samuel's estate at his death in 1781 was encumbered, and Washington carried the debt until his own death, when by the terms of his will it was forgiven. From 1784 to 1790 Battaile Muse, the son of Washington's troublesome old acquaintance from the French and Indian War, George Muse, served as rental agent for Washington's Bull-

skin and other western lands. Of the series of life tenants who occupied the Bullskin lands through the years, the most notable was John Ariss, Virginia's leading house builder before the Revolutionary War. Ariss, who may have taken part in redesigning Mount Vernon in the 1770s, leased a 700-acre tract "Near the white House" on Bullskin Run for £60 a year in 1786 and lived there until his death in the fall of 1799. A few days before his own death, Washington was contemplating the idea of employing Mount Vernon's "supernumerary hands" at Bullskin.

Related entries: Crawford Brothers; Washington's Bottom Tract

Suggestions for further reading:
"From Christopher Hardwick," 3 September 1758 (*Col. Ser.*, vol. 5).
"To James Nourse," 22 January 1784 (*Con. Ser.*, vol. 1).
"List of Tenants," 18 September 1785 (*Con. Ser.*, vol. 3).
"To Robert Lewis," 7 December 1799 (*Ret. Ser.*, vol. 4).

Bushnell, David (1742–1824)

Washington's hopes for the use of a man-propelled submarine, the *Turtle*, which David Bushnell designed in 1775, are the first example of modern submarine warfare. Washington described Bushnell's plan in September 1785 in reply to a query from Thomas Jefferson:

I am sorry I cannot give you full information respecting Captn Bushnals projects for the destruction of Shipping. No interesting experiment having been made, and my memory being treacherous, I may, in some measure, be mistaken in what I am about to relate.

Bushnel is a Man of great Mechanical powers—fertile of invention—and a master in execution—He came to me in 1776 recommended by Governor [Jonathan]

Trumbull (now dead) and other respectable characters who were proselites to his plan. Although I wanted faith myself, I furnished him with money, and other aids to carry it into execution. He laboured for sometime ineffectually, & though the advocates for his scheme continued sanguine he never did succeed. One accident or another was always intervening. I then thought, and still think, that it was an effort of genius; but that a combination of too many things were requisite, to expect much Success from the enterprise against an enemy, who are always upon guard. That he had a Machine which was so contrived as to carry a man under water at any depth he chose, and for a considerable time & distance, with an apparatus charged with Powder which he could fasten to a Ships bottom or side & give fire to in a given time (Sufft for him to retire) by means whereof a ship could be blown up, or Sunk, are facts which I believe admit of little doubt—but then, where it was to operate against an enemy, it is no easy matter to get a person hardy enough to encounter the variety of dangers to which he must be exposed. 1 from the novelty 2 from the difficulty of conducting the Machine, and governing it under Water on Acct of the Currents &ca. 3 the consequent uncertainty of hitting the object of destination, without rising frequently above water for fresh observation, wch when near the Vessel, would expose the Adventurer to a discovery, & almost to certain death—To these causes I always ascribed the nonperformance of his plan, as he wanted nothing that I could furnish to secure the success of it. This to the best of my recollection is a true state of the case—But [David] Humphreys, if I mistake not, being one of the proselites, will be able to give you a more perfect Acct of it than I have done.

Humphreys in fact later did give an extended account of Bushnell's "wonderful machine" in his life of Israel Putnam, as Bushnell himself did in an essay written for the American Philosophical Society in 1799.

Bushnell's plan came to a sudden and inglorious end in October 1776 when the British sunk the American sloop that was carrying the submarine up the Hudson River. In his report to Washington of the *Turtle*'s misfortune, Maj. Gen. William Heath wrote, "The Machine designed for blowing up the Enemy's Ships happened to be on board a Sloop which had the misfortune to be sunk by the Enemy—A Contrast this to blowing of them up." Bushnell successfully recovered the vessel, but, as he wrote after the war, "I found it impossible, at that time to prosecute the design any farther."

Bushnell was appointed a captain-lieutenant in the Continental army corps of sappers and miners in August 1779 and was promoted to captain in 1781. He experienced some difficulties with subordinates in late 1782, for which several of his men were tried and convicted at courts-martial. Washington must have been satisfied with Bushnell's handling of the insubordination, for he soon named him commander of the corps of sappers and miners, an office he held until the end of the war. Bushnell, who had been born in Saybrook, Connecticut, and educated at Yale College, settled farther south after the Revolutionary War and died in Warrenton, Georgia.

As novel as the idea of the *Turtle* may have seemed for the period, Bushnell was not the only person who attempted to build a submarine vessel during the Revolutionary War. Joseph Belton of Groton, Connecticut, a 1769 graduate of the College of Rhode Island, also secured Washington's permission to build a submersible vessel capable of attacking British warships in the Boston Harbor or the Hudson River. Belton, who Benjamin Franklin said appeared to be a "very ingenious Man" when introducing him to Washington, planned to "make a Machine by the help of which, I will carry a loaded cannon, two or three miles up or down any of our harbours without any other assistance, and all the way there should nothing appear above the surface much larger than a man's hat, and

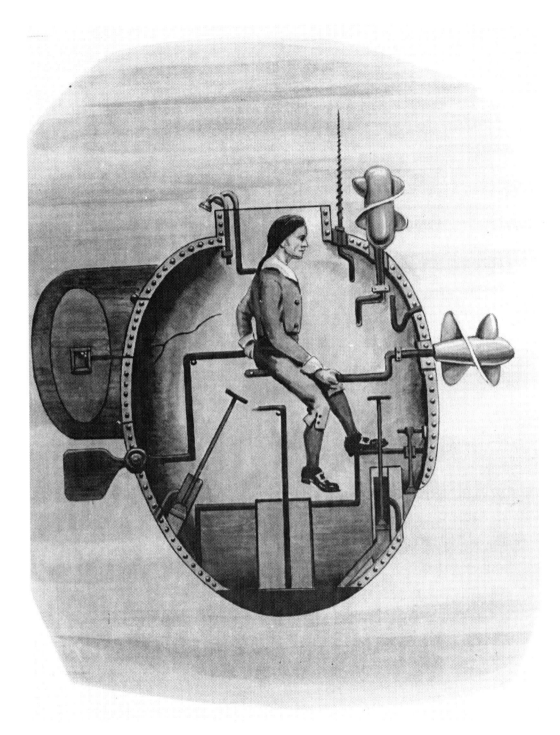

Francis Barber's 1875 rendering of David Bushnell's **Turtle,** *the first American submarine (Library of Congress)*

by attracting [contracting] my Machine, would wholely descend under water for some time, and by expanding, would rise to the surface at pleasure, and by this means, to avoid any discovery when I had arrived within an hundred and fifty, or two hundred yards of a Ship, I could descend under the surface, and go along side of her bottom against which, I could discharge the Cannon, that should be prov'd large enough to send a ball through any ships side." Like Bushnell, Belton was never able to build a successful submarine.

Related entry: Rumsey, James

Suggestions for further reading:
"From Benjamin Franklin," 22 July 1776 (*War Ser.,* vol. 5).
"From William Heath," 10 October 1776 (*War Ser.,* vol. 6).
"To Thomas Jefferson," 26 September 1785 (*Con. Ser.,* vol. 3).
Bushnell, David. 1799. "General Principles and Construction of a Submarine Vessel" (*Transactions of the American Philosophical Society,* vol. 4.).
Humphreys, David. 1788. *An Essay on the Life of the Honourable Major-General Israel Putnam.* Hartford, CT.

C

Carlyle, John (1720–1780)

John Carlyle, who immigrated to America from Dumfrieshire, Scotland, in 1740, was a prominent merchant in Alexandria, Virginia, and an original member of the Ohio Company. In 1747 he married Sarah Fairfax (1730–1761), a daughter of Col. William Fairfax of Belvoir and the sister-in-law of Washington's half brother Lawrence. When planning the 1754 expedition to the Ohio Country, Virginia governor Robert Dinwiddie appointed Carlyle, an officer in the Fairfax County militia since 1750, commissary of provisions and stores, with the rank of major, to be headquartered at Alexandria. Carlyle, who initially was jubilant at the prospect of earning £500 per year as commissary, soon found procuring provisions for the 500 men of the Virginia Regiment to be greatly troublesome and fatiguing (even with three assistants), and ultimately he proved a failure at the business.

In April 1755 the governors of five colonies met British army general Edward Braddock in the Blue Room of Carlyle's handsome new Georgian-style house on Fairfax Street in Alexandria (a museum since 1914) to coordinate their efforts for Braddock's campaign against the French and Indians. At the meeting was 23 year-old George Washington, recently commissioned an aide-de-camp to General Braddock.

Braddock appointed Carlyle "Storekeeper of all Provisions, Arms, Ammunition Bagage" for the campaign. Carlyle failed to find the needed stores for the Braddock expedition, leading Washington to complain to Governor Dinwiddie that he had been "extreamely ill used" but laying the blame upon Carlyle's deputies and saying that he was sorry for Carlyle, "as he is a Gentleman so capable of the Business himself and has taken so much pains to give satisfaction." The routine correspondence between Carlyle and Washington included brief reports about military stores, accounts, and bills of exchange; the shipping of crops, furniture, tools, and other goods, and occasionally military subjects; and usually enclosed letters to be passed on to other people. One interesting order that Carlyle placed for Washington in 1756 included "A fine strong Silver pierced, Boat Shell two edgd Sword Silver & gold gripe, spare & false Scabbard &ca." Carlyle also purchased slaves for Washington on at least one occasion, at the public sale of property belonging to a great planter in financial difficulties in January 1756.

Despite his failures in provisioning the military, Carlyle's reputation as a merchant and the prime mover of goods in the area increased. Carlyle became one of the leading merchants of Alexandria, and, with business partners John Dalton and William Ramsay, his hands were involved in nearly every local transaction. He more than anyone else, in fact, was the man responsible for founding the town and turning a few river warehouses into a thriving community. When it became evident that a new landing was needed for the area, for instance, Carlyle constructed it at his own expense and gave the public half-usage of it. Carlyle shipped wheat, tobacco, and other goods along the Potomac River in several vessels, including his sloop *Swift,* and on the eve of the Revolutionary War, he financed a brigantine, the *Fairfax* (*Anne and Elizabeth*), that sailed to the West Indies with a cargo that included herring and flour belonging to Washington. Washington purchased the latter vessel in 1774 and renamed it the *Farmer.* Carlyle was also one of the managers of the Potomac River Enterprise, an effort in the early 1760s to open the river to small craft to the Great Falls of the Potomac, about fifteen miles above Alexandria.

In addition to their business dealings, Carlyle and Washington met on social terms. Carlyle visited Mount Vernon numerous times, stopping to dine or spend the night while passing through the area, or to go foxhunting, discuss business plans, or compare notes on their respective flour mills. Washington in return often dined at Carlyle's home when in Alexandria. On one occasion Washington attended a ball, sponsored in part by Carlyle, which he mirthfully described in a diary entry:

> Went to a Ball at Alexandria—where Musick and Dancing was the chief Entertainment. However in a convenient Room detachd for the purpose abounded great plenty of Bread and Butter, some Biscuets with Tea, & Coffee which the Drinkers of coud not Distinguish from Hot water sweetned. Be it remembered that pocket handkerchiefs servd the purposes of Table Cloths & Napkins and that no Apologies were made for either. I shall therefore distinguish this Ball by the Stile & title of the Bread & Butter Ball.

> The Proprietors of this Ball were Messrs. Carlyle [Dr. James] Laurie & Robt. Wilson, but the Doctr. not getting it conducted agreeable to his own taste woud claim no share of the merit of it.
> We lodgd at Colo. Carlyles.

Washington apparently played cards at the Bread & Butter Ball, because on the next day he recorded the loss of seven shillings "By Cards" in his ledger accounts. A month later Carlyle and his wife were stranded at Mount Vernon for several days because of inclement weather. (Dr. Laurie, a local physician who had visited Mount Vernon the month before the Bread & Butter Ball to treat some of Washington's slaves for measles, showed up on Washington's doorstep in April of the same year, 1760: "Doctr. Laurie came here. I may add Drunk.") Carlyle also served as the principal administrator of the will of Washington's half brother Lawrence, whose estate descended in part to Washington after the death of Lawrence's daughter Sarah in 1754. On at least one occasion, in May 1761, Carlyle and Washington, joined by Charles Digges of Maryland, managed a horse race together at Alexandria.

Washington and Carlyle's business dealings were strained and their friendship tested in 1767 following a misunderstanding that arose over how to interpret Washington's January 1763 wheat contract with the partnership of Carlyle & Adam. Some years later, in 1770, Washington also purchased a slave, Bath, from the merchant firm of Carlyle & Adam.

Related entries: Braddock's Defeat; Dinwiddie, Robert; Fairfax, William; Washington, Lawrence

Suggestions for further reading:
Diaries, vol. 1.
"To John Carlyle," 14 May 1755 (*Col. Ser.,* vol. 1).
"From John Carlyle," 12 January 1756 (*Col. Ser.,* vol. 2).
"From John Carlyle," 25 July 1758 (*Col. Ser.,* vol. 5).

"To Carlyle & Adam," 15 February 1767 (*Col. Ser.*, vol. 7).

Munson, James D. 1986. *Colo. John Carlyle, Gent.: A True and Just Account of the Man and His House, 1720–1780.* Fairfax Station, VA.

Charles (Carlos) III, King of Spain

See Humor; Royal Gift.

Cherry Tree

"Cut down the two Cherry trees in the Court yard," wrote Washington in his diaries on 18 August 1785, long after the fabled event of his boyhood.

"Pa, (said George very seriously) do I ever tell lies?"

"No, George, I *thank God* you do not, my son; and I rejoice in the hope you never will. At least, you shall never, from me, have cause to be guilty of so shameful a thing."

The story:

The following anecdote is a *case in point.* It is too valuable to be lost, and too true to be doubted; for it was communicated to me by the same excellent lady to whom I am indebted for the last.

"When George," said she, "was about six years old, he was made the wealthy master of a *hatchet!* of which, like most little boys, he was immoderately fond, and was constantly going about chopping every thing that came in his way. One day, in the garden, where he often amused himself hacking his mother's pea-sticks, he unluckily tried the edge of his hatchet on the body of a beautiful young English cherry-tree, which he barked so terribly, that I don't believe the tree ever got the better of it. The next morning the old gentleman finding out what had befallen his tree, which, by the by, was a great favourite, came into the house, and with much warmth asked for the mischievous author, declaring at the same time, that he would not have taken five guineas for his tree. Nobody could tell him any thing about it. Presently George and his hatchet made their appearance. *George,* said his father, *do you know who killed that beautiful little cherry-tree yonder in the garden?* This was a *tough question;* and George staggered under it for a moment; but quickly recovered himself: and looking at his father, with the sweet face of youth brightened with the inexpressible charm of all-conquering truth, he bravely cried out, "*I can't tell a lie, Pa; you know I can't tell a lie. I did cut it with my hatchet.*"—Run to my arms, you dearest boy, cried his father in transports, *run to my arms; glad am I, George, that you killed my tree; for you have paid me for it a thousand fold. Such an act of heroism in my son, is more worth than a thousand trees, though blossomed with silver, and their fruits of purest gold.*

George Washington and the cherry tree (Library of Congress)

Parson Weems's story, which first surfaced in the fifth edition of his popular *Life of Washington* (1808), proved so popular that hardly an author failed to make mention of it when writing about Washington. Millions of children in nineteenth-century America were introduced to it through juvenile literature, McGuffey's *Readers,* or the ever-present Sunday School Union biographies, or, like Abraham Lincoln, they were lucky enough to own their own copy. Lincoln, whose own image eventually competed with that of Washington, remembered that "away back in my childhood, the earliest days of my being able to read, I got hold of a small book . . . Weems's Life of Washington." The story entered the twentieth century with embellishments, illustrating, it was supposed, something of the true greatness of Washington, both as a boy and a man: his character. At the same time Weems's detractors, skeptical of the story, condescendingly derided the fiddling "Rector of Mount Vernon" as a fraud. As Marcus Cunliffe observed, "all the more sober and ambitious" of Washington's nineteenth-century biographers studiously avoided Weems's "prize anecdotes": John Marshall (1804–1807), Aaron Bancroft (1807), David Ramsay (1807), Jared Sparks (1837), Washington Irving (1855–1859), Edward Everett (1860), and Woodrow Wilson (1897).

Despite scholarly dismissals, generations of Americans have half-believed the story, entirely plausible in essence, as one that might have happened to most any child of any era. What casts doubt upon the story is not anything unreasonable but, as one writer noted, the "exuberant morality of a thriftily parsonical book-agent." The silence of the documentary record for Washington's early years probably seals forever the possibility of knowing whether there is any basis for the story, although Weems claimed an "excellent lady" who also provided other anecdotes of Washington's youth. The cherry tree story epitomizes Weems's writing style: his subjects heroic; his purpose instructive; his tone decidedly moral, tinged with humor. He is religious but nonsectarian, patriotic but nonpolitical. Indiscriminately combining fact and tradition with fiction and romance, Weems was not afraid to appear ridiculous in order to advance his motive. Authenticity was not his aim. He described his reason for writing his *Life* to Mathew Carey within a month of Washington's death. "I've something to whisper in your lug," wrote Weems to the Philadelphia printer, "Washington, you know is gone! Millions are gaping to read something about him. I am very nearly primd and cockd for 'em. 6 months ago I set myself to collect anecdotes of him. My plan! I give his history, sufficiently minute—I accompany him from his start, thro the French & Indian & British or Revolutionary wars, to the Presidents chair, to the throne in the hearts of 5,000,000 of People. I then go on to show that his unparrelled rise & elevation were due to his Great Virtues." He would hold up for "the imitation of Our Youth" a virtuous Washington, said Weems, "enlivend with *Anecdotes apropos interesting and Entertaining.*"

The cherry tree story fits seamlessly into Weems's writings—although certainly not scrupulously historical in any sense, they are not altogether unreliable. They do not seriously distort the facts about their subjects, and they illustrate some truths about their subject, while inculcating some moral lessons, especially the urging to cultivate a love of truth and the warning to guard against vice. Weems's father of Washington, of whose relationship with his famous son little is known, took pains to carry out a plan of education aimed at counteracting the selfish spirit in children, which gives them the tendency to "fret and fight about trifles," and to reinforce the Christian emphasis that God is his "*true* Father." To the cherry tree story must be added others: his father's secret planting of cabbage seed that upon sprouting spelled "GEORGE WASH-

INGTON"; George's throwing a stone across the Rappahannock River; the Indian warrior's prophecy that Washington could not be killed by bullets; Mary Washington's dream of young George extinguishing the fire of her new house with water from an *American gourd* and a *wooden shoe;* and the prayer at Valley Forge. These stories, ranging from plausible to ludicrous, also must be seen in the context of the aims Weems set for himself.

Born in Anne Arundel County, Maryland, Mason Locke Weems (1759–1825) was by no means the only purveyor of Washingtonian anecdotes, only the most successful. He was ordained a deacon and in 1784 a minister in the Anglican Church, one of the first two candidates ordained for American service. He served as a minister in Maryland from 1784 to 1792. From 1794 to his death, he served as a book agent for Mathew Carey. Weems married Frances Ewell (1775–1843), a daughter of a sister of Washington's lifelong friend Dr. James Craik in July 1795. They lived in Dumfries in Prince William County, Virginia, and had ten children. Weems visited Mount Vernon overnight with his cousin Dr. James Craik, Jr., in March 1787 and corresponded with Washington in the 1790s. Weems is most famous for his *Life and Memorable Actions of George Washington,* which he began while Washington was still living. First published in 1800, it went through numerous editions and printings, with Weems adding additional material as often as he could. The ninth edition (1809) is the largest, more than 200 pages. Weems sent Washington copies of some of his publications, and at least one, *The Philanthropist, or, A Good Twenty-five Cents Worth of Political Love Powder, for Honest Adamites and Jeffersonians* (Dumfries, 1799), was dedicated to Washington. Weems also wrote several other works, including *God's Revenge Against Murder* (1807), *Life of General Francis Marion* (1809), *The Drunkard's Looking Glass* (1812), *God's Revenge Against Dueling* (1820), and *Bad Wife's Looking Glass* (1823). When he died in Beaufort, South Carolina, his body was brought back for burial to Bel Air, an estate near Dumfries.

Related entries: False Teeth; Ferry Farm; Washington Elm; "Whistling Bullets"

Suggestions for further reading:
Diaries, vol. 5.
"To Mason Locke Weems," 3 July 1799 (*Ret. Ser.,* vol. 4).
"To Mason Locke Weems," 29 August 1799 (*Ret. Ser.,* vol. 4).
Cunliffe, Marcus, ed. 1962. *The Life of Washington.* Cambridge, MA.
Onuf, Peter S., ed. 1996. *The Life of Washington by Mason Locke Weems: A New Edition with Primary Documents and Introduction.* Armonk, NY.
Weems, Mason Locke. 1809. 9th edition. *The Life of George Washington; With Curious Anecdotes, Equally Honourable to Himself and Exemplary to His Young Countrymen.* Philadelphia.

Chotank

The name Chotank (or Jotank) belonged to a creek, a Washington plantation, and a friendly neighborhood of tobacco plantations in Stafford (later King George) County, Virginia, that stretched peacefully to the east and west of the creek along the southern shore of the Potomac River. As a youth Washington spent many enjoyable days among the pleasant families who lived in the Chotank area, including memorable visits to some of his distant kinsfolk, recorded in his diary entries in 1747 and 1748, when he played billiards and whist and loo and made small loans to his cousins from the wages he was beginning to earn from his new occupation as a surveyor. (The "Chotank" branch of the Washington family descended from Lawrence, the immigrant brother of George's great-grandfather John Washington.) Washington, accompanied by Martha and her children, Patsy and Jacky Custis, took a fishing trip on the Potomac in Washington's schooner in the summer of 1768 that included stops in the Chotank area to visit some of those same relatives as well as his next-youngest brother, Samuel, who by 1755 had settled on a 600-acre farm at Chotank that he inherited from his father.

In later life Washington evidently recalled his youthful excursions to the Chotank area with great fondness, for when making his last will and testament in 1799, he remembered two of the cousins with whom he had amused himself in those early years, and with whom he had remained friends throughout his adult life, Lawrence Washington (1728–c.1809), the son of John and Mary Massey Washington, who lived on a bluff of the Potomac near the mouth of Chotank Creek; and Lawrence's first cousin Robert Washington (b. 1730), the son of Townshend and Elizabeth Washington of Chotank plantation and the eldest brother of the longtime manager of Mount Vernon's plantations, Lund Washington. To those "acquaintances and friends of my Juvenile years," Washington bequeathed "my other two gold headed Canes, having my Arms engraved on them; and to each (as they will be useful where they live) I leave one of the Spy-glasses which constituted part of my equipage during the late War."

Located on the Northern Neck (the peninsula between the Rappahannock and Potomac rivers), Chotank was noted for a series of great estates that had been settled by the time of Washington's birth: Hylton, Bedford, Albion, Barnsfield, Cedar Grove, Eagle's Nest, Litchfield, and Cleve.

Related entries: Ancestry; Ferry Farm; Washington, Augustine

Suggestions for further reading:
Diaries, vol. 2.
"To Jonathan Boucher," 19 August 1768 (*Col. Ser.*, vol. 8).
"From Buckner Stith," 22 March 1787 (*Con. Ser.*, vol. 5).
"Last Will and Testament," 9 July 1799 (*Ret. Ser.*, vol. 4).

Clinton, George (1739–1812)

*I*t has been stated that the exertions of few men of the American Revolution rank with those of George Clinton of Ulster County, New York. After a brief stint as a subaltern during the French and Indian War, Clinton studied law under William Smith of New York, one of the state's most able jurists. Although his public service began in 1768 when he was elected to the New York provincial assembly, Clinton did not come into Washington's sphere until he was elected a delegate to the Continental Congress in 1775. Clinton was appointed a brigadier general in the New York militia in December 1775, and in August of the next year, the New York convention instructed him to cooperate with the Continental army in New York. Under Washington's authority Clinton directed the vigorous efforts of the militia levies from Westchester, Dutchess, Ulster, and Orange counties to prepare for a British invasion of New York. "His acquaintance with the Country, abilites and zeal for the cause, were the motives that Induced me to make choice of him," Washington informed the New York convention at the time, adding, "I trust that Colo. Clinton will be equal to the command of both the Highland Fortifications [forts Montgomery and Clinton], they are under his direction at present." Clinton was the younger brother of James Clinton (c.1736–1812), a French and Indian War veteran and brigadier general in the Continental army who also spent much of the Revolutionary War commanding troops in the Hudson River Highlands.

Clinton was commissioned a brigadier general in the Continental army in March 1777, but his service in that capacity was limited by his election the following month to the offices of governor and lieutenant governor of New York under the state's new republican constitution. Nevertheless, of all the revolutionary governors, Clinton

Portrait of George Clinton (Library of Congress)

alone was entrusted with the government of his state and at the same time given direct command of the armed forces of his state. Clinton retained command of the aforementioned forts even after his election as governor, until early October 1777, when they were abandoned as untenable. Clinton proved an effective administrator and a capable politician and remained governor for eighteen years.

In the last months of the Revolutionary War, Clinton and Washington jointly purchased for speculation 6,071 acres of land along the Mohawk River in Montgomery County, New York, from Marinus Willett (1740–1830), a wealthy New York City merchant and former Continental army colonel who would later serve as mayor of New York City. Washington still owned about 1,000 acres of the Mohawk land at his death. The postwar correspondence between Clinton and Washington, often occasioned by concerns about the finances surrounding their land deal, reflects the cordial relationship that Clinton and his wife, Cor-

nelia Tappan Clinton, established with George and Martha Washington during the war. When a son was born, the Clintons named him for Washington, and young Washington's health frequently was among the topics considered noteworthy. From New York, Clinton assisted Washington's efforts to establish his garden at Mount Vernon by shipping "seed Corn & Pease," balsam and lime trees, and other "curious, and exoticks." In March 1789, before the results of the presidential election had been disclosed but with everyone knowing Washington would become the first president, Clinton invited the Washingtons to lodge at his home until suitable accommodations could be found. Washington, not wishing to impose such a burden on any private family, declined. After Washington became president, Clinton's position as governor often brought him and his family into contact with Washington at ceremonies and official functions.

Despite their warm friendship, Clinton and Washington differed on some key political issues, especially those relating to the role of federalism in the new republic. In June 1788 Clinton had been chosen president of the state convention that assembled at Poughkeepsie, New York, to consider ratification of the proposed Federal Constitution. Clinton's uncompromising opposition to the Constitution helped motivate fellow New Yorkers Alexander Hamilton and John Jay and Virginian James Madison to write *The Federalist* in an effort to counter his vocal resistance. Clinton remained an ardent anti-Federalist after the Constitution was ratified, leading him to oppose many of the policies of the new Washington administration. Washington nonetheless relied heavily on Clinton when negotiating with Indians in New York. When Washington was reelected in 1792, Clinton was among those receiving votes for the vice presidency, and later, from 1804 to 1812, he was vice president in the administrations of both Thomas

Jefferson and James Madison. Clinton died at Washington, D.C., and is buried in the Congressional Cemetery.

Related entry: Hamilton, Alexander

Suggestions for further reading:
"To Nathaniel Woodhull," 8 August 1776 (*War Ser.*, vol. 5).
"To George Clinton," 25 November 1784 (*Con. Ser.*, vol. 2).
Hastings, Hugh, and J. A. Holden, eds. 1899–1914. 10 vols. *The Public Papers of George Clinton.* Reprint, 1973. New York.
Kaminski, John P. 1993. *George Clinton: Yeoman Politician of the New Republic.* Madison, WI.

Clinton, Henry (d. 1795)

Henry Clinton, whose father, George Clinton (d. 1761), was governor of Newfoundland from 1732 to 1741 and of New York from 1741 to 1751, began his military career as a lieutenant in the New York militia in the mid-1740s. In 1751 he accompanied his father to England, where he secured a lieutenancy in the Coldstream Guards, but he apparently saw no active service until after he joined the Grenadiers near the end of the 1750s. During the Seven Years' War, Clinton was posted in Germany and rose to the rank of colonel, and in 1772 he was promoted to major general. He returned to America in May 1775, in time to distinguish himself at the Battle of Bunker Hill, and in 1776 he was placed second in command of the British forces in North America, under Gen. William Howe. A failed expedition against Charleston, South Carolina, in June 1776 threatened to diminish his reputation, but his prominent part in the Battle of Long Island and the capture of New York City the following August and September led to his promotion to lieutenant general and being made knight of the Bath.

Clinton captured Rhode Island in 1777 and advised Howe to unite his army with Gen. John Burgoyne's in New York, but the advice was ignored, with disastrous results for the British war effort. Howe took his army to Philadelphia instead, leaving Clinton in command at New York City. Clinton attempted to assist Burgoyne by making a diversion up the Hudson River, his troops capturing Forts Montgomery and Clinton in the process, but he was unable to prevent Burgoyne's defeat at Saratoga. In the spring of 1778, when Howe was recalled to England, Clinton became commander of all the British forces in America. He planned to evacuate Philadelphia, return the army to New York, and prepare for an expedition to the southern states, where large numbers of Loyalists supposedly were waiting to assist the British. The evacuation of Philadelphia was hindered by the arrival of the French fleet on the Atlantic coast, however, forcing most of the British troops to take a land route to New York, accompanied by a baggage train of 1,500 wagons hauling supplies. When Washington received intelligence of the British march, he ordered his army, with the help of the New Jersey militia, to shadow the British troops, harassing them with snipers, obstructing roads, and burning bridges at every turn. A major but indecisive battle took place in late June when the two armies converged at Monmouth Courthouse in New Jersey.

Clinton concentrated his forces at New York City, from which he conducted successful coastal raids while taking pains to avoid a general engagement, until late December 1779, when he set sail with several thousand troops for South Carolina. The expedition culminated in the American surrender of Charleston in May 1780, but rather than risk a follow-up expedition to the Chesapeake, as he had planned initially, he returned to New York, leaving Lord Cornwallis in command in the south. His defensive posture in New York combined with Cornwallis's strategic mistake of abandoning the Carolinas for Virginia opened the way for Washington's surprise march to Yorktown, where the most decisive battle of the war occurred. Following Washington's victory at Yorktown, Clinton resigned his command and returned to England, where he wrote "An Historical Detail of Seven Years Campaigns in North America from 1775 to 1782," published as *The American Rebellion . . .* in 1954.

Clinton, who is sometimes called "the elder" to distinguish him from his son Henry Clinton (1771–1829), who was also a general in the British army and a knight of the Bath, was promoted to full general in 1793 and served as governor of Gibraltar from July 1794 until his death in the following year.

Related entries: André, John; Asgill Affair; Cornwallis, Charles, Second Earl Cornwallis; Lee, Charles; Monmouth Courthouse, Battle of; Yorktown, Battle of

Suggestions for further reading:
Willcox, William B., ed. 1954. *The American Rebellion. . . .* New Haven, CT.
———. 1964. *Portrait of a General: Sir Henry Clinton.* New York.

Coat of Arms

The coat of arms of George Washington's ancestors made its way to the New World from Sulgrave Manor in Northamptonshire, England, in the seventeenth century, when Washington's great-grandfather Lawrence immigrated to Virginia. Several ancient depictions of the emblem have survived in England, including one carved in stone over a porch at Sulgrave, and a fourteenth-century stained-glass window in the south clerestory of the choir at Selby. The latter apparently commemorates John de Wessyngton (1416–1446), a prominent prior of Durham. Washington likely became familiar with the family crest in his childhood, since the emblem adorned his father Augustine's coach. The original coat of arms featured a raven on the seal, but a mythical griffin emerging from a ducal coronet, sometimes accompanied by a shield with stars and bands or with Washington's cipher, GW, is featured on most of the depictions commanded by Washington. Sprigs of wheat, a motif exemplifying the value Washington placed on agriculture, adorn some of the images.

Although Washington was not especially interested in his family's ancestry or origins, he did make use of the family coat of arms in ways typical for the eighteenth century. For example, in November 1771 he ordered from Robert Adams in England "A Neat Slip Cane, with a gold head (not expensive) with my Arms engravd thereon—Also a Plate with my Arms engravd & 4 or 500 Copies struck." The plate was engraved with a fashionable Chippendale design, and three hundred prints were struck, to be used for bookplates. The bookplates are accompanied with a motto, *Exitus Acta Probat,* translated "The end proves the deed." Washington also incorporated the coat of arms in the watermark of his writing paper and on his wax seal. The crest is incorporated twice in the elaborate chimneypiece in the west parlor at Mount Vernon. The pediment over the mantel exhibits a prominent painted representation of the seal carved of wood, and the cast-iron fireback of the fireplace contains a variation of the crest. The coat of arms also adorned Washington's pocket watch and much of the silver tableware ordered for Mount Vernon.

Washington's coat of arms has been incorporated into modern symbols, including the present design of the Purple Heart award and the official flag of the District of Columbia.

Related entry: Ancestry

Suggestion for further reading:
"To Robert Adam," 22 November 1771 (*Col. Ser.,* vol. 8).

Colvill Estate

Washington's promise to a dying man, he wrote in 1788, "has

occasioned more trouble and vexation to me engrossed as my time is with a multitude of other matters than any private circumstance of my life has ever done." By then, Thomas Colvill (d. 1766), the man to whom he made the pledge, had been dead for more than twenty years. Colvill had called Washington to his deathbed to ask him to serve as an executor for his estate. Washington's duties would be minimal, Colvill assured him, requiring only an occasional glance at the progress of the administration of the will. Colvill expected the administration to be managed by his wife, Frances (d. 1773), and John West, Jr. (d. 1777), the husband of Colvill's niece, Catharine. As it turned out, Colvill's estate was so complicated that Mrs. Colvill and West were incapable of performing their obligations, and Washington was forced to take an active part in its administration. It was a commitment that would plague him until 1797.

Colvill's will was a complex instrument that provided for the payment of numerous legacies to relatives living in England. Many obstacles stood in the way of identifying these heirs and verifying their claims. It was Colvill's wish, wrote Washington, to "leave the residue of his estate to—the Lord knows who, by description, which has stirred up a number of vexations and impertinent claims." Another hindrance was that Colvill had entangled his own affairs with those of his deceased brother John Colvill (d. 1756) while serving as executor for John's estate. In May 1765 Thomas sold his brother's estate, Merryland, a 6,300-acre tract in Frederick County, Maryland, to John Semple (d. 1773), a Scottish speculator living in Prince William County, Virginia, for £2,500 sterling. The proceeds from the sale would have cleared the lingering debts of John's estate, including £742 owed to Thomas. Semple gave a bond for the £2,500, which he later was unable to honor, and he assigned his rights to three

merchants in 1771, further complicating the matter. Although Washington was acquainted with Semple—both were active proponents of the scheme to make the Potomac River navigable at its falls—he could not prevail upon him to honor the bond or to give back to the estate a clear title to Merryland. "This Land was sold," wrote Washington, "to a Person neither very able, nor willing to pay for it. . . . ever since his [Thomas Colvill's] death we have been plagued with the letigeous person with whom the Contract was made." Thus, neither of the Colvill estates could be settled until some agreement could be reached with Semple, and with the merchants.

Frances Colvill died in 1773, and West in 1777, so when Washington returned home after the Revolutionary War he found himself the sole administrator of Colvill's estate. Although his hands in effect were tied, Washington renewed his efforts on behalf of Colvill's estate, which for the most part meant engaging in endless correspondence with various heirs and attorneys. The war had made it even more difficult to communicate with the parties in England, some of whom had died during the intervening period, and the "trouble and vexation" of writing letters and replies continued until May 1796, when the Virginia Court of Chancery finally laid down the terms of settlement. Washington was able to settle the estate in 1797, more than thirty-one years after giving his word to Colvill.

Related entry: Potomac River Navigation

Suggestions for further reading:
"To John West, Jr.," 4 July 1773 (*Col. Ser.*, vol. 9).
"From James Tilghman," 7 July 1786 (*Con. Ser.*, vol. 4).
"To James Keith," 24 January 1788 (*Con. Ser.*, vol. 6).
"To John Rumney, Jr.," 24 January 1788 (*Con. Ser.*, vol. 6).
"From Thomas Montgomerie," 24 October 1788 (*Pres. Ser.*, vol. 1).

"From George Pearson," 12 May 1797 (*Ret. Ser.*, vol. 1).

Commander in Chief's Guard

Washington's Life Guard, as the company was commonly called, was organized at the beginning of the New York campaign in 1776 for Continental army headquarters security. Washington was very specific about what he expected in the guard: "good Men" only who could be recommended by their commanding officers for their "sobriety, honesty, and good behaviour . . . five feet, eight Inches high, to five feet, ten Inches; handsomely and well made . . . neat, and spruce . . . perfectly willing, and desirous, of being of this guard. They should be drill'd men." Early on he wanted "none but Natives, & Men of some property," and later, only Virginians. Part of the reason for his caution was that "it is more than probable that in the Course of the Campaign, my Baggage, Papers, & other Matters of great public Import may be committed to the sole Care of these Men." Capt. Caleb Gibbs of Marblehead, Massachusetts, was appointed the first commander of the company; two of Washington's nephews, George Lewis (1757–1821) and George Augustine Washington, also served as officers. The lowest point in the guard's history took place about three months after its formation when one of its members, Thomas Hickey (d. 1776), became the first soldier of the Continental army to be hanged, after being tried and convicted of "Sedition and mutiny" for his part in a Loyalist conspiracy. The final act of the guard was to transport Washington's military papers from his Rocky Hill, New Jersey, headquarters to Mount Vernon after Washington resigned his commission in 1783.

Related entries: Gibbs, Caleb; Washington, George Augustine

Suggestions for further reading:
"General Orders," 11 March 1776 (*War Ser.*, vol. 3).
"General Orders," 27 June 1776 (*War Ser.*, vol. 5).
"To Caleb Gibbs," 22 April 1777 (*War Ser.*, vol. 9).
"To Alexander Spotswood, Alexander McClanachan, Abraham Bowman, and Christian Febiger," 30 April 1777 (*War Ser.*, vol. 9).
Godfrey, Carlos E. 1904. *The Commander-in-Chief's Guard*. Washington, DC.

Conotocarious

Conotocarious (Caunotaucarius) was the Indian name given to Washington in 1753 by the Half-King, a prominent Seneca chief allied with the British against the French in the struggle for control of the Ohio Country. The name, which means "town taker" or "devourer of villages," had been the Indian name of Washington's great-grandfather John Washington. In his "Biographical Memoranda" of 1786, written to assist a projected biography of Washington by David Humphreys, Washington recalled that during his journey to meet the commandant of the French forces on the Ohio River in the fall of 1753, he "was named by the half-King (as he was called) and the tribes of Nations with whom he treated, Caunotaucarius (in English) the Town taker; which name being registered in their Manner and communicated to other Nations of Indians, has been remembered by them ever since in all their transactions with him during the late War." Washington used the name when writing to the Half-King and other sachems of the Six Nations.

Related entries: Fort Necessity Campaign; Gist, Christopher; The Half-King

Suggestions for further reading:
"Washington's Journal" (*Diaries*, vol. 1).
"To Robert Dinwiddie," 25 April 1754 (*Col. Ser.*, vol. 1).
"To Andrew Montour," 10 October 1755 (*Col. Ser.*, vol. 2).

Constitutional Convention

After his return to Mount Vernon at the end of the Revolutionary War, Washington kept abreast of the affairs of the nation governed by the Articles of Confederation. A variety of economic problems challenged the country: repayment of the war debts, the scarcity of specie, the weakness of paper currency, and the inability to raise taxes. Added to this were the tendency of the states to act independently of one another, the inability to negotiate a badly needed trade treaty with Great Britain, problems on the western frontier, and after Shays's Rebellion in 1786–1787, the threat of anarchy. "It is clear to me as A, B, C," wrote Washington in 1786, "that an extension of federal powers would make us one of the most happy, wealthy, respectable, and powerful nations that ever inhabited the terrestrial globe. Without them we shall soon be everything which is the direct reverse. I predict the worst consequences from a half-starved, limping government, always moving upon crutches and tottering at every step."

Washington was initially skeptical that a "general Convention" could correct the present system. "I coincide perfectly in sentiment with you," he wrote John Jay in mid-May 1786, "that there are errors in our National Government which call for correction; loudly I will add; but I shall find myself happily mistaken if the remedies are at hand." He considered the situation delicate and feared that the people had not yet been "sufficiently misled" to retreat from their errors. "To be plainer," he informed Jay, "I think there is more wickedness than ignorance, mixed with our councils. Under this impression, I scarcely know what opinion to entertain of a general Convention. That it is necessary to revise, and amend the articles of Confederation, I entertain *no* doubt; but what may be the consequences of such an attempt *is* doubtful. Yet, something must be done, or the fabrick must fall. It certainly is tottering! Ignorance & design, are difficult to combat." The national character, he wrote Thomas Johnson a few months later, had sunk "much below par" and brought the country's politics and credit to the "brink of a precipice. A step or two more must plunge us into inextricable ruin."

After months of deliberation Washington finally decided to attend the Constitutional Convention in Philadelphia, where he hoped, he wrote James Madison, that the "most important of all objects—the fœderal governmt—may be considered with that calm & deliberate attention which the magnitude of it so loudly calls for." He left Mount Vernon for Philadelphia on 9 May, arriving in the city four days later. Once at Philadelphia he spent the next twelve days waiting for the arrival of the minimum number of delegates necessary to begin the meeting, spending many of his hours studying the proposals of James Madison and Edmund Randolph with the Virginia delegation and renewing his friendship with Benjamin Franklin, whom he had not seen since 1776. There was also time, however, for visiting country estates, attending parties and charity affairs, and other social events. When the Convention finally convened on 25 May, Robert Morris of the Pennsylvania delegation (in lieu of Franklin, who remained at home in the bad weather because of illness) proposed as the first order of business the appointment of Washington as president of the Convention. Washington was elected unanimously.

Washington's opening statement at the Convention, as recorded by Gouverneur Morris, reveals the gravity in which he held the proceedings: "It is too probable that no plan we propose will be adopted. Perhaps another dreadful conflict is to be sustained. If, to please the people, we offer what we ourselves disprove, how can we afterwards defend our work? Let us raise a standard to which the wise and the honest can repair. The event is in the hand of God." By lending his prestige to the Convention, Wash-

George Washington presiding at the signing of the Constitution of the United States in Philadelphia on 17 September 1787 (From the collections of the U.S. Capitol)

ington conferred a legitimacy upon its proceedings and the proposed Constitution. He was an advocate of a strong national government and a strong executive, which his voting record with the Virginia delegation reflects, and his presence at the meeting undoubtedly led the delegates to make the executive stronger than had he not attended the Convention. Washington contributed to the debates only once, on the last day of the Convention, when he urged the adoption of an amendment reducing the basis of representation in the House of Representatives from 40,000 to 30,000; the measure passed unanimously without further discussion. After the proposed Constitution had been accepted by the state delegations, all the papers of the Convention were entrusted to Washington's care, where they would remain until the new government, if adopted, was formed.

Washington found the final instrument acceptable and lent his vast influence toward its ratification. As he informed Lafayette while the ratification process was taking place, the fact that the delegates had united in forming a national government appeared to him a "little short of a miracle" given the differences of "manners, circumstances and prejudieces" among the states. "Nor am I yet such an enthusiastic, partial or undiscriminating admirer of it," he added, "as not to perceive it is tinctured with some real (though not radical) defects." The two great "pivots on which the whole machine must move," he thought, were simply that the general government be not "invested with more Powers than are indispensably necessary to perform [the] functions of a good Government," and that those powers be "so distributed among the Legislative, Executive, and Judicial Branches, into which the general Government is arranged, that it can never be in danger of degenerating into a monarchy, an Oligarchy, an Aristocracy, or any other despotic or oppressive form." According to Washington, the proposed Constitution contained "more checks and barriers against the introduction of Tyranny" than "any government hitherto instituted among mortals" and represented a contribution to the science of government, but, he warned, "we are not to expect perfection in this world."

For Washington the ratification of the Constitution was the completion of the Revolution; the result, in his discarded draft of his First Inaugural Address was:

I will not pretend to say that it appears absolutely perfect to me, or that there may not be many faults which have escaped my discernment. I will only say, during and since the Session of the Convention, I have attentively heard and read every oral & printed information on both sides of the question that could be procured. This long & laborious investigation, in which I endeavoured as far as the frailty of nature would permit to act with candour has resulted in a fixed belief that this Constitution, is really in its formation a government of the people; that is to say, a government in which all power is derived from, and at stated periods reverts to them—and that, its operation, it is purely a government of Laws made & executed by the fair substitutes of the people alone.

"Be assured," wrote James Monroe to Thomas Jefferson, "his influence carried this government." "I think that were it not for one great character in America," wrote U.S. Senator William Grayson, "so many men would not be for this government."

Related entry: Presidency

Suggestions for further reading:
"To John Jay," 18 May 1786 (*Con. Ser.,* vol. 4).
"To James Madison," 5 November 1786 (*Con. Ser.,* vol. 4).
"To Thomas Johnson," 12 November 1786 (*Con. Ser.,* vol. 4).
"To Charles Carter," 14 December 1787 (*Con. Ser.,* vol. 5).
"To Lafayette," 7 February 1788 (*Con. Ser.,* vol. 6).
"Undelivered First Inaugural Address: Fragments," 30 April 1789 (*Pres. Ser.,* vol. 2).

Rossiter, Clinton. 1966. *1787: The Grand Convention.* New York.
Van Doren, Carl. 1948. *The Great Rehearsal: The Story of the Making and Ratifying of the Constitution of the United States.* New York.

Conway, Thomas (1735–1800)

Thomas Conway, a native of Ireland who was educated and reared in France from the age of six, was a colonel in the French army when he engaged with the American representatives in Paris to travel to America and join the Continental army as an adjutant or a brigadier general. After arriving at Boston in early 1777, he traveled to Washington's headquarters at Morristown, New Jersey, where he sought to secure his commission. The Continental Congress appointed him a brigadier general the following May, and he was placed in command of four Pennsylvania regiments serving in Lord Stirling's division. After conducting himself well at the Battle of Germantown the following fall, Conway applied to Congress for a promotion to major general, but Washington opposed it on the ground that it would alienate the American brigadiers who had been in the service longer. "It will be as unfortunate a measure as ever adopted," he wrote Virginia delegate Richard Henry Lee. "I may add, and I think with truth, that it will give a fatal blow to the existence of the army."

By early November 1777 Conway had aligned himself with a handful of officers dissatisfied with Washington's leadership of the army. When Washington received the contents of a letter written by Conway offering foolish praise to Maj. Gen. Horatio Gates, "Heaven had been determined to save your country, or a weak general and bad counsellors would have ruined it," he sent a copy of it to Conway, who a few days later tendered the resignation of his commission to Congress. Congress rejected Conway's resignation, however, and on 13 December at the instigation of several prominent members dissatisfied with Washington's leadership, including Thomas Mifflin and Dr. Benjamin Rush (1746–1813), appointed him inspector general of the Continental army, with the rank of major general. After that, Conway, in league with Rush, Mifflin, and Gates, sought to have Washington superseded as commander in chief.

Washington was cool toward Conway. "That I did not receive him in the language of a warm and cordial Friend, I readily confess the charge," he informed the president of Congress, Henry Laurens. "I did not, nor shall I ever, till I am capable of the arts of dissimulation. These I despise, and my feelings will not permit me to make professions of friendship to the man I deem my Enemy, and whose system of conduct forbids it." At the same time Conway was received and treated at headquarters with "proper respect to his Official character" and had no reason for complaint. In fact Washington sought to keep the matter secret because "so desirous was I, of concealing every matter that could, in its consequences, give the smallest Interruption to the tranquility of this Army, or afford a gleam of hope to the enemy by dissentions therein."

After an expedition against Canada was abandoned, Conway was directed to join the army under Maj. Gen. Alexander McDougall at Fishkill, New York, and from there to Albany, where he wrote a "petulant letter" to Congress complaining of ill treatment, and offering his resignation once again. The letter's condescending tone alienated so many members of Congress that his resignation was accepted immediately, a reception that Conway had not expected. A hurried trip to York, Pennsylvania, where Congress was in session, failed to win a reinstatement. His continued criticism of Washington in Philadelphia after the British evacuated the city led him into a duel with Brig. Gen. John Cadwalader in July 1778. Shot in the mouth and neck and thinking himself mortally wounded, Conway wrote Washington that "I find myself just able to hold the pen during a few min-

utes; and take this opportunity of expressing my sincere grief for having done, written, or said any thing disagreeable to your excellency. My career will soon be over; therefore justice and truth prompt me to declare my last sentiments. You are in my eyes a great and good man. May you long enjoy the love, veneration, and esteem of these States, whose liberties you have asserted by your virtues." Conway survived, however, and returned to France.

Washington sarcastically characterized Conway as one who "possesses no other merit than of that after kind of sagacity, which qualifies a Man better for profound discoveries of errors, that have been committed, and advantages that have been lost, than for the exercise of that foresight and provident discernment which enable him to avoid the one and anticipate the other." The marquis de Lafayette described Conway "as a man sent by heaven for the liberty and happiness of America. . . . he told so to them and they are fools enough to believe it."

Related entries: Gates, Horatio; Mifflin, Thomas; Stirling, Lord

Suggestions for further reading:
"To Thomas Conway," 5 November 1777 (*War Ser.*, vol. 12).
"To Richard Henry Lee," 17 November 1777 (*War Ser.*, vol. 12).
"To Henry Laurens," 2 January 1778 (*War Ser.*, vol. 13).
"To Horatio Gates," 4 January 1778 (*War Ser.*, vol. 13).
"From Lafayette," 5 January 1778 (*War Ser.*, vol. 13).
"To Horatio Gates," 9 February 1778 (*War Ser.*, vol. 13).
Freeman, Douglas Southall. 1948–1957. 7 vols. *George Washington: A Biography.* New York.

Cornwallis, Charles, Second Earl Cornwallis (1738–1805)

After a successful military career that included service in Geneva and

Surrender of Lord Cornwallis. Painting by John Trumbull (Library of Congress)

Great Britain and appointments of aide-de-camp to the king, colonel of the Thirty-third British Regiment, and constable of the London Tower, Lord Cornwallis was promoted to major general in the British army effective 29 September 1775. He sailed from Cork, Ireland, in February 1776 with 2,500 troops to meet Gen. Henry Clinton at Cape Fear, North Carolina, to participate in Clinton's expedition against the southern colonies. After the short-lived campaign, Cornwallis led his army from South Carolina to Staten Island, New York, arriving in late July 1776.

Cornwallis took part in the New York campaign in 1776, participating in the Battle of Long Island and the capture of New York City in August and September 1776, and, more prominently, in the captures of Forts Washington and Lee on the Hudson River later that fall. His troops were then active in the pursuit of Washington's army in New Jersey. He was about to return home to England on leave when word came of Washington's stunning attack at Trenton. A week later he thought he had trapped Washington south of Trenton, only to be surprised again by Washington's attack on Princeton, which caused him, historians have suggested, to become much more aggressive in his military tactics. In September 1777 Cornwallis participated in the Battle of Brandywine and commanded the British forces that first occupied Philadelphia, and in early October he took part in the Battle of Germantown. Cornwallis returned to England in 1778 to attend his wife, who was seriously ill, and remained there until her death the following February. He returned to New York in August 1779, and the next spring he agreed to make an expedition to South Carolina, where at Camden on 16 August 1780 he completely routed an American force commanded by Maj. Gen. Horatio Gates. A setback occurred, however, at Cowpens in January 1781, when Lt. Banastre Tarleton's cavalry—nearly one-third of Cornwallis's army—was defeated by Continental army troops under the command of generals Daniel Morgan and Nathanael Greene. The defeat led Cornwallis to aggressively pursue the American troops across the Carolinas in a vain attempt to engage the Americans once again. Cornwallis finally succeeded in defeating Greene in mid-March, but the victory did not produce the hoped-for result of North Carolina giving way to British rule.

In May 1781 Cornwallis moved north from the Carolinas to reinforce generals William Phillips and Benedict Arnold in Virginia. Washington's correspondence, including letters from Virginia governor Thomas Jefferson and the marquis de Lafayette, kept him abreast of Cornwallis's movements in Virginia. Cornwallis joined forces with Arnold's troops at Petersburg in late May, and the combined British force, joined by some reinforcements sent by Clinton in New York City, marched on Richmond. Meanwhile, Washington took his army from New York to Virginia, and the French fleet blocked the Chesapeake, resulting in Cornwallis being trapped at Yorktown. On 17 October, after a siege of six weeks, during which his position became more and more precarious, Cornwallis opened negotiations for the surrender of his army. Terms of capitulation were quickly agreed upon, although Cornwallis avoided the humiliating ceremony of surrender on the 19th by pleading illness and sending Brig. Gen. Charles O'Hara (d. 1802) in his stead. Washington seemingly was unfazed by Cornwallis's failure to appear at the surrender of arms and extended an invitation to O'Hara for dinner, an offer which undoubtedly would have been made to Cornwallis had he been present, and which O'Hara accepted.

Cornwallis was paroled to England, where he was exchanged for Henry Laurens in May 1782. After the Revolutionary War Cornwallis had a distinguished public-service career that included appointments of governor general of India and viceroy of Ireland. He died in India.

Related entries: Clinton, Henry; Yorktown, Battle of

Suggestions for further reading:
Diaries, vol. 3.
"From Joseph Reed," 3 March 1776 (*War Ser.,* vol. 3)
Wickwire, Franklin, and Mary Wickwire. 1970. *Cornwallis: The American Adventure.* Boston.

Craik, James (1730–1814)

Of the many friendships that Washington made during his life, perhaps few were as intimate or as long as the one that began during the French and Indian War with the surgeon of the Virginia Regiment, Dr. James Craik. Their friendship was genuinely sincere, "seldom to be met with in those days," recalled Craik in December 1758. The extent to which that friendship developed early on can be seen in an affectionate letter that Craik wrote to Washington when the latter was seriously ill in the fall of 1757:

And I hope by the Assistance of God and the requesite care, that will be taken of you, where you now are: that tho. your disorder may reduce you to the lowest ebb; yet you will in a short time get the better of it—And render your friends here happy, by having the honour of serving once more under your Command—As nothing is more conducive to a Speedy recovery, than a tranquill easy mind, Accompanied with a good flow of Spirits—I would beg of you; not, as a Physician; but as a real friend who has your Speedy recovery Sincerely at heart; that you will keep up your Spirits, and not allow your mind to be disturbed, with any part of Publick bussiness; that perhaps may not be going on so well, as your concern for the

Publick could wish—Any little step of this kind, that might happen, would be triffling to the Neglect of yourself—The fate of your Friends and Country are in a manner dependent upon your recovery.

James Craik was born in Galloway, Scotland, and studied at the famous medical school at the University of Edinburgh. When he was 20 years old he emigrated to America, settling first in the West Indies, and then in Norfolk, Virginia, where he set up a medical practice. He was appointed a surgeon in the Virginia Regiment in March 1754 and was commissioned a lieutenant the following July, the same month that he served with Washington at the capitulation of Fort Necessity, where his "Doctor's Box" was destroyed by the French and Indians. Dr. Craik served as Washington's chief medical officer until the regiment was disbanded in 1762. He was one of the officers honored along with Washington by the Virginia House of Burgesses in September 1754 for "their late gallant and brave Behaviour in the Defense of their Country," and years later, in the fall of 1770, Craik accompanied Washington and the Crawford brothers on a journey to the Ohio Valley in search of good lands for the veterans' bounty rewards. (For his military service Craik was granted 1,374 acres on the Little Kanawha in Botetourt County and 4,232 acres on the Great Kanawha in Fincastle County. He also assisted Washington in administering control of the latter's western lands during the Revolutionary War.) After the French and Indian War Craik settled on his large plantation at Port Tobacco in Charles County, Maryland.

In 1760 Craik married Mariamne Ewell (1740–1814), the daughter of Sarah Ball Ewell, who was Washington's first cousin, and Charles Ewell of Prince William County. The Craiks and their nine children became frequent visitors to Mount Vernon, and Craik was summoned when illness struck among family or slave members,

since Craik was the physician for Martha and her children and the plantation's slaves. Much later, Washington contributed $100 per year toward the education of one of Craik's sons, his namesake George Washington Craik (1774–1808), who after finishing his schooling briefly practiced law in Alexandria before becoming a private secretary to Washington in 1796. In 1777 Washington named Craik assistant director of the general hospitals of the Continental army's middle department, an office he held until 1780. He also served as chief physician and surgeon of the Continental army from 1781 to 1783. During the war Craik seemed to be everywhere, treating Lafayette's wounds at the Battle of Brandywine; passing warnings to Washington about the so-called Conway Cabal; and trying to save the life of Washington's stepson, Jacky Custis, during his fatal illness at Yorktown. After the war Craik once again became one of the most frequent and welcomed visitors to Mount Vernon, especially after he moved his family to Alexandria in 1786. In February 1785 Craik sent Washington "Eight young Pair Trees" which the latter planted at Mount Vernon, and the following July some Chinese seeds for Washington to establish in his botanical garden. (Washington had called upon Craik to find him a gardener for Mount Vernon as early as May 1760.) In the fall of 1786 Craik treated Washington for a violent "ague & fever" that, in Washington's words, made "such havock of my mouth, nose & chin that I am unable to put a razor to my face." In addition to keeping a watch on Washington's health, Dr. Craik also often served as Washington's confidant about business and financial matters. In the fall of 1784 he accompanied Washington to the western lands once again; this time the two old-timers were accompanied by Craik's son William and Washington's nephew Bushrod Washington. When Washington became president Craik took into his home two of Washington's nephews while they received an education at Alexandria. Over the winter of 1791–1792, Washington selected Craik's son-in-law Richard Harrison to serve as the auditor of the Treasury Department, the only example of the period, noted historian Douglas Southall Freeman, of Washington permitting "personal considerations to weigh with him" in making official appointments. At Washington's urging, Craik in 1798 acceded to two posts, director of the general hospital for the U.S. Army and physician general, which he held until 1800. When recommending Craik for those posts, he wrote Secretary of War James McHenry that, "if I should ever have occasion for Physician or Surgeon to James McHenry, I should prefer my old Surgeon Doctr Craik, who from 40 years experience is better qualified than a dozen of them put together."

Although Washington called on Craik for medical assistance many times during their long friendship, none was so trying to his medical experience or so emotionally draining as when Craik was suddenly called upon to attend to Washington during his last illness, in 1799. According to the account left by Washington's secretary, Tobias Lear, Dr. Craik came in "and upon examining the General, he put a blister of Cantharides on the throat, took some more blood from him, and had a gargle of Vinegar & sage tea, and ordered some Vinegar and hot water for him to inhale the steam which he did;—but in attempting to use the gargle he was almost suffocated." When his other efforts and those of the two other doctors Craik had sent for likewise proved unsuccessful in alleviating Washington's sufferings, Washington told his old friend, *"Doctor, I die hard; but I am not afraid to go; I believed from my first attack that I should not survive it; my breath can not last long."* Craik, according to Lear, "pressed his hand, but could not utter a word. He retired from the bed side, & sat by the fire absorbed in grief." The doctor remained by the side of Washington until the very end, and afterward "tarried all day & all night" at Mount Vernon; the next day he assisted the family in making funeral arrangements. Craik was, with the family, one of the "Principal Mourners" at the funeral, and after the ceremony he "tarried here all night" once again.

Craik died at Alexandria, Virginia.

Related entries: Crawford Brothers; Death

Suggestions for further reading:
Diaries, vols. 1–6.
"From James Craik," 25 November 1757 (*Col. Ser.,* vol. 5).
"To James Craik," 10 July 1784 (*Con. Ser.,* vol. 1).
"To James McHenry," 5 July 1798 (*Ret. Ser.,* vol. 2).
Craik, James. 1938. "Boyhood Memories of Dr. James Craik, D. D., L. L. D." (*Virginia Magazine of History and Biography,* vol. 46).
Henriques, Peter R. 2000. *The Death of George Washington: He Died as He Lived.* Mount Vernon, VA.

Crawford Brothers

The endless obstacles faced by Washington in acquiring and settling large tracts of land beyond the Allegheny Mountains would have been even more relentless had it not been for the assiduous efforts on his behalf of Valentine (d. 1777) and William (1732–1782) Crawford, brothers who first crossed Washington's path about 1750 when he was surveying in what was then Frederick County, Virginia. The brothers settled not far from their stepfather Richard Stephenson's land on Bullskin Run, William at Stewart's Crossing (present-day Connellsville, Pennsylvania) on the Youghiogheny River, and Valentine a few miles to the north on Jacobs Creek. Both had come of age in a territory inhabited by Indians hostile to white settlers and disputed by the British and the French. During the French and Indian War they served with the British, Valentine as a wagoner and William as an officer commanding scouts in the Virginia Regiment. William also served as a captain in the Indian uprising of 1762–1763 known as Pontiac's Rebellion.

In the years following the French and Indian War William Crawford established himself as an Indian trader in the wilderness near Fort Pitt. During the late 1760s and early 1770s he surveyed a number of tracts for Washington, some of which lay in territory banned by the Proclamations of 1754 and 1763, including the Washington's Bottom tract on the Youghiogheny, one near Chartiers Creek, and several along the Kanawha and Ohio rivers. Crawford also accompanied Washington on his trip to visit his western lands in the fall of 1770. Valentine Crawford also served Washington in various ways, including overseeing Washington's Bullskin farms, transporting tobacco and other goods to Mount Vernon, purchasing servants, and finding a spinner. In the spring of 1774 Valentine contracted to serve as Washington's "Overlooker & manager of his business on the Ohio," and although laborers were recruited to clear and cultivate the land and erect fences and houses, Dunmore's War prevented Crawford from carrying out the agreement. Valentine Crawford died intestate in January 1777, causing his brother William, by then colonel of the Seventh Virginia Regiment in the Continental army, to lament to Washington, "I sopose by this time you may have herd of all my Misfortuns The loss of Hugh Stephensons [the Crawfords' half brother who died the previous fall] and Val Crawford [w]ho Died . . . without any will which is very hard on me, as his Afairs and mine are so Blend together that no man can Setle them but my self, and should I be Cut of[f] before they are Setled will ruin his Children and mine."

William Crawford took part in several Revolutionary War battles, including those at Brandywine and Germantown, Pennsylvania, where Washington relied on him to lead scouting parties. The following year Crawford commanded the militia defending the Virginia frontier from Indian attacks. In 1782, at Washington's request, Crawford led 500 frontiersmen raised for a militia expedition against the Wyandot and Delaware Indians in the region of Sandusky, in present-day northern Ohio. Intelligence about the expedition reached the Ohio first, however, and the troops were surprised by a strong force of Loyalists and Indians equipped with artillery. The militia scattered, and Crawford was captured, tortured, and killed. The official British report of Crawford's death, written by an eyewitness, read: "Crawford died like a hero; never changed his countenance, tho' they scalped him alive, and then laid hot ashes on his head; after which they roasted him by a slow fire." Washington, upon learning of the expedition's failure, wrote that he was "particularly affected" with the disastrous fate of his old friend, although "no other than the extremest Tortures which could be inflicted by Savages could, I think, have been expected, by those who were unhappy eno' to fall into their Hands."

Related entries: Bullskin Lands; Great Kanawha Tracts; Millers Run (Chartiers Creek) Tract; Washington's Bottom Tract

Suggestions for further reading:
Diaries, vols. 1–4.
"To William Crawford," 17 September 1767 (*Col. Ser.*, vol. 8).
"From William Crawford," 29 September 1767 (*Col. Ser.*, vol. 8).
"Articles of Agreement," 24 March 1774 (*Col. Ser.*, vol. 10).
"To Valentine Crawford," 30 March 1774 (*Col. Ser.*, vol. 10).
"To William Irvine," 10 July, 6 August 1782 (Fitzpatrick, *Writings*, vol. 24).

Cresap, Thomas (1694–1790)

*T*homas Cresap was born at Skipton in Yorkshire, England, and came to Maryland about 1717, where he became one of the colony's most prominent frontiersmen and land speculators. In 1734 he became a captain in the Maryland militia, and two years later he settled at Shawnee Old Town, on the Maryland side of the Potomac River, about fifteen miles overland from the future Fort Cumberland. A series of trails much traveled by Indians and whites intersected in the vicinity of Shawnee Old Town, and there Cresap erected a fortified trading post that became one of the leading posts on the frontier. Washington went to Old Town in 1748, noting in his diary that the route taken by his party on the Maryland side of the Potomac River was "I believe the Worst Road that ever was trod by Man or Beast." The following year Cresap became one of the original founders of the Ohio Company, and he helped lay out the company's road from Wills Creek to the Monongahela River. After Washington's defeat of Jumonville in 1754, Cresap, by now a colonel in the militia, was ordered to guard the French prisoners. In 1755 Washington came into contact with Cresap again, this time as an aide-de-camp to General Braddock, and Cresap's post served as an important rendezvous point for troops taking part in Braddock's expedition. Following Braddock's defeat Cresap was forced to retreat further down the Potomac River to the relative safety of the Conococheague settlement, which had been reinforced with militia from the Winchester area, but which also was abandoned in the late summer of 1756.

Washington visited Cresap on his trip to view his western lands in October 1770. Cresap, who had just returned from a lengthy stay in England on behalf of the Ohio Company, kept Washington apprised of the availability of cheap land in the west. Although he was too old for active service when the Revolutionary War began, he was a staunch supporter of the American side of the conflict. In 1775 Cresap began holding county court on his property on Redstone Creek, land which was claimed by both Pennsylvania and Virginia and which was adjacent to land owned by Washington's brother Augustine. (Cresap wanted to keep the land under Virginia jurisdiction.) On his second tour to his western lands, after the war, Washington again stayed at Cresap's settlement. The octogenarian, who had retained his mental capacities but was nearly blind, welcomed Washington with open arms. No doubt the two reminisced about their meeting four decades earlier, when the young surveyor had been introduced to life on the frontier and witnessed the Indian dance that he long ago recorded in his diaries. Cresap's son Michael Cresap (1742–1775), the controversial frontier leader during Dunmore's War in 1774, and his heirs quarreled with Washington over a large tract of land known as Round Bottom on the Ohio River.

Related entry: Croghan, George

Suggestions for further reading:
Diaries, vols. 1, 2, 4.
"To Thomas Cresap," 18 April 1754 (*Col. Ser.,* vol. 1).
"From Thomas Cresap," 21 March 1775 (*Col. Ser.,* vol. 10).
"To John Marshall," 17 March 1789 (*Pres. Ser.,* vol. 1).

Croghan, George (d. 1782)

George Croghan, an Irish immigrant who had settled near Carlisle, Pennsylvania, about 1741, was perhaps the leading Indian trader on the Pennsylvania frontier before the French and Indian War. He began speculating in western lands in the 1740s, purchasing 200,000 acres from the Iroquois in 1749 near the strategic fork of the Monongahela and Allegheny rivers where Fort Pitt (Pittsburgh) was later built. By 1754, when Washington used him as an interpreter to the Indians during the Fort Necessity campaign, Croghan had moved his business operations to a 4,000-acre tract on the banks of Aughwick Creek and to his plantation on Pine Creek, about four miles above the Forks of the Ohio. Croghan, whom the Indians called "the Buck," was appointed deputy superintendent of Indian affairs by Sir William Johnson in 1756, and two years later he settled on his lands near Fort Pitt. Around that time he also laid claim to 250,000 acres to the south of Lake Otsego in the Mohawk Valley of New York, where he settled some years later. To the network of trading posts and storehouses that Croghan set up on the frontier, which eventually extended from present-day West Virginia and eastern Kentucky to Lake Erie, the tribes of the Six Nations and other Indians brought furs and skins to exchange for European goods, and Croghan successfully rivaled the French for the lucrative Indian trade.

Croghan commanded a company of scouts and supplied flour and other provisions to British forces during the French and Indian War, and he came into contact with Washington during the Braddock and Forbes campaigns. Much of his commerce was ruined during the French and Indian War, and when the war ended Croghan began speculating heavily in Ohio and Illinois lands. Washington, while visiting his western lands in 1770, met White Mingo (Conengayote) and several other chiefs of the Six Nations at Croghan's residence on the Allegheny River. Croghan accompanied Washington on part of that journey, attempting to sell Washington land he claimed title to that was in the territory claimed by both Pennsylvania and Virginia, but Washington declined the offer, noting that "the unsettled state of this country renders any purchase dangerous." The Revolutionary War brought Croghan's western land schemes to an abrupt halt. His estate of nearly 500,000 acres, heavily encumbered with debts and mortgages, dwindled as Croghan, confined to his bed by lameness, attempted to settle his obligations. Near the end of the war he moved to Passyunk near Philadelphia, where he died in poverty.

Related entries: Cresap, Thomas; Fort Necessity Campaign; Half-King, The

Suggestions for further reading:
Diaries, vols. 1, 2.
Hanna, Charles A. 1911. 2 vols. *The Wilderness Trail, or The Ventures and Adventures of the Pennsylvania Traders on the Allegheny Path.* New York.
Volwiler, Albert T. 1926. *George Croghan and the Westward Movement, 1741–1782.* Cleveland.
Wainwright, Nicholas B. 1959. *George Croghan: Wilderness Diplomat.* Chapel Hill, NC.

Custis, Eleanor Parke ("Nelly")

See Lewis, Eleanor Parke Custis.

Custis, George Washington Parke (1781–1857)

Washington's grandson George Washington Parke Custis, known variously as "Tub," "Wash," and "Boy," was born at Mount Airy, the Maryland plantation of his mother's family. He was only about 6 months old when his father, Jacky Custis, died of camp fever at Yorktown, after which he went with his sister Nelly Custis to live with Martha Washington at Mount Vernon. After Wash recovered from an illness in 1784 Washington wrote that he was "as fat & saucy as ever," a remark alluding to why he was given the nickname Tub as well as to what extent the family had begun to spoil him. As early as 1786 Washington already seemed to be worrying about Wash's future, and much of Washington's role in his grandson's life revolved around the boy's education. "The boy, whom you would readily have perceived was the pet of the family," he wrote historian Catharine Sawbridge Macaulay Graham after her 1786 visit to Mount Vernon, "affords promising hopes from maturer age." Washington was

Engraved portrait of George Washington Parke Custis (Library of Congress)

determined that his grandson would receive the education that had not been offered to him and was neglected by the boy's father, although like his father, Wash's interests and passions seemed unsuited for a life of study. In 1785 Washington began to search for a tutor to live at Mount Vernon for Wash and his sister, resulting in the arrival of Gideon Snow, and later, of Tobias Lear, who would become Washington's secretary and close friend.

Lear enjoyed tutoring his young charges but soon found himself devoting less and less time to their lessons as his responsibility in the Washington household increased. Nevertheless, when Washington became president Tub's education was left to Lear's arrangement. While in New York Wash attended a private school near Trinity Church run by Patrick Murdoch at his house on Greenwich Street. After the government moved to Philadelphia in 1790, Washington and Lear thought the boy, not yet 10 years old, was ready for the rigors of a more highly structured school like the academy associated with the College of Philadelphia. The school operated year-round and took in students of all levels in preparation for their entry into the higher branches of education. At the academy Wash became familiar with the sons of the city's elite, but after a year's tutelage Lear considered the education received by Wash "by no means justifies the high Character given of that Seminary." After examining the boy Lear found that he had made no advances in Latin since leaving New York and had been given no instruction in math, with the result that "it is not to be wondered at now that he cannot tell 100 from 1000." What was worse, the head of the institution, Dr. William Smith (1727–1803), had lost control of the discipline of his charges, and their disrespect for him had become so great that the "lowest boys" in the school did not hesitate to speak of him in "the most disrespectful terms—there has been more than one instance lately of the subordinate masters being hissed by the boys—and one of them pelted with dirt and Stones as he came out of School." Despite this negative review, Wash remained in the school until it was decided to send him to the College of New Jersey at Princeton, New Jersey.

Washington soon became convinced that Wash was deriving "little or no benefit" from his attendance at the Princeton college. In November 1796 Washington wrote the first of a series of letters aimed at encouraging his ward to take his studies seriously. "You need nothing but the exertion of the talents you possess, with proper directions," he wrote, "to acquire all that is necessary; and the hours allotted for study, if properly improved, will enable you to do this. Although the confinement may feel irksome at first, the advantages resulting from it, to a reflecting mind, will soon overcome it." Many similar admonitions failed to make the hoped-for impression, although Wash received his grandfather's advice in the spirit that it was given and promised to reform. In fact, he seemed to understand the nature of his situation better than his guardian. "Permit me to make this humble confession," he wrote in June 1797, "sanctioned by reason and mature deliberation viz. That if in any way or by any mean I depart from your direction or guardianship—Let me suffer as I and such an unprudent act deserve—Unfortunately man never will beleive untill convinced perhaps too late, by his own situation." The president of the institution, Samuel Stanhope Smith (1751–1819), soon wrote a letter to Washington outlining Wash's poor performance at school. Washington's exasperation at his grandson was apparent in his reply to Smith: "From his infancy, I have discovered an almost unconquerable disposition to indolence in every thing that did not tend to his amusements: and have exhorted him in the most parental and friendly manner, often, to devote his time to more useful pursuits. His pride has been stimulated, and his family expectation & wishes have been urged, as inducements thereto. In short, I could say nothing to him now, by way of admonition—encouragement—or advice, that has not been repeated over & over again." Wash's education at Princeton ended in October 1797.

Back at Mount Vernon, Wash was given a regimented system by his grandfather, which no doubt shocked the youth, who was accustomed to living without much discipline. "Rise early," he wrote, "that by habit it may become familiar, agreeable—healthy—and profitable. It may for a while, be irksome to do this; but that will wear off." If Wash wanted to roam the Mount Vernon lands with a gun, he could, but only on the condition that he return in time for breakfast with the family, after which he would be confined to his studies until about an hour before dinner. Saturday alone was left for riding, hunting, or other proper amusements. It took Washington only two weeks to discover that he could keep Wash to his room, but he could not make him "attend to his Books if inclination, on his part, is wanting." Washington's own preference long had been for Wash to attend Harvard College in Massachusetts, and he briefly considered sending him to William and Mary College in Williamsburg before deciding that either route would be a waste of time and money. "What is best to be done with him, I know not," the disappointed grandfather wrote to Wash's stepfather, David Stuart (1753–c.1814), in search of advice. Stuart's reply was not encouraging. "I find it a subject far from easy, to say what I think had best be done with Washington—His habits and inclinations are so averse to all labour and patient investigation, that I must freely declare it as my opinion that not much is to be expected from any plan." Eventually they decided to enroll Wash in St. John's College in Annapolis, where the youth continued his by now well-ingrained habits of muddling through his studies, and where, to his grandfather's chagrin, he also discovered the opposite sex, although he would not marry until after Washington's death.

In 1798 Washington finally abandoned all hopes of keeping young Custis to "any literary pursuits, either in a public Seminary, or at home under the direction of any one." With a war with France possibly looming on the horizon, Washington decided that a military appointment might be good for his grandson, for it would serve as an honorable entrance into public life and possibly "divert his attention from a matrimonial pursuit (for a while at least) to which his constitution seems to be too prone." Custis was thrilled at the proposal, and his mother and grandmother consented, so with the help of his grandfather he received the appointment of aide-de-camp to Gen. Charles Cotesworth Pinckney, with the rank of colonel in the U.S. Army. Custis's time away from Mount Vernon seemed to be just what was needed to help him grow into maturity. The expected hostilities failed to materialize, so he did not have to encounter the hazards of war, but he later served as a volunteer during the War of 1812 when the British attacked Washington, D.C.

Custis and Lawrence Lewis were visiting Custis's New Kent, Virginia, plantation when Washington suddenly fell ill and died in December 1799. Shortly before his death Washington asked when the young men were expected to return and was told about a week later. "He made no reply" to the answer, undoubtedly saddened by the fact that he knew he would see neither his grandson nor his nephew again. Although Custis had come into vast landholdings when his own father died and would take control of Martha's property at her death, Washington nevertheless considered him as his own son and left him a 1,200-acre tract on Four Mile Run, in the vicinity of Alexandria, as well as his lots in the Federal City. Custis also was named as one of the executors of Washington's estate, and he and Lewis later erected the new tomb at Mount Vernon where Washington's remains were reinterred, as his will had directed.

Custis married Mary Lee Fitzhugh (1788–1858) in 1804, and together they had one daughter, Mary, who married Robert E. Lee. The Custises established their home at Arlington House, a beautiful Federal-style mansion built directly across the Potomac River from the Federal City on land inherited by Custis from his father, and since the Civil War the center of the Arlington National Cemetery. There Custis devoted himself to agriculture, painting, and literary pursuits. He published a drama based on an incident in Washington's life during the French and Indian War, *The Indian Prophecy* (Georgetown, D.C., 1828), and in 1859 the Washington, D.C., *National Intelligencer* compiled the first edition of his *Recollections and Private Memoirs of Washington*, containing curious anecdotes about Washington and life at Mount Vernon, which subsequently was expanded. Washington would have been proud of the praise heaped on his grandson in the *Intelli-*

gencer's obituary of Custis, reprinted in the introduction to the *Recollections*. "Mr. Custis," it began, "was distinguished by an original genius for eloquence, poetry, and the fine arts; by a knowledge of history, particularly the history of this country; for great powers of conversation, for an ever-ready and generous hospitality, for kindness to the poor, for patriotism, for constancy of friendship, and for a more than filial devotion to the memory and character of Washington."

Related entries: Custis, John Parke; Lear, Tobias; Lewis, Eleanor Parke Custis; Quasi-War

Suggestions for further reading:
"From Tobias Lear," 28 October 1790 (*Pres. Ser.*, vol. 6).
"To George Washington Parke Custis," 15 November 1796 (*Writings*, vol. 35).
"To Samuel Stanhope Smith," 24 May 1797 (*Ret. Ser.*, vol. 1).
"From George Washington Parke Custis," 8 June 1797 (*Ret. Ser.*, vol. 1).
"To George Washington Parke Custis," 7 January 1798 (*Ret. Ser.*, vol. 2).
Custis, George Washington Parke. 1860. *Recollections and Private Memoirs of Washington*. New York.

Custis, John Parke ("Jacky"; 1754–1781)

At the death of his father, Daniel Parke Custis (1711–1757), 3-year-old Jacky Custis became the principal heir to one of the most substantial estates in the Virginia colony. The property that would one day come under his control included large plantations in five counties—York, Hanover, Northampton, New Kent, and King William—as well as houses in Williamsburg and Jamestown. Although not much is known about Jacky Custis's very early life, one thing is certain: his mother's relentless anxiety about him. Martha simply could not bear to be apart from her son for any length of time. A two-week separation in 1762 left her miserable. "I carried my little patt [Patsy] with me," she informed a sister, "and left Jackey at home for a trial to see how well I could stay without him though we ware gon but wone fortnight I was quite impatient to get home if I at any time heard the doggs barke or a noise out I thought thair was a person sent for me I often fansied he was sick or some accident had happened to him so that I think it is impossible for me to leave him as long as Mr Washington must stay when he comes down." From that time until Jacky went away to school six years later, he was constantly by his mother's side.

Washington placed Jacky in Jonathan Boucher's school in Caroline County in 1768. For the next five years Jacky's progress, such as it was, is chronicled in the frequent correspondence between the schoolmaster and Washington. Jacky was Boucher's most important pupil and was treated accordingly, and Jacky apparently had no scruple about taking advantage of his tutor. By the time Jacky was old enough to leave Boucher's tutelage for King's College in New York City, Boucher had come to believe his happy-go-lucky charge was "exceedingly indolent" and "surprisingly voluptuous: one would suppose Nature had intended him for some Asiatic Prince." One valuable service that Boucher performed for Jacky at Washington's behest was to have the youth and his servant Joe surreptitiously inoculated against smallpox. Martha was not told of the event until after their recovery.

Jacky hardly had settled into King's College when he received the news that his sister, Patsy, had died suddenly. He wrote his mother an encouraging letter but confided to Washington that the "melancholy Subject" caused him so much uneasiness that "I myself could not withstand the Shock, but like a Woman gave myself up entirely to melancholy for several Days." He left school not long afterward to help ease his mother's grief, but soon after his return he found it more pleasant to spend his time with 16-year-old Eleanor Calvert ("Nelly"; c.1757–1811), the second daughter of Benedict and Elizabeth Calvert of Mount Airy in Maryland. Jacky entered into his engagement with Nelly without consulting either his mother or stepfather, and of course they both were disappointed that he had made so important a decision without enlisting their assistance. Washington's letter to his brother-in-law Burwell Basset says much about his view of Jacky's maturity: "I could have wish'd he had postpond entering into the engagement till his Studies were finishd, not that I have any objection to the Match, as she is a girl of exceeding good Character but because I fear, as he has discoverd much fickleness already." Washington was afraid that Jacky might change his mind "and therefore injure the young Lady; or, that it may precipitate him into a Marriage before, I am certain, he has ever bestowd a serious thought of the consequences."

When the time arrived for the marriage ceremony to take place in February 1774, Washington crossed the Potomac to Mount Airy without Martha, who felt that her lingering melancholy over the loss of Patsy might dampen the proceedings. Martha allegedly later wrote to her new daughter-in-law that "God took from me a daughter when June roses were blooming. He has now given me another daughter about her age when winter winds are blowing, to warm my heart again. I am as happy as one so afflicted and blest can be. Pray receive my benediction and a wish that you may long live the loving wife of my happy son and a loving daughter of your affectionate mother M. Washington." The letter may not be genuine, for the manuscript has never come to light, but the sentiments expressed certainly were. Five children were born to Jacky and Nelly, including an infant who died and three girls and a boy who survived to adulthood, each of whom was given the name Parke: Elizabeth Parke Custis ("Eliza"; 1776–1832), Martha Parke Custis ("Patty";

1777–1854), Eleanor Parke Custis ("Nelly"), and George Washington Parke Custis ("Wash"). Nelly and then Wash were adopted by Martha and George shortly after their birth.

Washington took command of the Continental army in June 1775, leaving Jacky to look after the welfare of his mother. "My great concern upon this occasion," he wrote Jacky from Philadelphia, "is the thoughts of leaving your Mother under the uneasiness which I know this affair will throw her into; I therefore hope, expect, & indeed have no doubt, of your using every means in your power to keep up her Spirits." He suggested that Jacky and his family live at Mount Vernon, where they were always welcome, and even more so now. Although they did not abandon their own home, from then until his death in 1781, Jacky's family was at Mount Vernon as often as not. In the spring of 1776 Martha finally consented to be inoculated with smallpox herself so that she could visit her husband at the Continental army encampment, where the disease was rampant. The complete success of the effort apparently left Jacky in a reflective mood, for the letter that he wrote to Washington to inform him of his mother's recovery was more than usually expressive of his love for his stepfather: "I am extremely desireous (but I am at Loss for Words sufficiently expressive) to return you Thanks for your parental Care which on all Occasions you have shewn for Me. It pleased the Almighty to deprive me at a very early Period of Life of my Father, but I can not sufficiently adore His Goodness in sending Me so good a Guardian as you Sir; Few have experience'd such Care and Attention from real Parents as I have done. He best deserves the Name of Father who acts the Part of one."

While Jacky was a minor, Washington had administered the Custis estate to the best future advantage for his stepson. He added two more large tracts of land to the estate, Romancoke in King William County and Pleasant Hill in King and Queen County, where it was supposed Custis would reside eventually. When Jacky came of age and began to handle his own affairs, Washington stepped back, although he continued to offer him fatherly advice. Jacky was not as good a business manager as his stepfather, however. In 1778 he purchased from a neighbor, Robert Alexander, a house and a 900-acre tract of land on the Potomac River, Abingdon, for £12 an acre. In what was becoming all too characteristic of Jacky's general mismanagement of his vast estate, he agreed to pay the principal and compound interest over a twenty-four-year period. The land was pleasantly situated and capable of great improvement, observed Washington when Jacky informed him of the purchase, for he thought the property worth owning, but, he decried, "No Virginia Estate (except a very few under the best management) can stand simple Interest how then can they bear compound Interest." Compound interest on the £12,000 purchase price would mean that Jacky would pay over £48,000 during the twenty-four years— more than £2,000 each year during the period of the agreement. "You may be led away with Ideal profits; you may figure great matters to yourself to arise from this, that, or t'other Scheme, but depend upon it they will only exist in the imagination, and that year after year will produce nothing but disappointment and new hopes; these will waste time, whilst your Interest is accumg." After Custis's death in 1781 it took the administrators of his estate more than a decade to negotiate an end to the transaction. Custis also purchased from Alexander's brother Garrard a nearby tract that became Arlington.

Historian Douglas Southall Freeman stated the consensus of everyone then and since concerning Martha's only surviving son and Washington's stepson when he said that Jacky Custis "was not morally bad by any test. He was good-natured and well-mannered and had no known vice worse than that of laziness and love of an easy life he knew from youth he could afford." Washington, he added, seems to have "made often the most frequent of parental mistakes—that of expecting much and of demanding nothing."

In 1778 Custis was elected to the Virginia House of Burgesses as a delegate from Fairfax County, along with George Mason. When Washington arrived in Virginia in 1781, Jacky decided to take part in the campaign against the British army in Virginia. He contracted camp fever during the siege of Yorktown, and died several days after the British surrender, robbing Washington of the joy of his stunning victory. He was buried at Eltham, the home of his uncle, Burwell Bassett.

At least five portraits of Jacky survive. He and his sister appear in two of them, one by the English portrait painter John Wollaston (b. c.1710) made in 1757 and located in the Lee Memorial Chapel at Washington and Lee University in Lexington, Virginia, and another, an oil on canvas by an unidentified artist, located in the Virginia Historical Society in Richmond. The other three portraits are miniatures, two painted by Charles Willson Peale in 1772 and 1776, located at Mount Vernon, and a copy of the first miniature painted in 1772 by Peale's brother, James Peale (1749–1831), which is in the Virginia Museum of Fine Arts in Richmond.

Related entries: Alexander, Robert; Boucher, Jonathan; Custis, George Washington Parke; Custis, Martha Parke; Peale, Charles Willson

Suggestions for further reading:
"To Jonathan Boucher," 30 May 1768 (*Col. Ser.*, vol. 8).
"To Burwell Bassett," 25 April 1773 (*Col. Ser.*, vol. 9).
"To John Parke Custis," 19 June 1775 (*War Ser.*, vol. 1).
"From John Parke Custis," 10 June 1776 (*War Ser.*, vol. 4).
"To John Parke Custis," 3 August 1778 (*Writings*, vol. 12).

Custis, Martha Parke ("Patsy"; 1756–1773)

Patsy Custis, the younger child of Martha Washington and her first husband, Daniel Parke Custis (1711–1757), was a small child when she was adopted by Washington after his marriage to Martha in January 1759. When Patsy was about 6 years old she began to suffer from epileptic seizures, which increased in severity and frequency as she entered adolescence. She was treated by many doctors, including Hugh Mercer, Washington's close friend and comrade-in-arms; James Carter, the distinguished surgeon in Williamsburg; John Johnson (b. 1745) of Frederick, Maryland; and William Rumney (d. 1783), an English surgeon who settled in Alexandria following his French and Indian War service with the British army. The treatments included "Hartshorne or other Drops commonly used to prevent faitiness and a small Bottle of Ointmt" to keep her body "cool and open"; the "Use of Barley Water and light cooling Food—Frumenty made of Barley or even of wheat"; the wearing of an iron ring; and trips to the baths at Warm Springs (now Berkeley Springs, West Virginia). Medicine was ordered from as far away as England. Washington diligently recorded the days on which her fits took place in a fruitless effort to establish a pattern that might be of benefit.

Washington kept a minute record of the expenditures of his young ward, who upon her father's death had become one of the richest young girls in the colony. Orders from England included silk, gloves, gauze caps with "Blond Lace borders," leather and satin pumps, a "Blewstrand Necklace," and "curls," as well as a "very handsome and fashionable" saddle with a "bridle and everything complete," and a parrot. Patsy occasionally attended plays in Alexandria with her mother and stepfather, and while she was still very young Washington purchased a spinet and songbooks for her. Later she was given lessons by music and dancing masters, and when a tutor was brought to Mount Vernon to begin her older brother Jacky's education, Patsy also received instruction.

On 19 June 1773, after a pleasant Sunday dinner with family and friends, Patsy had a seizure and was dead in two minutes. Her mother and stepfather were overwhelmed. Martha's sister was called to the house to comfort the grieving mother. Word was sent to James Connelly in Alexandria to fit a coffin, and a pall belonging to Washington that had been lent in Alexandria was recalled and prepared. The Reverend Lee Massey of Pohick Church

came to Mount Vernon to conduct the funeral. Condolence letters poured in, many containing kind but candid expressions that Patsy's suffering was now behind her. Washington wrote his wife's brother-in-law Burwell Bassett, expressing the family's sadness in typical eighteenth-century prose: "It is an easier matter to conceive, than to describe, the distress of this Family; especially that of the unhappy Parent of our Dear Patcy Custis, when I inform you that yesterday removd the Sweet Innocent Girl into a more happy, & peaceful abode than any she has met with, in the afflicted Path she hitherto has trod. She rose from Dinner about four Oclock, in better health and spirits than she appeard to have been in for

Patsy Custis, by Charles Willson Peale (Mount Vernon Ladies' Association of the Union)

some time; soon after which she was siezd with one of her usual Fits, & expird in it, in less than two Minutes without uttering a Word, a groan, or scarce a Sigh.—this Sudden, and unexpected blow, I scarce need add has almost reduced my poor Wife to the lowest ebb of Misery; which is encreas'd by the absence of her Son (whom I have just fixed at the College in New York, from whence I returnd the 8th Instt)."

At least three portraits of Patsy survive, two of which depict Patsy with her brother. One was painted by the itinerant English painter John Wollaston (b. c.1710) in 1757 and is located at the Lee Memorial Chapel at Washington and Lee University in Lexington, Virginia. The second portrait depicting the two children is by an unidentified artist and located in the Virginia Historical Society in Richmond. A miniature painted in 1772 by the renowned artist Charles Willson Peale is located at Mount Vernon.

Related entries: Custis, John Parke; Peale, Charles Willson

Suggestions for further reading:
"To Burwell Bassett," 20 April 1773 (*Col. Ser.,* vol. 9).
"From John Parke Custis," 5 July 1773 (*Col. Ser.,* vol. 9).

D

Dagworthy Controversy

*I*n the fall of 1755, John Dagworthy (d. 1784), a New Jersey native then living in Maryland, claimed that his king's commission of 1746 as a captain in a joint British-American expedition against the French at Montreal and Quebec entitled him to precedence over all colonial officers at Fort Cumberland, Maryland, including the senior officer at the fort, Lt. Col. Adam Stephen of the Virginia Regiment. Aware of Dagworthy's claims, Washington, colonel of the Virginia Regiment, stayed away from Fort Cumberland to keep Dagworthy from directly challenging his authority and began construction of another fort on the Virginia side of the Potomac River. "I can never submit to the command of Captain Dagworthy," he wrote Virginia governor Robert Dinwiddie, "since you have honoured me with the command of the Virginia regiment, &c." Dinwiddie agreed and allowed Washington to travel to Boston in February 1756 to get Gen. William Shirley, the commander of all the British forces in America, to settle the matter. Shirley's opinion was that Dagworthy's royal commission had expired when the expedition to Canada was abandoned in 1747 and that Dagworthy presently served as a provincial captain from Maryland and thus should submit to Washington's authority if the two should find themselves together. Dagwor-

thy cooperated, although he nevertheless assumed command of Fort Cumberland when the Virginians withdrew from it in the spring of 1757.

Related entry: Dinwiddie, Robert

Suggestions for further reading:
"From Adam Stephen," 4 October 1755 (*Col. Ser.*, vol. 2).
"To Robert Dinwiddie," 5 December 1755 (*Col. Ser.*, vol. 2).
"From William Shirley," 5 March 1756 (*Col. Ser.*, vol. 2).

Death

"*S*aturday, Decr. 14th. 1799. This day being marked by an event which will be memorable in the History of America, and perhaps of the World, I shall give a particular statement of it, to which I was an eye witness—" So began the fullest eyewitness account of the last illness and death of George Washington, made by his secretary Tobias Lear. Perhaps no other event in American history so well illustrates the precariousness of life in the centuries preceding the advent of modern medicine as the death of George Washington. When he died at age sixty-seven, Washington was the survivor of not only the dangers and hardships of two lengthy wars but also several major illnesses, including smallpox, malaria, and

"*Funeral Ceremonies*" *from F. L. Brockett.* The Lodge of Washington. *Alexandria, Va.: George E. French, 1876 (Library of Congress)*

pneumonia. Universally respected for his leadership roles in founding the new American republic, and quite possibly the wealthiest man on the continent, Washington took ill while riding about his farms and died two days later. His last anxieties were typical: ordering mundane affairs, such as arranging his accounts and his military papers, giving burial directions, apologizing for the trouble he was causing, and affectionately remembering his relatives.

Washington had developed a stoical attitude toward death at an early age, which was reinforced by his experiences in two wars. Although he did not dwell on death, and he certainly did not fear it, many statements in his writings, especially after the Revolutionary War, reveal that he had contemplated it and planned not to be surprised by it. Shortly after his return to Mount Vernon at the end of the war, he wrote to Adrienne, marquise de Lafayette, in the spring of 1784 that "I am now enjoying domestic ease under the shadow of my own Vine, & my own Fig tree; & in a small Villa, with the implements of Husbandry & Lambkins around me, I expect to glide gen-

tly down the stream of life, 'till I am entombed in the dreary mansions of my Fathers." Such phraseology appeared in his correspondence from time to time for the next fifteen years. On the occasion of the death of his sister, Betty, in April 1797, he wrote his nephew George Lewis (1757–1821), "The melancholy occasion of your writing has filled me with inexpressable concern. The debt of nature however sooner or later must be paid by us all, and although the seperation from our nearest relatives is a heart rending circumstance, reason religeon & Philosophy, teach us to bear it with resignation; while time alone can ameliorate, & soften the pangs we experience at parting." Of his brother Charles's death in September 1799, only three months before his own, Washington wrote to Burgess Ball, Charles's son-in-law, "The death of near relations, always produces awful, and affecting emotions, under whatsoever circumstances it may happen. That of my brother's, has been so long expected, and his latter days so uncomfortable to himself, must have prepared all around him for the stroke; though painful in the effect. I was the *first,* and am now the *last,* of my fathers Children by the second marriage who remain. when I shall be called upon to follow them, is known only to the giver of life. When the summons comes I shall endeavour to obey it with a good grace."

When the summons came the following December, Washington was busy planning for the future. As Lear recalled in his diary, the general had ridden about his farms from ten in the morning to after three in the afternoon, when he came in to dine. "Soon after he went out," said Lear, "the weather became very bad, rain, hail, and snow falling alternately with a cold wind." Washington franked some letters intended for the evening post, but refrained from sending a servant out in the severe weather. Lear, noticing that Washington's neck appeared to be wet, and that snow was hanging upon his hair, remarked on those facts, but Washington said no, his "great Coat" had kept him dry. He appeared at dinner without changing his clothes, and in the evening "he appeared as well as usual." He apparently took cold, however, for on Friday he complained of a sore throat. A heavy snowfall kept him inside Friday morning, but in the afternoon he left the mansion house to mark some trees that he wanted cut down. Despite a hoarseness that had developed during the course of the day, and that had grown worse in the evening, he was very cheerful, and spent what Lear described as an entertaining evening, reading aloud himself as well as listening to his secretary, who at Washington's request read the debates of the Virginia general assembly on the election of a senator and governor— "and on hearing Mr. Madison's observations respecting Mr. Monroe, he appeared much affected and spoke with some degree of asperity on the subject, which I endeavoured to moderate, as I always did on such occasions." On his retiring Lear suggested that he take something for his cold, but he answered no, "you know I never take any thing for a cold. Let it go as it came."

Between two and three o'clock on Saturday morning, he woke Martha and told her he was very unwell, that he had an ague. Observing that he could scarcely speak and that he breathed with difficulty, Martha wanted to call a servant, but he stopped her, lest she too should take cold. At dawn a servant woman, Caroline, went into the room to make a fire, and Martha sent her immediately to call Lear, who quickly dressed and went to their room. Washington asked Lear to send for his old friend and physician Dr. James Craik, and for George Rawlins, one of the overseers, to bleed him while they waited for Craik's arrival. Lear obeyed the requests before trying to administer to Washington "a mixture of Molasses, Vinegar & butter" that had been "prepared to try its effects in the throat; but he could not swallow a drop.

Whenever he attempted it he appeared to be distressed, convulsed and almost suffocated." Soon after sunrise the overseer came in and, against Martha's wishes but at Washington's firm insistence, bled him freely. Finding no relief from bleeding, and unable to swallow, an external bathing "with salvolatila" was applied "in the gentlest manner" to his throat, with Washington observing that "tis very sore." "A piece of flannel dip'd in salvolatila was put around his neck, and his feet bathed in warm water; but without affording any relief."

About eight o'clock in the morning, Washington expressed a desire to get out of bed. He was dressed and led to a chair by the fire but found no relief from the change, and after two hours returned to bed. In the meantime, a messenger, Cyrus, was sent for Dr. Gustavus Brown of Port Tobacco, whom Dr. Craik had recommended to be called in an emergency. Craik came in soon after, and upon examining Washington, put "a blister of Cantharides on the throat, took some more blood from him, and had a gargle of Vinegar & sage tea, and ordered some Vinegar and hot water for him to inhale the steam which he did;—but in attempting to use the gargle he was almost suffocated. When the gargle came from his throat some phlegm followed it, and he attempted to Cough, which the Doctor encouraged him to do as much as possible; but he could only attempt it." Craik then requested, about eleven o'clock, that Dr. Elisha Cullen Dick might be sent for, as he feared Dr. Brown was delayed. More bleeding and a blister afforded no relief. Dick arrived about three o'clock in the afternoon, and Brown soon after. Upon consultation the doctors decided to bleed him again, and administer a little "Calomel & tarter em.," but again without any effect.

About half past four o'clock, Washington requested that Martha bring from his desk two wills, one of which he remarked was useless, as being superseded by the other, and was burned by Martha at his request. After this was done, he spoke to Lear: "I find I am going, my breath can not last long. I believed from the first that the disorder would prove fatal. Do you arrange and record all my late military letters and papers. Arrange my accounts and settle my books, as you know more about them than any one else, and let Mr. Rawlins finish recording my other letters which he has begun." Lear assured him this would be done, and he then asked if he had omitted anything which it was essential for him to do, "as he," in Lear's words, "had but a very short time to continue among us. I told him I could recollect nothing; but that I hoped he was not so near his end; he observed smiling, that he certainly was, and that as it was the debt that all must pay, he looked to the event with perfect resignation."

In the course of the afternoon Washington appeared to be in great pain and distress, from the difficulty of breathing, and he frequently changed his position in the bed. He requested to leave his bed again, but the change offered no relief, and he returned to bed after only a half hour. He asked about his nephew Lawrence Lewis and stepgrandson George Washington Parke Custis, who were visiting New Kent and not expected back at Mount Vernon until the 20th of the month. About five o'clock he said to his old friend Craik, "*Doctor, I die hard; but I am not afraid to go; I believed from my first attack that I should not survive it; my breath can not last long.*" Craik, overwhelmed with grief, pressed his hand but could not utter a word. A few minutes later doctors Dick and Brown came in, and Washington told the three doctors, "I feel myself going, I thank you for your attentions; but I pray you to take no more trouble about me, let me go off quietly, I can not last long." Agreeing that "all which had been done was without effect," the younger doctors withdrew from the room, leaving Craik and the family alone. Washington continued in the same situation, "uneasy &

restless, but without complaining," until eight o'clock, when the physicians returned and "applied blisters and cataplasms of wheat bran to his legs and feet; after which they went out (except Dr. Craik) without a ray of hope." Lear then sent messages to nearby family members, requesting them to come to Mount Vernon as soon as possible.

With great difficulty Washington made several attempts to speak about ten o'clock. At length he said to Lear, "*I am just going. Have me decently buried; and do not let my body be put into the Vault in less than three days after I am dead.*" (In other accounts Lear wrote two days.) Lear nodded in assent but could not speak. Washington asked, "*Do you understand me?*" and Lear replied, "Yes." "*Tis well,*" Washington said, the last words he would utter. Before his death, which took place before eleven o'clock, "his breathing became easier; he lay quietly . . . and he expired without a struggle or a sigh! While we were fixed in silent grief, Mrs. Washington (who was sitting at the foot of the bed) asked with a firm & collected voice, *Is he gone?* I could not speak, but held up my hand as a signal that he was no more. *'Tis well,* said she in the same voice, *All is now over I shall soon follow him! I have no more trials to pass through!*" In addition to Martha, Craik, and Lear, the others in the room included Christopher Sheels, his bodyservant, who had been with him all day; servants Caroline, Molly, and Charlotte; and Mrs. Forbes, the housekeeper, who had been in and out of the room throughout the day and evening. Other family members apparently were downstairs.

About midnight Washington's remains were brought downstairs and laid out in the large room. When his body was measured for the coffin, it was "In length 6 feet 3½ inchs. exact." The funeral, directed by Washington's will to be private and without ostentation, was held four days later. It was attended by his relations (except Martha, who remained at the house), friends, neighbors, and official representatives from nearby Alexandria and the Federal City. The procession to the family tomb included his war horse, now riderless and equipped with his holsters and pistols and led by two slaves, and the local militia, accompanied by eleven pieces of cannon. A vessel in the Potomac River fired minute guns.

Modern medical diagnosis attributes Washington's death to acute epiglottitis caused by a virulent bacterium, probably *Hemophilus* influenza type b. Inflammation of the epiglottis, a cartilaginous plate at the base of the tongue near the entrance to the larynx, causes the symptoms exhibited during Washington's last illness, including its rapid onset; severe sore throat; difficulties in swallowing, speaking, and breathing; and restlessness.

Related entries: "First in War, First in Peace, and First in the Hearts of His Countrymen"; Last Will and Testament; Lear, Tobias; Papers

Suggestions for further reading:
"To Adrienne, Marquise de Lafayette," 4 April 1784 (*Con. Ser.,* vol. 1).
"To George Lewis," 9 April 1797 (*Ret. Ser.,* vol. 1).
"To Burgess Ball," 22 September 1799 (*Ret. Ser.,* vol. 4).
Henriques, Peter R. 2000. *The Death of George Washington: He Died as He Lived.* Mount Vernon, VA.
Lear, Tobias. 1906. *Letters and Recollections of George Washington.* New York.
Marx, Rudolph. 1955. "A Medical Profile of George Washington" (*American Heritage,* vol. 6).
"Last Illness and Death of Washington" (vol. 1, appendix 2). Jared Sparks. 1834–1837. 12 vols. *The Writings of George Washington.* Boston.
"Proceedings of Congress in Consequence of the Death of Washington" (vol. 1, appendix 3). Jared Sparks. 1834–1837. 12 vols. *The Writings of George Washington.* Boston.
Wells, Walter A. 1927. "Last Illness and Death of Washington" (*Virginia Medical Monthly,* vol. 53).

Declaration of Independence

Late in the summer after the Declaration of Independence was proclaimed, someone with intimate knowledge of Washington's life and family began to circulate a letter purporting to have been written by Washington in which he deplored the Continental Congress's decision to separate from the mother country. Washington suspected John Randolph, the former attorney general of Virginia who had fled to England, as the culprit. The letter fell on deaf ears in America, however, for Washington never had claimed to be an early advocate of independence. Indeed, the Fairfax County Resolves, a remonstrance to the king stating the colonists' grievances against the British government, passed at a public meeting over which Washington presided in July 1774, opened with the explicit statement that the inhabitants of the Virginia colony considered themselves to be "subject to all his Majesty's just, legal, and constitutional Prerogatives." It is "our greatest Wish and Inclination," stated the eighth resolution, "as well as Interest, to continue our Connection with, and Dependance upon the British Government." Resolve number nine did admit tacitly that the idea had crossed the minds of some, however, when it claimed that the British ministry was "artfully prejudicing our Sovereign, and inflaming the Minds of our fellow-Subjects in Great Britain, by propagating the most malevolent falsehoods, particularly that there is an Intention in the American Colonies to set up for independant States."

Tench Tilghman claimed to have heard similar statements after joining Washington's military family in 1776. In an April 1778 letter to his father, Tilghman wrote that he had heard Washington "declare a thousand times, and he does it every day in the most public company, that independence was farthest of anything from his thoughts, and that he never entertained the idea until he plainly saw that absolute conquest was the aim and unconditional submission the terms which Britain meant to grant." Tilghman, however, did not say

A painting by John Trumbull depicting the signing of the Declaration of Independence, 4 July 1776 (Library of Congress)

when Washington came to that fateful conclusion. A June 1777 letter to Washington from Arthur Lee (1740–1792) recollecting a visit to Mount Vernon nine years earlier suggests that Washington might have contemplated the idea of American sovereignty long before separation from Great Britain came to pass: "I never forgot your declaration when I had the pleasure of being at your House in [July] 1768 that you was ready to take your Musket upon your Shoulder, whenever your Country call'd upon you, I heard that declaration with great satisfaction, I recollect it with the Same, & have seen it verify'd to your Immortal honor & the eminent advantage of the Illustrious cause in which we are contending."

That Washington thought Congress's declaration irreversible, once made, is evidenced in his March 1777 letter to British army major Apollos Morris, who was thinking of joining the Patriot cause. "You are sensible that Independance has been declar'd by the United States," he wrote, "nor could they in my Opinion for the sake of Engaging the first Military Genius in Europe in their Service, recede a single Iota from it." By the following year he was even more adamant, writing that, to "discerning men, nothing can be more evident, than that a peace, on the principles of dependence, however limited, after what has happened, would be, to the last degree, dishonorable and ruinous." The same year he wrote, "Nothing short of independence, it appears to me, can possibly do. A peace on other terms would, if I may be allowed the expression, be *a peace of war.*"

It was on 9 July 1776 that Washington received word that Congress had been "pleased to dissolve the Connection which subsisted between this Country, and Great Britain, and to declare the United Colonies of North America, free and independent STATES," and his General Orders for that date directed the troops to assemble in the "evening on their respective Parades, at six OClock, when the declaration of Congress, shewing the grounds & reasons of this measure, is to be read with an audible voice." The orders expressed Washington's hope that "this important Event will serve as a fresh incentive to every officer, and soldier, to act with Fidelity and Courage, as knowing that now the peace and safety of his Country depends (under God) solely on the success of our arms." In the evening the Declaration was read, followed by "three Huzzas from the Troops," and later that night the troops in New York City pulled down and beheaded the large gilded lead statue of George III that stood on the bowling green at the south end of Broadway, "the troops having long had an inclination so to do, tho't this time of publishing a Declaration of Independence, to be a favorable opportunity." Washington mildly reprimanded the troops responsible in the next day's General Orders, and the 4,000-pound body of the statue was later sent to Connecticut to be melted into bullets for the American troops. In addition, ten ounces of gold was garnered from the statue's gold leaf.

Washington at least twice sought to reward his troops on the anniversary of the "important Event." In 1779 his desire "to distribute a portion of rum to the soldiers, to exhilerate their spirits upon the occasion" was thwarted because of the scantiness of the stock. In "remembrance of that auspicious Event," an extra gill per man was issued to celebrate the "Joyful Occasion" on 4 July 1782, however.

Related entries: Spirituous Liquors; Tilghman, Tench

Suggestions for further reading:
"Fairfax County Resolves," 18 July 1774 (*Col. Ser.*, vol. 10).
"From John Hancock," 6 July 1776 (*War Ser.*, vol. 5).
"To the Massachusetts General Court," 9 July 1776 (*War Ser.*, vol. 5).
"To Artemas Ward," 9 July 1776 (*War Ser.*, vol. 5).
"General Orders," 9, 10 July 1776 (*War Ser.*, vol. 5).
"To Apollos Morris," 1 March 1777 (*War Ser.*, vol. 8).
"From Arthur Lee," 15 June 1777 (*War Ser.*, vol. 10).
"American Independence" (vol. 2, appendix 10). Jared Sparks. 1834–1837. 12 vols. *The Writings of George Washington*. Boston.

Delaware Crossing

The departure and landing sites of Washington's famous crossing of the Delaware River from Pennsylvania into New Jersey on Christmas night 1776, for an early morning attack against the British, are both named Washington Crossing and are located respectively in Bucks County, Pennsylvania, and near Titusville in Mercer County, New Jersey. The orders of march directed the troops to assemble "one Miles back of [Samuel] McKonkeys ferry" about eight miles north of Trenton with his army of 2,400 men and eighteen cannon. Advance planning guaranteed that plenty of "Durham" boats, approximately fifty feet long and built to ferry fifteen tons each, were on hand. Hessian troops apparently were informed that boats were being brought down to the ferry, but did not act on the information. Mariners from Essex County, Massachusetts, were directed to handle the boats during the crossing. Washington's report to Continental Congress president John Hancock after the battle gives the details. "The Evening of the 25th," he wrote, "I ordered the Troops intended for this Service to parade back of McKonkey's Ferry, that they might begin to pass as soon as it grew dark, imagining we should be able to throw them all over, with the necessary Artillery, by 12 OClock, and that we might easily arrive at Trenton by five in the Morning, the distance being about nine Miles." By the time the boats began to ferry troops over the river, snow

Washington Crossing the Delaware, *Christmas 1776, after the painting by Emanuel Leutze (Library of Congress)*

was falling that changed to bitter sleet about eleven. "But the quantity of Ice, made that Night," reported Washington, "impeded the passage of Boats so much, that it was three OClock before the Artillery could all be got over, and near four, before the Troops took up their line of march." Following the battle the troops returned to their encampment across the river by way of McConkey's ferry.

Washington, genuinely satisfied with his troops' performance, thanked them in General Orders on 27 December, declaring that he "did not see a single instance of bad behaviour in either officers or privates." He rewarded the troops by having the captured field pieces, arms, horses, and accoutrements valued and the amount distributed proportionately among the officers and men who crossed the river. The commissary general also was ordered to provide rum for the soldiers.

On the Pennsylvania side of the river is a 478-acre state park, which contains a me-morial building and Emanuel Leutze's famous painting *Washington Crossing the Delaware* (c.1851). The Washington Crossing Monument, erected in 1916, overlooks the embarkation site. In 1918 the area, known since 1829 as Taylorsville and before that Tomlinson's Ferry, was renamed Washington Crossing. On the New Jersey side of the river is a 372-acre state park, including the McConkey ferry house, now a museum.

Related entry: Princeton, Battle of

Suggestions for further reading:
"General Orders," 25, 27 December 1776 (*War Ser.*, vol. 7).
"To John Hancock," 27 December 1776 (*War Ser.*, vol. 7).

Descriptions of Washington

Legion are the descriptions of Washington in his day cutting a "fine figure" and looking "truly noble and majestic; being tall and well proportioned." "You had prepared me to entertain a favorable opinion of General Washington," wrote Abigail Adams to her husband after first meeting Washington in 1775, "but I thought the half was not told me. Dignity with ease and complacency, the gentleman and soldier, look agreeably blended in him. Modesty marks every line and feature of his face." These and many like statements concerning Washington began to stream from the pens of his contemporaries while Washington was yet a young man, and, as his fame increased with his age, it was virtually assured that such sentiments would not diminish as his gray years approached. "Men caught their breath in admiration when they saw him on a spirited horse," noted biographer Douglas Southall Freeman of his subject's easy, soldierlike bearing. "Everything about him," Freeman continued, "suggested the commander—height, bearing, flawless proportions, dignity of person, composure, and ability to create confidence by calmness and by unfailing, courteous dignity." He was, as childhood friend Buckner Stith recalled in 1787, "a sound looking, modest, large boned young Man." What follows are perhaps the three most famous and often-quoted descriptions of Washington. The first is a depiction that focuses on the physique of Washington when he was in his late twenties, written by his close friend George Mercer in 1760. The second is from Thomas Jefferson's appraisal of Washington's character, written some fourteen years after the latter's death. The last is a series of anecdotes that Washington's stepgrandson George Washington Parke Custis narrated for posterity in his *Recollections and Private Memoirs of Washington*.

I. George Mercer to a Friend, 1760
He may be described as being straight as an Indian, measuring 6 feet 2 inches in his stockings, and weighing 175 lbs when he took his seat in the House of Burgesses in 1759. His frame is padded with well developed muscles, indicating great strength. His bones and joints are large as are his hands and feet. He is wide shouldered but has not a deep or round chest; is neat waisted, but is broad across the hips, and has rather long legs and arms. His head is well shaped, though not large, but is gracefully poised on a superb neck. A large and straight rather than a prominent nose; blue-grey penetrating eyes which are widely separated and overhung by a heavy brow. His face is long rather than broad, with high round cheek bones, and terminates in a good firm chin. He has a clear tho rather colorless pale skin which burns with the sun. A pleasing and benevolent tho a commanding countenance, dark brown hair which he wears in a cue. His mouth is large and generally firmly closed, but which from time to time discloses some defective teeth. His features are regular and placid with all the muscles of his face under perfect control, tho flexible and expressive of deep feeling when moved by emotions. In conversation he looks you full in the face, is deliberate, deferential and engaging. His demeanor [is] at all times composed and dignified. His movements and gestures are graceful, his walk majestic, and he is a splendid horseman.

II. Thomas Jefferson to Walter Jones, 2 January 1814
I think I knew General Washington intimately and thoroughly; and were I called on to delineate his character, it should be in terms like these.

His mind was great and powerful, without being of the very first order; his penetration strong, though not so acute as that of a Newton, Bacon, or Locke; and as far as he saw, no judgment was ever sounder. It was slow in operation, being little aided by invention or imagination, but sure in conclusion. Hence the common remark of his officers, of the advantage he derived from councils of war, where hearing all suggestions, he selected whatever was best; and certainly no General ever planned his battles more judiciously. But if deranged during the course of the action, if any member of his plan was dislocated by sudden circumstances, he was slow in re-adjustment. The consequence was, that he often failed in the field, and rarely against an enemy in station, as at Boston and York. He was incapable of fear, meeting personal dangers with the calmest unconcern. Perhaps the strongest feature in his character was prudence, never acting until every circumstance, every consideration, was maturely weighed; refraining if he saw a doubt, but, when once decided, going through with his purpose, whatever obstacles opposed. His integrity was most pure, his justice the most inflexible I have ever known, no motives of interest or consanguinity, of friendship or hatred, being able to bias his decision. He was, indeed, in every sense of the words, a wise, a good, and a great man. His temper was naturally high toned; but reflection and resolution had obtained a firm and habitual ascendency over it. If ever, however, it broke its bonds, he was most tremendous in his wrath. In his expenses he was honorable, but exact; liberal in contributions to whatever promised utility; but frowning and unyielding on all visionary projects and all unworthy calls on his charity. His heart was not warm in its affections; but he exactly calculated every man's value, and gave him a solid esteem proportioned to it. His person, you know, was fine, his stature exactly what one would wish, his deportment easy, erect and noble; the best horseman of his age, and the most graceful figure that could be seen on horseback. Although in the circle of his friends, where he might be unreserved with safety, he took a free share in conversation, his colloquial talents were not above mediocrity, possessing neither copiousness of ideas, nor fluency of words. In public, when called on for a sudden opinion, he was unready, short and embarrassed. Yet he wrote readily, rather diffusely, in an easy and correct style. This he had acquired by conversation with the world,

for his education was merely reading, writing and common arithmetic, to which he added surveying at a later day. His time was employed in action chiefly, reading little, and that only in agriculture and English history. his correspondence became necessarily extensive, and, with journalizing his agricultural proceedings, occupied most of his leisure hours within doors. On the whole, his character was, in its mass, perfect, in nothing bad, in few points indifferent; and it may truly be said, that never did nature and fortune combine more perfectly to make a man great, and to place him in the same constellation with whatever worthies have merited from man an everlasting remembrance.

III. George Washington Parke Custis
His Person and Personal Appearance.
Anecdotes of His Great Physical Prowess.
In person Washington was unique: he looked like no one else. To a stature lofty and commanding, he united a form of the manliest proportions, limbs cast in Nature's finest mould, and a carriage the most dignified, graceful, and imposing. No one ever approached the Pater patriæ that did not feel his presence.

So long ago as the vice regal court at Williamsburg, in the days of Lord Botetourt, Col. Washington was remarkable for his splendid person, the air with which he wore a small sword, and his peculiar walk, that had the light elastic tread acquired by his long service on the frontier, and was a matter of much observation, especially to foreigners.

While Col. Washington was on a visit to New York in 1773, it was boasted at the table of the British governor that a regiment just landed from England contained among its officers some of the finest specimens of martial elegance in his Majesty's service—in fact the most superb looking fellows ever landed upon the shores of the new world. "I wager your Excellency a pair of gloves," said a Mrs. Morris, an American lady, "that I will show you a finer man in the procession

to-morrow than your Excellency can select from your famous regiment." "Done,
madam," replied the Governor. The morrow came (the 4th of June,) and the procession in honor of the birthday of the
King advanced through Broadway to the
strains of military music. As the troops defiled before the Governor, he pointed out
to the lady several officers by name,
claiming her admiration for their superior
persons and brilliant equipments. In rear
of the troops came a band of officers not
on duty, of colonial officers, and strangers
of distinction. Immediately on their approach, the attention of the Governor was
seen to be directed toward a tall and martial figure, that marched with grave and
measured tread, apparently indifferent to
the scene around him. The lady now
archly observed, "I perceive that your Excellency's eyes are turned to the right object; what say you to your wager now,
sir?" "Lost, madam," replied the gallant
Governor: "When I laid my wager, I was
not aware that Col. Washington was in
New York."

To a question that we have been asked
a thousand and one times, viz., to what
individual, known to any who are yet living, did the person of Washington bear
the nearest resemblance? we answer, to
Ralph Izard, Senator from South Carolina, in the first Congress under the
Constitution. The form of Izard was cast
in Nature's manliest mould, while his air
and manner were both dignified and imposing. He acquired great distinction,
while pursuing his studies in England, for
his remarkable prowess in the athletic exercises of that distant period.

An officer of the Life Guard has been
often heard to observe, that the Commander-in-Chief was thought to be the
strongest man in his army, and yet what
thews and sinews were to be found in the
army of the Revolution. In 1781, a company of riflemen from the county of Augusta, in Virginia, reinforced the troops of
Lafayette. As the stalwart band of moun-
taineers defiled before the General, the
astonished and admiring Frenchman ex-

Portrait of Washington by Charles Willson Peale (Library of Congress)

claimed: "Mon Dieu! what a people are
these Americans; they have reinforced me
with a band of giants!"

Washington's great physical powers
were in his limbs: they were long, large,
and sinewy. His frame was of equal
breadth from the shoulders to the hips.
His chest, though broad and expansive,
was not prominent, but rather hollowed
in the centre. He had suffered from a pulmonary affection in early life, from
which he never entirely recovered. His
frame showed an extraordinary development of bone and muscle; his joints
were large, as were his feet; and could a
cast have been preserved of his hand, to
be exhibited in these degenerate days, it
would be said to have belonged to the
being of a fabulous age. During the last
visit by Lafayette to Mount Vernon,
among many and interesting relations of

events that occurred in olden days, he said to the writer, "It was in this portico that you were introduced to me in 1784; you were then holding by a single finger of the good General's remarkable hand, which was all that you could do, my dear sir, at that time."

In the various exhibitions of Washington's great physical prowess, they were apparently attended by scarcely any effort. When he overthrew the strong man of Virginia in wrestling, while many of the finest of the young athletæ of the times were engaged in the manly games, Washington had retired to the shade of a tree, intent upon the perusal of a favorite volume; and it was only when the champion of the game strode through the ring, calling for nobler competitors, and taunting the student with the reproach that it was the fear of encountering so redoubted an antagonist that kept him from the ring, that Washington closed his book, and without divesting himself of his coat, calmly walked into the arena, observing that fear formed no part of his being; then grappling with the champion, the struggle was fierce but momentary, for, said the vanquished hero of the arena, in Washington's lion-like grasp I became powerless, and was hurled to the ground with a force that seemed to jar the very marrow in my bones; while the victor, regardless of the shouts that proclaimed his triumph, leisurely retired to his shade, and the enjoyment of his favorite volume.

The power of Washington's arm was displayed in several memorable instances—in his throwing a stone across the Rappahannock river below Fredericksburg, another from the bed of the stream to the top of the Natural Bridge, and yet another over the Palisades into the Hudson. While the late and venerable C. H. Peale was at Mount Vernon in 1772, engaged in painting the portrait of the provincial colonel, some young men were contending in the exercise of pitching the bar. Washington looked on for a time, then grasping the missile in his master hand, whirled the iron through the air, which took the ground

far, very far, beyond any of its former limits—the Colonel observing, with a smile, "You perceive, young gentlemen, that my arm yet retains some portion of the vigor of my earlier days." He was then in his fortieth year, and probably in the full meridian of his physical powers; but those powers became rather mellowed than decayed by time, for "his age was like a lusty winter, frosty yet kindly," and, up to his sixty-eighth year, he mounted a horse with surprising agility, and rode with the ease and gracefulness of his better days. His personal prowess, that elicited the admiration of a people who have nearly all passed from the stage of life, still serves as a model for the manhood of modern times.

With all its development of muscular power, the form of Washington had no appearance of bulkiness, and so harmonious were its proportions, that he did not appear so passing tall as his portraits have represented. He was rather spare than full during his whole life; this is readily ascertained from his weight. The last time he weighed was in the summer of 1799, when having made the tour of his farms, accompanied by an English gentleman, he called at his mill and weighed. The writer placed the weight in the scales. The Englishman, not so tall, but stout, square built, and fleshy, weighed heavily, and expressed much surprise that the General had not outweighed him, when Washington observed that the best weight of his best days never exceeded from 210 to 220. In the instance alluded to he weighed a little rising 210.

Of the portraits of Washington, the most of them give to his person a fulness that it did not possess, together with an abdominal enlargement greater than in the life, while his matchless limbs have in but two instances been faithfully portrayed—in the equestrian portrait by Trumbull of 1790, a copy of which is in the City Hall of New York, and in an engraving by Laugier, from a painting by Cogniet, French artists of distinguished merit. The latter is not an original painting, the head being from Stuart, but the delineation of the limbs is the most perfect extant.

Of the remarkable degree of awe and reverence that the presence of Washington always inspired, we shall give one out of one thousand instances. During the cantonment of the American army at the Valley Forge, some officers of the 4th Pennsylvania regiment were engaged in a game of fives. In the midst of their sport they discovered the Commander-in-Chief leaning upon the enclosure and beholding the game with evident satisfaction. In a moment all things were changed. The ball was suffered to roll idly away, the gay laugh and joyous shout of excitement were hushed into a profound silence, and the officers were gravely grouped together. It was in vain the Chief begged of the players that they would proceed with their game, declared the pleasure he had experienced from witnessing their skill, spoke of a proficiency in the manly exercise that he himself could have boasted of in other days. All would not do. Not a man could be induced to move, till the General, finding that his presence hindered the officers from continuing the amusement, bowed, and wishing them good sport, retired.

Related entries: Custis, George Washington Parke; Jefferson, Thomas; Mercer, George; Natural Bridge, Virginia; Peale, Charles Willson

Suggestions for further reading:
"George Mercer to a Friend," 1760 (*Col. Ser.,* vol. 6).
"From Buckner Stith," 22 March 1787 (*Con. Ser.,* vol. 5).
"Thomas Jefferson to Walter Jones," 2 January 1814 (*Thomas Jefferson: Writings*).
Custis, George Washington Parke. 1860. *Recollections and Private Memoirs of Washington.* New York.

Diaries

See Papers.

Dinwiddie, Robert (1693–1770)

Virginia lieutenant governor Robert Dinwiddie had been in the American colonies for more than thirty years when he accepted 21-year-old George Washington's offer in the fall of 1753 to "go properly commissioned to the Commandant of the French Forces, to learn by what Authority he presumes to make Incroachments on his Majesty's Lands on the Ohio." Although Washington was adjutant general for the southern district, he had no military experience, but then neither had Dinwiddie, who was in charge of the military affairs of the Virginia colony and who was emerging as the leading proponent of intercolonial unity in matters of defense. Since leaving Glasgow, Scotland, for Bermuda in 1721, Dinwiddie's career consisted mostly of operating his mercantile and shipping business and holding the offices of admiralty agent and collector of the customs for Bermuda and surveyor general for the southern part of America. Nor had his service on the Virginia governor's council in the early 1740s before returning to England for five years in 1745 prepared him for possible hostilities on the frontier. Furthermore, there were no British army officers in the colony from whom he could seek assistance. The last communication from the Crown had commanded Dinwiddie to order any "Persons, whether Indians, or Europeans," encroaching on British settlements to depart in peace, or that failing, "to drive them off by Force of Arms."

The opportunity for Washington to begin a military career that he badly desired was also a chance for Dinwiddie to learn about the Ohio Country, the extent of French incursions there, and the disposition of the Indians toward the British settlements on the frontier. The mission was a complete success, for Washington discovered that the

French indeed had constructed a formidable fort near the Ohio on French Creek, Fort Le Boeuf, that the commandant, Jaques Le Gardeur Saint-Pierre, was defiant, and that both hostile and friendly Indians inhabited the region; among the latter the Half-King and Monacatoocha, two important chiefs of the Six Nations, could be depended on as allies against the French. Moreover, Washington was able to draw upon his surveying experience to produce a detailed plan of the fort and an adequate map of the river systems of the entire Ohio Country. Washington kept a journal while on his mission, which he presented to Dinwiddie upon his return to Williamsburg. Dinwiddie ordered it printed, instantly making Washington one of the most famous men in the colonies. Washington's success in carrying out the mission immediately led to another commission from Dinwiddie, to raise a company of 100 men to take part in the expedition to the Ohio that included both the defeat of Jumonville and Washington's capitulation of Fort Necessity at Great Meadows, Pennsylvania, in June 1754. Washington's subsequent involvement with the defense of the frontier, while commander of the Virginia Regiment and as an aide-de-camp during the Braddock campaign, brought him into continual contact with Dinwiddie for several more years, although by June 1757 Washington had become "convinced it wou'd give pleasure to the Governor to hear that I was involved in trouble: however underservedly, such are his dispositions toward me."

Related entries: Barbados; Braddock's Defeat; Carlyle, John; Dagworthy Controversy; Fort Necessity Campaign; Gist, Christopher; Great Kanawha Tracts; Half-King, The; Muse, George; Van Braam, Jacob

Suggestions for further reading:
Diaries, vol. 1.
"Commission from Robert Dinwiddie," 30 October 1753 (*Col. Ser.,* vol. 1).
"Appointment as Colonel of the Virginia Regiment," 14 August 1755 (*Col. Ser.,* vol. 2).

"To Robert Dinwiddie," 24 November 1756 (*Col. Ser.,* vol. 4).
"To Robert Dinwiddie," 17 September 1757 (*Col. Ser.,* vol. 4).
Alden, John R. 1974. *Robert Dinwiddie: Servant of the Crown.* Charlottesville, VA.

Dismal Swamp Company

The Great Dismal Swamp lies about twenty-five miles from the Atlantic coast in southeast Virginia and northeast North Carolina. It is underlain by peat. At its heart is Lake Drummond, a three- to five-mile pond discovered by the first governor of North Carolina, William Drummond, who was hanged in 1677 by Virginia governor William Berkeley for his role in Bacon's Rebellion. Water drains out of Lake Drummond rather than into it because its elevation is higher than the land around it. The swamp was a favorite source of lumber for shingles in the colony and an important source of fresh water for ships. In the twentieth century it remains a lush habitat for a variety of wild plant and animal life otherwise uncommon to eastern Virginia, including black bears, wildcats, rattlesnakes, and cottonmouth moccasins. Although Washington generally looked westward when contemplating future expansion in America, he recognized the potential value of the Dismal Swamp's 40,000 acres of land for settlement if it could be drained and cleared. With help from its proximity to the important markets of Norfolk, Virginia, the rich soil of the swamp would produce enormous wealth if it could be turned into productive cropland. He thus became a leading proponent in a bold venture to drain the swamp, the Dismal Swamp Company, which would require a series of small canals. Washington traveled to the swamp at least six times between 1763 and 1768.

Washington and three other self-proclaimed "Adventurers for Draining the Dismal Swamp," Thomas Walker (1715–1794), Fielding Lewis, and Burwell Bassett, first journeyed to the swamp in May 1763 to judge the feasibility of draining the land. On the same day the "Adventurers" left Williamsburg for the swamp, the deputy secretary of the Virginia colony, William Nelson (1711–1772), "in behalf of himself and many others" petitioned the Virginia council for a patent to the "considerable quantity" of unclaimed Dismal Swamp land in Norfolk and Nansemond counties. Washington subsequently made a detailed memorandum about the land and creeks of the Dismal Swamp and its subsidiaries for the first meeting of the Dismal Swamp Company, in November 1763. At the meeting the members each agreed to send by the following July five slaves for the "work of draining Improving and Saving the Land," and in July 1764 Washington bought three slaves to send to the swamp. In December 1764 the managers of the company purchased 1,119 acres of land on the road from Suffolk to Norfolk, part of which was in the swamp. John ("Jack") Washington (1740–1777), a distant cousin of Washington and a younger brother of Lund Washington, Mount Vernon's farm manager during the Revolutionary War, became resident overseer of the company's operations in the swamp in the fall of 1765. The company's small laborer force was insufficient for draining much of the swamp's 900 square miles, but it did produce a steady supply of shingles and clapboard.

Over time the company abandoned the idea of draining the swamp in favor of timber harvesting. Washington wanted to open "a communication between the rivers which empty into Albemarle Sound (thro' drummonds Pond) & the waters of Elizabeth or Nansemund Rivers." The Revolutionary War halted the company's efforts to connect the rivers, but after the war Washington took part in the company's renewed efforts to "prosecute the work with vigour," including inquiring into the possibility of

importing "300 able labourers, Germans or Hollanders, not more than eight women," for the purpose. In 1787 the Virginia general assembly passed an act to build the canals, and on the North Carolina side of the swamp the Lebanon Company was formed for the same purpose three years later. The cooperative venture began in 1793 and was not completed until 1828, although different sections of the canal system became operational as early as 1804. Washington sold his share of the company in 1795 to Henry Lee, but the share reverted to Washington's estate in 1809 after Lee failed to make the payments.

The old Dismal Swamp Company effectively closed in 1814.

Related entry: Mississippi Adventure

Suggestions for further reading:
Diaries, vol. 1.
"Dismal Swamp Land Company: Articles of Agreement," 3 November 1763 (*Col. Ser.*, vol. 7).
"To Hugh Williamson," 31 March 1784 (*Con. Ser.*, vol. 1).
"Resolutions of the Dismal Swamp Company," 2 May 1785 (*Con. Ser.*, vol. 2).
Royster, Charles. 1999. *The Fabulous History of the Dismal Swamp Company: A Story of George Washington's Times.* New York.

Distillery

Upon his return to Mount Vernon after retiring from the presidency, Washington entered into "a distillery, on a small scale," with his farm manager James Anderson, a business that he was "entirely unacquainted with." When Anderson proposed to enlarge the operation, Washington appealed to his old friend and Revolutionary War aide-de-camp John Fitzgerald for advice about whether the local market for distilled spirits would justify such an undertaking. Fitzgerald, himself a successful distiller of molasses, was sure that under Anderson's direction "the Distillation of Spirit from Grain" might be carried on to "great advantage" at Mount Vernon.

Anderson, with Washington's prodding, estimated that $520 would be required for "fixing a house for a Distillery 3 more Stills & a Boiler . . . Additional Mash Tubs—We have already one Stove which I bought and will do And the mash Tubs purchased are good as well as every other thing." The building of a "Still house a small malting house & Still," however, was a different matter. That, he said, "I could not well estimate—Our own people will do the whole excepting seting up the Stills, A Strong Cellar must be at hand to Lodge the Spirits in—And if such a Work be's carryd on, the constant Milling of Wheat, Buying Wheat &ca." Once the operation got under way, he added, "I then must move to the place of Action, as the most of the business will be done at that particular Spot."

Washington, convinced of the feasibility of the venture, erected a stone building near the existing gristmill at Mount Vernon's Dogue Run farm for the whiskey-making operation in the fall of 1797. It was described later by Washington as being "a pretty considerable Distillery," supplied with "five Stills, Boilers—&ca which, with the (Stone) House, has cost me a considerable Sum already, but I find these expenditures are but a small part of the advances I must make before I shall receive any return for them, having all my Grain yet to buy to carry on the business." A well was sunk for the use of the distillery "wch furnishes excellent water." A number of hogs were fattened for the slaughter in the rear of the distillery, which produced manure "over & above" what was needed for the gardens there.

Anderson's son John assisted his father in the management of the distillery from the beginning of its operation in early 1798. Anderson declined the opportunity to rent the mill and distillery together in the fall of 1799, and Washington rented the distillery along with the mill and Dogue Run farm to his nephew Lawrence Lewis. Another nephew, William Augustine Washington, in October 1798 agreed to supply corn for the distillery from Haywood, an estate further down the Potomac, on an annual basis.

In its best year Washington's distillery produced 12,000 gallons of whiskey and earned him £344—not bad considering, ironically, that one of the major tests of his presidency concerned the distilling of liquor.

Related entries: The Two James Andersons; Spirituous Liquors; Whiskey Rebellion

Suggestions for further reading:
"From John Fitzgerald," 12 June 1797 (*Ret. Ser.,* vol. 1).
"To John Fitzgerald," 12 June 1797 (*Ret. Ser.,* vol. 1).
"To James Anderson," 18 June 1797 (*Ret. Ser.,* vol. 1).
"From James Anderson," 21 June 1797 (*Ret. Ser.,* vol. 1).
"To Robert Lewis," 26 January 1798 (*Ret. Ser.,* vol. 2).

Dogue Run Farm

See Mount Vernon.

Duer, William (1747–1799)

Born in Devonshire, England, and educated at Eton College, William Duer served as an ensign in the British army and as an aide-de-camp to Lord Clive, whom he accompanied to India in 1764. Abandoning a military career, he moved to the American colonies in 1768 and entered the cotton-manufacturing business in New York and New Jersey. With the coming of the Revolution, he broke with the policies of his native country and in 1775 was elected to the New York provincial congress and appointed a colonel and deputy adjutant general in the New York militia. In 1776 he served on the drafting committee in the New York Constitutional Convention and was appointed to the New York committee of safety and the committee for detecting conspiracies. After traveling to Washington's headquarters to confer about American efforts to obstruct and defend the Hudson River in the summer of 1776, he opened a correspondence with Washington to convey items of secret intelligence. From 1777 to 1779 he represented New York in the Continental Congress, in which he became a member of the Board of War. Beginning in 1777 he also became the first judge of common pleas for Charlotte (now Washington) County, New York, an office he held until 1786. When Duer married Lady Kitty Alexander, the daughter of Lord Stirling, in 1779, Washington gave the bride away. Duer also was a signer of the Articles of Confederation and led the commission for conspiracies, established by Congress in 1780.

After the Revolution, Duer continued to play a leadership role in New York state. A founder of the Bank of New York in 1784, he was named to the state's Board of Treasury in 1786, and he also served in the New York general assembly in 1786. In 1787 he secured a tract for the Scioto Company of over 4 million acres north and west of the purchase of the Ohio Company and bounded on the west by the Scioto River. The speculative scheme was unable to sustain itself, however. In 1789 Washington appointed Duer assistant secretary of the newly founded U.S. Treasury Department. After holding the office for only six months, he resigned after being accused of using his office to speculate in government securities and army contracts. Duer spent the last years of his life imprisoned for debt in New York City after some land and business speculations failed. He was buried at Jamaica, Long Island, New York.

Related entry: Conway, Thomas

Suggestions for further reading:
"From William Duer," 28 January 1777 (*War Ser.,* vol. 8).

Dunmore, John Murray, Fourth Earl of (1732–1809)

"*I* am glad to find that our Noble Govr has, at length, met with a Check—was one of our Bullets A[i]md for him the World would be happily rid of a Monster without any person sustaining a loss. this is my opinion at least." Seldom, if ever, did George Washington express a like sentiment about anyone, as he did here about Lord Dunmore, a Scottish peer who sat in Parliament for several years and served as governor of New York before becoming governor of Virginia in September 1771. And this opinion had not been one that Washington had held very long. Only three months before making that statement while commanding the Continental army at Cambridge, Massachusetts, in the fall of 1775, Washington, in discussing the safety of his wife, Martha, had told his farm manager Lund Washington that "I can hardly think that Lord Dunmore can act so low, & unmanly a part, as to think of siezing Mrs Washington by way of revenge upon me." Despite "a Stir about Mrs Washingtons Continuing at Mt Vernon" and warnings from some friends and family members for Martha to leave her home, she and Washington remained convinced of her safety, and indeed it was the spring of 1781 before a British vessel was able to seriously threaten Mount Vernon. By then Dunmore long since had retreated to England.

Before the Revolutionary War the two men had been cordial if not intimate during Washington's frequent visits to Williamsburg. They often met at the governor's palace or at one of Dunmore's farms a few miles outside the bustling Virginia capital to discuss measures proposed in the Virginia general assembly or land-patent issues still lingering from the French and Indian War. In 1773 they even planned to make a summer trip together to the Ohio Valley so that the governor, in the words of historian Douglas Southall Freeman, "a hard-headed Scot of Washington's own age, who had a kindred appetite for land," could view firsthand the richness of his western lands. Disruption of legislative business the following year, when Dunmore suddenly dissolved the House of Burgesses in the spring, apparently was not meant by the governor to be taken as an unkind act aimed at any of the delegates in particular, nor was it interpreted as such by the members. On the contrary, both sides seemed eager to continue on friendly terms with the other, Washington included, who on the day after the dissolution attended a ball thrown by the delegates welcoming Lady Dunmore and the governor's family to Virginia. The correspondence between Washington and Dunmore abruptly ended in April 1775, however, with a quarrel over the governor's declaration making all western bounty land surveys carried out under the Proclamation of 1754 null and void, which affected several hundred thousand acres, including 20,000 belonging to Washington. Still, when Dunmore ordered the gunpowder magazine at Williamsburg seized only days later, Washington, numbered among the colony's moderates, advised against the use of arms as a response.

Washington's reaction to hearing the news that Dunmore had sought refuge on board the British warship *Fowey* at Yorktown to escape capture by a company of Hanover County volunteers in June 1775 has not been discovered. Nevertheless, the governor certainly had fallen low in Washington's estimation by the fall of 1775 as reports trickling into Continental army headquarters described Dunmore and "his Banditti" of "North British Tories" and "Negroe Soldiers . . . commanded by Scotchmen— proper Officers for Slaves" making incursions from the Chesapeake Bay on board royal ships against the towns, villages, and plantations bordering the navigable rivers of Virginia. The interception of a packet of Dunmore's letters to British army officers and various supporters of the king across the south scheming to bring together British army troops, Indians, and slaves for the purpose of invading the southern colonies sealed Washington's judgment of his former acquaintance and elicited the following prediction from Washington, made to Richard Henry Lee, a delegate to the Continental Congress from Virginia:

> Lord Dunmores Letters to General [William] Howe &ca wch very fortunately fell into my hands, & Inclosed by me to Congress, will let you pretty fully into his diabolical Schemes—If my Dear Sir that Man is not crushed before Spring, he will become the most formidable Enemy America has—his strength will Increase as a Snow ball by Rolling; and faster, if some expedient cannot be hit upon to convince the Slaves and Servants of the Impotency of His designs. You will see by his Letters what pains he is taking to invite a Reinforcement at all events there, & to transplant the War to the Southern Colonies. I do not think that forcing his Lordship on Ship board is sufficient; nothing less than depriving him of life or liberty will secure peace to Virginia; as motives of Resentment actuates his conduct to a degree equal to the total destruction of the Colony.

After failing to reestablish his authority in Virginia, Dunmore sailed for New York in the summer of 1776, adding nothing more to the strength of the British army than 106 sickly "Black & White" soldiers. He sailed for England in November 1776 and returned to the Americas some years later as governor of the Bahamas.

Related entry: Lewis, Andrew

Suggestions for further reading:
Diaries, vol. 3.
"To Lord Dunmore," 3 April 1775 (*Col. Ser.,* vol. 10).

"From Lord Dunmore," 18 April 1775 (*Col. Ser.,* vol. 10).
"To Lund Washington," 20 August 1775 (*War Ser.,* vol. 1).
"To Richard Henry Lee," 26 December 1775 (*War Ser.,* vol. 2).
Scribner, Robert L., and Brent Tarter, eds. 1977. *Revolutionary Virginia: The Road to Independence* (vol. 3). Charlottesville, VA.

August th 1745

George Washington

Geometry

One of the seven Sciences, and a very useful and Necessary Branch of the Mathematicks, whose subject is greatness: for as Number is the subject of Arithmatick, so that of Geometry is Magnitude, which hath its beginning from a Point, that is a thing supposed to be indivisible, and the original of all Dimension. By it is explained the Nature, kind and property of continued Magnitude that is a line, a superficies and a solid of which in their proper order.

Geometrical Definitions

1st A Point is void of Length Breadth and Dyth as the Point A.

2 A line is made by the moving of a Point and has length only as A B which is the first kind of Magnitude.

3 A Superficies is made by the moving of a line and has length and breadth as A B C D which is the second kind of Magnitude.

First page of Washington's school exercises, August 1745 (Library of Congress)

E

Education

David Humphreys's biography of Washington contains the tantalizing but cryptic statement that "his education was principally conducted by a private tutor." Although many have sought to identify the unnamed tutor, Washington himself edited Humphreys's draft in 1786 without commenting on the passage. It is known that Washington attended school with George Mason's "Neighbour & Your old School-fellow, Mr [David] Piper," a planter who lived in the vicinity of Washington and Mason's estates but who had been raised in Washington Parish, Westmoreland County, near Washington's birthplace, and a school stood at the nearby Lower Church of the parish. Old traditions, unsubstantiated by either word from Washington himself or by any other eighteenth-century documentary sources, have suggested that Washington was tutored first by a convict servant recruited by his father and by a local sexton in Truro Parish before attending the Reverend James Marye's Fredericksburg school, which opened in 1740. It was at Marye's school, or so the story goes, that young George discovered his natural inclination for ciphering and began to master mathematics, at which he eventually became quite proficient. Another plausible tradition says that, during much of the first five years after his father's death (1743–1748), he lived with his half brother Augustine, Jr. at Popes Creek and attended a day school several miles away operated by Henry Williams. From his school exercises that have survived in his papers at the Library of Congress, we know that, in addition to ciphering, Washington practiced writing, spelling, and grammar, all of which assisted the early development of a style of writing that can be characterized as clear, dignified, and effective, very well suited for the life of constant communication that was to become so essential. Even so, as his biographer Douglas Southall Freeman noted, that style developed gradually over time, making his earlier writings "wordy and sometimes vague."

Washington's school exercises, thought to have been finished by about age 15 (dates range from 1741 to 1747), consist mostly of copy work and mathematical lessons. Clearly written and neatly arranged, the topics cover a variety of subjects, especially mathematics and surveying, but also geography, poetry, the making of legal forms, and the well-known "Rules of Civility and Decent Behaviour in Company and Conversation," once thought to have been compiled if not composed by Washington himself but in the twentieth century shown to have come out of early Reformation Europe. Despite the traditions, however, there are no indications of who might have helped the young boy with these lessons. The copy work apparently included at least some oral instruction.

The school exercises consist of 218 pages—109 individual leaves bound together into three volumes after the papers passed into the possession of the Library of Congress. The first volume, consisting of 34 pages (17 leaves) that were bound together in 1892, contains a formula, "To Keep Ink from Freezing or Moulding" (1 page); two poems, "True Happiness" and "On Christmas Day" (2 pages); the above-mentioned "Rules of Civility" (10 pages); and a variety of legal forms (contracts, leases, conveyances, deeds, bills of sale and exchange, and wills; 21 pages).

The second volume, bound at the same time as the first volume, contains 58 pages (29 leaves) of school exercises on the following subjects: the "Mensuration of Plan Superfices" (4 pages); calculations surrounding the "Ecclesiastical and civil Kalender" (5 pages); lessons in geography (6 pages); surveying (8 pages); measuring solids and liquids (15 pages); and geometry lessons, including definitions, theorems, illustrations, and problems (19 pages).

The remaining volume, not bound until the 1930s, contains 122 pages (61 leaves) of mathematical and surveying problems: "Mensuration of Superficies" (2 pages); multiplication problems (2 pages); scratch paper (2 pages); money conversion and exchange (9 pages); simple and compound interest (15 pages); decimals (22 pages); lessons in geometry, trigonometry, and calculating square roots (29 pages); and surveying (39 pages).

The sources from which the above lessons were taken have been identified for some of the exercises. The formula for protecting ink and parts of the exercises concerning the measurements of solids and liquids, for instance, were taken directly from a book written by George Fisher and published in London in 1727, *The Instructor: Or, Young Man's Best Companion*. The second edition of William Leybourn's *The Compleat Surveyor* (1657) offered some of the lessons in geometry. The poem "On Christmas Day" most likely was copied by Washington shortly after it made its appearance in the February 1743 issue of *Gentleman's Magazine* (London). The poem "True Happiness," reprinted in the February 1734 issue of the same magazine, had appeared earlier in *Universal Spectator*. Most well known, perhaps, of all Washington's school exercises, are the ten pages of the first volume, the "Rules of Civility and Decent Behaviour in Company and Conversation." The copying of these maxims by the young lad did not merely fulfill a practice session for handwriting but also inculcated proper attitudes about personal comportment, language, manners, cleanliness, and other practices, and treatment of others expected of the Virginia gentry—care for the body, respect and consideration for others, and reverence for God. The best-known rule, or at least the one most often applied to Washington, is the last: "110th Labour to keep alive in your Breast that Little Spark of Ce[les]tial fire Called Conscience." But many others, more mundane, perhaps, are not to be neglected: "15th: Keep your Nails clean and Short, also your Hands and Teeth Clean yet without Shewing any great Concern for them"; or "90 Being Set at meat Scratch not neither Spit Cough or blow your Nose except there's a Necessity for it." Washington copied Francis Hawkins's seventeenth-century English translation of the rules. (Washington never mastered a foreign language.) Charles Moore, who traced these 110 maxims back through various English and French versions to the sixteenth century in his 1931 book on the subject, rightly summed up the long-held view on the subject: "These maxims were so fully exemplified in George Washington's life that biographers have regarded them as formative influences in the development of his character."

It is clear that Washington's formal education was of an elementary nature and

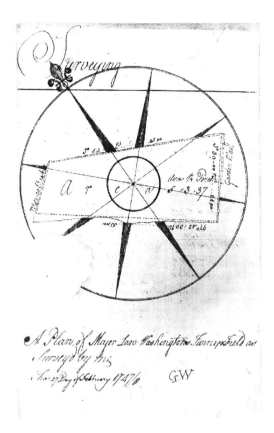

A *Plan of Major Law. Washington's Turnip Field as
Surveyed by me,
this 27 Day of February 1747/8*   GW

*An early drawing from George Washington's
surveying career (Library of Congress)*

opments in politics, agriculture, science, and
the arts, he also scanned the newspapers of
the day, receiving, says Freeman, more of
them than he read. His favorite seemed to
be Dunlap and Claypoole's daily (except
Sunday) *Pennsylvania Packet,* although he
also liked the *Pennsylvania Herald.* He of
course depended on the various editions of
the *Virginia Gazette* throughout his life for
business-related news close to Virginia. His
learning about the two subjects most important to him—agriculture and the military—was based as much on observation
and discovery as the books that he avidly
collected and read or the European magazines to which he subscribed. Freeman asserted that Washington's training in military
affairs was largely self-taught, based on his
experience before and during the French
and Indian War, until the time when he was
made commander in chief of the Continental army in 1775. He believed that Washington gave little attention to the final campaigns of the French and Indian War after
leaving the military in 1758, neglecting not
only to read the histories of that conflict as
they emerged but also to study the strategy
and tactics employed by the opposing
forces. Washington was schooled, as Freeman observed, "in those things an impatient
officer most disliked, the collection and custody of supplies, correspondence with officials, endless hard travel, the maintenance of
discipline, and the punishment of those who
defied it." Nevertheless, his correspondence
is sprinkled with allusions to the necessity
and value of supplementing experience
with knowledge, such as this one from
1755: "Remember, that actions, and not the
commission, make the Officer. More is expected from him than the title. Do not forget, that there ought to be a time appropriated, to attain knowledge, as well as to
indulge in pleasure. As we now have no opportunities to improve from example, *let us
read,* for this desirable end."

It is possible that, had his father lived
longer, Washington might have been sent

probably culminated with a short apprenticeship with an experienced land surveyor,
or at least someone knowledgeable about
surveying practices and skilled in the use of
surveying instruments. Washington likely
accompanied such a person on one or more
surveying field trips in order to learn how
to supplement his own written assignments
with the actual practice of fieldwork. The
22-acre survey near his birthplace at Popes
Creek, apparently made in 1747 when he
was 15 years old, was perhaps the final act
of his formal education. His diaries attest
many times to the fact that his surveyor's
eye never dimmed, however, as he often
noted the lay of the land across which he
traveled.

Washington's acquisition of knowledge,
however, did not end at age 15. As an adult,
in order to keep abreast of the latest devel-

across the sea for an English education like his father and older half brothers, Lawrence and Augustine, Jr., who all attended Appleby Grammar School in Cumberland, England. If that had been the case, it is not unlikely that Washington would have taken a degree at one of the colleges abroad or in America, as did a great number of his contemporaries in the revolutionary generation. The deficiency of education that Washington always keenly felt (and which was not compensated for by the many honorary degrees conferred on him after he became famous) no doubt contributed to the reasons that compelled him to assemble the magnificent library at Mount Vernon. More important for the country, however, was Washington's pursuit after he became president of a national education legacy not dissimilar to those designed by Benjamin Franklin, Thomas Jefferson, and Benjamin Rush (1746–1813). Washington's proposal to establish a national university failed, but his idea for a military academy came to fruition not long after his death. On a minor scale, the gift of his shares of the James River Company to Liberty Hall Academy at Lexington, Virginia, helped to endow what in time became a respected university, Washington and Lee, and he lent his name along with modest contributions to Washington College at Chestertown, Maryland, and Alexandria Academy at Alexandria, Virginia.

Related entries: Alexandria Academy; Tucker, St. George; Rules of Civility (Selected Writings)

Suggestions for further reading:
"School Exercises," 1744–1748 (*Col. Ser.*, vol. 1).
"From George Mason," 12 June 1756 (*Col. Ser.*, vol. 3).
Helderman, Leonard C. 1932. *George Washington: Patron of Learning.* New York.
Longmore, Paul K. 1988. *The Invention of George Washington.* Reprint, 1999. Charlottesville, VA.
Moore, Charles, ed. 1931. *George Washington's Rules of Civility and Decent Behaviour in Company and Conversation.* New York.
Potter, Eliphalet Nott. 1895. *Washington: A Model in His Library and Life.* New York.
Schroeder, John Frederick. 1854–1855. *Maxims of Washington: Political, Social, Moral, and Religious.* New York.

F

Fairfax, George William (1724–1787)

See Belvoir.

Fairfax, Sarah Cary ("Sally"; c.1730–1811)

See Belvoir.

Fairfax, William (1691–1757)

William Fairfax was born in Yorkshire, England, and served in the British army before receiving royal appointments in the colonies, first in the Bahamas and later in Massachusetts. He moved to Virginia in 1734 to become the agent for his cousin, Thomas, Lord Fairfax, the proprietor of the vast Northern Neck Proprietary, settling in King George County. In 1736 Fairfax began accumulating choice tracts of land further up the Potomac River and closer to the center of the proprietary, and in the early 1740s he built a grand mansion, Belvoir, not far from Mount Vernon. Fairfax's daughter Ann married George Washington's half brother Lawrence, and Fairfax's wife, Deborah Clarke, was a sister of Gedney Clarke

(1711–1764), the host of George and Lawrence in Barbados when the brothers went there in 1748 in search of a climate that might offer restoration to Lawrence's declining health. Two of Fairfax's three sons, George William and Bryan, became among Washington's closest friends. The third, William Henry, was a lieutenant in the British army who died at Quebec in 1759. A daughter, Hannah (1742–1808), married Washington's first cousin Warner Washington in 1764. Lawrence's marriage offered young George an entrance into the most prominent circles of the colony, as evidenced by Washington's advice to his younger brother John Augustine to visit the Fairfax family at Belvoir often, "as it is in their power to be very serviceable upon many occasion's to us as young beginner's . . . for to that Family I am under many obligation particularly to the old Gentleman."

Many have speculated that Fairfax, at the behest of his cousin the proprietor, obtained Washington's commission as the first surveyor of Culpeper County in 1749 from the president and masters of the College of William and Mary, the authorities responsible for issuing surveyorships. The fact that Leybourn's volume on surveying owned by Fairfax was included on a list of books at Mount Vernon made by Washington around 1764 tends to lend credence to such a belief. While in the office, between the ages of 17 and 20, Washington carried out more than 190 professional land surveys, allowing him to not only earn a good income but also meet some of the social elite of the colony and patent in his own name some of the best lands on the frontier. As a member of the provincial governor's council, Fairfax kept Washington informed of measures passed by the House of Burgesses as well as other news from the Virginia capitol in Williamsburg and beyond. Fairfax, who was also the county lieutenant of Fairfax County and lieutenant colonel of the Fairfax County militia, was on the committee appointed by Virginia governor Robert Dinwiddie in the fall of 1753 to draft the commission and instructions to Washington for his trip to warn the French off the Ohio. Later, when Washington was in command of the Virginia Regiment at Winchester, Fairfax made it a point to write him encouraging letters and to send him instructions on the construction of fortifications.

That Fairfax later took a special interest in offering Washington encouragement is undeniable, although it may be well-nigh impossible to properly estimate the influence Fairfax exerted on the life of young George. Of Fairfax Washington wrote, "whose memory and friendship, I shall ever retain a most grateful sense."

Related entries: Barbados; Belvoir; Fairfax of Cameron, Bryan Fairfax, Eighth Baron; Fairfax of Cameron, Thomas Fairfax, Sixth Baron

Suggestion for further reading:
"From William Fairfax," 9 May 1756 (*Col. Ser.,* vol. 3).

Fairfax Independent Company

Forty-nine prominent Fairfax County, Virginia, "Gentlemen & Freeholders" met at the county courthouse on 21 September 1774 to form a company of associators "not to exceed one hundred Men,

by the Name of The Fairfax independant Company of Volunties." The associators pledged to drill together to learn "military Exercise & Discipline" that they might be prepared to defend, ostensibly from Indian attacks, the "legal prerogatives" of King George III and the "Principles of the British Constitution." Furnished with "a good Fire-lock & Bayonet, Sling Cartouch-Box, and Tomahawk," members further promised to "constantly keep by us a Stock of six pounds of Gunpowder, twenty pounds of Lead, and fifty Gun-flints, at the least." The company was outfitted with assistance from Washington, who arranged to have arms, ammunition, drill manuals, and adornments for uniforms as well as "a pair of Colours, two Drums, two Fifes, and two Halberts," obtained in Philadelphia. Washington also, along with George Mason, advanced and collected money to pay for the supplies. The company settled upon blue uniforms "turn'd up with Buff; with plain yellow metal Buttons, Buff Waist Coat & Breeches, & white Stockings," more than likely the same uniform that Washington donned at the Second Continental Congress in 1775 when he was unanimously elected commander in chief of the Continental army. (An indentured tailor, Andrew Judge, made "1 Suite Regimentals" each for Washington, his farm manager Lund Washington, and his stepson, John Parke Custis.) The company also apparently decided to "take the Fashion of the Hunting Shirt Cap & Gaiters" from Washington.

The Fairfax Independent Company united with similarly formed companies of gentleman volunteers from Fauquier, Prince William, Richmond, and Spotsylvania counties in choosing Washington as field commander. Although a march to Williamsburg was proposed when Governor Dunmore seized the powder magazine in April 1775, neither the Fairfax Independent Company nor any of the other companies under Washington's direction saw actual military service, and all five were superseded the following August when the third Virginia convention reorganized the defense of the colony.

Related entry: Mason, George

Suggestions for further reading:
"From the Fairfax Independent Company," 19 October 1774 (*Col. Ser.,* vol. 10).
"Resolutions of the Fairfax County Committee," 17 January 1775 (*Col. Ser.,* vol. 10).
"From George Mason," 17 February 1775 (*Col. Ser.,* vol. 10).
"From the Fairfax Independent Company," 25 April 1775 (*Col. Ser.,* vol. 10).
"To the Officers of Five Virginia Independent Companies," 20 June 1775 (*War Ser.,* vol. 1).
"From the Fairfax Independent Company," 8 July 1775 (*War Ser.,* vol. 10).

Fairfax of Cameron, Bryan Fairfax, Eighth Baron (1736–1802)

Bryan Fairfax, the son of William and Deborah Clarke Fairfax of Belvoir, was Washington's lifelong friend and neighbor. He spent part of his youth living with his mother's relatives in Salem, Massachusetts. Upon his maturity in 1754 he joined an uncle's merchant firm in Barbados, but his stay proved short, and he returned to the mainland the same year to begin clerking for his brother-in-law, John Carlyle of Alexandria, Virginia. The young man's restlessness soon led him elsewhere for employment, and, with Great Britain on the brink of war with France, his eyes naturally fell upon the profession that his friend had chosen. With the assistance of his prominent father, who was not only Washington's friend and patron but also the senior member of the colonial council, Fairfax soon obtained a lieutenant's commission in Washington's regiment. "I am," wrote William Fairfax to Washington in May 1756, "therefore become a Solicitor in behalf of Bryan Fx who Seems now to like a Military

Life, that on a Vacancy You would please to appoint Him a Lieutenant in Some Company whereof the Captain is an exemplary worthy Officer, And if agreable to Bryan of which I am not certain; I persuade my Self He will diligently apply Himself to learn the Arts of War under your leading Example." A second letter soon followed, and from it Washington learned that the father had advised his son to "Study the Theory of Fortification and Gunnery as the Practice will be better understood—and is a Knowledge that adds much to a Soldier's Character." The elder Fairfax apparently also thought that Bryan was impressionable if not reckless, and added, "When I cautiond Bryan against Gaming, I told him, I imagind You would also discountenance it as a pernicious Tendency." Washington was able to place his young friend in Capt. George Mercer's company in July 1756, but Fairfax resigned his commission before the end of the year.

Less than a month after leaving Washington's regiment, Fairfax was partaking "of several merry Meetings and Dancings in Westmoreland and Essex" counties, apparently in search of a wife, and the following spring, after being "twice refused in his Love Addresses," he disappeared for a week, only to resurface in the Annapolis gaol under suspicions of being a wanted felon. He apparently had been snared while attempting to travel to New York to enlist in the British army. John Carlyle fortunately was able to redeem the captive and ease the minds of his family and of Washington. Fairfax's pretensions to a military career waned after this fiasco, although he did enter the Virginia militia service the following June as a captain, and briefly led his company to Fort Loudoun to reinforce Washington's Virginia Regiment.

Washington remained privy to gossip about Fairfax's love affairs, and in September 1758 Fairfax himself wrote Washington that "in Answer to your Enquiry I can scarce say whether I am alive or dead: I have been so long disorder'd both in Mind and Body that I am really between both. Disappointments in Love & repeated Colds have reduced me much; however tho' I am sensible of the Follies of this Life I am no ways desirous of leaving them: I had rather bear the Slings and Arrows of outrageous Fortune than venture upon the unknown Regions of Eternity. The Prospect is gloomy even when viewed by a Mind that thinks itself prepared for the Journey; but how dismal it must appear to those who are unprepared for it!" The same month, Washington, taking a hint from Sarah Cary Fairfax, Fairfax's sister-in-law, predicted that among the "Ladies upon a Matrimonial Scheme" wishing to be "transformed into that charming Domestick" was a Miss Cary. Fairfax did indeed win the hand of Sally Fairfax's younger sister Elizabeth, and they settled at Towlston Grange on Difficult Run in Fairfax County after their marriage in 1759. Washington later stood in as godfather for at least one of their children.

Fairfax, like Washington, was an avid fox hunter, and before the Revolutionary War the two men often engaged in the sport together. Fairfax also sold Washington a 600-acre tract, Chattins Run, on Goose Creek in Fauquier County in 1772. Early in the conflict with Great Britain the political sympathies of Fairfax and Washington diverged as Fairfax counseled a more moderate course of action, but they remained friends. In a passionate exchange of lengthy letters in August 1774 about the turn that political affairs were taking, Washington told his old friend that "I cannot conclude, without expressing some concern that I should differ so widely in Sentiments from you in a matter of such great Moment, & general Import; & should much distrust my own judgment upon the occasion, if my Nature did not recoil at the thought of Submitting to Measures which I think Subversive of every thing that I ought to hold dear and valuable—and did I not find, at the sametime, that the voice of Mankind is

with me." Fairfax in reply admitted that "I am very sorry we happen to differ in opinion. I hope however that our Sentiments will again coincide as in other Matters." Fairfax never became a supporter of the American cause.

A few months after Washington had taken control of the Continental army at Cambridge, Massachusetts, his farm manager and distant cousin Lund Washington wrote to inform him that Fairfax "is become a preacher he gave Public Notice that on such a Day he shoud preach at his own House Accordingly on that Day, Many Asembled to hear him, but to their great Confusion & surprize he Advise'd them to return to the Boosom of that Church in which they had been brought up (The Church of England) for he had been at much panes in Examineg the Scriptures, & the different modes of Worshipg the Supreme being, which was now adopted by many, to the disgrace of Christianity, & that he found none so pure & undefiled as that prescribed by the Canons of the Church of England." Washington probably wondered at his friend's newfound piety and may have frowned at his poorly veiled attempt to turn his neighbors toward the officially sanctioned church of the country that Washington himself was leading a war against, but unfortunately no response to Fairfax's actions has ever come to light. In 1789, when Washington was settling into the office of the presidency, Fairfax was ordained an Episcopal priest.

Fairfax never was able to harmonize his political views with those of his friends and neighbors, and when it became clear that the war would drag along he decided to go to England to live. In the fall of 1777 he visited the Continental army headquarters at Valley Forge, Pennsylvania, where he obtained Washington's consent to go to New York and a pass allowing him to cross enemy lines. Fairfax met disappointment at New York, however, for he was unwilling to swear the oaths required of him when applying for permission to board a vessel bound for England. His undertaking thus was a failure, but along with the thoughts about his lack of success that he carried back to Virginia, Fairfax bore a fresh perspective on his long friendship with Washington. "There are Times when Favours conferred make a greater Impression than at others," he wrote Washington after arriving home, "for, tho' I have received many, and hope I have not been unmindful of them, yet that, at a Time your Popularity was at the highest and mine at the lowest, and when it is so common for Men's Resentments to run high agst those that differ from them in Opinion You should act with your wonted Kindness towards me, hath affected me more than any Favour I have received; and could not be believed by some in N:York, it being above the Run of common Minds."

For his part, Washington affectionately reassured Fairfax that his friendship had "met with no diminution" because of the difference in their political sentiments. "I know the rectitude of my own intentions," Washington said, "and believing in the sincerity of yours, lamented, though I did not condemn, your renunciation of the creed I had adopted." Nor should any other person or power censure Fairfax, Washington told him, since his conduct was not opposed to the general interest of the people or the measures they were pursuing, for while conduct can be controlled, the "powers of thinking originating in higher causes, cannot always be moulded to our wishes." Washington then entered into yet one more discussion aimed at convincing Fairfax that from the "Tea Act to the present Session of Parliament" the British administration had not acted on principle in dealing with the American people. But before launching into his argument, Washington could not resist the opportunity to sermonize a little about how he regarded his friend's recent efforts to go to England: "The determinations of Providence are all

ways wise; often inscrutable, and though its decrees appear to bear hard upon us at times is nevertheless meant for gracious purposes; in this light I cannot help viewing your late disappointment; for if you had been permitted to have gone to england . . . your feelings as a husband, Parent, &ca. must have been considerably wounded in the prospect of a long, perhaps lasting seperation from your nearest relatives."

Although Fairfax remained unpersuaded of the justice of the American side in its dispute with Great Britain, he did live peaceably among his Virginia neighbors throughout the war, and his friendship with Washington was renewed after the latter returned to Mount Vernon in 1783. And Fairfax finally did manage to visit England, two times in fact, first in the 1780s, apparently to pursue the removal of the entail on his estate, and again in 1798 at the urging of physicians who suggested an exposure to sea air might help a lingering illness. When he sailed he had in his possession letters of introduction from Washington. While in England he assumed the title of Lord Fairfax, "which I should have done some years sooner had I known it was becoming to assume it," he wrote Washington, "& that it was not contrary to the American Constitution." (Fairfax's claim to succeed his cousin Robert Fairfax, who had died in 1793, as eighth Baron Fairfax of Cameron, was certified by the House of Lords in 1800.) Washington dined with Fairfax on 7 December 1799 at the latter's home, Mount Eagle, where he found "His Lordship greatly mended though still weak. . . . He has no legs left now, and indeed his whole body is greatly emaciated." Fairfax outlived his old friend, however, for only seven days after the visit Washington himself was dead from an unexpected illness. On the evening before Washington fell ill, Fairfax was among the small number of family and friends who unknowingly dined with Washington for the last time. Washington had remembered Fairfax when making his will the previous summer, bequeathing "a Bible in three large folio volumes, with notes" that had been sent to him from England in 1794.

Related entry: Fairfax, William

Suggestions for further reading:
Diaries, vols. 1–6.
"From William Fairfax," 9, 13–14, 20 May 1756 (*Col. Ser.,* vol. 3).
"From Bryan Fairfax," 15 September 1758 (*Col. Ser.,* vol. 6).
"From Bryan Fairfax," 3, 17 July 1774 (*Col. Ser.,* vol. 10).
"To Bryan Fairfax," 4, 20 July 1774 (*Col. Ser.,* vol. 10).
"From Bryan Fairfax," 5 August 1774 (*Col. Ser.,* vol. 10).
"To Bryan Fairfax," 24 August 1774 (*Col. Ser.,* vol. 10).
"To Bryan Fairfax," 1 March 1778 (*Writings,* vol. 11).
"From Bryan Fairfax," 17 June 1798 (*Ret. Ser.,* vol. 2).
"To Bryan Fairfax," 20 January 1799 (*Ret. Ser.,* vol. 3).

Fairfax of Cameron, Thomas Fairfax, Sixth Baron (1693–1781)

Lord Fairfax was born at Leeds Castle in Kent, England, and educated at Oriel College, Oxford. He came to America to take control of the Northern Neck Proprietary in Virginia, which he inherited from his mother, Catherine Culpeper (1670–1719). The original grant, which encompassed all the Virginia territory between the Rappahannock and Potomac rivers, across the Shenandoah Valley, had been given by King Charles II to a group of his companions in exile in 1649 that included Catherine's grandfather John, Lord Culpeper (1600–1660). Depending on where the boundaries were drawn, it was estimated to be a minimum of 1,400 square miles, or

nearly 1 million to 1.5 million acres. Thomas Fairfax became the sixth Lord Fairfax in 1710 following the death of his father, Thomas, Lord Fairfax (1657–1709), who was ironically a collateral descendant of Oliver Cromwell's second in command, Gen. Thomas, Lord Fairfax (1631–1690).

From 1734 to 1747, when Lord Fairfax settled permanently in Virginia, his cousin William Fairfax acted as his agent for the proprietary. Upon his removal to Virginia, Lord Fairfax made his home with his cousin at Belvoir, not far from Mount Vernon. Lord Fairfax soon moved to Frederick County in the Shenandoah Valley, where in 1749 he built his residence, Greenway Court. Washington's first surveys were for grants included in Lord Fairfax's proprietary, and it is probable that Fairfax was responsible for Washington's commission as surveyor of Culpeper County in 1749. Fairfax did not support the revolutionary cause that his protégé came to lead but was not disturbed—probably because of his connection to Washington. He died before the war's end. Washington wrote his close friend and Fairfax's kinsman George William Fairfax from Valley Forge, Pennsylvania, in March 1778 that he had heard that Lord Fairfax, "after having bowed down to the grave, and in a manner shaken hands with death, is perfectly restored, and enjoys his usual good health, and as much vigour as falls to the lot of Ninety." Upon the death of Lord Fairfax, Washington wrote his neighbor Bryan Fairfax that "altho' the good old Lord had lived to an advanced age, I feel a concern at his death."

Related entries: Belvoir; Fairfax, William; Greenway Court

Suggestions for further reading:
Diaries, vols. 1–4.
"To George William Fairfax," 11 March 1778 (Fitzpatrick, *Writings,* vol. 11).
"To Bryan Fairfax," 22 April 1782 (Fitzpatrick, *Writings,* vol. 24).
"The Northern Neck Proprietary to 1745" (vol. 1, appendixes 1, 2). Douglas Southall

Freeman. 1948–1957. 7 vols. *George Washington: A Biography.* New York.

False Teeth

Possibly the most enduring of all Washington-related myths is that he had a set of wooden teeth. He did not, although two segments of hippopotamus ivory that formed part of the lower teeth of one set of his dentures did rely on a half dozen little wooden pegs to hold them to their ivory base. Neither did Paul Revere, the famous night-riding silversmith of the Revolutionary War, fashion dentures for Washington, although the renowned portrait painter Charles Willson Peale did. Expert examination of the known dental relics attributed to Washington has determined that five types of teeth and tusks were used to prepare false teeth for Washington, including Washington's own and those of other humans, elephants, hippopotamuses, cattle, and probably walrus.

Washington was experiencing serious trouble with his teeth by 1772. He called upon John Baker (d. 1796), an English-born dental surgeon with a medical degree who recently had set up practice in Williamsburg. One of the first professionally trained dentists to practice in America, Baker had come to the colonies in the mid-1760s after honing his skills in England and on the continent. Baker extracted several of Washington's teeth, relieving some of the incessant pain that came after years of chronic decay. He also introduced Washington to the benefits of toothbrushes, although no remedy could reverse the effects of longtime neglect. Treatment, as primitive as it was, was not inexpensive, and Baker's charges for the period between March 1772 and November 1773 amounted to £14.6. Washington also relied on Baker's services after Baker moved to Philadelphia during the Revolutionary War.

In the spring of 1783, Washington, at his Continental army headquarters at Newburgh, New York, found himself in sore need of treatment for "some Teeth which are very troublesome to me at times, and of wch. I wish to be eased, provided I could substitute others (not by transplantation, for of this I have no idea, even with young people, and sure I am it cannot succeed with old,) and Gums which might be relieved by a Man of skill." He turned to a "particularly eminent" French dentist who had come to America three years earlier, Jean-Pierre Le Mayeur, and recommended as "a man of polished Manner, of strict Integrity, at the Head of his Profession and a friend" to the United States. Le Mayeur readily consented to work on Washington, which apparently meant extracting more teeth. Washington was so pleased with the dentist that he extended an invitation to "my House in Virginia," where he promised to show Le Mayeur "every Civility in my power in that State." Le Mayeur did visit Mount Vernon on several occasions, in time developing an intimacy with Washington and his family to the extent that he presented a little red horse to "little master George" (George Washington Parke Custis) as a token of Custis's frequently loaning his own blue horse to Le Mayeur. Martha Washington through the agency of Washington's secretary Tobias Lear sought Le Mayeur's services shortly after Washington's death when dentures made for her by Dr. Benjamin Fendall of Cedar Hill in Charles County, Maryland, proved inadequate. Le Mayeur eventually practiced dentistry across several states, from New York to South Carolina and to Santo Domingo, and especially Virginia, often sending gossipy news to Washington from wherever he had occasion to be.

By the time of his first inauguration, in 1789, Washington had only one tooth left, a lower left premolar. The following year, that single tooth served as the anchor for the base of a set of hippopotamus-tusk dentures

This Gilbert Stuart portrait of George Washington clearly demonstrates that he wore false teeth (Library of Congress)

made by dental surgeon John Greenwood (1760–1819) at his New York City office on Water Street. Pressure on the sole remaining tooth soon caused it to loosen and fall out, leaving nothing to fasten the base of the dentures to. The lower denture, containing one of Washington's own teeth, a lower right molar, has survived and is in the Fraunces Tavern Museum of the New York State Sons of the Revolution in New York City. Another set of dentures made by Greenwood is in the National Museum of

American History the Smithsonian Institution. The upper teeth of that set, carved from an upper canine tooth of a hippopotamus, are fastened to a swaged gold plate made to fit the palate of Washington's mouth. The lower denture was made from hippopotamus and elephant ivory, segments of which were, significantly, held together by a half dozen wooden pegs about the diameter of toothpicks. Greenwood was forced to rework this set of dentures, adding several clumsy braces when the dentures proved unsatisfactory. Despite the fact that Greenwood's dentures were ill-fitting and uncomfortable and in need of frequent alteration, Washington was very pleased with Greenwood's efforts on his behalf and continued to use the dentist for the remainder of his life.

The dentures Peale constructed for Washington formed a curious contraption. The base was made from a lead alloy connected by two strong spiral steel springs designed to press the plates firmly against the gums. The teeth in the lower denture, unusually white and once thought to be made of elk teeth, apparently were ground from cattle, and the upper teeth were shaped out of human teeth and elephant tusk. The often-repeated claim that these dentures weighed three pounds is ridiculous; altogether the teeth, springs, and lead base amount to less than four ounces.

Half of another lower denture, apparently hewn out of walrus tusks, is owned by the Medical College of the University of London, and its companion is missing but rumored to be in South America.

Related entry: Humor

Suggestions for further reading:
"Cash Accounts," April 1772, March, October, and November 1773 (*Col. Ser.*, vol. 9).
"From Jean-Pierre Le Mayeur," 20 January 1784 (*Con. Ser.*, vol. 1).
"To Richard Varick," 22 February 1784 (*Con. Ser.*, vol. 1).
"From Jean-Pierre Le Mayeur," 2 November 1785 (*Con. Ser.*, vol. 3).

"From John Greenwood," 28 December 1798 (*Ret. Ser.*, vol. 3).
"From Benjamin Fendall," 10 August 1799 (*Ret. Ser.*, vol. 4).
Sognnaes, Reidar F. 1973. "America's Most Famous Teeth" (*Smithsonian*, vol. 3).

Farewell Address

See Presidency; Selected Writings.

Father of His Country

Although many have noted the irony that the "Father of His Country" was himself deprived of offspring, who first bestowed this ancient title upon Washington is almost certainly lost in obscurity. A German-language newspaper or almanac printed in Lancaster, Pennsylvania, reputedly used it once in 1779. In his biography of Washington's artillery commander and secretary of war, historian North Callahan asserted that Henry Knox was the first "person of consequence" to use a similar phrase, when he wrote Washington on the eve of the Federal Convention in Philadelphia to consider revisions to the Articles of Confederation. Washington had written to Knox on 8 March 1787 seeking advice as to whether he should attend the Convention, and Knox's reply eleven days later urged Washington to do so:

> Were the convention to propose only amendments, and patch work to the present defective confederation, your reputation would in a degree suffer—But were an energetic, and judicious system to be proposed with Your signature, it would be a circumstance highly honorable to your fame, in the judgement of the present and future ages; and doubly entitle you to the glorious republican epithet—The Father of Your Country.

Knox, a former bookseller from Boston, it has been suggested, may have encountered the term in his vast reading, for it had been bestowed upon Cicero in 64 B.C., and on Peter the Great in 1721. As it turns out, however, the exact phrase already had been used in a poem composed in Washington's honor and sent to him by a "Lady in Holland," the Dutch poet Lucretia Wilhelmina van Winter of Leyden, at the end of the Revolutionary War. Amsterdam businessman Gerard Vogels, who himself upon seeing Washington acclaimed him the "greatest man who has ever appeared on the surface of this earth," said of van Winter when forwarding the twenty-stanza poem to Washington that the poet "thought it just to offer up her last poetical Breath in praise of an Hero who is esteemed by All to have equalled either ancient or modern Ones." Bearing a date of 20 October 1783 and located in the Washington Papers at the Library of Congress, "A Son Exelence, Monseigneur le General Washington," culminates with the final stanza:

Et que votre Statue, au Conseil etablie,
Soit par le grand Congres de ces nots
   honoré:
Contemplez Washington, Pere de la
   Patrie,
Defenseur de la Liberté.

The translation of the poem made for Washington by David Stuart (1753–c.1814), who recently had married the widow of Washington's stepson, Jacky Custis, reads: "May your Statue established by Council, be honored by Congress, with these honourable words—Lo! Washington! the Father of his Country, the Protector of Liberty!"

During Washington's first year as president correspondents writing Washington unabashedly addressed him as the "Father of our Country," the "Saviour of Your Country," the "Founder of a New Empire," and the "Great Father of thy people." Indeed, the country's newspapers began to popularize such language when writing about Washington's trip from Mount Ver-

non to New York City in April 1789 to take the helm of the new national government. The *Pennsylvania Packet* described the reaction of the tens of thousands who turned out to greet him at Philadelphia: "The joy of our whole city upon this august spectacle, cannot easily be described. Every countenance seemed to say, Long, long live George Washington, the Father of the people." The same was true upon Washington's arrival at New York: "All ranks and professions expressed their feelings, in loud acclamations, and with rapture hailed the arrival of the Father of his Country." The next month an address to Washington from the "Mayor, Aldermen, and Commonalty of the City of New York" claimed to have been "Long in the habit of revering you as the Father of our country." Similar addresses from the Connecticut legislature and the citizens of Newburyport, Massachusetts, as well as petitions from old soldiers and praises from children poured in the following fall. James Hardie in early 1792 sent a copy of his Latin grammar to Washington as a testimony of his "respect for one, who on account of his many & superiour virtues, is by all deservedly named *the Father of his Country.*"

Before Washington's death the title had entered the public consciousness, not only in America but also abroad. For instance, the wealthy and eccentric political and agricultural reformer and historian, David Steuart Erskine, eleventh earl of Buchan (1742–1829), of Dryburgh in Scotland, who had struck up a correspondence with Washington in the late 1780s, upon receiving word in January 1800 of Washington's death, recommended to the public "the constant remembrance of the moral and political Maxims conveyed to its citizens by the Father and Founder of the United States." Not everyone had shared Buchan's enthusiasm for Washington, however. Some Democratic-Republican critics of his political policies had spoken of Washington as the "stepfather of his country" during the second term of his presidency.

No doubt Mason Locke Weems boosted the title's popular currency in his *Life of Washington,* the runaway best-seller of the early nineteenth century. Weems, who used the exact phrase only twice, although his book was littered with allusions to Washington the father, seemed to indicate that the title was already in vogue, when he wrote, "That dearest and best of all appellations, '*the father of his country,*' was the natural fruit of that *benevolence* which he so carefully cultivated through life." Interestingly, Weems, who twice called Washington the "father of his army," labeled George III "the *expected father of his people,*" possibly alluding to an appellation bestowed on the king before the Revolution. Weems also called attention to the fact that the idea, if not the exact title, was used by French travelers to America. He noted that François-Jean de Beauvoir, chevalier de Chastellux, who visited Washington's Continental army headquarters during the war, had written that he was "astonished and delighted to see this great American living among his officers and men as a father among his children, who at once revered and loved him with a filial tenderness." The journalist Jacques-Pierre Brissot de Warville (1754–1793), another famous French traveler, who visited Mount Vernon in 1788, had assured his readers, said Weems, that, "throughout the continent, every body spoke of Washington as of a father."

Once fashionable, the term began to appear everywhere. The church divine William E. Channing eloquently wrote that "By an instinct which is unerring, we call Washington, with grateful reverence,— THE FATHER OF HIS COUNTRY." Henry Wadsworth Longfellow later referred to the title in lines written about the fine old colonial mansion that Washington used for his Continental army headquarters at Cambridge, Massachusetts, early in the Revolutionary War:

Once, ah, once within these walls
One whom memory oft recalls,
The Father of his country, dwelt.
★★★★★
Up and down these echoing stairs,
Heavy with the weight of cares,
Sounded his majestic tread.

Washington's step-grandson George Washington Parke Custis harkened back to the classical origins of the appellation "Father of His Country" when he described Washington's last illness and death many years later:

The last effort of the expiring Washington was worthy of the Roman fame of his life and character. He raised himself up, and casting a look of benignity on all around him, as if to thank them for their kindly attentions, he composed his limbs, closed his eyes, and folding his arms upon his bosom, the Father of his country expired, gently as though an infant died!

Related entries: Knox, Henry; Society of the Cincinnati

Suggestions for further reading:
"From Gerard Vogels," 10 March 1784 (*Con. Ser.,* vol. 1).
"From Nicholas Simon van Winter and Lucretia Wilhelmina van Winter," 10 April 1784 (*Con. Ser.,* vol. 1).
"From Henry Knox," 19 March 1787 (*Con. Ser.,* vol. 5).
"From the Citizens of New York," 9 May 1789 (*Pres. Ser.,* vol. 2).
"From the Connecticut Legislature," 17 October 1789 (*Pres. Ser.,* vol. 4).
"From John Coles," 27 October 1789 (*Pres. Ser.,* vol. 4).
"From the Citizens of Newburyport, Massachusetts," 27 October 1789 (*Pres. Ser.,* vol. 4).
"From James Hardie," 23 January 1792 (*Pres. Ser.,* vol. 9).

Federal City

Article 1, section 8, of the U.S. Constitution mandated the establishment of a permanent seat for the U.S. government, officially designated as the District of Columbia. The choice of a site on the Potomac River for the Federal City resulted from a political bargain between Washington's secretaries of treasury and state, Alexander Hamilton and Thomas Jefferson, in 1790. James Madison, a member of the House of Representatives closely aligned with Washington, took the lead in brokering the deal. Washington apparently was not privy to the negotiations, although every member of Congress knew that he privately preferred building the capital city on the Potomac. Hamilton was determined that Congress accept his proposals regarding the funding of the national debt and the federal assumption of state debts from the Revolutionary War. The southern states stood to gain little from assumption, however, for most of their debts had been paid by depreciated paper money. Jefferson, reflecting the views of most southerners and especially the influential Virginians, hoped to bring the capital closer to their region for the considerable benefits that would accompany it. Robert Morris, who had played the most important role in financing the Revolutionary War, was anxious for the federal government to leave New York City and ready as a senator from Pennsylvania to align with the south.

The compromise linking Hamilton's funding proposals with the seat of government resulted in the Residence Act, narrowly passed by Congress in July 1790, which located the permanent seat of the government in a new Federal City to be constructed within a ten-mile square between the mouths of the Eastern Branch and Conococheague Creek on the Potomac River. The choice of the Potomac site over New York City, Philadelphia, and various sites along the Susquehannah and Delaware rivers was certainly reasonable given Congress's earlier resolution that the new capital be "at some convenient place, as near the center of wealth, population, and

extent of territory, as may be consistent with convenience to the navigation of the Atlantic ocean, and having due regard to the particular situation of the western country." The Residence Act contained several other provisions. It gave the president authority to name commissioners to oversee the selection and acquisition of the specific site and the construction of public works. It moved the temporary location of the federal government from New York City to Philadelphia and set the time for moving to the permanent seat to after 1 December 1800. And, last, it appropriated funds to cover the expense of removal and authorized the president to request and accept grants of money and property to help defray those expenses.

Washington subsequently appointed Thomas Johnson, Daniel Carroll, and David Stuart (1753–c.1814) as the first commissioners to oversee the new city. The surveyor general of the United States, Andrew Ellicott (1754–1820), and his brother Joseph Ellicott (1760–1826) were sent to establish the city's boundaries. French-born Pierre-Charles L'Enfant was named chief architect and engineer. At its center, from an elevation known as Tiber Hill overlooking the lower lands along the Potomac, was the U.S. Capitol. A vast public parkway, known now as the Mall, extended from the Capitol to the river. It was bisected by another "grand avenu," at one end of which was located the "presidial palace," or the White House as it subsequently came to be called. The President's House was a mile from the Capitol, halfway toward Georgetown. Judiciary Square, to emphasize the independence of the Supreme Court from the legislative and executive branches, was situated on avenues that did not lead directly to either the Capitol or to President's Square. Forts were located at strategic points on the river.

The District of Columbia, L'Enfant promised, was to be "beautifull above what may be Imagined," but quarrels, controversies, inadequate funding, and the weak commitment of Congress impeded its progress for the next decade. Washington's last words on the city, written a week before his death to commissioner William Thornton, characterized its early history: "By the obstructions continually thrown in its way—by *friends* or *enemies*—this City has had to pass through a firey trial—Yet, I trust will, ultimately, escape the Ordeal with eclat. Instead of *a firey trial* it would have been more appropriate to have said, it has passed, or is on its passage through, the Ordeal of local interests, destructive Jealousies, and inveterate prejudices; as difficult, and as dangerous I conceive, as any of the other ordeals."

Related entries: L'Enfant, Pierre-Charles; Presidency; Thornton, William

Suggestions for further reading:
"From Pierre L'Enfant," 11 September 1789 (*Pres. Ser.*, vol. 4).
"From James Madison," 20 November 1789 (*Pres. Ser.*, vol. 4).
"Memorandum from Thomas Jefferson," 29 August 1790 (*Pres. Ser.*, vol. 6).
"Memorandum from James Madison," c.29 August 1790 (*Pres. Ser.*, vol. 6).
"To Thomas Jefferson," 2 January 1791 (*Pres. Ser.*, vol. 7).
"Proclamation," 24 January 1791 (*Pres. Ser.*, vol. 7).
"Memorandum from Thomas Jefferson," 11 March 1791 (*Pres. Ser.*, vol. 7).
"From Pierre L'Enfant," 22 June 1791 (*Pres. Ser.*, vol. 8).
"From Pierre L'Enfant," 17 January 1792 (*Pres. Ser.*, vol. 9).
Arnebeck, Bob. 1991. *Through a Fiery Trial: Building Washington, 1790–1800.* New York.
Scott, Pamela. 1995. *Temple of Liberty: Building the Capitol for a New Nation.* New York.

Ferry Farm

The family of 6-year-old George Washington moved in 1738 to Ferry Farm in King George (Stafford after 1776) County, Virginia, across the Rappahannock River from Fredericksburg. George's father, Augustine, purchased the farm from William Strother (d. c.1732) to be nearer his iron works on Accokeek Creek, eight miles northwest of Fredericksburg. Washington lived there for about fifteen years. The property actually was purchased by Washington's father as three separate tracts. The house stood on a tract of 165 acres, separated from the other two tracts. Adjacent to "the Home House," as Washington usually referred to the property, was a 300-acre parcel that Washington's father rented when he was living, which was later acquired by Washington. It was later called Pine Grove; the other eventually Ferry Farm, because of the ferry road that ran through the property to the riverfront on the Rappahannock. The original house caught fire on Christmas Eve 1740 but was rebuilt and apparently then disappeared by the 1830s. Parsons Weems described the house as a low frame building painted dark red. It was at Ferry Farm that, Weems says, Washington barked his father's cherry tree and threw a stone (not a silver dollar!) across the river.

Although Washington inherited Ferry Farm's land and ten slaves at his father's death in 1743, he yielded its income to his mother, who with the help of overseer Edward Jones operated it until 1772, when she moved to a house on Charles Street in Fredericksburg. Washington then rented the farm to William Fitzhugh for two years.

Washington advertised to sell the property in November 1772. "A TRACT of six hundred acres, including about two hundred of cleared land on the north side of *Rappahannock* river, opposite to the lower end of *Fredericksburg.* On this tract (a little above the road) is one of the most agreeable situations for a house that is to be found upon the whole river, having a clear and distinct view of almost every house in the said town, and every vessel that passes to and from it. Long credit, if desired, will be given."

Hugh Mercer, a Fredericksburg physician and Washington's close friend and later

Revolutionary War comrade, purchased the entire property in 1774 for £2,000 Virginia currency, to be paid in five annual installments. Mercer was killed at the Battle of Princeton in 1777, but his heirs held onto the property until 1829.

Ferry Farm was the scene of intense military activity during the Civil War. The ferry landing became a strategic crossing point for the Union army, which built pontoon bridges across the Rappahannock there during the campaigns in 1862, 1863, and 1864. Union soldiers occupying Ferry Farm during the battles of Fredericksburg reported that the Washington house had been torn down for fuel, although the house referred to apparently was a later building. Ferry Farm was acquired in 1996 by the George Washington's Fredericksburg Foundation, which also operates Kenmore, the Fredericksburg home of Washington's sister, Betty Washington Lewis.

Related entries: Lewis, Fielding, Sr.; Mercer, Hugh; Mount Vernon; Popes Creek; Washington, Augustine

Suggestions for further reading:
"Deed for Ferry Farm Land," 7 July 1748 (*Col. Ser.*, vol. 1).
"From Fielding Lewis," c.29 December 1772–February 1773 (*Col. Ser.*, vol. 9).
"From Hugh Mercer," 21 March 1774 (*Col. Ser.*, vol. 10).
"To Hugh Mercer," 28 March 1774 (*Col. Ser.*, vol. 10).
King, George H. S. 1937. "Washington's Boyhood Home" (*William and Mary Quarterly*, 2d ser., vol. 17).

"First in War, First in Peace, and First in the Hearts of His Countrymen"

First in war, first in peace, and first in the hearts of his countrymen, he was second to none in the humble and endearing scenes of private life. Pious, just, humane, temperate and sincere; uniform, dignified and commanding, his example was as edifying to all around him, as were the effects of that example lasting.

These remarkable words are taken from perhaps the most famous funeral oration in American history, delivered to the U.S. Congress on the occasion of Washington's death by Henry Lee, in December 1799. The opening phrase has entered into the consciousness of Americans' perceptions of Washington. Henry Lee ("Light-Horse Harry"; 1756–1818) was born near Dumfries in Prince William County, Virginia, and educated at the College of New Jersey, graduating in 1773. In 1776 he was commissioned a captain in Col. Theodorick Bland's regiment of light horse. Washington reputedly asked Lee to serve in his military family, but Lee refused because he preferred to remain with the light horse. "I am wedded to my sword," he wrote Washington when declining the appointment, "and my secondary object in the present war, is military reputation." Lee moved up the ranks, attaining the rank of lieutenant colonel in November 1780, and being sent to the southern department. In 1781 Lee's dragoons played an important role in assisting Maj. Gen. Nathanael Greene's famous retreat across the Carolinas from Lord Cornwallis and helping to prepare for the Battle of Guilford Courthouse. The Continental Congress gave Lee a medal for his wartime service. Lord Cornwallis supposedly said of Lee "that he came a soldier from his mother's womb." Lee's zeal also could be troublesome, as in the instance when he received Washington's reprimand for hanging a deserter and then sending the man's severed head "lopped and bleeding" into camp as an example to other troops.

In 1785 Lee was elected a delegate to the Confederation Congress, an office he held until the Federal Constitution was in place, and in 1792 he was elected governor of Virginia. He commanded the forces sent by Washington to quell the Whiskey Rebellion in Pennsylvania in 1794. He was elected to the U.S. Congress in 1799, and was there when asked to give Washington's funeral oration on 26 December to a joint session of Congress.

In 1808 Lee wrote his *Memoirs of the War in the Southern Department of the United States.* During the War of 1812 Lee was attacked by a mob while in a Baltimore prison, where he had been placed in protective custody after helping a friend disperse an attack on his home following the man's criticism of the American war effort. His wounds were severe and lingered on until his death. He visited the West Indies in 1817 for his health and died on the return voyage at Cumberland Island, near St. Mary's in Georgia, where he stopped to visit Mrs. James Shaw, the daughter of his old comrade-in-arms Nathanael Greene. He was buried there but reinterred at Washington and Lee University's Lee Chapel in 1913. His son Robert E. Lee was the commander of the Confederate Army during the Civil War.

Related entries: Death; Father of His Country

Suggestion for further reading:
Royster, Charles. 1981. *Light-Horse Harry Lee and the Legacy of the American Revolution.* New York.

Fisheries

When he was thinking about renting out his Mount Vernon estate in 1793, George Washington told English agriculturalist Arthur Young that his Potomac River plantation "is well supplied with various kinds of fish at all Seasons of the year; and in the Spring with the greatest profusion of Shad, Herring, Bass, Carp, Perch, Sturgeon &ca. Several valuable fisheries appertain to the estate; the whole shore in short is one entire fishery." As he later instructed a farm manager about ne-

gotiating with those wanting to contract to take the fish, "when the glut of the fish runs, he must be provided to take every one I do not want, or have them thrown on his hands: the truth of the case is, that in the height of the fishery, they are not prepared to cure, or otherwise dispose of them, as fast as they *could* be *caught.*" Because of the abundance of fish in the Potomac, the fisheries at Mount Vernon were conducted on a much grander scale than a simple farm industry and were crucial to the successful operation of the plantation.

The herring swam up the rivers of tidewater Virginia and Maryland every spring to spawn near the falls. Washington set out seines for catching herring on the Potomac as early as 1760. In March of that year he ordered two new fish seines described as "35 fathoms long each, each 20 feet deep all through, made of the best 3 thd. laid twine, small Inch Meshes, hung loose on the lines & well fixd with Leads & Corks." Washington's nets typically pulled in shad, white fish, and "a great Number of Cats" along with the herring. After cleaning, the catch was packed with salt into barrels and stored for use on the plantation, fish being a staple of the slaves' diet.

Over the next dozen years the seines used by Washington doubled in size as he increased the scale of his fisheries. The nets were purchased from John Bradshaw & James Davidson, makers of net, twine, and line at 27 Fishstreet in London, and sent to Mount Vernon by Washington's factor, Robert Cary & Co. His orders for seines contained detailed instructions for their manufacture. For example, in July 1772 he ordered seines ranging from 390 to 480 feet in length and "12 feet deep in the Middle & to decrease to 7 at the end when Rigged & fit for use." It was important for the nets to be "close Meshd in the Middle," wrote Washington, to prevent the herring from getting tangled in the net, the disengagement of which wasted valuable time and often led to the tearing of the mesh. Corks supporting the nets in the water should be "no more than 2 feet & half asunder & fixd on flat ways that they may Swim & bear the Sein up bettr." Furthermore, he instructed, fix a "float right in the middle" of the seine to guide its approach with greater certainty "in case the Corks should Sink." The leads were to be five feet apart. He also made suggestions on how to correct the faults of nets made the previous year, one of which was made with "the Meshes too open in the Middle; the other of being too strait rigd." And, he concluded, "I cd wish to have these Seins Tan'd but it is thought the one I had from you last yr was injd in the Vat for wch reason I leave it to you to have these Tan'd, or not, as you shall judge most expedient."

Running the fisheries involved more than maintenance of seines and the actual catching of fish. The river's depth had to be sounded at strategic points before the seines could be dropped. Fishing landings had to be constructed, as did houses for processing the catch. As the fisheries' operation increased, more boats were required. Barrels had to be found to pack the fish in, and salt had to be ferried in from Alexandria. The labor force had to be managed so that it could move to the river on short notice. Problems included bad weather—too cold, too stormy, or too rainy—which caused them to miss the ideal time for pulling in the fish; failure of the seines; shortage of barrels for packaging; and occasional poor packing resulting in spoiling. Once the catch was made it had to be disposed of. Some fish were shipped to Jamaica to be exchanged for West Indian goods like rum, spirits, coffee, sugar, sweetmeats, oranges, cocoa nuts, pineapples, and cash. The rest were stored for use on the plantation, and the offal used as fertilizer in Washington's fields. The catch and sales went in cycles. Typical of Washington's diary entries was one in April 1788: "At the fishing landing there was plenty of custom[ers] & no fish. Last week there was plenty of fish & no custom[ers]." Over the years Washington

tried a variety of ways to manage the business, from operating it himself, delegating it to a manager specified for the purpose, relinquishing control to his farm managers, as he did during the presidential years, or renting the entire manufactory out.

Related entries: Distillery; Mount Vernon

Suggestions for further reading:
Diaries, vol. 1–5.
"To Lawrence Sandford," 26, 29 September 1769 (*Col. Ser.,* vol. 8).
"From Robert Adam," 24 June 1771 (*Col. Ser.,* vol. 8).
"To John Bradshaw and James Davidson," 15 July 1772 (*Col. Ser.,* vol. 9).
"From James Davidson," 29 September 1772 (*Col. Ser.,* vol. 9).
"To James Davidson," 10 July 1773 (*Col. Ser.,* vol. 9).
"To Robert McMickan," 10 May 1774 (*Col. Ser.,* vol. 10).
"To Arthur Young," 12 December 1793 (*Writings,* vol. 33).

Fitzgerald, John (d. 1799)

John Fitzgerald served as one of Washington's Revolutionary War aides-de-camp, from 1776 to 1778. As a merchant in Alexandria, Virginia, where he had settled after leaving his native Ireland in 1769, Fitzgerald often came into contact with Washington, and before the war he stayed overnight at Mount Vernon on several occasions. Commissioned a captain in the Third Virginia Regiment in February 1776, Fitzgerald accompanied his regiment to New York the following summer when it was ordered to join the main Continental army under Washington's command. In October 1776, when the Third Virginia's major, Andrew Leitch (c.1750–1776), Fitzgerald's merchant acquaintance from Dumfries, died of wounds received at the Battle of Harlem Heights on 16 September, Washington named Fitzgerald acting major for the regiment. The next month Washington made Fitzgerald one of his aides-de-camp, with the rank of lieutenant colonel. In that capacity the "agreeable broad-shouldered Irishman" (as Martha Daingerfield Bland described Fitzgerald while visiting Washington's military family in the spring of 1777) served with Washington at the New Jersey Battles of Trenton, Princeton, and Monmouth Courthouse. Fitzgerald was wounded at the last of these battles, in June 1778, along with another of Washington's aides-de-camp, and he left the army shortly thereafter to resume his employment as a merchant in Virginia.

In the 1780s Fitzgerald became first a director and later the president of the Potomac Company. He visited Mount Vernon after Washington returned home from the war to discuss Potomac Company business with his former commander in chief and to reminisce about the war. Fitzgerald also handled some of Washington's personal business affairs, including improvements made to Washington's two lots in Alexandria, and he served as mayor of Alexandria from 1792 to 1794. In the 1790s he was port collector of Alexandria. Fitzgerald commanded one of the cavalry troops that met and escorted Washington into Alexandria "with Military honors" in November 1798 when Washington was leaving for Philadelphia to confer with other generals about organizing the defense against a possible invasion by the French.

Related entries: Aides-de-Camp; Monmouth Courthouse, Battle of; Potomac River Navigation

Suggestions for further reading:
Diaries, vols. 3–6.
"General Orders," 3 October 1776 (*War Ser.*, vol. 6).
"Martha Daingerfield Bland to Frances Bland Randolph," 12 May 1777 (*Proceedings of the New Jersey Historical Society* [1895], vol. 51).

Forbes Campaign

Following Braddock's defeat on the Monongahela River in July 1755 the British took three years to prepare another campaign against the French at Fort Duquesne. Scots medical doctor John Forbes (1707–1759), colonel of the Seventeenth British Regiment and adjutant general on Loudoun's staff, was given the rank of brigadier general to command the expedition. The large force he gathered for the expedition included the Virginia Regiment, which was under Washington's command. Next in command to General Forbes was Henry Bouquet (1719–1765), lieutenant colonel in the Royal American Regiment and Washington's immediate commander, who in 1763 became the commander of all the British forces in the southern colonies in America. Forbes decided to cut a road from Raystown, Pennsylvania, to the Forks of the Ohio by which his troops could march, but Washington opposed it, unsuccessfully insisting that the troops should use Braddock's Road, which led directly from Fort Cumberland to within a few miles of Fort Duquesne.

When Washington's efforts to win approval of the Braddock route failed, he became extremely pessimistic that the "Reduction of the Ohio" would ever take place. The British and colonial troops made a remarkable march through the Pennsylvania wilderness, however, and took post at Loyalhanna, about fifty miles from the French, in early September. On 12 September a "chosen Detachment" of 8,000 troops under the command of Maj. James Grant (1720–1806) of the Highlanders marched from Loyalhanna for Fort Duquesne. Two days later, according to Washington, "the enemy sallied out, and an obstinate Engagement began. . . . Our Officers and men have acquired very great applause for their gallant Behaviour during the action." When the encounter was over, the French and Indians had inflicted heavy casualties on Grant's force; the Virginia Regiment suffered a "heavy stroke," 62 killed of the "8 Officers & 166 Men" present, meriting

Washington, who had not been present at the engagement, Forbes's public comments in the coming days. Forbes ordered his troops to return to Raystown, where they spent the next two months recovering and testing the French in minor skirmishes. In mid-November a skirmish took place that resulted in two parties of the Virginia Regiment firing upon one another; several were killed and wounded, and Washington, he said, "never was in more imminent danger by being between two fires, knocking up with his sword the presented pieces." The culmination of the campaign took place on 23 November when Forbes summoned his entire force for another attack on Fort Duquesne. "The Enemy," Washington reported, "after letting us get within a days march of the place, burned the fort, and ran away (by the light of it) at night, going down the Ohio by water, to the number of about 500 men, from our best information." Forbes, seriously ill and with only a few months left to live, sent Washington to Williamsburg to report the victory. The French retreat from the Forks of the Ohio effectively ended the French and Indian War.

Related entries: Braddock's Defeat; Fort Loudoun

Suggestions for further reading:
"To John Forbes," 19 June 1758 (*Col. Ser.*, vol. 5).
"To Henry Bouquet," 3 July 1758 (*Col. Ser.*, vol. 5).
"To Henry Bouquet," 2, 6 August 1758 (*Col. Ser.*, vol. 5).
"To John Robinson," 1 September 1758 (*Col. Ser.*, vol. 5).
"To Francis Fauquier," 2 September 1758 (*Col. Ser.*, vol. 5).
"To John Forbes," 8 October 1758 (*Col. Ser.*, vol. 6).
"To Francis Fauquier," 28 November 1758 (*Col. Ser.*, vol. 6).

Fort Cumberland

See Wills Creek.

Fort Duquesne

See Forbes Campaign; Fort Necessity Campaign.

Fort Loudoun

"Desolation and murder still increase; and no prospects of Relief. The Blue-Ridge is now our Frontier." Such was Washington's assessment of the Virginia frontier in April 1756, ten months since the deadly French and Indian ambush of Braddock's forces near the Ohio River. Terrified settlers in the outlying areas had been pouring easterly across the mountains in search of refuge as hostile Indian raiders destroyed farm after farm, killing dozens of people. The little town of Winchester, where Washington had headquartered since the previous September after taking command of the colonial military forces in Virginia, was the rendezvous for many of the distraught families. Washington soon became convinced of the "great and absolute necessity" of erecting a "large and strong Fort" in the area, "to serve as a Receptacle for all our Stores, &c. and a place of Refuge for the women and Children in times of danger." Although "trifling in itself," Winchester enjoyed, because of its central location at the northern end of the Shenandoah Valley, a free and open communication with the surrounding country, with neighboring colonies as well as eastern Virginia, and with Fort Duquesne, from which it was vitally important to procure the earliest intelligence of enemy intentions. Washington had first visited Winchester and the surrounding countryside on his surveying trip of 1748, and in May 1753 he purchased property in the vicinity, which he held throughout his life, a half-acre lot in town and six acres on the town common.

Construction of the fort began in May 1756. It was named in honor of John

Campbell, fourth earl of Loudoun, the recently appointed commander of the colonial forces in North America. For the fort's site Washington chose the northernmost of several hills near the town, known since as Fort Hill, where the post road leading to Philadelphia crossed old Indian trails. Although he placed one of the Virginia Regiment's captains, William Peachey (1729–1802), in charge of the laborers building the fort, Washington soon "found as little of the matter as I know myself, the *work* could not be conducted if I was away." The fort when finished was considered a "Citadel" capable of sustaining a string of eighteen or twenty "lesser Fortresses" strung along the frontiers. In actuality, it was a tiny stockade, about fifty yards square, covering altogether about a half acre. Batteries mounted on its four bastions contained an impressive array of artillery pieces, including six 18-pounders, six 12-pounders, six 6-pounders, four swivel guns, and two howitzers. Its barracks could hold 450 men, and a deep stone well ensured a reliable source of water. "Every one that has Seen Fort Loudoun," wrote William Fairfax, "speak well of it's Structure, Situation & Commander." The French thought the fort impregnable and never attempted an attack on it.

It was at Fort Loudoun that Washington in August 1756 issued to the Virginia Regiment the formal British proclamation of war against France, instructing the "Commanders and Officers, to do and execute all Acts of Hostility in the Prosecution of this just and honorable War." Although it was on the route rejected by General Forbes when planning his successful campaign against Fort Duquesne, troops and stores routinely moved through Fort Loudoun during the French and Indian War. Fort Loudoun's presence made Winchester an even more important rendezvous for people and supplies on the Virginia frontier and led to a rapid increase in the town's population. Fort Loudoun was still an important post during the Revolutionary

War, and because of its relative remoteness from the main theater of war, British and Loyalist prisoners were often housed in the area.

Related entries: Braddock's Defeat; Forbes Campaign

Suggestions for further reading:
"To John Robinson," 24, 27 April 1756 (*Col. Ser.*, vol. 3).
"To Robert Dinwiddie," 27 April 1756 (*Col. Ser.*, vol. 3).

Fort Necessity Campaign

In late January 1754 Virginia governor Robert Dinwiddie commissioned Washington one of two captains to command companies of 100 men each to protect the Ohio Company's workmen at the Forks of the Ohio, the point where the Monongahela and Allegheny rivers meet to form the Ohio River. Two weeks later the House of Burgesses voted to enlarge the expedition to the Ohio by appropriating £10,000 for the defense of its settlers on the frontier, leading Dinwiddie to authorize the establishment of a regiment of 300 volunteers, designated the Virginia Regiment. Dinwiddie placed at its head the county lieutenant for Albemarle County, Col. Joshua Fry (c.1700–1754), an Oxford-educated immigrant and prominent burgess who taught mathematics at the College of William and Mary and who with Peter Jefferson produced the famous Fry-Jefferson Map of Virginia in 1751. Dinwiddie appointed Washington lieutenant colonel of the regiment.

Washington spent the next several weeks outfitting troops before setting out for the Ohio from Alexandria on 2 April with about 140 officers and men. It took more than a week to reach Winchester, about seventy miles away, where his force was augmented by the arrival of Capt. Adam

Stephen's company. "The difficulty of getting Waggons has almost been insurmountable" and had occasioned "so much inconvenience," Washington wrote after waiting a week at Winchester, "that I am determined to carry all our provisions &c. out on horse back." He hoped the workmen at the Forks of the Ohio would assist his march by sending packhorses to the Ohio Company's New Store at Wills Creek, about seventy miles northwest of Winchester, but when he arrived at Wills Creek he discovered that a French force of more than 1,000 men, backed by eighteen cannon, had compelled the surrender of the Forks on 17 April.

Upon receiving this news Washington decided to cut a wagon road by which "the heaviest Artillery" could be transported to the Ohio Company's storehouse at the mouth of Redstone Creek on the Monongahela, about thirty-seven miles south of his original destination, where he would encamp and await the arrival of Fry and the rest of the Virginia Regiment. With "great difficulty and labour" the expedition reached the Great Crossing of the Youghiogheny River in mid-May, where it encamped until the 24th, when it moved to Great Meadows, a "small marshy valley surrounded by sloping wooded hills." Washington's detachment was now about fifty miles west of Wills Creek; Colonel Fry and the remainder of the Virginia Regiment were still in Winchester, awaiting the arrival of a regiment from North Carolina under the command of Col. James Innes (d. 1759).

Meanwhile, on 23 May, Joseph Coulon de Villiers, sieur de Jumonville, a French army officer with more than fifteen years' service in America, left Fort Duquesne, the half-constructed French fortification at the Forks, with thirty-three men and an English interpreter to summon the Virginia troops to withdraw back across the mountains. Friendly Indians warned Washington of Jumonville's approach, and on 28 May,

after discovering the French "abt a half mile from the Road in a very obscure place surrounded with Rocks" (since named Jumonville's Rocks), Washington "formd a disposion to attack them on all sides, which we accordingly did and after an Engagement of abt 15 Minutes we killd 10, wounded one and took 21 Prisoner's." Among the dead was Jumonville, "killed by a Musket-Shot in the Head" or, depending on the source, tomahawked and scalped by the Indian chief Half-King. Among those taken prisoner were French ensign Pierre Jacques Drouillon, sieur de Macé (b. 1725), and the French commissary of stores on the upper Ohio, La Force (Michel Pépin). Casualties among Washington's detachment, which consisted of about fifty men, were "only one Man killd, and two or three wounded." Washington found the fifteen-minute engagement exhilarating, as he informed his brother John Augustine two days later: "I fortunately escaped without a wound, tho' the right Wing where I stood was exposed to & received all the Enemy's fire and was the part where the man was killed & the rest wounded. I can with truth assure you, I heard Bulletts whistle and believe me there was something charming in the sound."

Reports of the engagement were contradictory. The French claimed that Jumonville had been murderously ambushed while on a peaceful mission similar to Washington's own mission to the French commandant the previous fall, and that only the presence of the Indians kept the English from killing all the French. Washington and his officers justified the surprise attack on the basis that the French party had been stalking them for several days. They were "sent as spies rather than any thing else," he said, and never designed to "come to us but in a hostile manner." The Indians not only had discovered the enemy's "skulking place" and advocated an attack, but they also "scalped the Dead, and took away the most Part of their Arms," and afterward sent a young warrior with a "*French* Scalp" as a messenger to the Delaware Nation to "invite them to take up the Hatchet" against the French. Moreover, the Indians declared to Washington that if the English were "such fools" as to free their prisoners they would "never help us any more to take other *Frenchmen*." Washington sent the captured prisoners to Williamsburg.

Washington immediately fell back to his camp at Great Meadows, where he hastily began constructing a temporary defensive work of "small Pallisadoes, fearing that when the *French* should hear the News of that Defeat [of Jumonville], we might be attacked by considerable Forces." Washington originally had chosen the area for his camp because it was open and had a good source of water—reasons that would come back to haunt him later. The fort, dubbed Fort Necessity, was positioned on the narrow part of the meadow and surrounded by a ditch about eight yards out. A volunteer in the Virginia Regiment described Fort Necessity as "a smal Stocado Fort made in a circular Form round a smal House that stood in the Middle of it to keep our Provisions and Ammunition in, and was covered with Bark and some Skins and might be about 14 Feet square, and the Walls of the Fort might be about 8 feet distance from the said House all round." When the fort was declared "finished" on 3 June Washington optimistically declared that "with my small Number's I shall not fear the attack of 500 Men."

The month of June was spent finding provisions, conferring with Indians, shoring up the entrenchments at Fort Necessity, and preparing the road from Redstone to Great Meadows for heavy artillery. By the 10th Washington had received letters from Dinwiddie enclosing a medal for him to wear as a token of "His Majesty's Favo[r]" and, more important, promoting him to colonel as a result of Fry's death on 31 May. At the end of the month he regathered most of his force at Great Meadows to wait for a "Stock of provisions sufficient to serve us for some months." The troops had been without "meat & Bread for Six days already" and were uncertain when any would arrive. They had only about twenty-five head of cattle, most of them milch cows, for nearly 400 men. What's worse, the French were expecting reinforcements hourly and had been given intelligence of "our Starving Condition and our Numbrs & Situation." At the same time that Washington's men were returning to Fort Necessity, an enemy force consisting of 400 French soldiers and an unknown number of Indian allies under the command of Louis Coulon de Villiers, Jumonville's brother, was headed for Great Meadows from Fort Duquesne.

The French and Indians appeared before the fort about midmorning on 3 July and "began to fire upon us, at about 600 Yards distance," wrote Washington two weeks later, "but without any Effect: We immediately called all our Men to their Arms, and drew up in Order before our Trenches; but as we looked upon this distant Fire from us, we waited their nearer Approach before we returned their Salute." The attackers advanced in "a very irregular Manner" to within sixty yards of the fort, where they "made a second Discharge." The entire time the French and Indians remained secluded in the forest, "sheltered behind the Trees, ourselves without Shelter, in Trenches full of Water, in a settled Rain." The fight continued in this manner until "8 o'Clock at Night, when the French called to Parley . . . about Midnight we agreed that each Side should retire without Molestation, they back to their Fort at Monongehela, and we to Wills's Creek: That we should march away with all the Honours of War, and with all our Stores, Effects and Baggage."

Washington's men had behaved with "singular Intrepidity," he later reported, "and we determined not to ask for Quarter, but with our Bayonets screw'd, to sell our Lives as dearly as possibly we could." They had been overwhelmed by superior numbers and "could not hope for Victory; and from the Character of those we had to encounter, we expected no Mercy, but on Terms that we positively resolved not to submit to." The French terms of surrender were generous, however, and "no disagreeable News to us," for in reality Washington's troops were exhausted and hungry and their arms rendered useless by the rain. On top of that, as soon as it turned dark half of the men began to get drunk. The Virginia Regiment's losses were heavy—thirty killed and seventy wounded out of a force of less than 400 men—while French casualties were negligible—two deaths and seventeen seriously wounded.

Two final indignities accompanied the defeat of the Virginia Regiment. The first happened the next morning when a reinforcement for the French of about 100 Indians interrupted the march of the regiment and began to pilfer its baggage. The second was more serious for Washington and the officers of the Virginia Regiment, although not discovered until later: the articles of capitulation signed by them opened with a preamble stating that they had assassinated Jumonville. Although Washington and the other officers involved in discussing the terms of capitulation insisted that they never intended to admit to such and that the document was mistranslated as "death" by the translator, Capt. Jacob Van Braam, "a Dutchman, little acquainted with the English tongue," it was an embarrassment to them. Moreover, the terms of the capitulation also stipulated that Van Braam and another captain, Robert Stobo, were to be retained by the French as hostages until the prisoners captured with Jumonville were set free.

Despite the regiment's defeat, the House of Burgesses in mid-September officially thanked Washington and the officers and soldiers under his command "for their late gallant and brave Behaviour in the Defense of their Country." The resolution listed all the officers by name except for two, Captain Van Braam, who was suspected of mistranslating the articles of capitulation on purpose, and Maj. George Muse, who allegedly played the part of a coward during the attack. Washington resigned his commission in late October after Dinwiddie converted the Virginia Regiment to independent companies.

Great Meadows is now part of the Fort Necessity National Battlefield. Contemporary descriptions of the fort were confirmed by archeological excavations in 1952. The stockade, constructed of large white oak logs split in two, with the split sides facing out, was about fifty-three feet in diameter, with an outside perimeter three times that. The National Park Service reconstructed Fort Necessity on the original site in 1954. A museum is open to the public.

Related entries: Dinwiddie, Robert; Gist, Christopher; Indian Prophecy, The; La Force; Muse, George; Van Braam, Jacob; "Whistling Bullets"; Account of the Capitulation of Fort Necessity, 9 July 1754 (Selected Writings)

Suggestions for further reading:
"Washington's Journal" (*Diaries*, vol. 1).
"To Thomas Cresap," 18 April 1754 (*Col. Ser.,* vol. 1).
"To James Hamilton," c.24 April 1754 (*Col. Ser.,* vol. 1).
"To John Augustine Washington," 31 May 1754 (*Col. Ser.,* vol. 1).
"To Robert Dinwiddie," 3, 10 June 1754 (*Col. Ser.,* vol. 1).
"The Capitulation of Fort Necessity," 3 July 1754 (*Col. Ser.,* vol. 1).
"To Carter Burwell," 20 April 1755 (*Col. Ser.,* vol. 1).
"The Capitulation of Fort Necessity" (vol. 1, appendix 10). Douglas Southall Freeman. 1948–1957. 7 vols. *George Washington: A Biography.* New York.
Harrington, J. C. 1954–1955. "Metamorphosis of Fort Necessity" (*Western Pennsylvania Historical Magazine,* vol. 37).
Leduc, Gilbert F. 1943. *Washington and "The Murder of Jumonville."* Boston.
McDowell, William, Jr., ed. 1970. "Affidavit of John Shaw" (*Colonial Records of South Carolina: Documents Relating to Indian Affairs, 1754–1757,* 2d ser., vol. 2).

"Battle of the Great Meadows" (vol. 2, appendix 3). Jared Sparks. 1834–1837. 12 vols. *The Writings of George Washington*. Boston.

Fort Pitt

See Forbes Campaign; Fort Necessity Campaign.

Fort Washington (New York)

*T*he American Revolutionary War fort named for George Washington, "the very mention of which made officers blush and old soldiers groan" (or so said historian Douglas Southall Freeman), was built in the summer of 1776 as a simple pentagonal earthenwork from which to fire artillery shells at British warships in the Hudson River. Perched 230 feet above the river on the southern crest of the highest ridge on New York's Manhattan Island (now 184th Street), with Fort Lee on an opposing bluff in New Jersey, and river navigation obstructions consisting of chains, fire rafts, and row galleys in between, Fort Washington was considered a critical component of a three-pronged strategy aimed at preventing the British from gaining control of the river. Although its corners were set off by crude bastions, the fort had neither palisades, ditching, nor barracks. Construction began around 20 June, and by late August one general officer deemed it in such "Good order" that some of the fortification's cannon could be spared for the incomplete works to the north at King's Bridge, the island's only land link with the mainland. From 15 September to 21 October 1776, with his Continental army troops strung out on the heights between the two locations, Washington headquartered about a mile south of Fort Washington. He stayed at a house now known as the Jumel Mansion, built in the 1760s by Roger Morris, a native of Yorkshire, England, who had served with Washington on the Braddock campaign during the French and Indian War.

Unfortunately for the American war effort, the defensive river-security system that included Fort Washington failed to stop enemy vessels from running the river. Col. Joseph Phillips of the New Jersey militia levies wrote to inform Washington about 12 October that he "hath viewed with infinite regret, the Enemies Ships of War passing by us up the North River, opposite Mount Washington, with impunity: owing in a great measure, he humbly conceives, to the bad Construction of some of our Batteries, & the want of others in more suitable places." Phillips advised completing previously begun batteries and constructing more nearer the fort, measures sanctioned by Washington but in the end ineffective. The only consolation for the Americans was that the artillery fire from the fort inflicted considerable damage on British warships as they raced through the river obstructions, resulting in a number of casualties.

A council of war held in mid-October concluded that Fort Washington should be "retained as long as possible," reflecting the wishes of the Continental Congress recently expressed in a resolution directing Washington "if it be practicable, by every art, and whatever expence" to continue to place impediments to British navigation on the Hudson River. Washington thus instructed the fort's commander, Col. Robert Magaw of the Fifth Pennsylvania Regiment, to hold the post "as long as a good Officer ought to do," an order that was not reversed in the weeks following the Battle of White Plains on 28 October when Washington began to suspect that British general William Howe might be contemplating an attack on the fort.

On 16 November a concerted British assault employing four separate forces against the American outposts surrounding the fortifications ended with the British forcing the surrender of the fort and taking nearly 2,900 prisoners, including 230 officers. American casualties included 53 killed and 96 wounded, and British losses totaled 77 killed, 374 wounded, and 7 missing. Moreover, the Americans lost 43 pieces of artillery, a supply of ammunition, and in the words of Washington "some of the best" small arms in the possession of the Continental army. Four days later the British also took Fort Lee, but not before the Americans had fled with the garrison's gunpowder. The sudden and unexpected loss of so significant a number of American troops and a goodly amount of military equipment effectively ended Washington's hopes of a general engagement during the campaign and was a serious blow to American morale. Washington was mortified at the capture of Fort Washington, especially so since he had considered the advisability of holding the fort "repugnant to my own judgment" and since there had been time enough for its evacuation after it became clear that the Continentals could not seriously threaten British command of the Hudson River or that the fort could be of any use in prohibiting the British army from invading New Jersey. The British renamed Fort Washington for Freiherr Wilhelm von Knyphausen, the general who commanded the German troops that stormed the fort. The British army finally evacuated the fort in November 1783.

Washington's last connection with Fort Washington took place on Saturday, 10 July 1790, during his first term as president, when he and an entourage including the vice president; the secretaries of state, treasury, and war; and Washington's private secretaries, as well as some of the members of their families, "Having formed a party . . . visited the old position of Fort Washington and afterwards dined on a dinner provided by Mr. [William] Mariner at the House lately [owned by] Colo. Roger Morris but confiscated and in the occupation of a common Farmer."

Related entries: Harlem Heights, Battle of; Kip's Bay, New York; White Plains, Battle of

Suggestions for further reading:
Diaries, vol. 6.
"From Thomas Mifflin," 2 July 1776 (*War Ser.*, vol. 5).
"From Joseph Phillips," c.12 October 1776 (*War Ser.*, vol. 6).
"To John Augustine Washington," 6–19 November 1776 (*War Ser.*, vol. 7).
"To John Hancock," 16 November 1776 (*War Ser.*, vol. 7).
"To Joseph Reed," 22 August 1779 (*Writings*, vol. 16).
"To William Gordon," 8 March 1785 (*Con. Ser.*, vol. 2).
Bliven, Bruce, Jr. 1955–1956. *Battle for Manhattan*. New York.

Fraunces, Samuel ("Black Sam")

Samuel Fraunces came to New York from the West Indies in 1755 and in 1761 purchased a large four-story building on the corner of Pearl and Broad streets, built as a residence in 1719 by the DeLancey family. He opened it in 1762 under the name of Queen Charlotte or Queen's Head Tavern and turned it into one of the most popular meeting places in the city. Washington dined at Fraunces's Tavern on the day of his arrival in New York City from Cambridge, Massachusetts, on 13 April 1776, and four days later a court-martial sat there. In June 1776 Washington and his generals and staff were thrown "an elegant entertainment" in Fraunces's Tavern as part of the formal thanks of the New York provincial congress. The tavern's Long Room was the most spacious public hall in the city, and the place where Washington and the nearby officers bade one another an affectionate farewell at the end of the Revolutionary War on 4 December 1783, the day the British fleet sailed from the New York harbor. Washington apparently lodged there from 26 November to 4 December, during which time he gave "An Entertainment" on 30 November. Both the Continental Congress and the state of

New York awarded Fraunces money after the war as recompense for helping American prisoners held captive in New York City during the war. Fraunces, said one historian, "was always in the room, very resplendently dressed in wig and small-clothes, watching over the service provided by his assistants." The tavern was restored in 1907 by the Sons of the American Revolution and serves as their headquarters, and a restaurant on the first floor of the building carries on a tradition of 250 years.

Fraunces also served as steward of Washington's presidential household in New York City. As Tobias Lear described Fraunces to George Augustine Washington on 3 May 1789: "We have engaged Black Sam Frances as Steward & superintendent of the Kitchen, and a very excellent fellow he is in the latter department—he tosses up such a number of fine dishes that we are distracted in our choice when we set down to table, and obliged to hold a long consultation upon the subject before we can determine what to attack. Oysters & Lobsters make a very conspicuous figure upon the table and never go off untouched." When Washington complained of the extravagance of the table he set, Fraunces reputedly said, "Well, he may discharge me, he may kill me if he will, but while he is President of the United States, and I have the honor to be his Steward, his establishment shall be supplied with the very best of everything that the whole country can afford." Fraunces received twenty-five dollars a month for his services in the household, which in addition to purchasing and preparing food, also included taking care of dishes and linen, procuring firewood, and whitewashing on the premises.

Fraunces left Washington's employment in February 1790 and was replaced by John Hyde, who ironically spent considerably more running the president's household. Washington compared the two men the following year: "Francis, besides being an excellent Cook, knowing how to provide genteel Dinners, and giving aid in dressing them, prepared the Desert, made the Cake, and did every thing that Hyde & wife conjointly do; consequently the Services of Hyde alone is not to be compared with those of Frauncis's." Washington wanted to rehire Fraunces after the move of the presidential mansion to Philadelphia, and through Fraunces's son, Washington's secretary Tobias Lear negotiated his return, provided it be "understood that wine is not admissable at their Table . . . that Wine is not to be used at it again under any pretence whatsoever; for there can be no line drawn if it be once admitted; either as to the quantity or quality that will be drank at it." Fraunces was to be assisted by a new housekeeper, Ann Emerson, and a cook, Hercules, a Mount Vernon slave. Fraunces joined the presidential household at Philadelphia in November 1791 and remained there until the end of Washington's presidency.

At least two of Fraunces's children had some dealings with Washington while he was in New York, both Andrew G. Fraunces, a clerk with the Board of Treasury from 1785 to 1789 and the principal clerk of the Treasury Department from its creation in September 1789 until early 1793; and Andrew's sister, Elizabeth Fraunces Thompson.

Related entries: Lear, Tobias; Presidency

Suggestions for further reading:
"Expenses of Journey to New York," 4–13 April 1776 (*War Ser.,* vol. 4).
"To Tobias Lear," 20 September 1790 (*Pres. Ser.,* vol. 6).
"From Tobias Lear," 15 May 1791 (*Pres. Ser.,* vol. 8).
Decatur, Stephen, Jr. 1933. *Private Affairs of George Washington from the Records and Accounts of Tobias Lear, Esquire, His Secretary.* Boston.

Freemasonry

On 4 August 1753, George Washington became a Master Mason, the

Portrait depicting George Washington as a Freemason (Library of Congress)

highest rank in the Fraternity of Freemasonry, in the Masonic Lodge of Fredericksburg, Virginia. He had been initiated as an apprentice in the same lodge the previous November and "pass'd fellow Craft" in March 1753. Uniting Enlightenment ideals of reason, order, and fraternity with elements of the medieval guild system, Freemasonry gained popularity in the eighteenth century, particularly among the British, who exported it to the American colonies in 1731. Its cosmopolitan culture, aristocratic patronage, and general endorsement by men of social standing, supplemented by commercial connections, attracted widespread interest and led to its quick expansion, although its secret and mysterious rites aroused considerable suspicion in the early American republic.

For Washington, joining the Masons was a rite of passage, a formal entry into respectable and genteel if not elite society, and an expression of commitment to the public welfare. Initiates acknowledged their belief in God and in the immortality of the soul, and pledged themselves to the "true principles" of Masonry: fraternity, universal love, morality, acts of benevolence, and loyalty to civic laws and values. According to Washington, Freemasonry was just the type of social organization necessary to school the new republic in moral virture, one of the topics included in his Farewell Address. "To enlarge the sphere of social happiness," he wrote the Grand Lodge of Massachusetts in December 1792, "is worthy the benevolent design of the Masonic Institution; and it is most fervently to be wished, that the conduct of every member of the fraternity, as well as those publications which discover the principles which actuate them may tend to convince Mankind that the grand object of Masonry is to promote the happiness of the human race."

Washington's Masonic affiliation has been troublesome, however, to both Masons and non-Masons alike. Members proudly point to Washington's ties to the fraternity and to the complimentary language he used when referring to it, and to the fact that more than anyone in American history, Washington symbolizes the Masonic ideals of honor, honesty, and religious tolerance. For instance, when Washington made his northern and southern tours in 1790 and 1791, his replies to letters sent by Masonic lodges to welcome him to their cities express his desire for the "welfare of the fraternity," his willingness "to advance the interests" of the society, and his belief that he would "always be ambitious of being considered a deserving Brother." He took part

in a major Masonic ceremony, laying the cornerstone of the U.S. Capitol on 18 September 1793, in Masonic regalia. Detractors, on the other hand, stress that Washington's commitment to Freemasonry was as nominal as his church attendance was perfunctory, that he seldom broached the subject in his vast personal correspondence, and that he apparently was not very interested in attending lodge meetings even though throughout his life he routinely found time for ceremonial dinners and numerous amusements including foxhunting, balls, plays, and circuses.

The evidence that Washington did not often frequent lodge meetings comes from his own pen, in a September 1798 letter to George Washington Snyder, written to deny that the Masonic lodges in America were contaminated with the principles ascribed to the Society of the Illuminati. Washington made it a point to correct an error Snyder had "run into, of my Presiding over the English lodges in this Country. The fact is, I preside over none, nor have I been in one more than once or twice, within the last thirty years." None of the several instances in which Washington reputedly attended lodge meetings during the Revolutionary War has been substantiated, and Washington's declaration suggests that such rumors appeared later. After the war, various lodges bestowed honorary membership upon Washington, and some Masons down on their luck successfully appealed to him for charity. He attended celebrations and funerals where Masons took an active part, but continued to avoid lodge meetings. In short, Washington admired the principles and goals of Freemasonry and promoted them from a distance, declining to invest the time and effort necessary to become very familiar with them.

Washington himself received a Masonic funeral, although he had wished for a private burial. According to Washington's secretary, Tobias Lear, the family acquiesced to a request from the Alexandria "Militia,

Freemasons &c. [who] were determined to show their respect to the General's Memory by attending his body to the Grave." Washington's horse was "with his saddle, Holster, Pistols &c. led by his two grooms, Cyrus & Wilson in black. The Body borne by the Free Masons & Officers." At the vault the clergyman "read the service and gave a short extempore speech," after which the "Masons performed their ceremonies, & the Body was deposited in the Vault.!!!!"

Interestingly, the only references to the hereafter in Washington's writings are in letters addressed to Masons, such as this very uncharacteristic reference in his letter of January 1792 to the Grand Lodge of Pennsylvania: "I request you will be assured of my best wishes and earnest prayers for your happiness while you remain in this terrestial Mansion, and that we may hereafter meet as brethren in the Eternal Temple of the Supreme Architect." The insight into Washington's own beliefs is diminished, however, by the fact that he actually borrowed some of this text from the letter to which he is replying, a practice frequently used by him: "our *Prayer*— that you may be long continued to adorn the bright List of Master-Workmen which our Fraternity produces in the *terrestial Lodge;* and that you may be late removed to that *celestial Lodge,* where love and harmony reign, transcendent and divine; where the Great Architect more immediately presides."

Among the relics of Washington held by the Alexandria Lodge are a piece of cloth from the coat he wore at Braddock's defeat in July 1755, the apron and sash worn by Washington at the laying of the cornerstone of the U.S. Capitol, his field compass, his farm spurs, his cupping instruments, and pieces of his original coffin and the vault in which his remains were first laid.

Related entries: Death; Religious Beliefs

Suggestions for further reading:

"To William Herbert," 19 June 1784 (*Con. Ser.,* vol. 1).

"From John I. Sonnet," 10 January 1791 (*Pres. Ser.,* vol. 7).

"From John Brett Kenna," 14 July 1791 (*Pres. Ser.,* vol. 8).

"To the Grand Lodge of Pennsylvania," 3 January 1792 (*Pres. Ser.,* vol. 9).

"From G. W. Snyder," 22 August 1798 (*Ret. Ser.,* vol. 2).

"To G. W. Snyder," 25 September 1798 (*Ret. Ser.,* vol. 2).

Brockett, F. L. 1899. *The Lodge of Washington. A History of the Alexandria Washington Lodge, No. 22, A. F. and A. M. of Alexandria, Va., 1783–1876.* Alexandria, VA.

Callahan, Charles H. 1913. *Washington: The Man and the Mason.* Washington, DC.

Sachse, Julius F. 1915. *Masonic Correspondence of Washington as Found Among the Washington Papers in the Library of Congress.* Philadelphia.

Tatsch, J. Hugo. 1931. *The Facts About George Washington as a Freemason.* New York.

French and Indian War

See Braddock's Defeat; Carlyle, John; Conotocarious; Dinwiddie, Robert; Forbes Campaign; Fort Loudoun; Fort Necessity Campaign; Gage, Thomas; Great Kanawha Tracts; Indian Prophecy, The; La Force; Lewis, Andrew; Muse, George; Van Braam, Jacob; "Whistling Bullets"; Wills Creek.

Fry, Joshua (c. 1700–1754)

See Fort Necessity Campaign.

G

Gage, Thomas (c.1719–1787)

Thomas Gage, the second son of an Irish peer, was educated at Westminster School before entering the British army in the late 1730s. He took part in the Battles of Fontenoy and Culloden in 1745 and 1746 and was appointed lieutenant colonel of the Forty-fourth British Regiment in 1751. Nicknamed "Honest Tom," Gage was well liked and became a popular officer. His regiment was ordered to America in the fall of 1754, and he first became acquainted with Washington during their service together on the Braddock expedition of 1755. Gage commanded the vanguard of Braddock's advanced division when it left Little Meadows on 18 June 1755, and he was at the head of a column of more than 400 officers and men when it was surprised by French and Indian forces at Great Meadows on 9 July. In the subsequent fighting Gage narrowly escaped death. "I received a slight wound in my belly," he wrote, as well as "a graze of a slugg on my eye brow, some shots in my coat, and my horse twice wounded." At least one critic, Braddock's principal aide-de-camp, Capt. Robert Orme (d. 1790), accused Gage's troops of a precipitate retreat that caused "such Confusion, and struck so great a Panick among our Men, that afterwards no military Expedient could be made use of that had any Effect on them." Gage denied Orme's assertions, and others questioned the captain's motives, but all seemed to agree that Gage himself had bravely rallied several dozen of his troops to cover the retreat. Gage and his regiment afterward were sent to take part in the campaigns in the north. Gage subsequently raised a provincial regiment of light infantry and was promoted to colonel.

Washington and Gage remained on cordial terms after Gage left Virginia. When the commander in chief of the British forces in America, William Shirley, overlooked Washington when choosing a commander for the forces in the southern colonies, Washington complained to Gage, who was sympathetic to his claim to rank. "It's not at all Surprizing you should be disgusted at The Service," Gage wrote, "when a Command you was so justly entitled to, was given another; and your continuing to head The Virginia Troops after Such a Disappointment, is no small Instance of your Zeal for the Public Service, for which you have been ever remarkable." In the spring of 1758 Washington asked Gage to mention him to British general John Forbes, "not, Sir, as one, who has favors to ask of him," Washington assured his correspondent, but that he might be distinguished in some measure from the "motley herd" of provincial officers. Gage did what he could to promote Washington's name among the British leaders.

In 1760 Gage was appointed military governor of Montreal, an office he held for three years, and in 1761 he was promoted to major general. In the fall of 1763 he replaced Jeffery Amherst as commander in chief of the British forces in North America, first on a temporary basis, and permanently the following year. The signing of the Peace of Paris in February 1763 eased tensions with the French but not with the Indians, and Gage was forced to deal with Pontiac's Conspiracy during the first years of his tenure. George III's Proclamation of 1763 and Parliament's passage of a series of taxation and military measures over the next several years brought new tensions in the colonies, leading to the Boston Massacre in March 1770. Gage diffused the tension by withdrawing his regiments from Boston to Castle William and allowing the civil authorities to prosecute the British soldiers who had fired on the colonists. A relative calm settled on the colonies for the next three years. Gage, now colonel of the Twenty-second British Regiment as well as commander in chief, was promoted to lieutenant general in 1770.

In the spring of 1773 Gage took a leave of absence in England, which he had been away from for more than seventeen years. Washington happened to be in New York City on the eve of Gage's departure, taking his stepson, Jacky Custis, to King's College, and was able to attend the farewell dinner given by the citizens of New York City. Before returning to Virginia, Washington also accepted Gage's invitation to a private meal with Gage and his American wife. Despite the best intentions of leaders on both sides of the Atlantic, relations between the two sides deteriorated while Gage was in England, resulting in the establishment of committees of correspondence and culminating in the Boston Tea Party in December 1773. When Gage returned to America in May 1774, he brought with him additional powers as royal governor of Massachusetts, replacing Thomas Hutchinson (1711–1780)

and charged by Parliament with implementing its punitive measures against that colony.

Gage commanded the British army at Boston during the turbulent period that followed. His proclamation of the Coercive, or Intolerable, Acts, wrote Washington, "exhibited unexampled Testimony of the most despotick System of Tyranny that ever was practiced in a free Government." Washington also thought Gage was "exceedingly disconcerted at the quiet & steady Conduct" of the people of Massachusetts and of the measures pursued by other governments. Gage's attempts to fulfill the British ministry's order to take decisive actions to reassert royal authority at Boston led to Lexington and Concord and the bloody Battle of Bunker Hill but failed to slow the onslaught of rebellion. He was recalled not long after Washington took command of the American forces at Cambridge, being replaced by Gen. William Howe, and left America in October 1775, never to return. Before he left, Gage and Washington traded letters about the treatment of prisoners of war.

Related entry: Boston, Siege of

Suggestions for further reading:
Diaries, vol. 3.
"From Thomas Gage," 23 November 1755 (*Col. Ser.,* vol. 2).
"From Thomas Gage," 10 May 1756 (*Col. Ser.,* vol. 3).
"To Thomas Gage," 12 April 1758 (*Col. Ser.,* vol. 5).
"To Thomas Gage," 11 August 1775 (*War Ser.,* vol. 1).
Alden, John R. 1948. *General Gage in America.* Baton Rouge, LA.

Gates, Horatio (c.1728–1806)

Horatio Gates was born at Maldon in Essex, England, and entered the British army at a young age after being educated for the military. Between 1749 and

1754 he served in Nova Scotia, first as a lieutenant attached as an aide to the governor of the colony and later as a captain lieutenant in the Forty-fifth Regiment of Foot. In September 1754 he purchased a captaincy of one of New York's four independent companies. While serving in the latter capacity, he first came into contact with Washington when his company was ordered to join Braddock's disastrous campaign in 1755. Gates's company, slightly fewer than 100 men including officers, reached the Potomac River in late April 1755 and Fort Cumberland about three weeks later. Gates suffered a wound in the chest at the Battle of Monongahela on 9 July 1755 and spent several weeks recuperating. He was promoted to major in 1762 but sold his commission in 1769 when further advancement seemed unlikely. By 1770 he was known as a "red hot republican," an appellation he apparently wore with some pride, and he began to cast about for property in the colonies. At the urging of Washington and others, he decided to settle in Virginia in 1772, and a year later he bought a plantation in the lower Shenandoah Valley, which he named Traveller's Rest. At his Berkeley County, Virginia (now West Virginia), residence, he was a close neighbor of Washington's brother Samuel.

Gates visited Washington at Mount Vernon in early May 1775, shortly before Washington left for Philadelphia to attend the Continental Congress. Gates accompanied Washington to Cambridge, Massachusetts, the following July, as adjutant general of the Continental army, a position for which he was well qualified because of his administrative abilities. Washington appreciated Gates's accomplishments in that office and on numerous occasions attempted to persuade him to return to the office after he gave it up in the spring of 1776. At the time he received the appointment Gates probably had spent more years in active military service than any other officer in the American forces except for Maj. Gen.

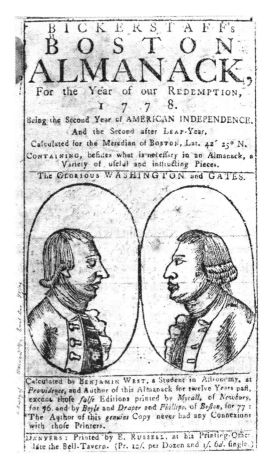

A page of "Bickerstaff's Boston Almanack" for 1778, with portraits of generals George Washington and Horatio Gates (Library of Congress)

Charles Lee. While on Washington's staff Gates was not only privy to the commander in chief's views on military strategy and tactics, but was also invited to voice his own, which usually fell on the side of caution. He was named a major general in May 1776 and placed in command of the northern department the following month. The following December he left the northern department to reinforce Washington's army in New York, and from there he was sent to Philadelphia to command the forces guarding the Continental Congress.

Gates's departure from the northern department created a void in command that was filled by Maj. Gen. Philip Schuyler, a respected and capable officer from New

York, but a man with enemies anxious to side with Gates in lobbying Congress to reappoint Gates as commander of the department. The struggle by Gates and his faction to have Schuyler relieved of his command revealed a spiteful and small-minded side to Gates's nature, and it left Schuyler vulnerable to the whims of Congress. Even Washington's confidence in Schuyler's management of the department could not save Schuyler from being recalled after Fort Ticonderoga in New York was taken by the British in July 1777, and Congress reappointed Gates commander of the northern department. The defeat of British general John Burgoyne a few weeks later at the Battle of Saratoga, New York, won Gates public applause, although Schuyler had laid much of the groundwork for success, and Maj. Gen. Benedict Arnold had directed the battle.

Following Saratoga the friends of Gates began to openly compare the regularly disciplined troops under his command to those of Washington, making thinly veiled hints that the Continental army and the American cause would be better served by having a new commander in chief. Gates, in the words of nineteenth-century historian Edward Meeks, "yielded to the whispers of ambition and the flattery of the injudicious, and at least connived at the attempt made to supersede Washington in the supreme command of the American army." Gates clearly broke protocol and alienated Washington by directly informing Congress of the victory instead of writing to Washington. To make matters worse, Congress honored Gates with the appointment as president of the newly constituted Board of War, a post well suited to take advantage of his administrative talents in reorganizing the army, but Gates used the office to squabble with Washington. Gates's silence and even complicity in the movement to have him replace Washington as commander in chief, culminating in the so-called Conway Cabal during the following winter, revealed the extent

of the vanity and weakness in Gates's character. Those weaknesses became more apparent when Congress appointed Gates commander of the southern department in 1780. In August of that year Gates's army suffered a disastrous defeat by Lord Cornwallis at the Battle of Camden, South Carolina. Washington's treatment of Gates following the battle was nothing less than magnanimous. Gates himself reputedly exclaimed "Great man! Noble, generous procedure!" upon receiving a kind letter from Washington after the disaster. Nineteenth-century historians were not so kind, however; they considered his slight against Washington mean and contemptible, and they also further censured Gates for not stirring from his camp during the bloody battles that gave rise to his fame.

Washington never again trusted Gates with a combat command. After the defeat Gates was replaced by Maj. Gen. Nathanael Greene as commander of the southern department. In the summer of 1782 he rejoined Washington at New York, where he apparently played a role in bringing forward the Newburgh Address, although he and Washington remained on cordial terms.

In 1783 Gates returned to Virginia, in time to bury his wife, Elizabeth Phillips Gates, whom he married in 1754, who died soon after he returned. (His only child, Robert, had died of illness on the same day the Continental Congress informed him he had been relieved of his command of the southern department.) Some historians have suggested that Gates's ambitious first wife caused him more problems than his own desire. Certainly a petty quarrel between her and Martha Washington, who was quite popular among the high-ranking officers in the Continental army, did nothing to help her husband. He married again in 1786, to Mary Vallance, a rich heiress, and in 1790, he sold Traveller's Rest, freed his slaves, and moved to Manhattan, New York. He was elected to the New York legislature for one term. He also served as president of the New York Society of the Cincinnati. He died at his Manhattan home in April 1806.

Despite his ambition, Gates was known as a warm and generous man with courteous manners, friendly to all.

Related entries: Newburgh Conspiracy; Schuyler, Philip

Suggestions for further reading:
"Horatio Gates: Professional Soldier," George Athan Billias. George Athan Billias, ed. 1964. *George Washington's Generals.* New York.
Knollenberg, Bernhard. 1940. *Washington and the Revolution.* New York.
Nelson, Paul David. 1976. *General Horatio Gates: A Biography.* Baton Rouge, LA.

Germantown, Battle of

The Battle of Germantown might be interpreted as either a hopeless, desperate attempt to oust the British army from Philadelphia or as a brilliant military stroke that nearly came off. Washington himself frequently asserted that ill luck alone averted success on 4 October 1777. Others compared the failure at Germantown with Maj. Gen. Horatio Gates's victory at Saratoga and concluded that poor leadership was to blame for the repeated defeats suffered by Washington's army in the summer and autumn of 1777. The truth lay somewhere between both points of view.

Washington was correct in believing that the first week of October provided what was perhaps the last good opportunity to defeat British general William Howe's army in the field and liberate Philadelphia. Howe had weakened the main encampment of his army at Germantown by detaching Lord Cornwallis with the British and Hessian grenadiers and two squadrons of light dragoons to occupy Philadelphia on 26 September, and on 29 September he sent two more regiments to attack the small American fort at Billingsport on the Delaware

River. Washington's intelligence services kept him informed of these developments, which were a major factor in convincing him to risk a general assault on Howe's army at Germantown.

The number of British and Hessian troops at Germantown on 4 October was probably about 7,000 or 8,000, compared with which Washington had 11,000 troops, including 3,000 militia. Howe had posted his army effectively, however, in terrain that strongly favored the defenders. The stone houses of Germantown were scattered for about two miles along Germantown Road, running northwest from Philadelphia toward Reading. Behind the houses stretched enclosed fields and orchards divided by walls, fences, hedges, and lanes perpendicular to the main road. The American attack along Germantown Road would inevitably become disorganized by the necessity of crossing those man-made obstacles as well as the area's numerous creeks, ravines, and low hills. Howe placed his troops at right angles to the Germantown Road, with advance detachments that would warn of any attack.

Washington devised a complicated four-pronged plan of attack. The two main columns, composed entirely of Continental troops, were commanded by major generals John Sullivan and Nathanael Greene. Sullivan's column of 3,000 men would attack the British left wing along Germantown Road, while Greene's column with 5,000 more was ordered to attack the British right wing along Lime Kiln Road. Washington apparently hoped that a successful attack by Greene on the British right wing would force Howe's army onto the Schuylkill River on the left, where it could be destroyed. The two other columns involved in the attack were composed entirely of militia under Maj. Gen. John Armstrong and Brig. Gen. William Smallwood. They would advance respectively along the Schuylkill River about two miles west of Germantown and the Old York Road, a similar distance east of the town. In the event, neither of the militia columns was seriously involved in the attack. Washington stayed with Sullivan's column throughout the battle.

Sullivan's column began the battle by attacking the Second British Regiment of light infantry at nearby Mount Airy and Mount Pleasant, and succeeded after a short time in pushing them back. For a time Sullivan's troops advanced confidently while the British light infantry betrayed some signs of surprise and confusion. Before long, however, they ran into more than 100 men of the Fortieth Regiment under Lt. Col. Thomas Musgrave, barricaded in Benjamin Chew's two-and-a-half-story stone house, Cliveden. The Chew house lay directly across Sullivan's line of advance and threatened to disrupt and delay the attack. Washington was on the scene almost immediately and conferred with his officers on the prudence of attempting to seize the British strong point before continuing the advance. Contemporary accounts indicate that, while Lt. Col. Alexander Hamilton and Col. Timothy Pickering argued for the detachment of a small regiment to guard the house while the rest of the force pressed the attack, Brig. Gen. Henry Knox insisted that permitting a British redoubt to remain in the American rear would be foolish. Knox's opinion prevailed with Washington, and the British easily beat back the attack subsequently launched by the Americans, who lacked artillery heavy enough to demolish the house.

The delay occasioned by this ill-advised attack provided Howe with an opportunity to organize a counterattack from his main line of defense. In addition, Greene's column advancing from the north had become disorganized in its advance and, coming late on the battlefield, met with British positions that were prepared to meet them. Smallwood's column, which had been designated to support Greene, never arrived. Perhaps more important (and Washington made much of this), a heavy fog descended on the battlefield just as the attack on the Chew house began. In the resultant confu-

sion, some soldiers in Sullivan's column apparently mistook each other for British troops and began to fire on each other. In a turn that Washington could not have foreseen, nervous American soldiers began to retire from the battlefield, and before long a full-fledged retreat was taking place. Washington's attempts to rally his troops proved of no avail, and he had no choice but to try to disengage the rest of his army. Greene's column had the most difficulty in pulling back and lost a Virginia regiment in the process, captured by the British.

American casualties at Germantown have never been precisely determined, but they were around 152 men killed, 521 wounded, and 400 men captured or missing, the figure reported by the Board of War. The British reported 70 killed, 450 wounded, and 14 missing. Though not as devastating as the Battle of Brandywine, the Battle of Germantown was clearly an American defeat. An overly complicated plan of attack that failed to make full use of the American numerical superiority, poor battlefield discipline, mistaken decisions by the officers in command, and plain bad luck had combined to scuttle Washington's plan for routing the British from Philadelphia.

Related entry: Brandywine, Battle of

Suggestions for further reading:
"General Orders for Attacking Germantown," 3 October 1777 (*War Ser.*, vol. 11)
"From Anthony Wayne," 4 October 1777 (*War Ser.*, vol. 11)
"To Benjamin Harrison," 5 October 1777 (*War Ser.*, vol. 11)
"To John Hancock," 5 October 1777 (*War Ser.*, vol. 11)
McGuire, Thomas J. 1994. *The Surprise of Germantown, or The Battle of Cliveden, October 4th 1777.* Philadelphia.

Gibbs, Caleb (c.1750–1818)

A "good natured Yankee who makes a thousand Blunders in the Yankee stile and keeps the Dinner table in constant Laugh" is how Martha Daingerfield Bland of Virginia described Caleb Gibbs of Marblehead, Massachusetts, to her sister-in-law when writing from Washington's headquarters at Morristown, New Jersey, in May 1777. Gibbs had given up the adjutancy of Col John Glover's Fourteenth Continental Regiment (the celebrated Marblehead Mariners) in March 1776 to enter Washington's military family at New York as captain of the Commander in Chief's Guard. He immediately became a trusted and popular member of the men who supported Washington daily, managing household tasks that regularly included procuring food, drink, lodging, and clothing; supervising the steward, cooks, and housekeepers, and the care of the horses; paying the bills; and assisting in the drafting and delivering of Washington's letters.

Promoted to major in July 1778, Gibbs was well liked and performed his duties with distinction, but he apparently had a misunderstanding with Washington in the fall of 1779 that resulted in his staying away from the latter's table. "Majr. Gibbs's present plan of separation" was an "act entirely of his own seeking," said Washington. "I mean to act coolly and deliberately myself, and will therefore give him an opportunity of recollecting himself. He has been guilty of a piece of disrespect; to give it no worse term; . . . and because I wou'd not suffer my orders to be trampled upon; a supercilious, and self-important conduct on his part is the consequence." Despite the dispute with Washington, Gibbs continued to supervise the headquarters household and maintain its accounts until the end of 1780, when he entered the Second Massachusetts Regiment in search of greater military distinction. In the spring of 1781 Washington commended Gibbs in General Orders for his past service in the guards corps. The following October Gibbs was wounded in the ankle during the American assault on British redoubt number 10 at the Battle of Yorktown.

After the war Gibbs served as major of Col. Henry Jackson's First American Regiment, and following that regiment's dissolution in June 1784, he lived by necessity in an "unsettled state," "œconomical in every instance," owing to the depreciated value of Continental certificates. "I have been floating about from Philadelphia to New Hampshire, negociating a little business partly on Commission," he informed Washington that October. "My Love and regard for you and Mrs Washington," he added, "has several times prompt me the last season to undertake a visit to Mount Vernon but on reconnoitreing my finances I have found it impossible to attempt the march." Gibbs managed to visit Mount Vernon for a few days at the end of June 1786; later that year he once again became a major, in Colonel Jackson's new regiment during Shays's Rebellion. Gibbs served in the Massachusetts convention that ratified the U.S. Constitution in February 1788, about which he kept Washington informed. After Washington was elected president, Gibbs made repeated but unsuccessful appeals to Washington and later to Alexander Hamilton for a federal appointment. When Gibbs's application for a commission in the army during the Quasi-War was vetoed by some of the Massachusetts congressional delegates, Washington vigorously but unsuccessfully objected to Gibbs's failure to receive an appointment.

Related entry: Commander in Chief's Guard

Suggestions for further reading:
"To Caleb Gibbs," 1 May 1777 (*War Ser.*, vol. 9).
"Martha Daingerfield Bland to Frances Bland Randolph," 12 May 1777 (*Proceedings of the New Jersey Historical Society* [1895], vol. 51).
"To William Colfax," 2 October 1779 (*Writings*, vol. 16).
"From Caleb Gibbs," 24 October 1785 (*Con. Ser.*, vol. 3).
"From Caleb Gibbs," 9, 24 February 1788 (*Con. Ser.*, vol. 6).
"To Caleb Gibbs," 6 March 1797 (*Ret. Ser.*, vol. 1).
"From Caleb Gibbs," 21 April 1799 (*Ret. Ser.*, vol. 4).

Wehmann, Howard H. 1972. "To Major Gibbs with Much Esteem" (*Prologue,* vol. 4).

Gist, Christopher (c.1706–1759)

"Christopher Gist," wrote historian Douglas Southall Freeman, was a man "who knew the art of the forests and knew, also, when to aid and when to leave Washington alone." A native of Maryland, Gist had become a leading explorer, surveyor, and Indian trader by the early 1750s. He was living in North Carolina in 1750 when the Ohio Company engaged him to explore west to what is now Pittsburgh and beyond to the mouth of the Scioto River, and between 1751 and 1753 he explored on the Great Kanawha and Ohio Rivers for the company. Thus he was the first American to explore southern Ohio and northeastern Kentucky from the Monongahela River to the Great Kanawha River. In 1753 he accompanied Washington as guide on his journey to Fort Le Boeuf to deliver Governor Dinwiddie's letter to Jacques Le Gardeur, sieur de Saint-Pierre (1701–1755), the commandant of the French forces in the Ohio Country. Washington apparently got along quite well with the rugged frontiersman, who suffered frostbite on the way back. At the time of their attack on Fort Necessity, in July 1754, the French destroyed Gist's plantation (known as Gist's Settlement) in the Monongahela Valley near Redstone Old Fort, forcing Gist to move his family to Opeckton, his property across the Potomac River from the Ohio Company's trading post at Wills Creek. Washington had been at Gist's New Settlement (where he had collected stores for his troops) when he first received word that the French were marching against him. Gist was with Washington at the surrender of Fort Necessity (near present-day Uniontown, Pennsylvania).

Gist later served as a guide in Braddock's expedition, and in fact, it was at Gist's plantation near present-day Mount Braddock, Pennsylvania, that the British general encamped his troops in June 1755. Beginning in that year Gist acted as a captain of scouts in the Virginia Regiment, commanded by Washington, and in 1757 he was appointed deputy superintendent of Indian affairs at Winchester, from which he often sent Washington "flying reports" (rumors) along with his own eyewitness accounts from the frontier. Gist, who entered land claims on the Ohio for Washington, George Mercer, and Robert Stewart, died of smallpox in July 1759 while returning to Winchester from Williamsburg. Gist's daughter Nancy lived for a time with the Fairfax family at Belvoir, their estate on the Potomac River a few miles from Mount Vernon. His son Nathaniel Gist commanded one of Washington's Sixteen Additional Continental Regiments during the Revolutionary War.

Gist kept a journal account of his travels with Washington to the French forces on the Ohio in 1753, which was published in the late nineteenth century.

Related entries: Braddock's Defeat; Croghan, George; Dinwiddie, Robert; Fort Necessity Campaign; Half-King, The; Virginia Regiment

Suggestions for further reading:
Diaries, vol. 1.
"From Christopher Gist," 15 October 1755 (*Col. Ser.,* vol. 2).
"From Christopher Gist," 10–12 July 1758 (*Col. Ser.,* vol. 5).
Darlington, William M., ed. 1893. *Christopher Gist's Journals with Historical, Geographical, and Ethnological Notes and Biographies of His Contemporaries.* Cleveland.

Graham, Catharine Sawbridge Macaulay (1731–1791)

The second daughter of Kentish landowner John Sawbridge and Elizabeth Wanley, the heiress of a London banker, Catharine Sawbridge was born at Olantigh House at Wye, Kent. Her father had her schooled at home along with her brother, who later became a supporter of the radical John Wilkes. In 1760 Catharine married Dr. George Macaulay, a Scottish physician in charge of a London hospital, who died six years later, leaving Catharine with a 6-year-old daughter. At the age of 57, she was remarried to 21-year-old William Graham, for which she was very much criticized.

The author of the celebrated eight-volume *History of England, from the Accession of James I to That of the Brunswick Line* (London, 1763–1783) and a staunch Republican, Macaulay supported deposing James I but considered Cromwell to be as depraved as the king he disposed. She denounced the Quebec Act and the taxation of the North American colonies in 1775 by replying to Burke's pamphlet *Thoughts on the Cause of the Present Discontents.* Her antimonarchical views and sympathies with radicals brought her public criticism but also supporters, including Horace Walpole, William Pitt, and the poet Thomas Gray. Mary Wollstonecraft was inspired by her work and said Macaulay was the "woman of the greatest abilities that this country has ever produced."

Armed with letters of introduction from Richard Henry Lee, Benjamin Lincoln, Henry Knox, Samuel Adams, and James Duane, among others, the Grahams arrived at Mount Vernon on 4 June 1783 for a ten-day visit. Washington was much taken with the author, "whose reputation among the Literati is so high, and whose principles are so much, & so justly admired by the friends to liberty and of mankind. It gave me pleasure to find that her sentimts respecting the inadequacy of the powers of Congress . . . concided with my own." He allowed her access to his military records "for her perusal & amusemt."

Graham wrote Washington a month after her visit saying that "we in vain search in the language of panigeric for some arrangement of words adequate to that superiority of praise which is due to the first character in the world. . . . I know the delicacy of your mind makes you as backward to meet applause as you are forward to deserve it. You must however give me leave to say that you above all the human race seem happily distinguished in the privilege of preserving and encreasing the esteem of mankind through the opportunity of a more intimate and correct knowledge of your character and talents."

Graham maintained a correspondence with Washington until her death, discussing among other things, the French Revolution and the politics of the United States. "The establishment of our new Government," Washington wrote Graham in January 1790, "seemed to be the last great experiment, for promoting human happiness, by reasonable compact, in civil Society. . . . That the Government, though not absolutely perfect, is one of the best in the World, I have little doubt. I always believed that an unequivocally free & equal Representation of the People in the Legislature; together with an efficient & responsible Executive were the great Pillars on which the preservation of American Freedom must depend." In her reply some months later, Graham expressed a hope "that the future Chief Majestrates of the United States, may in some measure partake of the wisdom, and virtue, of her first Chief Majestrate."

Graham sent Washington copies of her pamphlets *Letters on Education with Observations of Religious and Metaphysical Subjects* (London, 1790) and *Observations on the Reflections of the Right Hon. Edmund Burke, on the Revolution in France, in a Letter to the Right Hon. the Earl of Stanhope* (London, 1790), both of which were among the works in Washington's library inventoried after his death and now in the collection of the Boston Athenaeum.

Related entries: Education; Lincoln, Benjamin; Mount Vernon

Suggestions for further reading:
Diaries, vol. 4.
"From Richard Henry Lee," 3 May 1785 (*Con. Ser.,* vol. 2).
"From Catharine Sawbridge Macaulay Graham," 13 July 1785 (*Con. Ser.,* vol. 3).
"To Catharine Sawbridge Macaulay Graham," 10 January 1786 (*Con. Ser.,* vol. 3).
"To Catharine Sawbridge Macaulay Graham," 9 January 1790 (*Pres. Ser.,* vol. 4).
"From Catharine Sawbridge Macaulay Graham," June 1790 (*Pres. Ser.,* vol. 5).

A miniature depicting Col. William Grayson (Library of Congress)

Grayson, William
(c. 1736–1790)

William Grayson, a prominent lawyer from Dumfries, Virginia, who graduated from the College of Philadelphia in 1760, was one of Washington's aides-de-camp during the Revolutionary War. In the late 1760s he was among the circle of Washington's friends who frequented Mount Vernon for fox chases and evenings of card playing, and, in Grayson's case at least, to discuss business. Grayson also visited Washington at Mount Vernon in the 1770s and 1780s.

Grayson served as deputy king's attorney for several years—appointed by the governor at an annual salary of 3,000 pounds of tobacco—but by 1774 he had become an ardent supporter of the Patriot cause. In November 1774 he became captain of the Prince William County Independent Company, which was outfitted with assistance from Washington; he later became colonel of the county's regiment of minutemen, which marched to Hampton in December 1775. Grayson was unable to secure a Continental commission from the Virginia convention, however, and in August 1776 he accepted Washington's offer to join his staff as an aide-de-camp with the rank of lieutenant colonel. (Only two weeks earlier Grayson had led a party of about thirty Prince William volunteers in driving off a mischievous British landing party from the banks of the Potomac River not far from Mount Vernon.) Grayson spent the next four months by Washington's side as the Continental army headquarters moved through New York, Pennsylvania, and New Jersey, drafting official correspondence and accompanying the commander in chief on reconnoitering missions. In early January 1777 Washington nominated Grayson colonel of one of the Sixteen Additional Continental Regiments that Congress had authorized Washington to raise. Grayson took part in the Battles of Long Island, White Plains, and Brandywine, and he testified at the trial of Maj. Gen. Charles Lee after the Battle of Monmouth Courthouse, even though Lee previously had recommended Grayson for a Continental army commission, calling Grayson "a Man of extraordinary merit." Grayson retired from the army in April 1779 but continued to support the war effort by sitting on the Continental Board of War from December 1779 to September 1781.

After the war Grayson was elected to the Virginia House of Delegates, in which on the last day of 1784 he introduced Washington's Potomac River Company bill, which was passed by both the Virginia and Maryland legislatures. It was Grayson to whom Washington confided his misgivings about being given shares of Potomac Company stock by the state of Virginia. Grayson suggested that Washington could not well refuse the state's gift, but that he could assign the shares to some "public purposes of essential utility," a course which Washington eventually adopted, donating the shares to educational purposes.

In 1785 Grayson became a member of the Confederation Congress, and from its sessions in New York City he kept Washington apprised of its deliberations. Although he strongly supported southern interests, Grayson was influential in securing the passage of the most significant act of the Confederation government, the Ordinance of 1787, which organized the Northwest Territory. While at New York, Grayson also found time to arrange for "8 Yew & 4 Aspan trees" to be procured from Landon Carter's plantation on Bull Run and sent to Washington, in response to the latter's request that Grayson find some aspen and yew scions to "diversify the scene" at Mount Vernon.

Grayson also attended the Virginia Ratifying Convention for the Federal Constitution in the spring of 1788, where, according to Washington, he was "considered to be rather opposed to the new Constitution." Like many others in fact, Grayson's anxiety about ratifying the proposed Constitution was allayed only by Washington's presence at the Constitutional Convention in Philadelphia and the role that Washington was expected to play in the new system. "I think that were it not for one great character in America," Grayson told one correspondent, "so many men would not be for this government." In 1789 Grayson became one of Virginia's first U.S. senators, but he died the following year while at his home in Dumfries. Two years after his death, Virginia honored Grayson by naming a county

in the southwestern part of the state after him.

Related entries: Aides-de-Camp; Constitutional Convention

Suggestions for further reading:
Diaries, vol. 2.
"From William Grayson," 27 December 1774 (*Col. Ser.,* vol. 10).
"General Orders," 24 August 1776 (*War Ser.,* vol. 6).
"To William Grayson," 11 January 1777 (*War Ser.,* vol. 8).
"To William Grayson," 22 January 1785 (*Con. Ser.,* vol. 2).
"From William Grayson," 10 March 1785 (*Con. Ser.,* vol. 2).

Great Kanawha Tracts

The Great Kanawha River, for Washington, was an important link in the inland navigational scheme to connect the Great Lakes with the rivers of Virginia, especially the Potomac and the James, through the upper waters of the Ohio. The Kanawha is formed by the juncture, about two miles above its falls, of the Gauley River and the New, or Woods, River, which rises in North Carolina and flows north through southwest Virginia into present-day West Virginia. The Kanawha flows into the Ohio River about ninety-eight miles away. Washington early on recognized the potential value of the land along the Kanawha and sought to have it included among the 200,000 acres of land granted by Virginia lieutenant governor Robert Dinwiddie's Proclamation of 1754, which awarded land-bounty warrants to the officers and soldiers who had volunteered to serve in the expedition to the Monongahela River that concluded with the Battle of Great Meadows. In 1772, after years of uncertainty, the lands in the Kanawha and Ohio valleys were finally approved for inclusion under both Dinwiddie's proclamation and the royal proclamation of 1763, and from then to 1774 Washington sought to obtain choice tracts along the Kanawha River's shores.

Washington hardly had staked his claims in the area, however, before their legitimacy was thrown into confusion by Virginia governor Dunmore's 1774 declaration that all western bounty lands surveys carried out under the Proclamation of 1754 were null and void. Using military land-bounty warrants, Washington had claimed four tracts totaling 23,216 acres in the Great Kanawha Valley, not far upriver from where the Kanawha empties into the Ohio River, between 1772 and 1774. The first and largest tract, 10,990 acres claimed under the Proclamation of 1754, lay on the Kanawha's west, or north, bank "abt two Miles from the Mouth of that River and runs up the same, binding therewith, for Seventeen Miles." The second tract, 7,276 acres jointly granted to Washington and George Muse in November 1773, became Washington's in its entirety following a land-trade deal between the two men. A 2,000-acre tract on the Great Kanawha at the mouth of the Coal (Cole) River was claimed by Washington in 1774 on the basis of a land-bounty warrant purchased by him from Charles Mynn Thruston, who had been issued the warrant under the provisions of the Proclamation of 1763. The final tract, 2,950 acres claimed as part of the 5,000 acres entitled to Washington in his own right by the Proclamation of 1763, ran along the east, or south, bank of the Great Kanawha for about six miles.

In the fall of 1770, while it was yet uncertain whether the land along the Kanawha River would be allowed under the terms of the Proclamation of 1754, or even if the territory was in Virginia, Washington traveled to the Ohio to scout out bounty lands for the veterans of the Virginia Regiment. On the first day of November, a "little before eight Oclock," he wrote in his diary, "we set of[f] with our Canoe up the River to discover what kind of Lands lay upon the Kanhawa. The Land on both sides of this River just at the Mouth is very fine; but on the East side when you get towards the Hills (which I judge to be about 6 or 700 yards from the River) it appears to be wet, & better adapted for Meadow than tillage." Although the vastness of the land was great, its quality varied nearly every time Washington cast his eyes in a new direction. It was not what he had anticipated, but upon the whole he thought it "exceeding valuable" and about as satisfactory as could be found. His party spent several days exploring the land bordering the Kanawha, hunting and marking boundary trees along the river. "This Country abounds in Buffalo & wild game of all kinds," wrote Washington, "as also in all kinds of wild fowl, there being in the Bottoms a great many small grassy Ponds or Lakes which are full of Swans, Geese, & Ducks of different kinds." The woods teemed with a variety of trees also, including maple, elm, oak, ash, sycamore, walnut, poplar, and pine. By his own calculations, the mouth of the Kanawha River was 272 miles from Fort Pitt.

Settling the Kanawha tracts was not easy. Washington's old friend Valentine Crawford agreed to lead a party to seat the claims in 1774, but the expedition had to be aborted owing to Indian raids on the frontier. James Cleveland, Washington's overseer at his River farm on Clifton's Neck at Mount Vernon, organized another expedition in 1775. From the beginning Cleveland ran into difficulties. Renters were scarce, squatters had to be contended with, runaways among slaves and indentured servants had to be guarded against, and relations with Indians were unpredictable. Houses were nonexistent, and all supplies, tools, and livestock had to be transported to the area from great distances. The land was judged good for corn as a cash crop, but it was also expedient to establish potatoes, turnips, cucumbers, watermelons, and peaches. The first and most important task was to prepare fields for planting, which required a good deal of draining. Fences came later, in the off-seasons. Canoes, the most important means of transportation, and necessary for survival, had to be protected from sunlight and from theft. In spite of such obstacles a promising settlement was established on a Kanawha tract in Fincastle (Botetourt after 1776) County, only to be abandoned in 1776 because of renewed hostilities on the frontier.

During the Revolutionary War, Washington had scant time to devote to his western lands, and they were almost completely neglected. Therefore, in the fall of 1784 he made another trip to investigate his claims. While en route he discussed with everyone he encountered the possibility of opening up inland navigation for trade across the Alleghenies. Renewed Indian unrest prevented him from reaching the Kanawha, however, disappointing him in one of the main objects of the journey, "namely to examine into the situation quality and advantages of the Land which I hold upon the Ohio and Great Kanawha and to take measures for rescuing them from the hands of Land Jobbers & Speculators." New claimants, lumping his tracts together with other surveys, were offering them for sale at Philadelphia and in Europe. Washington nevertheless proclaimed himself "well pleased" with his journey, for the "more the Navigation of Potomack is investigated, & duely considered, the greater the advantages arising from them appear." He described the Great Kanawha as "a fine Navigable river to the Falls; the practicability of opening which, seems to be little understood; but most assuredly ought to be investigated."

Washington's renewed interest in the Kanawha was interrupted again by his call to the Constitutional Convention and his election to the presidency. After leaving office in 1797 Washington leased his lands on the Kanawha to James Welch, who in December 1797 agreed to find subtenants willing to settle and make substantial improvements on "convenient tenements of from 50 to 300 acres." Welch promised to pay $5,000 in rent for the first year, $8,000 for the second, $11,413 annually from thence until the expiration of thirty years, and "for 99 years *thereafter* on an annual Rent of $22,286," or, given the complicated transaction, Welch could purchase the tracts outright with four annual $50,000 payments beginning in 1804. Welch made no payments to Washington, and the Kanawha lands reverted to Washington's estate after his death.

Related entries: Crawford Brothers; Dinwiddie, Robert; Dunmore, John Murray, Fourth Earl of; James River Company; Millers Run (Chartiers Creek) Tract; Washington's Bottom Tract

Suggestions for further reading:
Diaries, vols. 2, 4.
"Petition to Botetourt," c.15 December 1769 (*Col. Ser.*, vol. 8).
"Advertisement," 16 December 1769 (*Col. Ser.*, vol. 8).
"To Botetourt," 5 October 1770 (*Col. Ser.*, vol. 8).
"Account of Expenditures for Trip to the Great Kanawha," 6 October–30 November 1770 (*Col. Ser.*, vol. 8).
"From James Cleveland," 12, 21 May 1775 (*Col. Ser.*, vol. 10).
"From James Cleveland," 16 November 1775 (*War Ser.*, vol. 2).
"Advertisement: Ohio Lands," c.10 March 1784 (*Con. Ser.*, vol. 1).
"To James Welch," 1, 7 December 1797 (*Ret. Ser.*, vol. 1).
"Schedule of Property," 9 July 1799 (*Ret. Ser.*, vol. 4).

Great Meadows

See Fort Necessity Campaign; The Indian Prophecy; "Whistling Bullets."

Greene, Nathanael (1742–1786)

Of the handful of general officers whose service proved absolutely essential to the Revolutionary War effort, perhaps none resembled his commander in chief more than Nathanael Greene, the son of a Quaker anchor-maker and small merchant from Warwick, Rhode Island. Greene's formal education, like that of Washington, was cut short, although he was introduced to Latin and taught geometry by his tutor, Adam Maxwell, and he had the benefit of discussing theology and philosophy with Ezra Stiles (later the president of Yale College). Greene apparently became disillusioned with Quakerism at an early age, and he eventually left the Society of Friends altogether. Greene, who was trained to follow in his father's footsteps, was not raised in poverty, but, like Washington, he had to supplement his natural ability with hard work in order to get ahead in life. As a young man Greene was witty and rather handsome, with blue-gray eyes, and was about five feet ten inches tall. His naturally candid and charitable disposition was said to appear stern whenever he was absorbed in a situation or a crisis that demanded his attention. A nineteenth-century historian noted that his "almost intuitive perception of character" resembled Washington's, and that he, like Washington, "seemed to take the exact measure of every man who approached him."

Again, like Washington, it has been said of Greene that he was athletic and excelled in many of the amusements of the day— throwing the bar, wrestling, and leaping, although in fact he limped slightly and suffered from asthma. Like his commander in chief, he enjoyed social events, especially balls and dancing, but, following the advice he sometimes offered to others, Greene was always careful to temper his fun, not to "check sociability but to render it natural." He was elected at a young age to the colonial legislature of Rhode Island. His involvement in politics led him to help form the Kentish Guards, a unit resembling the famed minutemen of the Revolutionary War, which in turn led him to an interest in military tactics. Like his commander in chief, Greene realized before most that the colonies' grievances with the mother country would lead to a final separation. Greene became known for his sense of duty, which like Washington's rested on the strength of his character and the confidence that what he was pursuing was aligned with the right.

The Continental Congress appointed Greene one of the first eight brigadier generals of the Continental army in June 1775, and in August 1776—long after Washington had recognized and come to depend on Greene's military abilities—Congress promoted him to major general. Henry Knox, Washington's famed artillery commander, is supposed to have said that within that single year Greene had transformed himself from "the rawest, the most untutored being" into the finest general officer in the Continental army. Indeed, by that time Washington's regard for Greene had grown so that he believed that if he were captured or killed in battle Greene should succeed him as commander in chief of all the American forces.

Greene accompanied Washington to New York in the spring of 1776 to face the expected British onslaught, but illness forced him to miss the ill-fated Battle of Long Island. Green supported Washington's decision to hold onto Forts Washington and Lee on the Hudson River, and he fortunately escaped capture when the forts fell to the British the following fall. The loss of the Hudson River forts made both Washington and Greene more cautious, and afterward the two generals tended to pursue strategies aimed at wearing down the enemy, exemplified by Greene's course of action later in the war with Lord Cornwallis in the south, which set the stage for the American victory at Yorktown. After the loss of New York and the Hudson River forts, Washington called upon Greene to help lead the Continental army's retreat across New Jersey. Greene's conspicuous roles in the American victories at Trenton on Christmas Day 1776 and at Princeton a week later caused him to boast in a letter to his wife, Catharine Littlefield ("Caty") Greene, that, as their affairs grew "more difficult and distressing," Washington had depended upon him more and more, and that he enjoyed Washington's "full confidence." Greene served very closely with Washington throughout 1777, and, in fact, for several days in August 1777 Washington left Greene in command of the entire army while he personally reconnoitered the American fortifications along the Delaware River. Greene also shared the criticism that fell upon Washington following the American losses at the Pennsylvania Battles of Brandywine and Germantown. Although his division played a crucial role in saving part of the American army at Brandywine, Greene received no public recognition for it, and he, along with Henry Knox, Joseph Reed, and Lafayette, increasingly came under bitter attack by those in and out of the army clamoring to elevate Maj. Gen. Horatio Gates to the position of commander in chief.

In March 1778, at Washington's persistent urging, Greene reluctantly assumed the office of quartermaster general. His service in that capacity literally saved the army from starvation. Greene took command of Maj. Gen. Charles Lee's division when Washington relieved Lee of his command at the Battle of Monmouth Courthouse the following June, and he also joined the Newport campaign in his home state, Rhode Island, later in 1778. Greene's successful use of the militia at the Battle of Connecticut Farms (Springfield) in 1780 so impressed the southern delegates to the Continental Congress that they petitioned Washington to give Greene the command of the Continental army in the southern department.

In December 1780, Washington in fact did choose Greene to replace Maj. Gen. Horatio Gates as commander of the southern department. Gates's army had been destroyed at Camden, South Carolina, in Au-gust 1780, and its surviving elements lay broken and scattered throughout the south. The decision was universally applauded, and Greene's skills for organization helped him to quickly reestablish the army. In February 1781 he made his famous "race to the Dan," a retreat across the Carolinas into Virginia that divided and weakened the pursuing British forces. Greene understood that pulling Cornwallis away from his base might provide an opportunity to attack and defeat him. Even one of his enemies, Col. Banastre Tarleton, recognized the wisdom of Greene's strategy during the historic retreat: "Every measure of the Americans during their march from the Catawba [River] to Virginia, was judiciously designed and vigorously executed." When Cornwallis's army began to fall back in search of supplies in late February, Greene recognized that the tables had turned in his favor, and he immediately dispatched the legendary cavalry unit commanded by Col. "Light-Horse" Harry Lee, along with Gen. Andrew Pickens's militia, to harass his former pursuers. Greene seized an opportunity on 15 March to attack Cornwallis at Guilford Courthouse in North Carolina; the ensuing battle was fierce, and Cornwallis emerged as the nominal victor, but the victory cost him an enormous price—one-fourth of his troops. Greene's strategy forced Cornwallis to retreat all the way to the Atlantic coast for supplies for his army and, more important, convinced him that the king's army could never hold onto its gains in the south until the rebel resistance in Virginia was destroyed. As a result Cornwallis made the fateful decision to take his army to Virginia, where it was trapped by Washington and Rochambeau.

Greene, meanwhile, turned southward, with the aim of clearing South Carolina and Georgia of royal troops. To accomplish this end Greene began a "war of the posts" aimed at capturing the British support posts that were essential for the British to maintain their army in the interior of South

Carolina and Georgia. Greene and the army kept the main British forces occupied while Lee's light horse and the militia attacked the supply posts and lines of communication. The strategy proved brilliant, quickly demoralizing the Loyalist militia and making the backcountry untenable for the British. In the spring of 1781 Greene's army suffered another defeat, this time at Hobkirk's Hill, South Carolina, but like the confrontation at Guilford Courthouse, the American losses were minor when compared to the costs the British paid for the victory. The Battle of Eutaw Springs, South Carolina, the following September proved a tactical draw, with the commanders of each side claiming to hold the field after the battle. Both sides suffered heavy casualties, and the British were forced to pull their forces from around the state, concentrating them at Charleston. The South Carolina government was reestablished as a direct result of Greene's maneuvers, and in Georgia a government was established when Greene successfully negotiated a deal to make Nathan Brownson governor instead of commander of the Georgia militia, as the state's delegates to Congress had directed. The Continental Congress presented Greene with a British standard and a gold medal for his important achievements in the South, while the states of North Carolina, South Carolina, and Georgia presented him with land and money.

A nineteenth-century biographer, Edward Meeks, observed of Greene, perhaps a little too uncritically, that he was "a man of method, industry, of calm, equable temper,—capable of bearing reverses without complaint, and of enjoying victory without exultation. He was a wise man, who could think in advance of the exigency, and thus provide against it;—a brave man, who could not be forced to fight, except when he thought proper;—a great man, who served his country with success and fidelity." Another writer of the period observed that Greene's keen ability to read men gave him a distinct advantage over his adversaries, allowing him to usually predict their movements and thus make his own plans accordingly, following an internal logic that seemed rash or confusing to those judging the relative strengths of his and his foe's armies. Greene was cautious but brave and willing to take decisive action when necessary; he was diligent and energetic and carried out his duties with ceaseless activity; his outmaneuvering of Cornwallis arose from clear thinking and resolution. A canny foe in New Jersey had earlier observed of him, "Greene is dangerous as Washington—he is vigilant, enterprising, and full of resources."

After the war Greene returned to Rhode Island, not to his two-and-a-half-story gabled frame house that he had built before the war near his family's ironworks in Coventry (called variously the Homestead and the Mount Vernon of the North) but to Newport, where he made plans to relocate to the south. In 1785 he traveled to Georgia to look after Mulberry Grove, his estate near Savannah, where he died in June 1786 of a "fever in the Head" after being "Sezed at table" with a "Violent pain in his Eye & Head" (apparently of stroke). Washington was devastated by his old friend's sudden death, following closely on the heels of two other close associates from the war, Tench Tilghman and Alexander McDougall. As late as the following spring he wrote Lafayette that Greene's passing was an "event which has given such genl concern and is so much regretted by his numerous friends that I can scarce persuade myself to touch upon it even so far as to say that in him you lost a man who affectionately regarded & was a sincere admirer of you."

Aware that Greene's financial situation had been desperate even before his death, Washington magnanimously offered to care for his namesake, George Washington Greene, by offering "to give him as good an education as this Country (I mean the United States) will afford and will bring him up to either of the genteel professions that his friends may choose, or his own inclination shall lead him to pursue at my own cost and expense." Almost five years later, Washington, while in Georgia on his southern tour as president, made it a point to visit Mulberry Grove to pay his respects to Greene's widow. He personally saw to it that Congress indemnified Greene's estate for old Revolutionary War bonds that Greene had given in order to supply clothing for the troops.

Related entries: Brandywine, Battle of; Gates, Horatio; Southern Tour

Suggestions for further reading:
"From Jeremiah Wadsworth," 1 October 1786 (*Con. Ser.,* vol. 4).
"To Jeremiah Wadsworth," 22 October 1786 (*Con. Ser.,* vol. 4).
"To Lafayette," 25 March 1787 (*Con. Ser.,* vol. 5).
Greene, George W. 1867–1871. 3 vols. *Life of Nathanael Greene.* New York.

Showman, Richard K. et al., eds. 1976—. 10 vols. to date. *The Papers of General Nathanael Greene.* Chapel Hill, NC.
Thayer, Theodore. 1960. *Nathanael Greene: Strategist of the Revolution.* New York.
"The Wartime Speculations of Nathanael Greene" (vol. 5, appendix 2). Douglas Southall Freeman. 1948–1957. 7 vols. *George Washington: A Biography.* New York.

Greenway Court

*L*ocated about four miles west of where Joseph Berry's ferry crossed the Shenandoah River in Frederick County, Virginia (or about one mile south of White Post in present-day Clarke County), Greenway Court was for three decades the home of Thomas, Lord Fairfax, the only English peer residing in the colonies. Fairfax, who had come to Virginia in 1747 to safeguard

Greenway Court, Lord Fairfax's western seat, as depicted in Woodrow Wilson's George Washington, New York, *1897 (Library of Congress)*

his interests in the Northern Neck Proprietary, a grant of 5 million acres of Virginia lands that came under his control following the deaths of his mother and grandmother, took up permanent residence at Greenway Court in 1749 and lived there until his death in 1781. His wilderness manor, referred to by Fairfax and others as the "lodge," has been described variously as a "great stone house" and a "modest stucco hunting lodge." It apparently stood on a beautiful knoll overlooking the lush forests and other charming scenes of the Shenandoah Valley. The lodge possessed a roof that ran long and sloping on one side, as was fashionable at the time, large dormer windows, and huge chimneys at opposing ends of the building. Of the original structures erected at Greenway Court, only the so-called land office remains, a little gray-stone house of two low stories, built about 1761 to conduct business related to Lord Fairfax's lands, such as collecting quit rents, platting surveys, and sheltering surveying instruments. Washington first visited Greenway Court in 1748, when he accompanied George William Fairfax (the son of Col. William Fairfax, cousin of the baron) on a monthlong surveying trip to the western part of the proprietary. Although Washington apparently did not return to Greenway Court during his brief career as a professional surveyor, when he surveyed dozens of grants for Lord Fairfax in the Shenandoah and valleys beyond, Washington did stay overnight at the lodge in March 1769 and again in March 1771. From time to time other prominent Virginians passed through Greenway Court, as Lord Dunmore, the royal governor of Virginia, did in 1774 while on the Shawnee campaign.

Related entry: Fairfax of Cameron, Thomas Fairfax, Sixth Baron

Suggestions for further reading:
Diaries, vols. 1–3.
"From George William Fairfax," 30 October 1761 (*Ret. Ser.,* vol. 7).
"To George William Fairfax," 20 July 1763 (*Ret. Ser.,* vol. 7).
Hughes, Sarah S. 1979. *Surveyors and Statesmen: Land Measuring in Colonial Virginia.* Richmond, VA.

H

The Half-King (c.1700–1754)

The Half-King, or Tanacharison, with what Washington's biographer Douglas Southall Freeman called "his irrepressible hatred of France and his ineradicable love of making speeches," was a prominent Seneca chief who advised the British on Indian affairs in the Ohio Country. At a meeting at Logstown on the Ohio River in 1752, he played an instrumental role in negotiating from the Six Nations permission for the British to construct a fort at the forks of the Allegheny and Monongahela Rivers. The following summer he led a delegation to warn the French that they were trespassing on Indian lands. The mission ended in failure, however, with the French, rejecting his demands and treating him contemptuously, ridiculing him by calling him an old woman. Virginia governor Robert Dinwiddie's instructions to Washington in October 1753 to investigate the extent of the French encroachment on British-claimed land in the Ohio Country specifically requested Washington to "address Yourself to the Half King" when meeting with the sachems of the Six Nations. Around that time the Half-King gave Washington the Indian name of Conotocarious (Caunotaucarius), signifying "town taker" or "devourer of villages." Washington later bestowed an English name on the Half-King when honoring him with a medal from Governor Dinwiddie, whom he wrote: "I

was also told an English Name wd please the Half King much, which made me presume to give him that of your Honour's, and call him Dinwiddie—Interpreted in their Language the head of all." Washington mistrusted the loyalty of the Half-King on a few occasions, but the chief rendered crucial support to the British during Washington's engagement with the French in May 1754, which resulted in the defeat of sieur de Jumonville. The Half-King kept faith with the British following the surrender of Fort Necessity, even when many of the other sachems went over to the French, and shortly before his death of alcoholism in October 1754, he declared that he "wou'd live and die with the English."

Related entries: Conotocarious; Croghan, George; Dinwiddie, Robert; Fort Necessity Campaign; Gist, Christopher

Suggestions for further reading:
"Washington's Journal" (*Diaries,* vol. 1).
"To Robert Dinwiddie," 29 May 1754 (*Col. Ser.,* vol. 1).
"To Robert Dinwiddie," 10 June 1754 (*Col. Ser.,* vol. 1).
"From Robert Dinwiddie," 27 June 1754 (*Col. Ser.,* vol. 1).

Hamilton, Alexander (1757–1804)

"I have been much indebted to the kindness of the General," wrote

Alexander Hamilton, as secretary of the treasury, presents the charter of the new Federal Bank to the cabinet members (Library of Congress)

Alexander Hamilton upon hearing of Washington's death, "and he was an Aegis very essential to me. But regrets are unavailing. . . . If virtue can secure happiness in another world, he is happy. In this the seal is now set upon his glory."

Hamilton was born in the British colony of Nevis, one of the Leeward Islands, the illegitimate son of James Hamilton and Rachel Fawcett Levine, and educated by a Presbyterian minister at St. Croix, where he was apprenticed as a clerk before coming to New York in 1772 to enter King's College. He left school in 1774 after hearing about the Boston Tea Party to join the New York Sons of Liberty and participate in the impending crisis with Great Britain. Over the next few months he wrote several essays, including "The Rights of the Colonies" and "Remarks on the Quebec Bill."

In March 1776, Hamilton was appointed captain of a New York provincial artillery company, just in time for him to join Washington's forces in the New York campaign. His conduct in supporting Washington's rear guard during the Continental army's retreat across New Jersey impressed Washington greatly, and in March 1777 Washington took him into his military family as an aide-de-camp with the rank of lieutenant colonel. The two soon developed a warm friendship and working relationship that lasted throughout Washington's two terms as president. His four years with Washington during the war gave him an opportunity to see firsthand the considerable weaknesses of the Confederation government. Always desirous of battlefield glory, Hamilton later sought and received permission from Washington to command a regiment in Lafayette's division, and at the Battle of Yorktown in October 1781, he commanded the successful assault on the British troops in redoubt number ten.

After the Battle of Yorktown, Hamilton returned to New York, where he was soon admitted to the bar, and in 1782 he was elected to the Continental Congress. In 1786 he entered the New York legislature and was one of his state's representatives at the convention that met in Annapolis to discuss commerce relations among the states. The failure of the Annapolis convention confirmed Hamilton's conviction that political unity was necessary for commercial harmony, and at his urging the convention's report included a call for another meeting in Philadelphia the following spring to consider revising the Confederation government. Although he was successful in leading the effort in his state to agree to send representatives to the Constitutional Convention, he had a more difficult time persuading the New York delegates to the Convention to sign the proposed Constitution. To win approval of the Constitution during the ratification process, Hamilton joined forces with James Madison and John Jay in writing *The Federalist,* a series of essays that forcefully set out the merits of the Constitution and convinced many across the country to support it. Hamilton himself was a member of the New York convention that ratified the Constitution in 1788.

Hamilton became Washington's secretary of the treasury when the new government was formed in 1789, implementing a financial program designed to fund the domestic debt by assuming state debts, raising excise taxes, imposing tariffs, and creating a national bank. The parts of his plan to handle the debt and charter a bank succeeded, and an impost was created for revenue, but the excise taxes infuriated many citizens and gave rise to the Whiskey Insurrection in Pennsylvania in 1794. Washington also relied on Hamilton's assistance in drafting many important documents, including his Farewell Address near the end of his second administration. Hamilton resigned as secretary of the treasury to practice law in New York City in 1795. "After so long an experience of your

public services," Washington wrote Hamilton after receiving his letter of resignation, "I am naturally led, at this moment of your departure from office, which it has always been my wish to prevent, to review them. In every relation, which you have borne to me, I have found that my confidence in your talents, exertions and integrity, has been well placed. I the more freely render this testimony of my approbation, because I speak from opportunities of information wch. cannot deceive me, and which furnish satisfactory proof of your title to public regard."

Over time, and more so after leaving Washington's administration, Hamilton became the central spokesman for the Federalist party. His political and philosophical differences with Thomas Jefferson led directly to the formation of the two-party system of government that eventually came to characterize American politics. The close association between Hamilton and Washington was renewed in 1798 when John Adams asked Washington to take the lead in preparing the provisional army for a possible war with France. Hamilton's role "as the principal & most confidential aid of the Commander in chief," wrote Washington to Adams when arguing that Hamilton should rank first among the generals of the army, "afforded him the means of viewing every thing on a larger scale than those whose attentions were confined to Divisions or Brigades; who knew nothing of the correspondences of the Commander in Chief, or of the various orders to, or transactions with, the General Staff of the Army." That some feared Hamilton's ambition was of no concern to Washington, because his ambition "is of that laudable kind which prompts a man to excel in whatever he takes in hand. He is enterprising, quick in his perceptions, and his judgment intuitively great; qualities essential to a great military character."

In 1800 Hamilton influenced many of the Federalists in the U.S. House of Representatives to vote to place Jefferson, his political rival, in the presidency when the election resulted in a tie between Jefferson and Aaron Burr. Four years later Hamilton ruined Burr's chances of becoming the Republican candidate for the New York governorship, ending Burr's political career. That year, as a result of their political animosity, Burr challenged Hamilton to a duel, in which the latter was mortally wounded.

Hamilton married Elizabeth Schuyler, the second daughter of Philip Schuyler of New York, in 1780.

Related entries: Clinton, George; Germantown, Battle of; Jefferson, Thomas; Knox, Henry; Presidency; Quasi-War; Schuyler, Philip; Spirituous Liquors; Whiskey Rebellion

Suggestions for further reading:
"To Alexander Hamilton," 2 February 1795 (*Writings*, vol. 34).
"To John Adams," 25 September 1798 (*Ret. Ser.*, vol. 3).
Mitchell, Broadus. 1957. 2 vols. *Alexander Hamilton*. New York.

Hancock, John (1737–1793)

John Hancock was born in Braintree (now Quincy), Massachusetts, and baptized there four days later by his minister father of the same name, who died when his little son was still quite young. Adopted and raised by his uncle Thomas Hancock, the richest merchant in Boston, Hancock attended Boston Latin School and, later, Harvard College before joining his uncle's shipping firm. In 1760 he sailed to England for a year to learn the business of trade from the British perspective, and on the first day of January 1763 he entered into partnership with his uncle. Thomas Hancock died the following year, however, leaving John as the heir of £70,000 and the head of Boston's leading mercantile house. He entered public service in 1766, when he became a member of the Massachusetts

general assembly, and two years later he began a protracted legal dispute with the Crown over the seizure of his ship *Liberty* and its cargo of Madeira wine for failure to pay a duty. In 1769 Hancock became a member of the Massachusetts General Court. Hancock's politics and his money made him popular with the people of New England, and he was elected president of the Massachusetts provincial congress in October 1774, and president of the second Continental Congress in May 1775, when Peyton Randolph left Congress to become speaker of the Virginia House of Burgesses. Hancock's marriage the following August to Dorothy Quincy at Fairfield, Connecticut, made him without a doubt the wealthiest New Englander to join the Patriot cause.

Hancock was presiding over Congress when Washington was commissioned commander in chief of the Continental army in June 1775. Early on, Hancock had desired the appointment for himself, but his lack of training and experience in military matters combined with recurring spells of gout ruled him out as a serious candidate for the office. In July 1775, shortly after Washington took command of the American forces at Cambridge, Massachusetts, Hancock wrote Washington to "beg the favour you will Reserve some birth for me, in such Department as you may Judge most proper, for I am Determin'd to Act under you, if it be to take the firelock & Join the Ranks as a Volunteer." Washington apparently was chagrined at Hancock's request, and in a diplomatically worded reply offered his regrets that "so little is in my Power to offer equal to Col. Hancock's Merits & worthy of his Acceptance." Despite his wounded pride at not being offered the command of the army, Hancock introduced Washington to his fellow Bostonians as a "fine man . . . a gentleman you will all like."

Hancock served as president of Congress until October 1777, when he was replaced by Henry Laurens of South Carolina. It was while serving in that capacity that Hancock affixed his famous signature on the Declaration of Independence. The letters Washington wrote to Hancock during the latter's tenure as president of Congress contain the most detailed descriptions of the movements of Washington's army during the eventful early years of the war. Always aspiring to military pretensions, Hancock commanded a force of Massachusetts militia in a maneuver against the British forces at Newport, Rhode Island, in 1778.

In September 1780 Hancock was elected the first governor of Massachusetts, an office he held for five years before resigning after a severe attack of gout. He presided at the Massachusetts convention that ratified the Federal Constitution in 1788 and was elected governor once again and died in office in October 1793.

When Washington made his presidential tour of the New England states in 1789, Hancock, ill again, did not go out to greet Washington but instead waited for Washington to come visit him. Washington did not do so, however, because he was concerned about setting a precedent whereby the chief executive of the United States might appear subservient to the chief executive of a state. Hancock relented and visited Washington first.

Related entry: New England Tour

Suggestions for further reading:
Diaries, vol. 5.
"To John Hancock," 16 September 1776 (*War Ser.,* vol. 6).
"To John Hancock," 5 January 1777 (*War Ser.,* vol. 7).

Harlem Heights, Battle of

The British army followed up its successful landing at Kip's Bay on 15 September 1776 by immediately occupying the area south from its beachhead to New York City, at the tip of Manhattan Island, and north to McGown's Pass (present-day 106th Street). Meanwhile, the Americans, humiliated by their poor performance in the face of the British cannonade at Kip's Bay, retreated to the plains of Harlem, where they extended a line of defense northward from a narrow valley known as the "Hollow Way" (present-day 125th Street) to above present-day 160th Street. Washington headquartered at the northernmost end of the American line at a Georgian-style mansion belonging to Roger Morris (1727–1794), an old acquaintance from the French and Indian War who had remained loyal to the Crown. Despite the natural defensive terrain of Harlem Heights, however, Washington's soldiers were in no way prepared to risk an engagement with the large British force that lay within sight.

The next morning, as Washington was finishing his report for Continental Congress president John Hancock about the ignominious events at Kip's Bay of the previous day, the British surprised a party of about 150 rangers that Washington had sent out before dawn under Lt. Col. Thomas Knowlton (1740–1776) of Connecticut to reconnoiter the British lines. Knowlton's scouts put up a strong resistance before beginning a systematic retreat in the face of overwhelming numbers. Meanwhile, Washington heard the sounds of gunfire at his headquarters and rode in the direction of the skirmishers. When he stopped to discuss the situation with officers in the vicinity of the Hollow Way, according to his aide-de-camp Joseph Reed, the "Enemy appeared in open view & in the most insulting manner sounded their Bugle Horns as is usual after a Fox Chase. I never felt such a sensation before, it seem'd to crown our Disgrace." Hearing the bugle and seeing that his "brave Fellows" had "behaved so well," Washington ordered reinforcements for Knowlton's party, which by then had returned to the safety of the American lines.

The counterattack included Knowlton's party and three rifle companies under the command of Maj. Andrew Leitch (c.1750–1776), a Dumfries, Virginia, merchant who had visited Mount Vernon before the war. A large diversionary force was dispatched toward the swampy cove where the Hollow Way ended at the Hudson River, near present-day Grant's Tomb.

By now it was about noon, an hour since the first volleys had been fired. The heaviest part of the skirmish ensued, lasting about another hour. The most intense fighting took place at a buckwheat field near present-day 120th Street between Broadway and Riverside Drive, just west of Columbia University. By two o'clock in the afternoon the Americans had redeemed their miserable showing of the previous day by driving the British back to about West 111th Street. Unprepared for a general engagement, Washington ordered his troops back to the American lines.

Washington's praise of his troops' behavior at Harlem Heights was as lavish as his condemnation had been severe of the militia's conduct at Kip's Bay. This time "our Troops behaved well, putting the Enemy to flight in open Ground, and forcing them from Posts they had siezed two or three times." Against seasoned Highlanders and Hessian riflemen, the Americans "behaved with great spirit and intrepidity." The American casualties amounted to about 150 killed, wounded, and taken prisoner, with the "greatest loss" sustained being the deaths of Knowlton and Leitch. Those officers had been ordered to get in the rear of the enemy, "while an apparent disposition was making as if to attack them in front; The Enemy ran down the hill with great eagerness to attack the party in front." Unluckily for Leitch and Knowlton, the parties under their command "began to fire on their flank instead of their rear," resulting in the death of the two officers. Their men acted with "the greatest resolution," however, and inflicted heavy casualties on the enemy. Official reports of British losses ranged from 92 to 235 killed and wounded.

When the day was over the Americans still controlled northern Manhattan, and they would for another month. The battle, although not much more than an indecisive minor skirmish with little military significance, was a great morale booster for the Americans. "This little advantage has inspired our troops prodigiously," wrote Washington. "They find it only requires resolution and good officers to make an enemy give way."

Related entries: Fort Washington; Kip's Bay, New York; White Plains, Battle of

Suggestions for further reading:
"General Orders," 17 September 1776 (*War Ser.*, vol. 6).
"To John Hancock," 18 September 1776 (*War Ser.*, vol. 6).
"To John Augustine Washington," 22 September 1776 (*War Ser.*, vol. 6).
"Robert Hanson Harrison to John Hancock," 20 October 1776 (*War Ser.*, vol. 6).
Bliven, Bruce, Jr. 1955–1956. *Battle for Manhattan.* New York.
Johnston, Henry P. 1897. *The Battle of Harlem Heights.* Reprint, 1970. New York.

Harrison, Benjamin, Sr. (c.1726–1791)

See Spurious Letters.

Heath, William (1737–1814)

William Heath was the son of a "plain farmer" from an old Roxbury, Massachusetts, family, and a farmer himself when not in military service. He held various public offices from 1761 to 1774, including a seat in the Massachusetts provincial congress. He became a strong advocate of military preparedness in the coming struggle with Great Britain, and he even wrote a number of essays for the newspapers advocating the importance of discipline in the military and the necessity of skill in the use of arms, signing the essays "A Military Countryman." Although he seems to have delighted in reading military treatises in his youth, he apparently did not join a military unit until he was almost 30 years old, when in 1765 he entered the Ancient and Honorable Artillery Company of Boston. After studying military tactics he became a captain, and over the next decade he gained respect for his knowledge of military matters although he had no real service experience before the British occupation of Boston. The Massachusetts provincial congress appointed Heath a brigadier general of militia in February 1775, and after the Battle of Bunker Hill he was promoted to major general. When his troops entered the Continental service, he became one of Washington's brigadier generals, and he brought his brigade of five regiments from Boston to New York in March 1776 to take part in the upcoming campaign. He was promoted to major general in August 1776.

In January 1777, Heath, with Washington's encouragement, commanded an attack on the British fort at King's Bridge, New York, in an effort to recapture the former American post. The expedition failed miserably, and criticism of Heath's abilities from both inside and outside the army began to mount, leading Washington to write him privately: "Your summons [for the British to surrender the fort], as you did not attempt to fulfil your threats, was not only idle but farcical, and will not fail of turning the laugh exceedingly upon us." The incident shows that Heath was anything but a great general, although he was a sincere Patriot and an honest man. Washington's correspondence with Heath remained cordial, but as soon as he could he quietly transferred Heath from the main army to the eastern department, which Heath commanded from Boston. Heath's exertions in the east-

ern department were valuable to the overall war effort but not critical. Nevertheless, Washington still considered Heath "an attentive, careful Officer."

Heath was transferred once again, in 1779, to the lower Hudson River Valley, where he remained until the end of the war, and after Arnold's defection to the British, Washington placed the trustworthy general in charge of West Point. The marquis de Chastellux accurately summed up General Heath in his *Travels* when he wrote: "His countenance is noble and open; and his bald head, as well as his corpulence, give him a striking resemblance to the late Lord Granby. He writes well, and with ease; has great sensibility of mind, and a frank and amiable character; in short, if he has not been in the way of displaying his talents in action, it may be at least asserted, that he is well adapted to the business of the cabinet. . . . During his stay at Newport, he lived honourably and in great friendship with all the French officers. In the month of September, General Washington, on discovering the treason of Arnold, sent for him, and gave him the command of West Point, a mark of confidence the more honourable, as none but the honestest of men was proper to succeed, in this command, the basest of all traitors."

Heath returned to his home in Roxbury after the war. In 1788 he served in the Massachusetts convention to ratify the Federal Constitution and later, in 1791 and 1792, in the state senate. Elected lieutenant governor of Massachusetts in 1806, he declined the honor. Heath published his memoirs in 1798, which proved to be a boon to historians: *Memoirs of Major-General Heath: Containing Anecdotes, Details of Skirmishes, Battles, and Other Military Events, During the American War, Written by Himself.*

Related entry: Boston, Siege of

Suggestions for further reading:
"General Orders," 12 August 1776 (*War Ser.,* vol. 5).

"To William Buchanan," 6 November 1777 (*War Ser.*, vol. 12).

Wilson, Rufus R., ed. 1798. *Heath's Memoirs of the American War.* Reprint, 1904. New York.

Hertburn, Chevalier William de

See Ancestry.

Horticulture

See Agriculture.

Houdon, Jean-Antoine (1741–1828)

*I*n June 1784 the Virginia general assembly directed Gov. Patrick Henry "to take measures for procuring a statue of General Washington, to be of the finest marble and the best workmanship." An appeal was made to Thomas Jefferson, then in France, to find an artist. Jefferson engaged Jean-Antoine Houdon, who, Jefferson wrote, had a reputation "unrivalled in Europe," for a thousand guineas plus expenses. Houdon and three assistants sailed to America with Benjamin Franklin, reaching Philadelphia in September 1785. "He comes now," Jefferson wrote to Washington, "for the purpose of lending the aid of his art to transmit you to posterity." Houdon and his assistants arrived at Mount Vernon with a French resident from Alexandria to serve as an interpreter, shortly before midnight on 2 October, and the following morning Houdon presented letters of introduction from Jefferson, Lafayette, Washington's former secretary David Humphreys, and Washington's old friend George William Fairfax.

Intending to stay in America less than thirty days, Houdon immediately made preparations for modeling, and four days later he was ready for Washington to pose for the first of two sittings. He made a life mask and from this fashioned a clay bust which he then duplicated. He carried the mask and one of the busts back to France; the other bust he left at Mount Vernon, where it became one of its most cherished possessions. Washington described in his diary how the artist prepared and applied his plaster:

> The Oven being made hotter than it is usually heated for Bread, the Plaister which had been previously broken into lumps— that which was hard, to about the size of a pullets egg; and that which was soft, and could be broken with the hands, larger; was put in about Noon, and remained until Night; when, upon examination, it was further continued until the Morning without any renewal of the heat in the Oven, which was close stopped. Having been sufficiently calcined by this operation, it was pulverized (in an Iron Mortar) & sifted for use through a fine lawn sieve, & kept from wet. When used, it is put into a Bason, or other Vessel with water; sifted through the fingers, 'till the Water is made as thick as Loblolly or very thick cream. As soon as the plaister is thus put into the Water, it is beat with an Iron spoon (almost flat) until it is well Mixed, and must be immediately applied to the purpose for which it is intended with a Brush, or whatever else best answers, as it begins to turn hard in four or five minutes, and in Seven or ten cannot be used, & is fit for no purpose afterwards as it will not bear wetting a second time. For this reason no more must be mixed at a time than can be used within the space just mentioned. The brush (common painters) must be put into water as soon as it is used, and the plaister well squeezed out, or this also becomes very hard. In this case to clean it, it must be beaten 'till the plaister is reduced to a powder, & then washed.

While at Mount Vernon Houdon also attended a funeral with Washington and the wedding of George Augustine Washington and Frances Bassett, Washington's nephew and Martha's niece.

Having finished his work, Houdon left Mount Vernon for Philadelphia on 17 October and was back in Paris by the new year. Years later Houdon's son-in-law wrote that the sculptor's visit to Mount Vernon "always shone with peculiar radiance" in Houdon's memory, for "the pleasure of having been close to Washington left memories he was fond of recurring to when others of various kinds had long been forgotten."

Houdon's statue is carved of Carrara marble and depicts the 53-year-old Washington with his exact measurements. Its symbolic elements depict the supremacy of the civil authority over the military, with Washington's right hand on a cane and his left hand on a fasces, which is made of thirteen rods representing the thirteen original states and rests on a plowshare. A sword hangs against the fasces. The statue bears Houdon's signature and the date of 1788, although it was not shipped to America until May 1796, after several years of exhibition at the Louvre in Paris. Many of his contemporaries attested to the statue's perfect likeness of Washington, including Lafayette, whose own bust carved by Houdon adorns the capitol at Richmond. "That is the man, himself," said Lafayette, "I can almost realize he is going to move."

Related entries: Jefferson, Thomas; Peale, Charles Willson; Trumbull, John

Suggestions for further reading:
Diaries, vol. 4.
"From Thomas Jefferson," 10 July 1785 (*Con. Ser.,* vol. 3).
Hart, Charles Henry, and Edward Biddle. 1911. *Memoirs of the Life and Works of Jean Antoine Houdon, the Sculptor of Voltaire and of Washington.* Philadelphia.

Howe, William (1729–1814)

See Brandywine, Battle of; Clinton, Henry; Fort Washington; Germantown, Battle of; Gage, Thomas; Morris, Robert; Princeton, Battle of; Spurious Letters; Trenton, Battle of; White Plains, Battle of.

Huddy, Joshua

See Asgill Affair.

Humor

Attention has often been drawn to Washington's aloof and serious nature, especially during the eight years of his presidency, when, aware that his conduct and style were setting precedents for the new nation, he governed his actions accordingly in order to endow the office with decorum and dignity. Washington, according to one recent observer, went so far as to suppress a natural and strong sense of humor. On the other hand, Washington's most consistently perceptive judge, Douglas Southall Freeman, wrote that the general had "no spontaneous sense of humor and while he occasionally indulged a laugh, it was over a bit of horseplay or some ludicrous harmless accident." Freeman did temper his testimony, however, by crediting Washington's statement that "it is assuredly better to go laughing than crying thro' the rough journey of life." Despite his austere persona, Washington's own letters and diary entries contain numerous examples of his amusing and often subtle sense of humor, and many of his contemporaries left anecdotes attesting to his spontaneous and sometimes caustic wit. The subjects of his humor encompassed, among others, military life, blundering subordinates, invitations to dinner, poetry written in his honor, sitting for portraits, money, false teeth, love, marriage, and births. That he appreciated amusing situations is beyond doubt, and accounts of numerous incidents have survived portraying Washington as laughing "very heartily," with "infinite glee," and "till the tears ran down his eyes," and upon occasion even throwing himself on the floor in fits of laughter.

One of the earliest examples of Washington's subtle sense of humor survives in a letter written to his brother John Augustine Washington from Fort Cumberland, Maryland, after the Battle of Monongahela (during the 1755 Braddock campaign). Anticipating Mark Twain's more famous quip, "The report of my death was an exaggeration," Washington writes: "As I have heard since my arrivl at this place, a circumstantial acct of my death and dying Speech, I take this early oppertunity of contradicting the first, and of assuring you that I have not, as yet, composed the latter."

In 1762, after chiding in jest his wife's brother-in-law Burwell Bassett about penning a letter on Sunday morning "when you ought to have been at Church, praying as becomes every good Christian Man who has as much to answer for as you have," Washington then accuses Bassett of sitting around "lost in admiration" of a newborn child to the neglect of "your Crops &c.— pray how will this be reconciled to that anxious care and vigilance, which is so escencially necessary at a time when our growing Property—meaning the Tobacco—is assailed by every villainous worm that has had an existence since the days of Noah (how unkind it was of Noah now I have mentioned his name to suffer such a brood of Vermin to get a birth in the Ark) but perhaps you may be as well of[f] as we are—that is, have no Tobacco for them to eat and there I think we nicked the Dogs, as I think to do you if you expect any more." This letter, humorous in its entirety and for a long time unavailable for examination, was considered by many to be fraudulent because it was deemed so out of character for Washington.

Annis Boudinot Stockton (1736–1801) of Princeton, New Jersey, an ardent admirer

of Washington who composed poetry in his honor, was frequently the recipient of some well-directed barbs of wit, as a letter written to her in September 1783 illustrates:

You apply to me, My dear Madam, for absolution as tho' I was your father Confessor; and as tho' you had committed a crime, great in itself, yet of the venial class[.] You have reason good, for I find myself strangely disposed to be a very indulgent ghostly Adviser on this occasion; and, notwithstanding 'you are the most offending Soul alive' (that is, if it is a crime to write elegant Poetry) yet if you will come and dine with me on Thursday and go through the proper course of penitence, which shall be prescribed, I will strive hard to assist you in expiating these poetical trespasses on this side of purgatory. Nay more, if it rests with me to direct your future lucubrations, I shall certainly urge you to a repetition of the same conduct, on purpose to shew what an admirable knack you have at confession and reformation; and so, without more hesitation, I shall venture to command the Muse not to be restrained by ill-grounded timidity, but to go on and prosper.

You see Madam, when once the Woman has tempted us and we have tasted the forbidden fruit, there is no such thing as checking our appetites, whatever the consequences may be. You will I dare say, recognize our being the genuine Descendents of those who are reputed to be our great Progenitors.

A letter to his Revolutionary War recording secretary Richard Varick, written in 1784, humorously reveals his incredulity upon receiving Varick's claim that the French dentist Jean-Pierre Le Mayeur had successfully provided Varick with new teeth. "I received great pleasure from the Acct which you have given me of Doctr La Moyeur's operations on you; and congratulate you very sincerely on the success. I shall claim your promise of relating the Sequel; for I confess I have been staggered in my belief of the efficacy of transplantation—being more disposed to think that, the *Operator* is partial to his own performances, and the *Operatee's,* in general, are inclined to compliment, or having submitted to the *Operations,* are somewhat unwilling to expose the truth—Your Acct I can—I shall rely upon."

Another letter, written to a neighbor in the spring of 1786, concerns the failure of Royal Gift, the Spanish jackass presented to Washington by the king of Spain, to perform stud service according to expectations. "Particular attention shall be paid to the Mares which your Servant brought," wrote Washington to William Fitzhugh, "and when my Jack is in the humour they shall derive all the benefits of his labours—for labour it appears to be. At present, tho' young, he follows what one may suppose to be the example of his late royal master, who cannot, tho' past his grand climacterick, perform seldomer, or with more majestic solemnity, than he does. However, I am not without hope, that when he becomes a little better acquainted with republican enjoyments, he will amend his manners, and fall into a better & more expeditious mode of doing business. If the case should be otherwise, I should have no disinclination to present his Catholic majesty with as good a thing, as he gave me." To another neighbor who sent his jenny to Mount Vernon for a like purpose, Washington said, "I feel myself much obliged by your polite offer of the first fruits of your Jenny. Tho' in appearance quite unequal to the match—yet, like a true female, she was not to be terrified at the disproportionate size of her paramour." To Royal Gift's credit, he eventually did produce offspring with a jenny belonging to Washington. Similar in kind was his remark to William Gordon about a Revolutionary War colonel getting married at an old age and needing to check his "ammunition, etc."

Washington also occasionally included subtle pieces of wit in his diary. Of a lazy overseer, he observed in one entry, "hard at work with an ax—very extraordinary this." While en route to Port Royal, Virginia, in January 1760, he stopped overnight at Dumfries, where he was informed that Col. Catesby Cocke had been "disgusted at my House, and left it because he see an old Negroe there resembling his own Image." Another diary entry, written when he was on the return trip of his presidential tour of the south, recounts Washington's attendance at a German Reformed Church in York, Pennsylvania, on Sunday, 3 July 1791. "Received, and answered an address from the Inhabitants of York town—& there being no Episcopal Minister *present* in the place, I went to hear morning Service performed in the Dutch reformed Church—which, being in that language not a word of which I understood I was in no danger of becoming a proselyte to its religion by the eloquence of the Preacher."

A story told by William Thornton, the architect of the U.S. Capitol, of dining with Washington after the presidency is typical of the anecdotes that began to circulate after Washington's death. "As he sat at table after dinner," said Thornton, "the fire behind him was too large and hot. He complained, and said he must remove. A gentleman observed it behooved the General to stand fire. 'Yes, said Washington, but it does not look well for a General to receive the fire behind'."

Related entries: Bassett, Burwell, Sr.; False Teeth; Royal Gift; Southern Tour

Suggestions for further reading:
Diaries, vols. 1, 6.
"To John Augustine Washington," 18 July 1755 (*Col. Ser.,* vol. 1).
"To Burwell Bassett," 28 August 1762 (*Col. Ser.,* vol. 6).
"To Annis Boudinot Stockton," 2 September 1783 (*Writings,* vol. 27).
"To Richard Varick," 22 February 1784 (*Con. Ser.,* vol. 1).
"To William Fitzhugh," 15 May 1786 (*Con. Ser.,* vol. 4).
"To Theodorick Bland," 15 August 1786 (*Con. Ser.,* vol. 4).

Henriques, Peter R. 1979. "George Washington: The Amiable Side" (*Northern Virginia Heritage,* vol. 1).

Zall, P. M. 1989. *George Washington Laughing: Humorous Anecdotes by and about our First President from Original Sources.* Hamden, CT.

Humphreys, David (1752–1818)

Of the thirty-two men who served as aides-de-camp and secretaries to Washington during the Revolutionary War, few perhaps were able to enter as fully into the friendship and trust of their commander in chief as David Humphreys, designated the "belov'd of Washington" by poet John Trumbull. Born in Derby, Connecticut, and educated at Yale College, where he took degrees in 1771 and 1774, Humphreys abandoned a brief career as a schoolmaster for the military life in 1776, when he volunteered to serve as an adjutant in the Connecticut militia. He entered the Continental army as an aide-de-camp to Maj. Gen. Israel Putnam in 1778, with the rank of major, and served in that capacity until May 1780, when Putnam suffered the debilitating stroke that ended his military career. Humphreys later wrote a biography of Putnam, *An Essay on the Life of the Honourable Major-General Israel Putnam,* published in Hartford in 1788. Humphreys next joined the staff of Maj. Gen. Nathanael Greene but scarcely had time to settle upon his new duties before Washington asked him to enter his own military family, with the rank of lieutenant colonel.

The degree of intimacy that eventually developed between Washington and his younger assistant is represented by the fact that Humphreys became Washington's solitary companion when the latter, while en route to Yorktown, "reached my own Seat at Mount Vernon" on 9 September 1781 after an absence of nearly six and a half years. Humphreys served bravely at the ensuing battle, for which he was later presented a sword by the Continental Congress, and Washington granted him the privilege of delivering to Congress the twenty-four captured British standards. Humphreys remained with Washington until the end of the war, faithfully drafting much of Washington's correspondence and attending to a myriad of other office duties.

At the end of the war, Congress, at the urging of Washington, gave Humphreys a diplomatic appointment, and in 1784 he traveled to Paris with Thomas Jefferson as secretary of the commission for negotiating treaties of commerce with foreign powers. In Paris one of his minor duties included making arrangements for the production of a gold medal for Washington that Congress had authorized years earlier after the British evacuation of Boston in March 1776. Around the same time Humphreys also began to "revolve in my own mind" the subject of a biography of Washington, "placing your actions in the true point of light in which posterity ought to view them," a subject he had broached to Washington shortly before setting sail for Paris. Washington enthusiastically supported the idea, and upon Humphreys' return to America in 1786 he accepted Washington's invitation to live at Mount Vernon while working on both the biography and a history of the Revolutionary War. Washington made detailed comments on many of the passages of the resulting biography, including his "Remarks," the only autobiographical recollections ever penned by Washington.

Humphreys' book established him as one of the soldier-poets of the Revolution, but only part of his "Life of General Washington" was published, and that anonymously in the "Notes" section of Jedidiah Morse's *The American Geography; or, A View of the Present Situation in the United States of America* (Elizabeth, New Jersey, 1789). Al-

David Humphreys (Library of Congress)

States of America (1782), *The Happiness of America* (1786), *The Anarchiad* (1786–1787), and *The Yankey in England* (1815).

After his return to America, Humphreys, when he was not at Mount Vernon, lived in Hartford. In 1787 he was elected to the general assembly, which appointed him commander of a regiment raised to fight Indians on the western frontier. From Hartford he kept up a constant correspondence with Washington, informing him of the deliberations taking place at the Connecticut Constitutional Convention and of Shays's Rebellion. Humphreys was back at Mount Vernon at the time Washington set off for New York City to assume the office of the presidency, and he accompanied Washington on his journey, along with the long-time secretary of the Continental Congress, Philadelphian Charles Thomson (1729–1824), who had brought confirmation of Washington's election to Mount Vernon. Three months later the new president named Humphreys a special commissioner to the Creek Indians. He next served as a special agent to gather information for the American government at London, Lisbon, and Madrid, and in 1793 he was commissioner at Algiers. Three years later he became envoy extraordinary and minister plenipotentiary to Spain, and while at Lisbon he married the daughter of a wealthy Englishman who lived in the city. Humphreys returned to America in 1801, bringing with him the first merino sheep to enter the country, and for the next decade devoted much of his time to the improvement of American agriculture. With the advent of the second war with Great Britain, in 1812, Humphreys, at the age of 70, commanded the Connecticut militia.

Related entries: Education; Natural Bridge, Virginia; Presidency; Trumbull, John

Suggestions for further reading:
"From David Humphreys," 30 September 1784 (*Con. Ser.,* vol. 2).

though the "Life" was reprinted several times while Humphreys was alive, it was not until the appearance in 1991 of Rosemarie Zagarri's *David Humphreys' "Life of General Washington" with George Washington's "Remarks"* that Humphreys' biography could be read in its entirety. Humphreys' straightforward narrative presents a sympathetic but accurate portrait and reveals a personal and private side of Washington that was available only to those as intimate with him as its author. Humphreys composed in 1786 a poem "expressive of the satisfaction" he experienced in his residence at Mount Vernon, the twelve-stanza "Mount Vernon: An Ode." A member of a literary group known as the "Hartford Wits," Humphreys also wrote or cowrote several other publications, including *A Poem Addressed to the Armies of the United*

"From David Humphreys," 11 February 1786 (*Con. Ser.*, vol. 3).

"From David Humphreys," 24 March 1787 (*Con. Ser.*, vol. 5).

"From David Humphreys," 10 October 1787 (*Con. Ser.*, vol. 5).

"Comments on David Humphreys' Biography of George Washington," c.1787–1788 (*Con. Ser.*, vol. 5).

"Mount Vernon: An Ode" (*The Miscellaneous Works of David Humphreys*). 1804. Reprint, 1968. Gainesville, FL.

Humphreys, David. 1788. *An Essay on the Life of the Honourable Major-General Israel Putnam.* Hartford, CT.

Zagarri, Rosemarie. 1991. *David Humphreys' "Life of General Washington" with George Washington's "Remarks."* Athens, GA.

I

The Indian Prophecy

Washington first met the Seneca Indian Kiashuta, or the Hunter (Guyasuta; c.1725–c.1794), in November 1753, when the chief, along with the Half-King and others, accompanied Washington to Venango. Kiashuta helped defend the French Fort Duquesne against Braddock's expedition in 1755 and led the Indians in the defeat of British major James Grant during the Forbes Campaign of 1758. He also fought against the British in Pontiac's War. After the French and Indian War, Kiashuta participated in many of the councils between the Iroquois and the English before the Revolution, during which he fought against the Americans.

During his tour of the Ohio Country in 1770, Washington met Kiashuta on the Little Kanawha River. "He expressed a satisfaction in seeing me," wrote Washington in his diary, "and treated us with great kindness, giving us a Quarter of very fine Buffalo." Kiashuta is perhaps the chief mentioned in a legend concerning Braddock's defeat on the Monongahela in 1755, which was started by Dr. Craik, Washington's lifelong friend and physician, who was with him at the battle. According to tradition, they traveled together on the 1770 expedition to explore the Ohio Country. While near the junction of the Great Kanawha and Ohio Rivers, a party of Indians approached them with an interpreter. At the head of the party was an aged and venerable chief, who, hearing that Washington was in the region, had come a long way to visit him. According to this chief, he had singled Washington out during the battle on the Monongahela as a conspicuous target. He and his compatriots fired their weapons at him many times, but to their utter astonishment Washington remained on the field unscathed. Persuaded that their youthful opponent was being guarded by the Great Spirit, they ceased firing at him. In his old age the chief now had come to pay homage to the man, who was the particular favorite of Heaven, and who could never die in battle.

The legend was popularized when Washington's grandson, George Washington Parke Custis, later dramatized Craik's story in *The Indian Prophecy: A National Drama in Two Acts* (Georgetown, D.C., 1828) and printed a version of the meeting in his *Recollections*. According to the legend, fifteen years after that event, on the night before the Battle of Monmouth Courthouse in 1778, a number of general officers resolved to petition Washington not to expose himself to enemy fire in the expected battle, as he had done at the Battles of Princeton and Germantown. The officers requested Craik to present their petition to Washington, but Craik at once assured the memorialists that, although their petition might be received as evidence of their regard for their commander's safety, it would not prevent Washington from jeopardizing himself as the situation required. Craik then related the romantic and imposing incident of the old Indian's prophecy as it supposedly took place on the banks of the Ohio in 1770. When on the next day an enemy artillery shell landed so close to Washington in the presence of some of the same officers that it blasted earth over him and his horse, Craik nodded to the officers and pointed toward heaven as if to say, in the words of the Indian prophet, "The Great Spirit protects him—he cannot die in battle."

Whether the legend is true or not, the theme of providential assistance was one that Washington returned to throughout his public career. For instance, during the Revolutionary War, on 20 August 1778, he wrote Brig. Gen. Thomas Nelson of Virginia: "The hand of Providence has been conspicuous in all this, that he must be worse than an infidel that lacks faith, and more than wicked that has not gratitude enough to acknowledge his obligations. But it will be time enough for me to turn preacher when my present appointment ceases; and therefore I shall add no more on the doctrine of Providence." Although he never developed this theme beyond such statements, he often repeated it during the war and his presidency.

Ironically, Washington's first opponent in the Revolutionary War, British general Thomas Gage, also was providentially protected at Great Meadows on 9 July, when he narrowly escaped death in the fighting. "I received a slight wound in my belly," Gage wrote, as well as "a graze of a slugg on my eye brow, some shots in my coat, and my horse twice wounded."

Related entries: Braddock's Defeat; Custis, George Washington Parke

Suggestions for further reading:
Diaries, vol. 2.
"To John Augustine Washington," 18 July 1755 (*Col. Ser.,* vol. 1).
Custis, George Washington Parke. 1828. *The Indian Prophecy: A National Drama in Two Acts. . . .* Georgetown, DC.

J

Jackasses

See Royal Gift.

James River Company

The James River Company was authorized by the Virginia general assembly in 1785 for the purpose of opening navigation on the James River above Richmond for "Communication between it & the Waters of the Great Kanawha . . . & opening a good road between it & Green-briar." (The Greenbriar River flows into the Kanawha River about 300 miles below Fort Pitt.) Washington began supporting the movement to extend navigation of the James in the early 1770s "in order to remove the jealousies which arose from the attempt to extend the Navigation of the Potomack." The Virginia general assembly, also desirous of preventing sectional rivalries, included both rivers in separate navigation bills introduced in late 1784. "We endeavoured to preserve an equal eye in this business to the interests of the two Rivers," he was informed by James Madison, who at Washington's behest had pushed both bills through the lower house of the general assembly. Washington was delighted with the passage of the bills, except for one provision—the general assem-

bly had voted to give him 100 shares of stock in the James River Company and fifty shares in the Potomac River Company in appreciation for his Revolutionary War service. Washington was greatly embarrassed by the gift, and agonized about whether to accept it. He steadfastly had refused to accept any remuneration for his role in the war, yet he did not want to do anything that might jeopardize the value of the stocks. He finally determined to hold the stocks in trust for "the use & benefit" of the public and in his will bequeathed the James River shares to Liberty Hall Academy in Rockbridge County.

Washington was pleased to be associated with the James River "business," which he thought "will be a source of great commerce with the Capitol, & in my opinion will be productive of great political consequences to this Country." He served as the titular president of the James River Company from 1785 to 1795. Edmund Randolph, one of the company's original directors, performed the actual duties of the president from 1785 to 1789, when Dr. William Foushee, another director, replaced him. In March 1786 the James River Company appointed James Harris, "a quaker, of good character, as a man, and a mechanic, formed by nature for the management of water, when applied to mills," to serve as company manager. Harris visited Mount Vernon twice in 1786 to consult with

Washington about company business. Washington viewed the "cut which had commenced between Westham and Richmond" in April 1786 while in Richmond on legal matters and again in April 1791, as he was setting off on his southern tour while president. Accompanied by the governor of Virginia and the manager and directors of the company, his second viewing of the "Canal, Sluces, Locks & other Works between the City of Richmond & Westham" was impressive enough for him to make extensive notes of what he saw in his diaries. "These together have brought the navigation to within a mile and half," he wrote, "or a Mile and ¾ of the proposed Bason; from which the Boats by means of Locks are to communicate with the tide water Navigation below. The Canal is of Sufficient depth every where but in places not brought to its proper width; it seems to be perfectly secure against Ice, Freshes & drift Wood. The locks at the head of these works are simple—altogether of hewn stone, except the gates & Cills and very easy & convenient to work."

Despite this auspicious beginning, it was 1808 before the James River Canal opened from Richmond to Crow's Ferry at Buchanan and 1830 before it reached Lynchburg. The James River Company was superseded by the James River and Kanawha Company in 1832.

Related entries: Education; Great Kanawha Tracts; Potomac River Navigation

Suggestions for further reading:
Diaries, vols. 4, 6.
"From James Madison," 1, 9 January 1785 (*Con. Ser.*, vol. 2).
"From Patrick Henry," 19 March 1785 (*Con. Ser.*, vol. 2).
"To Edmund Randolph," 16 September 1785 (*Con. Ser.*, vol. 3).
"To Patrick Henry," 29 October 1785 (*Con. Ser.*, vol. 3).
"From Washington Academy Trustees," 12 April 1798 (*Ret. Ser.*, vol. 2).
"Last Will and Testament," 9 July 1799 (*Ret. Ser.*, vol. 4).

Jay, John (1745–1829)

John Jay was born in New York City to a wealthy French Huguenot merchant family and graduated from King's College in 1764. In 1768 he was admitted to the New York bar, and the following year he was appointed secretary to the royal commission charged with settling the boundary dispute between New York and New Jersey. Jay married in April 1774 Sarah Van Brugh Livingston, the oldest daughter of New Jersey's wartime governor, William Livingston. An early supporter of the Patriot cause, Jay was one of New York's delegates to the Continental Congress from 1774 to 1779, serving as president for the last two years. In 1776 he was appointed a colonel in the New York militia but did not take command in the field because of his service in the New York provincial congress, where he helped draft the state constitution. In 1776 he also was appointed chief justice of New York, an office he held for two years.

In the spring of 1779, while Jay was still president of Congress, he sent Washington an extract of a letter respecting the "spurious Ambition" of Maj. Gen. Horatio Gates, whose relationship with Washington was strained to the breaking point. Washington wrote a lengthy and impassioned reply thanking Jay for the "distinguishing mark" of his "confidence and friendship" and expressing his confidence that "Things will come Right, and these States will be great and flourishing. The Dissolution of our Governments threw us into a political Chaos. Time, wisdom and Perseverance will reduce it into Form, and give it Strength, Order and Harmony. In this Work you are (in the Stile of one of your Professions) a *master builder,* and God grant that you may long continue a *free* and *accepted* one." Later that year Congress appointed Jay minister plenipotentiary to Spain, authorizing him to propose an alliance with the Crown, but delays in negotiation and the British sur-

Portrait of John Jay (Library of Congress)

render at Yorktown in 1781 ultimately rendered his mission unnecessary.

In 1782, Jay, still in Europe, was asked by Benjamin Franklin to assist him in Paris to negotiate a peace with Great Britain. After the peace, Jay served as secretary for foreign affairs, and he attempted to settle commercial disputes with Prussia and Morocco.

Upon his return to America he became an advocate of the Federal Constitution and joined James Madison and Alexander Hamilton in writing *The Federalist*. In 1790 Washington appointed him the first chief justice of the U.S. Supreme Court, an office he held until 1795. His major decisions on the bench included *Chisholm vs. Georgia*

(1793), which resulted in the Eleventh Amendment. Washington nominated Jay envoy extraordinary to England in April 1794 to negotiate a treaty to settle outstanding disputes on such matters as debts, boundaries, and navigation rights on the Mississippi River. He arrived in England in June and opened negotiations, which resulted in a treaty the following November that bears his name. When the terms of the treaty were made public in March 1795, hardly anyone was pleased. The Republicans were more vocal in their opposition than the Federalists, but even Washington was divided about what course to take. He nevertheless forwarded the treaty to the U.S. Senate for advice and consent in June 1795.

After the Senate considered Jay's Treaty, Washington's support was still lukewarm. "My opinion respecting the treaty," he wrote Secretary of State Thomas Jefferson, "is the same now that it was: namely, not favorable to it, but that it is better to ratify it in the manner the Senate have advised (and with the reservation already mentioned), than to suffer matters to remain as they are, unsettled." That the treaty "has received the most tortured interpretation," he next wrote Alexander Hamilton, "and that the writings agt. it . . . are pregnant of the most abominable mis-representations, admits of no doubt; yet, there are to be found . . . many well disposed men who conceive, that in the settlement of *old* disputes, a proper regard to reciprocal justice does not appear in the Treaty; whilst others, also well enough affected to the government, are of opinion that to have had *no* commercial treaty would have been better." Jay was accused of selling out his country and vilified across the nation, to the point, he said, that he could have found his way across America by "the light of his burning effigies." Yet the Senate ratified the treaty in August, the British in October, and Washington promulgated it

in February 1796. Despite the severe criticism that Jay's Treaty brought upon Washington's administration, Washington declared that he entertained a "very high opinion" of Jay's "judgment, candour, honor and discretion."

When Jay resigned from the Court in 1795 to become the governor of New York, Washington wrote him, "In whatever line you may walk my best wishes will always accompany you; They will particularly do so on the theatre you are about to enter upon; which I sincerely wish may be as smooth, easy and happy, as it is honorable." Jay served as governor until 1801. He then retired to private life. He died at Bedford, New York.

Related entry: Presidency

Suggestions for further reading:
"To John Jay," 14 April 1779 (*Writings*, vol. 14).
"From John Jay," 21 April 1779 (*Letters of Delegates*, vol. 12).
"To John Jay," 1–5 November 1794 (*Writings*, vol. 34).
"To the Secretary of State," 22 July 1795 (*Writings*, vol. 34).
Bemis, Samuel F. 1923. *Jay's Treaty*. New York.
Johnston, Henry P. 1890. 4 vols. *The Correspondence and Public Papers of John Jay*. New York.

Jefferson, Thomas (1743–1826)

Thomas Jefferson was born at Shadwell in Albemarle County, Virginia. After graduating from the College of William and Mary in 1762, he studied law for five years under the colony's most noted legal mind, George Wythe. Jefferson was admitted to the Virginia bar in 1767 and set up practice. He married Martha Wayles Skelton and began building his famous Italian country villa, Monticello, on a little mountain near his birthplace. In 1769 Jefferson was elected to the Virginia House of Burgesses, where he apparently

The first president of the United States, George Washington, confers with members of his first cabinet, including Thomas Jefferson (seated), secretary of state, and Alexander Hamilton, secretary of the treasury (Library of Congress)

met Washington for the first time, and he remained in that body until its demise in 1775, after which he was elected to the Continental Congress. In both bodies his talent for literary penmanship was repeatedly drawn upon by various committees. His two most famous writings were *A Summary View of the Rights of British America* (1774) and the Declaration of Independence. A month after leaving Congress in September 1776, he entered the Virginia House of Delegates, where he served until his election as governor in June 1779, leaving office in 1781. On the eve of the

Yorktown campaign, Washington commended Jefferson for his "readiness and Zeal" in assisting "every measure which I have had occasion to recommend thro' you, and . . . I shall esteem myself honored by a continuation of your friendship and corrispondence shou'd your Country permit you to remain in the private walk of life." In June 1783 he was sent back to Congress, where over a six-month period he drafted thirty-one reports and papers, the most important ones being his "Notes on the Establishment of a Money Unit," giving rise to the adoption of the dollar, divided in tenths and hundredths; a report on the treaty of peace with Great Britain that eventually was adopted; and a 1784 report containing the features of what became the Ordinance of 1787. His draft of a report outlining the procedures for negotiating treaties of commerce led to an appointment in the spring of 1784 to assist Benjamin Franklin and John Adams in treaty negotiations. Before Jefferson left for France, Washington asked Jefferson's opinion on the Society of the Cincinnati, to which Jefferson was opposed. Keeping the distinction between the civil and military was paramount in Jefferson's view, and in his counsel he reminded Washington that "the moderation and virtue of a single character has probably prevented this revolution from being closed as most others have been by a subversion of that liberty it was intended to establish: that he is not immortal, & his successor or some one of his successors at the head of this institution may adopt a more mistaken road to glory." Before Jefferson left for France, he and Washington also exchanged long letters about opening up western waterways to navigation, a subject they continued to discuss for several years. While in France, Jefferson wrote Washington about European developments, and at the behest of the Virginia general assembly, he engaged French sculptor Jean-An-

toine Houdon to carve the life-size marble statue of Washington that stands in the Virginia capitol. On the day after the "end to the business of the Fœderal Convention," Washington sent Jefferson a copy of the proposed Constitution.

Jefferson succeeded Franklin as minister to France in 1785 and remained in that country until October 1789. There he enjoyed the acquaintance of the French intellectual and social elite, including Lafayette, who wrote Washington about Jefferson with approval. Washington responded in May 1786, writing that "the favourable terms in which you speak of Mr Jefferson gives me great pleasure: he is a man of whom I early imbibed the highest opinion—I am as much pleased therefore to meet confirmations of my discernment in these matters, as I am mortified when I find myself mistaken."

Shortly after Jefferson's return to Virginia in late 1789, Washington appointed him secretary of state, an office he held throughout Washington's first administration. While serving in that capacity, his disagreement over the direction of the new government with the secretary of the treasury, Alexander Hamilton, became a source of concern for Washington. By February 1791, when Jefferson drafted a lengthy report for Washington arguing that Hamilton's bill to establish the Bank of the United States was not constitutional, Jefferson had begun to distrust Hamilton, and over the next two years the hostility between the two men increased to the point that they no longer could work together. Washington kept both men in office as long as possible, following neither's policies exclusively. "How unfortunate, and how much is it to be regretted," Washington wrote, "that whilst we are encompassed on all sides with avowed enemies and insidious friends, that internal dissensions should be harrowing and tearing our vitals. The last, to me, is the most serious, the most alarming, and the most afflicting of the two." Washington thought the breach between Jefferson and Hamilton so severe that it might bring down the whole republican experiment. "My earnest wish, and my fondest hope therefore is," Washington concluded, "that instead of wounding suspicions, and irritable charges, there may be liberal allowances, mutual forbearances, and temporising yieldings on *all sides.*"

Despite Washington's charitable belief that the views of both Jefferson and Hamilton were "pure, and well meant," he could never bring harmony to the relationship. By the time Jefferson left Washington's administration in late 1793, his rivalry with Hamilton had caused him to distrust Washington as well. "Naked he would have been sanctimoniously reverenced," he wrote of Washington to James Madison, "but enveloped in the rags of royalty, they can hardly be torn off without laceration." Nevertheless, Jefferson's pessimism about the political climate in the nation led him to encourage Washington to take a second term at the helm of government, writing, "North and South will hang together if they have you to hang on." Once he had left Washington's administration, he found it easier to criticize. Jefferson was vehement in his attack on Washington and Hamilton's decision to call out the military against the Whiskey Rebellion insurgents. "An insurrection was announced and proclaimed and armed against," Jefferson wrote, "but could never be found." He denounced Jay's Treaty as a betrayal of the American Revolution, attributing its passage to the "one man who outweighs them all in influence over the people"—meaning Washington. More and more he suspected the president's Federalist policies were not the product of his vision for the country but the result of schemes and plots perpetrated by Hamilton and others. So vehement was Jefferson's anti-Federalism that he included Washington among "the apostates who have gone over to these heresies, men who were Samsons in the field and Solomons in the council, but who have had their heads shorn by the harlot of England." When the letter with its obvious references to Washington later showed up in newspapers, it ended their correspondence forever. Jefferson was afterward more charitable of Washington, recalling in 1814, that "The whole of his character was in its mass perfect, in nothing bad, in a few points indifferent. And it may be truly said, that never did nature and fortune combine more perfectly to make a man great, and to place him in the same constellation with whatever worthies have merited from man an everlasting remembrance."

One important measure that Jefferson and Hamilton agreed on was the moving of the seat of the federal government to the new Federal City on the Potomac River. Jefferson took an active role in the city's establishment, both as secretary of state and during his own presidency, more so than any one senior federal official except Washington. Both Washington and Jefferson considered the location strategic to national unity and beneficent to their home state of Virginia. They consulted closely on the district's boundaries, the commissioners appointed to oversee the district, and the proposed sites and architectural designs for public buildings.

Jefferson's contributions to architecture in the young republic were not confined to his interest in the Federal City. In addition to his own two private houses, Monticello and Poplar Forest, he designed numerous public and private buildings, including the Virginia state capitol in Richmond and the University of Virginia at Charlottesville.

Jefferson died on same date as John Adams, the fiftieth anniversary of the signing of the Declaration of Independence.

Related entries: Descriptions of Washington; Hamilton, Alexander; Houdon, Jean-Antoine; Presidency

Suggestions for further reading:
"To Thomas Jefferson," 9 June 1781 (*Writings,* vol. 22).
"From Thomas Jefferson," 16 April 1784 (*Con. Ser.,* vol. 1).
"To Thomas Jefferson," 23 August 1792 (*Writings,* vol. 32).
"To Alexander Hamilton," 26 August 1792 (*Writings,* vol. 32).

Malone, Dumas. 1948–1982. 6 vols. *Jefferson and His Time.* Boston.
Peterson, Merrill D. 1970. *Thomas Jefferson and the New Nation: A Biography.* New York.

Jumonville

See Fort Necessity Campaign; The Half-King; La Force; Van Braam, Jacob; To Robert Dinwiddie, 29 May 1754 (Selected Writings).

Kip's Bay, New York

"He struck Several Officers in their flight, three times dashed his hatt on the Ground, and at last exclaimed 'Good God have I got such Troops as Those.' It was with difficulty his friends could get him to quit the field, so great was his emotions." So wrote Continental army general George Weedon of Washington's ineffectual efforts to rally his men to stand against an advanced landing party of British troops at Kip's Bay, a tiny inlet on the east side of Manhattan Island (now East Thirty-fourth Street), on 15 September 1776. Although eyewitness accounts seem to be lacking, the camp gossip that circulated in the days immediately following the event tended to confirm Weedon's account. Washington "threw his hat on the ground," wrote Maj. Gen. William Heath, "and exclaimed, 'Are these the men with which I am to defend America?'" Brig. Gen. William Smallwood of Maryland reported to the Maryland convention that "sixty Light Infantry, upon the first fire, put to flight two brigades of the *Connecticut* troops—wretches who, however strange it may appear, from our Brigadier-General down to the private sentinel, were caned and whipped by the Generals *Washington,* [Israel] *Putnam,* and [Thomas] *Mifflin,* but even his indignity had no weight, they

could not be brought to stand one shot." Washington's trusted aide-de-camp, Tench Tilghman, wrote of it in his diary: "I dont know whether the New Engd Troops will stand there [on the heights of Harlem], but I am sure they will not upon open Ground. I had a Specimen of that yesterday. Hear two Brigades ran away from a small advanced party of the Regulars, tho' the General did all in his power to convince them they were in no danger. He laid his Cane over many of the Officers who shewed their men the Example of running. These were militia, the New England continental Troops are much better."

These and other accounts substantially agree with Washington's own assessment of the unexpected landing of the British warships *Renown, Repulse,* and *Pearl,* and the schooner *Tryal,* which had sailed up the Hudson River to near Bloomingdale in order to give the appearance of landing at Harlem Heights, aiming to deceive the Americans from their true landing point at Kip's Bay. "On Sunday Morning," he informed the Massachusetts General Court three days later, "Six or Seven Ships of War which had gone up the East River above the City some few days before, began a most severe & Heavy Cannonade to Scour the Grounds and effect a Landing of their Troops. . . . I immediately on hearing the Canonade rode with all possible expedition towards the place of landing and where Breast Works had been thrown up to secure our Men, & found the Troops that had been posted there to my great suprize and Mortification retreating with the utmost precipitation . . . notwithstanding the exertions of their Generals to form 'em, running away in the most shamefull and disgracefull manner. I used every possible effort to rally them but to no purpose, & on the appearance of a small part of the Enemy (not more than Sixty or Seventy in Number) they ran off without firing a Single Shot. . . . this scandalous conduct occasioned a loss of many Tents, Baggage & Camp Equipage which would have been easily secured, had they made the least Opposition."

In fairness to the untrained militia, however, their entrenchments were, according to Continental army private Joseph Plumb Martin, "nothing more than a ditch dug along on the bank of the river with the dirt thrown out towards the water." Of the landing, Adm. Richard Howe's secretary, Ambrose Serle, wrote in his journal: "So terrible and so incessant a roar of guns few even in the [British] army and navy had ever heard before." But even Serle was amazed at the failure of nerve and hasty retreat of the Americans, adding that "the dastardly behaviour of the Rebels . . . sinks below remark."

After the British landed at Kip's Bay, Washington retreated and encamped at Harlem Heights, "so well calculated for defence, that I should hope If the Enemy make an Attack and our Men will behave with tolerable resolution, they must meet with a repulse it not a total defeat."

Related entries: Fort Washington; Harlem Heights, Battle of; White Plains, Battle of

Suggestions for further reading:
"To John Hancock," 16 September 1776 (*War Ser.,* vol. 6).
"To Nicholas Cooke," 17 September 1776 (*War Ser.,* vol. 6).

"To the Massachusetts General Court," 19 September 1776 (*War Ser.,* vol. 6).
"To John Augustine Washington," 22 September 1776 (*War Ser.,* vol. 6).
Bliven, Bruce, Jr. 1955–1956. *Battle for Manhattan.* New York.

Knight of Malta

See Royal Gift.

Knox, Henry (1750–1806)

Henry Knox was born in Boston. He was still a youth when, like Washington, his father died, and he was forced to drop out of the local common school to help support his mother and younger brother. He found employment in a local bookstore, where he was introduced to military tactics, especially artillery and engineering, and to the French language. Knox joined a grenadier company when he was 18 years old, and later he became second in command of the Boston Grenadier Corps. When he was about 20 years of age, he opened his own bookstore in Boston, known as the London Book Store. He married Lucy Flucker (c.1756–1824), a daughter of the royal secretary of Massachusetts, in June 1774.

At nearly 300 pounds, the "gregarious and extremely good-humored" and always elegantly dressed Knox made an imposing army officer. Knox and Washington became instant friends after Washington's arrival at Cambridge, Massachusetts, in June 1775, with their mutual interest in military subjects and dedication to a common cause. The new commander in chief, wrote Knox to his wife, "fills his place with vast ease and dignity, and dispenses happiness around him." Washington began to rely on Knox's independent judgment and was glad to ac-

Portrait of Maj. Gen. Henry Knox by Gilbert Stuart (Library of Congress)

cede to John Adams's suggestion that Knox head the Continental artillery, meager as it was at the time of his appointment in November 1775. Knox rapidly became one of Washington's most trusted generals, and their friendship outlasted the war.

Knox served as an engineer, assisting in planning and overseeing the building of the breastworks at Roxbury in 1775. When Washington and Gen. Charles Lee "viewd the works," wrote Knox with apparent satisfaction, "they express'd the greatest pleasure & surprize at their situation and apparent utility to say nothing of the plan which did not escape their praise." Six days after inspecting the works, Washington urged

Congress to place Knox in command of the Continental artillery, "knowing of no person better qualified . . . or whose appointment will give more general satisfaction." Without waiting for Congress to act, Washington sent Knox after the artillery captured from the British at Fort Ticonderoga, which was needed before Washington could undertake an attack on Boston. It was rather late in the season to undertake such an expedition, but within a month Knox was ready to leave New York with "a Noble train of Artillery"—eighty yoke of oxen dragging forty-two "exceeding strong sleds" across the hazardous frozen terrain. Knox delivered his trophies, fifty-five mortars and cannon of varying sizes, to Washington in early February 1776, making possible Washington's plan to drive the British from Boston. No doubt the expedition, which included a treacherous crossing of ice-filled Lake George, furnished valuable lessons that aided Knox when Washington called upon him the next December to perform the crucial task of transporting artillery across the ice-packed Delaware River for the Battle of Trenton.

Knox was promoted to brigadier general in December 1776, reporting directly to Washington himself, and he played crucial roles in the Battles of Trenton, Princeton, and Germantown. The arrival and commissioning by Congress of French artillerist and engineer Philippe-Charles-Jean-Baptiste Tronson du Coudray (1738–1777) threatened Knox's precedence in rank in the spring of 1777, provoking Washington to defend his general. "General Knox has deservedly acquired the character of one of the most valuable officers in the service, and . . . combatting the almost innumerable difficulties in the department he fills, has placed the artillery upon a footing that does him the greatest honor." Were Knox superseded, Washington continued, he "would not think himself at liberty to continue in the service," creating a scenario in which the whole train of artillery might collapse. Coudray's accidental drowning aborted that potential drastic outcome, however, and Knox was able to turn his full attention to assisting Washington with the Delaware River defense during the campaign for Philadelphia in the summer and fall of 1777.

"To accompany Knox through the Revolution," wrote his biographer North Callahan in 1958, "is to be in the fiery midst of every battle in which Washington himself took part, the genial and energetic artillery commander being constantly at his chief's side." Brave, cool in battle, and always optimistic, Knox never succumbed to despondency, no matter how dark the war effort seemed. He remained at Long Island following that disaster until the last artillery piece had been ferried safely away. He was at Valley Forge when Lucy Knox joined Martha Washington, Kitty Greene, and Lady Sarah Stirling to form a quorum to liven up the social life at headquarters. He was a member of the court-martial at Middlebrook, New Jersey, that tried Benedict Arnold in absentia after his defection. Knox and his officers commanding the artillery during the victory at Monmouth in 1778 were praised by Washington in General Orders with the comment that even "the Enemy have done them the Justice to acknowledge that no Artillery could be better served than ours." Likewise, the marquis de Lafayette paid the highest compliments to Knox at Yorktown in October 1781, when he declared to Knox that the "progress of your artillery is regarded by everyone as one of the wonders of the Revolution." After the battle of Yorktown, Washington commended Knox in glowing terms to Congress, writing of Knox that "His genius supplied the deficit of means." Urged by Washington, Congress soon promoted Knox to major general.

After that, he was with Washington at Wethersfield, Newburgh, and West Point. On 25 August 1783 he led the American

From a monument marking the trail over which Knox's artillery train passed from Fort Ticonderoga to Boston in the winter of 1775–1776 (New York State Conservation Department)

troops down from West Point to take formal possession of New York City. If Washington's praise and Congress's promotion were not enough, Washington, in his final official act as commander in chief, handed to Knox command of the Continental army. It is said that he embraced Washington with tears upon the latter's relinquishing command. It was Knox's additional honor to have fought in every battle where Washington fought. Knox also provided the original inspiration for the Society of the Cincinnati, the forming of which he suggested in May 1783, and he served as the organization's first vice president from the moment of its inception until his death. In 1785 he succeeded Benjamin Lincoln as secretary of war during the Confederation government, and held the office for eleven years, which included Washington's first term as president. While in office he instituted a plan for a national militia, negotiated several Indian treaties, and avidly supported the Federal Constitution. In fact, it was partly at Knox's urging in a letter in which he called Washington "the Father of Your Country" that Washington agreed to attend the Constitutional Convention in 1787. Knox also kept Washington abreast of Shays's Rebellion after those

events began to unfold in late 1786. Knox retired to private life in 1794, much against Washington's wishes. U.S. Senator William Maclay (1734–1804), comparing Knox with two other members of Washington's cabinet, Alexander Hamilton and Thomas Jefferson, wrote: "Knox is the easiest man and has the most dignity of presence. They retired at a decent time, one after another. Knox stayed the longest, as indeed suited his aspect best, being more of a Bacchanalian figure."

When war with France seemed to be on the horizon, John Adams appointed Knox a major general of the provisional army. Maclay wrote, "Give Knox an army and he will soon have a war." Knox had a disagreement in 1798 over rank with Washington, who too had been called out of retirement. Washington had ranked Alexander Hamilton, who had less military experience, as first major general of the army, ahead of Knox. They did reconcile before Washington's death the following year, although Knox felt very hurt by Washington's decision. In 1796 Knox settled at Montpelier, his estate on the St. Georges River at Thomaston, Maine, where he built an imposing nineteen-room mansion. He entered into several businesses, including farming, fishing, livestock, lumbering, brick making, and shipbuilding, and he built a wharf and several locks on the river. Although through his wife's inheritance and further purchase and grants he became one of the largest landholders in the country, he increasingly faced financial hardships with the passage of time. He died at Thomaston after swallowing a chicken bone at breakfast.

Related entries: Father of His Country; Hamilton, Alexander; Presidency; Quasi-War

Suggestions for further reading:
"To John Hancock," 8 November 1775 (*War Ser., vol. 2*)
"Instructions to Henry Knox," 16 November 1775 (*War Ser., vol. 2*).

"From Henry Knox," 5, 17 December 1775 (*War Ser.,* vol. 2).

"Inventory of Artillery," 17 December 1775 (*War Ser.,* vol. 2).

"To John Hancock," 31 May 1777 (*War Ser.,* vol. 9).

Brooks, Noah. 1900. *Henry Knox: A Soldier of the Revolution.* New York.

Callahan, North. 1958. *Henry Knox: General Washington's General.* New York.

Drake, Francis S. 1873. *Life and Correspondence of Henry Knox.* Boston.

L

La Force (Michel Pépin)

Michel Pépin, known as La Force, was the French commissary of stores on the upper Ohio on the eve of the French and Indian War. Washington first met La Force in December 1753 at Venango (now Franklin, Pennsylvania), an important French supply and trading post on the Allegheny River, while on his journey to Fort Le Boeuf to deliver Virginia lieutenant governor Robert Dinwiddie's letter to the commandant of French forces on the Ohio. In the spring of 1754, La Force, an able and experienced interpreter whom Washington called a "bold Enterprising Man, and a person of g[rea]t subtilty and cunning," was captured near Fort Necessity in the skirmish between Washington and the party of Frenchmen commanded by Jumonville. La Force claimed that he was unaware of the intentions of the French, whose officers after their capture insisted that they had been sent "on an Embassy," but Washington rejected their explanations as well as their pleas to be released. "Besides," Washington wrote Dinwiddie, "looseing La Force I really think wd tend more to our disservice than 50 other Men, as he is a person whose active Spirit, leads him into all parlys, and brought him acquainted with all parts, add to this a perfect use of the Indian Tongue, and g[rea]t influence with the Indian." La Force was sent to Williams-

burg and confined in the jail. Dinwiddie, calling La Force "a most wicked Fellow," blocked French efforts to secure his exchange. In August 1756, La Force, "by making a Hole in the Prison-Wall," escaped from Williamsburg, but he was recaptured less than forty miles away in King and Queen County after only two days. Upon his return to Williamsburg, La Force was placed in irons and chains to prevent future escapes. La Force later appealed to Washington for assistance, and he was paroled to New York in March 1759.

Related entries: Dinwiddie, Robert; Fort Necessity Campaign; Van Braam, Jacob

Suggestions for further reading:
Diaries, vol. 1.
"To Robert Dinwiddie," 29 May 1754 (*Col. Ser.,* vol. 1).
"To Robert Dinwiddie," 14 August 1756 (*Col. Ser.,* vol. 3).
"From La Force," c.March 1759 (*Col. Ser.,* vol. 6).

Lafayette (1757–1834)

Marie-Joseph-Paul-Yves-Roch-Gilbert du Motier, marquis de Lafayette, the highest-ranking foreign officer to serve in the American forces during the Revolutionary War, was born into a noble family at Chavaniac, in Auvergne, France. His father was killed at the Battle of

George Washington and the marquis de Lafayette on horseback at the winter quarters, Valley Forge (Library of Congress)

Minden when Lafayette was 2 years old, and his mother and maternal grandfather died when he was but 13, resulting in Lafayette's inheritance of a sprawling estate at an early age. When he was 17 years old Lafayette married Marie-Adrienne-François de Noailles (1759–1807), the daughter of the wealthy noble Noailles, an arranged marriage to be sure, but one eagerly entered into by the young bride and groom.

Lafayette decided to join the colonies' struggle with France's old enemy, Great Britain, and at the urging of Silas Deane, the Continental Congress's agent in Paris, he outfitted a ship to transport a group of French officers to America. In the third week of April 1777, the *Victoire* accordingly sailed from Bordeaux for Charleston, South Carolina. When Lafayette landed in South Carolina in June 1777 he had not yet celebrated his twentieth birthday. Ironically, at the time Lafayette arrived in America, Washington had become thoroughly disenamored with French glory seekers and their contracts with Deane. Congress, aware of Washington's views and even more unable than Washington to find a suitable place for their service, nevertheless was greatly impressed by Lafayette, and immediately commissioned him a major general effective 31 July 1777, and not from the date of his agreement with Deane, in order to keep him from outranking any existing major generals. On the same day Congress gave Lafayette his commission, Washington arrived at Philadelphia after a march of his troops from southern New York through New Jersey. He dined at City Tavern and for the first time met Lafayette. The two men immediately impressed each other, and Washington, to Lafayette's delight, invited the youth to mess at his headquarters and to reconnoiter the Delaware River fortifications with him the following day. From that time Lafayette traveled with the main army and participated in Washington's councils of war.

According to his agreement with Deane, Lafayette served the army without any command, but he was not in America long before he began to express a desire for command of a division. Although Congress did not rush to fulfill that request, Washington affectionately assured the young man that he wanted Lafayette to esteem him as both a "father and friend," and that alone satisfied Lafayette's quest for advancement during the intervening months before he was given a command, after the Battle of Brandywine.

Washington, however, did more than boost Lafayette's self-esteem, and he wrote Continental Congress delegate Benjamin Harrison of Virginia to clarify whether Lafayette's commission as major general was meant to include command of a division. Washington understood that the young Frenchman, not thinking his commission "merely honorary," expected to acquire practical experience in military matters, "but at the same time he has always accompanied it with a hint that so soon as *I* shall think him fit for the command of a Division, he shall be ready to enter upon the duties of it, and, in the meantime has offered his service for a smaller command." Harrison replied that Lafayette's "chief motive in going into our service was to be near you, to see service, and to give him an eclat at home where he expected he would soon return. . . . [He] could not have obtained the commission on any other terms."

Lafayette was shot in the left thigh while trying to rally the American troops at the Battle of Brandywine on 11 September 1777 and, after a brief stay at Philadelphia at Washington's urging, was nursed back to health at the Moravian settlement in Bethlehem. In early December he was given the command of Washington's old friend, Maj. Gen. Adam Stephen. By that time Lafayette had come to realize how indispensable Washington was to the Patriots' cause, and he told his mentor so directly, writing that, "if you were lost for America, there is nobody who could keep the Army and the Revolution for six months." Lafayette already was disenchanted with American politics and attributed dissension in Congress to "stupid men who without knowing a single word about war, undertake to judge you, to make ridiculous comparisons" between Washington and Maj. Gen. Horatio Gates. Washington, lamenting the difficulties of the army, reassured the youth by replying, "we must not, in so great a contest, expect to meet with nothing but sunshine." Lafayette also was quick to see through famed interloper Thomas Conway of the so-called Conway Cabal, describing Conway to Washington as a man styling himself before his fellow officers "as a man sent by heaven for the liberty and happiness of America." He added that Conway had told them so, "and they are fools enough to believe it."

Lafayette spent that winter with Washington at Valley Forge. He also took part in the Battle of Monmouth Courthouse on 28 June 1778, of which he later recalled seeing Washington in the battle scenes: he "seemed to arrest fortune with one glance. . . . I thought then as now that I had never beheld so superb a man." At Washington's urging Lafayette returned to France during the winter of 1778–1779 to negotiate support for the American cause, where he met the aged philosopher Benjamin Franklin for the first time. Lafayette's mission resulted in the French army under Rochambeau being sent to reinforce the Americans, with the stipulation that Rochambeau serve only at the discretion of Washington and not the Continental Congress. He also obtained badly needed supplies of munitions and clothing for the Continental forces. To the utter delight of Washington, Lafayette arrived at his commander in chief's headquarters in May 1780. Washington immediately sent his young protégé on another diplomatic mission, this time to win authorization from the Continental Congress to enlarge the army for a planned attack on New York.

In the spring of 1781 Lafayette was placed in command of 1,200 New England troops and was ordered to join Maj. Gen. Nathanael Greene in the Carolinas. Lafayette reached Richmond, Virginia, on 22 April in time to prevent the British from occupying the city. His army began to harass Cornwallis in his northward march and followed the British down the Virginia tidewater to Portsmouth. Lafayette then kept Cornwallis from escaping southward while Washington, De Grasse, and Rochambeau hurried to besiege Yorktown. Cornwallis finally surrendered on 19 October 1781.

Lafayette sailed for France the following December. During the next two years he corresponded with Washington, and in a letter of February 1783 he proposed to Washington the idea of jointly purchasing a small plantation to experiment with the freeing of slaves and "Use them only as tenants. Such an Exemple as Yours Might Render it a General Practice." Although Washington rejected the idea as impractical, Lafayette returned to it three years later, buying a plantation in Cayenne for the purpose. In August 1784 Lafayette returned to America, where he was affectionately welcomed everywhere he went, beginning at New York and including trips to Mount Vernon and to the Continental Congress, where he was honored with a reception at Trenton, New Jersey.

During his visit to Mount Vernon in August 1784, Lafayette described Washington in a letter to his wife: "I found him in the routine of his estate, where our meeting was very tender and our satisfaction completely mutual. I am not just turning a phrase when I assure you that in retirement General Washington is even greater than he was during the Revolution. His simplicity is truly sublime, and he is as completely involved with all the details of his lands and house as if he had always lived here." Lafayette noted that days at Mount Vernon began with breakfast followed by morning chats in which they "thoroughly discussed the past, the present, and the future" before Washington withdrew to take care of his affairs, leaving Lafayette alone to read. Dinner always included visitors from the neighborhood, and the "conversation at table turns to the events of the war or to anecdotes that we are fond of recalling." Tea followed, where private conversations were resumed.

When it was time for Lafayette to return to New York, Washington conducted him as far as Annapolis, Maryland, where he "left him proceeding on the road to Baltimore." It was a touching scene, recalled by Washington a week later in a letter to Lafayette. "In the moment of our separation upon the road as I travelled," he wrote, "& every hour since—I felt all that love, respect & attachment for you, with which length of years, close connexion & your merits, have inspired me. I often asked myself, as our Carriages distended, whether that was the last sight, I ever should have of you? And tho' I wished to say no—my fears answered yes." It was a melancholy moment for Washington. He continued:

> I called to mind the days of my youth, & found they had long since fled to return no more; that I was now descending the hill, I had been 52 years climbing—& that tho' I was blessed with a good constitution, I was of a short lived family—and might soon expect to be entombed in the dreary mansions of my father's—These things darkened the shades & gave a gloom to the picture, consequently to my prospects of seeing you again: but I will not repine—I have had my day.

Protesting from onboard the *Nymphe* in New York harbor, where he was waiting to return to France, Lafayette declared that "our late parting was Not By Any Means a last interview—My whole Soul Revolts at the idea—" and promised that "within the walls of Mount vernon we shall Yet often Speack of old times." The parting indeed proved to be their last, however, although the two carried on a frequent, detailed, and affectionate correspondence until Washington's death. From France Lafayette commented on the political situation in Europe, as well as personal matters like his travels and his opposition to slavery, which he called his "Hobby Horse." He sent Washington gifts of French hounds, Knight of Malta, a jackass and two jennets, birds, and toys for Washington's wards. In France he became involved in the French liberation movement, and, says one historian, he "consciously tried to model his deportment as a diplomat after Washington." On 12 July 1789 the Bastille was demolished, and Lafayette sent Washington the key to the famed prison, which still hangs in the main hall at Mount Vernon. Washington in turn kept him informed of affairs in the states, sending hams, a copy of the Constitution, and vocabularies of Indian languages. When Lafayette was denounced and imprisoned from 1792 to 1797, Washington as president wrote official letters on his behalf, but to no avail. Napoleon finally freed him, and after a period of exile in Denmark he settled at La Grange, his estate about forty miles from Paris.

In his will Washington bequeathed to Lafayette "a pair of finely wrought steel Pistols, taken from the enemy in the Revolutionary War." The pistols may have been returning a compliment that Lafayette had presented to Washington in 1779. A pair of pistols given to Gen. Andrew Jackson in 1824 by Congressman Charles Fenton Mercer, who received them from William Robinson, the son-in-law of Washington's nephew William Augustine Washington, were said to have been a gift from Lafayette and worn by Washington during the Revolution. Washington wrote that Lafayette "possesses uncommon Military talents, is of a quick and sound judgment, persevering, and enterprizing without rashness, and besides these, he is of a very conciliating temper and perfectly sober, which are qualities that rarely coincide in the same person."

At the invitation of President James Monroe, Lafayette returned to America in 1824, touring the country for more than a year, including a celebrated visit to Mount Vernon. When he died he was the last surviving general from the American Revolutionary War.

Related entries: Cornwallis, Charles, Second Earl Cornwallis; Lee, Charles; Royal Gift; "Vine and Fig Tree"

Suggestions for further reading:
"To Benjamin Harrison," 19 August 1777 (*War Ser.*, vol. 10).
"To Lafayette," 31 December 1777 (*War Ser.*, vol. 13).
"Lafayette to Adrienne Lafayette," 20 August 1784 (*Lafayette Papers*, vol. 5).
"To Lafayette," 8 December 1784 (*Con. Ser.*, vol. 2).
"From Lafayette," 21 December 1784 (*Con. Ser.*, vol. 2).
"From Lafayette," 23 August 1790 (*Pres. Ser.*, vol. 6).
"From Lafayette," 20–21 August 1798 (*Ret. Ser.*, vol. 2).
"To Lafayette," 25 December 1798 (*Ret. Ser.*, vol. 3).
"Marquis de Lafayette: Eager Warrior," Howard H. Peckham. George Athan Billias, ed. 1964. *George Washington's Generals.* New York.
Chinard, Gilbert. 1929. *The Letters of Lafayette and Jefferson.* Baltimore.
Gottschalk, Louis R. 1935–1950. 4 vols. *Lafayette Comes to America.* Chicago.

Last Will and Testament

"In the name of God amen I George Washington of Mount Vernon—a citizen of the United States, and lately President of the same, do make, ordain and

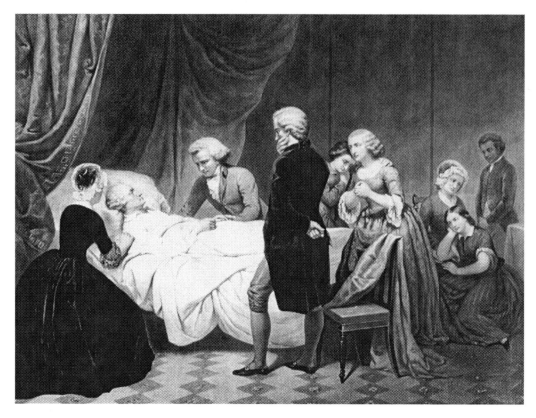

George Washington on his deathbed (Library of Congress)

declare this Instrument; which is written with my own hand and every page thereof subscribed with my name, to be my last Will & Testament, revoking all others." The will, twenty-nine pages apparently finished on 9 July 1799, reveals much about Washington's extensive landholdings, possessions, family, friends, dependents, and slaves. Appended to the will is a schedule of property describing the "landed property and other assets not specifically bequeathed to individual heirs." An earlier will, possibly written on the eve of his leaving to take command of the Continental army in 1775, was destroyed by Martha Washington at her husband's request on the afternoon of his death.

The will began with the customary ordering of all debts to be paid. To Martha he bequeathed the "use, profit and benefit" of his whole estate, "real and personal," for the term of her natural life. Upon Martha's decease it was his desire that all the slaves held by him in his *"own right"* should be freed. To emancipate them during her life, "tho' earnestly wished by me," would cause disagreeable consequences on account of their "intermixture by Marriages with the dower Negroes," whom he had no power to manumit. He included provisions for slaves who might from age or bodily infirmities be unable to support themselves, prohibited the sale or transport of any of his slaves out of state, and "most pointedly, and most solemnly enjoin[ed]" his executors to see that the clause respecting the slaves in "every part thereof be religiously fulfilled . . . without evasion, neglect or delay." His old servant Billy Lee was given an annuity of thirty dollars and his choice of being freed immediately or remaining at Mount Vernon.

Bank stock worth $4,000 was designated for the Alexandria Academy, and his shares in the James River and Potomac River canal companies were left respectively to Liberty Hall Academy in Lexington and for the establishment of a national university. He forgave the debts owed him by the estates of his brother Samuel Washington and brother-in-law Bartholomew Dandridge. His nephew Bushrod Washington was given all his manuscript papers, both public and private, as well as the books and pamphlets in his library. His brother Charles Washington was to receive the gold-headed cane left to Washington by Benjamin Franklin. The "acquaintances and friends of my Juvenile years," Lawrence and Robert Washington of Chotank, were each given a gold-headed cane and a spyglass used during the Revolutionary War. His old friend Dr. James Craik was bequeathed a "Tambour Secretary" and the circular chair from his study. Dr. David Stuart (1753–c.1814) was given a "large shaving & dressing Table, and my Telescope." Bryan Fairfax was given a Bible "in three large volumes, with notes." Lafayette was given a pair of "finely wrought steel Pistols, taken from the enemy" during the Revolutionary War. To his sisters-in-law Hannah and Mildred Washington and his friends Eleanor Stuart, Hannah Washington of Fairfield, and Elizabeth Washington of Hayfield he bequeathed each a mourning ring valued at $100, gifts made not "for the intrinsic value of them, but as mementos of my esteem & regard." Tobias Lear and his wife, Frances Bassett Washington Lear, were given use of the 360-acre Walnut Tree farm rent-free for their life, after which it would pass to Fannie's sons George Fayette and Charles Augustine Washington as part of the 2,077 acres east of Little Hunting Creek on the Potomac. Three hundred dollars was given to a distant relative, Sally B. Haynie, and $100 each to Sarah Green and to Ann Walker, daughters of Thomas Bishop (d. 1795), and John Alton (d. 1785) "in consideration of the attachment of their fathers

to me; each of whom having lived nearly forty years in my family." Five nephews—William Augustine Washington, George Lewis, George Steptoe Washington, Bushrod Washington, and Samuel Washington—were left each a sword "accompanied with an injunction not to unsheath them for the purpose of shedding blood, except it be for self defence, or in defence of their Country and its rights; and in the latter case, to keep them unsheathed, and prefer falling with them in their hands, to the relinquishment thereof."

Bushrod Washington and his heirs, "partly in consideration of an intimation to his deceased father [John Augustine Washington] while we were Bachelors, & he had kindly undertaken to superintend my Estate during my Military Services in the former War between Great Britain & France, that if I should fall therein," was given the main part of Mount Vernon, much larger when the will was written than when the promise was made during the French and Indian War. The residue of the Mount Vernon estate was given to Martha's granddaughter Eleanor Parke Custis Lewis and her husband, Lawrence Lewis, the son of Washington's sister, Betty. Martha's grandson George Washington Parke Custis, already the principal heir of the vast Custis estate, was given a 1,200-acre tract on Four Mile Run, in the vicinity of Alexandria, and Washington's "entire Square, number twenty one, in the City of Washington." The rest of his estate, vast tracts of land and some livestock, listed in an attached schedule and estimated by Washington to be valued at $530,000, was to be sold by the executors at the time and manner that they saw fit, with the proceeds divided into twenty-three equal parts and distributed to various family members.

The remainder of the will contained directions for the erection of a new family vault and an "express desire that my Corpse may be Interred in a private manner, without parade, or funeral Oration."

Washington named as executors his wife, Martha; George Washington Parke Custis; and five nephews: Lawrence Lewis, Bushrod Washington, George Steptoe Washington, Samuel Washington, and William Augustine Washington. The will was presented for probate on 10 January 1800 to the Fairfax County, Virginia, court. It was printed in Alexandria a few days later and circulated in pamphlet form. The court named as appraisers of the estate Washington's secretary Tobias Lear; a neighbor, Thomson Mason; Martha's grandson-in-law Thomas Peter; and William H. Foote, a nephew of the widow of his former plantation manager Lund Washington. The appraisers filed their report in the county clerk's office in 1810, and the estate was finally settled in June 1847.

Related entries: Death; Lee, William

Suggestions for further reading:
"Last Will and Testament," 9 July 1799 (*Ret. Ser.,* vol. 4).
"Washington's Will" (vol. 1, appendix 5). Jared Sparks. 1834–1837. 12 vols. *The Writings of George Washington.* Boston.
Prussing, Eugene E. 1927. *The Estate of George Washington, Deceased.* Boston.

Laurens, Henry (1724–1792)

Perhaps the most influential Patriot in the state of South Carolina, Henry Laurens was the owner of large plantations in Georgia and the Carolinas and the largest export business in Charleston, the city of his birth. Beginning in 1757 he began a distinguished career of public service when he was elected to the provincial house of commons in South Carolina. In 1761 he was commissioned a lieutenant colonel in the South Carolina militia. In 1774 he became president of the Charleston council of safety and was elected to the South Carolina provincial congress, of which he became president in

1775. He served as president of the Continental Congress for two years beginning in 1777, during which time he and Washington carried on an extensive correspondence about the war effort. Laurens was appointed minister to Holland in 1779 but was captured while on his way there and was imprisoned in the Tower of London until late 1781. In 1782, as one of Congress's appointed peace commissioners, he signed a preliminary peace. He was elected to represent South Carolina in the Constitutional Convention but did not attend. After returning to South Carolina from Britain in 1784, he retired from public life.

Laurens, whose son John served as an aide-de-camp to Washington, died and was buried at Mepkin, his estate on the Cooper River near Charleston.

Related entry: Laurens, John

Suggestion for further reading:
"To Henry Laurens," 10 November 1777 (*Laurens Papers,* vol. 12).

Laurens, John (1754–1782)

London and Geneva educated, John Laurens, the son of Henry Laurens of South Carolina, joined Washington's staff as a volunteer aide-de-camp in 1777. The Continental Congress commissioned him a lieutenant colonel after he distinguished himself during a raid in the Rhode Island campaign in August 1778, and Congress directed Washington to give him a field command commensurate to his rank. Laurens declined the commission, however. In 1779 Laurens, in search of greater glory on the battlefield, sought and received Congress's approval to travel to South Carolina and Georgia to raise a regiment of slaves to serve in the Continental army. When he left Washington's military family, the commander in chief was "unwilling to part with him," but did not try to retain him against his wishes. "The whole tenor of Laurens's conduct," he wrote, "has been such as to intitle him to my particular friendship and to give me a high opinion of his talents and merit. In the field he has given very distinguishing proofs of his bravery upon several interesting occasions." In fact Laurens participated in several important battles and was wounded twice, at Germantown and Monmouth, before being captured at Charleston in 1780.

Laurens also became a member of the South Carolina general assembly in 1779, and that same year Congress appointed him a secretary to Benjamin Franklin. Although he declined that appointment, he did accept a commission as special minister to France to seek assistance for the Patriot cause. After his return to America he was a participant in the siege of Yorktown, and there, in 1781, he and Lafayette's brother-in-law, Louis-Marie, vicomte de Noailles, served as the commissioners for drafting the terms of capitulation that were presented to Lord Cornwallis. In 1782 Laurens again proposed raising a corps of black levies for the defense of South Carolina, an idea Washington encouraged as "may be useful to the public cause."

Laurens was killed in 1782 in what Washington described as "a trifling skirmish" at Combahee Ferry in South Carolina, where he was attempting to round up enemy foragers intent on "plundering the Country of rice." "The Death of Colo Laurens," wrote Washington, "I consider as a very heavy misfortune, not only as it affects the public at large; but particularly so to his Family, and all his private Friends and Connections, to whom his amiable and useful Character had rendered him peculiarly dear." When describing Laurens after the war, Washington wrote that "no man possessed more of the amor patria—in a word, he had not a fault that I ever could discover, unless intripidity bordering upon rashness, could come under that denomination; & to this he was excited by the purest motives."

Related entries: Laurens, Henry; Yorktown, Battle of

Suggestions for further reading:
"To John Rutledge," 15 March 1779 (*Writings*, vol. 14).
"To John Laurens," 13 October 1780 (*Writings*, vol. 20).
"To John Laurens," 18 February 1782 (*Writings*, vol. 24).
Independent Chronicle (Boston), 2 December 1784.
Simms, William Gilmore, ed. 1867. *The Army Correspondence of John Laurens in the Years 1777–78.* New York.

Lear, Tobias (1762–1816)

When in 1793 the Father of His Country described Tobias Lear as a person who "possesses my entire friendship and confidence," Lear had been in Washington's service for about seven years. The Portsmouth, New Hampshire, native had come to Mount Vernon recommended by Benjamin Lincoln, Washington's close friend from the Revolutionary War, as a man "who supports the character of gentleman and scholar." Indeed, with a year's experience in Europe and a proficiency in French, the 1783 graduate of Harvard College seemed an ideal candidate for the position Washington had to offer: a private secretary who would live with the family and serve both as an assistant to his employer and a tutor to the two youngest children of Martha's deceased son Jacky, Nelly and George Washington Parke Custis. By the time Lear accepted the position, at $200 a year, one secretary, William Shaw, more interested in recreational forays into Alexandria than the daily grind of copying correspondence and arranging accounts, already had departed, as had a tutor for the children, Gideon Snow. Noah Webster also had visited Mount Vernon and determined that he was not suited for the position.

In addition to being intelligent and highly industrious, Lear was personable, or in Washington's words to Lincoln, "a genteel, well-behaved young man." Tutoring the children gave him more enjoyment than he had thought possible, but over time his responsibilities became more directly related to household management and to Washington himself, especially after Washington was elected president in 1789. In time Lear became Washington's closest associate and was entrusted implicitly with the affairs of state that Washington handled on a daily basis.

Lear left Washington's employment in 1793 to travel abroad on a business venture but returned the following year. He was elected president of the Potomac River Company in 1795, of which Washington was the major booster. In 1798 when it seemed war with France was likely, Washington appointed Lear his military secretary with the rank of colonel, and in 1802 Jefferson appointed him consul for Santo Domingo. Lear served as consul general at Algiers from 1804 to 1811, during which time he negotiated a peace treaty with Tripoli. For the last five years of his life he was an accountant with the War Department.

Lear probably is known more for writing the only eyewitness account of Washington's death than for either his role as Washington's secretary or his diplomatic service. "In the course of the afternoon," wrote Lear of his friend's last day, "he appeared to be in great pain and distress, from the difficulty of breathing, and frequently changed his position in the bed. On these occasions I lay upon the bed, and endeavoured to raise him, and turn him with as much care as possible. He appeared penetrated with gratitude for my attentions, & often said, I am afraid I shall fatigue you too much, and upon my assuring him that I could feel nothing but a wish to give him ease, he replied, *Well it is a debt we must pay to each other, and I hope when you want aid of this kind you will find it.*" Unfortunately, Lear died without the comforting hand of a friend— he committed suicide in Washington, D.C., in the fall of 1816 without explanation.

Lear and his first wife, Mary Long Lear ("Polly"; d. 1793), had a son named Benjamin Lincoln Lear (1791–1832), of whom Washington was godfather. Lear's second wife, Frances Bassett Washington Lear ("Fanny"; 1767–1796), was a niece of Martha Washington and a widow who had been married to the son of Washington's brother Charles, George Augustine Washington. When Fanny died Washington offered to "acquiesce in any plan which shall appear most conducive" to the "permanent interest" of Lear's stepchildren, Anna Maria (1788–1814), who later married Reuben Thornton (1781–1835), Charles Augustine (b. c.1790), and George Fayette Washington (1790–1867). Lear's third wife, Frances Dandridge Henley Lear (1779–1856), was also a niece of Washington's wife.

Related entries: Custis, George Washington Parke; Death; Lewis, Eleanor Parke Custis; Quasi-War

Suggestions for further reading:
"To Tobias Lear," 30 March 1796 (*Writings*, vol. 35).
Decatur, Stephen, Jr. 1933. *Private Affairs of George Washington from the Records and Accounts of Tobias Lear, Esquire, His Secretary.* Boston.
Lear, Tobias. 1906. *Letters and Recollections of George Washington: Being Letters to Tobias Lear and Others between 1790 and 1799.* New York.

Ledgers and Accounts

See Papers.

Lee, Charles (1731–1782)

Compared to George Washington, Charles Lee's military experience was extensive. Born in Dernhall in Cheshire, England, the son of a British general, Lee is said to have had a commission in his father's regiment at the age of 14, and undoubtedly his education was designed to facilitate his future career in the military. During the wandering of his early years, Lee studied the Greek and Latin classics; learned French and obtained a smattering of Spanish, German, and Italian; and read the military science of the day. Lee first came to America while still a lieutenant in the Forty-fourth British Regiment of Foot, and he was with the regiment when it took part in Maj. Gen. Edward Braddock's ill-fated 1755 expedition against Fort Duquesne, during which the regiment was attacked and Braddock killed. It was around that time that Lee and Washington probably met for the first time.

The following year Lee traveled with the Forty-fourth Regiment to the Iroquois country around Albany, New York, where he acquired the Mohawk name Ounewaterika, or "Boiling Water," which signifies "the spirit never sleeps," a name perhaps given to Lee because of his unpredictable temper. Lee was promoted to captain by 1758, when he was wounded at Ticonderoga, and he served in the British campaigns against Fort Niagara and Montreal. He then returned to England, joined a new regiment as a major, and in 1762 served under Brig. Gen. John Burgoyne on an expedition to the Iberian Peninsula, where he gallantly led the storming of the entrenched Spanish camp at Villa Velha. In 1765 Lee traveled to Poland, where he met King Stanislas Poniatowski, and became one of the king's aides-de-camp. When Stanislas lost power Lee went to Warsaw, where he was commissioned a major general in the Polish army. He was not given a command, however, so he joined the occupying Russian army in Moldavia against the invading Turks before returning to England by way of Hungary and Italy. Lee returned to America with a reputation as a conqueror, and he took every opportunity to remind Americans of his military accomplishments and experiences.

In June 1775, when Washington was commissioned commander in chief of the Continental army, he requested the Continental Congress to appoint Lee major general, for there were not many experienced officers in the Continental army. The soldier whom Abigail Adams called a "careless, hardy veteran" already had ingratiated himself with many members of Congress, as his reputation had preceded him, and he probably had indulged the secret hope that he himself might be appointed to the highest command. His indefatigable efforts at the siege of Boston helped impose order and complete the necessary engineering tasks at hand.

Washington expressed doubts about Lee early on, however, for in March 1776 he wrote in confidence to his brother Jack of the man whom Congress had just named his senior lieutenant: "He is the first Officer in Military knowledge and experience we have in the whole Army—He is zealously attachd to the Cause—honest, and well meaning, but rather fickle & violent I fear in his temper however as he possesses an uncommon share of good Sense and Spirit I congratulate my Countrymen upon his appointment."

From Boston Lee was dispatched to New York where he developed a plan of fortification consisting of redoubts and batteries along the waters extending around New York City and Long Island. He had barely begun to designate the sites for those defenses, however, when Congress sent him to take command of the Continental army's newly created southern department. Although both Lee and Washington thought that Lee's experience and talents, in Washington's words, would "have done more essential service to the common cause in Canada," Lee dutifully proceeded southward, making his way to Baltimore and Williamsburg and eventually South Carolina, where he won laurels for defending Charleston harbor against the British. Lee's scheme of defense for the New York area would not be implemented until after Washington's arrival in the area.

When Lee rejoined the Continental army at New York on the eve of the Battle of Long Island in August 1776, no one better recognized how sorely the main army needed his caliber of leadership than Lee himself. Eagerly anticipating more courageous deeds, most of the public applauded Congress's recall of Lee to the north, although the hullabaloo surrounding his return amused a few of his detractors. ("General Lee hourly expected, as if from heaven, with a legion of flaming swordsmen," wrote Col. William Malcom, a prominent New York City merchant in command of a regiment of militia levies.) Washington's own welcome of Lee displayed his confidence in Lee's abilities—upon his arrival he was immediately placed in command of the army north of King's Bridge. Lee, however, soon became sharply critical of Washington's troop dispositions.

Washington's losses between August and November 1776 served only to reinforce a growing feeling on Lee's part that Washington was unequal to the great task that lay before him. Indiscreet remarks about Washington and praise of Lee by Joseph Reed, Washington's trusted friend and aide-de-camp, only fueled Lee's tendency to place his own opinions before those of Washington, which in turn increased his hesitation in obeying Washington's orders. As a result he repeatedly disobeyed Washington's orders to cross the Hudson River and join the main army in New Jersey after the fall of the Hudson River forts. While allegedly spending the night of 13 December with "a woman of easy virtue" at White's Tavern in Baskingridge, New Jersey, Lee was captured by a British cavalry patrol and not exchanged until April 1778. In the meantime, Washington led the army to its striking victories at Trenton and Princeton, New Jersey, proving beyond a doubt that the commander in chief did not need Lee at his elbow to plan strategy. By the time Lee rejoined the army after his release, Washington was aware of the indiscreet correspondence between Lee and Reed, and he kept Lee at arm's length.

After his exchange Lee was offered the chance to lead a detachment to harass the British flank evacuating Philadelphia. He declined, however, and the marquis de Lafayette was placed in command of the detachment. Lee then changed his mind, asserted his right as senior major general, and was given the command. In late July 1778 he was ordered to attack the British rear guard over unfamiliar terrain at Monmouth, New Jersey, and he retreated when it seemed his attack was on the verge of failure after British general Henry Clinton anticipated the American maneuver. Washington arrived on the scene in time to witness Lee's retreat and rebuked him, although the exact exchange that passed between the two is not clear. Jared Sparks, the first editor of Washington's writings and the author of an early biography of Lee, claimed to have asked Lafayette about the occurrence years later, and Lafayette had replied that, though he had been very close to them both, he could not make out the exchange of words. According to Lafayette, it "was not the language, but the *manner*—no one had ever before seen Washington so terribly excited; his whole appearance was fearful."

In a letter written shortly after the battle, Lee accused Washington of uttering "very singular expressions" toward him during the fighting, implying that Lee was "guilty of disobedience of orders, or want of conduct, or want of courage." Washington was not inclined to argue with Lee about the matter, so Lee demanded an immediate court-martial in order that he might gain "some reparation for the injury" committed against him. Washington obliged, and a general court-martial convened on 4 July 1778 to try Lee on charges of disobeying orders and misbehavior on the day of the battle as well as showing disrespect to the commander in chief in his letters to Washington about the affair. The court found Lee guilty as charged on all three counts and sentenced him to be suspended from "any command in the armies of the United States of North America for the term of twelve months." Congress approved the sentence the following December.

After his court-martial Lee began a vigorous campaign to defend his actions at the Battle of Monmouth Courthouse, writing letters to army officers and members of Congress. Lee's efforts culminated in an article printed in the *Pennsylvania Packet* in December 1778, "General Lee's Vindication to the Public." The article contained so many "intemperate railings" against Washington that it provoked one of Washington's aides-de-camp, John Laurens, the son of Henry Laurens, the president of the Continental Congress, to challenge Lee to a duel in defense of the commander in chief's honor. Lee, accepting the challenge, was wounded seriously in the side but recovered. Lee retired to his farm in Virginia, from which he continued to circulate letters attacking not only Washington but also Alexander Hamilton, whom he claimed had perjured himself at Lee's trial. Washington, however, well aware of Lee's temperament, did not take much notice of Lee's peevishness. A disrespectful letter to Congress resulted in Lee's dismissal from the army in January 1780, and he died two years later. Washington in 1783 and 1784 magnanimously assisted in procuring a copy of General Lee's will for Lee's sister, Sidney Lee, who lived in Chester, England.

At Lee's death his manuscript papers came into the possession of the Revolutionary printer William Goddard, who informed Washington in May 1785 that he had prepared a three-volume edition of Lee's writings and correspondence for publication. "While it was my duty to preserve what was useful in military & political knowledge," Goddard explained, "I took the liberty to suppress such Expressions as appeared to be the Ebullitions of a disappointed & irritated mind; so that, I flatter myself, your Excellency will be convinced of the Candor of my Intention in the Execution of the work." Goddard further offered Washington the opportunity to make "any particular request" concerning the work before it was printed. In his reply Washington thanked Goddard for his overture but left the entire matter to the printer's "own good judgment," saying he had never had a difference with Lee except on public ground, and regretting that Lee had viewed it differently. "Should there appear in Genl Lee's writings anything injurious or unfriendly to me," Washington continued, "the impartial & dispassionate world, must decide how far I deserved it from the general tenor of my conduct. . . . conscious of my integrity, I would willingly hope that nothing would occur tending to give me anxiety; but should anything present itself in this or in any other publication, I shall never undertake the painful task of recrimination—nor do I know that I shall even enter upon my justification."

The printed prospectus for Goddard's edition of Lee's works included a lengthy statement claiming that the most difficult task of the editor had been to collect and arrange Lee's papers without giving offence to the men who had been the object of Lee's resentment, especially Washington. "Unhappily," the proposal read, "his Disappointments had soured his Temper . . . and so far got the better of his Philosophy, as to provoke him in the highest Degree, that he became, as it were, angry with all Mankind. To this exasperated Disposition we may impute the Origin of his *Political Queries,* and a Number of satirical Hints, thrown out both in his Conversation and Writing, against the Commander in Chief. Humanity will draw a Veil over the involuntary Errors of Sensibility, and pardon the Sallies of a suffering Mind, as its Presages did not meet with an Accomplishment." Goddard failed to attract enough subscribers to bring into print his planned *Miscellaneous Collections from the Papers of the Late Major General Charles Lee. . . .*

Related entries: Clinton, Henry; Lafayette;
Monmouth Courthouse, Battle of

Suggestions for further reading:
"To John Augustine Washington," 31 March 1776
  (*War Ser.*, vol. 3).
"To Charles Lee," 30 June 1778 (*Writings,*
  vol. 12).
"To Joseph Reed," 12 December 1778 (*Writings,*
  vol. 13).
"General Orders," 22 December 1778 (*Writings,*
  vol. 13).
"From William Goddard," 30 May 1785 (*Con.
  Ser.*, vol. 3).
"To William Goddard," 11 June 1785 (*Con. Ser.*,
  vol. 3).
"General Lee's Vindication to the Public"
  (*Pennsylvania Packet*, 3 December 1778).
Lee Papers. 1872–1875. 4 vols. New-York
  Historical Society Collections.
Alden, John R. 1951. *Charles Lee, Traitor or Patriot?*
  Baton Rouge, LA.

*Profile portrait of Richard Henry Lee, by Charles
Willson Peale (Library of Congress)*

Lee, Henry "Light-Horse Harry" (1756–1818)

See "First in War, First in Peace, and First in
the Hearts of His Countrymen."

Lee, Richard Henry (1732–1794)

Born at Stratford Hall in Westmoreland
County, Virginia, into one of the
colony's oldest and most prominent families, Richard Henry Lee was, along with his
younger brothers Arthur Lee (1740–1792)
and Francis Lightfoot Lee (1734–1797),
one of the most influential leaders in Revolutionary Virginia.

Lee entered the House of Burgesses in
1758, the same year Washington won his
first election, and served to 1775. Although
he had been schooled at Wakefield Academy in England, returning to his native
Westmoreland County in 1751, Lee was a
vocal opponent of the British Parliament
during the Stamp Act crisis and used his
considerable oratorical skills to incite his
compatriots to action. He cowrote the
Westmoreland Resolves, signed by several
relatives and the four brothers of Washington who lived in the area. He later organized Virginia's committee of correspondence to pass information on patriotic
activities from colony to colony, and he
took a prominent role in the first two Virginia conventions, of which Washington
was also a member. Lee was a Virginia delegate to the Continental Congress from
1774 to 1780 and from 1784 to 1787, serving as its twelfth president, from November
1784 to November 1785. While in Congress he served on the committee responsible for drafting Washington's commission as
commander in chief of the Continental
army and the instructions for Washington
to take command at Cambridge in 1775,
and he introduced the resolution of 7 June
1776 that led to the adoption of the Declaration of Independence, of which he was a
signer. He also wrote the first national
Thanksgiving Day proclamation, issued by

Congress on 31 October 1777, while at York, Pennsylvania, after the American victory at the Battle of Saratoga. He served on several important committees about which he frequently corresponded with Washington. Lee was also a colonel in the Virginia militia. Lee opposed ratification of the Federal Constitution but became one of Virginia's first U.S. senators under the new government, serving from 1789 to 1792. He died at his home Chantilly in Westmoreland County.

Although Lee and Washington frequently corresponded, a series of letters purported to have been written when they were both 9 years old is undoubtedly apocryphal.

Related entry: Declaration of Independence

Lee, William ("Billy")

Billy Lee (or Will as he was called also), was without a doubt the most famous slave of the eighteenth century. Washington acquired Billy when he was a teenager from Mary Smith Ball Lee, the widow of Col. John Lee of Westmoreland County, Virginia, in May 1768 for £61.15. Billy and his new owner soon became inseparable, with the young slave accompanying Washington on his many forays across the Virginia countryside for pleasure, foxhunting, or business trips to Alexandria, Fredericksburg, and Williamsburg.

George Washington Parke Custis in his *Recollections* fondly described Washington's famed body-servant accompanying his owner on foxhunts: "Will, the huntsman, better known in Revolutionary lore as Billy, rode a horse called *Chinkling,* a surprising leaper, and made very much like its rider, low, but sturdy, and of great bone and muscle. Will had but one order, which was to keep with the hounds; and, mounted on *Chinkling,* a French horn at his back, throwing himself almost at length

on the animal, with his spur in flank, this fearless horseman would rush, at full speed, through brake or tangled wood, in a style at which modern huntsmen would stand aghast."

Custis also recalled anecdotes of Billy during Revolutionary War episodes in which Billy appeared, including the Battles of Monmouth Courthouse and Yorktown, as well as the more famous attempt by the British for propaganda of some forged letters attributed to Washington as coming from Billy. Custis wrote also of Billy's later years at Mount Vernon:

> Billy carefully reconnoitred the visitors as they arrived, and when a military title was announced, the old body-servant would send his compliments to the soldier, requesting an interview at his quarters. It was never denied, and Billy, after receiving a warm grasp of the hand, would say, "Ah, colonel, glad to see you; we of the army don't see one another often in these peaceful times. Glad to see your honor looking so well; remember you at headquarters. The new-time people don't know what we old soldiers did and suffered for the country in the old war. Was it not cold enough at Valley Forge? Yes, was it; and I am sure you remember it was hot enough at Monmouth. Ah, colonel, I am a poor cripple; can't ride now, so I make shoes and think of the old times; the gineral often stops his horse here, to inquire if I want anything. I want for nothing, thank God, but the use of my limbs."

These interviews were frequent, as many veteran officers called to pay their respects to the retired chief, and all of them bestowed a token of remembrance upon the old body-servant of the Revolution.

Billy's faithful service to Washington during the Revolutionary War gave him a special place at Mount Vernon after the war.

In July 1784 Washington appealed to Clement Biddle, his purchasing agent in Philadelphia, to arrange to have Lee's wife, Margaret Thomas Lee, sent to Virginia:

"The Mulatto fellow William who has been with me all the War is attached (married he says) to one of his own colour a free woman, who, during the War was also of my [military] family—She has been in an infirm state of health for sometime, and I had conceived that the connection between them had ceased—but I am mistaken— they are both applying to me to get her here, and tho' I never wished to see her more, yet I cannot refuse his request (if it can be complied with on reasonable terms) as he has lived with me so long & followed my fortunes through the War with fidility." Although Washington asked Biddle to procure Margaret Thomas, or Margaret Lee, passage to Alexandria either by sea or stage, no evidence has ever been found that she came to Mount Vernon.

In April 1785 Billy fell and broke his knee while helping bear the chain on a surveying trip with Washington. The slow recuperation left him partly lame, but the accident was only the beginning of Billy's misfortunes. Three years later Lee fell while in Alexandria and broke the other knee. The new break had not healed properly by the time Washington traveled to New York to accept the presidency. Billy set out for New York with Washington's party but was forced to halt at Philadelphia for medical treatment for two months. Washington instructed his secretary to allow Billy to return to Mount Vernon or come on to New York. "He has been an old & faithful Servt," wrote Tobias Lear to Biddle, who was looking after Billy's welfare in Philadelphia. "This is enough for the Presidt to gratify him in every reasonable wish."

Forced to cease serving as Washington's butler and valet after becoming lame, Billy took up cobbling shoes at Mount Vernon. When Washington died he remembered Billy in his will, giving him the choice of his immediate freedom or to remain at Mount Vernon; in either case an annuity of thirty dollars independent of his victuals and clothes, "as a testimony of my sense of his attachment to me, and for his faithful services during the Revolutionary War." Billy opted to continue in his situation at Mount Vernon, cobbling shoes and chatting with war veterans who passed by the manor house for another quarter century. Bushrod Washington, the inheritor of Mount Vernon upon Martha's death, later increased Billy's annuity to $150 a year, and gave him a house. Lee died at Mount Vernon and was buried at a small cemetery where the bodies of slaves and free blacks were interred in the eighteenth and nineteenth centuries.

Billy Lee was featured prominently in several contemporary paintings of Washington, including John Trumbull's *George Washington* (London, 1780), now in the Metropolitan Museum of Art, and Edward Savage's *The Washington Family* (1796), in the National Portrait Gallery in Washington, D.C.

Related entry: Biddle, Clement

Suggestion for further reading:
"To Clement Biddle," 28 July 1784 (*Con. Ser.,* vol. 2).

L'Enfant, Pierre-Charles (1754–1825)

A native of Paris, France, with training in architecture and art, Pierre-Charles L'Enfant came to America in 1777 to serve as an engineer in the Continental army. He was wounded severely at the Battle of Savannah in October 1779 but had recovered in time to be taken prisoner at the fall of Charleston the following year. He was exchanged in 1782 and breveted major at the end of the war. In 1783 he returned to Paris briefly on personal business and to secure for the American Society of the Cincinnati a number of diplomas and medals, of his design, before settling in New York City. When Congress took up the matter of the new Federal City in the fall of 1789, L'Enfant's "Embition" and desire to become a "usefull Citizen" led him to solicit a "share in the Undertaking" from Washington. Washington appointed L'Enfant surveyor and designer for the proposed Federal City in January 1791, and L'Enfant left New York for Georgetown, Maryland, a few weeks later.

It was not L'Enfant's first involvement with a seat of the federal government, for when the Continental Congress left Philadelphia for New York City in 1785, it had employed L'Enfant to supervise the conversion of New York's City Hall into Federal Hall. The scale of the present business was incomparably grander, however, and L'Enfant recognized the necessity of pushing on with the utmost urgency. "I indulge the Idea of seeing soon the progress of the Establishment become the wonder of all," he wrote. The "grand Improvements of publique magnitude" that he planned would serve as models for all the subsequent work as well as "stand to future ages a monument to national genious and munificence." Washington and Jefferson, who were closely involved in setting up the new city on the Potomac, along with Congress, approved L'Enfant's plan to divide the city into simple squares overlaid with a multitude of broad avenues on the scale of a large European city.

Executing the ambitious plan required more delicacy than the talented Frenchman was capable of, however. In addition to architectural conception, where L'Enfant's real genius lay, the work included the tedium of negotiating contracts with numerous landowners in the vicinity and overseeing surveying and construction. The commissioners responsible for the Federal City's public works found him arbitrary and unconciliatory, and in turn L'Enfant considered them men so "little versed in the minutia of such operations" that he refused to work with them—leaving Washington no alternative but to find a replacement. L'Enfant's design for the Federal City was retained, however, and for many years he watched the city develop from a rented room at Rhodes Tavern on Fifteenth Street, where he lived in poverty. He died in Prince George's County, Maryland.

Related entries: Federal City; Thornton, William

Suggestions for further reading:
"From Pierre-Charles L'Enfant," 29 April 1784 (*Con. Ser.*, vol. 1).
"From Pierre-Charles L'Enfant," 6 December 1786 (*Con. Ser.*, vol. 4).
"From Pierre-Charles L'Enfant," 11 September 1789 (*Pres. Ser.*, vol. 4).
"From Pierre-Charles L'Enfant," 22 June 1791 (*Pres. Ser.*, vol. 8).
"From Pierre-Charles L'Enfant," 19 August 1791 (*Pres. Ser.*, vol. 8).
Kite, Elizabeth S. 1929. *L'Enfant and Washington, 1791–1792.* Baltimore.

Lewis, Andrew (1720–1781)

His father was of French Huguenot descent but had lived in Ulster as a Scots-Irishman, his mother came from Loch Lynn in Scotland; together John and Margaret Lewis "furnished five sons to fight the battles of the American revolution," as John Lewis's carved headstone read. (The Lewises found refuge in Virginia with Governor Gooch, a friend of Margaret Lewis's family, in 1732 after John Lewis killed his Irish landlord in a dispute over rents.) Andrew Lewis and his four brothers, including baby Charles, the only "New World child" among the five, all became distinguished for defending English settlers against Indians. Andrew and his brothers grew to adulthood in Staunton, the town founded by their father that became the seat of Augusta County, which extended (or so claimed the burgesses of Virginia) west from the mountains clear to the Mississippi River and up into the Ohio Country.

Andrew, often called "Paddy," had been active in the Augusta militia for several years before receiving a captain's commission in Col. George Washington's Virginia Regiment in 1754. One of his first duties as a new officer was to clear a road to the mouth of Redstone Creek on the Monongahela River for the heavy artillery that was being sent from Alexandria to Washington at Great Meadows, and he was still performing that and other duties when Fort Necessity was surrendered to the French in July 1754. His next major assignment came from Virginia governor Robert Dinwiddie during Braddock's campaign, when he was ordered to protect the citizens living on the Augusta County frontier from incursions of small parties of Indians and French. By the end of 1754 Lewis and his men had erected a fort on Jackson's River in Augusta County, five miles west of Warm Springs (present-day Bath County), christened Fort Dinwiddie.

After Braddock's defeat in July 1755 Washington made Lewis the major of the new Virginia Regiment, sending him to Fredericksburg on a mission to receive new recruits for the regiment. In 1756 Lewis supervised the building of a Virginia fort, commonly called the Cherokee Fort, in the Upper Cherokee Country, for the women and children of the Cherokee and Catawba allied with the British. He was appointed county lieutenant of Augusta County in 1757. In July 1758 Washington adopted "Indian dress" (hunting shirts and leggings) for Lewis and 200 men, whom he sent to Lt. Col. Henry Bouquet of the Royal American Regiment to serve in the Forbes expedition, to the delight of both Bouquet and Gen. John Forbes.

In September 1758 Lewis was recognized for his conduct at Fort Duquesne, where, in Washington's words, marching "up the Virginians with great dispatch and Intrepidity," he saved the Highlanders under British army major James Grant from being cut to pieces, but was captured by the French with Grant and most of his men and taken prisoner to Montreal. After a brief stay at Montreal, the French sent Lewis to Quebec for a year before allowing him to return to Virginia. Unaware at first that Lewis had been taken alive, Washington wrote that Lewis's death was "a great loss to the Regiment, & Colony we have the Honr to serve; he opposd that Expedition to the utmost, unavailingly, but went chearfully upon it after his Sentiments were known, he desired his Friends however to remember (as he went out) that he had opposd it, forseeing I imagine the Disaster that woud happend." When Grant attempted to blame Lewis for the defeat, Lewis challenged him to a duel, which was refused, and Lewis labeled Grant a coward for refusing to fight. Washington supported Lewis's efforts to refute the charges against him.

Given Lewis's knowledge of Native Americans, it was no surprise when in 1768 he was named one of the Virginia commissioners to treat with the Six Nations at Fort Stanwix, along with commissioners from Pennsylvania, New York, and New England. Lewis's unusual "strength, stature, and grave and commanding demeanour" reputedly led the governor of New York at the time to say that "the earth seemed to tremble under him as he walked." After settling in Botetourt County near present-day Salem, Lewis served in several sessions of the Virginia colonial legislature; in fact he was elected to the same session of the House of Burgesses with Washington on the eve of the Revolutionary War, and served in the Virginia conventions of March and December 1775.

Lewis's reputation in Virginia as one of the state's leading military commanders was sufficient for him to be one of the handful of men who were considered candidates to head the Virginia forces at the outbreak of the Revolutionary War. Washington certainly had formed a very high opinion of Lewis's character and abilities and was very pleased when the Continental Congress confirmed Lewis's appointment as brigadier general, as expressed in a letter to his brother John Augustine Washington in March 1776: "The appointment of Lewis I think was also judicious, for notwithstanding the odium thrown upon his Conduct at the Kanawha I always look'd upon him as a Man of Spirit and a good Officer—his experience is equal to any one we have." Not everyone shared Washington's enthusiasm about his old friend's appointment, however. Lewis, observed historian Douglas Southall Freeman, was a good fighter, but he was also "distant and taciturn in manner and lacked art in dealing with persons of station." Lewis had been the commanding general of the Virginia forces that defeated the Indians under Cornstalk at the Battle of Point Pleasant near the mouth of the Kanawha River in May 1774. Despite the victory, Lewis was criticized by some for remaining in the rear during the fighting while his troops suffered heavy casualties. A contemporary ballad encapsulated the views of his critics:

Old Andrew Lewis in his tent he did set
With his cowards around him, alas he did
    sweat,
His blankets spread over him and hearing
    the guns roar,
Saying was I at home I would come here
    no more

Others blamed the heavy casualties at Point Pleasant on Lord Dunmore, however, and Lewis redeemed himself in the eyes of many Virginians in July 1777 when he defeated Lord Dunmore's forces at Gwynn Island near the mouth of the Rappahannock River, causing Dunmore finally to flee the colony altogether.

When Congress failed to promote Lewis to major general in the spring of 1777, Washington tried to soothe Lewis's wounded pride by reminding him that he too "was much disappointed at not perceiving your name in the list of major-generals, and most sincerely wish that the neglect may not induce you to abandon the service. Let me beseech you to reflect that the

period has now arrived when our most vigorous exertions are wanted, when it is highly and indispensably necessary for gentlemen of abilities in any line, but more especially in the military, not to withhold themselves from public employment, or suffer any small punctilios to persuade them to retire from their country's service. The cause requires your aid; no one more sincerely wishes it than I do." Lewis nevertheless resigned his commission in mid-April 1777. He afterward was appointed a commissioner to treat with the Indians at Fort Pitt, and he served on the Virginia executive council from 1780 until his death in Bedford County, Virginia, in September 1781. One of Lewis's sons, Thomas Lewis (1754–1824), occasionally corresponded with Washington in the 1780s and 1790s about land settlement on the Great Kanawha and Ohio Rivers.

Related entries: Braddock Expedition; Dunmore, John Murray, Fourth Earl of

Suggestions for further reading:
"To George William Fairfax," 25 September 1758 (*Col. Ser.*, vol. 6).
"From Andrew Lewis," 31 October 1758 (*Col. Ser.*, vol. 6).
"To John Augustine Washington," 31 March 1776 (*War Ser.*, vol. 3).
"To Andrew Lewis," 30 March 1777 (*War Ser.*, vol. 9).
Johnson, Patricia Givens. 1980. *General Andrew Lewis of Roanoke and Greenbrier.* Christiansburg, VA.

Lewis, Betty Washington (1733–1797)

Betty Lewis was born at Popes Creek, her brother George's birthplace, in the year following his birth and brought up at Ferry Farm, the family farm near Fredericksburg, Virginia. She married Fielding Lewis, Sr., in 1750, and they settled on the outskirts of Fredericksburg, where they erected a handsome mansion, later known as

Kenmore. Washington became good friends and a business associate of his brother-in-law, and he frequently stayed at his sister's home when visiting Fredericksburg on business or traveling to and from Williamsburg.

Fielding Lewis died in 1782, leaving Betty and her children in somewhat reduced circumstances. Betty's stepson John Lewis (1747–1825), the son of her husband's first wife, Catherine Washington Lewis, and a partner in his father's gunpowder manufacture during the Revolutionary War, was to inherit, after his stepmother's death, his father's property in Fredericksburg and Spotsylvania County. Washington helped the family with the settlement of the estate, and in the coming years, he took on the responsibility of seeing that Betty's sons got a start in life. Two of the youngest boys, Robert and Howell, he took into his presidential household as clerks, similar to the way he had taken their older brother George (1757–1821) into his military family at the beginning of the Revolutionary War. Another son, Lawrence, whose first wife, Susannah Edmundson, died in childbirth in 1790 after a year of marriage, was hired in the 1790s to help manage his uncle's property. Lawrence married Martha Washington's granddaughter, Nelly Custis, in 1799.

In turn, Washington sought Betty's assistance in raising the child of another sibling, his niece, Harriot Washington (1776–1822), a daughter of Samuel Washington and his fourth wife, Anne Steptoe Allerton Washington (1739–1777), who became largely dependent on her uncle George after Samuel's death in 1781 and who, after living several years at Mount Vernon, was sent to live with Betty, where she remained for several years until her marriage to Andrew Parks in July 1796. Betty also increasingly took on the responsibility of caring for her aging mother, who had moved from Ferry Farm in early 1772 to a small house on Charles Street in the center of Fredericksburg, about 300 yards from her own home. As Mary Ball Washington's life slowly ebbed away from the ravages

of breast cancer, the responsibility for meeting the doctors, procuring medicine, and generally looking after her welfare fell to Betty. When Mary finally succumbed to her illness in August 1789, Washington was in New York City serving as the country's first president, and Betty's own sons were absent, so the funeral arrangements and the settling of her estate largely fell to Betty.

Betty's own health began to deteriorate in the 1790s, and she found it more and more difficult to maintain the house. In 1796 she went to live with her son George and his wife, Catherine Daingerfield Lewis (1764–1820), at Marmion in King George County, Virginia. She died the following spring while visiting her daughter Betty Lewis Carter (1765–1830) and son-in-law Charles Carter, Jr. (1765–1829), at Western View in Culpeper County, where she had carried her granddaughter Nancy (b. 1790), the daughter of Fielding, Jr., "for the advantage of her education." The "melancholy occasion" of Betty's death, wrote Washington, "filled me with inexpressable concern." No doubt it gave him pause, for the passing of "my *only* sister" left only him and his alcoholic brother Charles of all his siblings.

Related entries: Lewis, Fielding, Sr.; Lewis, Howell; Lewis, Lawrence; Lewis, Robert

Suggestions for further reading:
"To Betty Lewis," 15 March 1789 (*Pres. Ser.*, vol. 1).
"From Betty Lewis," 24 July 1789 (*Pres. Ser.*, vol. 3).
"From Burgess Ball," 25 August 1789 (*Pres. Ser.*, vol. 3).
"From Betty Lewis," 18 May 1790 (*Pres. Ser.*, vol. 5).
"From Betty Lewis," 16 September 1790 (*Pres. Ser.*, vol. 6).
Felder, Paula S. 1998. *Fielding Lewis and the Washington Family*. Fredericksburg, VA.

Lewis, Eleanor Parke Custis ("Nelly"; 1779–1852)

Nelly Custis's close ties with her grandfather began almost at the time of her birth, when, because of the poor health of her mother, Eleanor Calvert Custis ("Nelly"; c.1757–1811), she was sent to Mount Vernon to be nursed, as was her younger brother George Washington Parke Custis ("Wash") after his birth two years later. The tragic death of her father, John Parke Custis, of camp fever contracted during the Battle of Yorktown in 1781, combined with her mother's remarriage in late 1783 to David Stuart (1753–c.1814), a widower who recently had set up a medical practice in Alexandria, resulted in Nelly and Wash's remaining with their grandparents. Giving up the children led their mother to later remark that "there is not an hour in the Day that I do not accuse myself of a failure."

At Mount Vernon, Nelly was exposed to a myriad of visitors that included family, neighbors, former army officers, foreign travelers, and others, but most of her time was spent with her grandmother. The two became particularly close as Martha began to teach Nelly the domestic art of running a refined plantation household and to pass on to her grandchild her own favorite passions of needlework and religious devotion. A tutor, William Shaw, was engaged to teach Nelly and Wash in 1785. Shaw left after a brief stay and was replaced the following year by Tobias Lear, a New Hampshire native who had attended Harvard College. Lear became a permanent fixture in the family, eventually marrying in succession two of Martha's nieces. Lear was satisfied with his charges: "A little Grandson of Mrs. Washington's, by a former husband, and his Sister, the one of 6 and the other of 8 years old afford me no small pleasure & amusement in instructing them, they are, without partiality, as fine children as were ever seen, I never thought I could be so much attached to children as I am to them." Nelly enjoyed learning, especially poetry, which she took delight in composing.

Nelly's life began to change significantly in 1789 when Washington became presi-dent. She and her brother and grandmother joined Washington in New York City, by then a bustling city of more than 20,000 people, about a month after Washington's arrival there. Martha enrolled her in Isabella Graham's school at Number 5 Maiden Lane, one of the most prominent girls' schools in the nation. Her studies became more intense but were supplemented by private lessons in dancing, music, singing, and art taught by the best teachers in the country, and she was exposed to the social life enjoyed by the city's elite—balls, plays, comedies, and museums. When the presidential household moved to Philadelphia, her world grew even larger. In Philadelphia she was introduced to Elizabeth Bordley, the daughter of Washington appointee John Beale Bordley, and the two girls struck up a friendship that lasted more than sixty years. In one of her last letters to "my dear Betsey," written in 1851, Nelly reflected on their early friendship: "Memory still restores to me the dear scenes of our youth, Union Street where I have passed so many happy hours, where the *Sun always appears to shine* as it did in our hearts in those happy days."

Nelly's closest friend in Philadelphia remained her grandmother. Over the years the two had become so inseparable that they found it painful to part company even for a short time. A summer visit with her mother left Nelly nearly panic-stricken. "To part from Grandmama is all I dread," she confided to Bordley. "I have lived with her so long—& she has been more than a Mother to me. It is impossible to love any one, more than I love her, & it will grieve me extremely to part from her." Nelly reminisced about the depth of that love a quarter century after Martha's death: "I prefer'd a *room* in my Beloved Grandmama's house, to a Palace away from her. I was never so happy as when with her—never so *safe,* so secure from misfortune, as when under her maternal eye. I never felt any love so powerful as that which I entertained for the best & most

Beloved of Parents—not even for my children have I ever felt so much as for her."

As for her grandfather, Nelly genuinely loved and esteemed him as the "most affectionate of Fathers." Washington doted on Nelly and her brother, although her friends usually found themselves uncomfortable in the general's presence. "I have often made him laugh heartily at the relation of my frolics and difficulties," she recalled, but "I have never felt that awe of him which others did." Washington purchased a harpsichord for Nelly in 1793, resulting in, wrote Wash in his *Recollections,* untold hours of practice, during which she would "play and cry, and cry and play." Her playing greatly pleased her grandfather, however, and it gratified Nelly to give him pleasure. Washington did not hesitate to mingle his affection for his granddaughter with practical advice, as illustrated by a letter to Nelly written on the occasion of the engagement of an older sister, when Nelly was about 15 years old. "Do not then in your contemplation of the marriage state," he warned, "look for perfect felicity before you consent to wed. Nor conceive, from the fine tales the Poets and lovers of old have told us, of the transports of mutual love, that heaven has taken its abode on earth: Nor do not deceive yourself in supposing, that the only mean by which these are to be obtained, is to drink deep of the cup, and revel in an ocean of love. Love is a mighty pretty thing; but like all other delicious things, it is cloying; . . . love is too dainty a food to live upon alone, and ought not to be considered farther than as a necessary ingredient for that matrimonial happiness which results from a combination of causes."

When it came time for Nelly to think about her own marriage she undoubtedly remembered her grandfather's advice. She had many suitors before Cupid took her by surprise when he "slyly called in Lawrence Lewis to his aid, & transfixed me with a Dart." What's more, it happened "in the *very moment* that I had (after mature considera-

tion) made the *sage* and prudent resolve of passing through life, as a *prim starched Spinster.*" She was pleased with the prospect of marrying. "The Man I have chosen to watch over my future happiness," she said, "is in every respect calculated to ensure it. . . . he is universally esteemed for those virtues which do honour to the Head and Heart." By all accounts her choice of a husband could not have pleased her grandparents more, for Lawrence, a widower twelve years her senior, was a son of Washington's sister, Betty, and said to be the favorite nephew of Washington. The wedding took place on Washington's birthday *new style,* 22 February. Washington gave the newlyweds his gristmill and distillery and his 2,000-acre Dogue Run farm, where they began building Woodlawn, an elegant federal-style brick mansion designed by William Thornton, the architect of the Capitol, about four miles from Mount Vernon on Gray's Hill, the property's highest elevation. The Lewises eventually had eight children, but Nelly outlived all but one, Frances Parke (1799–1875), who was born less than three weeks before Washington's unexpected illness and death. Although Nelly was confined with her infant at Mount Vernon, she was unable to visit her grandfather as he lay dying or attend his funeral, and he was unable to see his infant great-granddaughter.

The next few years were difficult ones for Nelly, and indeed, the rest of her life was characterized more by pain than joy. Her beloved "Grandmama" died in May 1802 when Nelly and her two children were sick with the measles. Less than three weeks later her second daughter, 10-month-old Martha Betty Lewis, died. Nelly was already carrying a third child, Lawrence Fielding Lewis, who was born and died in early August. If losing Martha and two children within a few months was not enough, at Martha's death Mount Vernon became the property of Nelly's brother Wash, and Nelly and Lewis were forced to move to Woodlawn before it was completed. At the new house she delivered five more children over the next decade, all of whom she outlived: Lorenzo (1803–1847), Eleanor Agnes Freire (1805–1820), Fielding Augustine (1807–1809), George Washington Custis (1810–1811), and Mary Eliza Angela (1813–1839). In the 1820s and 1830s the productivity of the Dogue Run farm declined seriously, forcing the Lewises to spend more and more of their time at Audley, their plantation in western Virginia. In 1839 Nelly's youngest child, Angela, died in childbirth, and two months later Lawrence was dead, too. Nelly lived the last decade of her life at Audley, suffering increasingly from arthritis, gradually losing her hearing, and generally declining in health. Woodlawn gradually fell into disarray and was sold in 1846. The following year Lorenzo, of "apparently robust health in the midst of his usefulness," suddenly fell ill and died after a two-week illness. Nelly's remaining child, Frances Parke Butler, was with her husband and family in New Orleans, living "a life," from Nelly's perspective, "of sorrow, privation, anxiety, almost always." Nelly found consolation in the habits of religious devotion that her "Grandmama" had instilled in her more than a half century before. "I live in my own room," she wrote her old friend Elizabeth Bordley in 1848, "except at meals, seldom go out of the front door—work until candle light, & read as long as I can keep my eyes open. I rise always before the Sun & read my prayer Book & Bible until breakfast is ready. Is not *this* a *regular life*." One source of comfort in her last years was the elevation to the presidency of Zachary Taylor. After a two-week stay with the Taylors at the White House she was convinced that the current president was "the *only one worthy* to be the successor of Washington." She looked upon his election as "a peculiar mercy from the Giver of all good." She predicted Taylor would become the "Regenerator of his Country," but her expectations were cut short by Taylor's sudden death in July 1850.

After suffering a stroke in July 1850 Nelly was mostly confined to a wheelchair for the next year, although she was able to receive visitors and keep up her correspondence with her family and friends, especially Elizabeth Bordley. Nelly died after a second stroke. In accordance with her wishes, Nelly's remains were taken back to Mount Vernon for burial alongside her grandparents. Woodlawn is now owned by the National Trust for Historic Preservation and is open to the public.

Related entries: Custis, George Washington Parke; Custis, John Parke; Lear, Tobias; Lewis, Lawrence

Suggestions for further reading:
"To Elizabeth Parke Custis," 14 September 1794 (*Writings,* vol. 33).
Bourne, Miriam Anne. 1982. *First Family: George Washington and His Intimate Relations.* New York.
Brady, Patricia, ed. 1991. *George Washington's Beautiful Nelly.* Columbia, SC.
Ribblett, David L. 1993. *Nelly Custis: Child of Mount Vernon.* Mount Vernon, VA.

Lewis, Fielding, Sr. (1725–1782)

Fredericksburg merchant and storekeeper Fielding Lewis, who was born in Gloucester County, Virginia, was a widower with one son, John (1747–1825), when he married Washington's only sister, Betty, in 1750. In February 1752 Washington surveyed for Lewis an 861-acre tract in Spotsylvania County that adjoined the town of Fredericksburg and was conveyed to Lewis a month later. In 1756, when Washington was fighting the French and Indians on the frontier, Lewis acted as a commissary for a company of associators temporarily attached to the Virginia Regiment and handled the movement and sale of Washington's tobacco crop. He also sought to purchase a slave carpenter for

Washington. In the summer of 1757 Washington relied on Lewis to supply him with a "looking Glass," and "Salt—Molasses," and the next spring he supplied Washington with sixty blankets. Lewis was a Spotsylvania County representative to the Virginia House of Burgesses, in which he chaired several important committees, and he was also county lieutenant for Spotsylvania County. During his frequent trips to Williamsburg, Lewis often conducted business transactions for Washington. In fact, the two men shared a long business association that included speculating in Virginia and North Carolina lands bordering on the Great Dismal Swamp, investing in a scheme for building improvements at the Hot Springs in Augusta County, and buying shares in the agricultural experiment of Italian wine merchant Philip Mazzei (1730–1816) in Albemarle County. Their correspondence is full of mundane matters, exhibiting the easy familiarity that characterized their relationship.

In April 1775, on the eve of his leaving to take command of the Continental army, Washington gave Lewis power of attorney to negotiate all his business at Williamsburg. Lewis, who served on the committee of correspondence and as chairman of the Spotsylvania County committee, played an instrumental role in preparing the state militia's defense against the British by operating, with his son John's help, a gunpowder manufacture. In addition to being empowered with six other men to contract for gunpowder, lead, and flints for the use of the militia, he was commissioned to open a small-arms factory at Fredericksburg, where at his own expense he repaired old muskets, equipped soldiers for service, and financed the construction of the vessel *The Dragon* to guard the entrance of Chesapeake Bay. He was not reimbursed for his expenditures on behalf of the colony, however, and his Fredericksburg home, known later as Kenmore, was sold to pay the debts of his estate in 1796. Washington lamented Lewis's death, and "my concern is encreased by the information . . . of his dying much indebted." After Fielding's death Washington helped educate and find positions for some of the ten surviving children of Fielding and Betty, including Lawrence, Robert ("Bob"), and Howell. Kenmore is now owned by the George Washington's Fredericksburg Foundation and is open to the public.

Related entries: Ferry Farm; Lewis, Betty Washington; Lewis, Howell; Lewis, Lawrence; Lewis, Robert

Suggestions for further reading:
"To Fielding Lewis," 20 April 1773 (*Col. Ser.*, vol. 9).
"From Fielding Lewis," 8 March 1775 (*Col. Ser.*, vol. 10).
"From Fielding Lewis," 23 April 1775 (*Col. Ser.*, vol. 10).
"Memorandum to Fielding Lewis," 30 April 1775 (*Col. Ser.*, vol. 10).
Felder, Paula S. 1998. *Fielding Lewis and the Washington Family.* Fredericksburg, VA.

Lewis, Howell (1771–1822)

Described by his mother as a boy of "very Slender Education" with an "exceeding Good disposition," the eleventh child of Washington's sister, Betty, and her husband, Fielding, entered the protective care of his illustrious uncle in the spring of 1792. The president hoped that having Howell Lewis under his own tutelage in Philadelphia for a few months would be enough to "impress him with ideas, and give him a turn to some pursuit or other that might be serviceable to him hereafter." Tobias Lear, the president's secretary, predicted a longer apprenticeship. "Mr. Lewis possesses excellent dispositions," wrote Lear, "but unfortunately he has been too much in the habits of a young Virginian; but I trust a few years with the President will correct them." In any event, Washington confided to a friend, the young man was spending his time "rather idly," and although he had "no *real* want" of Howell in the presidential household business, he could put him to work as "a writer in my office (if he is fit for it)," copying letters "from breakfast until dinner—Sundays excepted." A similar arrangement had helped Howell's brother Bob get his start in life three years earlier, and Washington was anxious to see the last of his sister's sons overcome the disadvantages resulting from their father's early death.

Lewis worked as a copyist in 1793 and 1794, earning, like his brother before him, $300 a year plus room and board in the presidential mansion. Many of the copies made by Lewis, covering the period between February 1787 and early October 1790, contain mistakes ranging from errors in spelling and punctuation to more serious blunders of misreading and omission, helping to give rise to the "mistaken impression shared by some," says historian and recent editor of Washington's papers W. W. Abbot, "that the mature [Washington] was a bad speller and careless writer."

Although his nephew was still very young and inexperienced in business matters, Washington called upon Howell to take temporary control of Mount Vernon when its farm manager died suddenly in 1793. The resulting correspondence between Washington and Lewis about affairs at the estate, rich in detail about every facet of farm life, reveals the extent to which Washington was concerned not only with occurrences at the farm but also with the development of his nephew's abilities. Reproof, though infrequent, was instructive. The first lesson? Reports are for conveying information, so make them "plain and correct" and above all else full, keeping in mind also that "one part should always corrispond or at least not be inconsistent with, the other part." It might be "well always, when a matter is directed," Washington taught his nephew, "to say whether it is complied with; for the mind is never as-

sured of this until informed." More advice followed. He directed him to consider that there "are two paths always to an order; to wit: giving and executing it, and these always are in distinct persons; and the giver never knows what the receiver does, until it is reported." To assist general conduct and reduce reliance on memory, Washington advised carrying at all times a small "Pocket book" in which notations could be written on the moment. Guidance about moving an empty corn house while the ground was still hard evolved into a discourse about an old saying: "And speaking of this I will mention a proverb to you which you will find worthy of attention all the days of your life; under any circumstances, or in any situation you may happen to be placed; and that is, to put nothing off 'till the Morrow, that you can do to day. the habit of postponing things is among the worst in the world; doing things in season is always beneficial; but out of season, it frequently happens that so far from being beneficial, that oftentimes, it proves a real injury. It was one of the sayings of the wise man you know, that there is a season for all things, and nothing is more true; apply it to any occurence or transaction in life." Such admonitions were given, Washington assured his nephew, "not with a view to find fault, but to shew you the advantages of correctness; and, as you are a young man just advancing into life and business, to impress you with the propriety and importance of giving attention, and doing whatever you undertake, well."

Lewis eventually left his uncle's patronage, married Ellen Hackley Pollard (1776–1859), and settled in Culpeper County, Virginia. Washington's diary entries indicate that his nephew sometimes returned to Mount Vernon for visits, for five days in January 1798, for instance, and for ten days ending on 9 December 1799, just five days before Washington's unexpected death. Lewis later wrote of his uncle, who had named him a beneficiary in his will, "I have sometimes thought him decidedly the handsomest man I ever saw; and when in a lively mood, so full of pleasantry, so agreeable to all with whom he was associated, that I could hardly realize that he was the same Washington whose dignity awed all who approached him."

Related entries: Lewis, Betty Washington; Lewis, Fielding, Sr.; Lewis, Robert

Suggestions for further reading:
Diaries, vol. 6.
"To Betty Lewis," 8 April 1792 (*Writings,* vol. 32).
"To Charles Carter," 19 May 1792 (*Writings,* vol. 32).
"To Howell Lewis," 18 August 1793 (*Writings,* vol. 33).
"To Howell Lewis," 25 August 1793 (*Writings,* vol. 33).
"To Howell Lewis," 3 November 1793 (*Writings,* vol. 33).
Bourne, Miriam Anne. 1982. *First Family: George Washington and His Intimate Relations.* New York.
Felder, Paula S. 1998. *Fielding Lewis and the Washington Family.* Fredericksburg, VA.

Lewis, Lawrence (1767–1839)

Lawrence Lewis, a son of Washington's sister, Betty, was often said to be the favorite nephew of the master of Mount Vernon. Lawrence's first wife, Susannah Edmundson, whom he married in 1789, died in childbirth in 1790. He served as an aide-de-camp to Gen. Daniel Morgan during the Whiskey Rebellion and, after being recommended by his uncle to the secretary of war, James McHenry, was offered a captaincy in the light dragoons in January 1799, which he declined.

In the summer of 1797 Washington asked Lawrence to make his home at Mount Vernon, an offer Lewis accepted, arriving at the estate to take up residence on 31 August 1797. From the outset Washington made it clear to the younger man, who was suffering from failing health as well as melancholy, "that you, servant (if you bring one) and horses, will fare in all respects as We, & mine do; but that I shall expect no Services from you for which pecuniary compensation will be made. I have already as many on wages as are sufficient to carry on my business, and more indeed than I can find means to pay, conveniently. As both your Aunt and I are in the decline of life, and regular in our habits, especially in our hour of rising & going to bed, I require some person (fit & Proper) to ease me of the trouble of entertaining company; particularly Nights, as it is my inclination to retire (and unless prevented by very particular company, always do retire) either to bed, or to my study, soon after candle light. In taking these duties (which hospitality obliges one to bestow on company) off my hands, it would render me a very acceptable Service. And for a little time *only,* to come, an hour in the day, now and then, devoted to the recording of some Papers which time would not allow me to complete before I left Philadelphia, would also be acceptable. Besides these, I know nothing at present, that would require any portion of your time, or attention: both of which, if you have inclination for it, might be devoted to Reading, as I have a great many instructive Books, on many subjects, as well as amusing ones; or, they might be employed in sporting, there being much game of all sorts here; or in riding, & viewing the management of my farms, from whence something useful may be drawn, as I think Mr [James] Anderson in many things could give you useful lessons and a better insight into husbandry than your opportunities have, Hitherto, presented to you." Washington hastened to make sure Lawrence understood that none of the foregoing was meant to "restrain you from attending to your own affairs, or restrain you from visiting your friends at pleasure; all I have in view by making this communication is to guard against misconception on either side."

Lawrence's residence at Mount Vernon provided him with one benefit not foreseen by his uncle: on 22 February 1799, Washington's sixty-seventh birthday, Lawrence married Martha Washington's granddaughter Nelly Custis at Mount Vernon. Shortly before the nuptials Washington wrote to another nephew, Bartholomew Dandridge, about the impending event. "Lawrence Lewis," he wrote, "is appointed a Captn in the Corps of light Dragoons; but before he enters the Camp of Mars, he is to engage in that of Venus with Nelly Custis, on the 22d of next month; they having, while I was at Philadelphia, without my having the smallest suspicion that such an affair was in agitation, formed their Contract for this purpose."

Washington rented his Dogue Run farm, mill, and distillery to Lewis in the fall of 1799, and he later informed Lawrence that he was leaving him in his will the outlying farm land, along with the improvements, totaling, he estimated, about 2,000 acres, that the young couple might settle permanently adjacent to Mount Vernon. Washington also named Lewis one of the executors of his estate. Shortly after Washington's death Lawrence built Woodlawn, designed by architect William Thornton, who also designed the U.S. Capitol. Woodlawn, now owned by the National Trust for Historic Preservation and open to the public, Lewis later declared to be "worse than nothing" because of the expense of maintaining the house and operating the plantation in the face of poor harvests and declining profits. Lewis took little interest in farming. In fact, Lewis never was a very energetic person and, according to Nelly, could not be expected to struggle much against the difficulties of life, for, she later wrote, he "loves to be a *genuine Virginian,* that is, to have plenty of servants for every purpose."

In his last hours Washington expressed a desire to see Lawrence and his step-grandson George Washington Parke Custis, who were away in New Kent County, and who together in 1831 erected the new family tomb in which Washington's remains rest today.

Related entries: Lewis, Betty Washington; Lewis, Eleanor Parke Custis; Lewis, Fielding, Sr.; Lewis, Howell; Lewis, Robert

Suggestions for further reading:
Diaries, vol. 6.
"From Lawrence Lewis," 24 July 1797 (*Ret. Ser.,* vol. 1).
"To Lawrence Lewis," 4 August 1797 (*Ret. Ser.,* vol. 1).
"From Lawrence Lewis," 21 November 1798 (*Ret. Ser.,* vol. 3).
"To Lawrence Lewis," 2 December 1798 (*Ret. Ser.,* vol. 3).
"To Lawrence Lewis," 20 September 1799 (*Ret. Ser.,* vol. 4).
Felder, Paula S. 1998. *Fielding Lewis and the Washington Family.* Fredericksburg, VA.

Lewis, Robert ("Bob"; 1769–1829)

On the eve of leaving Mount Vernon to take the helm of the new national government at New York in 1789, Washington anticipated the need to take in "a young person in my family of a good disposition, who writes a good hand, and who can confine himself a certain reasonable number of hours in the 24 to the recording of letters in books, which will be provided for their reception from the separate papers on which they now are, and will be first draughted." Washington's thoughts immediately turned to Robert Lewis, the tenth child of his sister, Betty, and her husband, Fielding. Robert was a likeable young man of twenty who had grown up at Kenmore, the family plantation on the outskirts of Fredericksburg, Virginia, and schooled at the academy in town. "If Bob is of opinion that this employment will suit his inclination," Washington wrote his sister, "and he will take his chance for the allowance that will be made (which cannot be great as there are hundreds who would be glad to come in) I should be very glad to give him the preference. He will be at no expence (except in the article of clothing) as he will be one of the family and live as we do." Bob Lewis eagerly accepted the offer, telling his uncle that "I shall ever consider myself under a thousand obligations for the proffered post, and think the confinement you speak off rather a pleasure, and hope from my assiduous attention to merit the station." Young Lewis's salary was set at $300 a year plus, as his uncle promised, room and board—he even was instructed not to bring a horse, unless he should be willing to sell it after his arrival in the city. Lewis accompanied Martha Washington to New York the following May, where his dual position as a family member and a trusted assistant on Washington's staff gave him ample opportunity to meet influential persons passing through the presidential mansion. "I am, of so much more consequence here, than when at home," he wrote his mother after settling into his new situation, "that I believe, I shall never be content to live anywhere else." His initial enthusiasm waned over time, however, and before the end of two years he left his uncle's employment and returned to Virginia.

In January 1791, in an affectionate letter, written, he said, to "avoid the Embarassment which I apprehended to myself from personal communications of this matter in the first instance," Lewis informed his uncle of his engagement to Judith Carter Browne (1773–1830) of Elsing Green in King William County, Virginia. Aware of the "consequence which might attend My connexion with you, Sir," he promised to discuss the matter at length in a future conversation, hinting that he planned to continue to profit from the patronage of "an Uncle whom I love with the purest affection." At the same time he professed himself to be just as pleased to "carry me into the retirement of a Country life," so long as he took along the "continuance of your regards, which I value far above all price."

Lewis soon left the presidential household, by then relocated in Philadelphia, for Virginia. In the summer of 1791 Lewis assumed temporary management of Mount Vernon when the estate's farm manager became ill. Washington must have approved of the way his nephew acted that season, for by the following year Lewis was managing Washington's landholdings in western Virginia (Fauquier, Loudoun, Frederick, and Berkeley counties, and Winchester), a position filled with responsibilities such as making leases, collecting rents, and buying and selling tracts and house lots. Lewis and his young wife settled at Spring Hill in Fauquier County. In the spring of 1793 Washington gave Lewis a 400-acre tract in Stafford County that he had inherited from his mother (handed down from her father), lying on the road near the "Accocreek old Furnace" [Accokeek Iron Works] about eight miles from Falmouth, across the Rappahannock River from Fredericksburg. Long overrun with trespassers, Lewis encountered numerous difficulties gaining control of the property. A larger gift followed in 1796, Washington's long-neglected tract of 1,369 acres in Fauquier County left to him by his father more than a half century before, located about fifteen miles northwest of Fredericksburg on Deep Run, a creek flowing into the Rappahannock River. The second gift, said Washington, was presented to Lewis "in Consideration of natural affection and the sum of ten pounds Current money." Washington also remembered Bob Lewis (along with the rest of Betty's children) when making his will in July 1799.

Lewis served several terms as mayor of Fredericksburg later in his life.

Related entries: Lewis, Betty Washington; Lewis, Fielding, Sr.; Lewis, Howell

Suggestions for further reading:
Diaries, vols. 5–6.
"To Betty Lewis," 15 March 1789 (Pres. Ser., vol. 1).

"From Robert Lewis," 18 March 1789 (*Pres. Ser.*, vol. 1).

"From Robert Lewis," 10 January 1791 (*Pres. Ser.*, vol. 7).

"To Robert Lewis," 29 April 1793 (*Writings*, vol. 32).

"To Robert Lewis," 18 May 1794 (*Writings*, vol. 32).

"From Robert Lewis," 26 October 1797 (*Ret. Ser.*, vol. 1).

"To Robert Lewis," 23 January 1799 (*Ret. Ser.*, vol. 3).

Bourne, Miriam Anne. 1982. *First Family: George Washington and His Intimate Relations.* New York.

Felder, Paula S. 1998. *Fielding Lewis and the Washington Family.* Fredericksburg, VA.

Liberty Hall Academy

See Education; James River Company.

Lincoln, Benjamin (1733–1810)

Benjamin Lincoln, a farmer from Hingham, Massachusetts, educated in the common schools, served as town clerk (after his father and grandfather), justice of the peace, and a representative in the Massachusetts provincial congress. He began his Revolutionary War military service as a lieutenant colonel in the Suffolk County militia, which he marched to Cambridge in April 1775. The provincial congress soon elected him mustermaster of Massachusetts, and in July he even stood in as president of the provincial congress. When the Massachusetts General Court superseded the provincial congress, he was in July 1775 elected to its governing inner circle, the Massachusetts council. He was appointed brigadier general of the militia in February 1776 and promoted to major general the following May. The next month he experienced combat for the first time when he took part in breaking the British blockade at Boston. In September 1776 the Massachusetts House of Representatives placed him in command of about 5,000 men drafted from the state as "temporary forces" to reinforce the Continental army at New York. Lincoln mustered his troops in time to join the main American line at the Battle of White Plains on 28 October 1776, and after the Continental army fled New York across New Jersey, Lincoln traveled to Providence for more militia reinforcements. He was back at Peekskill, New York, in time to assist Maj. Gen. William Heath's unsuccessful attempt to recapture Fort Independence from the British in January 1777. Lincoln afterward crossed the Hudson River with his reinforcements and led them to Morristown, New Jersey, the site where Washington had chosen to winter the main army.

A few days later the Continental Congress commissioned Lincoln a major general in the Continental army on the strength of Washington's recommendation: "I should not do him justice, were I not to add, that he is a Gentleman well worthy of notice in the Military line. he commanded the Militia from Massachusetts last Summer or Fall rather, and much to my satisfaction, having proved himself on all occasions, an active, spirited, sensible man. I do not know whether it is his wish, to remain in the military line, or whether if he should, any thing under the rank he now holds in the State he comes from, would satisfy him— how far an appointment of this kind might offend the Continental Brigadiers, I cannot undertake to say."

It was not long before Washington called upon Lincoln to assist Maj. Gen. Philip Schuyler in the northern department. He wrote Schuyler about Lincoln: "This Gentleman has always Supported the Character of a judicious, brave, active Officer, and as he is exceeding popular and much respected in the State of Massachusetts . . . he will have a degree of influence over the Militia, which cannot fail being very advantageous. I have destined him more particularly to the command of them, and I promise myself it will have a powerful tendency to make them turn out with more cheerfulness, and to inspire them with perseverance to remain in the field." Lincoln may not have been one of Washington's brilliant generals, in the way that Nathanael Greene was, but, like Washington, Lincoln's integrity earned for him the love and respect of his men. Lame and undramatic, without any pompousness, it was not so much his kind and amiable countenance, his gentle wit, or his gracious manner that endeared him to the soldiers. Rather, like Washington, his obvious integrity commanded respect. Everyone knew that he was reliable, methodical, sober, frugal, pious, and temperate. One writer from the nineteenth century said he was "almost too good a man for a warrior."

In the Saratoga campaign in the fall of 1777, Lincoln led militia troops in attacks on the British supply lines in and around Fort Ticonderoga, finally assuming command of Maj. Gen. Horatio Gates's right wing. Lincoln's right ankle was shattered during a reconnaissance of the front lines after the battle of Bemis Heights, effectively keeping him from active service until August 1778. For their roles in that battle, Washington presented generals Lincoln and Benedict Arnold with "shoulder and sword knots." When Lincoln returned to active service, Congress ordered him to the southern department, where his experience commanding militia would be especially useful. He became extremely popular with not only the soldiers but also the political leaders of the region, and he was forced to remain in service long after he sought to relinquish his command. A series of British maneuvers combined with the chronic uncertainty of American support for the Continental army prevented Lincoln from achieving any major successes in the south. He was captured when Charleston fell to the British after a six-week siege in the spring of 1780, paroled to Philadelphia, and exchanged the following November.

When Massachusetts wrote a new constitution in 1780 many clamored for Lincoln to become the first governor, but he modestly declined, unwilling to enter politics. After a winter in Massachusetts he rejoined Washington in New York. He led the Continental army on its desperate 400-mile march to Virginia, where he took part in the Yorktown campaign; in fact Washington directed Cornwallis to receive his instructions regarding surrender from Lincoln. Lincoln conducted the royal troops to the field selected for laying down of arms and there received Cornwallis's sword. While at Yorktown he was appointed the first secretary at war, an office he held until the fall of 1783. At the peace he returned to his home in Hingham, where he supplemented his modest income from farming with various commercial ventures and modest land speculation. In 1786 he briefly left private life to command the volunteer militia raised to disperse the insurgents taking part in the rebellion led by Daniel Shays (1747–1825). In 1788 Lincoln was elected lieutenant governor of Massachusetts, a largely ceremonial post he held with competency and dignity, but his postwar political career in the state was hampered by his strong Federalist stance and the petty jealousy of Gov. John Hancock. In the fall of that same year, while ratification of the Constitution was being discussed across the country, Lincoln kept Washington informed of the political mood in his state, which was unanimous, he declared, in its approval of Washington as the future first president, as well as the national political aspirations of Hancock and John Adams.

In 1789 Lincoln appealed to Washington for a position in the new federal government, and Washington named him collector of the port of Boston, a lucrative office he held until a year before his death. Washington also called on Lincoln to treat with the Indians in the south and in the northwest in the early 1790s.

Related entry: Opinion of the General Officers, 9 March 1792 (Selected Writings)

Suggestions for further reading:
"To John Hancock," 20 December 1776 (*War Ser.*, vol. 7).
"To John Hancock," 14 January 1777 (*War Ser.*, vol. 8).
"To Benjamin Lincoln," 26 October 1788 (*Pres. Ser.*, vol. 1).
"From Benjamin Lincoln," 20 February 1789 (*Pres. Ser.*, vol. 1).
"Opinion of the General Officers," 9 March 1792 (*Writings*, vol. 31).
Lawrence, Alexander A. 1951. *Storm over Savannah*. Athens, GA.
Mattern, David B. 1995. *Benjamin Lincoln and the American Revolution*. Columbia, SC.
Uhlendorf, Bernhard A., ed. 1938. *Siege of Charleston*. Ann Arbor, MI.

Livingston, William (1723–1790)

William Livingston, a 1741 graduate of Yale College from Albany, New York, and an early and avid supporter of the American cause against Great Britain, studied law in New York City, where he was admitted to the bar in 1748. In 1772 he resettled in Elizabeth, New Jersey, where he penned anti-British tracts and satire, sharpening a talent he had exercised since the early 1750s, when he published *The Independent Reflector*, a weekly New York newspaper. Livingston also published the first of two editions of *A Digest of Laws of New York* in 1752, and he wrote poetry during the decade before.

Livingston's first contact with Washington occurred during the spring of 1776, when as a member of the New Jersey delegation to the Continental Congress, he served on a congressional committee appointed to confer with Washington about the current state of the American war effort. Livingston also took an active part in the ensuing military campaign as brigadier general of the New Jersey militia and was responsible for raising reinforcements from his state for the New York campaign. Elected governor of New Jersey in 1776 to replace the ousted William Franklin, the Loyalist son of Benjamin Franklin, Livingston was engaged in constant communication with Washington after the Continental army evacuated New York and went into winter quarters at Morristown, New Jersey. His former service in the militia made Livingston sensitive to the difficulties faced by Washington as commander in chief of the American forces, and as governor Livingston goaded an often-reluctant legislature to undertake measures advocated by Washington.

Although his responsibilities as a wartime governor allowed little time for literary pursuits, Livingston did find time to occasionally write for the newspapers. Livingston arranged for one lengthy composition, "The Impartial Chronicle," a satire of Hugh Gaine's Loyalist newspaper, the *New-York Gazette: and the Weekly Mercury*, to be printed in the Philadelphia *Pennsylvania Packet* in February 1777. He sent a copy of the "Chronicle" to Washington with the design of affording him "a little Diversion in a Leisure moment," and Washington's reaction was favorable. "Fraught with the most poignant Satire," is how Washington described the piece, adding, "it afforded me real pleasure."

Correspondence between Livingston and Washington ended with the Revolutionary War, although Livingston attended the Federal Constitutional Convention in 1787. He did send Washington a polite address upon the latter's ascension to the presidency in 1788. Livingston held the governor's office until his death at Elizabeth in 1790.

Related entry: Constitutional Convention

Suggestions for further reading:
"From William Livingston," 28 June 1776 (*War Ser.*, vol. 5).
"To William Livingston," 28 June 1776 (*War Ser.*, vol. 5).

"From William Livingston," 27 November 1776 (*War Ser.*, vol. 7).

"To William Livingston," 24 January 1777 (*War Ser.*, vol. 8).

"To William Livingston," 14 March 1778 (*Writings*, vol. 11).

"The Impartial Chronicle," the *Pennsylvania Packet* (Philadelphia), 18 February 1777.

Prince, Carl E., et al., eds. 1979–1988. 5 vols. *The Papers of William Livingston*. New Brunswick, NJ.

Long Island, Battle of

After moving his army from Boston to the New York area in the spring of 1776, Washington initially stationed half of his troops in the string of forts and redoubts erected the previous year by the Americans along the shore of Manhattan Island. The other half of his force, about 9,000 men, he concentrated on Long Island's Brooklyn Heights, a strategic eminence commanding New York City. The Americans spent the summer fortifying Brooklyn Heights, but it remained vulnerable to a British attack because of the ease with which Gen. William Howe could move the main body of his army from its Staten Island encampment to Long Island. The similarity between the American position in New York and the British in Boston was not lost on Howe, whose failure to control Bunker Hill and Dorchester Heights had led to his army being driven out of Boston. Accordingly, on 22 and 23 August, Howe landed 20,000 men on Long Island at Gravesend Bay, about ten miles from the American works. Washington wrote four days later that the British "Marched through the Flat & level Land, which is quite free of Wood, till they (or part of them) got within abt three Miles of our Lines, where they are now Incampd; A Wood & broken ground lying between Us. What there real design is I know not."

Expecting an attack on New York City, Washington thought the enemy force on Long Island much smaller than it actually was, and he sent over only minor reinforcements to Brooklyn Heights. By the time it became clear to Washington, on the evening of 26 August, that "the grand push" was intended for Brooklyn Heights, British and Hessian troops secretly had outflanked the only American troops sent out from the American works, about 5,000 Continental army troops in two divisions, commanded by major generals Lord Stirling and John Sullivan. Stirling's troops were the first to be surprised, when between two and three o'clock in the morning of 27 August they encountered 5,000 British Highlanders under Maj. Gen. James Grant advancing up the Gowanus Road, one of the main roads leading to Brooklyn Heights from the British disembarkation point. After a four-hour fight most of the American troops made it back to Brooklyn Heights, although Lord Stirling was taken prisoner.

Meanwhile, Sullivan's troops at Flatbush Pass were cannonaded by a corps of Hessians under Lt. Gen. Leopold Philipp, Freiherr von Heister (d. 1777), and driven into a larger British force marching against them from Old Jamaica Road. General Sullivan, too, was captured. By eight o'clock in the evening Howe had concentrated his whole force within striking distance of Washington's forces at Brooklyn Heights, where "they mean to attack and force us from our Lines by way of regular approaches rather than in any other manner." Strong winds and ebbing tides had prevented five British warships from joining the fray, which undoubtedly would have worsened the predicament of the American troops. When it was all over Washington's forces had lost 200 to 300 men killed and nearly 1,100 captured, while British and Hessian casualties amounted to 63 men killed, 283 wounded, and 21 taken prisoner.

Reluctant to follow up his victory by immediately storming the American defenses, Howe on the day after the battle di-

Washington's retreat from Long Island, 1776 (Library of Congress)

rected his troops to begin digging trenches and building breastworks. On the same day, some "pretty smart" skirmishing took place between American and British riflemen before an incessant rain rendered their weapons useless. At a council of war on the 29th Washington and his generals unanimously agreed to abandon Long Island for New York City, and the withdrawal began under the cover of darkness that same evening. The British began to suspect something was awry during the early-morning hours of 30 August, but by the time they entered the American breastworks at half past four, a dense fog had settled over the area, concealing the Americans as they were ferried across the East River. Washington reputedly was the last man to step in the last boat that left the landing.

Related entries: Boston, Siege of; Kip's Bay, New York

Suggestions for further reading:
"To John Hancock," 26, 29 August 1776 (*War Ser.*, vol. 6).
"Robert Hanson Harrison to John Hancock," 27 August 1776 (*War Ser.*, vol. 6).
"Council of War," 29 August 1776 (*War Ser.*, vol. 6).
"From Lord Stirling," 29 August 1776 (*War Ser.*, vol. 6).
"To Lund Washington," 29 August 1776 (*War Ser.*, vol. 6).
Manders, Eric I. 1978. *The Battle of Long Island.* Monmouth Beach, NJ.

Alexander McDougall, from a miniature by John Ramage (New-York Historical Society)

M

McDougall, Alexander
(1732–1786)

Alexander McDougall was born at Islay, on the southern tip of the Inner Hebrides, Scotland, about four or five months after the birth of Washington. When he was 6 years old his family immigrated to America and settled at New York City, where as a youth McDougall began to engage in trade under the tutelage of his father, who got his own start in the city by peddling milk. During the French and Indian War, McDougall briefly united his mercantile interests with a seafaring life by commanding two privateering vessels, the *Tyger* and the *Barrington*.

When war loomed on the horizon between the American colonies and Great Britain, McDougall, by then a successful merchant known for his bold espousal of revolutionary principles, was indicted and jailed for writing anti-British tracts, including "A Son of Liberty to the Betrayed Inhabitants of the City and Colony of New York" (1769), in which he contrasted the legislature of New York with the legislatures of the other colonies. Every member of the colonial New York legislature censured McDougall's tract as "an infamous and seditious libel," except for Philip Schuyler, his future comrade-in-arms. Imprisonment in 1770 and 1771 did not

dampen McDougall's courage, however, and his admirers among the colony's citizens soon outnumbered his critics. After months in jail, the undaunted McDougall could exclaim, "I rejoice that I am the first sufferer for liberty since the commencement of our glorious struggle." After his release from confinement he was elected to the New York provincial congress, where he became a leader among the radicals, and in late June 1775, that body appointed him colonel of the First New York Regiment.

Although Washington expected McDougall to join the Continental army at Cambridge, Massachusetts, to assist in the siege of Boston, McDougall recognized that he was needed more in the New York provincial congress to counter the conservatives who were seeking reconciliation with Great Britain. Washington, declaring to Philip Schuyler that McDougall's "Zeal is unquestionable," agreed, and instead relied upon McDougall to scavenge the New York area for cannon and ammunition badly needed by the American forces at Cambridge.

McDougall was promoted to brigadier general in August 1776, and later that same month, Washington, because of McDougall's nautical experience, chose him to superintend the embarkation of the troops retreating from Brooklyn after the Battle of Long Island. McDougall's health rapidly deteriorated during the fall of 1776, and by mid-December 1776, while headquartered at Morristown, New Jersey, he was hinting to Washington that he wanted to resign his commission and leave the army. Washington persuaded McDougall to "try whether a little Rest might not contribute to the Cure of a Disorder which is generally brought on by Colds and Fatigue." The suggestion seemingly was enough, for only two weeks later McDougall was writing back expressing confidence in his full recovery. In fact, McDougall's exertions during the ensuing campaign so satisfied Washington that he was moved to write and commend him: "I wish every officer in the army could appeal to his own heart, and find the same principles of conduct that I am persuaded actuate you: we should then experience more consistency, zeal, and steadiness, than we do now, in but too many instances." That zeal and consistency prompted Washington to praise McDougall several more times during the course of the war, and years later Washington lamented McDougall's passing in a letter to Thomas Jefferson, calling McDougall "a brave Soldier and a disinterested patriot."

After the Battle of Germantown in 1777, Washington recommended McDougall for promotion to major general, writing to the president of the Continental Congress, "From his abilities, military knowledge, and approved bravery, he has every claim to promotion. If I mistake not, he was passed over in the last appointments of major-generals, and younger officers preferred before him; but his disinterested attachment to the service prevented his acting in the manner that is customary in like circumstances." Congress duly promoted him. In the spring of 1778, Washington ordered McDougall to superintend the construction of the Hudson River fortifications in the highlands of New York, and he served as the commanding general in the highlands until the fall of 1780, when he became a delegate to the Continental Congress. Washington advised McDougall to

accept the post, writing that "I think your presence there, at this juncture, while all the arrangements for the next Campaign are before them, would be of so much utility, that I cannot but take the liberty to urge your immediate compliance with the pleasure of the State. It appears to me, you can in no way at this time, so essentially serve the public as by going there; the moment is singularly critical; and the determinations depending must have the greatest influence upon our future affair." Congress later appointed McDougall secretary of marine affairs, but he declined the post.

After the Revolutionary War, McDougall was elected to a second term in the Continental Congress as well as to the New York Senate, an office he held at his death. He also played prominent roles in the establishment of the Bank of New York and in the Society of the Cincinnati, serving as president of both organizations. McDougall died in his adopted city and was buried at the First Presbyterian Church.

Related entry: Boston, Siege of

Suggestions for further reading:
"From Alexander McDougall," 2 January 1776 (*War Ser.*, vol. 3).
"To Alexander McDougall," 21 December 1776 (*War Ser.*, vol. 7).
"To Alexander McDougall," 9 February 1779 (*Writings*, vol. 14).
"To Alexander McDougall," 8 May 1779 (*Writings*, vol. 15).
"To Alexander McDougall," 24 October 1780 (*Writings*, vol. 20).
"To Thomas Jefferson," 1 August 1786 (*Writings*, vol. 28).
Champagne, Roger J. 1975. *Alexander McDougall and the American Revolution in New York*. Schenectady, NY.

McHenry, James (1753–1816)

James McHenry, a Scots-Irish native of Antrim County, Ireland, was classically educated in Dublin before emigrating to Baltimore in 1771. His father and brother soon followed him to Maryland and established a thriving import business, the assets of which McHenry inherited in 1790. McHenry enrolled in Newark Academy in Delaware in 1772 and later studied medicine under Dr. Benjamin Rush (1746–1813). He became a surgeon in the Continental army hospital at Cambridge, Massachusetts, in 1776, and the following August he was appointed surgeon of the Fifth Pennsylvania Regiment. Captured at the fall of Fort Washington in New York on 16 November 1776 and paroled in early 1777, McHenry was allowed to care for other sick paroled prisoners, under Washington's direction. Washington was so pleased with McHenry's care of the prisoners that when McHenry was exchanged in 1778 he asked him to join his military family as an aide-de-camp. McHenry served in that post until 1780, when he joined the staff of Lafayette. McHenry was promoted to major a few months before retiring from the service in 1781.

That year McHenry was elected to the Maryland Senate, a seat he held for five years. Washington, always pleased to have an ally in elected office, congratulated McHenry's election to the senate seat with a paraphrase of a Latin proverb: "You know it is an old and true Maxim that to make a good peace, you ought to be well prepared to carry on the War." McHenry was a Maryland delegate to the Continental Congress from 1783 to 1786, and in 1787 he was a member of the Constitutional Convention. Washington appointed McHenry secretary of war in 1796 when Timothy Pickering became Washington's new secretary of state. Later, during the preparation for a possible war with France in 1798, Washington came to regret McHenry's appointment "*sorely*. . . . I early discovered . . . that his talents were unequal to great exertions, or deep resources. In truth they were not expected; for the fact is, it was a Hobson's choice." John Adams finally forced McHenry's resignation in May 1800, and he

retired to his country estate near Baltimore, where he wrote a number of books and engaged in philanthropic work. A fort in Maryland that McHenry was instrumental in constructing was later renamed in his honor and made famous by Francis Scott Key during the War of 1812. In 1807 McHenry published a Baltimore city directory, and in 1813 he was president of the first Bible society founded in the city. McHenry died in Baltimore.

When recommending McHenry for a diplomatic secretaryship in 1783, Washington called him "a man of Letters and Abilities, of great integrity, sobriety and prudence. In a word, a Man of strict honor; possessing all those good qualities (without a bad one with which I am acquainted) necessary to fit him for such an Office. . . . he is of an amiable temper; very obliging, and of polished manners."

Related entries: Pickering, Timothy; Presidency; Quasi-War

Suggestions for further reading:
"To James McHenry," 11 December 1781 (*Writings,* vol. 23).
"To James Madison," 22 April 1783 (*Writings,* vol. 26).
"To James McHenry," 5, 14 September 1798 (*Ret. Ser.,* vol. 2).
Steiner, Bernard C., ed. 1907. *The Life and Correspondence of James McHenry.* Cleveland.

Mackay, James (d. 1785)

See Account of the Capitulation of Fort Necessity (Selected Writings).

Madison, James (1751–1836)

George Washington first met James Madison in Philadelphia in August 1781 while Washington was on his march to Yorktown and Madison was serving in the Continental Congress. Washington was immediately impressed by the delegate from Virginia, nineteen years his junior, whom he recognized, in the words of a recent historian, as "a rising, competent, and dedicated public servant on whom he could count as an ally." Two years later the men began one of the most important collaborations of the early republic when they worked together to enlist support from the states for Congress's proposal to create a revenue sufficient to support the Confederation government. The result of their efforts, in 1783, Madison's "Address to the States" of 25 April, an explanation of Congress's plan, and Washington's "Circular to the Governors" of 8 June, his exhortation for the plan's acceptance, would not be the last time the men worked in tandem to buttress an increasingly weak federal government.

The collaboration between Madison and Washington continued after the Revolutionary War when Madison, as a member of the Virginia general assembly, secured, with Washington's guidance, legislation for improving the navigation of the Potomac and James Rivers—projects that had interested Washington for nearly as long as Madison had been alive. The genuine friendship that developed during the months they worked on the navigation bill soon had important repercussions, for it placed Madison in a position where he could make the case to Washington that his attendance at the Constitutional Convention was crucial for its chances of success and could urge him to head the Virginia delegation to the Convention. As it turned out, both men made important contributions at the Convention, Washington by bestowing legitimacy on the proceedings with his presence and prestige and Madison by drafting and arguing for important provisions in the Constitution.

As president, Washington relied on Madison primarily for drafting important messages, although he often sought Madison's advice about constitutional questions, federal appointments, and executive etiquette. One interesting example of the ex-
tent to which Madison and Washington worked together is Washington's first inaugural address. Not only did Madison prepare the draft of the address and, as a member of the new Congress, the reply to the address from the House of Representatives, but he also drafted Washington's reply to Congress's reply! By the end of his first term, however, Washington had become more dependent on his cabinet, and thus he consulted Madison less frequently. Madison increasingly found himself at odds with the president's policies as they were more and more influenced by Alexander Hamilton, especially the policies regarding the nation's finances. During Washington's second administration Madison's opposition to Washington's Neutrality Proclamation, the Jay Treaty, and Washington's stance on the Whiskey Insurrection, among other things, sealed the end of their friendship.

Near the end of his first administration Washington asked Madison to draft for him a farewell address that would serve as his legacy to the people of the United States. When Washington made the decision to serve a second term, he set aside Madison's draft, but in 1796 he sent it to Madison's political enemy, Hamilton, for incorporation into a revised farewell address. Hamilton discarded much of Madison's work, but nevertheless, about one-third of the final address was based on Madison's original draft.

On the day Washington became sick with the illness that killed him in December 1799, he asked his secretary, Tobias Lear, to read from the public papers "the debates of the Virginia Assembly on the election of a Senator and Governor;—and on hearing Mr. Madison's observations respecting Mr. Monroe, he appeared much affected and spoke with some degree of asperity on the subject." Ironically, after Washington died, Madison was the delegate to propose that the members of the Virginia general assembly wear mourning badges throughout the session. "Death has robbed our country," he said, "of its most distinguished ornament, and the world of one of its greatest benefactors. George Washington, the Hero of Liberty, the father of his Country, and the friend of man is no more. The General Assembly of his native state were ever the first to render him, living, the honors due to his virtues. They will not be the second, to pay to his memory the tribute of their tears."

Related entries: Constitutional Convention; Hamilton, Alexander; Presidency; Farewell Address (Selected Writings)

Suggestions for further reading:
Brant, Irving. 1941–1961. 6 vols. *James Madison*. New York.
Hutchinson, William, and William Rachal, Robert Rutland, and J. C. A. Stagg, et al., eds. 1962—. 3 sers. 25 vols. to date. *The Papers of James Madison.* Chicago and Charlottesville, VA.
Leibiger, Stuart. 1999. *Founding Friendship.* Charlottesville, VA.

Mansion House Farm

See Mount Vernon.

Marshall, Thomas Hanson (1731–1801)

See Alexander, Robert.

Mason, George (1725–1792)

George Mason lived south of Mount Vernon at Dogue's Neck (also Mason's Neck) in Fairfax County, Virginia, where in the 1750s he built an ornate Georgian-style mansion, Gunston Hall. When his father, George Mason (1690–1735), died, young George was left to the guardianship of his uncle, John Mer-

cer of Marlborough, Washington's occasional attorney and the father of three sons with whom Washington was closely connected. Mason was associated with Washington's half brother Lawrence in the Ohio Company, of which Mason served as treasurer, or cashier, from 1752 to 1773, and the earliest correspondence between Mason and Washington is a letter from Mason apologizing for missing Lawrence's funeral in the summer of 1752. As treasurer of the Ohio Company, Mason was involved with assisting the British and provincial troops raised to defend the Virginia frontier, so in 1755 when Washington was commissioned colonel of the Virginia Regiment, Mason wrote to assure him "that Nothing wou'd give Me more sensible pleasure than an Opportunity of rendering You any acceptable Service."

Their proximity as neighbors brought Mason and Washington into frequent contact before the Revolutionary War. They each owned several tracts of land near one another that at one time had belonged to larger grants, including, in separate parcels, about two-thirds of a 584-acre tract between Dogue's Neck and Little Hunting Creek that originally had been granted to George Brent (c.1640–1700) in the seventeenth century. In 1759 they joined George William Fairfax and others in subscribing to invest in the establishment of Maurice Pound's vineyard at nearby Colchester. Both men served on the vestry of Truro Parish before the Revolution. Although a vehement disagreement took place in 1767 about whether to change the location of the parish's Pohick Church, which was in dire need of a new building, the matter did not disrupt their friendship. Mason also was a trustee of the town of Alexandria from its founding in 1754 to its incorporation in 1779.

Mason and Washington also shared a mutual interest in politics, and both were elected to the House of Burgesses in the late 1750s. In 1769 the neighbors consulted about how to best respond to the other colonies' calls for Virginia merchants to join the nonimportation association. In 1774 they took the lead in Fairfax County's preparation for the proposed Virginia convention; Washington presided over the meeting where Mason drafted the Fairfax Resolves. Both men advanced and collected money to pay for the supplies needed for the Fairfax Independent Company. The following year Mason was a delegate to the Virginia convention and a member of the council of safety. At the convention he drafted the ordinance for raising an armed force to defend the colony, which he sent to Washington. In 1776 Mason took the lead in drafting a major part of the Virginia Constitution as well as the Declaration of Rights. Mason also shared Washington's interest in Potomac River navigation, and in the spring of 1775 he wrote a legislative bill directed at establishing a company that would raise capital by subscription, but the matter was dropped because of the outbreak of hostilities with Great Britain. When the navigation issue was revisited after the war, Mason served as one of several commissioners from Virginia and Maryland charged with framing "liberal and equitable regulations" concerning the river who conferred at Mount Vernon in March 1785. It was regarding a political issue that Washington made one of the more revealing of his few prepresidential remarks about religion, when he wrote Mason in October 1785 about James Madison's anonymous Memorial and Remonstrance against the religious assessment bill that had been introduced in the Virginia general assembly. While not philosophically opposed to assessments, he declared that "no mans sentiments are more opposed to *any kind* of restraint upon religious principles than mine."

When it came to the matter of framing a new Federal Constitution, Mason and Washington parted company. After the adoption of the Constitution, Mason led the opposition to its ratification, writing in 1787 his "Objections to the Federal Constitution," which outlined his insistence that the Constitution should contain a condemnation of slavery as well as a Bill of Rights. Mason sent his neighbor a manuscript copy of his "Objections" to the Constitution, "which a little Moderation & Temper, in the latter End of the Convention, might have removed. . . . You will readily observe, that my Objections are not numerous . . . tho' in my mind, some of them are capital ones." Although Mason sent his "Objections" to interested parties across the country, he avoided having it printed, and it was not until Washington's secretary, Tobias Lear, without his employer's knowledge, sent a copy to a Virginia newspaper, that the "Objections" was made public.

After Washington's election under the new government, rumors circulated in Stafford that Mason had declared that "we shoud have a very pretty President at the head of our new Government, one Who had pd of[f] his Debts within the time of the war with paper money altho it had been lent to him in specia." It was true that Washington's Mount Vernon farm manager, Lund Washington, had paid a debt for his employer to Mason in paper, although at the time of payment, according to Lund's explanation, Mason had "made no objection to receiveg it, yet some time after he mention'd in a Letter to me his haveg sustained a loss by that payment." Washington took little notice of the allegation, although he certainly was offended. He considered Mason's continued opposition to the Constitution unreasonable. His old friend's "Pride on the one hand," Washington wrote, "and want of manly candor on the other, will not I am certain let him acknowledge an error in his opinions respecting it though conviction should flash on his mind as strongly as a ray of light." Mason made no attempt to conceal his contempt for the Constitution yet did not hesitate to write Washington on behalf of friends and family members seeking federal appointments, and he declared to Washington, who was now in New York, his willingness to render in Virginia any service "without Reserve; as I can truly say there is not a man in the World, who more sincerely wishes You every Felicity." Although Mason and Washington occasionally corresponded about land matters until shortly before Mason's death, their friendship would never be renewed.

Mason, who suffered from severe gout throughout his adult life, was married twice, to Anne Eilbeck (d. 1773) of Mattawoman in Charles County, Maryland, in 1750, with whom he had five sons and four daughters; and to Sarah Brent (c.1730–1806) of Woodstock, Virginia, in 1780.

Related entries: Constitutional Convention; Pohick Church, Truro Parish; Religious Beliefs

Suggestions for further reading:
"From George Mason," 5, 28 April 1769 (*Col. Ser.,* vol. 8).
"To George Mason," 3 October 1785 (*Con. Ser.,* vol. 3).
"From George Mason," 7 October 1787 (*Con. Ser.,* vol. 5).
Miller, Helen Hill. 1975. *George Mason, Gentleman Revolutionary.* Chapel Hill, NC.
Rutland, Robert A., ed. 1970. 3 vols. *The Papers of George Mason, 1725–1792.* Chapel Hill, NC.

Mercer, George (1733–1784)

George Mercer, the eldest son of the legal scholar John Mercer of Stafford County, Virginia, was educated at the College of William and Mary. He was one of the lieutenants appointed by Virginia governor Robert Dinwiddie in February 1754 to recruit men for a proposed expedition to the Forks of the Ohio. He became a captain at the same time that Washington became a colonel following the death of Col. Joshua Fry and was present at the capitulation of Fort Necessity in July 1754. When Washington reorganized the Virginia Regiment following Braddock's defeat, in September 1755, he made Mercer his aide-de-camp. Mercer subsequently served as a company commander in Washington's regiment before being sent to South Carolina with a detachment of Virginia troops in 1757. The following year Mercer became lieutenant colonel of the Second Virginia Regiment, which was raised by Col. William Byrd III for British general John Forbes's expedition against Fort Duquesne.

After their French and Indian War service, Mercer and Washington entered a partnership with two other former officers, Robert Stewart and Nathaniel Gist (1733–1789), to secure land in the west under Dinwiddie's Proclamation of 1754. Rivalry between their partnership and one formed by two other veterans of the 1754 campaign, Adam Stephen and Thomas Bullitt, resulted in Mercer and Washington becoming fellow burgesses from Frederick County in 1761. Mercer was also a manager of the Potomac River Company as well as the London agent for the Ohio Company, which took him to England from 1763 to 1770. While in England, Mercer secured the post of stamp collector for the colony and returned to Virginia briefly in the fall of 1765, arriving at Williamsburg just two days before the Stamp Act went into effect. An angry mob demanded his resignation, which he tendered the following day. Beginning in the fall of 1767, George and Martha Washington spent at least two seasons at a house in Warm Springs (now Berkeley Springs, West Virginia) owned by Mercer.

While in England, Mercer's financial status deteriorated, and in the early 1770s he mortgaged pieces of his substantial Virginia landholdings to pay debts he had incurred in England. Mercer's brother James, who had been left with a power of attorney to manage George's affairs in America, without knowing of the English liens pledged some of the same property in order to pay debts

Painting by George Trumbell of George Washington on horseback during the Battle of Princeton, at which Hugh Mercer was killed, c.1900. (Library of Congress)

incurred in Virginia. George Mercer soon became suspicious of his brother's role in the matter and empowered Washington, George Mason, and John Tayloe to sell his interest in the disputed property in an attempt to raise money to straighten out his affairs. Mason and Tayloe subsequently refused to act, leaving Washington to manage the sales. To complicate matters, some of the property was tied up in the estate of their deceased father, who had died insolvent, and some of the property was owned jointly with a half brother, John Francis Mercer (1759–1821), who was a minor. Thousands of acres of George Mercer's land, lying in four counties, was sold in 1774, including two lots totaling 571 acres that Washington purchased out of 6,500 acres on the Shenandoah River in Frederick (now Clarke) County, near present-day Berryville, Virginia. By 1775 Washington had bought more of the entangled property, paying £892 for two tracts totaling 1,168 acres on

Four Mile Run, a stream that flows into the Potomac River about four miles north of Hunting Creek in Fairfax County, Virginia. Washington refused to serve as a trustee for Mercer's estate when the Revolutionary War came, although after the war he once again became embroiled in the affair. Mercer moved to Paris in 1776, partly to escape his creditors in England, and lived there for the remainder of his life.

An early and often-quoted description of Washington in which he is portrayed as "being straight as an Indian" and "a splendid horseman" is attributed to a letter written by Mercer in 1760.

Related entries: Descriptions of Washington; Dinwiddie, Robert; Mercer, James; Mercer, John

Suggestions for further reading:
"From George Mercer," 16 September 1759 (*Col. Ser.*, vol. 6).
"Description of Washington," 1760 (*Col. Ser.*, vol. 6).

"To James Mercer," 28 March 1774 (*Col. Ser.*, vol. 10).

"To John Tayloe," 28 March 1774 (*Col. Ser.*, vol. 10).

"To James Mercer," 26 December 1774 (*Col. Ser.*, vol. 10).

"To James Mercer," 21 February 1777 (*War Ser.*, vol. 8).

"To John Francis Mercer," 8 July 1784 (*Con. Ser.*, vol. 1).

"Statement concerning George Mercer's Estate," 1 February 1789 (*Pres. Ser.*, vol. 1).

Mercer, Hugh (c.1725–1777)

Fredericksburg apothecary and physician Hugh Mercer was born at Aberdeenshire, Scotland. He studied medicine at the University of Aberdeen from 1740 to 1744, and in April 1746 he served as an assistant surgeon in Charles Stuart's forces at the Battle of Culloden, where the prince's army was destroyed. Mercer immigrated to Philadelphia the following year. After that not much is known of his life except that he settled at what became Mercersburg in Franklin County, Pennsylvania, until he became a captain in the provincial forces during the French and Indian War. Mercer was seriously wounded in the shoulder during an attack on the Indian town of Kittanning on the Allegheny River in 1756. Surviving alone on roots and berries, he managed over a period of weeks to find his way back to Fort Cumberland at Wills Creek. Mercer was promoted to lieutenant colonel in 1758 and soon found himself accompanying another Scots physician, British general John Forbes, on an expedition to Fort Duquesne. Mercer was placed in charge of the garrison and during the campaign became close friends with Washington, who was then colonel of the Virginia Regiment.

When Mercer retired from the service, he settled in Virginia at Fredericksburg, where he opened an apothecary shop and built up a lucrative medical practice. Beginning in January 1769, Mercer's role as a physician brought him to Mount Vernon to treat Martha's ill-fated daughter, Patsy, who died of epilepsy in 1773. In April 1774 Mercer purchased Ferry Farm, Washington's boyhood home near Fredericksburg, for £2,000 Virginia currency, agreeing to make five annual payments. Ferry Farm remained in Mercer's family until 1829.

In the spring of 1775 Mercer organized volunteers to defend the Virginia colony after marines from the British armed schooner *Magdalen* ferried off the powder from the Williamsburg magazine to HMS *Fowey*. The Virginia convention commissioned Mercer colonel of the Third Virginia Regiment in early 1776—"old officers was the Cry, and have them they would"—Washington's friend Andrew Lewis said of the appointment, which exceedingly pleased Washington. In fact, Washington thought Mercer competent to serve immediately as a brigadier general, but, he wrote, "I question (as a Scotchman) whether it would have gone glibly down." Mercer was promoted to brigadier general on 5 June 1776 and at Washington's request ordered by the Continental Congress to join the main army at New York. Upon his arrival he took command of the flying camp, a "mobile strategic reserve" formed to defend the area between New York and Philadelphia.

Washington relied on his old friend often during the New York campaign to help plan strategy and to reconnoiter the British outposts on Staten Island. Mercer accompanied Washington in the retreat across New Jersey and helped plan the Christmas night surprise attack on Trenton in 1776. At the Battle of Princeton he led one of the columns of soldiers along the main road running out of the town in order to cut off a possible enemy retreat. His horse was killed from under him, and he encountered alone a detachment of enemy troops that savagely beat him with their musket butts and stabbed him with bayonets. Upon receiving word that Mercer was still alive, Washington sent his nephew and fellow Virginian, Capt George Lewis (1757–1821), to Lord Cornwallis under a flag of truce with a request that Lewis might be allowed to wait upon the wounded general. Cornwallis permitted Lewis to stay with Mercer and ordered his own surgeon to assist Dr. Benjamin Rush (1746–1813) in tending to his wounds. The "brave & worthy" Dr. Mercer lingered for a few days and was buried at Christ Church in Philadelphia. Nearly seventy years later he was reinterred at Laurel Hill Cemetery, where a monument was erected in his honor.

Related entries: Ferry Farm; Forbes Campaign; Princeton, Battle of

Suggestions for further reading:
Diaries, vols. 2–3.
"From Hugh Mercer," 21 March 1774 (*Col. Ser.,* vol. 10).
"To Hugh Mercer," 28 March 1774 (*Col. Ser.,* vol. 10).
"From General Hugh Mercer," 16 July 1776 (*War Ser.,* vol. 5).
"From General Hugh Mercer," 27 July 1776 (*War Ser.,* vol. 5).
"Benjamin Rush to Richard Henry Lee," 7 January 1777 (*Letters of Benjamin Rush,* vol. 1).

Mercer, James (1736–1793)

James Mercer, the third son of legal scholar John Mercer of Stafford County, Virginia, practiced law in Fredericksburg after graduating from the College of William and Mary. Mercer's relationship with Washington was a varied and long-standing one. From 1762 to 1776 Mercer was a member of the Virginia House of Burgesses from Hampshire County (now West Virginia). In 1769 he purchased five lots in Fredericksburg, two from Washington and three from Washington's brother-in-law, Fielding Lewis. Washington dined at Mercer's house in August 1770. Mercer served as an attorney for the Custis estate suit in 1771 at Washington's behest and ap-

peared before the Virginia council to petition for land grants due for French and Indian War claims. In 1774 and 1775 Washington paid £892 for two patents of land totaling 1,168 acres from Mercer and his brother George on Four Mile Run, a stream that flows into the Potomac River about four miles north of Hunting Creek. Mercer served in the Virginia conventions from 1774 to 1776, was named to the committee of correspondence in 1774 and to the Virginia committee of safety in 1775. He served in the Virginia Constitutional Convention of 1776, and in 1779 and 1780, he was a Virginia delegate to the Continental Congress. From 1786 to 1790 he was a trustee and president of the Fredericksburg Academy. From 1789 until his death he served as a judge of the Virginia Court of Appeals. He died in Richmond and is buried at St. John's historic churchyard.

In February 1777 Mercer and Washington exchanged letters about the complicated affairs of Mercer's brother George, of which Washington had acted as a trustee before the Revolutionary War. In answer to Mercer's queries about bonds, Washington, deeply involved in the war effort at his Continental army headquarters at Morristown, New Jersey, drawing on his memory, which he admitted "indeed is of the very worst kind," referred to the estate being taken out of Mercer's hands. Mercer's reaction was irate, as indicated by memorandums that he wrote in the margins of Washington's letter: "Memo: the Generals Memory—really does fail him egregiously—No Man ever told him that this Estate was taken out of my Hands from any suspicions—& therefore he shou'd not have trusted to a bad memory . . . instead of appologizing for misprentals on a/c of bad memory—really is so inventive as to assert what is not true! see that Let. let it be asked is there that man in the world who ever imputed such Conduct to me except the writer—nay more—I have been honoured with the intimacy of the writer from our Youth upwards—I pray him to vouch one instance of his proving my heart depraved! . . . This is the most extraordinary Let. I ever saw—The Genl's memory is at least *bad!* . . . as to the Genls memory. N.B. it is very extraordinary." Unfortunately, this did not prove to be the last word on the subject. In the late summer of 1779 Mercer's failure to pay outstanding debts led Washington to write to his distant cousin and farm manager, Lund Washington: "If Mr. M. possessed so little honor, I may say honesty, as to attempt paying me two shillings in the pound for a debt he was greatly indulged in (the depreciation at the time he made the offer not exceeding this), I must be content; for knowing nothing of your Laws, and being unwilling that any act of mine should injure the currency, I chose to make no difficulties in the case if the loss of the whole debt should be the consequence of it. . . . But in all matters of this kind . . . I had much rather you would advise with, and pursue the advice of, some sensible Whigs who are known to be men of discernment, and of honor and probity (that are acquainted with the laws and practises of the State in like cases) than to consult, and refer things to me, who am totally unacquainted with both." That did not end the matter, however, and before the war was over Washington found himself involved in a chancery court suit with Mercer. In November 1782 the general court ordered Washington to turn over to Mercer all the bonds and papers relating to George Mercer's estate. Even so, Washington occasionally still was drawn into the estate's lingering legal problems. After the war Washington and Mercer maintained a cordial relationship, visiting each other a few times, and Mercer sent Washington some "everlasting (or Lady Pease)" to plant at Mount Vernon. In 1786 Washington got Mercer to subscribe to William Gordon's *History,* and during his presidency Washington sought Mercer's advice about political appointments.

Washington may have gotten wind of the memorandums Mercer wrote on his letter, for in 1792 he wrote Mercer asking about the execution of the deeds for land purchased from his brother's estate in Frederick County in 1774: "If so, your memory, (much better I am persuaded than mine) may furnish you with the fact; and with the circumstances attending it." Their last letters to one another were cordial.

Related entries: Mercer, George; Mercer, John

Suggestions for further reading:
"To James Mercer," 21 February 1777 (*War Ser.,* vol. 8).
"To Lund Washington," 14 September 1779 (*Writings,* vol. 16).
"To Lund Washington," 11 April 1780 (*Writings,* vol. 18).
"To James Mercer," 3 October 1792 (*Writings,* vol. 32).

Mercer, John (1704–1768)

John Mercer, originally from Ireland, lived at his estate Marlborough in Stafford County, Virginia, a few miles up the Potomac River from the Chotank neighborhood Washington frequented as a youth. Mercer practiced law until 1734, when his aggressive courtroom tactics led to disbarment. He then pursued the scholarly study of law, built one of the best libraries in the colony, and compiled the first edition of Virginia's laws, *An Exact Abridgement of All the Public Acts of Assembly, of Virginia, in Force and Use* (Williamsburg, 1737). Mercer speculated in large tracts of land in Fauquier and Loudoun Counties and was instrumental in founding the Ohio Company to speculate in lands in the Ohio River Valley. He served as secretary of the Ohio Company when Washington's half brother Lawrence was its president, and Washington called on Mercer for legal advice about his deceased brother's Mount Vernon estate as early as 1754. Mercer also represented the Custis family in a lengthy legal battle, which Washington was brought into after his marriage to Martha Custis in 1759. Three of John Mercer's sons, George, James, and John Fenton (1735–1756), served with Washington in the Virginia Regiment during the French and Indian War. The latter was killed by Indians while on scouting duty for Washington in April 1756. In November 1774 Washington was in charge of auctions to settle the estate of John Mercer, bringing him into contact with George and James and their younger brother, John Francis (1759–1821), Mercer's young son from a second marriage who later served in the Virginia and Maryland general assemblies, the Continental Congress, and the U.S. House of Representatives. John Mercer's complicated estate became entangled with that of his son George and plagued Washington for more than a quarter century.

Related entries: Mercer, George; Mercer, James

Mifflin, Thomas (1744–1800)

Thomas Mifflin, one of the youngest and most radical delegates to serve in the Continental Congress, was brought up in a strict Philadelphia Quaker home and educated at the College of Philadelphia. He spent two years in Europe before entering into the merchant trade with his brother George in 1765. In 1772 he became a member of the provincial assembly, and from that time until shortly before his death, he was one of Pennsylvania's most prominent political figures. Washington came to know Mifflin quite well during the first and second Continental Congresses, dining at his home on several occasions. In May 1775 Mifflin and Washington were named with several other delegates to a committee charged with finding ways to supply the colonies with military stores

and ammunition. The handsome and articulate Mifflin moved comfortably among the colony's business leaders and was instrumental in carrying out the committee's charge.

Mifflin's military service began after the Battles of Lexington and Concord when he became a major in the Philadelphia Associators. Washington, after Congress appointed him commander in chief in June 1775, invited Mifflin to serve as his aide-de-camp with the rank of lieutenant colonel. Mifflin served in that capacity for a brief period only, for in August 1775 he became quartermaster general of the Continental army, an office that required a combination of management and business skills as well as commercial connections. He was promoted to colonel the same December, to brigadier general the following May, and to major general in February 1777. Washington especially relied upon Mifflin's knowledge of Philadelphia and his influence in the area when procuring boats and wagons necessary for American forces posted near the Delaware River.

Mifflin later became one of the chief participants in the so-called Conway Cabal, although the exact extent of his involvement or even the reasons for it have never been discovered. Thomas Conway himself, while denying that he had used the expression "*Weak General*" to refer to Washington, admitted that he had given his sentiments about him "in private conversation with some General officers, and in particular to General Mifflinn." Benjamin Rush (1746–1813), a partner in the attempt to topple Washington, said Mifflin "possessed genius, knowledge, eloquence, patriotism, courage, self-government and an independent spirit in the first years of the war," but Rush left no clues to Mifflin's motives. When Mifflin wanted to leave the Board of War and return to active command in May 1778, Washington, aware of Mifflin's feelings and behavior toward him, declared to a delegate of Congress that he had "nothing *personally* to oppose to it" if Mifflin himself could reconcile "such conduct to his own feelings as an *Officer* and Man of *honour* and Congress hath no objection to his leaving his Seat." And yet, said Washington, "I must think, that Gentleman's stepping in, and out, as the Sun happens to beam forth or become obscure is not *quite* the thing, nor *quite* just with respect to those Officers who take the bitter with the Sweet." Although Mifflin continued to harbor an unfriendly attitude toward his commander in chief, the collapse of the so-called cabal prevented Mifflin from openly displaying any ill feelings.

Mifflin resigned from the army in February 1779 following charges of negligence and corruption in carrying out his duties as quartermaster general. He was reelected to the Continental Congress in 1782 and became its president the following year. Thus, ironically, it was to Mifflin that Washington tendered his resignation at the end of the war. Mifflin became a member of the Pennsylvania general assembly in 1785, and in 1787 he was a delegate to the Constitutional Convention. He served as president of the Pennsylvania supreme executive council from 1788 to 1790, when he was elected the first governor of Pennsylvania under the new state constitution, an office he held for nine years. During his tenure as governor Mifflin personally assisted in putting down the Whiskey Insurrection, one of the most serious crises of Washington's presidential administrations, and a final irony considering his long-standing lack of enthusiasm for Washington.

Mifflin died in Lancaster, Pennsylvania, and is buried in the Lutheran cemetery there.

Related entry: Conway, Thomas

Suggestions for further reading:
"From Thomas Conway," 5 November 1777 (*War Ser.*, vol. 12).
"To Gouverneur Morris," 18 May 1778 (*Writings*, vol. 11).

Millers Run (Chartiers Creek) Tract

Of the 37,000 acres of land that Washington acquired in western Virginia and in the Ohio Valley before the Revolutionary War, none caused him so much trouble as the 2,813-acre tract lying on Millers Run, a tributary of Chartiers Creek, near present-day Canonsburg, Pennsylvania. Washington acquired the property with a 3,000-acre land-bounty warrant that had been assigned to him by John Posey for payment of a £2,000 debt Posey had amassed during the 1760s. (Under the provisions of the Proclamation of 1763, Posey, a veteran of the French and Indian War who operated a ferry downriver from Mount Vernon, was entitled to that amount of land for his wartime military service as a captain of artificers in the Second Virginia Regiment.)

This tract was claimed for Washington in the summer of 1771 by William Crawford, the frontiersman and land surveyor looking after Washington's concerns in the west. "I have found som at about 15 or 16 miles distance from Fort pitt," Crawford wrote Washington that August, "which is very good farming Land and good Medow Land as any, the up Land Level or no more hilly in common to Lay the ground dry." At the time of Crawford's letter the area was considered to be in Augusta County, Virginia, but by the time Washington finally visited the property in 1784, the Pennsylvania-Virginia boundary dispute had been settled, and it lay in Washington County, Pennsylvania.

Unfortunately for Washington, Crawford was not the only one to recognize the high quality of the land. Squatters began to occupy the property as early as the spring of 1772, when Crawford ran off several men who had built cabins there in anticipation of beginning a permanent settlement, some of whom owned land nearby on Chartiers

Creek. Crawford had several houses erected on the land in an attempt to strengthen Washington's claim. In mid-November 1772 Crawford wrote to assure Washington that "Your Land on Chertees is Safe yeat but how Long they may Continue so I dont [k]now as the People at that time going to setle on them that we com down was Driven of[f] and attempt to Return in the Spring, I Shall Setle Som man on them if Posable and hop[e] by that means to Secure them Every thing in my Power shall be don."

One chief obstacle in securing Washington's claim at Chartiers Creek was his old acquaintance from the French and Indian War, George Croghan, who was claiming tens of thousands of acres in the region. Washington's claim still was not properly surveyed or titled by December 1773, when Crawford wrote Washington about Croghan's activities in the area, enclosing a sketch of the tract and outlying properties. "Som People about 10 or 12 in number has gon on your Cherter Land within this few days," said Crawford, "and there is no geting them of[f] without by Force of Arms They are in Couraged by Majr [Edward] ward [half-]Brother to Colo. Croghan [w]ho Claims the Land and says he has a Grant from the Crown for that Land and he will undemnefie them, if they will set in any house whare no Person is Living and also offers the Land for Sail warrenting the Purcher a Lawfull title . . . I co[u]ld Drive them away but they will com back Emedetly as soon as my back is turnd. They man I put on the Land they have drove away and Built a house so Colse to his dore he cannot get into the house at the dore." Although Crawford surveyed the property twice in efforts to validate Washington's claim, Crawford's prediction that the settlers would be difficult to remove proved true, and Washington ultimately went to court to legitimize his claim. That did not occur until after the Revolutionary War, however, when Washington engaged Penn-

sylvania attorney Thomas Smith to bring an ejectment case against a recalcitrant group of squatters, about fifteen families belonging to the Associate Presbyterian Church (Seceders Church), who had moved onto the property in October 1773.

Washington visited his Millers Run tract in September 1784 when he and Dr. James Craik made an extensive tour of their western landholdings. A meeting with the squatters failed to give satisfaction to either party. In his diary Washington summarized his discussion with the settlers, who, after dining with him, "began to enquire whether I would part with the Land, & upon what terms; adding, that tho' they did not conceive they could be disposed, yet to avoid contention, they would buy, if my terms were moderate. I told them I had no inclination to sell; however, after hearing a great deal of their hardships, their religious principles (which had brought them together as a society of Cececders) and unwillingness to seperate or remove; I told them I would make them a last offer and this was—the whole tract at 25/. pr. Acre, the money to be paid at 3 annual payments with Interest; or to become Tenants upon leases of 999 years, at the annual Rent of Ten pounds pr. ct. pr. Ann[um]." When the sectarians, none of whom was interested in renting, asked Washington if he would sell for the same price at a longer credit and without interest and were "answered in the negative they then determined to stand suit for the Land."

The ensuing litigation consumed much of Washington's time for the remainder of the winter after his return to Mount Vernon. Lawyer Smith began ejectment proceedings in Washington County in December 1784 but at Washington's instruction had the case removed from the lower court to the Pennsylvania Supreme Court the following spring. It was October 1786 before the case actually was tried, and by then Washington had come to believe the settlers were "willful & obstinate Sinners" intent on robbing him of his land for ten or twelve years, if not altogether. Although the defendants hired noted jurist Hugh Henry Brackenridge to represent them, the verdict was decided entirely in Washington's favor, forcing the squatters to leave the land permanently. Smith cautioned Washington to go easy on the settlers, however: "You have now *thirteen* Plantations—some of them well improved—I take it for granted that the improvements increase the value of the Land much more than all the expences of the Ejectments—those who mad[e] them are now reduced to indigence—they have put in Crops this season, which are now in the ground—they wish to be permitted to take the grain away—to give this hint may be improper in me—to say more would be presumptuous." Washington magnanimously—though grudgingly—left it to Smith's discretion whether to eject the settlers immediately or allow them to remain at their respective farms as tenants paying an "equitable rent." The squatters remained as tenants for a few years, but in the end they were forced to leave behind their "cultivated fields, meadows, orchards, and buildings," as their attorney Brackenridge described them nearly three decades later, without any compensation from Washington.

Washington rented the Millers Run lands to new tenants until Col. Matthew Ritchie, a former member of the Pennsylvania general assembly, purchased the entire 2,813 acres in June 1796 for the sum of $12,000 for himself and Alexander Addison (1759–1807), a Presbyterian minister, writer, and Federalist judge in Pennsylvania. When Washington died in 1799 he was still due money on the property. In 1801 the executors of Washington's estate brought an action against the mortgage, forcing the Washington County sheriff to sell the land once again.

Related entries: Crawford Brothers; Dinwiddie, Robert; Great Kanawha Tracts; Washington's Bottom Tract

Suggestions for further reading:
Diaries, vols. 2, 4.
"From William Crawford," 2 August 1771 (*Col. Ser.,* vol. 8).
"From William Crawford," 15 March 1772 (*Col. Ser.,* vol. 9).
"To Thomas Lewis," 5 May 1774 (*Col. Ser.,* vol. 10).
"From Thomas Smith," 17–26 November 1785 (*Con. Ser.,* vol. 3).
"To Thomas Smith," 22 September 1786 (*Con. Ser.,* vol. 4).
"From Alexander Addison," 11 July 1798 (*Ret. Ser.,* vol. 2).
"To Alexander Addison," 29 July 1798 (*Ret. Ser.,* vol. 2).

Mississippi Adventure

On his way home from a trip in May 1763 to inquire into the feasibility of opening 40,000 acres in the Dismal Swamp, a great coastal swamp bordering Virginia and North Carolina, Washington attended a meeting in Stafford County, Virginia, to organize a land company to "explore and settle some Tracts of Land upon the Mississippi and its Waters." The Mississippi Adventure, as Washington called it, was one of a number of such ventures springing up to lay claim to the frontier lands east of the Mississippi River, denounced by France only four months earlier in the Treaty of Paris. The company aimed to secure a patent from the king for 2.5 million acres west of the Appalachian Mountains embracing part of the watersheds of the Wabash, Ohio, and Tennessee Rivers. Largely the work of four sons of Thomas Lee—Richard Henry, Thomas Ludwell, Francis Lightfoot, and William—the Mississippi Land Company was organized by nineteen prominent Potomac River Valley Virginians, most of whom Washington probably knew well. The company's membership was limited to fifty men, including nine slots reserved for London members, but it never numbered more than about forty. The company's fifty "Adventurers" would each own 50,000 acres separately, not jointly, "anything in the said Grant to the Contrary notwithstanding."

By the terms of the company's memorial to the king requesting the grant, the company hoped to get this tract without cost for twelve years or longer. During that time it promised to settle 200 families on the land "at the least, if not interrupted by the savages or any foreign enemy." Several partners had formed "determined resolution . . . to be themselves among the first settlers." The settlers would engage in agriculture and the production of raw materials, cultivating commodities most wanted by Great Britain—"such as Hemp, Flax, Silk, Wine, Potash, Cochineal, Indigo, Iron &c. . . . especially naval stores so essential to the very being of a commercial state." They would not interfere with "Manufactures but afford a never failing demand for them." The company would ease the expense and difficulty the "poorer sort" of settlers normally encountered when attempting to secure patents, in effect making the land cheaper for them because they would not have to hire surveyors or pay cash for patents. The memorial asked for a "small Fort" to be garrisoned at the confluence of the Cherokee and Ohio Rivers to protect the "Infant Settlement from the insults of the Savages" and another at the junction of the Ohio and the Mississippi "to check the French settlers on the West side of the latter River." It asserted that settlement of the region would provide a buffer between the "friendly disposition of the Southern Indians" and the "fierce and warlike Irocois, with their six nations ever accustomed to War and sheding of blood." One month after drafting its petition, and before it could be acted on by the British ministry, the king issued the Proclamation of 1763, prohibiting any settlement west of the Appalachian range. Five years later the company resubmitted the 1763 memorial, but it was refused on the basis that some of the territory it sought was protected by the 1768 Treaty of Hard Labor with the Cherokee. The company then drafted a new petition with different boundaries that was read by the king's council and referred to the Board of Trade for consideration in March 1769. Before the board took it up, however, it was learned that the proposed territory was included in the 20 million acres likely to be granted to the Walpole Company.

Washington decided to write off his £27.13.15 investment in the Mississippi Land Company as a loss at the beginning of 1772.

Related entry: Dismal Swamp Company

Suggestions for further reading:
"Mississippi Land Company: Articles of Agreement," 22 May 1763 (*Col. Ser.*, vol. 7).
"Mississippi Land Company: Memorial to the King," 9 September 1763 (*Col. Ser.*, vol. 7).
"Mississippi Land Company: Minutes of Meeting," 22 November 1765 (*Col. Ser.*, vol. 7).
"Mississippi Land Company: Minutes of Meeting," 22 May 1767 (*Col. Ser.*, vol. 7).
"Mississippi Land Company's Petition to the King," December 1768 (*Col. Ser.*, vol. 8).
Carter, Clarence Edwin. 1910–1911. "Documents Relating to the Mississippi Land Company, 1763–1769" (*American Historical Review*, vol. 16).

Monmouth Courthouse, Battle of

"Yes, sir, he did once," was Brig. Gen. Charles Scott's answer to whether he had ever heard Washington swear. "It was at Monmouth and on a day that would have made any man swear. Yes, sir, he swore that day till the leaves shook on the trees. Charming! Delightful! Never have I enjoyed such swearing before or since. Sir, on that memorable day he swore like an angel from heaven!" The object of Washington's reputed wrath at the Battle of Monmouth Courthouse in June 1778 was Maj. Gen. Charles Lee, whom Washington had discovered retreating from what had been planned as a vigorous American as-

George Washington at the Battle of Monmouth Courthouse, 28 June 1778 (Library of Congress)

sault against the rear guard of the British baggage train as it passed through Monmouth County, New Jersey, on its way to New York following the British evacuation of Philadelphia. Washington learned of the evacuation as it was taking place and immediately threw his own forces in pursuit of the British army with orders to harass and delay the enemy's progress across New Jersey. At first British general Henry Clinton marched his army by two parallel routes, but the Americans' vigilance began to wear on the British troops, unaccustomed to carrying heavy packs in temperatures that often rose above 100 degrees, and Clinton decided to avoid a major confrontation with Washington's forces by combining his two lines of march into a single column, which ironically made his troops even more vulnerable to skirmishes, raids, and abuses.

After ten days, on the morning of 28 June, Washington's forward column was in position to attack the rear guard of the British baggage train, whose three divisions stretched more than five miles across Monmouth County. Washington ordered Lee to lead an advance attack, "unless there should be very powerful reasons to the contrary," while Washington set the main army in motion to support Lee's division. Lee made no preparations for the battle, however, and once the fighting began, he issued a series of confused orders and counterorders that resulted in the chaotic retreat of his troops "without having made any opposition, except one fire." At the same time the marches and countermarches of the Americans alerted Clinton that Washington intended a full-scale engagement. Clinton wasted no time in attempting to seize the advantage,

Monmouth Courthouse, Battle of   *223*

ordering Lord Cornwallis to pursue the fleeing Americans. Only Washington's sudden appearance at the front halted the withdrawal of his bewildered troops. After confronting Lee, whom he ordered to make a stand at a nearby hedgerow, Washington assembled the American troops to face the fire of their pursuers. Shaken by Washington's rebuke, Lee declared that he would "not be the first man to quit the field," and he seems to have fought bravely and skillfully during the ensuing battle, although a court-martial subsequently found him guilty of "a breach of orders and of misbehaviour before the enemy."

"I never saw the General to so much advantage," wrote Alexander Hamilton of Washington's leadership during the fighting. "His coolness and firmness were admirable. He instantly took measures for checking the enemy's advance, and giving time for the army, which was very near, to form and make a proper disposition." "His presence stopped the retreat," Lafayette remembered years later. "His fine appearance on horseback, his calm courage, roused to animation by the vexations of the morning, gave him the air best calculated to excite enthusiasm. . . . I thought then, as now, that never had I beheld so superb a man." The measures included a spirited counterattack led by Brig. Gen. Anthony Wayne that penetrated almost to the British artillery. By the time enemy reinforcements forced Wayne's troops to fall back, Washington had organized a defensive position strong enough to resist assault. The two armies clashed into the late afternoon, when exhaustion from the oppressive heat forced both sides to withdraw from the field. Washington expected to resume the battle the next morning, but shortly after midnight Clinton's army slipped away undetected and resumed its march, reaching the safety of the high ground near Sandy Hook before the Americans could renew their pursuit.

Neither the Americans nor the British emerged a clear winner at Monmouth, although both sides claimed victory. American casualties amounted to more than 365, including 72 killed, 161 wounded, and 132 missing. British casualties were more than 1,200 and included more than 250 killed, 174 wounded, and more than 600 deserters—440 of them German. The two sides together lost about 100 men to sunstroke. The battle proved to be a political triumph for Washington, and the Continental army's formidable resistance against professional soldiers in the field made Clinton, already cautious, even more unwilling to send his men into combat. The battle also proved to be the last major battle to take place in the northern department during the war.

Related entries: Clinton, Henry; Cornwallis, Charles, Second Earl Cornwallis; Lee, Charles

Suggestions for further reading:
"Council of War," 17 June 1778 (*Writings,* vol. 12).
"To Henry Laurens," 29 June 1778 (*Writings,* vol. 12).
"To Henry Laurens," 1 July 1778 (*Writings,* vol. 12).
"Nathanael Greene to Jacob Greene," 2 July 1778 (*Greene Papers,* vol. 2).

Morris, Gouverneur (1752–1816)

"The *finish* given to the style and arrangement of the Constitution fairly belongs to the pen of Mr. Morris . . . a better choice could not have been made, as the performance of the task proved." That was James Madison's assessment in 1831 of Gouverneur Morris, the indefatigable penman whose unsigned phrases grace perhaps the most historic document of modern times. Ironically, Morris's economy of words in that document seems at odds with his vocal participation in its creation, as he indeed was the most active delegate at the Constitutional Convention besides Madi-

The leaders of the Continental Congress, including Gouverneur Morris (second from left) (Library of Congress)

son himself. At the convention Morris frequently conversed and dined with Washington, who would have been at the center of a much stronger central government under the constitution that Morris argued for—with a president elected for life, and a lifetime Senate chosen by the president. Morris had been a strong advocate for Washington and the army during his service in the Continental Congress, and he became the most informative contact in Europe during Washington's presidential administrations. In 1789 he traveled to France as an agent for Robert Morris (no relation), whom he had served as assistant superintendent of finance for several years, and to England as a special commissioner for Washington, "to inquire into British intentions concerning their treaty violations as well as the possibility of negotiating a new commercial treaty." Morris sent Washington frequent detailed reports of political

events taking place all over Europe, and in 1792 Washington appointed him minister to France. He was the only foreign minister to remain in Paris during the Reign of Terror. Morris took an active part in a plot to rescue Louis XVI from the revolutionaries, and he saved Lafayette's wife from the guillotine. From 1794 to 1798 Morris traveled throughout Europe. He returned to New York and was elected to the U.S. Senate in 1800. He died at Morrissania, the family estate on the east side of the Harlem River in Westchester County, New York, where he had been born. Morris, who lost a leg to amputation as a result of leaping from a runaway carriage in Philadelphia, was brother of Lewis Morris (1726–1798), a New York signer of the Declaration of Independence.

Related entries: Constitutional Convention; Madison, James

Suggestions for further reading:
"From Gouverneur Morris," 12 November 1788 (*Pres. Ser.*, vol. 1).
"From Gouverneur Morris," 13 October 1789 (*Pres. Ser.*, vol. 4).
"From Gouverneur Morris," 24 January 1790 (*Pres. Ser.*, vol. 5).
"From Gouverneur Morris," 1 December 1790 (*Pres. Ser.*, vol. 7).
"To Gouverneur Morris," 28 January 1792 (*Pres. Ser.*, vol. 9).
Davenport, Beatrix Cary, ed. 1939. 2 vols. *A Diary of the French Revolution by Gouverneur Morris*. Boston.

Morris, Robert (1734–1806)

The Financier of the Revolution, as he is known, and a signer of the Declaration of Independence and the U.S. Constitution, Robert Morris was born at Liverpool, England, and came to America when he was about 14 years old. Six years later, in 1754, he became a partner in the shipping firm of Willing, Morris and Company of Philadelphia, where in 1765 he signed the nonimportation agreement. In 1775, while a member of the Pennsylvania council of safety and a member of the final session of the provincial assembly, his company contracted with a secret committee of the Continental Congress to import arms and ammunition for the Patriot cause. At the same time he was a Pennsylvania delegate to Congress and served on several important committees, including the executive committee and a secret committee charged with procuring munitions, both of which led to frequent communication with Washington, and the committee of secret correspondence responsible for drafting instructions for the envoy to France, Silas Deane (1737–1789). Beginning in 1778 he and Deane were accused of fraudulent financial dealings and became the subject of several congressional inquiries, all of which exonerated both men. In 1781 Morris was appointed superintendent of finance; he was authorized to fit out ships for the U.S.

government and assume the responsibility for purchasing supplies for the Continental army. Morris reorganized the civil administration by borrowing money from France in 1781 and from the Netherlands in 1783 and 1784, earning him the title of Financier of the Revolution.

During the Constitutional Convention, Washington stayed at Morris's home, and when Washington moved the seat of the federal government from New York to Philadelphia in 1790, a city committee rented the house for the presidential mansion. The house had served as British general William Howe's headquarters when his army occupied the city during the war and subsequently was gutted by fire but rebuilt and occupied by Morris. The Morris family moved to a nearby house when the Washingtons moved in, becoming their nearest neighbors. It was, wrote Washington, "the best *single House* in the City," yet it required alteration before it could be made adequate for "the *commodious* accomodation" of his family. John Adams occupied the same house during his presidency.

Morris's fortunes collapsed in 1798 as a result of failed land speculations. He spent three years in debtor's prison, and died in poverty.

Related entries: Constitutional Convention; Declaration of Independence; Presidency

Suggestion for further reading:
"To Tobias Lear," 5 September 1790 (*Pres. Ser.*, vol. 6).

Morristown, New Jersey

After successfully routing the British at the Battles of Trenton and Princeton in late December 1776 and early January 1777, Washington retreated to the safety of Morristown in the hills of north-central New Jersey. Situated on the banks of the Whippany River about twenty-six miles west of New York City and halfway between Philadelphia and West Point, New York, Morristown was considered by the British to be invulnerable to a winter attack. At Morristown, Washington could monitor the movements of the British and threaten New Brunswick, Perth Amboy, and Newark. Washington headquartered at Morristown from 6 January to 28 May 1777, staying in a three-story tavern on the town square owned by Jacob Arnold, a captain in the Morris County light horse. Washington headquartered at Morristown again during the winter of 1779–1780, staying at a mansion house built by Jacob Ford on the eve of the war.

Related entries: Princeton, Battle of; Trenton, Battle of

Suggestion for further reading:
"To the Continental Congress Executive Committee," 7 January 1777 (*War Ser.,* vol. 8).

Mount Vernon

"I can truly say," wrote Washington in 1790, "I had rather be at Mount Vernon, with a friend or two about me, than to be attended, at the Seat of Government, by the Officers of State, and the Representatives of every Power in Europe." Named after Admiral Edward Vernon, the former commander of Washington's half brother Lawrence, Mount Vernon was Washington's home for his entire adult life, and the home to which he brought his wife, Martha, after their marriage in 1759. The frequency with which the "friend or two"—relatives, Revolutionary War veterans, foreign dignitaries, and curiosity seekers—dropped by Mount Vernon led Washington to call his home a "well-resorted tavern." It was eighteen months after his homecoming from the war, in fact, before George and Martha dined alone at Mount Vernon. Although he spent extended peri-

ods away from the estate, including a nearly eight-year stretch during the Revolutionary War and briefer periods as president, Washington always "kept a picture of Mount Vernon in his mind's eye" and longed for the tranquility that only his home could provide. Following his retirement from the presidency, granddaughter Nelly Custis informed a friend, "grandpapa is very well and much pleased with being once more Farmer Washington."

Washington's home was the center of a group of plantations owned by Washington, and as much a small village as a family home. The Mount Vernon estate, eventually amounting to more than 8,000 acres, consisted of five main farms, namely, the Mansion House farm, the Union farm, the Dogue Run farm, the Muddy Hole farm, and the River farm, as well as some outlying tracts. One of Washington's three mills was also at Mount Vernon, near the mouth of Dogue Run. "No estate in United America," wrote Washington to Arthur Young in 1793, "is more pleasantly situated than this. It lies in a high, dry, and healthy country, 300 miles by water from the sea, and . . . on one of the finest rivers in the world."

The Mansion House farm takes its name from Washington's residence, a two-story white-frame Georgian mansion overlooking the Potomac River about seven miles south of Alexandria. The original house was built by Lawrence Washington, who had inherited the plantation at the death of their father in 1743. Washington inherited the property, consisting of 2,126 acres on Little Hunting Creek, after the death of Lawrence and his heirs. In addition to the mansion house, which Washington subsequently enlarged to include a spacious banquet hall with a Palladian window and Italian marble chimneypiece, the farm had numerous other buildings, including a separate kitchen, smokehouse, dairy, wash house, coach house, greenhouse, barns, slave quarters, and beautiful English gardens. The

An aquatint depicting George Washington's home, Mount Vernon (Library of Congress)

handsome exterior of the mansion is sided with beveled pine slabs painted with sand to simulate stone blocks, and a graceful cupola caps the hip roof midway between two large brick chimneys at the ridge ends. A number of dormer windows also jut out of the roof. The east front, with its tall-columned piazza, overlooks the Potomac River. The west front faces the road leading to Alexandria and is joined to the nearest outbuildings on either side by curving arcades. The interior of the mansion still is furnished with many original possessions of Washington and his family, including portraits by Charles Willson Peale and Gilbert Stuart, the harpsichord imported for Nelly Custis, the key to the Bastille, and surveying tools. At his death Washington left the Mansion House farm and some smaller tracts subsequently added to it to his nephew Bushrod Washington, along with the Muddy Hole and Union farms. The man-

sion, America's first national shrine and perhaps one of the most well-known residential houses in America, was acquired from Washington's great-grandnephew by the Mount Vernon Ladies' Association of the Union in 1858. Sitting on about 500 of the original acres, the house, grounds, and museums are open to the public. Both George and Martha Washington are buried in the nearby family vault.

Just west of the Mansion House farm was the Union farm, so named because it consisted of the Ferry and French's tracts, 928 acres of arable and meadow land. Corn, wheat, and rye were rotated primarily at Union farm, although smaller amounts of oats, clover, alfalfa, peas, turnips, potatoes, and pumpkins were raised there also. Livestock was restricted severely at this farm for the most part, except for sheep, which were allowed to graze the pasture ground. The buildings included a house of four rooms for the farm manager as well as quarters for nearly five dozen slaves and a rectangular brick barn and stable complex erected between 1788 and 1791. The barn, based on a plan sent to him by English agriculturalist Arthur Young, was, in Washington's words, "equal, perhaps, to any in America, and for conveniences of all sorts, particularly for sheltering and feeding horses, cattle, &c. scarcely to be exceeded any where." On the farm's Potomac River frontage was a landing for the ferry to Maryland and a fishery purchased from John Posey.

North of Union farm and northwest of the Mansion House farm lay the 650-acre Dogue Run farm, named after the creek it bordered. Washington considered it the best of all his lands. The buildings included a two-room house for the farm's overseer, quarters for more than forty slaves, and sheds sufficient for thirty workhorses and oxen. At the mouth of Dogue Run was a gristmill, to which Washington added a distillery after his retirement from the presidency. The famous sixteen-sided "new circular barn" was constructed at Dogue Run farm in 1793. Designed as a building for treading wheat in all weather, the barn, reconstructed in the early 1990s, was, wrote Washington, "well calculated, it is conceived, for getting grain out of the straw more expeditiously than the usual mode of threshing." Inherited by Nelly Custis and her husband, Lawrence Lewis, at Washington's death, Dogue Run farm is also the site of Woodlawn, the Federal-style mansion erected by the Lewises shortly after they inherited the property.

The River farm lay east of the Mansion House farm along the Potomac, being separated from the others by the stream known as Little Hunting Creek. It contained about 1,200 acres of tillable ground, on which were grown, by rotation, wheat, oats, peas, rye, corn, turnips, clover, potatoes, timothy, pumpkins, and melons. The farm also had standing pastures for calves, milch cows, oxen, and ewes. A variety of other stock was kept on the farm at times as well—including workhorses, mules, oxen, and other horned cattle, sheep, and hogs. Improvements on the property included a two-story overseer's house containing about five rooms, quarters for about fifty or sixty slaves, a large barn, and stables. Because of its location on the river, the plantation provided plenty of mud for compost.

Muddy Hole farm lay across Little Hunting Creek from the River farm and directly north of the Mansion House farm, away from the Potomac. The crops raised on its 476 acres of tillable soil included oats, wheat, rye, clover, timothy, corn, peas, potatoes, pumpkins, squash, and "Turnips, and such like things as may be useful for Stock." Improvements included a small house for the overseer, quarters for about 30 slaves, and a "tolerable good barn, with stables for the work-horses." The land at Muddy Hole, which was prone to gully washing, was manured with plaster. Stock was restricted primarily to sheep and calves.

Over the decades Washington made substantial improvements to the Mount Vernon estate. After the Revolutionary War he enlarged the house from a small building of eight rooms into a commodious two-story mansion of more than a dozen rooms and passageways, ninety-six feet long by thirty-two feet in depth, complete with a large attic and cellar, a portico, and a columned piazza. He made improvements to the gardens and grounds around the house, sowing the lawn with English grass seeds, planting hedges, replacing dead trees in the serpentine walks and shrubberies, and established orchards in the outlying farms. During the last decade of his life Washington experimented with modern agricultural methods and was constantly receiving and planting evergreens and flowering trees and shrubs from various parts of the world.

Related entry: Ferry Farm

Suggestions for further reading:
"To Charles Lee," 20 February 1785 (*Con. Ser.*, vol. 2).

"Building Instructions for a Barn," 1792 (*Writings,* vol. 32).
"To Anthony Whiting," 6 January 1793 (*Writings,* vol. 32).
"To William Pearce," 23 November 1794 (*Writings,* vol. 34).
"To Lawrence Washington," 20 September 1799 (*Ret. Ser.,* vol. 2).
"Washington's Plans for His River, Union, and Muddy Hole Farms," 10 December 1799 (*Ret. Ser.,* vol. 4).
"Growth of the Mount Vernon Tract" (vol. 6, appendix 1). Douglas Southall Freeman. 1948–1957. 7 vols. *George Washington: A Biography.* New York.
Dalzell, Robert F., Jr., and Lee Baldwin Dalzell. 1998. *George Washington's Mount Vernon: At Home in Revolutionary America.* New York.

Muddy Hole Farm

See Mount Vernon.

Muse, George (1720–1790)

*I*t is not the lot of great men to always deal only with other great men, and perhaps that was more true during the time when George Washington lived than at the present. George Muse, an Englishman who first crossed Washington's path in the 1740s, certainly was not a great or a noble man, and that he was a contrary one, at least where Washington was concerned, and given to alcohol, cannot be disputed, although he might not have been the perfect scoundrel that some regarded him as after his apparently cowardly behavior at the capitulation of Fort Necessity in July 1754. Though he was not cut from the same cloth as Lord Dunmore or Benedict Arnold or even Charles Lee, three other men who provoked Washington's ire, he nevertheless disgusted Washington as few others ever did.

Muse, who was Washington's senior by twelve years, had been among the Virginia troops, including Washington's half brother Lawrence, who served in the Cartagena campaign of 1741. He subsequently became deputy adjutant general under Lawrence for the Virginia colony, taking upon himself the duties of adjutant general during the illness that finally took Lawrence's life in 1752. He was already a captain in the provincial forces when Virginia lieutenant governor Robert Dinwiddie decided to make him major on the 1753 expedition against the French on the Ohio. He afterward served under Washington as a captain, major, and lieutenant colonel in the first Virginia Regiment.

Of his infamous behavior at the capitulation of Fort Necessity, one report said Muse "instead of bringing up the 2d division to make the Attack with the first, he marched them or rather frightened them back into the trenches," a move exposing the Carolina Independent Company to French fire and forcing them to fall back also. Another report denounced Muse for halting his troops and running them "back in the utmost Confusion. happy he that could get into the Fort first." Washington omitted Muse's name when praising his officers and men in his report to Dinwiddie, as did the House of Burgesses when making an address thanking the officers for their role. One of the four officers in the Virginia Regiment wounded at Fort Necessity, William La Péronie, a Frenchman who was killed the following year in Braddock's defeat, informed Washington from Williamsburg that many had enquired of him "about Muses Braveries; poor Body I had pity him ha'nt he had the weakness to Confes his Coardise him self, & the inpudence to taxe all the reste of the oficiers withoud exeption of the same imperfection. for he said to many of the Cousulars and Burgeses that he was Bad But th' the reste was as Bad as he." To speak "francly," declared La Péronie, "had I been in town at the time I Coun't help'd to make use of my horse's wheup for to vindicate the injury of that vilain." Furthermore, Muse had "Contrived his Business" so that several men in Williamsburg had asked La Péronie if it were true that Muse had challenged Washington to a "fight: my answer was no other But that he Should rather chuse to go to hell than doing of it. for had he had such thing declar'd: that was his Sure Road—I have made my particular Business to tray if any had some Bad intention against you here Below: But thank God I meet allowais with a goad wish for you from evry mouth each one enterting such Caracter of you as I have the honour to do my Self."

No, Washington was not thought badly of by anyone because of Muse. Muse himself, however, was universally accused of cowardice and resigned his commission, moving Dinwiddie to remark that, "as he is not very agreeable to the other Officers, I am well pleas'd at his resignatn." But the world was smaller then, and that was not the end of Washington's association with Muse. Two years later Muse was a colonel of the militia and as such attended councils of war in Winchester to consider the defense of the frontier. Muse then disappears from Washington's records until one snowy evening in January 1768 when he came to Mount Vernon with Washington's brother Charles and the supplier for the Virginia Regiment in 1754 and 1755, Charles Dick, for what turned into a week of playing cards.

Muse's resignation might have pleased Dinwiddie, but it also prevented Muse from losing any of the bounty land promised to him as an officer under Dinwiddie's Proclamation of 1754—15,000 acres—to the consternation of some. In August 1770 he agreed to convey one-third of it to Washington if the latter would pay all the costs arising from the "Surveying and securing" of the land. Thus when a patent was issued

to Muse for 3,323 acres the following November, Washington was owner of one-third, and he secured the rest of the property by exchanging it for 2,000 acres that he purchased from across the Kanawha River. In March 1771 Muse attended a meeting of former officers of the original Virginia Regiment to hear Washington's report about his trip to examine the lands lying on the Kanawha River that had been allotted to the officers.

When the acreage was finally approved by the council, Muse apparently concluded that he had been shortchanged and somehow threw the blame upon Washington in an "impertinent Letter" written in December 1773. The letter has not survived, but Washington's acerbic response, written in late January 1774, has. "As I am not accustomed to receive such from any Man," Washington wrote, "nor would have taken the same language from you personally, without letting you feel some marks of my resentment; I would advise you to be cautious in writing me a second of the same tenour; for though I understand you were drunk when you did it, yet give me leave to tell you, that drunkenness is no excuse for rudeness." Except for Muse's "stupidity & sottishness," said Washington, he might have read in the newspapers that 10,000 acres of land had been approved for him. "& all my concerns is, that I ever engag'd in behalf of so ungrateful & dirty a fellow as you are. . . . I wrote to you a few days ago concerning the other distribution, proposing an easy method of dividing our Lands; but since I find in what temper you are, I am sorry I took the trouble of mentioning the Land, or your name in a Letter, as I do not think you merit the least assistance from G: Washington."

Despite Washington's anger, he and Muse carried through on their previous agreement concerning the land swap. Muse turned over his interest in the property to his son Battaile Muse in January 1775.

Muse married Elizabeth Battaile (d. 1786) in 1749 and settled in Caroline County, and Battaile Muse (1751–1803), who settled in Berkeley County, was rental agent for Washington's western lands in the 1780s.

Related entries: Dinwiddie, Robert; To George Muse, 29 January 1774 (Selected Writings)

Suggestions for further reading:
"From William La Péronie," 5 September 1754 (*Col. Ser.,* vol. 1).
"Agreement with George Muse," 3 August 1770 (*Col. Ser.,* vol. 8).
"To George Muse," 29 January 1774 (*Col. Ser.,* vol. 9).
"From George Muse," 6 January 1775 (*Col. Ser.,* vol. 10).
"From George Muse," 3 March 1784 (*Con. Ser.,* vol. 1).

National University

See Education; Potomac River Navigation; Tucker, St. George.

Natural Bridge, Virginia

Scant but undeniable evidence reveals that Washington on at least once occasion visited the Natural Bridge of Virginia, a massive 215-foot stone arch spanning a 93-foot-wide gorge, through which runs a shallow tributary of the James River, Cedar Creek. When making remarks on David Humphreys' proposed biography of himself, Washington silently passed over Humphreys' statement that Washington was "remarkably robust & athletic. I have several times heard him say, he never met any man who could throw a stone so great a distance as himself; and, that when standing in the valley beneath the natural bridge in Virginia, he has thrown one up to that stupendous arch." Tradition, unusually mute on the subject, adds nothing to Humphreys' story other than unsubstantiated accounts that Washington himself carved the initials "GW" twenty-five feet above the streambed that runs beneath the bridge.

When those initials first appeared remains a mystery, although they were there by the mid-nineteenth century. A historian of the Natural Bridge conjectured that Washington visited the Natural Bridge at the same time he inspected a chain of forts to the west. "General Washington is known to have been at Buchanan, twelve miles south of Natural Bridge; it is hardly likely that he would not take advantage of his close proximity to visit his comrade-in-arms, Captain Audley Paul," a fellow veteran of the Braddock campaign who lived at "Spreading Spring," four miles south of the Natural Bridge, and later, the stone house at Springfield, a mile closer to the bridge.

Long venerated by area Indians before Thomas Jefferson succeeded in acquiring the "rock bridge" with 157 surrounding acres in July 1774 for a mere twenty shillings, the truly awe-inspiring natural wonder attracted a myriad of visitors in the eighteenth and nineteenth centuries, including, in addition to Washington and Jefferson, Light-Horse Harry Lee, Daniel Boone, Davy Crockett, Andrew Jackson, Henry Clay, Stonewall Jackson, Sam Houston, Robert E. Lee, Matthew Fontaine Maury, and countless lesser-known individuals.

Porte Crayon drew the arch as early as 1855; a page from Crayon's "Virginia Illustrated" (1871) has Crayon and some heroines traveling the fourteen miles south from Lexington to the Natural Bridge and climbing it. "Porte went on to point out the spot where Washington is said to have written his initials. After considering the spot attentively

Photograph of the Natural Bridge, Virginia (Library of Congress)

Fannie declared she did not believe any mortal could have reached it without a ladder; and Dora said that, while she knew from her history that Washington was a great general and statesman, she never heard that he could climb any better than other people. Minnie observed, for her part she had always felt averse to hearing such stories about Washington, or to believing he could have done anything so childish." After these musings Crayon and his entourage left the Natural Bridge for another county attraction, Rockbridge Alum Springs.

Charles Dudley Warner (1829–1900), a frequent writer for *Harper's Weekly*, mentioned Washington's initials in his description of the Natural Bridge. "The arch is quite regular," wrote Warner, "and both arch and abutments are smooth as if cut with a chisel. On one side, about twenty-five feet above the stream, are natural tablets, or smooth surfaces, upon which are cut or scratched with sharp instruments hundreds of names. Among them is that of G. Washington. I confess that this exploit gave me a new feeling about the 'Father of our Country,' as I saw him in imagination in his stocking feet, clinging by his fingernails and eyelids, risking his life to carve in an inaccessible place his immortal name. But then he was not the Father of his Country when he did it."

Legends about Washington and the Natural Bridge have continued in the twentieth century. In his "Sketch of Natural Bridge," essayist Albert F. Gilmore asserted that Washington himself had surveyed the Natural Bridge, although Washington's surveying records do not substantiate the claim. "Interest in Natural Bridge," wrote Gilmore, "is historic as well as geologic. Associated with it are two names foremost in American history, George Washington and Thomas Jefferson; the latter as owner of the Bridge and adjoining territory by virtue of a grant from King George III; the former as surveyor, when, in the service of Lord Fairfax, he not only examined the structure and measured its lofty height, but left enduring evidence by a surveyor's mark now apparent on a recently uncovered stone by the stream side, and by his own initials hewn in the wall, up which he had climbed with a daring characteristic of his venturesome nature." Despite the latter claim, however, no evidence has ever surfaced showing that Washington surveyed the Natural Bridge or any other land in the area.

Related entries: Descriptions of Washington; Humphreys, David

Suggestions for further reading:
Tompkins, E. P., and J. Lee Davis. 1939. *The Natural Bridge and Its Historical Surroundings.* Natural Bridge, VA.
Zagarri, Rosemarie. 1991. *David Humphreys' "Life of General Washington" with George Washington's "Remarks."* Athens, GA.

New England Tour

*I*n the fall of 1789 Washington began consulting with his cabinet and others about the propriety of "makg. a tour through the Eastern states during the recess of Congress to acquire knowledge of the face of the Country the growth and Agriculture there of and the temper and disposition of the Inhabitants towards the new government." Washington's advisers thought the idea highly appropriate, provided he would later tour the southern states as well, which he did in the spring of 1791, and after several weeks of preparation he informed his sister, Betty Lewis, that in two or three days he intended to "set out for Boston by way of relaxation from business and reestablishment of my health." There was a light rain falling when he departed for Boston from the seat of government in New York City on 15 October, accompanied by his secretaries Tobias Lear and William Jackson and six servants.

Along the way there were the requisite ceremonies—some of which could not "be avoided though I had made every effort to do it"—and addresses involving town officials and representatives of various groups of veterans, civic organizations, and religious bodies. Several cities on his itinerary asked him to sit for portraits. He also was importuned to taste a sample of inventor Thomas Fielder's "suppos'd improvmt in the Article of American Rum" and see Fielder's exhibition of an "apparatus for facilitating navigation," a device described by one detractor as "a boat to work by— Magic, I suppose." Ever conscious of the precedent-setting nature of his actions, his arrival in Boston occasioned some disagreements and embarrassment regarding the protocol of how the president should be received by local and state officials. In Boston he became "much disordered by a Cold and inflamation in the left eye," giving the name "Washington influenza" to the cold and flu epidemic that afflicted not only the citizens of Boston but also the entire country that fall.

There was much merriment, too. At Boston the streets were filled with a "vast concourse of people" cheering before an elaborately ornamented arch stretched across the street near the State House, bearing the inscription "To the Man who unites all hearts" on one side and "To Columbia's favourite Son" on the other. "There followed an ode composed in honor of the President; and well sung by a band of select Singers." At Faneuil Hall the governor and council honored him with "a large & elegant dinner." At Cambridge the president and leaders of Harvard College showed him the 13,000-volume library and the museum's newly acquired orrery, "a curious piece of Mechanism for shewing the revolutions of the Sun, Earth and many other of the Planets." At Newburyport and Portsmouth he was similarly received. During a voyage in Portsmouth Harbor with dignitaries of New Hampshire, he was saluted by thirteen guns as the vessel sailed by the Old Fort (Fort William and Mary) and lighthouse on Newcastle Island; there was even time to visit the fishing banks to drop the lines for cod. At Lexington he took time to contemplate the "Spot on which the first blood was spilt in the dispute with Great Britain."

Washington recorded his impressions of the people and the countryside. He found the road from Boston to Marblehead "very pleasant," but the town itself was a different matter, for it "has the appearance of antiquity. The Houses are old—the streets dirty—and the common people not very clean." Salem, on the other hand, was "a neat Town." In Portsmouth there were some "good houses . . . but in general they are indifferent; and almost entirely of wood." The roads of Massachusetts were generally "amazingly crooked, to suit the convenience of every Mans fields; & the directions you receive from the People equally blind & ignorant"; "intolerable" was the word used most often to describe the roads of Connecticut. Typical of the taverns and inns along the way was one in Connecticut where for breakfast Washington ate "only bread and meat." It was "not a good House," he wrote, "though the People of it were disposed to do all they cou'd to accomodate me." Everywhere he went Washington noted the dwellings and church buildings, their situation and appearance, whether their chimneys were of brick or stone. He paid particular attention to the land and inquired about the livestock and crop yield; he collected information about manufacturing as well, especially as it related to the usage of cotton.

Washington, "having earnestly entreated that all parade & ceremony might be avoided on my return," made the trip back to New York City in less than half the time, arriving at his house on 13 November, where he "found Mrs. Washington and the rest of the family all well." He had visited nearly sixty towns and villages in Massachusetts, Connecticut, and New Hampshire. Rhode Island, which was deliberately left off the president's itinerary because it had not called a convention to ratify the U.S. Constitution, was toured briefly by Washington in August 1790 following the state's passage of a ratification resolution. It too was a success, reported newspapers, for "every individual thought he beheld a friend and patron; a father or brother after a long absence; and, on his part, the President seemed to feel the joy of a father on the return of the prodigal son."

Related entries: Hancock, John; Presidency; Southern Tour

Suggestions for further reading:
Diaries, vol. 5.
"To Betty Washington Lewis," 12 October 1789 (*Pres. Ser.*, vol. 4).
"From John Hancock," 26 October 1789 (*Pres. Ser.*, vol. 4).
"To the Citizens of Boston," 27 October 1789 (*Pres. Ser.*, vol. 4).
"To the Society of Quakers," October 1789 (*Pres. Ser.*, vol. 4).
"To the Clergy of Newport, Rhode Island," 18 August 1790 (*Pres. Ser.*, vol. 6).
"To the Inhabitants of Providence, Rhode Island," 19 August 1790 (*Pres. Ser.*, vol. 6).

New York Lands

See Clinton, George.

Newburgh Conspiracy

Newburgh, New York, Washington's Continental army headquarters from April 1782 to August 1783, was the location of several significant events. It was at Newburgh that Washington announced to the army the cessation of hostilities with Great Britain, and where he condemned a proposal that he head a constitutional monarchy. It was at Newburgh that the Order of the Purple Heart and the Society of the Cincinnati were established. And it was at Newburgh that Washington suppressed the Newburgh Conspiracy.

Despite the sorely deficient state of the Continental treasury in 1782, Washington successfully fielded another army, but the troops' discontent simmered all summer and showed no signs of diminishing with the coming of fall and winter. Their patience could not be expected to last forever. As Washington put it, "The Army, as usual, are without pay; and a great part of the Soldiery without shirts; and tho' the patience of them is equally thread bear, the States seem perfectly indifferent to their cries." As a pressure group a standing army was a double-edged sword, a fact not lost to its senior officers, or to financier Robert Morris, or to the more perceptive delegates in the Continental Congress—it might prove to be as unwieldy as it was powerful. Fortunately for the fledgling republic, discussions among general officers during the winter about how to best exert the army's influence were tempered by the officers' determination to safeguard the army's "immaculate" reputation at any cost. Nevertheless, everything came to a head on 10 March 1783, when an anonymous address called on the officers at Newburgh to "redress their own grievances" at a meeting the following day.

The writer of the address, Maj. John Armstrong, Jr., proposed that the officers deliver to Congress an ultimatum to the effect that its demands be met or that the officers would refuse to disband the army at the end of the war, or if the war did not end, that they would leave Congress defenseless by taking the army to "some unsettled country." The moment of crisis was averted only by Washington's personal and dramatic intervention. He had been warned that trouble was in the offing and that the army must be heard. In his General Orders of 11 March, Washington sternly forbade the officers to meet as proposed in the anonymous address, but he promptly and wisely arranged for another meeting to be held a few days later, on 15 March, at which the officers' grievances could be voiced. When issuing the order, he did not plan to be present at the meeting, but he subsequently changed his mind and attended, probably as a result of another anonymous paper, of 12 March, which interpreted the language of his General Orders as favoring the ideas expressed in the first address.

The story, as passed down, has been told many times. The officers, who had not expected their commander in chief to attend their meeting, listened nervously while Washington explained the principles upon which he had opposed the anonymous summons to convene an "irregular and hasty meeting" of the officers, declaring pointedly that he considered his own "Military reputation as inseperably connected with that of the Army." After exhorting the officers to maintain their loyalty to Congress, Washington pulled out a letter from a congressional delegate and began to read, but so haltingly that he reached into his pocket for his spectacles, commenting while doing so, "Gentlemen, you must pardon me. I have grown gray in your service and now find myself growing blind." Minutes later he was gone, his departure as unexpected as his arrival had been. The effect on the officers of his simple remark regarding his eyesight was so powerful that they immediately passed resolutions expressing confidence in Congress and rejecting the Newburgh Addresses "with disdain." The Newburgh affair was not without consequences, however, for it so shocked Congress that the following week it promised the officers five years of pay in lieu of the half-pay pensions already approved but not provided for.

The Newburgh headquarters, the house of Jonathan Hasbrouck, is now a museum open to the public.

Related entries: Nicola, Lewis; To the Officers of the Army, 15 March 1783 (Selected Writings)

Suggestions for further reading:
"General Orders," 11, 18 March 1783 (*Writings*, vol. 26).
"To Joseph Jones," 12, 18 March 1783 (*Writings*, vol. 26).

"To the President of Congress," 12, 16, 18
March 1783 (*Writings*, vol. 26).
"To the Officers of the Army," 15 March 1783
(*Writings*, vol. 26).
"To Benjamin Harrison," 19 March 1783
(*Writings*, vol. 26).
"To John Armstrong, Jr.," 23 February 1797
(*Writings*, vol. 35).

Nicola, Lewis (1717–1807)

ewis Nicola, a former British army officer who served as colonel of the Continental army Invalid Regiment during the Revolutionary War, is best known for advocating in 1782 the creation of a constitutional monarchy with Washington as king, "which I conceive would be attended with some material advantage." Washington's "mixture of great surprise and astonishment" was followed by a strong rebuke: "If I am not deceived in the knowledge of myself," he wrote Nicola, "you could not have found a person to whom your schemes are more disagreeable. . . . Let me conjure you then, if you have any regard for your Country, concern for yourself or posterity, or respect for me, to banish these thoughts from your Mind, and never communicate, as from yourself, or any one else, a sentiment of the like Nature." Nicola was so taken aback at Washington's response that he wrote three separate letters of apology.

Nicola had come to America from Dublin, Ireland, in the 1760s, settling in Philadelphia as a merchant. Prominent in the cultural circles of Philadelphia, he was proprietor of a circulating library and curator of the American Philosophical Society. During the Revolutionary War he published three military manuals, including *A Treatise of Military Exercise, Calculated for the Use of the Americans* (Philadelphia, 1776). He spent his last years at Alexandria, Virginia, where he died.

Related entries: Descriptions of Washington; Newburgh Conspiracy

Suggestion for further reading:
"To Lewis Nicola," 22 May 1782 (*Writings*, vol. 24).

Northern Neck Proprietary

See Fairfax of Cameron, Thomas Fairfax, Sixth Baron; Greenway Court.

Ohio Country

See Braddock's Defeat; Carlyle, John; Craik, James; Cresap, Thomas; Croghan, George; Dinwiddie, Robert; Dunmore, John Murray, Fourth Earl of; Forbes Campaign; Fort Necessity Campaign; Gist, Christopher; Great Kanawha Tracts; Half-King, The; La Force; Mercer, George; Mercer, John; Potomac River Navigation; Van Braam, Jacob; Wills Creek.

Cover of a pamphlet created for a 1999 exhibition at the University of Virginia demonstrating the process of documentary editing (The Papers of George Washington)

P

Papers

The public and private papers of America's most famous citizen are a true national treasure. Washington the surveyor, planter, and land speculator would have become a prolific letter writer even if the French and Indian War had not catapulted him into the public eye, but his involvement in that war and the ensuing revolutionary struggle ensured that his papers would number among the largest of any individual of the eighteenth century. Washington himself began to consider his papers as one of his most important legacies long before completing his role in the great events that they chronicle. Early on he began to save all his incoming correspondence, and after a time he began the practice of retaining copies of most of his outgoing letters as well. Near the end of the Revolutionary War, Congress approved the appointment of a recording secretary who, with a team of copiers, arranged his wartime papers, copying Washington's own letters, orders, and instructions into bound books, thirty large folio volumes deposited upstairs at Mount Vernon. After the war Washington became the first editor of his papers when he went over his French and Indian War letter books, cleaning up mistakes in spelling and grammar. He then engaged a number of individuals, including some family members, to copy his corrected letter books. Following his earlier practice, Washington carefully preserved his presidential papers and sent them to Mount Vernon for safekeeping at the end of his second administration, except for a group left in the possession of his successor, John Adams. During his retirement Washington used a letter press that he had acquired while president for copying letters.

The priority that Washington placed on the preservation of his papers is illustrated by his wish to erect a separate building to house them at Mount Vernon, which if carried out would have set in effect a precedent for the modern presidential library. Although he died before acting on that idea, Washington expressed concern for his papers during the last hours of the unexpected illness that took his life in late 1799. He instructed his private secretary Tobias Lear to settle his financial accounts and "*arrange and record all my late military letters and papers. . . . let Mr.* [Albin] *Rawlins finish recording my other letters which he has begun.*" Washington in his will bequeathed his papers to his nephew Bushrod Washington, who subsequently proved to be less interested in their preservation than his uncle. Bushrod left the papers at Mount Vernon until 1803, when he sent most of them to Richmond, Virginia, to Chief Justice John Marshall, who was writing a multivolume biography of Washington. By that time the letters between Martha and

George Washington had been destroyed, reputedly by Martha herself before her death.

Bushrod's casual attitude toward his uncle's papers ultimately led to their dispersement. He returned many of Washington's incoming letters to their original authors and gave others away as souvenirs. He allowed about 1,500 more to be carted off beginning in 1815 by the tutor of Nelly Custis's children, William B. Sprague, who left inferior copies in their place, and Bushrod gave carte-blanche permission to the editor of the first published edition of Washington's papers, Jared Sparks, to use them as he saw fit. Sparks's sins against what had been among the most valuable of his subject's possessions were particularly egregious in that he not only dispensed documents as if they were his own but also mutilated some in the process to satisfy autograph hunters and other curious persons anxious to obtain a piece of something once owned by Washington.

The legal ownership of George Washington's papers at Bushrod's death in 1829 passed to his nephew George Corbin Washington, who sold those in his possession to the U.S. government in two series, those of a public nature in 1834, for $25,000, and those regarded as private in 1849, for $20,000. The papers transferred to the U.S. government, cared for by the Department of State until the Library of Congress took over their administration in 1904, consist of about 60,000 documents. Although that is by far the single largest collection of Washington's papers, tens of thousands of other manuscript papers written by or to Washington have survived and are scattered around the world in nearly 300 American and more than seventy foreign repositories. A substantial number also remain in private hands.

The earliest manuscripts that Washington chose to retain consist of schoolwork he made as a child, more than 200 pages of mostly math and surveying exercises, legal forms, and the often-published "Rules of Civility & Decent Behaviour in Company and Conversation," which comprise only ten pages. The lessons, which would have been especially useful to an eighteenth-century middle-class planter, appear to have been copied between 1744 and 1748, although they may have been begun as early as 1741. The surveying and geometry lessons are particularly interesting in that they probably prepared Washington for his brief but important career as a professional surveyor, during which he made more than 190 surveys. The records of these surveys included field books in which surveying field notes were made, finished surveys complete with plats and descriptions of boundaries, notebooks with surveys without plats, warrants, and accounts. In addition, deeds for many of his properties have survived.

Some fifty-one surviving manuscript volumes collectively called Washington's "diaries" by scholars span Washington's entire life. Neither introspective nor literary, they are not diaries in any conventional sense. The vast majority are more like daybooks in which Washington made very brief notations about the routines of agriculture, livestock, the weather, amusements, and visitors to Mount Vernon or the presidential mansions. A number of manuscripts best described as "travel journals" are grouped among the diaries: the surveying trip "over the Mountains" in the spring of 1748; the trip to Barbados with his older half brother Lawrence in the winter of 1751–1752; his journey to the French commandant at Fort Duquesne beginning in October 1753; the expedition to the Ohio in the spring of 1754; his tours of western lands in the falls of 1770 and 1784; the Yorktown campaign of 1781; his northern and southern tours as president in 1790 and 1791; and his trip to western Pennsylvania during the Whiskey Rebellion of 1794. Distinct from the diaries but similar in nature is Washington's journal of the proceedings of the president, a daily account of Washington's official activities and correspondence, kept by his secretaries but written in the first person.

In addition to Washington's school exercises, surveying records, and diaries, a variety of other "miscellaneous"-type documents are contained in his papers. Financial records covering the span of Washington's public and private life, although incomplete, include more than 6,000 pages of ledgers, accounts, invoices, and receipts. Among his pre-Revolutionary War papers are such financial records from the private sphere as well as a number of orders, instructions, memorandums, and army returns related to the French and Indian War, and a large amount of material related to the estate of John Custis (1678–1749) and Daniel Parke Custis (1711–1757) and their heirs, of which Washington assumed the management after marrying Martha Custis in 1759. Typical among such Revolutionary War–era documents are general orders, official reports, army returns, prisoner returns, sketches and maps, courts-martial proceedings, minutes from councils of war, congressional and state resolutions, commissions, resignations, and financial accounts related to Washington's headquarters. Of special interest after the war are the inventory of the livestock, farm implements, and slaves on the farms of his Mount Vernon estate and the detailed weekly farm reports that he required of his farm managers beginning in 1785. The presidential period contains large numbers of official reports, a variety of circulars, congressional bills and acts, treaty negotiations, documents on Indian affairs, petitions for federal office, material on the planning of the Federal City, presidential household accounts, and agriculture-related papers. His retirement papers also have their share of unusual documents, including Washington's lengthy comments in his annotated copy of James Monroe's *A View of the Conduct of the Executive, in the Foreign Affairs of the United States* . . . (Philadelphia, 1797); his lists of candidates for army appointments and other documents related to the Quasi-War with France; elaborate plans for the management of his Mount Vernon farms; slave lists; a schedule of his extensive landholdings; and his last will and testament.

The majority of Washington's papers consists of his correspondence. Covering a fifty-year period, the letters written by and to Washington number in the tens of thousands. The correspondents include some of the most celebrated figures of the age in America and Europe. Their subjects cover Washington's participation in the most important arenas of the eighteenth century—the French and Indian War, the Revolutionary War, the Constitutional Convention, the establishment of the American presidency, the French Revolution, and the Quasi-War with France. The correspondence also offers the most intimate look possible at the private Washington, his plantation and business affairs, and his family life. Some two-thirds of all the documents in Washington's papers were generated during the eight-year period of the Revolutionary War.

Several attempts have been made to edit Washington's papers in the two centuries since his death, including Jared Sparks's *The Writings of Washington: Being His Correspondence, Addresses, Messages, and Other Papers* . . . (12 vols., 1834–1837), Worthington Chauncey Ford's *The Writings of George Washington* (14 vols., 1889–1893), and John C. Fitzpatrick's *The Writings of George Washington from the Original Manuscript Sources, 1745–1799* (39 vols., 1931–1944). Fitzpatrick also edited *The Diaries of George Washington, 1748–1799* (4 vols., 1925). As their titles imply, these editions included only documents generated by or for Washington and did not include those written to him. All were sparsely annotated. In 1969 the Mount Vernon Ladies' Association of the Union and the University of Virginia jointly sponsored an ambitious effort to assemble copies of all of Washington's papers, including letters written to him as well as by him, in preparation for a comprehensive modern scholarly edition of Washington's papers. Over half of a projected 90 volumes of *The Papers of George Washington,* edited by a team led successively by W. W. Abbot, Dorothy Twohig, and Philander D. Chase, has been published so far (2001). When complete, the fully annotated edition will include Washington's *Diaries* (6 vols.) and the *Journal of the Proceedings of the President* (1 vol.) and five chronological series of his correspondence, the *Colonial Series* (10 vols.), the *Revolutionary War Series* (40 vols.), the *Confederation Series* (6 vols.), the *Presidential Series* (20 vols.), and the *Retirement Series* (4 vols.), as well as an electronic edition of the papers and a yet-to-be-determined number of volumes of school exercises and financial records.

Related entries: Education; Rawlins, Albin; Varick, Richard

Suggestions for further reading:
"Introductory Note" (*Writings,* vol. 1).
"Preface" (*Col. Ser.,* vol. 1).
"School Exercises," 1744–1748 (*Col. Ser.,* vol. 1).
"The Letter Book for the Braddock Campaign," 2 March–14 August 1755 (*Col. Ser.,* vol. 1).
"Preface" (*War Ser.,* vol. 1).
"Instructions to Bezaleel Howe," 9 November 1783 (*Writings,* vol. 27).
"To Richard Varick," 1 January 1784 (*Con. Ser.,* vol. 1).
"To James Craik," 25 March 1784 (*Con. Ser.,* vol. 1).
"Last Will and Testament," 9 July 1799 (*Ret. Ser.,* vol. 4).
Abbot, W. W. 1989. "An Uncommon Awareness of Self: The Papers of George Washington" (*Prologue: Quarterly of the National Archives,* vol. 21).

Peale, Charles Willson (1741–1827)

The only likeness of George Washington before the Revolutionary War was rendered in oil by Charles Willson

The only likeness of George Washington painted before the Revolutionary War, by Charles Willson Peale (Courtesy of Washington and Lee University)

Peale in 1772. In the portrait Washington is wearing his colorful military uniform from the French and Indian War, complete with three-cornered hat, elegant sash, and decorative officer's gorget. The blue coat and red vest are trimmed in silver; the buttons also are of silver, and a medallion graces the hat. His right hand, gloved, is resting inside his vest. A folded document stuffed in the vest pocket is labeled "Order of March." He is carrying weapons, an English-made sword ordered in 1757, and, oddly enough, an ordinary fowler used for hunting. The landscape scene in the background—a mountain range, a river with falls, and an Indian camp—seems to evoke the west that Washington was familiar with during the French and Indian War. Particularly striking is Peale's youthful rendering of his subject's face. Although Washington already had passed his fortieth birthday, he might easily be mistaken for half that age. Combined with the details of the uniform and the landscape, it is obvious that the artist and his subject conspired to depict the colonel of the Virginia Regiment, the commission of which Washington had resigned fourteen years earlier. The portrait's younger-looking Washington also paired well with the companion for which it was intended, a portrait of Martha Washington painted by John Wollaston in 1757. The Peale portrait, for which the artist was paid £18.4.0, now hangs in the Robert E. Lee Memorial Chapel at Washington and Lee University in Lexington, Virginia. While at Mount Vernon, Peale also painted miniatures of Martha Washington and her children, Jacky and Patsy, for which he charged £13 each.

By the time Peale arrived at Mount Vernon in May 1772, he had become perhaps the most promising portrait painter in the colonies, having studied in England under the famous artist Benjamin West from 1767 to 1769. Peale's practice was to tour sections of Virginia, Maryland, and Pennsylvania where he would paint miniatures for planters and merchants. The miniatures were popular because they could be painted quickly, were less expensive, and were less demanding of the subjects than larger paintings. At this time Peale, who was born in Charleston, Maryland, was residing in Annapolis, where he had served a lengthy apprenticeship to a saddle maker as a youth. He was introduced to Washington by Jacky Custis's tutor, Jonathan Boucher, who recently had moved his boys school to Annapolis.

Washington allowed Peale to take his portrait several more times, beginning in December 1773, when the artist returned to Mount Vernon. Peale had resettled in Philadelphia during the first year of the Revolutionary War, and in 1776 Washington sat for Peale while at Philadelphia after John Hancock commissioned him to paint portraits of George and Martha. In that portrait a bareheaded Washington was pictured in his Continental army uniform against a background of Boston and its har-

bor. Mezzotint engravings based on the painting were the means by which most of Washington's contemporaries came to know his image. The original painting, which hung in the Hancock house at Boston until 1863, when it was sold at auction, is now in the Brooklyn Museum. Peale served as a recruiting officer for Pennsylvania and later as a Continental army captain, taking part in the Battles of Trenton, Princeton, Germantown, and Monmouth Courthouse. Other portraits followed, perhaps drawing on Peale's own military experience: a picture of Washington after the Battles of Trenton and Princeton in late 1776 and early 1777; a portrait of Washington at Valley Forge during the winter of 1777–1778, commissioned in 1779 by the Pennsylvania supreme executive council; a painting of Washington and his generals at Yorktown painted between 1781 and 1783; and a portrait of Washington at the Constitutional Convention in 1787, from which Peale engraved his last mezzotint. Altogether, counting the oil paintings and engravings based on them, Peale rendered some sixty portraits of Washington.

One little-known illustration of Washington made by Peale was done in June 1777, when Peale traveled to the Continental army headquarters at Quibbletown, New Jersey, to see Washington, "who promised to sit for his Miniature but at this Time he had not Leisure." Peale accompanied Continental troops to a mountaintop in the area "overlooking the country as far as my Eyes could see—Brunswick Amboy and Staten Island—and even beyond the Bay at Amboy," from which he watched, about six miles distant, a skirmish between Lord Stirling's brigade and the British. Shortly after Peale came to the spot "where I spent the whole day," Washington arrived there, and Peale drew a rough sketch in his diary of himself and Washington perched on the edge of the cliff, viewing the skirmish in the valley below. Peale returned home the following day without taking a likeness of

Washington, however, other than the rough sketch.

Peale was deeply interested in natural history, and after the war he opened a museum in Philadelphia that he filled with a wide assortment of fossils, rocks, minerals, and exotic animals, birds, and fish. "Mr. Peale's animals reminded me of *Noah's Ark,*" wrote a minister, "into which was received every kind of beast and creeping thing in which there was life. But I can hardly conceive that even Noah could have boasted of a better collection." Peale delivered lectures on natural history at the museum and took the leading part in founding the Philadelphia Academy of Fine Arts.

The favorite of every visitor, young and old, was Peale's wax models, an unheard-of novelty in America. The lifelikeness of the wax portrayals astonished one and all. Washington himself supposedly was startled into bowing to Peale's double portrait of his sons, Raphaelle and Titian I. Advertisements in the *Pennsylvania Packet* in March 1787 list among the exotic animals, birds, and reptiles on exhibit at the museum a golden pheasant that had been sent to Washington by the marquis de Lafayette. Two months later Peale invited Washington to a private showing of his exhibition on changing perspective views. The same year, the Reverend Manasseh Cutler, after visiting Peale's museum and describing the collection of distinguished characters who graced its walls, said that, "at the upper end of the room, General Washington, at full length and nearly as large as life, was placed, as President of this sage and martial assembly."

In the spring of 1789, when Washington was about to make his triumphal entry into Philadelphia while en route to New York City to take office as U.S. president, Peale was called upon to help prepare the surprise decoration of the bridge at Gray's Ferry across the Schuylkill River. Each end of the bridge was outfitted with an arch of laurel, the sides lined with laurel and cedar,

and large flags marking the roads that read "The New Era," "May Commerce Flourish," a third with a Liberty cap and the slogan, "Don't Tread on Me," and the fourth the rising sun of empire. Flying banners representing each of the eleven states that had ratified the Constitution were strewn along the north side of the bridge, and on its south side waved the flag of the American union. Across the river, "every fence, field and avenue" was lined with 20,000 spectators welcoming Washington as a hero with shouts and cheers and clapping, while in the background cannon pealed, ships sounded, and church bells rang.

In 1792 Washington donated a feather cloak and hat, probably from Hawaii, to Peale's museum, the "first government deposit," which influenced Rembrandt Peale's later portrait, *Man in a Feathered Helmet.* Rumors that George and Martha were expected to attend Peale's so-called "New Theatre" in May 1794 gave the enterprise extra clout. Washington's name routinely headed the annual subscription list for the museum, followed by Vice President John Adams and dozens of other dignitaries. In 1798 Peale designed a medal with a relief of Washington on one side, encircled by his name, and with the arms of the United States on the reverse, with the motto, "Liberty and Security," and on the trilled edge, "An asylum for the oppressed of all nations."

Peale kept an extensive diary, and authored several published works, including *An Essay on Building Wooden Bridges* (1797), *Introduction to a Course of Lectures on Natural History* (1800), and *An Epistle to a Friend on the Means of Preserving Health* (1803). He died at Philadelphia and is buried in St. Peter's Churchyard.

A younger brother of Peale, James Peale (1749–1831), studied art under his more famous brother from 1762 to 1770, when he began painting in earnest, concentrating on historical figures, still lifes, and landscapes. His most famous work was a series of miniatures of Washington. Charles Willson Peale's children also became artists, including Raphaelle, Titian Ramsay I, Rubens, Titian Ramsay II, and Rembrandt. Rembrandt Peale's lost *Apotheosis of General Washington* (1800) served as the inspiration for many copies.

Related entries: Custis, John Parke; Custis, Martha Parke; False Teeth; Houdon, Jean-Antoine; Trumbull, John; Washington, Martha Dandridge Custis

Suggestions for further reading:
"To Jonathan Boucher," 21, 23 May 1772 (*Col. Ser.,* vol. 9).
"Cash Accounts," May 1772 (*Col. Ser.,* vol. 9).
"To Lafayette," 25 September 1778 (*Writings,* vol. 12).
"From Charles Willson Peale," 6 January 1788 (*Con. Ser.,* vol. 6).
Brigham, David R. 1995. *Public Culture in the Early Republic: Peale's Museum and Its Audience.* Washington, DC.
Miller, Lillian, ed. 1983–1996. 4 vols. *The Selected Papers of Charles Willson Peale and His Family.* New Haven, CT.
Sellers, Charles Coleman. 1969. *Charles Willson Peale.* New York.

Pickering, Timothy (1745–1829)

Timothy Pickering, a native of Salem, Massachusetts, and a 1759 graduate of Harvard College, practiced law in his hometown after being admitted to the Massachusetts bar in 1768. From 1772 to 1777 he held several public offices, including selectman, town clerk, and assessor, and representative to the more important Massachusetts General Court. At the start of the Revolutionary War he was colonel of the Essex County militia and author of a drill manual, *An Easy Plan of Discipline for a Militia* (1775), a copy of which he gave to Washington. In late March 1777 Washington offered Pickering the post of adjutant general of the Continental army, which he accepted, beginning duties the following July. He accompanied Washington at the Battles of Brandywine and Germantown before the Continental Congress appointed him to the Board of War near the end of the year. He became quartermaster general of the Continental army in August 1780, an office he held to 1785. Pickering's efforts in supplying the army were instrumental during Washington's march from New York to Yorktown in 1781, and he also played an important role in the demobilization of the army in 1783. Contrary to many other veterans, Pickering's judgment of Washington was less than flattering. He reputedly told Maj. Gen. Nathanael Greene one night while watering their horses at a ford that, "Before I came to the Army, I entertained an exalted opinion of General Washington's military talents, but I have since seen nothing to enhance it." Pickering continued to hold Washington in low esteem despite the fact that Washington subsequently gave him several important posts in the federal government.

At the war's end Pickering moved to Philadelphia and entered into a mercantile partnership with Samuel Hodgdon, the Continental army's commissary general of military stores. The firm of Pickering & Hodgdon also speculated in land and depreciated soldiers' notes, but by 1786 it was running into trouble, and Pickering decided to settle on his lands in the Wyoming Valley of western Pennsylvania. Before he left Philadelphia in early 1787, he managed to garner several important offices of the newly created county of Luzerne. Life on the frontier proved to be even more financially unstable for Pickering, however, and in 1789 he began to petition for various state and federal appointments without success.

Pickering's fortunes began to change in 1790 when Washington sent him to Tioga Point, Pennsylvania, to treat with representatives of the Seneca tribe. After hearing complaints about fraudulent land deals and the killing of Indians by "white savages" from Farmer's Brother and Red Jacket, two important Seneca chiefs, Pickering sided with the Indians in their grievances with the U.S. government. "I have found that they are not difficult to please," he wrote Washington. "A man must be destitute of humanity, of honesty, or of common sense, who should send them away disgusted: He must want sensibility, if he did not sympathize with them on their recital of the injuries they have experienced from white men." The eye-opening experience led Pickering to draft a plan to introduce the "art of husbandry, and civilization, among our Indian neighbours," a well-meaning but misguided proposal aimed at assimilating Indians into the white culture. Recognizing that Pickering was particularly adept in Indian diplomacy, Washington offered him the office of superintendent of Indian affairs for the northern department. Pickering, holding out for a better office, declined the appointment but offered to continue to negotiate with leaders of the Six Nations, to Washington's great satisfaction.

In August 1791 Pickering finally received a federal appointment when Washington gave him the lucrative office of postmaster general. His efficient management of the department allowed him time to continue to advise the president about Indian relations, resulting in the improvement of the administration's Indian policy. He became Washington's principal and most successful Indian diplomat, and in January 1795 his services were rewarded when Washington named him secretary of war following the resignation of Henry Knox. Later that year Pickering became embroiled in the controversy to ratify the Jay Treaty. Pickering endorsed the treaty because of the positive effect it would have on U.S.-Indian relations when the British abandoned their posts in the northwest. Unfortunately, his labors to secure the treaty's ratification included a deliberate attempt to ruin the reputation and political career of Edmund Randolph, Washington's old friend and secretary of state. When Randolph, the sole cabinet member to oppose

the Jay Treaty, resigned, Washington named Pickering his replacement. Although political animosity and public disputes characterized Pickering's tenure as Washington's chief adviser, John Adams kept Pickering in office when he succeeded Washington as president in 1797.

Pickering's last connection with Washington was to make preparations for the so-called Quasi-War in 1797 and 1798 when Adams asked the former president to lead the provisional army. Pickering eventually returned to Massachusetts and was elected to the U.S. Senate in 1803 and the House of Representatives in 1813, where he adamantly opposed America's new war with Great Britain. Pickering retired from public life in 1817 and died twelve years later in his native Salem. He spent his last years contending for scientific agriculture, Unitarianism, the abolition of slavery, and his place in history—which meant to him puncturing the burgeoning myth of the founding generation by exposing the mediocrity and ineptness of Washington, the vanity and calumny of John Adams, the overrated reputation of Samuel Adams, and the "supreme" hypocrisy of Jefferson.

Related entries: Presidency; Quasi-War

Suggestions for further reading:
"To Timothy Pickering," 30 March 1777 (*War Ser.*, vol. 9).
"From Timothy Pickering," 9, 14 April 1777 (*War Ser.*, vol. 9).
"To Timothy Pickering," 4 September 1790 (*Pres. Ser.*, vol. 6).
"From Timothy Pickering," 5 September 1790 (*Pres. Ser.*, vol. 6).
"From Timothy Pickering," 4, 23, 31 December 1790 (*Pres. Ser.*, vol. 7).
Clarfield, Gerard H. 1980. *Timothy Pickering and the American Republic*. Pittsburgh.

Pohick Church, Truro Parish

Located a dozen miles south of Alexandria and about five miles from

Mount Vernon, in Fairfax County, Virginia, is historic Pohick Church, the church of George Washington. In 1762 Washington was elected a vestryman of Truro Parish, an office concerned less with ecclesiastical affairs than with temporal ones, such as caring for the neighborhood's poorer citizens, overseeing the maintenance of local roads, and policing the movements of indentured servants and slaves from among the area's many plantations. By far the most important parish issue during Washington's thirteen-year tenure was a proposal in 1767 to move the location of the parish meetinghouse from the south side of Pohick Creek to a more central location on the main thoroughfare on the other side of the creek. Many, including Washington's neighbor and fellow vestryman George Mason of Gunston Hall, were disinclined to abandon the old site because the bones of their ancestors were resting in the churchyard. Washington, who at the time was one of the parish's two church wardens, allegedly brought to the parochial meeting a plat drawn by himself delineating all the roads and houses in the parish and showing that the proposed location was more accessible than the old to every single one of the church's worshipers. When the issue was decided in favor of the new location, Mason purportedly donned his hat and stalked out of the meeting, exclaiming, "That's what gentlemen get for engaging in debate with a d—d surveyor!"

Daniel French (1723–1771), a wealthy planter who lived at Rose Hill, his plantation west of Alexandria, contracted with the vestry to build the new church for £877, Virginia currency. (French also owned land in the vicinity of Mount Vernon, including a plantation on Dogue Run adjacent to Mount Vernon that Washington purchased in 1786.) In 1772 the vestry voted to construct an eighteen-by-twenty-four-foot brick vestry house near the church.

The old Pohick Church building was of simple wooden construction. By contrast the new church, a substantial 3,000-square-foot brick structure, is typical late Georgian parish architecture; its simple rectangular plan includes a low-pitched hip roof with no tower, resembling its northern neighbor, Christ Church, Alexandria, as originally built. Its symmetrical facades contain an unusual feature—rectilinear windows on the first floor and arched windows on the second. The interest and beauty of the building are further enhanced by the use of sandstone to construct the modillioned cornices, angle quoins, and door trim. The church was occupied and badly treated by Union soldiers during the Civil War, but has since been restored and is used for regular services.

The new church was still under construction when the Washington family had to call upon its rector, Lee Massey, to read the funeral service of the family's youngest member, Patsy Custis, who died of epilepsy on 19 June 1773. The new building was completed the following February, and Washington made known his intentions to frequent the church by having his monogram attached to the door of his pew and by having the pew equipped with drawers in which to set his prayer books and papers. His regular attendance at the church was soon halted by the coming of the Revolutionary War, however, which ended his career as a vestryman as well, although he did not formally resign until February 1784.

Related entries: Mason, George; Religious Beliefs

Suggestions for further reading:

"Minutes of Truro Parish Vestry," 21 September 1769 (*Col. Ser.*, vol. 8).
"Cash Accounts," February 1774 (*Col. Ser.*, vol. 9).
"Cash Accounts," August 1774 (*Col. Ser.*, vol. 10).
"From Daniel McCarty," 22 February 1784 (*Con. Ser.*, vol. 1).
"To Daniel McCarty," 22 February 1784 (*Con. Ser.*, vol. 1).
Minutes of the Vestry: Truro Parish Virginia, 1732–1785. 1974. Lorton, VA.
Slaughter, Philip. 1908. *The History of Truro Parish in Virginia.* Philadelphia.

Popes Creek

"Came up to Popes Creek & staid there all day." Thus reads Washington's diary entry for 24 May 1768, of the tidewater estate where he had been born some thirty-six years before. Located in Westmoreland County, Virginia, Popes Creek (later called Wakefield) was part of the Bridges Creek plantation, the original seat of the Washington family in Virginia. Washington's father, Augustine Washington, Sr., built a house on the west side of Popes Creek about three-quarters of a mile from the Potomac River, in the mid-1720s. From the gentle slope where the house was situated one could easily see across the creek and the river to the wooded Maryland shore, dotted here and there with farms and plantations. At Popes Creek, Washington spent the first three years of his life, until Augustine decided to move his growing family to another plantation about sixty miles further up the Potomac River near Little Hunting Creek, later known as Mount Vernon. The elder Washington apparently entrusted the administration of the Popes Creek property to his second son, Augustine, Jr. (Austin), who at the time was barely 17 years old, the age at which his own son William Augustine assumed administration of the estate nearly thirty years later, in 1774.

At the time of the elder Augustine's death in 1743, the Popes Creek plantation consisted of the residence house; kitchen and pantry, and other storerooms; a dairy; a stable; a barn; other outbuildings; and a number of tobacco houses. A handful of slaves lived and worked at the site, no doubt taking care of the livestock, including 30 sheep, 62 cattle, 75 hogs, 140 geese, as well as such common fowl as chickens.

Washington returned to the site of his birth numerous times during his youth, to visit Augustine, Jr. and his family, but by the time the few words in the aforementioned diary entry were jotted down, Washington's half brother had been dead for six years, and the plantation was occupied by his widow, Anne Aylett Washington, and their four children. Upon her death in 1773 Popes Creek was inherited by Anne and Augustine's only son, William Augustine Washington, who renamed it Wakefield and lived there until the plantation house burned during the Revolutionary War, in 1779. Rather than rebuilding the house after the fire, Washington's nephew abandoned the site for one a mile to the west, and the ruins of the house deteriorated into rubble in the following decades. Washington's step-grandson George Washington Parke Custis marked the site in 1816 with an inscribed stone slab that stated simply:

HERE
ON THE 11th OF FEBRUARY, 1732,
WASHINGTON
WAS BORN

A small but steady number of curiosity seekers and souvenir hunters made pilgrimages to the site of Washington's birth in the ensuing decades. The heirs of Popes Creek deeded the house site to the state of Virginia on the eve of the Civil War, but the state failed to rescue the site from neglect, and it passed into federal hands in 1882. The Wakefield National Memorial Association immediately began to acquire additional surrounding land, and efforts to erect a large monument at the site culminated in the erection in 1896 of a fifty-one-foot granite shaft that is plainly visible from vessels passing on the Potomac River at a distance of five miles. A memorial mansion intended to represent the typical eighteenth-century Virginia plantation house was erected there in honor of the bicentennial of Washington's birth. At the same time the U.S. Congress designated the area as the George Washington Birthplace National Monument and incorporated it into the National Park Service. A mile northwest of the memorial house is the Washington family burial ground containing the graves of many of Washington's ancestors.

Archeological excavations of the remains of the house (most completely in the 1970s) have revealed a large original building that was added onto until it became a U-shaped building. The bottom of the U contained the building's largest section, which included a two-room cellar extending under the entire section, with a fireplace in each room. This section measured about nineteen feet wide by fifty-eight feet long. The appendages were about eighteen feet by sixteen feet, one of which also contained a cellar with a fireplace. Overall the entire structure was nearly seventy feet long. The central section of the structure easily could have contained two very large rooms and a large hall, or four rooms and a corridor. The eighteen-inch-thick foundations of the main section and thirteen-inch-thick foundations of the wings were more than adequate to support a second story. Remnants of several outbuildings also have been excavated at the site, including a detached kitchen and a smokehouse, as well as a garden area and an ice pond.

Related entries: Ancestry; Birthday; Ferry Farm; Mount Vernon; Washington, Augustine; Washington, Augustine ("Austin")

Suggestions for further reading:
Hatch, Charles E., Jr. 1979. *Popes Creek Plantation: Birthplace of George Washington.* Washington's Birthplace, VA.
Hoppin, Charles Arthur. 1926. "The House in which George Washington was Born" (*Tyler's Quarterly Historical and Genealogical Magazine,* vol. 8).
"The Cost of Washington's Birthplace" (vol. 1, appendix 6). Douglas Southall Freeman. 1948–1957. 7 vols. *George Washington: A Biography.* New York.

Portraits

See Houdon, Jean-Antoine; Peale, Charles Willson; Trumbull, John.

Potomac River Navigation

Washington first explored the Potomac River with a view toward opening its navigation in the summer of 1754, at the urging of Charles Carter (1707–1764), the member of the Virginia House of Burgesses charged with handling the expenditures for the military expedition of that year to the Forks of the Ohio. He found the Potomac full of such obstacles as shallow water, narrow channels, "swift and ugly" falls, and clusters of small islands. Except for the major impediment, the seventy-six-foot descent in a little over a mile at the Great Falls of the Potomac, he thought all the obstructions could be surmounted. Despite his judgment that crossing the Great Falls "is not practacable till great alterations are made," Washington concluded that the Potomac was the "more convenient least expensive and I may further say by much the most expeditious way" to the Ohio Country.

Others agreed with Washington's assessment. British general Edward Braddock saw the utility of opening a water route from the Potomac to the Ohio and in fact made use of the Potomac for transporting artillery, ammunition, and provisions partway through Virginia for his expedition of 1755. Braddock's death and John Forbes's choice of another route for his campaign in 1758 temporarily curtailed interest in the Potomac route. In 1762 twenty-two men living "convenient" to the Potomac, eleven each from Virginia and Maryland, formed an enterprise to open the river to "Small-Craft" down to the Great Falls, which "will be of the greatest Advantage to *Virginia* and *Maryland,* by facilitating Commerce with the Back Inhabitants." Although Washington copied the "Remarks" that he had saved from his 1754 trip for a member of the enterprise, he apparently had few dealings with it. The group folded when the future settlement of the west was called into question by the land-acquisition restrictions of King George III's Proclamation of 1763. When those restrictions were lifted at the end of the decade, a new enterprise was formed, with Washington and Thomas Johnson, Jr. (1732–1819), an attorney and later governor of Maryland, assuming the leadership roles. Washington's efforts for the new venture culminated in the Virginia general assembly's passage in 1772 of an act opening navigation of the Potomac from the tidewater to Fort Cumberland at Wills Creek. On the other side of the Potomac, however, Johnson's attempt to secure passage of a similar bill in the Maryland provincial assembly was defeated by the strong opposition of merchants in Baltimore. Before any progress could be made, the Revolutionary War halted all efforts to extend navigation of the Potomac.

After the war, in 1784 and 1785, Washington personally led renewed efforts to open the Potomac. He used the influence afforded him by his postwar stature to oversee the simultaneous passage of nearly identical navigation bills in the Virginia and Maryland general assemblies. The dual acts created the Potomac River Company, and the Virginia legislature passed an additional act giving Washington fifty shares of Potomac River Company stock as well as 100 shares in the new James River Company as a "compliment" to commemorate his Revolutionary War service. Washington was unwilling to accept the gift but uncertain as to how to reject it. After agonizing about the matter for several months, he requested the Virginia legislature to redirect the shares of both companies to "objects of a public nature." The result was a new act appropriating the "said shares with the tolls and profits hereafter accruing therefrom . . . to such objects of a public nature" decreed by Washington. In the mid-1790s Washington decided to contribute the fifty Potomac River Company shares toward an endowment to form a national university in the new Federal City, and stipulated to that effect in his will.

Washington served as the first president of the Potomac River Company, and under his leadership works commenced at Shenandoah Falls, Seneca Falls, and the Great Falls. Several of the smaller obstructions to navigation soon were removed, and considerable progress was made on the major obstructions. In the late 1780s the company found it increasingly difficult to collect subscriptions, however, and the works were "suffered to progress so limpingly" through the 1790s. The Maryland general assembly stepped in to shore up the company in 1799, supplying the impetus to finally complete the construction of the series of locks and canals necessary to bypass the Great Falls that opened in February 1802.

Related entries: James River Company; Mississippi Adventure

Suggestions for further reading:
Diaries, vols. 4, 5.
"Notes on the Navigation of the Potomac River above the Great Falls," July–August 1754 (*Col. Ser.,* vol. 1).
"To Charles Carter," August 1754 (*Col. Ser.,* vol. 1).
"To a Participant in the Potomac River Enterprize," c.1762 (*Col. Ser.,* vol. 7).
"John Semple's Proposal for Potomac Navigation," 1769 (*Col. Ser.,* vol. 8).
"From John Semple," 8 January 1770 (*Col. Ser.,* vol. 8).
"To Benjamin Harrison," 10 October 1784 (*Con. Ser.,* vol. 2).
"From James Madison," 1 January 1785 (*Con. Ser.,* vol. 2).
"To William Grayson," 22 January 1785 (*Con. Ser.,* vol. 2).
"Report of the Potomac Company Directors," 8 November 1787 (*Con. Ser.,* vol. 5).
Bacon-Foster, Corra. 1912. *Early Chapters in the Development of the Patomac Route to the West.* Washington, DC.

Powel, Samuel (1739–1793), and Elizabeth Willing (1742–1830)

Samuel and Elizabeth Willing Powel were among the Washington family's closest friends during the first family's years in Philadelphia. Samuel, who had been an enthusiastic supporter of the Revolution, subscribing £5,000 to the war effort, was for many years the mayor of Philadelphia as well as a founder of the University of Pennsylvania, a manager of the Pennsylvania Hospital, and a member of the American Philosophical Society. Elizabeth Powel, or Eliza as she was commonly called, was the sister of Thomas Willing, a Philadelphia banker, and Mary Willing Byrd, widow of William Byrd III of Westover, Virginia. During the Constitutional Convention, Washington frequently accepted Eliza's invitations to tea or dinner at the Powels' home on Third Street, and attended various agricultural experiments with Samuel, who owned a country estate outside Philadelphia on the Schuylkill River and who was the president of the Philadelphia Society for Promoting Agriculture.

Related entry: Presidency

Suggestions for further reading:
Diaries, vol. 5.
"Stanzas on the Presidents Birth-Day," 22 February 1792 (*Pres. Ser.,* vol. 9).

The inauguration of George Washington (Library of Congress)

Presidency

Washington's primary goals as first president were threefold: first, the establishment of a national government strong enough to administer domestic affairs to the satisfaction of the people in all thirteen states and to command the respect of foreign countries; second, the settlement of the nation's finances, which meant protecting the new government's credit while paying the debts left over from the Revolutionary War; and third, the management of foreign affairs, which consisted of maintaining the peace with Great Britain, wresting control of the Northwest Territory while pacifying the numerous Indian nations scat-

tered on the western frontier, and opening navigation of the Spanish-controlled Mississippi River to American shipping. Later, and only ancillary to these goals, was the establishment and design of the Federal City on the banks of the Potomac River.

The first goal was perhaps the hardest initially, for late-eighteenth-century Americans were for the most part still very suspicious of executive authority. In fact, the only reason the proponents of the new Constitution were able to secure a majority at the federal convention was that the executive office was designed with an eye toward Washington as its first occupant. Washington realized that the trust of the people in the executive branch would be invested in him personally, and he took increased pains to guard the reputation that he long had cultivated as a disinterested public servant of unimpeachable moral character. Washington was aware of the precedent-setting nature of his conduct while in office, many instances of which could be cited but perhaps none better than his own words of caution to his nephew Bushrod Washington, the heir to Mount Vernon and a future Supreme Court justice, who in vain had sought a federal appointment from his uncle: "My political conduct must be exceedingly circumspect and proof against just criticism, for the eyes of Argus are upon me, and no slip will pass unnoticed." Washington knew that the American populace, from the altruistic and paternalistic guardians of liberty down to every self-interested grubber for petty office, would cry foul at the first hint of unfair executive patronage. Argus, the hundred-eyed guardian of the gods in classical mythology, could never act so annoyingly as its envious modern republican rivals. "It is the nature of Republicans, who are nearly in a state of equality," Washington wrote, "to be extremely jealous as to the disposal of all honorary or lucrative appointments."

There was a downside to having a weak central government, as Washington had learned firsthand during the Revolutionary War and in the years following the peace under the Confederation government. The constitution of the latter in fact had provided no central executive authority at all, and little evidence could be found to suggest that a very weak government was any less of an evil than one too strong. Washington optimistically believed that the United States would become a great nation, and although he studiously avoided the ostentatious trappings of monarchy, he emphatically insisted that even a republican head of state must conduct himself and his household with proper decorum. Unsure of how and where to draw the line that would command the respect of foreign dignitaries while preserving the sense of decorum acceptable to the people, he ultimately relied on the people's regard for his reputation as a

person of integrity and honesty as the final arbiter when making such distinctions. Shortly after taking office, the unexpected and unwanted intrusions on his time by an endless array of callers and invitations forced Washington to host weekly receptions at the presidential mansion. These levees soon turned into "stiff, ceremonial affairs" that usually were as dissatisfying to the visitors as they were dreaded by Washington, but at least the public was given the semblance of open access to the president.

Even more important to the sound establishment of the office of presidency than the precedents Washington set concerning the dignity and formality of the office was the path he marked by making judicious federal appointments. Departing from the traditional patronage system of European powers was only the first step; he went to great lengths not only to balance sectional interests but also to find appointees acceptable to local and regional inhabitants. He surprised some in Congress when he ignored overtures to use patronage to build a coalition in that body. In addition to his own cabinet officials, he appointed all the Supreme Court justices (the only president to do so), territorial governors, foreign ministers, customs and revenue officials, Indian commissioners, lighthouse keepers, federal marshals, district attorneys, and judges. By the end of his second term as president the names of almost 400 nominees had been sent to Congress by Washington for Senate confirmation, and in no instance could he be accused of sacrificing the public interest by proposing a nominee for reasons of personal preference. He adhered to his rule of balancing various sectional and political interests when choosing his own cabinet, evidenced by his selection of Henry Knox, Alexander Hamilton, Thomas Jefferson, and Edmund Randolph to lead, respectively, the Departments of War, the Treasury, State, and Justice, the four most important posts in his government. He dealt with the department heads in his administration much as he had with the general officers under his command during the Revolutionary War: on important matters he consulted each for advice but reserved for himself the making of decisions. The result of this style of executive administration quickly gave rise to Vice President John Adams's oft-repeated observation that "No man, I believe, has influence with the President. He seeks information from all quarters, and judges more independently than any man I ever knew."

Although he surrounded himself with men of the highest caliber in order to ensure that the executive branch would become a fundamentally powerful one within the confines of the Constitution, Washington was extremely circumspect and deferential in his dealings with Congress. He had scrupulously submitted to the prerogatives of the Continental Congress while commander in chief of the army during the Revolutionary War, and as president he adopted the same strategy. He understood that the surest way to counter lingering suspicions that executive authority tended toward corruption was to execute the laws Congress passed without interfering in the legislative process. Thus he seldom recommended to Congress specific items for its legislative agenda, and only twice in eight years did he exercise his power to veto bills, both presidential prerogatives under the Constitution. At the same time Washington expected Congress not to encroach on the constitutional mandates of the presidency, especially his authority to make federal appointments, regulate the military, and conduct foreign affairs. The relationship between Washington and Congress for the most part was an amicable one throughout his two terms as president, and halfway through his second term, Washington could boast that "the powers of the Executive of the U. States are more definite, and better understood perhaps than those of almost any other Country; and my aim has been, and will continue to be, neither to stretch,

nor relax from them in any instance whatever, unless imperious circumstances shd. render the measure indispensible."

Once his system of executive management began to function efficiently Washington could turn his attention to the major domestic priority of his administration, putting the economic system of the country on a sound basis. The outstanding Revolutionary War debts of the United States amounted to about $75 million— more than $50 million owed by the federal government (some $40 million owed to American citizens and $11 million owed to the French government and Dutch financiers) and another $25 million owed by the states to various domestic concerns. At the going rates, 4 to 6 percent, the annual interest on the total debt was by itself more than several times the revenue the federal government expected to generate from all its sources combined. Ever the optimist when contemplating the country's economic and commercial potential, especially when considering America's vast natural resources and the inevitable westward expansion of the country's citizens, Washington was confident that a just solution to the debt crisis could be found that would retire the debt quickly without repudiating any of it or without burdening the people with unfair taxation—the cause of the Revolution in the first place. Both Washington and Congress delegated the responsibility of developing a sophisticated financial plan to Alexander Hamilton, who drew up a series of reports between 1790 and 1792 that were as abstruse as his scheme was brilliant.

The main features of Hamilton's plan included refinancing both federal and state debts (which the federal government would assume) at a standard interest rate; monetizing the new securities (in effect increasing the money supply); increasing federal revenue by raising custom duties on imports of coffee, tea, and spirits, and by placing an excise tax on domestically distilled spirits; and establishing a national bank. The intricacies of Hamilton's plan made many citizens nervous and resulted in controversy and acrimony. Although Washington approved of his secretary's plan, he could not publicly endorse it without breaking his rule of noninterference in the legislative process. Congress passed a funding bill based on Hamilton's proposals in June 1790—minus the provision calling for the assumption of state debts, which was done later—as well as an act to incorporate the Bank of the United States in February 1791. Once implemented, Hamilton's financial system met with immediate success, allowing the administration to turn its attention to enhancing the development of the country's burgeoning commercial interest in agriculture and manufacturing. The final part of Hamilton's system, an elaborate plan to encourage manufacturing, was finished in December 1791 and presented to Congress the following month, but never was enacted.

Foreign policy during Washington's administration consisted of several interrelated components. When Washington envisioned the United States, he saw a nation bounded by Canada on the north and water on three sides—from the Great Lakes down the Mississippi River to the Gulf of Mexico and back up the Atlantic seaboard—with the potential to extend across the continent. Unfortunately, several obstacles stood in the way of making that vision a reality. The British, claiming that the Americans had violated the Treaty of Paris by failing to settle the legitimate prewar debts owed to British citizens, had declined to relinquish control of a line of important military forts in the Northwest Territory. The continued occupation of these posts by the British seriously curtailed American influence on the Indians along the frontier and at the same time kept open an extensive and profitable fur-trading network operating out of Canada. Spain controlled most of the Mississippi, the province of Louisiana, including the valuable port at New Orleans, as well as both East and West Florida. The Spanish,

after successfully prohibiting American shipping on the mighty Mississippi, were making incursions into Kentucky and Tennessee. Diplomacy with both Spain and Great Britain had failed, and the Indian nations from Pennsylvania south to Georgia, secretly armed by both the Spanish and the British, were openly hostile to Americans seeking to push their country's frontier west.

To the south, the powerful Creek Nation, under the leadership of Alexander McGillivray, the son of a half-Creek, half-French mother and a fur-trading Scots father, had allied with the Spanish after the British evacuation of West Florida at the end of the Revolutionary War. The Confederation government had not been able to stop the Creeks from raiding American settlements in the northeastern part of the tribe's territory, which included parts of Tennessee, Georgia, and Alabama. When negotiations between federal commissioners and the Creeks broke down, Washington invited McGillivray to New York so the two could negotiate directly. There he adopted the same policy he had practiced as early as 1753, when he treated with the Half-King and other chiefs of the Six Nations at Logstown, while on his way to deliver Virginia governor Robert Dinwiddie's ultimatum to the French to leave the Ohio Valley, and which he had polished during the Revolutionary War when he entertained northern chiefs at Continental army headquarters in order to impress upon them the grandeur and military might of the American forces. He received the Creek chief as a visiting head of state, bestowing upon him lavish gifts and respectfully discussing the mutual advantages that would result from an alliance. The resulting Treaty of New York in August 1790 contained concessions on the part of both the Creeks and the Americans, as well as the appointment of McGillivray as U.S. agent to the Creeks with an annual salary of $1,500. The treaty did not bring to end all hostilities on the frontier, of course, but it did prove that the president's administration was capable of negotiating treaties with foreign powers. The following year another treaty was signed, with the Cherokee Nation.

While an all-out war with the southwest Indians was prevented by the treaties of 1790 and 1791, the Indians in the northwest, with British encouragement, were harassing settlements across the Ohio frontier. Back-to-back victories by Miami Indians against American forces under the command of generals Josiah Harmar and Arthur St. Clair, in late summer 1790 and early winter 1791, respectively, resulted not only in severe criticism of Washington's Indian policy but also a congressional inquiry into the latter loss. Washington's bid for Congress's approval of a third expedition passed by a narrow margin only, for many delegates now insisted that the president must negotiate a settlement. His choice of another former Revolutionary War general from Pennsylvania (also the home state of Harmar and St. Clair), Anthony Wayne, while not greeted with enthusiasm by Congress, proved decisive. After two years of preparation, during which negotiations failed to ameliorate the hostility of the Northwest Indians, Wayne's forces completely routed a large Indian force under the command of Little Turtle at the Battle of Fallen Timbers (Ohio) in August 1794, resulting in the Treaty of Greenville (Ohio) in August 1795. Two months later the Spanish gave up their demands on the east side of the Mississippi and opened the river to American commerce by signing Pinckney's Treaty. Meanwhile John Jay had successfully negotiated a new treaty with Great Britain in which the British agreed not only to relinquish finally their possession of the long-held posts but also to drop their claim to any territory south of Canada. Winning the battle for the frontier both militarily and diplomatically had immediate and far-ranging repercussions for the expansion of the republic.

The securing of peace on the American continent, which also included putting down the uprising caused by the excise tax placed on domestic spirits, was only part of the challenge faced by Washington in the arena of foreign affairs. Washington's taking office coincided with the French Revolution and the advent of a new and serious war between France and Great Britain, a conflict that before the end of his first term had spread across Europe and threatened U.S. neutrality. Initially enthusiastic at France's move toward republicanism, Washington soon became wary of the ability of America's wartime ally to halt its reform before plunging into chaos and violence. When his assessment proved correct, Washington increased his efforts to maintain a neutral policy, with an especial eye to America's own interest, a course that became increasingly difficult to pursue as the partisan bickering between Alexander Hamilton and Thomas Jefferson turned rancorous. Adding to Washington's difficulty was the arrival of the new French ambassador, Edmund Genet. Charged with winning the total allegiance of the United States to the side of the French, Genet's efforts to enlist popular support for the French proved to be nothing more than enthusiastic bumbling, but at the same time British interference with American shipping on the open seas was pushing the country to the brink of war. Washington's Proclamation of Neutrality, issued in April 1793, elicited more fury on the part of his political opponents perhaps than any of his other actions as president. Washington sent Chief Justice John Jay to negotiate a treaty, which was completed in November 1794 and signed by Washington the following August, bringing Washington and his administration severe criticism across America. In the end it was approved narrowly by Congress. Most important, the British recognized American neutrality in the European war and confirmed the peace that Anthony Wayne had won with arms on the frontier.

The self-styled "closing act" of Washington's administration took place on 19 September 1796, when the Philadelphia *American Daily Advertiser* printed a personal message from the president to his "Friends, & Fellow—Citizens," the people of the United States. Known since as the Farewell Address, its drafting spanned many months—years if you count the intervening time between James Madison's first draft in 1792 and Washington's renewed interest in it in 1796—and the result is a thoughtfully crafted valediction filled with fatherly advice for his country. "My wish is that the whole may appear in a plain style," he told Alexander Hamilton when enlisting his help in finishing the address, "and be handed to the public in an honest, unaffected, simple part." Its publication, less than two months before the next presidential election and deliberately timed to coincide with Washington's annual fall departure for Mount Vernon, served the immediate purpose of informing the public of Washington's refusal to stand for a third term. The Farewell Address looks beyond the past and present to the more distant future, however, for Washington conceived it as a lasting testimony of what his near half century of public service had taught him. It is both a warning and an exhortation.

The principal theme of the Farewell Address is the same as that visited by Washington in his Farewell Address to the Continental army in November 1783—the importance of a strong American Union, now established under the Constitution.

> The Unity of Government which constitutes you one people is also now dear to you. It is justly so; for it is a main Pillar in the Edifice of your real independence, the support of your tranquility at home; your peace abroad; of your safety; of your prosperity; of that very Liberty which you so highly prize. . . . it is of infinite moment, that you should properly estimate the immense value of your national Union to

your collective & individual happiness; that you should cherish a cordial, habitual & immoveable attachment to it.

The dangers to national unity, said Washington, are many: sectional divisions, foreign influences, disobedience to constitutional government, and political factions; its supports sufficient: self-interest, education, religion and morality, financial responsibility, and neutrality. The individuals entrusted with the authority to administer the union, however, are susceptible to the universal tendency that "predominates in the human heart," to love and abuse power. Happily, the Constitution has provided "reciprocal checks in the exercise of political power," but to "preserve them must be as necessary as to institute them." The preservation of these safeguards will limit the consolidation of powers—"a real despotism"—if public servants confine themselves to operate within their respective spheres.

Washington's "counsels of an old and affectionate friend," his guiding political principles developed over the decades, end with an affectionate adieu:

> I anticipate with pleasing expectation that retreat, in which I promise myself to realize, without alloy, the sweet enjoyment of partaking, in the midst of my fellow Citizens, the benign influence of good Laws under a free Government—the ever favourite object of my heart, and the happy reward, as I trust, of our mutual cares, labours and dangers.

Related entries: Hamilton, Alexander; Knox, Henry; Jay, John; Jefferson, Thomas; Madison, James; New England Tour; Pickering, Thomas; Southern Tour; Whiskey Rebellion; Farewell Address (Selected Writings); Farewell Address to the Army (Selected Writings)

Suggestions for further reading:
"To Bushrod Washington," 27 July 1789 (*Pres. Ser.*, vol. 3).
"To the U.S. Senate and House of Representatives," 7 August 1789 (*Pres. Ser.*, vol. 3).
"To the U.S. Senate," 22 August 1789 (*Pres. Ser.*, vol. 3).

"To the Commissioners to the Southern Indians," 29 August 1789 (*Pres. Ser.,* vol. 3).

"Report Relative to a Provision for the Support of Public Credit," 14 January 1790 (Syrett, *Hamilton Papers,* vol. 6).

"Proclamation," 14, 26 August 1790 (*Pres. Ser.,* vol. 6).

"Second Report on the Further Provision Necessary for Establishing Public Credit," 13 December 1790 (Syrett, *Hamilton Papers,* vol. 7).

"Opinion on the Constitutionality of the Bank," 12 February 1791 (*Pres. Ser.,* vol. 7).

"From James Madison," 21 February 1791 (*Pres. Ser.,* vol. 7).

"Opinion on the Constitutionality of an Act to Establish a Bank," 23 February 1791 (*Pres. Ser.,* vol. 7).

"To the Secretary of State," 2 July 1794 (*Writings,* vol. 33).

De Conde, Alexander. 1958. *Entangling Alliance: Politics and Diplomacy under George Washington.* Durham, NC.

Smith, Richard Norton. 1993. *Patriarch: George Washington and the New American Nation.* New York.

Warren, Jack D., Jr. 2000. *The Presidency of George Washington.* Mount Vernon, VA.

Princeton, Battle of

When word of the surprise American attack on Trenton, New Jersey, on Christmas Day 1776 reached British headquarters at New York City, Lord Cornwallis abandoned plans to embark for England and rode to Princeton, where he found earthworks being prepared. On the morning of 2 January Cornwallis advanced with 8,000 men toward Trenton, where he arrived in the late afternoon after being harassed along the way by American sharpshooters. By that time Washington, who had reentered Trenton that morning, had moved his force to a ridge across Assunpink Creek overlooking Trenton. After several unsuccessful attempts by the British to cross the creek, Cornwallis decided to rest his troops until the following day and to bring 2,000 reinforcements from Princeton. Washington, however, correctly ascertained that, with the large British force concentrated before him,

their stores back at New Brunswick and Princeton must be inadequately guarded and boldly decided to attack one or both of those posts. Accordingly, with campfires burning and the sounds of entrenchments being thrown up, Washington moved his entire force toward those destinations. When the sun rose Cornwallis was astonished to find that the entire American force had disappeared. After his surrender at Yorktown in 1781 Cornwallis reputedly told Washington that his march from New York to Virginia, although costly, was not so surprising, for "after all, your Excellency's achievements in New Jersey were such that nothing could surpass them."

Near sunrise some of Cornwallis's reinforcements met Washington's army as it approached Princeton. A brief fight occurred during which the British lost about 18 killed, 58 wounded, and 300 captured, along with their cannon. The American casualties, about 25 killed and 40 wounded, included the mortal wounding of Washington's old friend Maj. Gen. Hugh Mercer. Washington's army evacuated Princeton after two hours, and rather than proceed toward New Brunswick it crossed the Delaware yet another time. Cornwallis's troops began to arrive at Princeton about an hour after the departure of the Americans, and from Princeton the British marched to New Brunswick. On the morning of 4 January Washington put his army in motion toward New Brunswick, but after deciding that his men were too fatigued, he directed them to march for the safety of Morristown in the hills of north-central New Jersey.

In Mercer County, New Jersey, on the southern edge of Princeton, at the original site where the heaviest fighting took place, is a 40-acre state park.

Related entries: Morristown, New Jersey; Trenton, Battle of

Suggestions for further reading:
"To John Hancock," 5 January 1777 (*War Ser.,* vol. 7).

A monument honors George Washington's victory at the Battle of Princeton, 1777 (Library of Congress)

Smith, Samuel S. 1967. *The Battle of Princeton.* Monmouth Beach, NJ.

Stryker, William S. 1898. *The Battles of Trenton and Princeton.* Reprint, 1967. Spartanburg, SC.

Proclamations of 1754 and 1763

See Crawford Brothers; Dinwiddie, Robert; Dunmore, John Murray, Fourth Earl of; Great Kanawha Tracts; Millers Run (Chartiers Creek) Tract; Muse, George; Van Braam, Jacob; Washington's Bottom Tract.

Putnam, Israel (1718–1790)

Israel Putnam, observed nineteenth-century historian Charles J. Peterson in his *Heroes of the Revolution,* was "one of the most daring spirits of the Revolution. He had not the comprehensive mind required for a great strategist; but in leading a column to the storm, or in any emergency requiring indomitable valor, possessed no rival. He needed some one to plan, but he was a Paladin to execute. His name was almost miraculous. Other military leaders distinguished themselves in battle; Putnam was the battle itself." Peterson's hyperbole may have been exaggerated only slightly, for by the time these remarks were penned, Putnam's boldness and daring had long since entered the realm of legend.

"Old Put," as Washington and others referred to Putnam during the Revolutionary War, had been born in Danvers (Salem), Massachusetts. Little about his education and childhood has been discovered, although his writing and spelling indicate that he received next to no formal education. He moved to Pomfret, Connecticut, after his marriage in 1739, where he became a respectable farmer known for his industriousness and acknowledged as a candid man with good sense who could be trusted as a man of integrity.

By the time of the French and Indian War, Putnam had gained enough financial independence to serve as a captain in Robert Rogers's Rangers. Captured by a detachment of French soldiers and Indians, he was brutally tortured and on the verge of being burned alive when he was rescued at the last moment. He eventually was exchanged. After that Putnam was sent with a contingent of Connecticut troops to square off against the Spanish in Cuba, where he survived shipwreck and disease. When he retired from military service in 1764, hardly a man in the colonies could equal Putnam's military reputation. His troops especially respected Putnam's willingness to share their hardships and not to shrink from the perils of service.

After his return home Putnam became active in the Sons of Liberty, and in 1766 he was elected to the Connecticut general assembly. In 1773 he joined an expedition to explore West Florida, sailing first to the West Indies, then through the Gulf of Mexico up the Mississippi River. In October 1774, with war on the horizon, he was appointed lieutenant colonel of the 11th Connecticut Regiment. The story is told that he was plowing in his field when news of the Battle of Lexington reached him and that, without stopping to unyoke his oxen, change his clothes, or say good-bye to his family, he left the field directly to offer his assistance to the American cause, traversing the 100-mile distance to Cambridge in twenty-four hours. A week later he had visited the Connecticut general assembly and returned to Boston as a brigadier general of the Connecticut militia.

Putnam was soon appointed a major general in the Continental army and was involved in the planning and fighting at the Battle of Bunker Hill. When the Continental Congress solicited Washington's advice on whom it should appoint to command in Canada, Washington replied that Putnam "is a most valuable man, & a fine executive Officer, but I do not know how he would conduct in a separate department." Putnam remained attached to the main army under Washington's command. He accompanied the Continental army to New York, where he took part in the Battle of Long Island and the evacuation of New York City, as well as the retreat across New Jersey. He was with Washington at the Battle of Princeton in January 1777, but the following May, after Washington apparently had decided that Putnam was now better suited to command a post away from the center of action rather than to lead troops in the field, Washington sent him to command the Hudson Highlands. He retired from the army in 1779 after suffering a paralytic stroke, although he lived for another decade before dying in Brooklyn, Connecticut.

Although Washington sometimes criticized Putnam for being too cautious in obeying his orders, he wrote an affectionate letter commending him at the end of the war: "For I can assure you, that, among the many worthy and meritorious Officers, with whom I have had the happiness to be connected in Service, through the Course of this War, and from whose cheerful Assistance and Advise, I have received much support and Confidence in the various and trying Vicissitudes of a Complicated Contest, the Name of a Putnam is not forgotten; nor will it be, but with that Stroke of Time which shall obliterate from my Mind, the remembrance of all those Toils and Fatigues, through which we have struggled for the preservation and Establishment of the Rights, Liberties and Independence of our Country."

Putnam also became a posthumous author of *Two Putnams—in the Havana Expedition 1762 and in the Mississippi River Exploration 1772–73,* published in 1931.

Related entries: Boston, Siege of; French and Indian War

Suggestions for further reading:
"To Joseph Reed," 1 April 1776 (*War Ser.,* vol. 4).
"To Israel Putnam," 2 June 1783 (*Writings,* vol. 26).
Humphreys, David. 1788. *An Essay on the Life of the Honourable Major-General Israel Putnam.* Hartford, CT.

Q

Quasi-War

Washington was deeply involved in military preparations for the so-called Quasi-War with France and was not without political influence despite his retirement from the presidency in 1797, for he was still the best-known and most-respected military and political leader in the United States. As the first president and hero of the Revolutionary War, many Americans looked to him for military leadership and even solicited his political advice on matters properly in the purview of President John Adams.

On 11 July 1798, Secretary of War James McHenry arrived at Mount Vernon with a letter from Adams and a commission, already approved by the U.S. Senate, for Washington as "*Lieutenant General and Commander in Chief of all the Armies raised or to be raised for* the service of the United States." Although Washington felt no compunction in preparing for war against "intoxicated and lawless France," he accepted the commission with reluctance. In his letter of acceptance to Adams of 13 July, Washington mourned the potential necessity of abandoning his "peaceful abode" for "the boundless field of public action—incessant trouble—and high responsibility." Convinced of the "justice of our cause," however, he agreed to serve on condition that he not be called into the field from Mount Vernon unless his presence was indispensable.

Almost immediately after his appointment, Washington became involved in an ugly controversy over the appointment and ranking of the three major generals who would serve under him. In July 1798 John Adams nominated, and the Senate confirmed, Alexander Hamilton as inspector general and highest-ranking major general, to be followed by Charles Cotesworth Pinckney and Henry Knox. Washington had suggested this arrangement to Adams and correctly anticipated opposition from Knox, who had been senior to both Hamilton and Pinckney in the Continental army, but he was determined to have Hamilton as his second in command even if Knox declined his commission. As expected, Knox made his bitter disappointment known to both Washington and Adams, but to Washington's surprise Adams determined in September to reverse the ranking, placing Knox at the top and Hamilton at the bottom. With the support of McHenry, Secretary of State Timothy Pickering, and Secretary of the Treasury Oliver Wolcott, Jr., and the implied threat of resigning his own commission, Washington succeeded by October in forcing Adams to return to the original ranking. By that time, however, Knox had declined the commission, and Adams's relations with his cabinet had been damaged badly. Although he absolved

Washington of any wrongdoing, the president deeply resented what he viewed as the hidden intrigues of his cabinet to undercut him.

The content of Washington's private correspondence sometimes went beyond the range of affairs for which he was actually responsible. McHenry and Pickering kept Washington informed of cabinet proceedings unrelated to military matters, dwelling at times on the shortcomings of their colleagues or of the president himself. For his part, Washington wrote of Republican diplomatic and political views in increasingly bitter terms in 1798 and 1799, and in letters to cabinet members he expressed his disapprobation of Adams's diplomatic policies when they appeared too conciliatory to Republican sentiments. Washington was also critical of some of Adams's subordinates, suggesting to McHenry in one extraordinary letter that he was improperly carrying out his duties as secretary of war.

Washington did not have to leave Mount Vernon on military business except for a trip to Philadelphia in November and December 1798. Nevertheless, for the last eighteen months of Washington's life, much of his time would be taken up in correspondence related to the formation of a military force to deal with a possible French invasion. The regular army of 3,000 men, which had been reorganized in 1796, was clearly inadequate to the task, and Congress had resolved on 28 May 1798 to create a provisional army of 10,000 men in the event of actual war with France. In addition, on 16 July, Congress authorized the creation of a "New Army," adding twelve regiments and six troops of dragoons to the four regiments of the regular army already in existence.

It was the appointment of officers for the New Army with which Washington was most concerned. While the newly created major generals Hamilton and Pinckney took responsibility for recruiting officers in New England and much of the South respectively, Washington's acquaintance with prominent Virginians, including Revolutionary War comrades like Daniel Morgan, made him the natural choice to oversee the solicitation and collection of applications for military office from that state. Washington met with Hamilton and Pinckney in Philadelphia late in 1798 to choose officers from among the dozens of applications, and in the first six months of 1799, he corresponded with McHenry on matters relating to the actual appointment of these officers.

It was a complicated and time-consuming business, and in the autumn and winter of 1799, problems of quartering the New Army and finding prospective officers for the provisional army disturbed Washington's repose at Mount Vernon. He tried to delegate as much responsibility as he could to Hamilton and Pinckney, especially as it became increasingly clear that a military conflict with France was unlikely. To his annoyance, however, correspondence relating to the Quasi-War would occupy Washington until the last weeks of his life.

Related entries: Adams, John; Custis, George Washington Parke; Hamilton, Alexander; Knox, Henry; Lear, Tobias; McHenry, James; Pickering, Timothy

Suggestions for further reading:
"To John Adams," 4 July 1798 (*Ret. Ser.*, vol. 2).
"To James McHenry," 4 July 1798 (*Ret. Ser.*, vol. 2).
"Suggestions for Military Appointments," 14 July 1798 (*Ret. Ser.*, vol. 2).
"Candidates for Army Appointments from Virginia," November 1798 (*Ret. Ser.*, vol. 3).

R

Ramsay, David (1749–1815)

"It is no exaggeration" wrote his biographer, "to say that David Ramsay created American history." Writers can be expected to be extravagant when praising their subjects, but in this instance the observer was not excessive. Ramsay's detailed, chronological narratives, extensively drawn from letters and other documents generated during the period he chronicled, were the first of their kind in America. His numerous writings include the *History of the Revolution of South Carolina* (Trenton, New Jersey, 1785) and the *History of the American Revolution* (Philadelphia, 1789), two volumes each, copies of which Ramsay sent to Washington, plus his *Life of Washington* (New York, 1807), and the posthumous three-volume *History of the United States* (Philadelphia, 1816–1817).

Ramsay, who was born in Lancaster, Pennsylvania, graduated from the College of New Jersey in 1765 and taught school briefly before taking a medical degree from the College of Philadelphia in 1773. He set up a medical practice in Charleston, South Carolina, where he remained the rest of his life, outliving two wives, Frances Witherspoon, the daughter of John Witherspoon, and Martha Laurens, the daughter of Henry Laurens, and raising eight children to adulthood. Ramsay rose to prominence in his adopted state during the Revolutionary War, when he served as a member of the South Carolina council of safety and the state assembly, as well as a surgeon in the Continental army. He was one of forty Charleston citizens taken by the British to St. Augustine, Florida, and held for eleven months as hostages. From 1782 to 1786 he served in the Confederation Congress, and later he served in the South Carolina Senate, including a seven-year stint as president of that body. In addition, he served as president of the state medical society, the Hamilton Steamboat Company, and the Reciprocal Insurance Company. When he was 66 years old, he was shot in the back with a pistol by a Charleston tailor disgruntled at Ramsay for having declared him legally insane; he lingered for two days before dying.

Ramsay's was one of the earliest biographies of Washington. Devoting most of its pages to Washington the Revolutionary War hero, Ramsay portrayed his subject as a man of "sound judgment and upright principles" with "mild conciliatory manners" who exhibited the "most perfect subjection of his passions to reason"—in short, a necessary symbol for republican government of virtuous civic and political leadership. "Rome with all her heroes—Greece with all her patriots, could not produce his equal." Thus, he declared, "learn from Washington wherein true glory consists—Restrain your ambition—Consider your power as an obligation to do good."

Ramsay's funeral oration on the death of Washington, delivered at St. Michael's Church in Charleston on 15 January 1800, was subsequently printed the same month.

Related entries: Death; Humphreys, David; Laurens, Henry

Suggestions for further reading:

Shaffer, Arthur H. 1991. *To Be an American: David Ramsay and the Making of the American Consciousness.* Columbia, SC.

Smith, William Raymond. 1966. *History as Argument: Three Patriot Historians of the American Revolution.* The Hague, the Netherlands.

Rawlins, Albin (b. 1775)

"In Albin Rawlins," noted a recent scholar, George Washington "finally had found a copyist who could alter his spelling for the better rather than the worse." The employment of Rawlins as a copying clerk at Mount Vernon in February 1798 coincided with Washington's plan to erect a small separate building on his plantation to house his papers, a plan still under consideration at the time of Washington's sudden death in late 1799. Rawlins had first come to Washington's attention in October 1797 when Washington's friend and frequent correspondent Alexander Spotswood proposed the young man as a candidate for the office of household steward at Mount Vernon. According to Spotswood, Rawlins was "Recommended to me by his brother; who Says, he is 22 years of age, writes a fine hand, and well acquainted with figures, haveing been brought up in a Store, and the last year lived with him; he also gives me every assurance, of his Sobriety, and good Moral character; and Says if Necessary; he can bring with him a Recommendation." By the time he received Spotswood's letter, however, Washington had hired Eleanor Forbes as housekeeper and had changed his mind about the need for a steward at Mount Vernon. Nevertheless, Spotswood apparently led Rawlins to believe that he might still enter Washington's employment, and in January 1798 Rawlins wrote directly to Washington from the courthouse in Hanover County expressing his preference for "living with you to any other" and presenting his services for "Writing, riding abt for you &c."

Upon receiving Rawlins's letter, and seeing his neat, careful handwriting, Washington decided to tell Rawlins of another situation he had been contemplating, "To copy & record letters & other Papers; to keep Books (if required) & an account of articles received from, & delivered to the Farms; and such other matters & things as relate thereto; to go (by land or water, at my expence, when expence is necessary) to such places as my business may require. To receive grain, and attend to the measurement of it, and other things when it is necessary to send a trustworthy person to see it done, would constitute your principal employments." The two men struck a bargain, with Washington agreeing to pay Rawlins $150 per year plus room and board for his services. Rawlins arrived at Mount Vernon in mid-March 1798, and a few weeks later successfully underwent inoculation for smallpox. Before the summer passed, Rawlins was not only copying his new employer's letters into letter books but also assisting Washington with surveys of his farms and taking part in the management of the plantation's farm implements.

Rawlins and his brother, George, who was hired by Washington as overseer of his Union farm in September 1798, both appear in Tobias Lear's account of Washington's last illness and death in December 1799. George Rawlins, "who was used to bleeding the people," was sent for at Washington's own urging early on the morning of the 14th, that Washington might receive a bleeding while waiting for the doctor to arrive. The overseer came in soon after sunrise and reluctantly bled his employer. Later that afternoon, only a few hours before his death, Washington instructed Lear to arrange his letters and accounts and "let Mr Rawlins finish recording my other letters, which he has begun." The last letter that Albin Rawlins entered in Washington's letter book was from Washington to Timothy Pickering of 10 February 1799.

Related entries: Death; Papers

Suggestions for further reading:
"From Alexander Spotswood," 28 October 1797 (*Ret. Ser.,* vol. 1).
"From Albin Rawlins," 26 January 1798 (*Ret. Ser.,* vol. 2).
"To Albin Rawlins," 31 January 1798 (*Ret. Ser.,* vol. 2).
"From Albin Rawlins," 7, 16 February 1798 (*Ret. Ser.,* vol. 2).
"To Albin Rawlins," 12 February 1798 (*Ret. Ser.,* vol. 2).
Letters and Recollections of George Washington: Being Letters to Tobias Lear and Others between 1790 and 1799. 1906. New York.

Reed, Joseph (1741–1785)

Joseph Reed was born and raised at Trenton, New Jersey, and took degrees at the College of New Jersey before reading law and being admitted to the New Jersey bar in 1763. He spent the next two years at the Middle Temple at London's Inns of Court, studying and frequenting the House of Commons to follow debates on American affairs. While in London he also met and courted his future wife, Ester De-Berdt (1746–1780), the daughter of a city merchant. Upon his return to America, Reed set up a law practice in Trenton (and later Philadelphia) and entered into other business concerns. By mid-1766 he had built up a busy and widespread law practice. In 1767 he was appointed deputy secretary of the colony of New Jersey, which included the duty of personally serving as clerk of the council. Reed married in 1770 and settled in Philadelphia with his English

bride and her widowed mother. Within two years Reed was well on his way to becoming one of the most prominent attorneys in the city.

Reed became an early and fierce Patriot, serving on the Philadelphia committee of correspondence in 1774 and as president of the Pennsylvania provincial congress in 1775. That year he also was appointed lieutenant colonel of a regiment of Pennsylvania associators. Reed met Washington during the first Continental Congress, and the two became close friends immediately. When Washington was appointed commander in chief of the Continental army, he brought Reed into his military family as his first secretary. He wanted, said Washington, a person with whom he could "live in unbounded confidence," who could "think for me, as well as execute Orders." Reed acted in that capacity until early 1776, when Washington prevailed upon him to accept the office of adjutant general of the army, a post he held until January 1777. Reed was by Washington's side throughout the New York campaign, and Washington later drew upon Reed's knowledge of the Delaware River when preparing for the Battles of Trenton and Princeton and for the campaign for Philadelphia.

The friendship between Reed and Washington was severely strained for several months beginning in late November 1776 by Washington's chance reading of a letter from Maj. Gen. Charles Lee to Reed charging Washington with being indecisive during the New York campaign. The breach was healed a few months later, however, when Reed wrote to Washington professing that he always had "cherished unfeigned affection and admiration" for him. "True it is," confessed Washington in reply, "I felt myself hurt by a certain Letter, which appear'd at that time to be the eccho of one from you—I was hurt, not because I thought my judgment wrong'd by the expressions contain in it, but because the same Sentiments were not communicated immediately to my Self." Washington was perfectly satisfied, however, "that matters were not as they appeared from the Letter alluded to."

Although their friendship was renewed, the circumstances of war prevented their association from being as close as it was in 1776. They corresponded regularly, especially after Reed was elected president of the Pennsylvania supreme executive council, the highest executive office in the state, in 1778. While in office Reed presided over the abolition of slavery in Pennsylvania and served as the prosecutor in the trial of Benedict Arnold on charges of misusing his military authority for personal gain while commanding at Philadelphia. In 1780 Reed received a severe personal shock when his wife, not yet 35 years old, suddenly fell ill and died, leaving him alone with their five young children. Reed himself lived less than five more years, dying before the age of 45.

Related entries: Delaware Crossing; Lee, Charles; Princeton, Battle of; Trenton, Battle of

Suggestions for further reading:
"To Joseph Reed," 23 January 1776 (*War Ser.*, vol. 3).
"To Joseph Reed," 30 November 1776 (*War Ser.*, vol. 7).
"To Joseph Reed," 11 June 1777 (*War Ser.*, vol. 10).
"To Joseph Reed," 27 April 1777 (*Writings*, vol. 14).
Reed, William Bradford. 1847. 2 vols. *Life and Correspondence of Joseph Reed*. Philadelphia.
Roche, John F. 1957. *Joseph Reed: A Moderate in the American Revolution*. New York.

Religious Beliefs

As a practicing Christian, or more specifically, Episcopalian, Washington's behavior is known with some exactitude. He was a lifelong member of the Anglican church in Virginia, in which he was baptized, married, and served as godfather for the children of various relatives and friends. From 1763 to 1784 he was a member of the Truro Parish Vestry, taking an active part in its affairs until 1774 and serving as a churchwarden on three occasions. Yet despite his support of the church, Washington attended religious services sparingly. According to his diaries, he went to church about once a month while at Mount Vernon, choosing instead to read, ride, hunt, and entertain on Sundays. During his presidency, perhaps more conscious of his example, he went more frequently, attending St. Paul's Chapel and Trinity Church in New York City and Christ Church and St. Peter's in Philadelphia. Even then he did not partake of the sacrament of the Lord's Supper, although his wife was a "habitual communicant." One minister, Dr. James Abercrombie, recalled in 1831 the Washington family's attendance at Christ Church, observing that "on Sacrament Sundays, Gen'l Washington immediately after the Desk and Pulpit services, went out with the greater part of the congregation, always leaving Mrs. Washington with the communicants, she *invariably* being one, I considered it my duty, in a sermon on Public Worship, to state the unhappy tendency of *example,* particularly those in elevated stations, who invariably turned their backs upon the celebration of the Lord's Supper. I acknowledge the remark was intended for the President, as such, he received it." Indeed, Washington understood that the minister referred to him and discussed the matter with an unnamed U.S. senator during the following week. The senator, Abercrombie continued, "told me he had dined the day before with the President, who in the course of the conversation at the table, said, that on the preceding Sunday, he had received a very just reproof from the pulpit, for always leaving the church before the administration of the Sacrament; that he honored the preacher for his integrity and candour; that he had never considered the influence of his example; that he would never again give cause for the repetition of the reproof; and that, as he had never been a communicant, were he to become one of them, it would be imputed to an ostentatious display of religious zeal arising altogether from his elevated station. Accordingly, he afterwards never came on the morning of Sacrament Sunday, tho' at other times, a constant attendant in the morning." The most astute observer to date of Washington's religious preferences, Paul F. Boller, suggested that Washington's reluctance to take communion arose from the feeling that his mind and heart were not in "a proper condition to receive the sacrament," and that he was unwilling to indulge in hypocrisy.

As for other rituals, Washington on occasion observed the custom of having a blessing pronounced at mealtime, especially if there was a clergyman present to say grace. He apparently did not take the same delight in reading religious pamphlets or sermons as his wife, who did so daily with her granddaughter, Nelly Custis. Perhaps Washington's attitude about his personal practice of religion may be seen in his behavior, as recorded in his diaries, while on the presidential tour of New England in November 1789: "It being contrary to Law & disagreeable to the People of this State (Connecticut) to travel on the Sabbath day and my horses after passing through such intolerable Roads wanting rest, I stayed at [Isaac] Perkins's Tavern (which by the bye is not a good one) all day—and a meeting House being with in a few rod of the Door, I attended Morning & evening Service, and heard very lame discourses from a Mr. [Enoch] Pond."

It is difficult to trace over time any changes in Washington's religious beliefs. He seems from an early age to have developed the attitudes toward religion and habits of church attendance that he would carry throughout his life. By the time of his earliest surviving writings he apparently had imbibed generously of Stoic philosophy, either directly through his own study,

or indirectly, perhaps by his association with the Fairfax family at Belvoir, said to be given to Stoicism, which thereafter filtered his religious and philosophical opinions. As a philosophy of life Stoicism is simple, practical, reasonable, and humanitarian. As such it had elements in common with the fraternal organizations familiar to Washington, such as Freemasonry. The Stoic philosophy embraced the classical virtues and reinforced the Deist beliefs current in the eighteenth century. Boller notes that Washington relied upon "a Grand Designer along Deist lines." His conception of the subject apparently was not as complex or as subtle as that of Benjamin Franklin, Thomas Jefferson, or James Madison, but it was, said Boller, "as deep-seated and meaningful for his life." He formed his religious vocabulary after his usual fashion of borrowing, using, and discarding phrases of language from others as the occasion arose. More often than not Washington referred to God as "Providence" or "Heaven," although he sometimes appealed to the "Director of Human Events," the "Great Ruler of Events," the "Supreme Ruler," the "Governor of the Universe," the "Author of the Universe," the "Supreme Architect of the Universe," the "Grand Architect," the "Author of all good," the "supreme arbiter of events," the "beneficent Being," the "Sovereign Dispenser of life and health," the "Higher Cause," and the "Great Creator."

The qualities attributed to Providence by Washington reveal that he conceived of Providence as an "Omnipotent," "benign," and "beneficient" Being that by "invisible workings" in "Infinite Wisdom" dispensed justice in the affairs of mankind. Astonishment and gratitude were owed this Being. The "ways of Providence" were, he confessed on many occasions, ultimately "inscrutable." Such beliefs are exemplified in Washington's calm, almost detached, acquiescence to the *irreversible* acts of Providence, such as terminal illness or the death of a loved one. An early letter consoling Burwell

Bassett for the death of his daughter, for instance, was not dissimilar to condolences that he would write ever after: "The ways of Providence being inscrutable, and the justice of it not to be scanned by the shallow eye of humanity, not to be counteracted by the utmost efforts of human power or wisdom, resignation, and as far as the strength of our reason and religion can carry us, a cheerful acquiescence to the Divine Will, is what we are to aim." Although he tempered his submission with hope as long as there was the chance that Providence might decree otherwise, once the will of Providence had been manifested there would be no protest from Washington. Where it was yet unknown what course would be taken, however, Washington insisted that individuals had both a need and an obligation to discover and work with Providence. Even his occasional use of the terms "Fate," "Fortune," and "Destiny" were linked with the role of individuals in their own affairs, playing down the fixed nature implied by those words.

What Washington once styled as his "Doctrine of Providence" played a central role in the outcome of not only individuals, but also of peoples and nations. Washington's encounters with enemy gunfire in July 1755 during the disastrous Braddock campaign of the French and Indian War left him convinced that he had been left in the land "of the livg by the miraculous care of Providence, that protected me beyond all human expectation." He had survived despite having two horses shot from under him and four bullets pass through his coat. Providence was involved in defeat, too, for British general Edward Braddock was killed and his troops beaten by a handful of men who only intended to molest and disturb their march. "Victory was their [the enemy's] smallest expectation," he wrote, "but see the wondrous works of Providence! the uncertainty of Human things!" That same uncertainty seemed to characterize the changing fortunes of the Revolu-

tionary War, although Washington held firmly to the justness of the American cause and to a belief that Providence ultimately would favor that cause. His General Orders frequently contained appeals to the Almighty for assistance, expressions of thanksgiving for the "remarkable interpositions of Providence," and reminders for the troops to attend divine services.

As time progressed, Washington's faith in the intervention of Providence on behalf of American arms seemed to grow. "It is not a little pleasing, nor less wonderful to contemplate," he wrote while at White Plains, New York, in August 1778, "that after two years Manœuvring and undergoing the strangest vicissitudes that perhaps ever attended any one contest since the creation both Armies are brought back to the very point they set out from and, that that, which was the offending party in the beginning is now reduced to the use of the spade and pick axe for defence. The hand of Providence has been so conspicuous in all this, that he must be worse than an infidel that lacks faith, and more than wicked, that has not gratitude enough to acknowledge his obligations, but, it will be time enough for me to turn preacher, when my present appointment ceases; and therefore, I shall add no more on the Doctrine of Providence." After Lord Cornwallis surrendered his army at Yorktown in the fall of 1781, Washington ordered divine services to be attended universally "with that seriousness of Deportment and gratitude of Heart which the recognition of such reiterated and astonishing interpositions of Providence demand of us." In his farewell orders to the army on 2 November 1783, Washington again declared that the "singular interposition of Providence in our feeble condition were such, as could scarcely escape the attention of the most unobserving."

Although Washington often wrote about the intervention of Providence in human affairs, he only rarely mentioned his beliefs about an afterlife. When a friend named a son after him, Washington wrote to express the hope that "he will live long to enjoy it, long after I have taken my departure for the world of Spirits." On the eve of his leaving Mount Vernon for Philadelphia for the Constitutional Convention, he confided in Robert Morris of his internal conflict about whether to become involved again in a public life: "My first remaining wish being, to glide gently down the stream of life in tranquil retirement till I shall arrive at the world of Sperits." When his mother died in August 1789, at the age of 83, he wrote to console his sister, Betty, expressing the "hope that she is translated to a happier place." To another he referred to being "translated to a happier clime." How literally Washington meant these references to a "happier clime" and a "land of Spirits" is unclear. Certainly there is a detached and almost fatalistic tone about them. In short, he did believe in immortality, but it is unclear whether he held the classical version of one's life and deeds living on in the effects and memory of subsequent generations or the more literal land of spirits, so totally "other worldly" as to be unknowable and hence not worth troubling oneself over. The mention of a happier clime and meeting in the future indicates that he leaned more in favor of some sort of literal afterlife.

For Washington, toleration and liberty of conscience coincided with the civil and social roles of religion. In roles of authority and leadership, both military and civil, Washington invariably appealed to the twin pillars of "human happiness"—religion and morality—to buttress the civil authority and uphold the social underpinnings. He supported chaplains in the army during both the French and Indian and the Revolutionary wars. Appeals to Providence and days of thanksgiving were frequent during the Revolutionary War and afterward. The latter were ordered by both the Continental and U.S. Congresses, but there were also special thanksgiving services ordered by Washington on his own, without any prompting from Congress. Nor was he opposed to public support of religion. When writing George Mason in October 1785 about James Madison's anonymous Memorial and Remonstrance against the religious assessment bill in the Virginia general assembly, Washington expressed his view that, "Altho' no mans sentiments are more opposed to *any kind* of restraint upon religious principles than mine are; yet I must confess, that I am not amongst the number of those who are so much alarmed at the thoughts of making people pay towards the support of that which they profess, if of the denominations of Christians; or declare themselves Jews, Mahomitans or otherwise, & thereby obtain proper relief." Organized religion was, Washington believed, indispensable to the maintenance of morality, which in turn was one of the supports of the social order.

Washington's most public statement on the relationship between religion and society, as he saw it, was included in his Farewell Address to the people of the United States, made shortly before he retired from his second term as president. "Of all the dispositions and habits which lead to political prosperity," Washington wrote, "Religion and morality are indispensable supports. In vain would that man claim the tribute of Patriotism, who should labour to subvert these great Pillars of human happiness, these firmest props of the duties of Men & citizens. The mere Politician, equally with the pious man ought to respect & to cherish them. A volume could not trace all their connections with private & public felicity. Let it simply be asked where is the security for property, for reputation, for life, if the sense of religious obligation desert the Oaths, which are the instruments of investigation in Courts of Justice? And let us with caution indulge the supposition, that morality can be maintained without religion. Whatever may be conceded to the influence of refined education on minds of peculiar structure—reason & experience both forbid us to expect that National morality can prevail in exclusion of religious principle."

It is worth noting that in his Farewell Address Washington declined to ascribe any attributes to either the religion or the morality that he referred to. His travels across the country had exposed him to the religious and cultural diversity of the people in the United States, and he apparently gave little thought to the particulars of the beliefs held by any of those people. He long had been a champion of freedom of conviction, or conscience, and he did not hesitate to wish "every temporal and spiritual felicity" to Baptists, Quakers, Catholics, and Jews alike. To the latter he wrote that the new government gave "to bigotry no sanction." To what extent religious opinion entered Washington's changing view of slavery is not known, however.

As president Washington followed the same policy he had when he served as commander in chief of the Continental army—he recognized the importance of organized religion and encouraged participation in it. The theme that America was under the special agency of Providence was stressed in his first inaugural address:

> It would be peculiarly improper to omit in this first official Act, my fervent supplications to that Almighty Being who rules over the Universe, who presides in the Councils of Nations, and whose providential aids can supply every human defect, that his benediction may consecrate to the liberties and happiness of the People of the United States, a Government instituted by themselves for these essential purposes: and may enable every instrument employed in its administration to execute with success, the functions allotted to his charge. In tendering this homage to the Great Author of every public and private good, I assure myself that it expresses your sentiments not less than my own; nor those of my fellow-citizens at large, less than either. No People can be bound to acknowledge and adore the in-

visible hand, which conducts the Affairs of men more than the People of the United States. Every step, by which they have advanced to the character of an independent nation, seems to have been distinguished by some token of providential agency. And in the important revolution just accomplished in the system of their United Government, the tranquil deliberations and voluntary consent of so many distinct communities, from which the event has resulted, cannot be compared with the means by which most Governments have been established, without some return of pious gratitude along with an humble anticipation of the future blessings which the past seem to presage.

Throughout his presidency Washington repeated this theme, whether in annual addresses to Congress, official messages to state and local governments, or in letters to civic organizations. Providence also was invoked frequently in Washington's private correspondence.

From time to time Washington also made references not only to religion in general but also to Christianity. His circular letter to the governors of the thirteen states, written at his headquarters in Newburgh, New York, shortly before the end of the war, is perhaps the most explicit:

> That God would have you, and the State over which you preside, in his holy protection, that he would incline the hearts of the Citizens to cultivate a spirit of subordination and obedience to Government, to entertain a brotherly affection and love for one another, for their fellow Citizens of the United States at large, and particularly for their brethren who have served in the Field, and finally, that he would most graciously be pleased to dispose us all, to do justice, to love mercy, and to demean ourselves with that Charity, humility, and pacific temper of mind, which were the Characteristicks of the Divine Author of our blessed Religion, and without an humble imitation of whose example in

these things, we can never hope to be a happy Nation.

Part of the text of the address, with minor modifications and with the words "Almighty God" placed at the beginning and "Through Jesus Christ Our Lord" at the end, has circulated as "Washington's Prayer."

Related entries: Death; Pohick Church, Truro Parish

Suggestions for further reading:
"To Thomas Nelson," 20 August 1778 (*Writings*, vol. 12).
"To George Mason," 3 October 1785 (*Con. Ser.*, vol. 3).
"To Robert Morris," 5 May 1787 (*Con. Ser.*, vol. 5).
"From Jonas Phillips," 7 September 1787 (*Con. Ser.*, vol. 5).
Boller, Paul F. *George Washington and Religion*. 1963. Dallas, TX.

Revolutionary War

See Aides-de-Camp; Appointment as Commander in Chief; Boston, Siege of; Brandywine, Battle of; Commander in Chief's Guard; Delaware Crossing; Fairfax Independent Company; Fort Washington; Germantown, Battle of; Harlem Heights, Battle of; Kip's Bay, New York; Long Island, Battle of; Monmouth Courthouse, Battle of; Morristown, New Jersey; Newburgh Conspiracy; Princeton, Battle of; Society of the Cincinnati; Spirituous Liquors; Trenton, Battle of; Valley Forge; Washington Elm; White Plains, Battle of; Yorktown, Battle of.

River Farm

See Mount Vernon.

Robert Cary & Co.

Robert Cary & Co. was a large London firm involved in the Virginia trade and long one of the principal agents for handling the Custis family's business affairs in London, receiving regular consignments of tobacco from Custis plantations and shipping British goods and supplies that the family required. After his marriage to Martha Custis, Washington continued the connection with the Cary house, not only sending most of the Custis tobacco to Cary and ordering goods and supplies for Mount Vernon, but consigning much of his own Potomac tobacco to them as well. Washington kept in his business letter book copies of his letters to Cary & Co., his orders for goods enclosed in the letters, and the invoices for the goods shipped by Cary. He kept separate accounts for goods charged to his wife's children, Martha Parke Custis and John Parke Custis, and John Parke's plantations.

Related entries: Spirituous Liquors; To Robert Cary & Co., 1 May 1759 (Selected Writings)

Suggestions for further reading:
"To Robert Cary & Co.," 1 May 1759 (*Col. Ser.*, vol. 6).

Rochambeau (1725–1807)

Jean-Baptiste-Donatien de Vimeur, comte de Rochambeau, was born at Vendôme, France, the son of a French lieutenant general and governor of Vendôme. Rochambeau himself was made a lieutenant general in 1780 and placed in command of the French forces sent to reinforce the Continental army. He arrived in America in March 1780 and headquartered at the Vernon House in Newport, Rhode Island, until June 1781. Washington and Lafayette joined Rochambeau there in March 1781 to plan the upcoming campaign.

Washington seriously considered attacking New York with Rochambeau's assistance in August 1780. "In the idea of an operation against New York," he wrote the

An undated painting by Charles Willson Peale of Jean-Baptiste-Donatien de Vimeur, comte de Rochambeau (Library of Congress)

Frenchman, "it has always been a fundamental principle with me, that there ought to be a naval superiority to give such a prospect of success as would justify the undertaking." The size of the collective force "requisite to act with vigor and confidence" was lacking in Washington's opinion, however, so the idea was abandoned. The frequent correspondence between the two generals over the next few months led first to mutual respect and then to genuine friendship, as exhibited by Rochambeau's order for an early celebration of Washington's birthday in February 1781, which included a parade of French troops, an artillery salute, and a day of rest for the troops.

In June 1781 Rochambeau finally marched toward the Hudson River, attacking a detachment of British general Henry Clinton's army on Manhattan Island on the way in a feint designed to deceive the enemy as to the army's real intentions. He crossed the Hudson as if he intended to march into New Jersey, but instead joined Washington's army at Phillipsburg, nine miles from Kingsbridge. This movement caused Clinton to abandon his planned expedition to the Chesapeake to reinforce Lord Cornwallis, with disastrous results for Cornwallis and the British war effort. The combined forces of Washington and Rochambeau moved toward Williamsburg, Virginia, where they united with Lafayette's in mid-September. For the next two weeks the three generals planned strategy, and the siege of Yorktown began on 29 September, forcing Cornwallis to surrender on 19 October. The following day Washington personally thanked Rochambeau for his part in the victory, and later that month the Continental Congress recognized his efforts in a resolution of thanks, directing Washington to present him with "two of the Field pieces taken at York, with an inscription engraved on them expressive of the occasion," an order that Washington, with "infinite satisfaction," complied with.

Several months later Rochambeau returned to his estate near Vendôme. Washington, not long after his return to Mount Vernon, which Rochambeau had visited while en route to Yorktown, wrote Rochambeau: "The tranquil walks of domestic life are now unfolding to my view; & promise a rich harvest of pleasing contemplation—in which my dear Genl you will be one of my most agreeable themes—as I shall recollect with pleasure, that we have been Contemporaries & fellow-labourers in the cause of liberty, and that we have lived together as Brothers should do—in harmony & friendship."

Rochambeau took an active part in forming the French Society of the Cincinnati, about which he corresponded with Washington. Rochambeau's memoirs were published posthumously in 1809 and translated into English in 1838.

Related entries: Clinton, Henry; Yorktown, Battle of

Suggestions for further reading:
Diaries, vol. 3.
"To Rochambeau," 21 August 1780 (*Writings,* vol. 19).
"General Orders," 20 October 1781 (*Writings,* vol. 23).
"To Rochambeau," 1 February 1784 (*Con. Ser.,* vol. 1).
Rice, Howard C., Jr., and Anne S. K. Brown. 1972. *The American Campaigns of Rochambeau's Army.* Princeton, NJ, and Providence, RI.

Royal Gift

Shortly after the Revolutionary War, Washington decided to obtain a Spanish jackass, thought the best in the world, to begin breeding mules at Mount Vernon, hoping to "secure a race of extraordinary goodness" from which to stock the country. He apparently had become convinced during the war that horses and oxen were inferior as draft animals to mules.

King Charles III of Spain presented Washington with a pair, one of which died during the rough voyage to America. The surviving animal, later named Royal Gift, was described by Massachusetts lieutenant governor Thomas Cushing, who received him in Boston, as "a fine Creature, just fifty Eight Inches high, & the largest that I beleive ever came into this Country, As he has been something Bruised upon the Passage by the frequent tossing of the Vessell, although no ways essentially hurt." A Spaniard who could not speak English, sent along to care for and deliver the jack, walked the animal from Boston to Mount Vernon. Meanwhile, the marquis de Lafayette also acquired an additional two jacks, one at Cadiz and one at Malta, and shipped them to America in two different vessels. The jack from Cadiz was lost at sea, but the one from Malta arrived safely at Mount Vernon in November 1786. Washington named it Knight of Malta and described it as "light & active," suitable for the road. In August 1791 three of Washington's jacks were described thus: "Royal Gift 14 hands 1½ Inch. his Ears 14 Inches[.] Knight Malta. 13 hands. 1½ Inch. his Ears. 12½ Inches[.] Young Jack 3 Years old this spring—12 hands. 1¼ I: Ears 12 I." That same year Washington sent Royal Gift to his kinsman William Washington in South Carolina.

In a newspaper advertisement placed by Washington's farm overseer John Fairfax offering to cover mares and jennies at Mount Vernon in the spring of 1786, Royal Gift was said to be "A JACK ASS of the first race in the kingdom of Spain . . . four years old, is between 14 ½ and 15 hands high, and will grow, it is said, till he is 20 or 25 years of age. He is very bony and stout made, of a dark colour, with light belly and legs." The advertisement went on to discuss the advantages to be derived from the propagation of "this mongrel race"— namely their "great strength, longevity, hardiness and cheap support."

In February 1786 Washington sent twenty-five barrels of fine flour to Surinam to buy a jenny for the purpose of preserving the "breed of the valuable Jack" sent by the "Catholic Majesty." The jenny arrived at Mount Vernon by the middle of the following November. By the end of 1788 Washington had set aside upwards of twenty of his best mares for the sole purpose of breeding mules, an activity he engaged in during his presidency and retirement years. The number of mules kept at Mount Vernon at any given time had climbed to more than fifty by 1798.

Royal Gift died in 1796, but his offspring Young Royal Gift continued to spawn offspring until beyond Washington's death.

Related entry: Humor

Suggestions for further reading:
Diaries, vols. 4, 5.
"From Thomas Cushing," 7 October 1785 (*Con. Ser.,* vol. 3).
"Advertisement," 23 February 1786 (*Con. Ser.,* vol. 3).

"To Arthur Young," 4 December 1788 (*Pres. Ser.*, vol. 1).

"From George Augustine Washington," 1 August 1791 (*Pres. Ser.*, vol. 8).

"To Robert Lewis," 23 January 1799 (*Ret. Ser.*, vol. 3).

"From Robert Lewis," 13 February 1799 (*Ret. Ser.*, vol. 3).

Pennsylvania Packet, 7 March 1786.

Rules of Civility and Decent Behaviour in Company and Conversation

See Education; Selected Writings.

Rumsey, James (1743–1792)

James Rumsey, an uneducated but "handsome and engaging jack-of-all-trades" particularly fascinated with mechanical invention, was born at Bohemia Manor in Cecil County, Maryland. About 1782 he resettled at the springs in Bath, Virginia (now Berkeley Springs, West Virginia), where he engaged in the building trade, operated a sawmill and bloomery, and became a partner in a new boardinghouse and general store. Rumsey and Washington apparently first met in late summer 1784, when Washington and his old friend Dr. James Craik lodged at the boardinghouse for a couple of nights while on a trip to visit their western lands. At the boardinghouse Washington apparently learned of Rumsey's design for a mechanical boat that could be propelled upstream by means of poles pushing against the riverbed when given force by a paddle wheel that was turned by the current against which the boat was to move. Washington became absolutely enthralled as he watched Rumsey demonstrate a small model of how his invention worked (described in Washington's lengthy diary entry for 6 September 1784),

and on the following day, at Rumsey's request, he gave the inventor a written certificate of what he had seen. "The discovery," wrote Washington, "is of vast importance—may be of the greatest usefulness in our inland navigation—&, if it succeeds, of which I have no doubt, that the value of it is greatly enhanced by the simplicity of the works; which when seen & explained to, might be executed by the most common Mechanic's." Rumsey wasted no time in arranging to have Washington's statement printed in the *Virginia Gazette,* although in fact by that time he already had begun contemplating the likely success of a steam-powered vessel and the important question of whether steam engines could be produced simply and cheaply enough "as to make them of public benefit." John Fitch, a competitor also experimenting with steam power, contemptuously dismissed Rumsey's invention as a "Pole Boat" and stingingly asserted that Washington's endorsement of it was "one of the most imprudent acts" of his life. Washington, however, retained his optimism that Rumsey in time would perfect this or a similar invention and that sooner or later steam vessels would pass regularly up and down the Potomac. Impressed with Rumsey's mechanical abilities, Washington on the date of the demonstration contracted with the storekeeper to build him a two-story house, complete with kitchen and stable, near the springs in Bath, although Washington was unable to make much, if any, use of the house or its dependencies, which were, according to eyewitnesses, poorly constructed. (Washington recorded a detailed description of the proposed dwelling house in his diary entry for 6 September 1784.) Rumsey later was hired to manage the Potomac Company, of which Washington served as president.

In 1787 Rumsey exhibited on the Potomac River near what is now Shepherdstown, West Virginia, a boat propelled by streams of water forced out through the

PROPOSALS

For forming a Company, to enable
JAMES RUMSEY
To carry into Execution, on a Large and Extensive Plan, his
STEAM·BOAT
And sundry other Machines herein after mentioned.

Whereas JAMES RUMSEY, of Berkeley county, in the state of Virginia, has been several years employed, with unremitted attention and at a great expence, in bringing to perfection the following machines and engines, namely, one for propelling boats on the water, by the power of steam, which has already been accomplished in experiments, on a boat of about six tons burthen; another machine, constructed on similar principles, for raising water at a small expence, to be applied to the working of mills of different kinds, as well as to various useful purposes in agriculture; and also others, by means of which, grist and saw-mills may be so improved in their construction, by a very cheap and simple mechanism, as to require the application of much less water than is necessary in the common mode: And whereas the expenditures that the said *James Rumsey* has necessarily incurred in the prosecution of these important discoveries, and in endeavouring to bring the machines and engines which he has so invented to perfection, have rendered him incapable, without assistance, to carry his said plans fully into effect: Therefore, he, the said James Rumsey, hereby doth, by the advice of sundry gentlemen of reputation, propose to form a company on the following plan, to enable him to complete and carry into execution his aforesaid inventions; being anxious to evince the great utility, which he is confident, will result to his country therefrom. For this purpose, he proposes.

1st. To reserve, subject to his own disposal, one moiety or half part of the interest, and property, in his said discoveries and machines.

2nd. That the other moiety of the interest and property in the same, be divided into fifty equal shares, to be disposed of to such gentlemen as may choose to encourage so laudable and beneficial an undertaking.— The purchasers to pay at the time of subscribing, twenty Spanish milled dollars, for each share, into the hands of the said James Rumsey, or of the trustees hereafter to be appointed, who will be authorised by him to receive subscriptions.

3d. The said James Rumsey, hereby engages to convey to the said Trustees, for the use and benefit of the company, Lands, of considerable value, as a security for the faithful appropriation of the monies so to be subscribed; which monies shall be applied to the immediate purposes of perfecting the before mentioned machines, and obtaining grants from the legislatures of the several states, vesting in the said James Rumsey, his executors administrators and assigns, an exclusive right to, and interest in the said discoveries and machines, for a certain term of years.

4th The said James Rumsey farther engages, that, at the expiration of one year from the date hereof (at which time he expects to have his machines completed) he will convey to each subscriber, his executors, administrators, or assigns, the share or shares by them respectively subscribed for, on his or their paying the said James Rumsey the additional sum of forty Spanish milled dollars, on each share so subscribed. And that, should any subscriber, or his legal representative, then wish to relinquish his share or shares, the money advanced by him for the same, shall be refunded to him. But should it so happen, that all, or a great number of the subscribers, or their representatives, should not be desirous of retaining their respective shares, and that the said James Rumsey should thereby, be disabled from refunding to them, out of the fund arising from the original subscriptions, the sum of twenty dollars advanced for each share; in that case he agrees that the lands, so as aforesaid to be conveyed in trust, shall be sold by the trustees aforesaid, for the express purpose of reimbursing the monies, advanced by those persons so declining to retain their shares; the surplus to be refunded to the said James Rumsey or his representatives.

5th. That those persons who may think proper to pay the additional sum of forty dollars for each share, and thereby be invested with a complete proprietorship in the concern, shall form themselves into a company, which shall hold their meetings at such times and places as may be by them agreed upon, for the purpose of promoting the interest of the proprietors, and for directing the mode, in which the business of the company shall, from time to time be conducted. That at all such meetings of the company, each proprietor shall be entitled to one vote for every share he shall possess, to the number of five (inclusive) and one vote for every five additional shares. That the said James Rumsey, so long as he shall continue a proprietor of one moiety (equivalent to fifty shares) or of a lesser number, shall be entitled to a proportionable number of votes, with the other proprietors; and that every person who may purchase from the said James Rumsey a share or shares (each of which shall be one equal fiftieth part of his the said James Rumsey's proprietorship, hereby reserved) shall have the same right of voting as other proprietors.

That, so soon as twenty shares shall be subscribed for, the subscribers shall meet, in order to appoint trustees, for the purposes before specified: and that when the company shall be completely organized, every person entitled to give a vote in person, shall also, in case of absence, have a right to vote by proxy.

In Witness of the premises, We the Subscribers, have hereunto set our Names, this   day of   1788.

George Washington's copy of Rumsey's proposal to form a steamboat company, May 1788 (Library of Congress) stern, a steam engine being employed to operate the force pump. Rumsey's experiments resulted in "five pamphlets Respecting My Boat and other plans," which he sent to Washington in March 1788, printed as *A Plan, Wherein the Power of Steam Is Fully Shewn, by a New Constructed Machine, for Propelling Boats or Vessels, of Any Burthen, against the Most Rapid Streams or Rivers with Great Velocity. Also, a Machine, Constructed on Similar Philosophical Principles, by Which Water May Be Raised for Grist or Saw-Mills, Watering of Meadows, &c. &c.* (Shepherdstown, 1788); the pamphlet was still in Washington's library at his death. About this time Rumsey published another pamphlet containing a discussion of his method for applying steam to propel vessels, *A Short Treatise on the Application of Steam* (Philadelphia, 1788). He also formed a company, the Rumseyan Society, to promote his projects, which included improved versions of a sawmill, a gristmill, and a steam boiler. The society, which consisted of about twenty shareholders, Benjamin Franklin being the most prominent, subscribed $1,000 to send Rumsey to Europe to apply for patents for his improvements and to interest foreign capital. Rumsey kept Washington informed of his decision to "throw myself upon the wide world in persuit of my plans," and ventured to express his wish that Washington "Could with propriaty mention me in a Line the first oppertunity to the Marquis La Fayette Mr Jefferson or any other Gentleman that you may think proper." Washington apparently did not write letters on Rumsey's behalf, however. Rumsey managed to secure British patents on his boiler and steamboat shortly after his arrival in England, and similar protections were obtained in America three years later. Rumsey died in London shortly before his second steamboat was completed, and he was buried in St. Margaret's churchyard near Westminster.

Related entry: Potomac River Navigation

Suggestions for further reading:

Diaries, vol. 4.
"Certificate for James Rumsey," 7 September 1784 (*Con Ser.,* vol. 2).
"To James Rumsey," 31 January 1786 (*Con. Ser.,* vol. 3).
"From James Rumsey," 5, 19 September 1786 (*Con. Ser.,* vol. 4).
"From James Rumsey," 17 December 1787 (*Con. Ser.,* vol. 5).
"From James Rumsey," 15 May 1788 (*Con. Ser.,* vol. 6).
Virginia Gazette, and Winchester Advertiser, 11 January 1788.
Beltzhoover, George M., Jr. 1900. *James Rumsey, the Inventor of the Steamboat.* Charleston, WV.
Turner, Ella May. 1930. *James Rumsey, Pioneer in Steam Navigation.* Scottdale, PA.

S

St. Clair, Arthur (1737–1818)

Arthur St. Clair was born in Edinburgh, Scotland, where he studied medicine at the famous university after a childhood of which scant record remains. He apparently became dissatisfied with the life of a physician, however, and entered the military during the French and Indian War. Service as a subaltern in the Royal American Regiment brought St. Clair to Canada in 1759, where he served as a lieutenant under Gen. James Wolfe (1727–1759). Following the siege of Quebec, St. Clair married, and after the peace he was made commander of Fort Ligonier in western Pennsylvania. He then resigned his commission, purchased a tract of land in the area (in fact the largest "beyond the mountains" in western Pennsylvania), and began farming. Like Washington, St. Clair also turned his mathematical mind to surveying.

Patriotic, brave, and respected by his fellows, St. Clair was appointed colonel of the Second Pennsylvania Regiment in January 1776. He rose rapidly in rank, being promoted to brigadier general in August 1776 and to major general the following February. In June 1777 he was sent to command Fort Ticonderoga, which he evacuated shortly after his arrival after receiving intelligence that Canadian, Indian, and British and Hessian troops were converging in the area for an attack. He was severely criticized for the evacuation and recalled by Congress. A court-martial subsequently cleared St. Clair of any blame, however, and although Washington did not lose confidence in him either, his military reputation suffered until July 1779, when the successful assault on the British at Stony Point, New York, took place under his command. When Washington moved toward Yorktown in 1781, St. Clair remained in Philadelphia with newly recruited Pennsylvania troops to protect the Continental Congress. He later joined the main army at Yorktown during the siege, and from there he traveled south to unite with Maj. Gen. Nathanael Greene near Savannah. St. Clair remained on active duty until November 1783.

After the war St. Clair continued to live in Pennsylvania, where he was elected to the Confederation Congress in 1785, serving as its president in 1787. He was appointed governor of the Northwest Territory in 1788, an office he held until 1802, when Ohio was admitted to the union. He also was president of the Pennsylvania Society of the Cincinnati. In 1791 he led an expedition to establish a chain of military posts and a road through the wilderness from Fort Washington on the Ohio River to Kekionga, a Miami village at the forks of the Miami, St. Marys, and St. Joseph Rivers. The expedition had progressed about two-thirds of the way when it was attacked and overwhelmed by about 1,500 Indian warriors from ten tribes under the leadership of Little Turtle of the Miami, Blue Jacket of the Shawnee, and Buckongahelas of the Delaware. St. Clair's forces suffered heavy casualties—some 900 of 1,400 officers and troops were killed or wounded—and St. Clair himself, severely ill with gout, was surrounded twice during the "very precipitate" retreat. The defeat was a bitter disappointment to Washington, who had warned St. Clair to be on guard against a surprise attack. An enquiry into the fiasco by a committee of the House of Representatives eventually exonerated St. Clair.

St. Clair died a few days after being injured from a fall from a horse at Laurel Hill in western Pennsylvania.

Related entries: Society of the Cincinnati; Yorktown, Battle of

Suggestions for further reading:
"From Arthur St. Clair," 17, 25 July 1777 (*War Ser.*, vol. 10).
"From Arthur St. Clair," 20 April 1784 (*Con. Ser.*, vol. 1).
"From William Darke," 9–10 November 1791 (*Pres. Ser.*, vol. 9).
"To the U.S. Senate and House of Representatives," 12 December 1791 (*Pres. Ser.*, vol. 9).
Smith, William Henry, ed. 1882. 2 vols. *The St. Clair Papers.* Cincinnati.

Schuyler, Philip (1733–1804)

A deep and abiding friendship between Philip Schuyler and George Washington began when the two met for the first time in mid-May 1775 at Philadelphia, where Schuyler had come to serve as a New York delegate to the second Continental Congress. Less than a year apart in age, equal in height and commanding presence, the two men instantly recognized common interests. Each had served in the French and Indian War and thus had seen firsthand how the British army administered

tered itself and solved logistical problems. Likewise, both had dealt with Indians on the frontier. Colonial politics were not unfamiliar to the men either, both of whom enthusiastically supported the revolutionary activities of their respective provincial governments. Although Schuyler, unlike Washington, was the scion of one of the great landed aristocratic families of New York and had received an education quite superior to that generally thought to have been Washington's lot, both men were proficient in mathematics, had studied military tactics, and had proved themselves adept in managing large estates and varied business interests. Schuyler, like Washington, had lost his father while still young and had been taken under the wings of supportive family members, whose estate, again like Washington's Mount Vernon, eventually came under his control. By the time Schuyler and Washington first met, Schuyler commanded a vast estate in the Mohawk Valley and along the Hudson River, and his schooner and three sloops regularly plied the Hudson for trade. These and other similarities probably accounted for their immediate friendship.

The New York provincial congress's unanimous recommendation of Schuyler as its first choice to serve as commander of the northern department could have been substituted as a letter of recommendation for Washington:

Courage, prudence, readiness in expedients, nice perception, sound judgment, and great attention, these are a few of the natural qualifications which appear to us to be proper. To these ought to be added an extensive acquaintance with the sciences, particularly the various branches of mathematical knowledge, long practise in the military arts, and above all a knowledge of mankind. On a general in America, fortune also should bestow her gifts that he may rather communicate lustre to his dignities than receive it and that his country, his property, his kindred and connections, may have sure pledges that he will faithfully perform the duties of his high office and readily lay down his power when the general weal requires it. . . . And therefore you will not be surprised to hear that we are unanimous in the choice.

Acting upon this recommendation, and Washington's as well, Congress on 19 June 1775 resolved to appoint Schuyler one of Washington's first four major generals. The two men traveled together from Philadelphia to New York City, where they separated, Washington continuing on to Cambridge, Massachusetts, and Schuyler to Albany, where he would, in the words of Washington's instructions to him, "see that the Orders of the Continental Congress are carried into Execution with as much precision and Exactness as possible. . . . Your own good Sense must govern in all Matters not particularly pointed out, as I do not wish to circumscribe you within too narrow Limits." Washington never wavered in his trust of Schuyler's judgment and abilities when it came to handling the military matters of his department, and their mutual friendship and esteem grew as the men kept up a steady wartime correspondence.

Schuyler's efficient and energetic efforts, reinforced by his ample fortune and extensive influence, at times almost single-handedly kept the army in the field in the northern department. The abandonment of the American fort at Ticonderoga, New York, to the British in early July 1777 without a defense (and without Schuyler's knowledge or approval) placed Schuyler, as commanding general of the department, in a difficult and unfortunate position. His enemies used the event to convince Congress to replace him as commander of the northern department. Washington wisely refused to become embroiled in the matter, and Congress was forced to recall Schuyler on its own authority. (A court-martial in October 1778 acquitted Schuyler with honor against charges that he had neglected his duty concerning Ticonderoga.) Before the arrival of his successor, Maj. Gen. Horatio Gates, however, Schuyler managed to implement what proved to be a successful strategy to impede the British march across New York, delaying and harassing Burgoyne's army at every step and setting the stage for Burgoyne's defeat two months later at the Battle of Saratoga. His reaction to Gates's vindictive attitude toward him, said a nineteenth-century historian, was "one of the noblest triumphs of patriotism and virtue over envy, jealousy, and the consciousness of being wronged" exhibited during the war. Another historian of the same period observed that, although Schuyler "suffered a greater injury than was inflicted on any other individual during the war, he did not allow his exertions in behalf of his country to be affected by it. He was the same noble-hearted patriot, whether in retirement or surrounded by power."

Although Schuyler resigned his Continental army commission in the spring of 1779, Washington still sought his advice that same year when planning the expedition led by Gen. John Sullivan against the Iroquois Indians in New York State. In 1780 Schuyler headed a Continental Congress committee at Washington's headquarters that helped reorganize the army's staff departments and foster cooperation with the French forces in America. Washington tried to get Schuyler to rejoin the army in a new capacity in 1781, but Schuyler politely refused the overture. Schuyler did heed Washington's July 1781 entreaty to oversee the construction of 100 bateaux to transport troops down the Hudson River. (The same year Washington stood as godfather to Schuyler's daughter.) At Washington's urging Schuyler also assisted in keeping a watchful eye on a movement within Vermont to realign with the British Crown. He served several terms in the New York state senate in the 1780s and 1790s, as well as two terms in the U.S. Senate, being elected in 1789 and again in

1797. Like Washington he was keenly interested in the potential of canals to enhance inland navigation.

Schuyler's last years were shrouded in grief. In a few short years his wife, Catherine Van Rensselaer, a daughter, and his son-in-law Alexander Hamilton all preceded him in death. One of his last acts was to manumit all his slaves, with sufficient property for them to support themselves. He died and was buried at Albany.

Related entries: Gates, Horatio; Hamilton, Alexander

Suggestions for further reading:
"Philip Schuyler: The General as Aristocrat," John H. G. Pell. George Athan Billias, ed. 1964. *George Washington's Generals.* New York.
Gerlach, Don R. 1964. *Philip Schuyler and the American Revolution in New York.* Lincoln, NE.
Lossing, Benson J. 1872–1873. 2 vols. *Life and Times of Philip Schuyler.* New York.

Simpson, Gilbert, Jr.

See Washington's Bottom Tract.

Slavery

"It is one of the strange inconsistencies of history," wrote an early-twentieth-century student of George Washington, "that one of the foremost champions of liberty of all times should himself have been the absolute owner and master of men, women and children." Indeed, George Washington, who grew up with slavery, shared the fundamental quandary of Virginia's slaveholding elite: reconciling slavery with the prevalent natural-rights theories with their emphasis on liberty, the watchword of the American Revolution. Before the Revolutionary War, Washington viewed slavery from the perspective of the typical eighteenth-century Virginia planter. He was barely 11 years old when he inherited about a quarter of his father's more than four dozen slaves, and as a young man he occasionally added to that number, apparently without compunction. His marriage to Martha Dandridge Custis in 1759 greatly increased the number of slaves under his immediate control, although the slaves owned by Martha and her children did not and would never belong to him. The intermarriage of the Custis slaves with Washington's own slaves eventually created difficulties for Washington when he made the decision to free the slaves owned outright by him.

The slaves at Mount Vernon did not live particularly well. One visitor to Mount Vernon, the Polish aristocrat Julian Ursyn Niemcewicz (1758–1841), was shocked by the roughness of their quarters. "We entered one of the huts of the Blacks," he wrote, "for one can not call them by the name of houses. They are more miserable than the most miserable of the cottages of our peasants. The husband and wife sleep on a mean pallet, the children on the ground; a very bad fireplace, some utensils for cooking, but in the middle of this poverty some cups and a teapot. . . . A very small garden planted with vegetables was close by, with 5 or 6 hens, each one leading ten to fifteen chickens. It is the only comfort that is permitted them; for they may not keep either ducks, geese, or pigs." Their rations, chiefly maize, herring, and occasional salt meat, seemed inadequate. Of an estimated 300 slaves at Mount Vernon, 100 worked in the fields without a "single day for themselves except for holidays." (Occasionally slaves were given a day off to travel to Alexandria to conduct some small private business or attend the horse races.) Despite these conditions, Niemcewicz observed that the slaves seem "disposed to gaiety" and on Sundays participated in games "as if they had rested all week." The slaves also spoke "very good English," much in contrast to the French spoken by slaves in the French colonies vis-

After retiring from the presidency, George Washington supervises the work of two of his slaves at his Virginia plantation, Mount Vernon (Library of Congress)

ited by Niemcewicz. Altogether, Niemcewicz concluded, Washington treated his slaves "far more humanely than do his fellow citizens of Virginia. Most of those gentlemen give to their Blacks only bread, water and blows." Other foreign visitors to Mount Vernon concurred with Niemcewicz's assessment.

Despite his reputation for being kind to his slaves, Washington had no illusions about his relationship with his slaves. "The Gen'l never called his negroes *his children,* I know for a certainty," recalled his step-granddaughter Nelly Custis in 1823. "He was a generous & noble master & they feared & loved him." Washington resorted to corporal punishment on occasion, although he personally did not administer it. His directions regarding one runaway represent his attitude: "Let Abram get his deserts when taken, by way of example; but do not trust to [Hyland] Crow to give it him; for I have reason to believe he is swayed more by passion than judgment in

all his corrections." Individuals even more unruly than Abram were given an opportunity to rehabilitate themselves at another of Washington's plantations, but if they remained recalcitrant, they might be sent further away. In 1766 Washington placed one such fellow, Tom, onboard a merchant vessel sailing for the West Indies, instructing the captain of the ship to sell him "in any of the islands you may go to, for whatever he will fetch, and bring me in return for him" molasses, rum, limes, and other goods. Another of Washington's slaves committed an offense so serious that he was tried under state law, found guilty, and executed.

Some of the slaves at Mount Vernon and Washington's other plantations occupied positions of some trust and responsibility. Davy, for instance, managed Washington's Muddy Hole farm for many years. Washington considered him as capable as most of his white overseers and better than some, although he distrusted Davy's honesty regarding livestock. For his efforts Davy was rewarded with special quarters, two or three hogs at killing time, and other privileges. Slaves with special skills—carpenters, masons, gardeners, spinners, millers—fared better than field workers. Domestic and personal servants were also more fortunate than other slaves. Usually mulattoes, they formed the aristocracy of the plantation's slave society. Their clothing was more decent than the annual "jacket and a pair of homespun breeches" allotted to field hands, and most learned to read and write. The most famous, William Lee ("Billy"), Washington's body-servant during the Revolutionary War, was the subject of special provisions in Washington's will.

Washington recognized that slaves experienced the same range of emotions as the unenslaved and attempted to make accommodations where possible. He instructed an agent, for instance, not to conclude an agreement for the purchase of a mason if the sale would "hurt the man's feelings" by disrupting his family. When family separation resulted in runaways, his attempts to recapture them were often halfhearted. Christopher Sheels, who had replaced Billy Lee as Washington's body-servant during the presidential years, went unpunished after his plan to escape with his young wife was exposed; retained as Washington's personal servant, Christopher attended Washington in his final illness. On the other hand, Washington was genuinely stunned when Ona Judge, his wife's servant in the presidential household, absconded to the north, and he did not abandon his efforts to have her returned even after he discovered that she had married a free mulatto in New Hampshire, John Staines. When his nephew Lawrence Lewis lost a servant in a like manner in 1797, Washington confided to him that "it is my opinion these elopements will be *much more,* before they are *less* frequent; and that the persons making them should never be retained, if they are recovered, as they are sure to contaminate and discontent others. I wish from my Soul that

the Legislature of this State could see the policy of a gradual abolition of Slavery; It might prevt much future mischief." Washington had shown a concern for keeping slave families intact as early as 1779, when he expressed a reluctance to offer "these people at public venue . . . if these poor wretches are to be held in a State of Slavery I do not see that a change of masters will render it more irksome, provided husband & wife, and Parents & children are not separated from each other, which is not my intention to do."

The health of his slaves was of particular concern to Washington, for reasons both humane and economic. While at Mount Vernon, Niemcewicz had observed a boy of 15 years "lying on the ground, sick, and in terrible convulsions." Washington already had sent to Alexandria for a doctor. "It is foremost in my thoughts," he wrote a Mount Vernon manager, "to desire you will be particularly attentive to my Negros in their sickness; and to order every Overseer positively to be so likewise; for I am sorry to observe that the generality of them, view these poor creatures in scarcely any other light than they do a draughthorse or Ox; neglecting them as much when they are unable to work; instead of comforting & nursing them when they lye on a sickbed." Christopher, his servant, had received special treatment from his master when he had been sent to Pennsylvania in search of medical treatment after being bitten by a rabid dog.

Over the decades Washington became disillusioned with the institution of slavery. His travels in the other colonies, especially the northern ones where slavery seemed to be declining, convinced him that slavery was not an efficient labor system. The moral and ethical considerations apparently troubled him as well, although he continued to purchase slaves as required by necessity. As a member of the Virginia House of Burgesses he supported a 1772 petition to the Crown that attacked the trafficking of slaves as a "trade of great inhumanity" that threatened the "very existence of your Majesty's American dominions." Two years later he presided over the public meeting that resulted in the drafting of the Fairfax Resolves, including a resolution attacking the slave trade by "declaring our most earnest Wishes to see an entire Stop forever put to such a wicked cruel and unnatural Trade."

A few months after taking command of the Continental army in 1775 Washington issued orders that declared blacks as well as young boys and old men unfit for military service because of their supposed inability to "endure the fatigues of the campaign." The policy was modified in December 1775, since "Numbers of free Negroes are desirous of inlisting, he gives leave to the recruiting Officers, to entertain them, and promises to lay the matter before the Congress, who he doubts not will approve of it." A further modification took place in 1778 when Washington permitted Rhode Island officer Joseph Varnum to raise a regiment of free blacks. Similarly, in 1778 and 1779, Washington tentatively approved a scheme devised by his aide-de-camp John Laurens of South Carolina to raise a regiment of slaves in his home state and Georgia for Continental army service.

During the war years Washington became more and more disillusioned with the slave system. Early on he received Phillis Wheatley's inspiring poem in his honor and was so favorably impressed that he invited the former slave to his headquarters. By 1778 he had developed an aversion to owning slaves and was desirous of exchanging them for land. When one land purchase was contemplated he instructed his farm manager, Lund Washington, to attempt to swap slaves for land. "I had rather give Negroes—if Negroes would do. for to be plain I wish to get quit of Negroes." When he resumed the management of his plantations shortly after the war, his opinion of the system's inefficiency grew stronger. By 1786 he had

come to a strong resolution on the subject, expressed in a letter to John Francis Mercer: "I never mean (unless some particular circumstance should compel me to it) to possess another slave by purchase; it being among my first wishes to see some plan adopted by the legislature, by which slavery in this Country may be abolished by slow, sure & imperceptible degrees." He declared to Robert Morris that "I can only say, that there is not a man living who wishes more sincerely than I do, to see a plan adopted for the abolition of it—but there is only one proper and effectual mode by which it can be accomplished, & that is by Legislative authority; and this as far as my suffrage will go, shall never be wanting." He encouraged Lafayette's experimental settlement in Cayenne for freed slaves, although he rejected overtures to participate in the experiment. "Would to God a like spirit would diffuse itself generally into the minds of the people of this country," he wrote, "but I despair of seeing it. . . . To set the slaves afloat at once would, I really believe, be productive of much inconvenience and mischief; but by degrees it certainly might, and assuredly ought to be, effected, and that too, by legislative authority."

During the course of his presidency Washington became convinced that economic necessities would force the slave issue at some point, and the potential danger of the system for the republic weighed heavily on his mind. In 1794 he informed his secretary Tobias Lear that he wanted to dispose of his western lands, partly so that "the remainder of my days may, thereby, be more tranquil & freer from cares," but also for a more private reason. "Besides these, I have another motive which makes me earnestly wish for the accomplishment of these things, it is indeed more powerful than all the rest. namely to liberate a certain species of property—which I possess, very repugnantly to my own feelings; but which imperious necessity compels . . . until I can substitute some other expedient, by which expences not in my power to avoid (however well disposed I may be to do it) can be defrayed." Later that year he discussed the subject with fellow Virginian and war veteran Alexander Spotswood: "With respect to the other species of property, concerning which you ask my opinion, I shall frankly declare to you that I do not like even to think much less talk of it. However, as you have put the question, I shall, in a few words, give you my ideas of it. Were it not then, that I am principled agt selling Negroes, as you would Cattle in the market, I would not, in twelve months from this date, be possessed of one as a slave." He concluded with a prophecy that the system might eventually disrupt the union. "I shall be happily mistaken, if [slaves] are not found to be a very troublesome species of property ere many years pass over our heads."

Washington's expectation that the slave issue would loom larger and larger in the republic led him to make provisions for the freedom of his slaves in his will. He could not free the Custis-owned slaves, but he stipulated that all the slaves held by him in his "*own right*" should be freed upon his wife's decease. He recognized the "most painful sensations, if not disagreeable consequences" that would arise by giving freedom to only some of the slaves under his control, but there was nothing he could do. Provisions were included for the aged, the infirm, and others unable to support themselves; young slaves were to be taught to read and write; and strict prohibitions were placed on the sale or transporting of any of them outside Virginia. A pointed and solemn enjoinder was placed on his executors to fulfil "religiously" every clause respecting his slaves without "evasion, neglect or delay." Washington obviously did not want any of his slaves to become a liability to the community, nor did he want the slaves to continue in servitude.

Related entries: Last Will and Testament; Wheatley, Phillis

Suggestions for further reading:
"To Lawrence Lewis," 4 August 1797 (*Ret. Ser.,* vol. 4).
"Washington's Slave List," June 1799 (*Ret. Ser.,* vol. 4).
"Last Will and Testament," 9 July 1799 (*Ret. Ser.,* vol. 4).
"To Robert Lewis," 17 August 1799 (*Ret. Ser.,* vol. 4).
Haworth, Paul Leland. 1915. *George Washington: Farmer.* Indianapolis.
Hirschfeld, Fritz. 1997. *George Washington and Slavery: A Documentary Portrayal.* Columbia, MO.

Society of the Cincinnati

The Society of the Cincinnati was established in 1783 amidst Washington's ever-present concern for civil-military relations, the daily expectation of an announcement of peace with Great Britain, Congress's reluctance to settle the long-standing debts owed to the army, and the discontent among the officers and troops after Washington's successful suppression of the Newburgh Conspiracy. It began when Maj. Gen. Henry Knox introduced his proposal to form a military society whose membership would be open to the whole officer corps, including the officers of foreign allies serving in America. The idea was not new to Knox, at least not in all its elements, for as early as September 1776 he had expressed a desire that he might have "some ribbon to wear in his hat, or in his button hole, to be transmitted to his descendants as a badge and a proof that he had fought in defence of their liberties." For his chief collaborators in planning the society, Knox relied on two men from New England, his own aide-de-camp, Capt. Samuel Shaw of Massachusetts, and Brig. Gen. Jedediah Huntington of Connecticut, as well as the major general Baron von Steuben. Other prominent early supporters at Washington's encampment included Engineer Rufus Putnam, also of Massachusetts, and Alexander Mc-

Dougall and Philip Van Cortlandt of New York.

The name of the society could not have been better chosen. Like the noble Cincinnatus, who left his plow to lead the Roman war against the Aequi in 458 B.C., many of the officers serving in the Continental army had suspended their own agricultural pursuits to go off to war. Washington himself epitomized the disinterested and selfless sacrifice the officers had made, for like the Roman general Washington not only had abandoned his farms but also had been entrusted with dictatorial powers by his government, and he would very soon willingly resign his commission and return to private life. Washington was named president of the society by its organizers.

There were several good reasons for forming such an organization. First, it would be a benevolent society. Many officers were unprepared to return to civilian life after being in the service of their country for so long, and they faced an uncertain if not a bleak future. It was likely that substantial help would be necessary to support needy officers, widows, and orphans, and in Knox's words, the society would "erect some lone shelter for the unfortunate, against the storms and tempests of poverty." The society would attempt to fill the void left by Congress's failure to settle the army's accounts. This mutual concern for the future welfare of the officers and their families was the result of the intimacy that had developed over the years between men who shared a common sacrifice of suffering and fighting while in the army. Their bond was not something that could be shared with those who had not experienced it, and they were loath to abandon it. As surgeon William Eustis later recalled, the society "grew naturally out of the affections of the officers from a desire to perpetuate their friendships." Also, likely as not, many other officers shared Knox's wish to transmit to descendants some proof of wartime service. Congress had awarded medals and swords to a few officers of special distinction, and Washington had established chevrons and purple ribbons for deserving noncommissioned officers and men, but as yet nothing had been proposed to recognize the "regular officer of long meritorious service." The eagle-shaped badge and the medal designed by Pierre L'Enfant and adopted by the society were appropriate for an organization borrowing motifs from the Roman Empire and proved immensely popular.

At the same time, it is certain that the founders of the Society of the Cincinnati hoped that a national organization of former officers would be able to exert leverage in favor of their own interests on a recalcitrant Congress. If Congress had neglected the army during the war, what incentive would it have to settle its accounts with the troops once the fighting had ended and the men had returned home? Once back in their respective states, members of the Cincinnati could pressure both their delegates to Congress and their state lawmakers to seek a meaningful final settlement. What other influence the founders expected to bring to bear on the national political scene is unknown, although the officers who formed the nucleus of the Cincinnati tended to be men whose war experiences had given them a national vision; most in fact would be avid supporters of the Constitution, and many later gravitated toward the Federalist party.

On the other hand, the American public still retained its old fears of a standing army, and the legitimacy of the Cincinnati's claims for existence was not adequate in the public's eye to make it feel comfortable about an organized national society of former army officers. There was more than one aspect of the Cincinnati that caused some consternation among the public when its existence became known in the months after the end of the war. Clauses in the society's Institution (its constitution) permitting frequent meetings, the raising of large sums of money, and the enrolling of foreign and honorary members could be construed as means to disguise more sinister intentions. A hereditary clause allowing members of the Cincinnati to pass on their membership to their eldest sons was particularly troublesome. To many Americans a hereditary military society smacked of European aristocracy, which was opposed by the principles of the republican ideology of the Revolution.

Washington himself was skeptical about the society, although he very much wanted to support his former army officers. He did not want to risk his reputation needlessly, however, and so, characteristically, he took his time in making up his mind about whether to lend his name to the organization. The first national assembly of the Cincinnati was planned for May 1784, and as the time drew near Washington sought opinions from trusted friends and advisors.

In April 1784, still undecided about what course to pursue, Washington asked Jefferson to give him his opinion on the Institution of the society. After studying the document Jefferson replied that he thought it originated from the officers' natural desire to foster the friendships that had developed during the war. That was the only positive thing he had to say about the Institution or the society. He went on to attack the hereditary- and foreign-membership provisions. More serious, said Jefferson, the society tended to blur the proper relationship between the civil and military, giving rise to the risk that when assembled it might exercise its power in a way antithetical to the welfare of the nation. The latter assertion alone would have been enough to persuade Washington without Jefferson's additional observation that "the moderation & virtue of a single character has probably prevented this revolution from being closed as most others have been by a subversion of that liberty it was intended to establish: that he is not immortal, & his successor or some one of his successors at the head of this institution may adopt a more mistaken road

to glory." No doubt these last statements clinched the argument, for Washington knew firsthand that some Americans still harbored a desire for a king.

The extent to which Washington accepted Jefferson's criticism can be seen in his "Observations on the Institution of the Society," drafted around 4 May 1784:

> Strike out every word, sentence, and clause which has a political tendency.
> Discontinue the hereditary part in all its connexions, *absolutely*. . . .
> Admit no more honorary Members into the Society.
> Reject subscriptions, or donations from every person who is not a Citizen of the United States.
> Place the funds upon such a footing as to remove the jealousies which are entertained on that score.
> . . .Abolish the General meetings altogether, as unnecessary . . . District meetings might also be discontinued as of very little use . . .
> No alterations short of what is here enumerated will, in my opinion, reconcile the Society to the Community. . . .

Washington's observations about the Institution of the Society of the Cincinnati coincided with the society's first national assembly, at which Washington himself was to preside. It is impossible to know whether Jefferson's opinion convinced Washington to oppose the society as so conceived, or whether he had already come to that conclusion on his own and conveniently relied on Jefferson's arguments when drawing up his observations. Either way, Washington was persuaded that enough of the public was so firmly against the society as a hereditary and military organization that its Institution must be so altered as to make the existence of the society fundamentally unnecessary. When the society's delegates finally assembled at City

Tavern in Philadelphia, Washington threatened to withdraw from the organization altogether if the Institution was not revised according to his demands. And accordingly it was, but as each state organization had to approve the revision, and not all did, discussions continued.

At the very moment Washington was presenting his argument that the delegates consider the society's disbandment, sudden and unexpected news arrived from France that forced him to make an about-face. At this critical point L'Enfant arrived from France with the badges and with the news that the French officers, among them d'Estaing and Rochambeau, had eagerly formed a French society, with the approbation of the French king himself. Moreover, L'Enfant brought with him from France a gift for Washington, a golden eagle studded with diamonds, given in the name of the French navy. He also brought news that the French members had pledged substantial sums to the American society. It was now impossible to abolish the society without insulting the Americans' allies in victory. Aware that his reputation was involved in the controversy, Washington no longer could use the threat of withdrawing his membership as a bargaining chip to gain the passage of the amendments he wanted. And he certainly no longer could suggest that the society consider abolishing itself. In the end, he was forced to compromise, but the amendments to the Institution that were adopted included some of his proposals. The hereditary aspect was removed, but honorary memberships were allowed within state societies. General meetings would still be held every three years, but only for regulating the distribution of surplus funds. And finally, the badges were retained because of the allies' esteem for them, "not as ostentatious marks of discrimination, but as pledges of our friendship, and emblems, whose appearance will never permit us to deviate from the paths of virtue." Taken together, the amendments

buttressed the benevolent purposes of the organization. The amended Institution was accepted immediately by eight of the state branches, but it was unclear how many state societies had to approve the amendments before the revised Institution became effective. Before the year was out, some of the state societies were considering rescinding their adoption of the amended Institution and proposing to reintroduce the hereditary principle on new grounds. That unsettled state of affairs continued until after Washington's death.

In the final analysis, Washington's initial skepticism about the society and his sudden reversal from advocating its abolition to supporting it to the extent of lending his name to it is completely in keeping with his character. It was after all a necessary and pragmatic political move aimed at pacifying the officers and the public. Perhaps he also had in mind his vision for the future of the United States, enabling him to see the positive aspects of a national organization, and he seized the opportunity to help define it. Peace had come, but completing the Revolution would require, he later wrote James Madison, that "prejudices, unreasonable jealousies, and local interest yield to reason and liberality. Let us look to our National character and to things beyond the present period."

Today, the Society of the Cincinnati is headquartered at the Anderson House in Washington, D.C., where it maintains an extensive archive on the society.

Related entries: Knox, Henry; L'Enfant, Pierre-Charles

Suggestions for further reading:
"Circular Letter to the State Societies of the Cincinnati," 1 January 1784 (*Con. Ser.,* vol. 1).
"From Thomas Jefferson," 16 April 1784 (*Con. Ser.,* vol. 1).
"General Meeting of the Society of the Cincinnati," 4–18 May 1784 (*Con. Ser.,* vol. 1).
"Observations on the Institution of the Society," c.4 May 1784 (*Con. Ser.,* vol. 1).
"Winthrop Sargent's Journal," 4–18 May 1784 (*Con. Ser.,* vol. 1).

Gardiner, Asa Bird. 1905. *The Order of the Cincinnati in France. . . .* Providence, RI.

Hume, Edgar Erskine. 1941. *General Washington's Correspondence concerning the Society of the Cincinnati.* Baltimore.

Mattern, David B. 1995. *Benjamin Lincoln and the American Revolution.* Columbia, SC.

Myers, Minor, Jr. 1983. *Liberty without Anarchy: A History of the Society of the Cincinnati.* Charlottesville, VA.

Southern Tour

Washington's determination, upon assuming the presidency, to visit every state in the United States began with his tour of New England in the fall of 1789 and concluded with his tour of Virginia, the Carolinas, and Georgia in the spring of 1791. Before making the latter trip Washington had never traveled farther south than the Great Dismal Swamp on the eastern border of Virginia and North Carolina. The tour, "being in the nature of a short visit" by design, consisted of long days of dusty riding and short nights spent in unfamiliar hostels, punctuated by rapid meetings with local dignitaries in the little towns that the presidential entourage passed through on its way to Charleston, South Carolina, the intended highlight of the tour. The most exciting moments of the whole trip occurred on the day of his departure, 7 April, when at the Colchester ferry on Occoquan Creek, about eight miles from Mount Vernon, the four horses hitched to his chariot "one after another and in quick succession" all jumped "over board harnessed & fastened as they were and with the utmost difficulty they were saved & the Carriage escaped been dragged after them as the whole of it happened in swimming water & at a distance from the shore."

Washington's assessment of the trip was that it was a complete success. "I performed a journey of 1887 miles without meeting with any interruption by sickness, bad weather, or any untoward accident," he wrote. "Indeed so highly were we favored that we arrived at each place, where I proposed to make any halt, on the very day I fixed upon before we set out—The same horses performed the whole tour, and, altho' much reduced in flesh, kept up their full spirits to the last day." The horses included Prescott, a white parade steed that Washington would mount for ceremonial purposes along the way, and a dozen others—four each for his coach, baggage wagon, and escort. The trip enabled Washington to see the lands and towns of the south firsthand and to judge the disposition of the people. "The country appears to be in a very improving state," he wrote at the journey's end, "and industry and frugality are becoming much more fashionable than they have hitherto been there—Tranquillity reigns among the people." The citizenry was generally pleased with the central government: "The farmer finds a ready market for his produce, and the merchant calculates with more certainty on his payments." The region was behind in manufacturing only and likely would remain so for a long time to come, he thought. Moreover, twenty-three official addresses had been presented to him, assuring him that his popularity in the south was as great as that in New England.

Washington arrived back at Mount Vernon on 12 June 1791.

Related entries: New England Tour; Presidency

Suggestions for further reading:
Diaries, vol. 6.
"Itinerary for the Southern Tour," c. February 1791 (*Pres. Ser.,* vol. 7).
"To David Humphreys," 20 July 1791 (*Pres. Ser.,* vol. 8).
Henderson, Archibald. 1923. *Washington's Southern Tour, 1791.* Boston and New York.

Spirituous Liquors

We cleaned ourselves (to get Rid of the Game we had catched

the Night before) & took a Review of the Town & then return'd to our Lodgings where we had a good Dinner prepar'd for us Wine & Rum Punch in Plenty & a good Feather Bed with clean Sheets which was a very agreeable regale.

This earliest surviving reference to intoxicating spirits in Washington's writings appears as the entry for the sixth day of his "Journal of my Journey over the Mountains," a small notebook in which he kept a brief account of the daily movements of a surveying party running boundary lines for Thomas, Lord Fairfax's lands in the lower Shenandoah Valley of Virginia, which Washington accompanied in March and April 1748, when he was 16 years old. A similar record survives from Washington's Barbados diary, written while at sea on Christmas Day 1751, when the voyagers celebrated the holiday by eating "Irish goose" and drinking "a health to our absent friends."

Drinking to the health of friends probably carried more meaning in the eighteenth century than it does today. In any event, Washington was familiar with the medicinal use of distilled spirits. In November 1757, after suffering from a lingering illness for about three months, he wrote Sally Fairfax requesting to borrow recipes and "materials to make Jellys" and a "bottle or two of Mountain, or Canary Wine[.] Mr [Charles] Green [rector of Truro Parish, who also practiced medicine] directs me to drink a Glass or two of this every day mixd with Water of Gum Arabic." A recipe in Washington's papers from the same period for making thirty gallons of "Small Beer" from boiled "Bran Hops" and molasses may have been kept for its medicinal value. A cookbook at Mount Vernon in the writing of Martha Washington's first mother-in-law, Frances Parke Custis, included recipes for ordinary medicinal waters of cinnamon, wormwood, and raisin, or black, cherry wine sealed in sterilized bottles, as well as for shrub, a mixture of brandy, wine, and water.

Although Mrs. Custis's cookbook contained recipes for making a variety of wines, including blackberry, cherry, lemon, and gooseberry as well as hippocras, a cordial drink made of wine and spices that was in vogue, Washington did not hesitate to order spirits from outside the colony. Beginning in late 1757, and continuing until he left to take command of the Continental army in 1775, his orders to English merchants Thomas Knox of Bristol and Robert Cary & Co. of London often included requests for "1 Cask bottled Beer" and "1 Cask best bottled Cyder," "1 Hogshead best Porter" and "1 Groce best Bottled Porter," and more frequently for wine, "3 Galn of Rhenish in pt. Bottles," "a Pipe of good old Madeira from that Island, let it be well securd," and "from the best House in Madeira a Pipe of the best Old Wine, and let it be Secur'd from Pilferers." The latter instructions were necessary ones, for not all shipments arrived intact; on at least one occasion a cask of cider failed to arrive; on another, some ordered goods had arrived "in bad order—The Porter entirely Drank out"; and in yet another instance "there was a good deal of ullage indeed, and what I dislikd still more was, a large Tap in the head of the Cask which left me in doubt whether it was done on the Passage (which occasiond the difficiency) or was in the cask before Shipping of it."

One typical eighteenth-century custom regarding spirits that Washington was well acquainted with was their employment at elections, when candidates were expected to treat the public. In July 1758, for example, when his name was put forward for a seat in the Virginia House of Burgesses, Washington's account of the money spent for alcohol-related electioneering efforts on his behalf amounted to £39.6. The amount of refreshments distributed by his agents included nearly 47 gallons of beer, more than 70 gallons of rum punch, about 34½ gallons of wine, 2 gallons of cider, and 3½ pints of brandy. As a result of these efforts 310 voters cast their ballots for Washington, seventy more than the second-place candidate and enough to give Washington a victory. Nevertheless, Washington had feared that those engineering his election had "spent with too sparing a hand," as they had during his first campaign for the Virginia House of Burgesses, which ended in defeat when an opponent treated the voters better.

Spirits also served as an important commodity in the commercial affairs of the eighteenth century. In 1767 Washington placed a slave, Tom, "both a Rogue & Runaway," on board a schooner bound for St. Christopher's in the West Indies with instructions to the vessel's captain to sell him "for whatever he will fetch" and bring back, among other items, a hogshead of "best Rum," some molasses and sweetmeats, and the "residue, much or little, in good old Spirits." In 1770 Washington sought to trade a shipment of herring for, among other things, a hogshead of rum and a barrel of good spirits. He instructed Daniel Jenifer Adams to sell his "Superfine Flour" in Barbados and use the money to purchase either "Negroes, if choice ones can be had" or "Rum and Sugar from Barbadoes, or any of the Windward Islands," and to find him a "Cask of about 50 or 60 Gallns of the best old Spirits especially from Barbadoes." Upon their arrival at Mount Vernon spirits could be used on the plantation, shared with family and friends, stored indefinitely, or traded for other items as necessary. Spirits-related goods served as symbols of comfort and status. In July 1772, for instance, Washington ordered from England "4 Neat & fashe Cut glass Decanters wt. brd Bottms—that they may stand firm on the Table 6 Neat & fashe Cut Beer Glasses to suit Ditto 2½ dozn Do Do Wine Do to Suit Do to be rather low, & strong, as well as Neat."

Washington also was interested in the establishment of vineyards in the colonies. In 1759 he joined George Mason, George William Fairfax, and others in subscribing to assist Maurice Pound, a German immigrant attempting to make a success of his fledgling vineyard at Colchester, Virginia, a small settlement about eight miles from Mount Vernon. In 1773 Washington subscribed to an agricultural venture begun by Italian wine merchant Philip Mazzei (1730–1816), in Albemarle County, Virginia, for the purpose of "raising and making Wine, Oil, agruminous Plants and Silk." Pound's venture failed, and Mazzei's collapsed during the Revolutionary War. Washington later contemplated planting his own vineyard at Mount Vernon, asking a merchant when ordering 150 gallons of "your choicest" Madeira wine "if there is nothing improper, or inconsistent in the request a few setts or cuttings of the Madeira Grape (that kind I mean of which the Wine is made)." Although Washington, too, failed to establish a viable vineyard, he later built a distillery where he processed his neighbors' surplus grain and in 1798, his best year, earned £344.

After the Revolutionary War wine consumption at Mount Vernon increased, as evidenced by the number of orders made. His careful instructions to farm manager William Pearce about serving it to visitors while the Washingtons were away presumably were the guiding principles for when they were at home. "It is not my intention that it should be given to every one who may incline to make a convenience of the house in traveling," Washington wrote, "or who may be induced to visit it from motives of curiosity." There were three "descriptions of people" to whom it could be given—Washington's *particular* and intimate acquaintances, in case business should call them there, Dr. James Craik, for instance; some of the "*most* respectable foreigners" who may be brought down from Alexandria or the Federal City or introduced by letter from some "particular acquaintance before mentioned"; or to "persons of some distinction (such as members of Congress &ca) who may be travelling through the Country from North to South or from South to North." Furthermore, provide the guests with claret rather than Madeira, except on extraordinary occasions. "I have been thus particular," Washington concluded, "that you may have a full view of my ideas on this subject, and conform to them; and because the knowledge I have of my servants is such, as to believe, that if opportunities are given them they will take off two glasses of wine for every one that is drank by such visitors."

Wine was always served at the presidential mansion. Washington's personal preference was for Madeira, and it was always available at his table. On special occasions visitors had a choice of up to four kinds. The number of entertainments and official functions was large, and the expenditures on wines and liquors were considerable. Shortly after assuming office Washington commissioned the making in France of some "handsome and useful coolers for wine *at* and *after* dinner. . . . *eight* double ones (for madeira and claret wines usually drank at dinner) each of the apertures to be sufficient to contain a pint decanter, with an allowance in the depth of it for ice at bottom so as to raise the neck of the decanter above the cooler." Similar decanters were ordered for the wine "*after* dinner, *four* quadruple coolers," with apertures the "size of a *quart* decanter or quart bottle for four sorts of wine." Both sets, Washington directed, must have central handles for easy movement between tables as well as one other requirement, "that is in whole or part to avoid extravagance. For extravagance would not comport with my own inclination, nor with the example which ought to be set." When Washington left the office of president he presented one each of the silver-plated coolers to Timothy Pickering, James McHenry, and Oliver Wolcott, respectively the secretaries of state, war, and treasury, as keepsakes by which to remember him.

Ironically, considering the pervasiveness of spirits in Washington's milieu, one of the most critical tests of his presidential administration was the implementation of Alexander Hamilton's excise tax on the domestic manufacture of distilled liquors. The levy imposed a heavy burden on frontier farmers dependent on distilling for disposal of their surplus grain, especially those of the south and the west, and protests arose almost immediately. Sentiments against the measure remained unchanged despite attempts by Congress to lessen its impact. An attempt to enforce the collection of the excise tax led to armed resistance in western Pennsylvania and forced Washington call out thousands of troops to suppress the rebellion.

Also while president Washington made a memorandum containing his opinions of the general officers from the Revolutionary War who were to be considered candidates for the commander in chief of the U.S. Army. The memorandum, considered at a cabinet meeting on 9 March 1792 that was attended by Thomas Jefferson, Alexander Hamilton, and Henry Knox, listed by name three generals who in Washington's opinion could not handle liquor too well. Charles Scott he described as "Brave and means well; but is an officer of inadequate abilities for extensive command; and, by report, is addicted to drinking." Anthony Wayne he considered "More active and enterprising than Judicious and cautious. No œconomist it is feared. Open to flattery; vain; easily imposed upon; and liable to be drawn into scrapes. Too indulgent (the effect perhaps of some of the causes just mentioned) to his Officers and men. Whether sober, or a little addicted to the bottle, I know not." And of his old acquaintance George Weedon he wrote, "Not supposed to be an Officer of much resource though not deficient in a competent share of understanding; rather addicted to ease and pleasure; and no enemy it is said to the bottle; never has had his name brot. forward on this acct."

The impressions, whether merry or melancholy, conjured up by the recounting of such scenes contrast sharply with those produced by the reading of the orders issued by Washington, when colonel and commander of the Virginia Regiment, at Fort Cumberland in September 1755: "Any Soldier who is guilty of any breach of the Articles of War, by Swearing, getting Drunk, or using an Obscene Language; shall be severely Punished, without the Benefit of a Court Martial." Moreover, in the orders Washington publicly rebuked a soldier who kept "a Disorderly and riotous Assembly, constantly about him," warning the soldier of dire consequences if he presumed to sell "any Liquor to any Soldier or any other Person whatsoever." That such orders were necessary became apparent the following spring when rumors surfaced in the Virginia general assembly that the "greatest Immoralities & Drunkenness have been much countenanced and proper Discipline neglected" in the Virginia Regiment. Although Washington protested that he had "by Threats and persuasive means, endeavoured to discountenance Gaming, drinking, swearing, and irregularities of every other kind," he admitted that some officers had the "seeds of idleness very strongly ingrafted in their natures." He issued an orderly shortly afterward that "Any Soldier found Drunk, shall immediately receive one hundred lashes; without Benefit of a court-martial."

Other regulations were set in place: sutlers furnishing the regiment were required to fix reasonable prices for all liquors, and troops were not allowed to drink at the public houses at Winchester, nor were the townspeople allowed to sell the troops liquor or allow them to visit their homes drunk. Nevertheless, by August 1756 the regulations had proved so "ineffectual to restrain the paltry tippling houses and Ginn-shops" in the town from selling liquor to the troops that the men were ordered to encamp in tents outside the town, and fifty lashes were promised to any soldier found drinking or purchasing any liquor other than that officially provided the troops by designated sutlers. Another order a few weeks later offered a 5 percent bounty from an offending soldier's pay to anyone who "detects another in committing this crime." Nevertheless, the number of tippling houses kept in the town multiplied, and the rates of liquor distribution remained "immoderately high." Indians were never to be given liquor either, except a "little rum mixed with water" when they "behave in a mild discreet manner." For their encouragement "to behave well," workmen were promised, "so long as they deserve it, four gallons of rum, made into punch, every day."

Washington's earlier troubles with alcohol abuse among the troops of the Virginia Regiment were not forgotten when he became commander in chief of the Continental army. One of his first General Orders at Cambridge, Massachusetts, contained warnings for offenders against the orders of the Continental Congress that the troops be supplied with spirituous liquors only upon written order by the captain of companies. "Some persons are so daring as to supply the Soldiers with immoderate Quantities of Rum, and other spirituous Liquors," and they would be severely punished, whether a "Sutler, Tavernkeeper, or licenced Innholder." Before the month ended a soldier was court-martialed and found guilty of "forgeing an Order of General [Israel] Putnams to obtain a quart of Rum" and sentenced to receive twenty lashes, to be "executed after prayer time" the following day. Nevertheless, abuses continued, and in September Washington issued new orders, confining sales to regimental sutlers and threatening not only to arrest but also to confiscate and redistribute the liquor and stores of any persons "not regularly authorized and appointed" who sold them to the troops in camp. Even that order was misconstrued to mean that regimental sutlers could sell to soldiers in other regiments, and had to be clarified a few weeks later. The following February the situation became so bad that orders were issued directing sutlers to "see that they shut up their houses at Taptoo beating, and do not offer, upon any Account, to sell a drop of Liquor after that hour."

Abuses continued after the Continental army left Cambridge for New York, and Washington regularly issued orders for punishments of troops convicted by courts-martial for being intoxicated. A soldier convicted of "leaving his guard, getting drunk, and damning the Officer of the guard," for instance, was whipped "Thirty-nine Lashes on his bare back." A corporal convicted of "getting drunk, when on duty," was "reduced to the Ranks, and whipped Thirty Lashes on his bare back." Despite such problems, rum was regularly issued as a part of the provisions for working parties, and the commissary general was directed to distribute to the colonels of each regiment enough rum "for the refresment of their men, in time of action," to the allowance of a half a pint per man, to be "properly dealt out, by putting it under the care of a very discreet officer." When the army moved to Morristown, New Jersey, in 1777, spirits became more difficult to procure and were issued only to "fatigue parties, scouting parties, or to such troops as are necessarily employed in any extraordinary piece of duty." Instances of drunkenness declined, but rum and other stores sometimes were taken and used without proper authorization. Punishments became more severe: a soldier received 100 lashes for being drunk on post, and another, for "Deserting his post, being drunk, and suffering others to desert to the enemy," was sentenced to "suffer *Death*." Perhaps Washington's opinion is best summed up by his statement that "there can not be a greater failing in a Soldier than drunkenness."

Even general officers were not immune from charges of alcohol abuse. In the fall of 1777 Brig. Gen. William Maxwell was tried at a court-martial on the charges that he commanded his troops while "disguised with liquor in such a manner as to disqualify him in some measure, but not fully, from doing his duty; and that once or twice besides, his spirits were a little elevated with liquor." The court acquitted Maxwell. Maj. Gen. Adam Stephen, Washington's old comrade-in-arms from the French and Indian War, was not so lucky, however. Court-martialed with three charges against him—misbehavior on the army's march from Smith's Clove, New York; unofficerlike behavior at the Battles of Brandywine and Germantown; and "Drunkenness"—Stephen was found guilty of "unofficerlike behaviour, in the retreat from Germantown, owing to inattention, or want of judgement; and that he has been frequently intoxicated since in the service, to the prejudice of good order and military discipline" and was sentenced to be dismissed from the army.

As late as 1792, when Washington was president, he informed the secretary of war that "So long as the vice of drunkenness exists in the Army so long I hope, Ejections of those Officers who are found guilty of it will continue; for that and gaming will debilitate and render unfit for active service any Army whatsoever." Despite problems with abuse of alcohol, wine was regularly consumed at headquarters, often sent as gifts, and used in the hospital department. It was also used to celebrate important occasions. On New Year's Day 1778 Washington ordered "a gill of spirits to be Served to each noncommission'd Officer and soldier," and a gill of rum was issued to each soldier on the day of celebration in May 1778 when news of the official French alliance reached the army. Washington's desire "to distribute a portion of rum to the soldiers, to exhilerate their spirits upon the occasion" of the anniversary of independence in 1779 was thwarted because of the scantiness of the stock. An extra gill per man was issued to celebrate the "Joyful Occasion" on 4 July 1782, however, and on Thanksgiving

Day 1782 each soldier received a gill of West India rum. And finally on 18 April 1783, the day before Congress's proclamation for a cessation of hostilities with Great Britain, an extra ration of liquor was ordered to be issued "to *every* man tomorrow, to drink Perpetual Peace, Independence and Happiness to the United States of America."

Related entries: Distillery; Whiskey Rebellion; Recipe for Small Beer, c.November 1757 (Selected Writings)

Suggestions for further reading:
"Orders," 19 September 1755 (*Col. Ser.,* vol. 2).
"To Robert Dinwiddie," 18 April 1756 (*Col. Ser.,* vol. 3).
"Orders," 7, 30 August 1756 (*Col. Ser.,* vol. 3).
"Recipe for Small Beer," c.November 1757 (*Col. Ser.,* vol. 4).
"To Sarah Cary Fairfax," 15 November 1757 (*Col. Ser.,* vol. 5).
"To Lawrence Sanford," 26 September 1769 (*Col. Ser.,* vol. 8).
"General Orders," 11, 29 July 1775 (*War Ser.,* vol. 1).
"General Orders," 4, 20 November 1777 (*War Ser.,* vol. 11).
"To William Pearce," 23 November 1794 (*Writings,* vol. 34).
"From James Anderson," 21 June 1797 (*Ret. Ser.,* vol. 1).
"To Robert Lewis," 26 January 1798 (*Ret. Ser.,* vol. 2).
Decatur, Stephen, Jr. 1933. *Private Affairs of George Washington from the Records and Accounts of Tobias Lear, Esquire, His Secretary.* Boston.
Rorabaugh, W. J. 1979. *The Alcoholic Republic: An American Tradition.* New York.

Spurious Letters

The most famous attempt to discredit Washington during the Revolutionary War took place in London in 1776 when J. Bew, a bookseller in Paternoster Row, printed a small pamphlet of political propaganda, *Letters from General Washington, to Several of His Friends in the Year 1776. . . .* The letters portrayed Washington as disgusted with the Continental Congress, disheartened with the war effort, and eager for a reconciliation with England. The idea for the publication apparently was inspired by the British capture of some of Washington's genuine correspondence, among which was a letter to Martha Washington that Gen. William Howe returned unopened to the sender. When the pamphlet reached the American shores, New York Loyalist printer James Rivington struck off as a separate broadside one of the letters therefrom to Martha Washington, and in 1778 Rivington reprinted the entire pamphlet, apparently with the goal of stirring up sectional strife between the inhabitants of New England and those of the southern states. The expected reaction failed to materialize, however, for a number of British magazines by then had cast doubts on the letters' authenticity.

The "editor" of the pamphlet claimed to have discovered the letters after he "espied" Washington's body-servant Billy among the American prisoners captured at the fall of Fort Lee. Billy (who in fact was not taken prisoner), said he, gave him "a small portmanteau of his master's; of which, when he found that he must be put into confinement, he intreated my care. It contained only a few stockings and shirts; and I could see nothing worth my care, except an almanack, in which he had kept a journal, or diary, of his proceedings since his first coming to New York; there were also two letters from his lady, one from Mr. [John Parke] Custis, and some pretty long ones from a Mr. Lund Washington [Washington's wartime farm manager], and in the same bundle with them, the first draughts, or foul copies, of answers to them." Upon reading a copy of the pamphlet, Washington observed that the letters were written with a great deal of art. "The intermixture of so many family circumstances (which, by the by, want foundation in truth)," he wrote, "gives an air of plausibility, which renders the villainy greater; as the whole is a contrivance to answer the most diabolical purposes. Who the author of them is, I know not.

From information, or acquaintance, he must have had some knowledge of the component parts of my family; but he has most egregiously mistaken facts in several instances; Tho' the design of his labors is as clear as the sun in its meridian brightness." Washington later attributed the contents of the letters to John Randolph, the last royalist attorney general of Virginia.

Although the spurious letters were not taken seriously during the war, an attempt to use them to injure Washington's political reputation was made near the end of his presidency when the letters were reprinted, along with many genuine ones, by Benjamin Franklin Bache under the title *Epistles Domestic, Confidential, and Official, from General Washington* . . . (New York, 1796). The new reprinting elicited a response that was, said John C. Fitzpatrick, "unsparing in its castigation of the forgeries"—and approved of by Washington. Washington himself even took the trouble to refute their authenticity, which he did in a letter to the secretary of state, Timothy Pickering, pointing out their discrepancies at some length. Washington wrote to Connecticut executive council member Jeremiah Wadsworth (1743–1804) of the printer, "I shall thank you (when re-published) for the refutation of the impudent forgeries of letters, carrying my signature, which Mr Bache has taken so much pains to impose on the public as genuine productions. This man has celebrity in a certain way, for His calumnies are to be exceeded only by his Impudence, and both stand unrivalled." Washington at the time also wrote to Benjamin Walker (1753–1818), a former aide-de-camp, that, "of all the mistakes which have been committed in this business, none is more palpable, or susceptible of detection than the manner in which it is said they were obtained, by the capture of my Mulatto Billy, with a Portmanteau. *All the Army,* under my immediate command, could contradict this; and I believe most of them know, that no Attendant of mine, or a particle of my baggage ever fell into the hands of the enemy during the whole course of the War." Moreover, Washington informed Walker, it would be a "singular satisfaction to me to learn, who was the Author of these letters; and from what source they originated. No person in this country can, I conceive, give this information, but Mr. Rivington: If, therefore, you are upon terms of familiarity with that Gentleman, and see no impropriety in hinting this desire to him, it would oblige me. He may comply to what extent his own judgment shall dictate, and I pledge my honor that, nothing to his disadvantage, or the disadvantage of any of the Actors at that time, shall result from it."

On the day before he left office in March 1797, Washington sent a list of the spurious letters to Pickering, noting that the original forgeries were "supposed to be of some consequence to strike at the integrity of the motives of the American Commander in Chief, and to paint his inclinations as at variance with his professions and his duty. Another crisis in the affairs of America having occurred, the same weapon has been resorted to, to wound my character and deceive the people." He repeated that during the war the whole army knew that neither Billy nor any of Washington's baggage had ever been in the possession of the enemy. "These well-known facts made it unnecessary, during the war," he wrote, "to call the public attention to the forgery, by any express declaration of mine: and a firm reliance on my fellow-citizens, and the abundant proofs they gave of their confidence in me, rendered it alike unnecessary to take any formal notice of the revival of the imposition, during my civil administration. But as I cannot know how soon a more serious event may succeed to that which will this day take place, I have thought it a duty that I owed to Myself, to my Country and to Truth, now to detail the circumstances above recited; and to add my solemn declaration, that the letters herein described are a base forgery, and that I never saw or heard of them until they appeared in print. The present letter I commit to your care, and desire that it may be deposited in the office of the department of state, as a testimony of the truth to the present generation and to posterity."

Related entry: Papers

Suggestions for further reading:
"From John Hancock," 28 October 1776 (*War Ser.*, vol. 7).
"To John Hancock," 14 November 1776 (*War Ser.*, vol. 7).
"To Richard Henry Lee," 15 February 1778 (*Writings,* vol. 10).
"To Richard Henry Lee," 25 May 1778 (*Writings,* vol. 11).
"To the Secretary of State," 3 March 1797 (*Writings,* vol. 35).
"To Jeremiah Wadsworth," 6 March 1797 (*Ret. Ser.*, vol. 1).
"To William Gordon," 15 October 1797 (*Ret. Ser.*, vol. 1).
Fitzpatrick, John C. 1929. *The George Washington Scandals.* Alexandria, VA.
Ford, Worthington Chauncey. 1889. *The Spurious Letters Attributed to Washington.* New York.

Stephen, Adam (c.1718–1791)

Adam Stephen was born in Scotland and trained for a career in medicine at the University of Edinburgh. After temporarily abandoning his medical career for what proved to be an unsatisfactory stint in the British navy, he decided to renew his medical practice in the colonies, settling in Virginia. He still found the military life alluring, however, and in 1754 he secured a captain's commission in the Virginia Regiment, commanded at that time by Washington. Stephen was with Washington, serving as major, during the Virginia Regiment's skirmish with the French in July 1754, which resulted in the capitulation of Fort Necessity.

Promoted to lieutenant colonel shortly after the defeat at Fort Necessity, Stephens

was left as the senior Virginia military officer when Washington resigned his commission the following fall. Both men accompanied British general Edward Braddock on his ill-fated expedition in the summer of 1755, and when Washington took command of the new Virginia Regiment in September 1755, Stephen, then commandant at Fort Cumberland, once again became Washington's second in command, a position he held until Washington left the military at the end of 1758. Stephen became the Virginia Regiment's colonel in September 1761, shortly before it was disbanded.

Around that time Stephen carried on a vigorous but unsuccessful political campaign in Frederick County to gain one of its two seats in the Virginia House of Burgesses, one of which was held by Washington. The campaign apparently led to some animosity between Stephen and Washington, but the circumstances surrounding their quarrel remain obscure. Their contact from that time to the beginning of the Revolutionary War was restricted to matters concerning western lands. In June 1763, for instance, Stephen and Washington both became shareholders in the Mississippi Company, a speculative land venture, and in October 1770, while on his western tour to scout out lands for the veterans of the French and Indian War, Washington stopped off at Stephen's farm in Frederick County, near present-day Martinsburg, West Virginia. Stephen did dine at Mount Vernon once during the period, in August 1769.

When hostilities broke out between Great Britain and the colonies, Washington and Stephen both were elected to the Virginia convention, where they served together on the committee charged with drafting men to defend the colony. Stephen was appointed colonel of the Fourth Virginia Regiment in February 1776 and promoted to brigadier general the following September and then to major general in February 1777. His division was attached to the Continental army under Washington. In May 1777 Washington reprimanded Stephen for inflating the casualties inflicted on the enemy by a detachment of troops under his command during a skirmish and for describing, in the words of Washington, the "disorderly rout" of his own soldiers after the enemy gained "notice of your coming and was prepared for it, as I expected."

At the Battle of Brandywine in September of the same year, Stephen led his division in the column facing the enemy, and is said to have conducted himself with great spirit and good judgment. He reputedly "behaved again with gallantry" during the attack on the British army at the Battle of Germantown the next month, but his military career ended suddenly in November 1777, when he was dismissed from the army after being tried and found guilty of "unofficerlike behaviour, in the retreat from Germantown, owing to inattention, or want of judgement; and that he has been frequently intoxicated since in the service, to the prejudice of good order and military discipline." Stephen's complaint to the president of the Continental Congress that his dismissal had resulted simply from "my misfortune to become the object of hatred of a person of high rank" fell on deaf ears. The marquis de Lafayette took command of Stephen's division in December 1777.

After the war Stephen settled on his farm in Berkeley County (now West Virginia), and in 1788 he was a member of the Virginia convention called to ratify the Federal Constitution. He apparently had no further contact with Washington, however.

Related entry: Fort Necessity Campaign

Suggestions for further reading:
Diaries, vols. 1, 2.
"To Henry Laurens," 7 October 1777 (*War Ser.,* vol. 11).
"General Orders," 20 November 1777 (*War Ser.,* vol. 11).
"General Orders," 4 December 1777 (*War Ser.,* vol. 11).
Ward, Harry M. 1989. *Major General Adam Stephen and the Cause of American Liberty.* Charlottesville, VA.

Stirling, Lord (William Alexander; 1726–1783)

William Alexander, or Lord Stirling as he is usually known, was the son of James Alexander, a native of Scotland who fled to America in 1716 after taking part in the plot to place the pretender James Edward on the British throne. Stirling's claim to be the sixth earl of Stirling was rejected by a committee of the House of Lords in 1762, but he nevertheless was known as Lord Stirling both in America and abroad.

Stirling was born in New York City, where he was given the best education the country then afforded and like his father became proficient in the "exact sciences," including astronomy, but especially mathematics. Upon his father's death Stirling and his mother took over the commercial ventures his father had started, and through a contract to supply the king's troops Stirling became acquainted with the commissariat of the British army and became an aide-de-camp and private secretary to Gen. William Shirley, the commander of the British forces in America and later governor of New Jersey. He accompanied Shirley to England for what was supposed to be a short trip but did not return to America for several years. Upon his return Stirling settled first at New York and then, permanently, at Baskenridge, New Jersey, after marrying Sarah, the eldest daughter of Philip Livingston, thus becoming the brother-in-law of future New Jersey governor William Livingston. Stirling became surveyor general of New Jersey (a post previously held by his father) and served as a governor of King's College in New York. His economic ventures included iron manufacture and the cultivation of hemp and vines. Stirling first met Washington during the French and Indian War.

After the outbreak of hostilities between the Americans and the British, Stirling was elected to the New Jersey provincial congress. In the summer of 1775 he began raising a regiment of volunteers in New Jersey, and the New Jersey provincial convention appointed him colonel of the First New Jersey Regiment the following November. From that time until Stirling's death from illness in January 1783, Washington relied on Stirling's firm commitment to the American cause and his abilities as general. In March 1776 Stirling was appointed a brigadier general and placed in command at New York. He took part in the Battle of Long Island in August 1776, commanding a division of about 1,600 troops from Delaware and Maryland that bravely defended itself against a British force of about 7,000 for several hours before it was forced to surrender.

Stirling was exchanged for the governor of the Bahamas about a month after his capture and rejoined Washington. He was promoted to major general in February 1777, and during the winter of 1777–1778 he manifested his loyalty to Washington by exposing the so-called Conway Cabal to his commander in chief, to whom he declared Conway's disaffection "such wicked duplicity of conduct I shall always think it my duty to detect." Stirling served in the main army under Washington's command until the summer of 1781, when he was sent to Albany, New York, to command the northern department in anticipation of an impending attack by the British forces quartered at Ticonderoga, New York, and Canada.

Washington's biographer, Douglas Southall Freeman, noted of Stirling that, although rumors circulated of him spending "convivial evenings over a nest of bottles or an unpretending jug," there was never a whisper that he was drunk when gunfire was heard. Freeman also observed that field operations directed by Stirling, for reasons never made clear to either Stirling or Washington, were usually "apt to get snarled." Stirling's honor or favor with the other officers never suffered from the mishaps, however, for they all admired him, enjoyed his company, and considered him a brave and faithful officer. But then, they did not expect of him either the "strategical sense" of Nathanael Greene or the "fierce, unrelenting combat" of Benedict Arnold. Stirling was, concluded Freeman, in that large category of soldiers whom Washington would not ever "think of demoting—or of advancing."

Stirling died at Albany in January 1783 from complications brought on by gout, which he had long suffered from. Interestingly, by the time of his death Stirling had commanded at one time or another every brigade in the Continental army except those of South Carolina and Georgia. Upon receiving word of Stirling's passing, Washington, at his Newburgh, New York, headquarters, sent his and Martha's condolences to Stirling's wife, Sarah, and notified the president of the Continental Congress of the general's death, observing that the "remarkable bravery, intelligence, and promptitude of his Lordship to perform his duty as an Officer, had endeared him to the whole Army; and now make his loss the more sincerely regretted." Since his death took place away from the army Stirling did not have a funeral "attended with the Military honors due to his rank." Washington then issued the following notice to the army in General Orders: "The death of Major General Lord Sterling having happened at such a distance from this Army, that his funeral could not be attended with the Military honors due to his rank, the Commander in chief however wishes as a testimony of respect to the memory of his Lordship, that the General officers and such others as think proper, would go into mourning, one Month on the occasion, by wearing a Crape, or weed during that time." Washington also later placed in General Orders the Continental Congress's resolution honoring Stirling for his "early and meritorius" exertions to the common cause. At his death Stirling's vast estate had dwindled to nearly nothing.

Related entries: Conway, Thomas; Morristown, New Jersey

Suggestions for further reading:
"To Lady Stirling," 20 January 1783 (*Writings,* vol. 26).
"To the President of Congress," 20 January 1783 (*Writings,* vol. 26).
"General Orders," 22 January 1783 (*Writings,* vol. 26).
"General Orders," 4 February 1783 (*Writings,* vol. 26).
Nelson, Paul David. 1987. *William Alexander, Lord Stirling.* University, AL.
Valentine, Alan. 1969. *Lord Stirling.* New York.

Stobo, Robert (1717–1770)

See Van Braam, Jacob.

Strother Farm

See Ferry Farm.

Stuart, David (1753–c.1814)

See Alexander, Robert; Custis, George Washington Parke; Father of His Country; Federal City; Last Will and Testament; Lewis, Eleanor Parke Custis.

Sullivan, John (1740–1795)

The "fiery fighting Irishman," as one historian described John Sullivan, received a classical education from his father, an immigrant schoolteacher, in preparation for his career as a small-town New Hampshire attorney, which began when he was only 18 years of age. His prewar years were characterized by confrontation and contention, and his wartime experience with the Continental Congress was in no way less controversial. He also was overly ambitious, and his craving for glory led to unnecessary errors on the battlefield and, ultimately, ended his military career prematurely. He was not brilliant by any means, but he was competent and dependable within his proper sphere, which Washington tended to use to the advantage of the Continental army. Washington always thought highly of Sullivan, even while recognizing his failings, and Sullivan stood loyal to Washington to the last.

Sullivan first met Washington while attending a session of the first Continental Congress. Appointed a brigadier general in the Continental army by the second Continental Congress, he was ordered to Boston in June 1775 to join Washington in the siege of Boston. In strategy sessions with the commander in chief, Sullivan became an advocate of waiting until winter before attacking the British, and when the time finally came for an attack, he volunteered to lead the assault on the enemy barracks, although the assault ended in failure. Washington ordered Sullivan to lead reinforcements to the northern department for the Canadian campaign. He was called upon to assume command of the army there shortly after his arrival, owing to the death of Gen. John Thomas from smallpox. Although his force was weak, Sullivan ordered a raid at Trois Rivières. A defeat ensued, and only the fact that the troops were infested with smallpox kept him from making another attempt. After much delay he reluctantly ordered a retreat back to Crown Point.

Meanwhile, in mid-May 1776, the Continental Congress had appointed Gen. Horatio Gates commander of the northern department and requested Washington to send him to Canada. Sullivan responded negatively to the news of Gates's appointment and wrote Washington a private letter insinuating that he was unwilling to continue in the department unless Washington himself or Maj. Gen. Charles Lee took command of it. Washington forwarded the letter to the president of Congress, John Hancock, with his appraisal of Sullivan: "That [Sullivan] is aiming at the Command in Canada, is obvious—whether he merits it or not is a matter to be considered; and that it may be considered with propriety I think it my duty to observe—as of my own knowledge—that he is active, spirited, and zealously attach'd to the Cause; that he does not want Abilities, many Members of Congress, as well as myself, can testify—But he has his wants; and he has his foibles—The latter are manifested in a little tincture of vanity, and in an over desire of being popular, which now and then leads him into some embarrassments. His wants are common to us all; the want of experience to move upon a large Scale; for the limited, and contracted knowledge which any of us have in Military Matters stands in very little stead; & is greatly overbalanced by sound judgment, and some knowledge of Men and Books; especially when accompanied by an enterprizing genius, which I must do genl Sullivan the justice to say, I think he possesses. . . . The Character I have drawn of Genl Sullivan is just, according to my Ideas of him."

Gates assumed command according to Congress's desires, and Sullivan traveled south to Philadelphia to submit his resignation. Once there, however, his friends dissuaded him from following through with his intentions. Sullivan rejoined Washington at New York and was promoted to major general. When Maj. Gen. Nathanael Greene became ill on the eve of the Battle of Long Island, Washington gave his command to Sullivan. The Americans were positioned behind their breastworks on Brooklyn Heights, and Sullivan ordered all the approaches to the area guarded save one, the pass on the Jamaica Road opening on the Americans' rear. It was this route the enemy took. Sullivan surrendered to three Hessian soldiers while hiding in a cornfield. Before his exchange Sullivan further embarrassed himself before Congress by delivering to it a peace overture from Lord Richard Howe.

After joining Washington's army once again, Sullivan managed to partly redeem himself at the Battles of Trenton and Princeton, New Jersey. He now began to suffer from a digestive disorder that was complicated by his heavy use of alcohol. When Maj. Gen. Arthur St. Clair was given the command at Ticonderoga, Sullivan again thought himself offended and offered his resignation to Washington, who replied: "Do not, my dear General Sullivan, torment yourself any longer with imaginary Slights, and involve others in the perplexities you feel on that Score. No other officer of rank, in the whole army, has so often conceived himself neglected, Slighted, and ill treated, as you have done, and none I am sure has had less cause than yourself to entertain such Ideas. Mere accidents, things which have occurred in the common course of Service, have been considered by you as designed affronts."

Sullivan continued with Washington's army, and once again led a less-than-successful expedition against the enemy, this time to Staten Island in August 1777. The following month, in movements reminiscent of Long Island, he played a prominent role in the American defeat at the Battle of Brandywine. Many in Congress blamed him for the defeat and called for an inquiry into the Staten Island raid. The Battle of Germantown followed soon after, and although Sullivan was not able to distinguish himself, it was at least clear this time that he was in no way responsible for the defeat. The inquiry on Staten Island completely and publicly exonerated Sullivan, and the criticism of his conduct at Brandywine faded in the coming year. (Washington described Sullivan's role in the affair as "spirited and active," and the marquis de Lafayette wrote of Sullivan that "such courage as he showed that day will always deserve the praise of every one.")

In the summer of 1778 Washington gave Sullivan the independent command that he had long craved—he would command the American forces in joint operations with the French on a campaign to Rhode Island. Everything came off as planned until the British fleet suddenly appeared, causing the French fleet to abandon Sullivan's forces. He competently gave battle to the British and afterward perfectly executed an amphibious retreat. Thwarted again, to be sure, but praised again for his efforts, this time by Greene, one of the best generals in the army, who wrote: "If I am to judge, the expedition has been prudently and well conducted; and I am confident there is not a general officer, from the commander-in-chief to the youngest in the field, who would have gone greater lengths to have given success to it, than General Sullivan." Greene added that Sullivan was "sensible, active, ambitious, brave, and persevering in his temper."

In the spring of 1779 Washington decided to place Sullivan in command of a retaliatory expedition against marauding Indians in western New York state. After spending the summer building up his force and accumulating supplies, he finally took the offensive in late August. Before the campaign was over Sullivan's troops had razed more than forty Indian villages belonging to the Iroquois confederacy (Mohawks, Oneidas, Onondagas, Cayugas, Senecas, and Tuscaroras), destroyed or confiscated their crops, and effectively put a temporary halt to the raids. Sullivan, while finally successful in a campaign, at the same time managed to alienate the Board of War and many members of Congress. He offered to resign in November 1779 for health reasons, thinking that Congress would grant him temporary leave. Congress instead accepted his resignation, and his military career ended. Washington seized the opportunity to reassure Sullivan of his affection: "I flatter myself it is unnecessary for me to repeat to you, how high a place you hold in my esteem. The confidence you have experienced and the manner in which you have been employed on several important occasions testify the value I set upon your military qualifications and the regret I must feel that circumstances have deprived the army of your services."

Ironically, in September 1780 Sullivan was elected to the body that he had often criticized. After a year of less-than-distinguished service in the Continental Congress, he returned to his native New Hampshire, where, in addition to resuming a successful law practice, he served three terms as president of the state. Washington appointed him a federal judge for the district of New Hampshire in 1789, an office he held for three years before declining health forced him to retire from public service.

Related entry: Long Island, Battle of

Suggestions for further reading:
"To John Hancock," 17 June 1776 (*War Ser.,* vol. 5).
"From John Sullivan," 9 March 1777 (*War Ser.,* vol. 8).
"To John Sullivan," 15 March 1777 (*War Ser.,* vol. 8).
"To John Sullivan," 15 December 1779 (*Writings,* vol. 17).
Hammond, Otis G., ed. 1930–1939. 3 vols. *Letters and Papers of Major-General John Sullivan, Continental Army.* Collections of the New Hampshire Historical Society.
Whittemore, Charles P. 1961. *A General of the Revolution: John Sullivan of New Hampshire.* New York.

Surveying Career

See Bullskin Lands (Mountain Quarter); Chotank; Crawford Brothers; Cresap, Thomas; Dinwiddie, Robert; Education; Fairfax of Cameron, Thomas Fairfax, Sixth Baron; Fairfax, William; Greenway Court; Lewis, Fielding, Sr.; Papers; Washington, Augustine ("Austin"); Washington, Lawrence.

T

Thompson, Elizabeth (b. c.1704)

Throughout most of the Revolutionary War, Washington's Continental army headquarters was kept comfortable by an elderly civilian retainer, Elizabeth Thompson. Hired in July 1776 for "50£ New York money" a year, Thompson kept house for the commander in chief's military family until late 1781. That she was illiterate is evidenced by her mark on receipts, but the "very worthy Irish woman" was shrewd when it came to bartering for extra provisions for Washington's dining pleasure among the local people of whatever town the headquarters happened to be near. By August 1781 it was evident that Thompson could not continue to meet the needs of the headquarters' officers and staff much longer, so Washington directed Lt. William Colfax of his guard to ease her transition back into civilian life. "From Trenton you will contrive [to forward] Mrs. Thompson to Newtown," he wrote, "or such other place as she wishes to go to." Thompson made her mark on a receipt of that date, but Martha Washington apparently was dissatisfied with her husband's decision to let the aging lady go and asked him to look into the possibility of hiring Thompson as a housekeeper. "What did you pay Mrs Thompson a Month, and where is she?" wrote Washington to the manager of the headquarters household. "Mrs Washington wishes I had mention'd my Intentions of parting with the old Woman, before her, as she is much in want of a Housekeeper—How do you think she would suit?" Thompson did not reenter Washington's employment, however, and he apparently had trouble finding an adequate replacement for her for his headquarters. While at Newburgh, New York, in June 1783 Washington wrote to a correspondent: "Pray let me know whether old Mrs. Thompson (our former Housekeeper) is in Town or not." And in September 1783 he wrote a correspondent in New York City: "You will do me a favor by requesting Mr. Fraunces to enquire if a *good* Cook, German I should prefer, could be obtained, and sent to me immediately. Mrs. Thompson, formerly my Housekeeper and lately gone to the City probably can assist in the enquires and examination. I want a Person that has understanding in the business. who can order, as well as get a dinner; who can make dishes, and proportion them *properly,* to any Company which shall be named to him to the amount of 30."

Related entry: Gibbs, Caleb

Suggestions for further reading.
"To Caleb Gibbs," 1 May 1777 (*War Ser.,* vol. 9).
"To William Colfax," 28 August 1781 (*Writings,* vol. 23).

"To William Stephens Smith," 18 June 1783 (*Writings,* vol. 27).

"To Daniel Parker," 18 September 1783 (*Writings,* vol. 27).

Thornton, William (1759–1828)

Known primarily as the architect of the U.S. Capitol, William Thornton was born in the West Indies to a British Quaker family who apprenticed him for four years to a surgeon and apothecary in Cumbria, England in 1777. He took a medical degree from the University of Edinburgh in 1783 and lived in Paris for a time before settling in Philadelphia in 1786, where he became the principal director of the Philadelphia Steam Boat Company. His incorporation of the Roman Pantheon into his drawings for the competition to design the Capitol in January 1793 won the enthusiastic support of the judges, and, more important, of Washington, who formally approved his winning entry the following April. In the fall of 1794 Washington appointed Thornton to the Federal City's three-member board of commissioners, which had the oversight of planning the city and developing its public works, including the construction of the federal buildings. Despite disputes about designs and other controversies and difficulties arising from Congress's unwillingness to adequately fund the various projects that it sanctioned, Thornton executed his duties to the general satisfaction of all, including Washington. Thornton served as a Federal District commissioner until Thomas Jefferson dissolved the board in 1802. By then Thornton also had become deeply involved in the construction of the President's House on President's Square and taken up another subject close to Washington's heart, the establishment of a "grand national university" in the Federal City.

Thornton often opposed the policies of Washington's administration, but he was completely awed by the president. "His mind dwells in the midst of great things, and mingles in trifles with difficulty," he wrote one friend. "He is a man of great accuracy, of great forbearance, firm in his friendships, chaste in his opinions and words, correct in his judgment, free from affectation, mild and even meek in his manners, respectful to the meanest person, whose salute he never fails to return." The two men became great friends after Washington's retirement from the presidency. Thornton shared Washington's fears about the Federal City, and only one week before his death, Washington confided his worries that the city had to "pass through a firey trial" before its completion. Thornton rushed to Mount Vernon upon hearing of Washington's sudden illness, hoping to save the general's life by performing a tracheotomy, but arriving too late, he proposed to "attempt his restoration, in the following manner. First to thaw him in cold water, then to lay him in blankets, and by degrees and by friction to give him warmth, and to put into activity the minute blood vessels, at the same time to open a passage to the lungs by the trachæa, and to inflate them with air, to produce an artificial respiration, and to transfuse blood into him from a lamb." Thornton reasoned that Washington had died from loss of blood and the want of air, the replenishing of which could recall him to life. "If these means had been resorted to and had failed all that could be done would have been done, but I was not seconded in this proposal; for it was deemed unavailing."

Thornton became the leader of an unsuccessful movement to entomb Washington's remains in a sepulchral monument in the Federal City, preferably in a mausoleum incorporated into the U.S. Capitol.

Related entries: Federal City; L'Enfant, Pierre-Charles

Suggestions for further reading:
"From William Thornton," 12 March 1795
  (*Thornton Papers,* vol. 1).
"William Thornton to John Coakley Lettsom,"
  26 November 1795 (*Thornton Papers,* vol. 1).
"On National Education," 1795–1797 (*Thornton
  Papers,* vol. 1).
"To William Thornton," 8 December 1799 (*Ret.
  Ser.,* vol. 4).

Tilghman, Tench (1744–1786)

"There is a Gentleman . . . at Baltimore who I *know* to be as worthy a man in *every* point of view as any that lives." Washington's opinion of his trusted aide-de-camp Tench Tilghman was formed over a five-and-a-half-year period beginning in August 1776 when he entered Washington's military family. Born at Fausley, the Tilghman family estate in Talbot County, Maryland, Tench graduated from the College of Philadelphia and then became a merchant in Philadelphia. Washington had become acquainted with Tilghman's younger brother James Tilghman, Jr. (1748–1796), of Alexandria, Virginia, during the early 1770s, and he visited the home of their father, James Tilghman, Sr. (1716–1793), a prominent Philadelphia attorney originally from Talbot County, Maryland, at least three times while serving as a delegate to the Continental Congress in 1774 and 1775. These family connections and Tilghman's able performance during the summer of 1775 of his duties as secretary and treasurer to the Continental Congress Indian commissioners for the northern department undoubtedly brought him to the attention of Washington, who was in great need of assistance at headquarters at the time Tilghman arrived in the summer of 1776.

After meeting Washington at New York, Tilghman volunteered to serve as one of Washington's aides-de-camp without rank or pay, although he currently was a captain of a Philadelphia company serving in the flying camp. He was greatly impressed with Washington from the beginning, as illustrated by a letter to his father written in August 1776. "You can have no Idea of the Generals Merit and Abilities without being with him," he wrote. "Few Words serve him, but they are to the purpose, and an Order once given by him is implicitly obeyed thro' every Department. His civilities to me have been more than I had a right to expect, but I endeavour to make it up by my Assiduity in executing his Commands, in some of which I have given him very particular Satisfaction." Tilghman quickly became an indispensable member of Washington's military family, involved in writing much of the general's correspondence. His congenial nature and unflagging zeal to do whatever task he was called upon to perform made him a great favorite at headquarters. Martha Daingerfield Bland when visiting headquarters summed him up as "a modest, worthy man who, from his attachment to the General lives in his family and acts in any capacity that is uppermost, without fee or reward."

Tilghman was not officially appointed one of Washington's aides-de-camp until June 1780, nor did he receive an army commission until May 1781, when at Washington's request the Continental Congress resolved to commission him a lieutenant colonel, to rank from 1 April 1777. "If there are men in the Army deserving the commission proposed for him," wrote Washington to a member of Congress, "he is one of them. . . . he joined my family and has been a zealous servant and slave to the public, and a faithful assistant to me for near five years, great part of which time he refused to receive pay. Honor and gratitude interests me in his favor and makes me solicitous to obtain his commission." Washington did Tilghman the honor of sending him to Congress with dispatches announcing the British surrender at Yorktown in October 1781, and the delegates expressed their gratitude by directing the Board of War to present him with "a horse properly caparisoned, and an elegant sword, in testimony of their high opinion of his merit and ability." Tilghman took an extended leave of absence from the army in the spring and summer of 1782, and retired from the army the following December. Upon receiving Tilghman's resignation Washington wrote him that "I have often repeated to you that there are few Men in the World to whom I am more attached by inclination than I am to you." Tilghman married his cousin Anna Maria Tilghman of Maryland in June 1783, and resumed his merchant business, resettling in Baltimore. From then until his death less than three years later, he acted as Washington's agent in business matters in Baltimore, and his frequent correspondence with Washington during that period reveals much about Washington's postwar activities at Mount Vernon.

Washington was deeply affected at Tilghman's declining health and death. He wrote Tilghman's brother, Thomas Ringgold Tilghman (1765–1789) that "there were few men for whom I had a warmer friendship, or greater regard than for your Brother— Colonel Tilghman—when living; so with much truth I can assure you, that, there are none whose death I could more sincerely have regretted." Similarly, he wrote Tilghman's father, James, that, of "all the numerous acquaintances of your lately deceased son, and amidst all the sorrowings that are mingled on that melancholy occasion, I may venture to assert (that excepting those of his nearest relatives) none could have felt his death with more regret than I did because no one entertained a higher opinion of his worth, or had imbibed sentiments of greater friendship for him than I had done." He was moved to write Thomas Jefferson that Tilghman had "left as fair a reputation as ever belonged to a human character."

Related entry: Jefferson, Thomas

Suggestions for further reading:
"Martha Daingerfield Bland to Frances Bland Randolph," 12 May 1777 (*Proceedings of the New Jersey Historical Society* [1895], vol. 51).
"To John Sullivan," 11 May 1781 (*Writings*, vol. 22).
"To Tench Tilghman," 10 January 1783 (*Writings*, vol. 26).
"To John Augustine Washington," 30 June 1784 (*Con. Ser.*, vol. 1).
"To Tench Tilghman," 11, 18 August 1784 (*Con. Ser.*, vol. 2).
"To Thomas Ringgold Tilghman," 10 May 1786 (*Con. Ser.*, vol. 4).
Tilghman, Tench. 1876. *Memoir of Lieut. Col. Tench Tilghman, Secretary and Aid to Washington. . . .* Reprint, 1971. New York.

Trenton, Battle of

"You can form no Idea of the perplexity of my Situation," wrote Washington to his brother John Augustine on 18 December 1776. "No Man, I believe, ever had a greater choice of difficulties & less means to extricate himself from them." The inauspicious performance of the American forces in New York during the campaign of 1776, concluding with the Battle of White Plains on 28 October and the capture of Fort Washington on 16 November, was followed by a hasty retreat across New Jersey to the Delaware River. By the time Washington set up his headquarters in Bucks County, Pennsylvania, on 8 December, the effective force directly under his command had dwindled to fewer than 3,000 men, although it was augmented by 2,000 militia in the coming weeks. Beleaguered by the rigors of the march, inadequate supplies, the onslaught of winter, and the expiration of the troops' terms of enlistment, the survival of Washington's army seemed doubtful. "When I reflect upon what our situation in this Quarter will be in ten days from this time," wrote Washington on 21 December, "I am almost led to despair." Meanwhile, the British, with a fighting force twice the size of the Ameri-

Washington at Trenton, New Jersey, 2 January 1777 (Library of Congress)

cans, had secured every post that Washington's army had passed through in New Jersey and were, Washington assured John Hancock, "daily gathering strength from the disaffected; This strength, like a Snowball by rolling, will increase, unless some means can be devised to check effectually, the progress of the Enemy's Arms."

The means that Washington hit upon was an audacious plan to overwhelm the British army garrison at Trenton, New Jersey, by a surprise attack on Christmas Day, only a week before most of his troops were scheduled to return home. Three crossings of the Delaware were planned. One crossing would take place directly opposite Trenton, under the command of Brig. Gen. James Ewing, while Washington crossed eight miles above Trenton at McConkey's Ferry and marched down. Another, under Col.

John Cadwalader's command, was to cross downriver and attack the Hessians at Burlington. Washington crossed the ice-laden river as planned with more than 2,500 men, but both Ewing and Cadwalader failed, preventing the "whole of the Enemy" from falling into American hands. After marching to Trenton Washington's troops forced the guards "& enter'd the Town with them pell-mell," wrote Maj. Gen. Henry Knox, "& here succeeded a scene of war of Which I had often Conceived but never saw before. The hurry fright & confusion of the enemy was inlike that which Will be when the last Trump shall sound—They endevord to form in streets the heads of which we had previously the possession of with Cannon & Howitzers, these in the twinkling of an eye cleard the streets . . . finally they were driven through the Town into an open plain beyond the Town . . . Completely surrounded . . . & were oblig'd to Surrender." The Hessian casualties included at least twenty-two killed, eighty-four wounded, and more than 900 taken prisoner, while the Americans lost two men killed, said to have frozen to death, and four wounded. Washington recrossed the Delaware with his prisoners and headquartered at Newton, Pennsylvania, until 2 January 1777, when, upon receiving intelligence of an enemy advance, he crossed the Delaware once again and reentered Trenton briefly before marching to Princeton.

Related entries: Delaware Crossing; Fort Washington; Princeton, Battle of; White Plains, Battle of

Suggestions for further reading:
"General Orders," 25 December 1776 (*War Ser.,* vol. 7).
"To John Cadwalader," 27 December 1776 (*War Ser.,* vol. 7).
"To John Hancock," 27 December 1776 (*War Ser.,* vol. 7).
Smith, Samuel S. 1965. *The Battle of Trenton.* Monmouth Beach, NJ.
Stryker, William S. 1898. *The Battles of Trenton and Princeton.* Reprint, 1967. Spartanburg, SC.

Trumbull, John (1756–1843)

*T*he precocious youngest son of Connecticut governor Jonathan Trumbull, Sr. was born at Lebanon, Connecticut. At his father's insistence he delayed pursuing a career in art until after his graduation from Harvard College in 1773. He barely had embarked upon his career as an artist, however, when he felt compelled to join the American war effort. He entered military service as an adjutant and aide-de-camp to Connecticut brigadier general Joseph Spencer in May 1775. A few days after Washington's arrival at Cambridge, Massachusetts, to take control of the American forces, Trumbull caught Washington's attention by executing a much-needed view and plan of the British works at Roxbury. The map led to Trumbull's appointment as Washington's second aide-de-camp on 27 July 1775. The 19 year old suddenly found himself, he later recalled, in the family of "one of the most distinguished and dignified men of the age; surrounded at his table, by the principal officers of the army, and in constant intercourse with them." Trumbull "soon felt myself," he admitted, "unequal to the *elegant* duties of my situation," and at the end of three weeks he left Washington's household to become Spencer's brigade major. Around that time Trumbull also drew for Washington another map, encompassing the entire Boston area.

In June 1776 Maj. Gen. Horatio Gates appointed Trumbull deputy adjutant general for the northern department, with the rank of colonel; he executed his duties with great vigor at Albany, Ticonderoga, Crown Point, and Providence before resigning in February 1777 during a dispute with the Continental Congress about the dating of his commission. He returned to Lebanon, "resumed my pencil" for some time, and then set off for Boston in search of a teacher to supervise his instruction in the fine arts. His progress in painting, he wrote in his autobiography some sixty years later, was impeded by the "often desultory" manner in which he pursued the craft at that time. A "deep and settled regret" over forsaking the army led him to reenter the military service as a volunteer aide-de-camp to Maj. Gen. John Sullivan during the unsuccessful campaign to recapture Rhode Island in 1778. Another year of studying painting with "great assiduity" in Boston led him to conclude that his prospects of future advancement in art necessitated his placement under the tutorage of some great master, and he returned to Lebanon to make preparations for a voyage to England to study painting under the American Benjamin West, the historical painter for King George III. Permission to travel at length was secured from Lord George Germain, the British secretary of state for the colonies, and he left for London in May 1780. (By that time Trumbull had executed by his count sixty-eight drawings and pictures.) Armed with a letter of introduction from Benjamin Franklin, Trumbull was received kindly by West, who was instructing another pupil destined to paint famous portraits of Washington, Gilbert Stuart.

When news reached London in November 1780 of Benedict Arnold's treason and the resulting execution of British major John André, Trumbull was arrested as a rebel spy and confined to Tothill Field Prison (where he continued painting) until the following June, when Edmund Burke obtained his bail on condition that he leave the country within thirty days. He returned to America by way of Antwerp, Amsterdam, and Bilbao, arriving in Massachusetts in January 1782. Trumbull returned to Lebanon briefly and then traveled to the Continental army's main headquarters at New Windsor, New York, to present himself to Washington as resident agent to assist his brother Joseph Trumbull in supplying the Continental army.

When the war ended Trumbull embarked for London again, in December

1783, arriving the next month at West's residence, where he busily engaged himself in painting by day and attending classes at the Royal Academy at night. Under West's tutelage Trumbull began painting Revolutionary War and other historical subjects. His paintings from the period include *Battle of Bunker Hill,* his spirited and successful portrayal of the battle that from a distance he witnessed firsthand, and several other now famous paintings, including *Death of General Montgomery in Attack of Quebec, Death of General Mercer at Battle of Princeton,* and *Sortie Made by the Garrison of Gibraltar.*

Upon his return home to Connecticut, Trumbull joined David Humphreys, Joel Barlow, and Timothy Dwight in publishing pro-Federalist satiric prose and verse, *The Anarchiad,* in the *New-Haven Gazette and the Connecticut Magazine* in 1786 and 1787, under the pseudonym the Connecticut Wits. He took another voyage to Europe in 1787, this time to Paris; he returned to America in 1789 and began painting portraits of Washington and other prominent leaders.

In 1790 Trumbull was commissioned to paint a full-length portrait of President Washington. He represented Washington in his full military uniform, standing by a white horse, leaning his arm upon the saddle, with scenes of the British evacuation of New York in the background. One interesting anecdote is told of the finished painting, *Washington and the Departure of the British Garrison from New York City,* by Trumbull in his *Autobiography:*

At this time, a numerous deputation from the Creek nation of Indians was in New York, and when this painting was finished, the President was curious to see the effect it would produce on their untutored minds. He therefore directed me to place the picture in an advantageous light, facing the door of entrance of the room where it was, and having invited several of the principal chiefs to dine with him, he, after dinner, proposed to them a walk. He

was dressed in full uniform, and led the way to the painting-room, and when the door was thrown open, they started at seeing another "Great Father" standing in the room. One was certainly with them, and they were for a time mute with astonishment. At length one of the chiefs advanced toward the picture, and slowly stretched out his hand to touch it, and was still more astonished to feel, instead of a round object, a flat surface, cold to the touch. He started back with an exclamation of astonishment—"Ugh!" Another then approached, and placing one hand on the surface and the other behind, was still more astounded to perceive that his hands almost met.

The painting (108 by 72 inches), every detail of which was copied from real objects, still stands in the Governor's Room at City Hall in Philadelphia.

In 1792 Trumbull journeyed to Philadelphia to paint another portrait of Washington, commonly celebrated as the best existing portrait of Washington in his "heroic military character," to borrow Trumbull's phrase. The city of Charleston, South Carolina, had commissioned Trumbull to paint the portrait to commemorate Washington's 1791 visit to the city. Trumbull began with more than his unusual enthusiasm:

I undertook it *con amore,* (as the commission was unlimited,) meaning to give his military character, in the most sublime moment of its exertion—the evening previous to the battle of Princeton; when viewing the vast superiority of his approaching enemy, and the impossibility of again crossing the Delaware, or retreating down the river, he conceives the plan of returning by a night march into the country from which he had just been driven, thus cutting off the enemy's communication, and destroying his depot of stores and provisions at Brunswick. I told the President my object; he entered into it warmly, and, as the work advanced, we talked of the scene, its dangers, its almost desperation. He *looked* the scene again, and I happily transferred to the canvass, the lofty expression of his animated countenance, the high resolve to conquer or to perish. The result was in my own opinion eminently successful, and the general was satisfied.

Charleston's representative objected to the finished painting, *Washington Before the Battle of Princeton,* however, on the grounds that the city wanted a more matter-of-fact likeness of the recent Washington—"calm, tranquil, peaceful"—so the artist reluctantly asked the president to sit again. Although it was an imposition, Washington cheerfully submitted to a "second penance." Another portrait was commenced, with a view of Charleston in the background, complete with "a horse, with scenery, and plants of the climate." The latter painting was more agreeable to its patrons and was sent to hang in Charleston City Hall; the former painting (92½ by 63 inches) was presented to the Connecticut Society of the Cincinnati and went to Yale College in 1806. Trumbull also painted several small portraits of Washington, including a full-length portrait 20 inches high painted in England from memory for Martha Washington in 1780; the head of the portrait was used for the United States bicentennial issue postage stamp in 1932.

Trumbull in 1793 became private secretary to John Jay, who was envoy extraordinary to Great Britain. For the next decade Trumbull was involved in diplomatic work and a series of business ventures. From 1808 to 1815 he lived in Europe. In 1817, the year he became the president of the American Academy of Fine Arts, the U.S. Congress commissioned him to paint four large murals inside the Rotunda of the Capitol Building in Washington. The murals, or more accurately enlarged easel pictures, the *Declaration of Independence,* the *Surrender of General Burgoyne at Saratoga,* the *Surrender of Cornwallis at Yorktown,* and the *Resignation of*

General Washington, still adorn the walls of the Dome Room.

Trumbull was in Europe during the last years of Washington's life, and their correspondence concerned Washington's subscription to a series of engravings produced from Trumbull's paintings and Trumbull's accounts of events in Europe. He later painted a picture of a gallery in which all of his historical pictures (fifty-seven) were represented, which eventually became the property of Yale College. Trumbull died at New York City and was buried at New Haven beneath his great full-length military portrait, *Washington at the Battle of Trenton* (1784), with the inscription on a black marble tablet, "Colonel John Trumbull, Patriot and Artist, Friend and Aid of Washington . . . To his Country he gave his SWORD and his PENCIL." Trumbull's estate included a breast pin given to him by General and Mrs. Washington, containing "a lock of the hair of that illustrious man, set with pearls."

Related entries: Houdon, Jean-Antoine; Peale, Charles Willson; Trumbull, Jonathan, Sr.

Suggestions for further reading:
Diaries, vol. 6.
"From John Trumbull," 6 March 1798 (*Ret. Ser.,* vol. 2).
"From John Trumbull," 18 September 1798 (*Ret. Ser.,* vol. 3).
"To John Trumbull," 6 February 1799 (*Ret. Ser.,* vol. 3).
"From John Trumbull," 24 March 1799 (*Ret. Ser.,* vol. 3).
Sizer, Theodore, ed. 1953. *The Autobiography of Colonel John Trumbull.* Reprint, 1970. New York.

Trumbull, Jonathan, Sr. (1710–1785)

Jonathan Trumbull, Sr., of Lebanon, Connecticut, the only colonial governor to champion the Patriot cause, served as Connecticut's chief executive from 1769 to 1784. He trained for the Christian ministry as a young man, graduating from Harvard College in 1727, but abandoned his preferred path before ordination when an elder brother died unexpectedly and he was called upon to join his father's mercantile business. He was first elected to the Connecticut general assembly in 1733, and despite his business failure in 1766, over the next four decades Trumbull emerged as one of the most prominent men in the commercial and political affairs of the colony. Elected lieutenant governor in 1766, and governor in successive terms after 1769, Trumbull proved to be a very effective and popular chief executive. As wartime governor he managed the movement of manpower, munitions, and other supplies from his state for the Continental army. From his "War Office," a simple frame structure next to his home in Lebanon that had been erected by his father in 1732, Trumbull kept up a frequent and cordial correspondence with Washington throughout the war.

Typical of the succor that Trumbull gave to Washington during the war was his response to Washington's plea in August 1776 for reinforcements for the New York campaign. Trumbull issued an urgent call that raised nine regiments of 350 men each. As Maj. Gen. Horatio Gates told Washington later that month, Governor Trumbull "has, from the beginning of the Misfortunes of this Army, done every thing in his Power to reestablish it in Health and Power. Too much cannot be said in his Praise." As the relationship between Trumbull and Washington matured, Washington came to hold the governor in great esteem. The story that Washington reputedly gave Trumbull the name "Brother Jonathan," which served as the collective symbol of America until it was replaced by "Uncle Sam," seems to have been made up in the mid-1840s, however.

At war's end Washington sent Trumbull a message expressing his wish that their mutual friendship and esteem, which had been "planted and fostered in the tumult of public life, may not wither and die in the serenity of retirement." When Trumbull gave up the governor's office a few months later, he expressed his desire that the correspondence between them that had "commenced under the pressure of disagreeable circumstances, may not wholly cease when we find ourselves in a happier situation—Altho enveloped in the shades of retirement, the busy Mind cannot suppress its activity, but will be seeking some employment, which will indeed be necessary to dispel that languor, which a Scene of Inactivity would be apt to produce. Subjects will not be wanting; far different, & more agreable I trust, than those we have been accustomed to dwell upon."

Their peacetime correspondence proved to be scant, however, for Trumbull's health was failing fast, and he had only another year to live. Upon receiving word of Trumbull's death in 1785, Washington wrote to his son, Jonathan Trumbull, Jr., that "A long, & well spent life in the Service of his Country, placed Govr Trumbull amongst the first of Patriots. In the social duties he yielded to none—and his Lamp, from the common course of Nature, being nearly extinguished—worn down with age & cares, but retaining his mental faculties in perfection, are blessings which rarely attend advanced life. All these combining, have secured to his memory universal respect & love here, and no doubt immeasurable happiness hereafter."

Trumbull and his wife, Faith Robinson Trumbull, had several famous children, including John Trumbull the painter; Jonathan Trumbull, Jr. (1740–1809), Washington's military secretary from 1781 to 1783 and later prominent in politics; and Joseph Trumbull (1737–1778), Washington's initial choice for commissary general of the Continental army.

Related entry: Trumbull, John

Suggestions for further reading:
"To Jonathan Trumbull, Sr.," 20 April 1784 (*Con. Ser.,* vol. 1).
"From Jonathan Trumbull, Jr.," 1 September 1785 (*Con. Ser.,* vol. 3).
"To Jonathan Trumbull, Jr.," 1 October 1785 (*Con. Ser.,* vol. 3).
The Trumbull Papers. 1902. 3 vols. Collections of the Massachusetts Historical Society (5th ser.). Boston.
Buel, Richard, Jr. 1980. *Dear Liberty: Connecticut's Mobilization for the Revolutionary War.* Middletown, CT.

Tucker, St. George (1752–1827)

St. George Tucker, legal scholar, essayist, astronomer, and inventor, was born in Bermuda and came to Virginia in 1771. He married in 1777 the daughter of Theodorick and Frances Bolling Bland, Frances Bland Randolph (1752–1788), who was the widow of John Randolph, thus becoming the stepfather of the eccentric John Randolph of Roanoke (1773–1833).

An early and avid supporter of the colonies' fight for independence from Great Britain, Tucker was an eyewitness to the events at Yorktown and described Washington's arrival at Williamsburg on 14 September 1781: "He approached without any pomp or parade attended only by a few horsemen and his own servants."

In the mid-1780s Tucker authored a "sensible pamphlet" on commerce (in the words of James Madison, who sent a copy to Washington) entitled *Reflections on the Policy and Necessity of Encouraging the Commerce of the Citizens of the United States of America, and of Granting Them Exclusive Privileges of Trade* (Richmond, 1785) and was named by the Virginia legislature one of five commissioners appointed to attend the Annapolis Convention on interstate commerce in 1786. Tucker and his wife spent a weekend at Mount Vernon in September while en route to the meeting in Annapolis.

Tucker became prominent in Virginia in jurisprudence (in 1790, upon George Wythe's death, he became professor of law at the College of William and Mary) as did his two sons, Henry St. George and Nathaniel Beverly. In the 1790s he was a judge of the state's general court. Tucker set forth an emancipation and colonization scheme in his *Dissertation on Slavery* (Philadelphia, 1796).

In April 1797 Tucker sent Washington his "Sketch of a Plan for the Endowment, & Establishment of a National University," written to buttress Washington's own arguments for creating and supporting a national university. Washington, who during his presidency had unavailingly asked Congress to consider the subject, had repeated his arguments for endowing such an institution in his final annual message to Congress and in his Farewell Address. Tucker decided to write his essay upon hearing that Congress once again had ignored Washington's plea, despite Washington's promises to contribute his fifty shares of Potomac Company stock toward its endowment. Washington thanked Tucker for his essay, saying that he had postponed further consideration of the subject until he could more leisurely devise some plan to effect his wishes on the subject. Alas, however, that moment never came.

Tucker became a strong anti-Federalist, and by 1798 he was teaching his law students to take the same course, a fact that Washington lamented, noting as he did so that many government officers were "the highest toned democrats." Tucker also published the first American text on law, an annotated edition of *Blackstone's Commentaries* (1803), which included essays on political theory in the appendix, "Of Several Forms of Government" and "Of Right of Conscience." These and other essays consistently revealed Tucker's belief in the virtues of liberal, Jeffersonian Republican principles. This publication helped earn Tucker the title of "American Blackstone."

Tucker, who wrote dramatic and farcical plays, characterized in his words as "political farce," was a poet of some renown (he even has been credited with popularizing "Yankee Doodle"), leaving behind more than 200 lyrical compositions, two of which, "Resignation" and "Days of My Youth," regularly appear in American anthologies. In his "On General Washington," a series of rhyming couplets using imagery drawn from Roman mythology written in 1780, Tucker extols Washington as the savior of liberty. Another, "To a Truly Great Man," was penned to remind Washington that he had no right to create a bank.

Tucker's house, a simple white clapboard structure, which he purchased from Edmund Randolph in 1788 and subsequently enlarged, is one of the few original buildings in colonial Williamsburg to survive from the period.

Related entries: Education; Potomac River Navigation

Suggestions for further reading:
"From St. George Tucker," 24 April 1797 (*Ret. Ser.,* vol. 1.)
"To St. George Tucker," 30 May 1797 (*Ret. Ser.,* vol. 1.)
Coleman, Mary Haldane. 1938. *St. George Tucker, Citizen of No Mean City.* Richmond, VA.
Cullen, Charles. 1987. *St. George Tucker and Law in Virginia 1772–1804.* New York.
Prince, William S., ed. 1977. *The Poems of St. George Tucker of Williamsburg, Virginia 1752–1827.* New York.
Riley, Edward M., ed. 1948. "St. George Tucker's Journal of the Siege of Yorktown, 1781" (*William and Mary Quarterly,* 3d ser., vol. 5).

Turtle

See Bushnell, David.

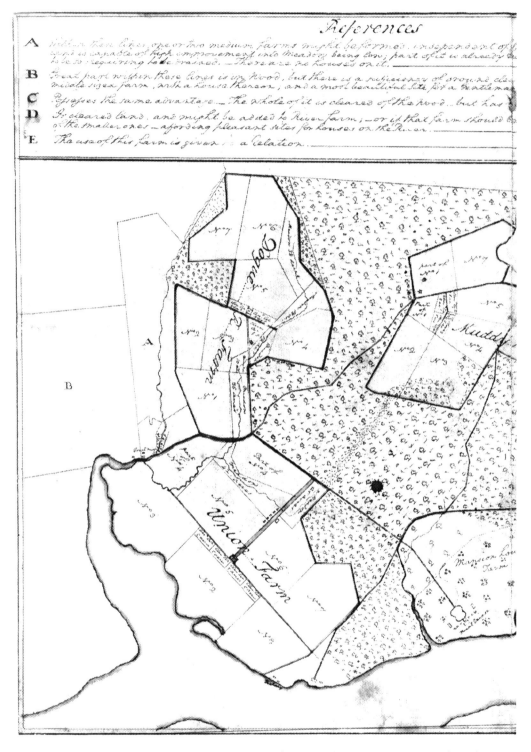

George Washington's map showing Mount Vernon's Union farm, 1799 (Henry E. Huntington Libarary)

Union Farm

See Mount Vernon.

George Washington praying at Valley Forge (Library of Congress)

Valley Forge

"It is with infinite pain & concern," wrote Washington after moving his headquarters to Valley Forge in December 1777, "that I transmit Congress the inclosed Copies of Sundry Letters respecting the state of the Commissary's Department. In these matters are not exaggerated. I do not know from what cause this alarming deficiency, or rather total failure of Supplies arises: But unless more vigorous exertions and better regulations take place in that line and immediately, This Army must dissolve." In one of the enclosed letters referring to the hardship at Valley Forge, an officer writes, "I have used every Argument my Imagination could invent to make the Soldiers easy, but I despair of being able to do it much longer—When they *have* their Allowance, the Beef has no Fat and the Proportion of Bone so great that it does not suffice Men who have been used to be full fed, the Spirit of stealing and robbing, which God knows was great enough before, must increase if no other bad Consequences follow." Conditions at Valley Forge only got worse as the winter progressed, even though the weather of 1777–1778 was moderate compared with other winters during the Revolutionary War.

Valley Forge, Pennsylvania, took its name from an iron forge situated on the Schuylkill River about twenty miles northwest of Philadelphia in Chester and Philadelphia (now Montgomery) Counties. Washington chose the location for strategic reasons. It was a natural defensive position that would be difficult for the British, then headquartered at Philadelphia, to attack without warning. With the Continental army relatively near Philadelphia, British general William Howe would think twice before dispatching troops too far from the city during the winter. And the proximity of Valley Forge to York and Lancaster, where the Continental Congress and the Pennsylvania legislature had fled, would afford Washington an opportunity to assist those bodies if necessary.

Washington reputedly headquartered near the mouth of Valley Creek in Philadelphia County, at a stone mill house that was owned by Quaker Isaac Potts and was occupied at the time by his aunt Deborah Pyewell Potts Hewes, the widow of Thomas Potts II and the wife of Caleb Hewes. The quarters were "exceedingly pinched for room." The headquarters house is shown on an early plan of the Valley Forge encampment drawn by the French engineer Brig. Gen. Duportail. Despite the severe hardships associated with the encampment at Valley Forge, the Continental army stayed there until 19 June 1778.

Related entries: Howe, William

319

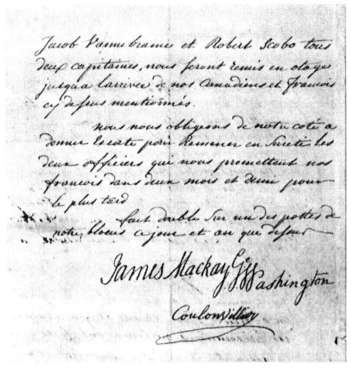

The capitulation at Fort Necessity, signed on 3 July 1754 (Royal Ontario Museum, Toronto)

Suggestions for further reading:
"To Henry Laurens," 22 December 1777 (*War Ser.*, vol. 12).
Bodle, Wayne K., and Jacqueline Thibaut. 1980. 3 vols. *Valley Forge Historical Research Report.* Valley Forge, PA.
Weedon, George. 1902. *Valley Forge Orderly Book.* New York.

Van Braam, Jacob (1725–1784)

A native of Holland who had served as a lieutenant in the Dutch army, Jacob Van Braam came to America in 1752 and settled in Fredericksburg, Virginia. He was appointed a lieutenant and interpreter on Washington's trip to the French commandant on the Ohio River in the winter of 1753–1754. Washington was calling him captain by May, and in June 1754 he informed Robert Dinwiddie that "Captn Vanbra'am has acted as Captn ever since we left Alexandria and an experienc'd good

Officer he is and very worthy the Command he has enjoy'd." He translated the terms of the surrender of Fort Necessity, which included a provision that he be held hostage, along with another of the regiment's captains, Robert Stobo, to ensure the performance of the treaty as well as the exchange of prisoners held by the English who had been captured at the engagement in May 1754 where Jumonville was killed.

Some controversy soon arose over Van Braam's translation of the articles of capitulation, which the French interpreted to be an admission that Jumonville had been assassinated. Adam Stephen, the regiment's major at the time of its defeat, later recalled that when Van Braam returned with the French proposals for surrender, "we were obliged to take the Sense of them by Word of Mouth: It rained so heavily that he could not give us a written Translation of them; we could scarcely keep the Candle light to read them; they were wrote in a bad Hand, on wet and blotted Paper, so that no Person could read them but Van Braam, who had heard them from the Mouth of the French Officer. Every Officer, then present, is willing to declare, that there was no such Word as Assassination mentioned; the Terms expressed to us, were 'the Death of Jumonville.' If it had been mentioned, we could have got it altered, as the French seemed very condescending, and willing to bring Things to a Conclusion, during the whole Course of the Interview." Stephen also claimed that Van Braam had mistranslated by "evil Intention or Negligence" the article concerning hostages. Washington agreed: "That we were wilfully, or ignorantly, deceived by our interpreter in regard to the word *assassination,* I do aver, and will to my dying moment; so will every officer that was present. The interpreter was a Dutchman, little acquainted with the English tongue, therefore might not advert to the tone and meaning of the word in English; but, whatever his motives were for so doing, certain it is, he called it the *death,* or the *loss,* of the Sieur Jumonville. So we received and so we understood it, until, to our great surprise and mortification, we found it otherwise in a literal translation." Van Braam, who upon his arrival in Maryland in 1752 had advertised himself in the *Maryland Gazette* as a teacher of French, hardly can be faulted for his hasty translation of the surrender, but Stephen and many others in the colony accused Van Braam of deliberately mistranslating the articles of capitulation, and aside from George Muse, the lieutenant colonel of the regiment accused of cowardice during the engagement, Van Braam was the only officer omitted from the list of officers commended by the Virginia House of Burgesses. Landon Carter, for instance, who often sent Washington unsolicited advice throughout Washington's life, said Washington's "only unpardonable blunder" in the affair at Fort Necessity was "making a Confidant" of Van Braam.

The French carried Van Braam to Fort Duquesne and then to Montreal, where he remained until he was exchanged in September 1760, by which time anger at him in Virginia had subsided somewhat. Upon his return to Virginia, the House of Burgesses awarded Van Braam £828.11 in salary while a prisoner and £500 as compensation for "his Sufferings during a long and painful Confinement." (Stobo likewise was compensated for his confinement, from which he escaped in 1759 to avoid being executed by the French after their discovery that he had smuggled plans of Fort Duquesne to General Braddock.) Under the terms of Dinwiddie's Proclamation of 1754, Van Braam's service as a captain in the Fort Necessity campaign also entitled him to receive 9,000 acres of bounty land, which he did, on the Little Kanawha River. Although Washington offered to buy Van Braam's shares in the fall of 1771, Van Braam later sold two-thirds of his share to John Didsbury, a boot maker in London who had made shoes for Washington in the 1750s and 1760s. Rather than return to service in the Virginia Regiment, which the other officers would not have accepted, Van Braam decided to return to Europe, where he secured a captain's commission in the Royal American Regiment. He retired to a farm in Wales on half-pay at the end of the French and Indian War but was recalled to his regiment in 1775 because of new hostilities in the colonies. He accompanied the Royal Americans to St. Augustine in East Florida, and he took part in the British campaign against Georgia before selling his commission in 1779. He returned to Europe once again, this time to settle in France.

Related entries: Dinwiddie, Robert; Fort Necessity Campaign; La Force; Muse, George

Suggestions for further reading:
Diaries, vol. 1.
"To Robert Dinwiddie," 10 June 1754 (*Col. Ser.,* vol. 1).

"The Capitulation of Fort Necessity," 3 July 1754 (*Col. Ser.,* vol. 1).
"From Robert Stewart," 6 April 1761 (*Col. Ser.,* vol. 7).
"To Jacob Van Braam," 22 November 1771 (*Col. Ser.,* vol. 8).
"To Jacob Van Braam," 30 December 1773 (*Col. Ser.,* vol. 9).
"From Jacob Van Braam," 20 December 1783 (*Con. Ser.,* vol. 2).
"From Thomas Pleasants, Jr.," 2 June 1788 (*Con. Ser.,* vol. 6).
"To Thomas Pleasants, Jr.," 8 June 1788 (*Con. Ser.,* vol. 6).

Varick, Richard (1753–1831)

Washington's "recording secretary," Richard Varick, was born in Hackensack, New Jersey, but had opened a law office in New York City by the Revolutionary War. He was commissioned a captain in the Continental army, in the First New York Regiment, but detached to Gen. Philip Schuyler as his military secretary in June 1775. The Continental Congress appointed Varick deputy mustermaster general for the northern department in September 1776, and the following year, when the mustermaster's department was reorganized, Congress promoted him to lieutenant colonel. He served in the northern department, taking part in the New York Battles of Stillwater and Saratoga, until his office was abolished in January 1780. After 1780 he was made inspector general of West Point, and in August 1780 he became one of Maj. Gen. Benedict Arnold's aides-de-camp. After Arnold's defection to the British army, a court of inquiry cleared Varick of any complicity, and he joined Washington's military family as recording secretary in May 1781.

Washington had wanted to employ "a Man of character in whom entire confidence can be placed" to supervise a team of writers in copying the thousands of loose sheets generated during the war. In that capacity, for the next two and a half years, Varick and his team of clerks at Poughkeepsie, New York, arranged, classified, and copied Washington's Revolutionary War papers. Washington, after receiving the completed copybooks, commended Varick for his achievement in a letter written on New Year's Day 1784: "I take this first opportunity of signifying my entire approbation of the manner in which you have executed the important duties of recording Secretary, and the satisfaction I feel in having my Papers so properly arranged, & so correctly recorded—and beg you will accept my thanks for the care and attention which you have given to this business. I am fully convinced that neither the present age or posterity will consider the time and labour which have been employed in accomplishing it, unprofitable spent." After the war Varick held several public offices in New York State, including speaker of the assembly and attorney general. He also served as mayor of New York City for seven years, being elected in 1790. From 1806 to 1831 he served as president of the Society of the Cincinnati. Varick died in Jersey City, New Jersey.

Related entry: Papers

Suggestions for further reading:
"To Samuel Huntington," 4 April 1781 (*Writings,* vol. 21).
"To Richard Varick," 25 May 1781 (*Writings,* vol. 22).
"To Richard Varick," 1 January 1784 (*Con. Ser.,* vol. 1).

"Vine and Fig Tree"

Of the various metaphors that Washington used when alluding to his retirement following both the Revolutionary War and his presidency, none was so favored as this famous biblical phrase. After an eight-year absence from Mount Vernon—which he visited only once during the Revolutionary War, in 1781, while en route from New York to Yorktown—can there be any wonder that his mind filled with reassuring thoughts of at long last dwelling in the peace and security of his home?

Washington's fullest use of this metaphor (first used in November 1776) appears in a letter to Lafayette in early 1784. "At length my Dear Marquis," he began, "I am become a private citizen on the banks of the Potomac, & under the shadow of my own Vine & my own Fig tree, free from the bustle of a camp & the busy scenes of public life, I am solacing myself with those tranquil enjoyments, of which the Soldier who is ever in pursuit of fame—the Statesman whose watchful days & sleepless Nights are spent in devising schemes to promote the welfare of his own—perhaps the ruin of other countries, as if this Globe was insufficient for us all—& the Courtier who is always watching the countenance of his Prince, in hopes of catching a gracious smile, can have very little conception." To return to his domestic affairs had been the yearning of Washington's heart for eight years, and now that it was upon him, it was satisfying, but there was more. "I am not only retired from all public employments," he declared, "but I am retireing within myself; & shall be able to view the solitary walk, & tread the paths of private life with heartfelt satisfaction—Envious of none, I am determined to be pleased with all. & this my dear friend, being the order for my march, I will move gently down the stream of life, until I sleep with my Fathers."

To Adrienne, Lafayette's wife, Washington used the same language two months later: "From the clangor of arms & the bustle of a camp—freed from the cares of public employment, & the responsibility of Office—I am now enjoying domestic ease under the shadow of my own Vine, & my own Fig tree; & in a small Villa, with the implements of Husbandry & Lambkins around me, I expect to glide gently down the stream of life, 'till I am entombed in the dreary mansions of my Fathers."

But there was more to Washington's use of this metaphor than his personal feelings; he latched onto the phrase because of what it represented for the country. The Americans had waged a long and expensive war with the greatest military power on earth and had emerged victorious because God, or Providence, as Washington usually styled it, was on its side. Moreover, Washington already was being compared with the heroes of ancient times, and he and others could not fail to find biblical and classical figures to look to. (The biblical quotes that follow are taken from the version of the Bible printed in Philadelphia in 1782 by Robert Aitken and approved and recommended by the Continental Congress, the first complete Bible printed in English on the American continent.) The phrase is first mentioned in connection with the peace that ensued after King Solomon inherited his father's throne: "And Judah and Israel dwelt safely, every man under his vine, and under his fig-tree, from Dan even to Beer-sheba, all the days of Solomon" (1 Kings 4:25). The unknown author of Kings was making a pointed reference to the usage of the metaphor in the Psalms by Solomon's father, David, who himself was looking back to God's dealing with the Egyptians as Moses led the people of Israel out of Egypt: "He smote their vines also and their fig-trees; and brake the trees of their coasts" (Ps. 105:33).

The biblical prophets Isaiah, Jeremiah, Hosea, Micah, and Zechariah also used the metaphor, and perhaps it is appropriate to quote the latter two as well, as one of them may have served as the actual basis for Washington's use of the phrase: "But they shall sit every man under his vine, and under his fig-tree, and none shall make *them* afraid: for the mouth of the LORD of hosts hath spoken *it*" (Mic. 4:4). And Zechariah: "In that day, saith the LORD of hosts, shall ye call every man his neighbour under the vine, and under the fig-tree" (Zech. 3:10). He certainly referred to the Micah text when he wrote his old friend Sarah Cary Fairfax that he had become "Worn out in a manner by the toils of my past labour, I am again seated under my Vine & Fig tree, and wish I could add that there are none to make us afraid; but those whom we have been accustomed to call our good friends and allies, are endeavouring if not to make us affraid, yet to despoil us of our property; and are provoking us to Acts of Self-defence, which may lead to War."

Related entries: Lafayette; Mount Vernon

Suggestions for further reading:
"To Lafayette," 1 February 1784 (*Con. Ser.,* vol. 1).
"To Adrienne, Marquise de Lafayette," 4 April 1784 (*Con. Ser.,* vol. 1).
"To Sarah Cary Fairfax," 16 May 1798 (*Ret. Ser.,* vol. 2).

Virginia Regiment

See Braddock's Defeat; Forbes Campaign; Fort Necessity Campaign; Muse, George; Stephen, Adam.

Wakefield

See Popes Creek.

Ward, Artemas (1727–1800)

Artemas Ward, a storekeeper and justice of the peace in Shrewsbury, Massachusetts, entered the Massachusetts General Court shortly after graduating from Harvard College in 1748, and during the French and Indian War he served as colonel of the Third Regiment of Massachusetts militia. In October 1774 the Massachusetts provincial congress commissioned Ward a brigadier general, and in May 1775 he was made commander in chief of the state's armed forces. While serving in the latter capacity, Ward was nominally in command at the Battle of Bunker Hill, but, as he remained at his Cambridge headquarters all day, his contribution to the outcome of the battle was of little consequence. In June 1775 the Continental Congress appointed Ward first major general of the Continental army, and in that capacity he commanded the American forces besieging the British in Boston until Washington's arrival on 2 July, when Ward became second in command.

Ward received Washington at Cambridge perfunctorily but without "personal cordiality," and although he carried out his duties professionally, he kept his distance. Ward could reasonably expect to be the main contender for the position occupied by Washington. Not only did Ward have the requisite experience from his service as a colonel during the French and Indian War, but he also knew the land, the people, and the militia of the region that was supplying the largest number of troops to the new Continental establishment. Ward sought to resign his officer's commission in the spring of 1776, ostensibly for reasons of ill health, as the army was preparing for its march from Boston to New York. He was suspected by Washington, however, of "finding that there was a probability of his removing from the smoke of his own Chimney." Washington was not overly impressed with Ward's military abilities. Washington was aware, as much for reasons political as military, of the propriety of asking Ward to take command of the Continental forces left behind in Massachusetts after the evacuation. Ward, although his health was still declining rather than improving, apparently was not averse to yielding to the request. When Ward relinquished command of the eastern department to another major general of the Continental army from Massachusetts, William Heath, in March 1777, Washington thanked Ward for his "zeal & services." Ward in return offered his "most devout and ardent Wishes that Heaven may crown your future Efforts with complete and glorious Success," but beyond one or two inconsequential letters written in the summer of 1777, that was the final correspondence between the two men.

Ward continued in public service after leaving the Continental army. His membership on the Massachusetts council from 1776 to 1780 included a stint as president; he was elected chief justice of the court of common pleas of Worcester County; and in 1779 he was elected to the Continental Congress, in which he served on committees appointed to consider Washington's correspondence with Congress. In the postwar years Ward served in the state legislature. Ward died in his native Shrewsbury, and his home is owned now by Harvard University, which maintains it as a memorial.

Related entry: Boston, Siege of

Suggestions for further reading:
"From Artemas Ward," 22 March 1776 (*War Ser.*, vol. 3).
"To Artemas Ward," 29 March 1776 (*War Ser.*, vol. 3).
"Orders and Instructions for Artemas Ward," 4 April 1776 (*War Ser.*, vol. 4).
"To Charles Lee," 9 May 1776 (*War Ser.*, vol. 4).
"To Artemas Ward," 3 March 1777 (*War Ser.*, vol. 8).
"From Artemas Ward," 20 March 1777 (*War Ser.*, vol. 8).

Washington, Augustine (1694–1743)

Augustine Washington's grandson (and George Washington's nephew) Robert Lewis handed down a description of his grandfather made by a "Mr. Withers of Stafford a very aged gentleman" who remembered Augustine as being six feet tall, "of noble appearance, and most manly proportions, with the extraordinary development of muscular power for which his son [George] was afterward so remarkable." According to Withers's recollections, when Augustine was the agent for the Principio Iron Works, he had been known to "raise up and place in a wagon a mass of iron that two ordinary men could barely raise from the ground." Despite such physical prowess, Withers also remembered Augustine as a gentle man, "remarkable for the mildness, courtesy, and amiability of his manners."

Augustine Washington, the father of George Washington, was only about 4 years old when his own father, Capt. Lawrence Washington, died in 1698 at Bridges Creek in Westmoreland County, Virginia. Lawrence, who was only 38 years old when he died, divided his estate between his wife and three children, including little Augustine, with the declaration that it was his desire for his estate to be kept intact and not appraised, and for his children to remain under the "care & Tuition" of their mother, Mildred Warner Washington, until their majority or the day of their marriage. In the spring of 1700 Mildred Washington remarried, to George Gayle of Whitehaven, Cumberland, England, where they decided to live. Tragedy struck the new family the following January when Mildred died after delivering a little girl, Mildred, who also died not long afterward. Augustine's stepfather then enrolled Augustine at Appleby School in Westmoreland, England, where he remained for several years. Augustine must have retained fond memories of his few years in England, because he later elected to have his two eldest sons, George's half brothers Lawrence and Augustine, Jr., educated at the same school, where, if he had lived, he might possibly have sent George and his younger brothers.

Augustine returned to Virginia in 1704 after his father's cousin, John Washington of Chotank, who was an executor of his father's estate, was awarded custody of Augustine and his two siblings, an older brother also named John and a younger sister. For much of the next decade Augustine resided at Chotank (then in Stafford County but now in King George County), which was not far from his father's plantation at Bridges Creek, which would be his when he came of age in 1715, and near where his illustrious son George would be born. Augustine's inheritance included more than 1,000 acres of land (much of it under cultivation by that time); a sizeable amount of tobacco; a half dozen slaves; farm implements and other tools; and livestock consisting of four horses, six sheep, twenty-two cattle, and forty-four hogs. In addition he received a large assortment of household goods and eleven books. Almost immediately upon receiving this property, Augustine married Jane Butler (1699–1729) of Westmoreland County in April 1715, and their combined estates meant that the young man began his married life with about 1,740 acres of land under his control.

Augustine quickly became active in the civic and political affairs of Westmoreland County and began speculating in land in the neighborhood. His deals included buying, selling, trading, and leasing tracts of timberland as well as cultivated farms complete with houses, outbuildings, fences, gardens, orchards, and pasturage. He soon built a substantial residence at a site on Popes Creek that contained a sweeping picturesque vista of the creek and the Potomac River, which lay beyond. It was at this house that George, the eldest of Augustine's five children by his second wife, Mary Ball Washington, was born in 1732. (Augustine and Mary had four sons and a daughter who survived infancy—George, Samuel, John, Charles, and Elizabeth.) Although the family lived in the new house only a few years before settling near Fredericksburg on the Rappahannock River, it turned out that Augustine lived at Popes Creek longer than anywhere else in his life, for nearly seventeen years. Augustine left the estate to his namesake, Augustine, Jr., who had settled there permanently before the death of his father.

Concerning Augustine's death, tradition says he caught cold while riding in a storm and died of complications shortly afterward, on 12 April 1743. This reminds us much of his famous son's death nearly fifty-seven years later. George Washington Parke Custis wrote of his step-great-grandfather's death in 1851: "The father of the Chief made a declaration on his death-bed that does honor to his memory as a Christian and a man. He said, I thank God that all my life I never struck a man in anger, for if I had I am sure that, from my remarkable muscular powers, I should have killed my antagonist, and then his blood at this awful moment would have lain heavily on my soul."

Augustine's will divided his 10,000 acres and more than four dozen slaves among his heirs, providing for his wife and children and leaving the bulk of his estate to his oldest three sons, Lawrence, Augustine, Jr., and George. The younger Augustine received the original home place at Popes Creek (George's birthplace), where he already was living. Lawrence, too, already had been in possession of the Little Hunting Creek plantation (Mount Vernon) for three or four years. George, under the capable guardianship of his mother, was left the Strother farm near Fredericksburg (later called Ferry Farm), which Augustine had purchased in November 1738, and where he had lived with his family since the fall of 1739.

According to George Washington, his father was "intered in the family Vault," established at Bridges Creek in the seventeenth century, where Augustine's father, grandfather, son Augustine, Jr., and some six generations of the Washington family were buried before the cemetery fell into disuse and neglect.

Related entries: Ancestry; Ferry Farm; Popes Creek; Washington, Mary Ball

Suggestion for further reading:
Hatch, Charles E., Jr. 1979. *Popes Creek Plantation: Birthplace of George Washington.* Washington's Birthplace, VA.

Washington, Augustine ("Austin"; 1720–1762)

Washington's half brother Augustine, the second-eldest son of Augustine and Jane Butler Washington (1699–1729), was educated at Appleby School in Westmoreland County, England. At age 17 he took over the management of the Popes Creek plantation in Westmoreland County, Virginia, where George had been born, in anticipation of later coming into the property, which took place at his father's death in 1743. In August 1750, while surveying in western Virginia, George surveyed for Austin a 500-acre tract at the head of Flowing Springs Run, not far from George's Bullskin lands. By the mid-1750s Austin was well on his way to becoming one of the prominent residents of the Popes Creek neighborhood; he had been elected to the House of Burgesses and, along with his elder brother Lawrence, had become a shareholder in a venture formed to speculate in lands even farther to the west, the Ohio Company. Austin's health was not strong, however, and he died at Popes Creek of an illness that "had pursued him for years" despite going to England to seek treatment in late winter or early spring 1762. At his death Austin was survived by a wife, Anne Aylett Washington (d. 1773), and several young children, including daughters Elizabeth (1750–1814), Jane (1756–1833), and Ann (1752–1777), and sons William Augustine (1747–1810) and George (b. c.1758). He left a £4,617 estate that included seventy slaves valued at £2,900 and personal property worth £1,694.

The few letters that have survived between Austin and George Washington, such as those written during the Braddock campaign of 1755, when Austin was in the House of Burgesses and George on the frontier, indicate a genuine concern for each other.

Related entries: Popes Creek; Washington, Augustine; Washington, Lawrence

Suggestions for further reading:
"To Augustine Washington," 14 May 1755 (*Col. Ser.*, vol. 1).
"To Augustine Washington," 2 August 1755 (*Col. Ser.*, vol. 1).
"From Augustine Washington," 16 October 1756 (*Col. Ser.*, vol. 3).

Washington, Bushrod (1762–1829)

The son of George Washington's favorite brother, John Augustine, and his wife, Hannah Bushrod (c.1773–1808), Bushrod Washington was also a great favorite of his famous uncle. Bushrod was born and raised in Westmoreland County, Virginia, and graduated from the College of William and Mary in 1778. After leaving William and Mary he read law, during which time he enlisted to serve in the siege of Yorktown. He went to Philadelphia in 1782 to study law under James Wilson. After returning to Virginia he traveled with Washington to visit his western lands in 1784 and the following year married Julia Ann Blackburn ("Nancy"; 1768–1829), settling at Bushfield in Westmoreland County. After becoming an attorney he sometimes did legal work for his uncle, especially in the years following Washington's retirement from the presidency. In 1787 Bushrod was elected to the Virginia House of Delegates and admitted to the Virginia bar, and the following year he was elected to the Virginia convention that ratified the Federal Constitution.

When Bushrod was 27 years old, he sought from his uncle the office of U.S. district attorney for Virginia. Washington's frank reply left his nephew little doubt of his prospects: "However deserving you may be of the [office] you have suggested, your standing at the bar would not justify my nomination of you . . . in preference of some of the oldest, and most esteemed General Court Lawyers in your own State." Furthermore, said the uncle, his political conduct in making nominations "even if I was uninfluenced by principle, must be exceedingly circumspect and proof against just criticism, for the eyes of Argus are upon me, and no slip will pass unnoticed that can be improved into a supposed partiality for friends or relatives." Bushrod did not receive a federal appointment until 1798, when John Adams appointed him associate justice of the U.S. Supreme Court. While on the Court he rendered the majority opinion in several important early cases, including *Marine Insurance Company v. Tucker* (1806), *Dartmouth College v. Woodward* (1819), *Green v. Biddle* (1823), and *Ogden v. Saunders* (1827).

Bushrod was the executor of his uncle's vast estate and the principal heir to Mount Vernon, where he was later buried. He also had custody of Washington's papers. In 1816 he became the first president of the American Colonization Society.

Related entries: Papers; Washington, Charles; Washington, George Augustine

Suggestions for further reading:
"To Bushrod Washington," 9 November 1787 (*Con. Ser.*, vol. 5).
"To Bushrod Washington," 27 July 1789 (*Pres. Ser.*, vol. 3).

Washington, Charles (1738–1799)

Washington's youngest brother, Charles, lived in Fredericksburg, Virginia, where tradition says he built and operated a local watering hole, the Rising Sun Tavern. He married a cousin, Mildred Thornton (b. c.1739) of Spotsylvania County, in 1757. Charles resettled his family in 1780 at Happy Retreat, a house he built near Evitts Run in the Shenandoah Valley on land he inherited from his older half brother Lawrence. Present-day Charles Town, West Virginia, was established on Charles's land in 1786.

Charles owned two tracts totaling 345 acres on the Potomac River between Mount Vernon and Dogue Run, which he sold to John Posey in 1759. Washington eventually purchased the larger tract, 200 acres, in 1769. Charles also became a shareholder in the Mississippi Land Company, along with his brothers George, John Augustine, and Samuel.

Charles and George together were executors of their brother Samuel's estate, but Charles, because he was nearer, took the larger role, not altogether agreeable to Washington. "I labour under Many Afflictions On Acct of the Orphans," Charles wrote Washington in January 1789. "Money is Such a Scarce Article amongst us, that there are scarcely coming at any . . . Fortitude & Patience is my only resource." Washington suspected that Charles frequently drew on another resource, however, as he instructed his nephew Bushrod, who had questions about Samuel's estate: "I much fear that the management of [Samuel's estate] is in very bad hands; as the hours of your Uncle Charles are—I have reason to believe—spent in intoxication. This circumstance, added to a natural indolence, leaves too much to the Steward to expect *industry* and *fair dealing;* unless he differs widely from the generallity of his class."

Charles died three months before George, after several months of illness. His last days, "so uncomfortable to himself," led Washington to contemplate his own mortality. "I was the *first,* and now the *last,* of my fathers Children by the second marriage who remain," he wrote, and "when I shall be called upon to follow them, is known only to the giver of life. When the summons comes I shall endeavour to obey it with a good grace." Washington in his will had bequeathed to Charles the gold-headed cane that Benjamin

Franklin had left to Washington in his will. The cane has been in the possession of the U.S. government since 1845 and is now on deposit at the Smithsonian Institution.

Related entries: Washington, Bushrod; Washington, George Augustine

Suggestions for further reading:
"To Charles Washington," 15 August 1764 (*Col. Ser.*, vol. 7).
"To Charles Washington," 31 January 1770 (*Col. Ser.*, vol. 8).
"To Bushrod Washington," 17 November 1788 (*Pres. Ser.*, vol. 1).

Washington, George Augustine (c.1758–1793)

The eldest son of Washington's brother Charles, George Augustine Washington twice served as an aide-de-camp to his famous uncle during the Revolutionary War, from September 1779 to May 1781 and from December 1781 to May 1782. By 1782 he was already suffering from the chronic "fever and pain in the Breast" that took his life a decade later. George Augustine married Martha Washington's niece Frances Bassett ("Fanny"; 1767–1796) in 1785. Their first child, a son, George Fayette, named after his uncle and Lafayette, died as an infant in 1787. Several other children followed, including Anna Maria (1788–1814), who married Reuben Thornton (1781–1835), Charles Augustine (b. c.1790), and another George Fayette (1790–1867). After her husband's death, Fanny married Washington's secretary Tobias Lear, whose first spouse also had died.

George Augustine operated Mount Vernon for Washington when his uncle left to occupy the presidency. "The general superintendence of my Affairs is all I require of you," Washington told his nephew, "for it is neither my desire nor wish that you should become a drudge to it—or, that you should refrain from any amusements, or visitings which may be agreeable either to Fanny or yourself to make or receive. . . . Nor is it my wish that you should live in too parsimonious and niggardly a manner. Frugality & œconomy are undoubtedly commendable and all that is required." George Augustine sent detailed weekly farm reports to his uncle while Mount Vernon was under his management and in every way pleased his uncle, but by August 1790 he was forced to take periodic trips in search of a cure for the tuberculosis that eventually took his life. Dr. James Craik, Washington's old friend, recommended a trip to the West Indies as early as 1782, a voyage George Augustine subsequently took to "Burmuda & the West Indies in pursuit of health which he had but imperfectly recovered," at his uncle's expense, who must have thought back to his own voyage with his sick elder half brother Lawrence thirty-five years earlier. After hearing of George Augustine's death at Eltham, the home of his wife's family, Washington wrote from Philadelphia to another wartime aide, David Humphreys, that "perhaps in no instance of my life have I been more sensible of the sacrifice than in the present; for at my age the love of retirement grows every day more and more powerful, and the death of my nephew, the poor Major, will, I apprehend, cause my private concerns to suffer very much. This melancholy event . . . Altho' it had been long expected: and indeed, to me, of late appear'd inevitable; yet I have felt it very keenly." Upon his return to Mount Vernon he called his old friend and now the Reverend Bryan Fairfax to perform "funeral obsequies" for a few friends of the deceased. In his will Washington left legacies to the children of George Augustine and Fanny: "as on account of the affection I had for, and the obligation I was under to, their father when living, who from his youth had attached himself to my person, and followed my fortunes through the viscissitudes of the late Revolution—afterwards devoting his time to the Superintendence of my private concerns for many years . . .

thereby affording me essential Services, and always performing them in a manner the most felial and respectful."

Related entries: Bassett, Burwell, Sr.; Washington, Bushrod; Washington, Charles

Suggestions for further reading:
"To George Augustine Washington," 31 March 1789 (*Pres. Ser.*, vol. 1).
"From George Augustine Washington," 5, 19, 26 March 1790 (*Pres. Ser.*, vol. 4).
"To Frances Bassett Washington," 24 February 1793 (*Writings*, vol. 32).
"To David Humphreys," 23 March 1793 (*Writings*, vol. 32).
"To Bryan Fairfax," 9 April 1793 (*Writings*, vol. 32).

Washington, John Augustine ("Jack"; 1736–1787)

Washington's closest brother, John Augustine, or Jack as he was usually called, served as resident manager of Mount Vernon while Washington served as colonel of the Virginia Regiment in the years following Braddock's defeat during the French and Indian War. It was in the postscript to the earliest surviving letter to Jack that Washington described the engagement with the French in May 1754 that has become so famous: "I fortunately escaped without a wound. . . . I can with truth assure you, I heard Bullets whistle and believe me there was something charming in the sound."

Jack married Hannah Bushrod (c.1738–c.1801) and settled at Bushfield in Westmoreland County, Virginia. Together they had several children, including Bushrod, who inherited the bulk of his uncle George's Mount Vernon lands; Corbin (1765–c.1799); George Augustine (1767–1784); and Jane ("Jenny"; 1759–1791), who married John Thornton.

Jack and George were very close friends, although most of the details of their rela-

tionship have been lost to history because of the paucity of their surviving correspondence. Washington did assist in the education of Jack's sons, and he also helped Jack financially. Jack suffered from severe gout for several years before his sudden death in 1787. Jack's premature death shocked Washington, who lamented bidding farewell to the "much loved Brother who was the intimate companion of my youth and the most affectionate friend of my ripened age." Washington declined to serve as an executor for his brother's estate because he thought his nephew Bushrod was capable of discharging those duties alone, but he offered to assist the family by rendering occasional services.

Related entries: Lewis, Betty Washington; Washington, Augustine; Washington, Bushrod; Washington, Charles; Washington, Mary Ball; "Whistling Bullets"

Suggestions for further reading:
"To John Augustine Washington," 31 May 1754 (*Col. Ser.*, vol. 1).
"From John Augustine Washington," 4 April 1784 (*Con. Ser.*, vol. 1).
"To Bushrod Washington," 10 January 1787 (*Con. Ser.*, vol. 4).

Washington, Lawrence (c.1718–1752)

"George has been with us," wrote Col. William Fairfax to Lawrence Washington in September 1746, "and says He will be steady and thankfully follow your Advice as his best friend." George Washington's half brother Lawrence Washington, his senior by fourteen years, was his surrogate father and role model after their father died. He was named after his grandfather Lawrence, who had received the name from the Reverend Lawrence Washington, M.A., Fellow of Brasenose College, Oxford, and later a country rector allegedly ousted by the Puritans for drunkenness.

Lawrence attended Appleby School in England with his brother Augustine, the same school his father had attended as a child. Lawrence returned to Virginia in 1738 and was commissioned a captain in one of the Virginia companies raised to fight in the War of Jenkins' Ear. He served with the Virginia troops in the siege of Cartagena in March 1741 under Vice Adm. Edward Vernon and returned to Virginia in late 1742 or early 1743, when he was appointed adjutant general of the colony. Lawrence's military service undoubtedly contributed to George's inclination toward a military career. Lawrence married Ann Fairfax (d. 1761), the daughter of Col. William Fairfax of Belvoir, in July 1743. About that time he began rebuilding a house earlier erected by his father on Little Hunting Creek, renaming it Mount Vernon in honor of his former commander. Lawrence's marriage brought him into the powerful Fairfax family and introduced young George to the social life of the Virginia elite at the Fairfax estate at Belvoir, four miles from Mount Vernon. In the summer of 1746 Lawrence attempted to persuade his stepmother, Mary Ball Washington, that young George's future lay in the sea, but the idea was abandoned after Mary's own half brother Joseph Ball wrote her from England advising against it, saying that George "had better be put apprentice to a Tinker" than be sent to sea, where "they will . . . Cut him & Slash him and use him like a Negro, or rather, like a Dog."

By 1749 Lawrence had become a prominent planter and had served seven years as burgess for Fairfax County, but he was forced to give up his seat in the House of Burgesses because of rapidly deteriorating health, apparently tuberculosis. Lawrence also began to accumulate extensive tracts of land, some of which were surveyed by his younger half brother. The earliest surviving letter written by young George Washington was addressed to Lawrence shortly before the latter sailed for England in search of medical advice and to conduct business for the Ohio Company,

of which he was a prominent member. Opening with an expression of concern for Lawrence's health, the letter mainly concerns the possible effects of a proposed establishment of a ferry on the Rappahannock River. Lawrence's ill health offered George the only occasion of his life to travel out of what would become the United States, when they sailed to Barbados in 1751. Lawrence remained in Barbados three months after George's return to Virginia. The warm tropical air failed to bring any relief to his health. Lawrence then determined to try Bermuda, but it too offered no restorative cure. Lawrence returned to Virginia in June 1752, only weeks before his death at Mount Vernon, where he was buried.

Lawrence at his death bequeathed to "his Loving Brother George" three vacant "lotts of Land Containing half an acre each, Situate Lying and being in the Town of Fredericksburg [Virginia] . . . the same three Lotts of Land being now the Property of the sd George Washington as tenant for Life (by the Last will and Testament of the sd Augustine Washington Deceased)." More important, Lawrence made George the residuary heir of his Mount Vernon estate, consisting of two tracts, 2,126 acres along Little Hunting Creek upon which the house was situated, and 172 acres on nearby Dogue Run, where a gristmill was already in operation. George also received from Lawrence a small number of slaves and Lawrence's land in Berkeley County, Virginia (now West Virginia). Mount Vernon eventually came to George after the death of Lawrence and Ann's only surviving child, Sarah Washington, at age 4 in 1754.

Related entries: Ancestry; Barbados; Fairfax, William; Mount Vernon; Washington, Mary Ball

Suggestions for further reading:
Diaries, vol. 1.
"To Lawrence Washington," 5 May 1749 (*Col. Ser.,* vol. 1).
"To Ann Fairfax Washington," September–November 1749 (*Col. Ser.,* vol. 1).

Henriques, Peter R. 1992. "Major Lawrence Washington Versus the Reverend Charles Green: A Case Study of the Squire vs. the Parson" (*Virginia Magazine of History and Biography,* vol. 100).

Washington, Lund
(1737–1796)

*L*und Washington of Fairfax County, Virginia, served as Washington's business agent and farm manager at Mount Vernon from late 1764 to 1785. Lund's service to Washington during the Revolutionary War was particularly important when he ran the plantation, assisted Washington's family, and oversaw Washington's western landholdings. When Lund left his employment Washington wrote Lund that "I shall always retain a grateful sense of your endeavours to serve me; for as I have repeatedly intimated to you in my Letters from Camp, nothing but that entire confidence which I reposed, could have made me easy under an absence of almost nine years from my family & Estate; or could have enabled me, consequently, to have given not only my time, but my whole attention to the public concerns of this Country for that space."

Lund's great-grandfather Lawrence Washington (1635–1677) was a brother of George Washington's great-grandfather, John (1632–1677).

Related entry: Mount Vernon

Suggestion for further reading:
"To Lund Washington," 20 November 1785 (*Ret. Ser.,* vol. 3).

Washington, Martha
Dandridge Custis
(1731–1802)

*T*he oldest of eight children in a family of relatively modest means,

Martha Washington was the daughter of John and Frances Jones Dandridge of New Kent County, Virginia. John Dandridge was the grandson of an immigrant merchant. Her mother was the granddaughter of the first pastor of the Bruton Parish Church in Williamsburg, Rowland Jones.

She married Daniel Parke Custis (1711–1757) in June 1749 after he at long last had secured the blessings of his eccentric father, John Custis (1678–1749) of Williamsburg. When John Custis died in November 1749, he left his son heir to one of the wealthiest estates in the colony. They settled at Custis's White House plantation on the Pamunkey River and had four children, all with the middle name of Parke—Daniel, Frances, Martha ("Patsy"), and John ("Jacky"). The first two children died in early childhood, Patsy at age 17, and Jacky when he was 27. After eight years of marriage, in July 1757, Daniel Parke Custis died intestate, leaving Martha to administer the vast estate, which by law would pass to her and the children. Only eighteen months later, on 6 January 1759, she married Washington, reputedly at the White House plantation but possibly at nearby St. Peter's Church, in a ceremony conducted by the Reverend David Mossom. She and Washington first met at the house of Martha's neighbor, William Chamberlayne, while Washington was en route from western Virginia to Williamsburg in May 1758. The newlyweds resided at the White House for three months before resettling with Martha's two surviving children at Mount Vernon. Several months after their move Washington wrote a distant relative that "I am now I beleive fixd at this Seat with an agreable Consort for Life and hope to find more happiness in retirement than I ever experiencd amidst a wide and bustling World." By all accounts, Martha and George Washington had a good marriage. Their relationship was affectionate and filled with mutual respect and dependence. "In my estimation," he once wrote a recently married

George and Martha Washington with Martha's grandchildren, Eleanor Parke Custis and George Washington Parke Custis (Library of Congress)

French correspondent, "permanent & genuine happiness is to be found in the sequestered walks of connubial life, than in the giddy rounds of promiscuous pleasure, or the more tumultuous and imposing scenes of successful ambition."

Martha and her new husband tended to indulge their children, and Martha became worrisome whenever either was separated from her. When Patsy suddenly fell dead while having an epileptic seizure in 1773, she was stricken with grief and became more protective of Jacky, who by then was nearly grown and soon to be married to Eleanor Calvert Custis ("Nelly"; c.1757–1811).

When Washington took command of the Continental army in 1775, Martha joined him during each campaign. Her periodic visits to Washington's headquarters were, in the words of Mercy Otis Warren, "to soften the hours of private life, to sweeten the cares

of a hero, and smooth the rugged paths of war." One visitor to Continental army headquarters wrote after meeting Martha that she "combines in an uncommon degree great dignity of manner with the most pleasing affability, but possesses no striking marks of beauty. I learn from the Virginia officers that Mrs. Washington has ever been honored as a lady of distinguished goodness, possessing all the virtues which adorn her sex, amiable in her temper and deportment, full of benignity, benevolence, and charity, seeking for objects of affection and poverty, that she may extend to the sufferer the hand of kindness and relief." The rugged paths of war included the death of her last remaining child, Jacky, who died at Yorktown of camp fever in 1781. She and George raised Jacky's two youngest children, Eleanor Parke ("Nelly") and George Washington Parke Custis, spoiling them just as they earlier had her son and daughter.

Martha and George enjoyed only a few years of retirement at Mount Vernon before it was interrupted in 1789 when Washington was called to the presidency. Despite her reluctance to leave Mount Vernon, she supported her husband's difficult decision to serve. In the conduct of her precedent-setting role as first lady, she was, wrote Washington's secretary Tobias Lear, "one of those superior beings who are sent down to bless good men." Although not dissatisfied with the role, she wrote that her "grand-children and domestic connections make up a great portion of the felicity which I looked for in this world, I shall hardly be able to find any substitute that will indemnify me for the loss of such endearing society." She had "learned too much of the vanity of human affairs to expect felicity from the scenes of public life. I am still determined to be cheerful and happy in whatever situation I may be; for I have also learned from experience that the great part of our happiness or misery depends on our dispositions and not on our circumstances. We carry the seeds of the one or the other about with us in our minds wherever we go." She afterward called the eight years spent in New York and Philadelphia her "lost years."

One visitor to Mount Vernon after the Revolutionary War described her as "Rather fleshy, of good complexion, has a large portly double chin and an open and engaging Countenance, on which a pleasing smile sets during conversation, in which she bears an agreeable part." Another said she was "hearty, comely, discreet, affable." Another visitor was less charitable: "Small and fat."

Martha Washington insisted on sitting for portraits in the decorated caps that were the fashion of the day, but she does appear without the headdress in a miniature painted by Charles Willson Peale. She died and was buried at Mount Vernon. Before her death she burned nearly all her correspondence with her husband.

Related entries: Bassett, Burwell, Sr.; Custis, Eleanor Parke; Custis, George Washington Parke; Custis, John Parke; Custis, Martha Parke; Last Will and Testament; Peale, Charles Willson

Suggestion for further reading:
Lossing, Benson J. 1886. *Mary and Martha, the Mother and the Wife of George Washington.* New York.

Washington, Mary Ball (c.1708–1789)

The daughter of Joseph Ball (c.1649–c.1712) of Lancaster County, Virginia, and his second wife, Mary Johnson Ball (d. 1721), Mary Ball married Augustine Washington of Popes Creek in Westmoreland County, Virginia, a widower with three children, on 6 March 1731. George Washington was the first of Mary and Augustine's five children. In 1738 the family settled at the Strother farm (Ferry Farm), which lay across the Rappahannock River from Fredericksburg in King George (later Stafford) County. Mary was called the "the rose of Epping Forest," the name of her father's estate in Virginia.

Mary showed a mother's natural concern for the safety of her first son, which he apparently in the exuberance of youth felt was misplaced. When Lawrence Washington attempted to steer his younger half brother into the British navy, for instance, she withheld her consent. While on the Braddock campaign, Washington wrote her several letters to reassure her of his safety, including one detailing the disastrous battle on the Monongahela where Braddock was killed. After receiving his account of having survived "four Bullets through my Coat, and two Horses shot under me," she must have requested him not to return to the arena again, for his next letter began "If it is in my power to avoid going to the Ohio again, I shall, but if the Command is press'd upon me by the genl voice of the County, and offerd upon such terms as can't be objected against, it would reflect dishonour upon me to refuse it; and that I am sure must, or ought, to give you greater cause of uneasiness than my going in an honourable Comd."

Historians have characterized the relationship between the son and his mother as one devoid of affection, although the documentary references are meager. Washington did give Mary the use and income of the Ferry Farm plantation, which he inherited in 1743, until the early 1770s, when she decided to move into Fredericksburg, and after that he took on the burden of handling all her financial accounts. In Fredericksburg, Mary lived comfortably and was seen often in a "riding chair" that Washington purchased for her in Philadelphia while attending the first Continental Congress in 1774. During the Revolutionary War there was little communication between the two, but Washington did make sure that other family members offered her assistance. After the war there were occasional visits and correspondence. Washington's final visit to his mother at her Fredericksburg home, made on the eve of his leaving for his inauguration in 1789, he described as the "last act of personal duty" that "I may (from her age) ever have it in my power to pay." At 80 years of age she still lived alone with a handful of servants, slowly declining of breast cancer. Her daughter Betty Lewis lived nearby, available to help when necessary. Although Washington at the time urged his mother to "break up housekeeping" and move in with one of her children, he discouraged her from coming to Mount Vernon, which would not "answer purposes in any shape whatsoever. . . . to be compared to a well resorted tavern, as scarcely any strangers who are going from North to South, or from South to North, do not spend a day or two at it. . . . Nor, indeed, could you be retired in any room in my house; for what with the sitting up of company, the noise and bustle of servants, and many other things, you would not be able to enjoy that calmness and serenity of mind, which in my opinion you ought now to prefer to every other consideration in life." The following July her condition began to deteriorate more quickly, and she expressed a desire to hear from her son once again, but she died on 25 August before getting the chance. "Awful and affecting as the death of a parent is," wrote Washington when he received the word of her death, "there is consolation in knowing that Heaven has spared ours to an age beyond which few attain, and favored her with the full enjoyment of her mental faculties and as much bodily strength as usually falls to the lot of fourscore. Under these considerations and a hope that she is translated to a happier place, it is the duty of her relatives to yield due submission to the decrees of the Creator. When I was last at Fredericksburg, I took a final leave of my Mother, never expecting to see her more." Washington of course could not attend her burial.

After his mother's death Washington wrote of her to his sister that "She has had a great deal of money from me at times, as can be made appear by my books . . . and over and above this had not only had all that was ever made from the Plantation but got her provisions and every thing else she thought proper from thence. In short to the best of my recollection I have never in my life received a copper from the estate—and have paid many hundred pounds (first and last) to her in cash—However I want no retribution—I conceived it to be a duty whenever she asked for money, and I had it, to furnish her notwithstanding she got all the crops or the amount of them, and took every thing she wanted from the plantation for the support of her family, horses &ca besides."

Mary Ball Washington's house in Fredericksburg is still standing and open to the public. A fifty-foot granite obelisk erected near her grave a few blocks from her house was dedicated by President Grover Cleveland in 1894, and a state college in the city is named after her.

Related entries: Ancestry; Ferry Farm; Lewis, Betty Washington

Suggestions for further reading:
"To Mary Washington," 18 July 1755 (*Col. Ser.*, vol. 1).
"To Mary Washington," 14 August 1755 (*Col. Ser.*, vol. 1).
"To Mary Washington," 30 September 1757 (*Col. Ser.*, vol. 4).
"Account with Mary Washington," 27 April 1775 (*Col. Ser.*, vol. 10).
"From Betty Lewis," 24 July 1789 (*Pres. Ser.*, vol. 3).
"From Burgess Ball," 25 August 1789 (*Pres. Ser.*, vol. 3).
"To Betty Lewis," 13 September 1789 (*Pres. Ser.*, vol. 4).
"Mary Washington's Move to Fredericksburg" (vol. 3, appendix 4). Douglas Southall Freeman. 1948–1957. 7 vols. *George Washington: A Biography.* New York.
Lossing, Benson J. 1886. *Mary and Martha, the Mother and the Wife of George Washington.* New York.

Washington, Samuel (1734–1781)

Married five times, with children by his second and fourth wives, Samuel Washington was George's next-youngest brother, separated by their sister Betty. By 1770 he lived at Harewood, his house in the Shenandoah Valley in Berkeley County, near present-day Charles Town, West Virginia, not far from his younger brother Charles and near George's western lands.

George sometimes unburdened himself to Samuel, as he did in a letter written on the last day of August 1780: "We are always without an Army, or have a raw and undisciplined one, engaged for so short a time that we are not fit either for the purposes of offence or defence, much less is it in our power to project schemes and execute plans which depend upon well disciplined Troops. One half the year is spent in getting Troops into the Field, the other half is lost in discharging them . . . In a word short enlistments has been the primary cause of the continuance of the War, and every evil which has been experienced in the course of it. . . . It is impossible for any person at a distance to have an idea of my embarrassments, or to conceive how an Army can be kept together under any such circumstances as ours is."

Washington took part in administering Samuel's debt-ridden estate after his death. "In God's name," he wrote his brother Jack in January 1783, "how did my Brothr. Saml. contrive to get himself so enormously in debt? Was it by purchases? By misfortunes? or shear indolence and inattention to business?" Washington in the early 1770s had lent Samuel £400 to buy a tract of land, which was still unpaid at his demise. He felt obligated to look after the children of his brother's fourth wife, Anne Steptoe Allerton Washington (1739–1777), who died while taking the smallpox inoculation during the Revolutionary War. He sent Lawrence Augustine (1775–1824) and George Steptoe (c.1773–1808) to Alexandria Academy and the University of Pennsylvania. Their sister Harriot (1776–1822) lived at Mount Vernon from about 1782 until 1792, when he placed her with his sister Betty Lewis, where she remained until she married Andrew Parks of Fredericksburg. According to Washington, Harriot had been spoiled since coming to Mount Vernon after her mother's death. She "has sense enough," he informed Betty, "but no disposition to industry nor to be careful of her Cloaths," which without admonition and proper restraints "will be (I am told) dabbed about in every hole & corner." Washington considered Samuel's sons "incorrigible" in their youth, although each turned out well. The two boys read law under Edmund Randolph, Washington's attorney general. George Steptoe married Lucy Payne, a sister of Dolley Madison, and Lawrence married Mary Dorcas Wood (d. 1835). Another son, Ferdinand (or Ferdinando; 1767–1788), the eldest, whom Washington attempted to find a "berth in the navy or on a merchant ship," so displeased Washington by his "extravagance and bad conduct" that he refused him any further assistance.

Related entries: Lewis, Betty Washington; Washington, Charles; Washington, John Augustine; Washington, Mary Ball

Suggestions for further reading:
"To Samuel Washington," 31 August 1780 (*Writings,* vol. 19).
"To John Augustine Washington," 16 January 1783 (*Writings,* vol. 26).

Washington Elm

*O*f the many unsubstantiated stories told about Washington, few have been so persistent and yet so plausible as the tradition handed down of Washington taking formal command of the Continental army beneath an elm tree on Cambridge Common. The tree was certainly standing there at the time—its rings showed that when it fell in 1924—but Washington's biographer Douglas Southall Freeman contended there was no evidence that the transfer of command from Artemas Ward took place there or nearby. Not only was there no "passing mention of the 'Washington elm' or of the Cambridge Common" in any contemporary account, said Freeman, but the event also did not even "impress itself on witnesses as ceremonious." No one present at the exchange, in fact, felt the need to record it, and stories of drumrolls, shouting soldiers, and booming cannon came later.

A 4 July 1775 entry from the journal of an unidentified chaplain printed in 1864, if genuine, would constitute a contemporary account and contradict Freeman, however. "I have seen the new general appointed by Congress to command the armies of the colonies," the entry begins. "On seeing him I am not surprised at the choice. I expected to see an ardent, heroic-looking man; but such a mingled sweetness, dignity, firmness, and self-possession I never before saw in any man. The expression 'born to command' is peculiarly applicable to him. Day before yesterday, when under the great elm in Cambridge he drew his sword and formally took command of the army of seventeen thousand men, his look and bearing impressed every one, and I could not but feel that he was reserved for some great destiny." The manuscript journal upon which this excerpt is founded, if it exists, has not been identified.

What is known with certainty is that Washington and Maj. Gen. Charles Lee arrived at Cambridge on Sunday 2 July 1775, where they were greeted by the troops in the camp with the "greatest civility and attention." The troops had assembled on the parade ground early in the day but dispersed following the onset of a drenching rain that continued all afternoon. The next day the troops turned out once again; the scene is described by Joseph Hodgkins, a lieutenant in a Massachusetts regiment, in a letter to his wife: "I have nothing Remarkebel to rite Except that geaneral Washington & [Charles] Leas got into Cambridge yesterday and to Day thay are to take a vew of ye Army & that will be attended with a grate deal of grandor there is at this time one & twenty Drummers & as many feffors a Beting and Playing Round the Prayde." James Stevens, a private from Andover, Massachusetts, however, recorded in his journal on the same date that "nothing hapeng extroderly we preaded thre times."

Related entry: Appointment as Commander in Chief

Suggestions for further reading:
"General Orders," 3 July 1777 (*War Ser.*, vol. 1).
Batchelder, Samuel F. 1925. *The Washington Elm Tradition: "Under This Tree Washington First Took Command of the American Army?"* Cambridge, MA.

Washington's Bottom Tract

Washington's Bottom, on the Youghiogheny River in Fayette County in western Pennsylvania, about thirty-five miles southeast of Fort Pitt, was Washington's first land acquisition west of the Alleghenies. William Crawford began the process of procuring the 1,644-acre tract (actually five contiguous tracts of approximately 330 acres each), located "in the Forks of Monongahela and Yaughyaughgany," for Washington beginning in 1767. Although the formal patent for Washington's Bottom was not issued until February 1782, the tract was surveyed in late 1768. Crawford declared of the survey that he had "done it as if for my self taking all the good Land and Leveing all that was sory only som Joyning the Mill seat."

Washington first viewed his grant at Washington's Bottom while on a trip to his western lands in October 1770. In a diary entry written during the tour, he said the tract "Includes some as fine Land as ever I saw—a great deal of Rich Meadow and in general, is leveller than the Country about it. This Tract is well Waterd, and has a valuable Mill Seat (except that the stream is rather too slight, and it is said not constant more than 7 or 8 Months in the Year; but on acct. of the Fall, & other conveniences, no place can exceed it)."

In October 1772, Gilbert Simpson, Jr., the son of one of Washington's longtime tenants, proposed farming the Washington's Bottom tract. After "perposeing and thinking of perposeing to you as you have a plenty of good lands lying out at red Stone and unsetled," Simpson wrote, "I would undertak to Settle it in pardnership with you." Washington entered into an agreement with Simpson by Christmas of that year, and in April 1773 Simpson and three slaves began clearing land and planting corn as the first step in settling the land. When Simpson's wife refused to join him in the venture, he became disillusioned and vowed to quit. In early fall 1773, however, Simpson suddenly informed Washington—without explanation—that he had moved his family to the tract.

Simpson's inauspicious career as a planter is chronicled in a somewhat humorous series of letters he wrote to Washington between 1773 and 1775, when Washington went to Boston to take command of the Continental army, and in 1784, after Washington returned from the war. The letters reveal that Simpson not only struggled to keep his wife living in the remote area, but also became exasperated at the slaves who worked the land, fell into disputes with the contractors engaged in carpentry work at the property, and was threatened by bands of marauding "Shanee Indens [who had] Left there towns in order to Cut of[f] the frounteer Inhabetance." The latter so frightened Simpson and his neighbors that Valentine Crawford, William's brother, in May 1774 felt compelled to let Washington know of it: "Mr Simson yester day Seemed verey Much Sceard But I Cheard him up all I Could Butt him and his Nabours Seemed to Con Clude to Build a fort if times growd aney worse." Simpson and his neighbors indeed did begin building a stockade fort at Washington's Bottom a few days later.

After the war, Washington made it his main priority to gain control over his property and personal business affairs, all of which had been completely in the hands of others for eight long years. The land at Washington's Bottom, in fact, really never had been under his control, as he indicated to Simpson in a letter written in February 1784. "Having closed all my transactions with the public," Washington wrote, "it now behooves me to look into my own private business, no part of which seems to call louder for attention, than my concerns with you." Washington informed Simpson that he had determined to advertise the mill and land for rent and to travel to the property to settle his account with Simpson, both of which he did before the end of that year.

The notice offering the Washington's Bottom tract for lease, which Washington placed in the *Virginia Journal and Alexandria Advertiser* the following July, indicates that Simpson had made improvements to 600 of the 1,644 acres, including "about 150 Acres of cleared Land in Meadow, Pasture and tillage, under good Fencing, a good Dwelling-House, Kitchen, Barn, Stable, and other necessary Buildings, 120 bearing Apple-Trees, &c.—The Quality of the Soil is inferior to none in that Country, and the situation advantageous for a Tavern." Also, the advertisement indicated that a large number of horses, cattle, sheep, and hogs, as well as the slaves at the property, could be hired. In addition to the property, its improvements, the livestock, and the slaves, the notice emphasized another prominent feature at the tract: the gristmill that had been erected about a mile from the farm on the bank of Washington's Run, a small stream flowing into the Youghiogheny River about three-quarters of a mile below the mill. Washington had decided to spare no expense in constructing the mill, and Simpson in December 1774 had admitted to Washington that "it is True She has alreydy Cost you double The Money I Ever Expect She Was To Cost and She Will Cost a Great deel More yet." At that time, even more irritating to Washington than the cost of building the mill was the fact that, after more than a year and a half of construction, it was still unfinished. Even the momentous events of the war could not mask Washington's dis-

gust with Simpson, of whom he wrote while at his Continental army headquarters at Cambridge, "I never hear of the Mill under the direction of Simpson, without a degree of warmth & vexation at his extreame stupidity." The final tally for the mill amounted to more than £1,200.

Moreover, what the newspaper notice did not reveal, and what Washington did not fully realize, although he should have from Simpson's letters, was the acute state of disrepair at the plantation. Washington's second trip to his Washington's Bottom tract took place in September 1784. He described Simpson's farm in his diary entry for 13 September 1784:

I visited my Mill, and the several tenements on this Tract (on which Simpson lives). I do not find the Land in *general* equal to my expectation of it. Some part indeed is as rich as can be, some other part is but indifferent—the levellest is the coldest, and of the meanest quality— that which is most broken, is the richest; tho' some of the hills are not of the first quality.

The Tenements, with respect to buildings, are but indifferently improved—each have Meadow and arable [land], but in no great quantity. The Mill was quite destitute of Water. The works & House appear to be in very bad condition and no reservoir of Water—the stream as it runs, is all the resource it has. Formerly there was a dam to stop the Water; but that giving way it is brought in a narrow confined & trifling race to the forebay, wch. and the trunk, which conveys the water to the Wheel are in bad order. In a word, little rent, or good is to be expected from the present aspect of her.

To make matters worse, according to Simpson, all the fruit trees at Washington's Bottom had been killed by the severity of the previous winter. Ultimately, rather than bringing significant benefits to Washington, as he hoped, his Washington's Bottom tract was a drain on his resources. In closing the partnership account with Simpson, he did not even bother to balance the figures, an unusual step for Washington, ordinarily punctilious about such matters. Instead he just curtly noted: "Settled by a payment in depreciated paper Money."

Washington held onto his land at Washington's Bottom until 1795, when he sold it to Revolutionary War veteran Israel Shreve (1739–1799), who had rented the property since 1787. Shreve soon sold part of the tract and made substantial improvements on the land he retained, but he failed to make his payments when due, and after three years of excuses, Washington brought a suit against the mortgage. Unfortunately, Shreve's indebtedness did not amount to the sums owed to him by his own debtors or the value of his whole estate, and he was severely strapped for cash. Washington's suit threatened to send him to debtor's prison, and elicited from Shreve a pathetic plea to be allowed more time to remit the payments, and promising to call on his brother for assistance in honoring the agreement. "But after all the Exertions I could make," Shreve informed his former commander in chief in December 1798, "a Cassa [Ca. sa., i.e., writ of capias] was Served upon me the 11th Inst. Returnable next week when I must Lie in a poor dirty Misurable Loathsom prison as a Punishment for not paying money at a time when there is next to none in Circulation, I have known your Excellency Several times repreave Crimanals who had forfited their lives & restore them again to be Citizens I have a good Wife and Several dear Little Children Round me who has Committed no fault to merit So greavious a turn in Life If your Excellency Could Condisend to pass by this grevious punishment it would be hundreds to my advantage and prehaps not one cent to your Disadvantage." Shreve's request did not fall upon deaf ears, for Washington upon receiving his letter, authorized the sheriff to stay the proceedings against him, although his delinquency in making the payments on the Washington's Bottom land brought about even more difficulties for Washington's own financial affairs. Shreve's health already was failing by this time, and he died the next year before securing clear title to the property.

Related entries: Bullskin Lands; Crawford Brothers; Dinwiddie, Robert; Great Kanawha Tract; Millers Run (Chartiers Creek) Tract; Washington's Bottom Tract

Suggestions for further reading:
Diaries, vol. 4.
"To William Crawford," 17 September 1767 (*Col. Ser.,* vol. 8).
"From William Crawford," 7 January 1769 (*Col. Ser.,* vol. 8).
"From Gilbert Simpson," 5 October 1772 (*Col. Ser.,* vol. 9).
"To Lund Washington," 20 August 1775 (*War Ser.,* vol. 1).
"To Gilbert Simpson," 13 February 1784 (*Con. Ser.,* vol. 1).
"From Gilbert Simpson," 27 April 1784 (*Con. Ser.,* vol. 1).
"From Israel Shreve," 22 June 1785 (*Con. Ser.,* vol. 3).
"From Israel Shreve," 30 July 1797 (*Ret. Ser.,* vol. 1).
"To Israel Shreve," 10 January 1799 (*Ret. Ser.,* vol. 3).
Virginia Journal and Alexandria Advertiser, 15 July 1784.

Wayne, Anthony (1745–1796)

As one biographer described, a "braver man, perhaps, never lived. His name, indeed, has passed into a synonym for all that is headlong and unapproachable in courage." Anthony Wayne was born at Waynesboro (near Paoli) in Chester County, Pennsylvania, and educated first by his uncle, Gilbert Wayne, who was exasperated at his nephew's lack of attention to his studies. His uncle thought Wayne a born leader, however, and predicted that his nephew one day might "perhaps make a soldier. He has already distracted the brains of two-thirds of the boys under my charge by rehearsals of battles,

Anthony Wayne standing in uniform with his horse (Library of Congress)

sieges, etc. During noon, in place of the usual games of amusement, he has the boys employed in throwing up redoubts, skirmishing, etc." Later Wayne attended the Philadelphia Academy. Like Washington, Wayne studied mathematics, became a surveyor, and kept up his interest in military affairs.

As he grew into manhood, Wayne developed a commanding presence, and his merits, including his courage and decisiveness and his "blunt familiarity" with his troops, made him one of the more popular generals in the Continental army. Still, contemporaries and historians alike have never found it difficult to come up with less-flattering adjectives to describe Wayne: vain, impulsive, proud, quick-tempered, impetuous, arrogant, and passionate. Washington's description in 1792 seems to catch Wayne's true spirit, however, and probably accounts for Wayne's popularity with his men: "More active & enterprizing than Judicious & cautious. No economist it is feared: open to flattery—vain—easily imposed upon and liable to be drawn into scrapes. Too indulgent . . . to his Officers and men—Whether sober—or a little addicted to the bottle, I know not . . . under a full view of *all* circumstances, he appeared most eligible. . . . has many good points as an officer, and it is to be hoped that time, reflection, good advice, and above all a due sense of the importance of the trust which is committed to him, will correct his foibles, or cast a shade over them." Washington's judgment proved correct, as evidenced by the praise he offered Wayne in December 1779 when writing to honor Wayne's troops for the successful completion of a military operation: "With pleasure I add to this testimony that your own conduct on every occasion has justified the confidence which induced me to appoint you to the command."

Wayne served in the Pennsylvania general assembly and the committee of safety before being commissioned colonel of the Fourth Pennsylvania Regiment in January 1776. Washington sent him to Canada in the spring of 1776, and his performance in the Battle of Trois Rivières the following June, combined with his personal aggressiveness and the rigid discipline he required of his troops, soon earned him a reputation as one of the Continental army's best young officers. Over the winter of 1776 and 1777,

he held an independent command at Ticonderoga, New York. In February 1777 he was promoted to brigadier general, and two months later Washington ordered him to rejoin the main army, with which he participated in the Philadelphia campaign, and the Battles of Brandywine, Germantown, and Monmouth Courthouse.

During the Philadelphia campaign, his opinions given to Washington concerning the Delaware River defense indicate a sound knowledge of the terrain, conciseness, and good judgment. His vigorous defense at Chadds Ford against Gen. Wilhelm von Knyphausen's larger force during the Battle of Brandywine showed remarkable courage, and the skillful disengagement of his troops under the cover of darkness revealed an amazing ability to adapt to events as required. The so-called Paoli Massacre, a surprise attack against his camp nine days later at the hands of British general Charles "No-flint" Grey, so named because the British didn't fire a single shot during the attack but used bayonets only, taught Wayne a lesson in warfare that he never forgot.

At the Battle of Germantown a few weeks later Wayne took part in leading the attack in the thick Pennsylvania fog, encouraging his men to avenge the Paoli Massacre. For a time he tended to doubt Washington's ability to lead the Continental army—thinking his superior too cautious. Following Washington's abrupt dismissal of Maj. Gen. Charles Lee at the Battle of Monmouth Courthouse in June 1778, Wayne gallantly stepped forward to face a series of bitter enemy assaults, giving Washington valuable time to organize the main defense at the West Ravine and in the process winning for himself the praise of his commander in chief, who in his report of the affair to Congress said: "The catalogue of those who distinguished themselves is too long to admit of particularizing individuals. I cannot, however, forbear to mention Brigadier-General Wayne, whose good conduct and bravery throughout the action deserves particular commendation." Wayne became one of the central witnesses against Lee at the latter's court-martial.

Wayne's role in the successful assault on Stony Point, New York, in July 1779 earned him universal admiration and a medal from the Continental Congress. Washington's initial plan for the surprise attack on the 150-foot-high rocky promontory supposedly led Wayne to utter the famous line, "General, I'll storm hell if you will plan it." Washington judiciously let Wayne handpick the soldiers he wanted for the daring after-midnight assault; some 1,350 well-disciplined Continental infantry were chosen, supplemented by a guard consisting of Maj. Henry Lee's light horse. During the attack, which began shortly after midnight, Wayne received a minor injury that only increased the vigor of his men. According to Washington's report of the operation to Congress, Wayne "improved upon the plan recommended by me and executed it in a manner that does signal honor to his judgment and to his bravery. In a critical moment of the assault he received a flesh wound in the head with a musket-ball; but continued leading on his men with unshaken firmness." The brilliant and stunning victory instantly catapulted Wayne into legend and earned for Washington's army a respect by the British that it had hitherto been denied. In praising Wayne's achievement, Washington claimed the victory had a "good effect" on the minds of the American people, and gave the Continental troops greater confidence in themselves, as well as tending to "depress the spirits of the enemy proportionately."

In 1781 Wayne led the Pennsylvania line south to Virginia; he served with Lafayette, saving his army from a surprise attack at Green Spring in July and then taking an active part in the siege and attack at Yorktown. After the surrender of Cornwallis he was sent to Georgia, where he also served with distinction, gathering militia and winning back the allegiance of many disaffected residents, making, in his words, "*Whigs* out of *Tories.*" Also in 1781 he was branded with his famous nickname, "Mad Anthony," by an eccentric soldier who considered Wayne insane. The nickname was quickly adopted by other soldiers as a tribute to his impetuosity in battle. In September 1783, as the war drew to a close, Congress breveted him a major general.

Wayne served in the Pennsylvania convention that ratified the Federal Constitution but then returned to Georgia, which he had seen and liked during the war, and settled on a rice plantation the state had awarded him for his wartime service. Georgia elected him to the U.S. House of Representatives in 1791, but the election was voided shortly after he took office. In 1792, after the humiliating defeats of expeditions commanded by Josiah Harmar (1753–1813) and Arthur St. Clair, Washington chose Wayne to succeed Major General St. Clair as commander of the American forces employed against the Indians in the Northwest Territory. He led the army to a decisive victory at Fallen Timbers in August 1794 and concluded the Treaty of Greenville in August 1795, opening the territory to settlement. Wayne died at Presque Isle, now Erie, Pennsylvania.

Related entries: Germantown, Battle of; Whiskey Rebellion

Suggestions for further reading:

"To the President of Congress," 21 July 1779 (*Writings*, vol. 15).
"To Anthony Wayne," 28 December 1779 (*Writings*, vol. 17).
"Opinion of the General Officers," 9 March 1792 (*Writings*, vol. 31).
"Anthony Wayne: Military Romanticist," Hugh F. Rankin. George Athan Billias, ed. 1964. *George Washington's Generals.* New York.
Boyd, Thomas. 1929. *Mad Anthony Wayne.* New York.
Knopf, Richard C. 1960. *Anthony Wayne, a Name in Arms: Soldier, Diplomat, Defender of Expansion Westward of a Nation.* Pittsburgh.
Stillé, Charles J. 1893. *Major-General Anthony Wayne and the Pennsylvania Line in the Continental Army.* Philadelphia.

Webb, Samuel Blachley (1753–1807)

Samuel Blachley Webb of Wethersfield, Connecticut, was the stepson and private secretary of Continental Congress member Silas Deane. Webb was but 21 years old when he led a company of local militia to Boston to join in the American attempt to drive out the British. He was wounded at the Battle of Bunker Hill in June 1775, and a month later he was appointed an aide-de-camp to Maj. Gen. Israel Putnam. Around the same time, Webb first came into contact with Washington; he was favorably impressed by the new commander in chief, of whom he wrote to his stepfather: "Our General and the other gentlemen from the southward will be the means of disciplining the army, which was much needed."

Webb became more closely associated with Washington in the summer of 1776 after Washington appointed him an aide-de-camp in his own military family. Washington in late winter had instructed his secretary and friend Lt. Col. Joseph Reed to recruit an assistant to help in the myriad affairs of the headquarters office, and Reed had recommended Webb in a letter written at Philadelphia in early March: "Mr Webb has long had an Inclination to be in your Family if the Post should be agreeable to him & he is agreeable to you I believe I should prefer him to any other." Washington's reply contained his notions of Webb as well as what he expected from the new secretary: "You mention Mr Webb in one of your Letters as Assistant—he will be agreeable enough to me if you think him qualified for the business—what kind of a hand he writes I know not—I believe but a crampt one; latterly none at all, as he has either the Gout or Rhumatism in both—He is a Man fond of Company—of gaiety—and of a tender Constitution; whether therefore, such a person would answer yr purpose so well as a plodding, methodical Person, whose sole business shd be to arrange his Papers &ca in such order as to produce any one, at any Instant it is called for, & capable at the sametime of composing a Letter, is what you have to consider. I can only add that I have no one in view myself, & wish you success in your choice."

Washington appointed Webb an aide-de-camp in June, with the rank of lieutenant colonel, and Webb's position on Putnam's staff was filled by Aaron Burr. Webb turned out to be a competent assistant, tending to correspondence and other office work and accompanying Reed in meeting British flags. He remained on Washington's staff throughout the New York campaign and was wounded at the Battle of White Plains. He was with Washington in his retreat across New Jersey, and was wounded a third time at the Battle of Trenton. In early 1777 Washington named Webb colonel of one of the Sixteen Additional Continental Regiments that Congress recently had authorized to be raised. Webb was captured by the British while on an expedition to Long Island, New York, in December 1777, exchanged a year later, and returned to his regiment, which he commanded until the end of the war. Washington may have breakfasted at a tavern owned by Webb's family in Litchfield, Connecticut, while en route to Yorktown in May 1781.

Related entry: Aides-de-Camp

Suggestions for further reading:
Diaries, vol. 3.
"General Orders," 22 July 1775 (*War Ser.,* vol. 1).
"From Joseph Reed," 3 March 1776 (*War Ser.,* vol. 3).
"To Joseph Reed," 25 March 1776 (*War Ser.,* vol. 3).
"General Orders," 21 June 1776 (*War Ser.,* vol. 5).
Ford, Worthington Chauncey, ed. 1893–1894. 3 vols. *Webb Correspondence and Journals.* New York.

Weedon, George (c. 1734–1793)

George Weedon kept an inn at Fredericksburg, Virginia, known as the Rising Sun Tavern, where Washington frequently stayed. One lodger, Dr. Smyth, an Englishman who in 1784 published in London a book of travels in America, noted that on the eve of the Revolutionary War the Rising Sun's owner "was then very active and zealous in blowing the flames of sedition." A close friend of Washington, Weedon served with Washington in the Virginia Regiment as an ensign beginning in September 1755. He was promoted to lieutenant in July 1757 and to captain-lieutenant in May 1762. After the French and Indian War, Weedon became a captain in the Spotsylvania County militia. In December 1774 he was named captain of the Spotsylvania Independent Company.

In January 1776 the Virginia convention appointed Weedon lieutenant colonel of the Third Virginia Regiment. The following August he was promoted to colonel and ordered to lead his regiment to the northward, arriving at Washington's New York headquarters on 11 September 1776. Washington in January 1777 called upon Weedon to accept the post of acting adjutant general, and the following month Congress conferred upon him the rank of brigadier general. Optimistic sometimes to a fault, he became known to the Continental army troops as "Joe Gourd" or "Old Joe Gourd" because of his reputed propensity to serve the patrons of his tavern back in Fredericksburg rum punch from a gourd. Weedon wrote of Washington to fellow Virginian John Page in April 1777 that "no other man but our present General, who is the greatest that ever did or ever will adorn the earth, could have supported himself under the many disappointments and disgraces he was subjected to from this singular system of carrying on a war against the most formidable enemy in the world." He was with Washington and the main army at the Battles of Brandywine and Germantown, Pennsylvania. He commanded a brigade in Maj. Gen. Nathanael Greene's division during the Battle of Brandywine. Weedon left active service after the winter of Valley Forge, in the spring of 1778, dissatisfied with his rank but retaining his commission. Back in Virginia he helped supervise the militia's resistance to British raids along the Potomac and James Rivers, and he later commanded the Virginia militia at Gloucester, Virginia, during the siege of Yorktown, after which Washington called on him to secure the arms and accoutrements surrendered by the British on 19 October. Weedon's last act of consequence in the military was to guard the British and German convalescents that Washington ordered to be quartered at Fredericksburg until they could rejoin their respective corps.

Weedon resigned his commission in July 1783, and after the war he and Washington corresponded about agricultural matters and the Society of the Cincinnati. Washington's opinion of his general officers written in 1792 says of Weedon: "Not supposed to be an Officer of much resource though not deficient in a competent share of understanding; rather addicted to ease and pleasure; and no enemy it is said to the bottle; never has had his name brot. forward on this acct." Weedon died at Fredericksburg.

Related entry: Brandywine, Battle of

Suggestions for further reading:
"To George Weedon," 23 September 1781 (*Writings,* vol. 23).
"To George Weedon," 19, 20 October 1781 (*Writings,* vol. 23).
"To George Weedon," 3 November 1781 (*Writings,* vol. 23).
"Opinion of the General Officers," 9 March 1792 (*Writings,* vol. 31).
Weedon, George. 1902. *Valley Forge Orderly Book.* New York.

Weems, Mason Locke (1759–1825)

See Cherry Tree.

Wessyngton, Chevalier William de

See Ancestry; Coat of Arms.

Western Lands

See Crawford Brothers; Great Kanawha Tracts; Millers Run (Chartiers Creek) Tract; Washington's Bottom Tract.

Wheatley, Phillis (c.1753–1784)

Phillis Wheatley was about 7 or 8 years old when she was kidnapped near her home in present-day Senegal, Africa, in 1761 and placed on board a slave ship destined for America. Upon her arrival at Boston she was purchased by John Wheatley, a local tailor, as a personal servant for his wife, Mary, who gave the young girl her name and tutored her in the Scriptures and ancient classics. Wheatley began writing poetry by age 13; her earliest surviving poem, "To the University of Cambridge in New England," was composed in 1766. Four years later she published *An Elegiac Poem on the Death of A Celebrated Devine . . . George Whitefield,* and in 1773 Wheatley accompanied John Wheatley's son Nathaniel on a three-year voyage to London, where a volume of her poems was printed under the title *Poems on Various Subjects, Religious and Moral* (1773). In October 1775 the poet sent Washington a poem written in his honor, enclosed in a brief letter entreating his acceptance of it, "though I am not insensible of its inaccuracies. Your being appointed by the Grand Continental Congress to be Generalissimo of the armies of North America, together with the fame of your virtues, excite sensations not easy to suppress. Your generosity, therefore, I presume, will pardon the attempt."

Celestial choir! enthron'd in realms of
   light,
Columbia's scenes of glorious toils I
   write.
While freedom's cause her anxious breast
   alarms,
She flashes dreadful in refulgent arms.
See mother earth her offspring's fate
   unknown!
See the bright beams of heaven's
   revolving light
Involved in sorrows and the veil of night!
The goddess comes, she moves divinely
   fair,
Olive and laurel binds her golden hair:
Wherever shines this native of the skies,
Unnumber'd charms and recent graces
   rise.
Muse! bow propitious while my pen
   relates
How pour her armies through a
   thousand gates:
As when Eolus heaven's fair face
   deforms,
Astonish'd ocean feels the wild uproar,
The refluent surges beat the sounding
   shore;
Or thick as leaves in Autumn's golden
   reign,
Such, and so many, moves the warrior's
   train.
In bright array they seek the work of
   war,
Where high unfurl'd the ensign waves in
   air.
Shall I to Washington their praise recite?
Enough thou know'st them in the fields
   of fight.
Thee, first in place and honours,—we
   demand
The grace and glory of thy martial band.

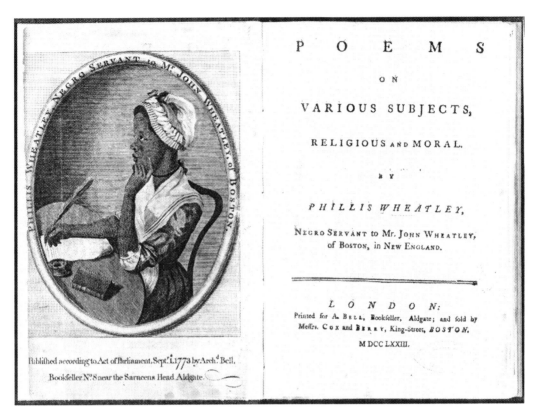

Portrait of Phillis Wheatley, which appears on the title page of her book of poems (Library of Congress)

Fam'd for thy valour, for thy virtues
    more,
Hear every tongue thy guardian aid
    implore!
One century scarce perform'd its destined
    round,
When Gallic powers Columbia's fury
    found;
And so may you, whoever dares disgrace
The land of freedom's heaven-defended
    race!
Fix'd are the eyes of nations on the scales,
For in their hopes Columbia's arm
    prevails.
Anon Britannia droops the pensive head,
While round increase the rising hills of
    dead.
Ah! cruel blindness to Columbia's state!
Lament thy thirst of boundless power too
    late.
Proceed, great chief, with virtue on thy
    side,
Thy ev'ry action let the goddess guide.

A crown, a mansion, and a throne that
    shine,
With gold unfading, Washington! be
    thine.

Washington's reaction to Wheatley's poem was so favorable that he later sent a copy to his friend Joseph Reed in Philadelphia, saying that, "at first, With a view of doing justice to her great poetical Genius, I had a great Mind to publish the Poem, but not knowing whether it might not be considered rather as a mark of my own vanity than as a Compliment to her I laid it aside till I came across it again." Reed arranged to have the poem printed in the "Poetical Essays" section of the April 1776 issue of Tom Paine's *The Pennsylvania Magazine: Or, American Monthly Museum.* The letter and poem also appeared in the 30 March 1776 issue of Dixon and Hunter's Williamsburg newspaper, the *Virginia Gazette,* although it is not known whether Reed placed it there. On the last day of February 1776, Washington wrote Wheatley a letter in which he apologized for his delay in acknowledging her letter and thanked her for the "elegant Lines," adding that he was undeserving "of such encomium and panegyrick" and that he would "be happy to see a person so favour'd by the Muses, and to whom nature has been so liberal and beneficent in her dispensations." Washington apparently met the poet at his headquarters in Cambridge, Massachusetts, sometime in March 1776.

Wheatley had obtained her freedom by the time she married John Peters, a free black jack-of-all-trades of Boston, in 1778, with whom she had several children. She died in poverty at Boston. Many of her writings were published posthumously, including *Memoir and Poems of Phillis Wheatley* (1834) and *The Letters of Phillis Wheatley, the Negro-Slave Poet of Boston* (1864).

Related entry: Slavery

Suggestions for further reading:
"From Phillis Wheatley," 26 October 1775 (*War Ser.*, vol. 2).
"To Joseph Reed," 10 February 1776 (*War Ser.*, vol. 3).
"To Phillis Wheatley," 28 February 1776 (*War Ser.*, vol. 3).
The Pennsylvania Magazine: Or, American Monthly Museum. April 1776. Philadelphia.
Renfro, Herbert G. 1916. *Life and Works of Phillis Wheatley.* Washington, DC.

Whiskey Rebellion

One of the most controversial components of the fiscal plan drafted by Alexander Hamilton and passed by the U.S. Congress during Washington's first administration in 1791 was the excise tax on distilled spirits. Immediately opposed by back-country settlers on the western frontiers of the southern and middle states because it interfered with the most efficient way of shipping grain to eastern markets, discontent became so vocal by the following year that Washington was compelled to issue a proclamation in mid-September against "certain violent and unwarrantable proceedings . . . lately taken place, tending to obstruct the operation of the laws of the United States." The hostility, wrote Washington, "is become too open, violent & serious to be longer winked at by Government, without prostrating it's authority, and involving the Executive in censurable inattention to the outrages which are threatened." Washington expected to be severely criticized for enforcing the excise law, but, he wrote, "I shall disregard any animadversions upon my conduct when I am called upon by the nature of my office, to discharge what I conceive to be a duty—and none, in my opinion, is more important, than to carry Laws of the United States into effect."

Opposition festered for the next two years, with much of the agitation centered in the four western counties of Pennsylvania—Washington, Westmoreland, Fayette, and Allegheny. The dissent manifested itself peacefully in petitions and memorials to legislators, but violence erupted in July 1794, when federal revenue officers attempted to serve papers against distillers in the western counties who had not registered according to law the previous year. When word of the violence reached Philadelphia, Washington and members of his cabinet met with Pennsylvania governor Thomas Mifflin and other state officials. After much discussion it was decided that "a competent force" should be called forth and employed to "suppress the insurrection and support the Civil Authority." On 7 August, Washington reluctantly issued a proclamation commanding the insurgents "to disperse and retire peaceably to their respective abodes" by the 1 September. Mifflin issued a supporting proclamation on the same date, and Secretary of War Henry Knox sent a circular letter to the governors of Pennsylvania, New Jersey, Maryland, and Virginia requesting 12,950 militia.

Before sending the militia, however, Washington made a final effort to restore order peacefully. He appointed three federal commissioners to meet with the insurgents—U.S. attorney general William Bradford, Federalist senator James Ross of Washington County, and Jasper Yeates, associate justice of the Pennsylvania Supreme Court. In the third week of August and again in early September, the commissioners met in Pittsburgh with a committee representing the western Pennsylvania counties, which assured the commissioners that it would assist in restoring order. It soon became evident, however, that the committee could not fulfill its promises of conciliation. The violent opposition continued, and the resistance appeared to be spreading into western Maryland and Virginia and creeping eastward in Pennsylvania. The report filed by the federal commissioners after their return to Philadelphia signaled that it was "absolutely necessary that the civil authority should be aided by a military force in order to secure a due execution of the laws."

After reading the commissioners' report, Washington resolved to no longer defer decisive action, and on 15 September he issued a proclamation admonishing and exhorting the insurgents "to refrain and desist from all unlawful combinations and proceedings whatsoever" and requiring "all Courts, Magistrates and Officers whom it may concern" to use their powers to strictly enforce the laws to preserve the public peace. Ten days later Washington issued a second proclamation, which called out the militia and explained his reasons for resorting to force. Washington wrote that, since he had hoped that alliances in western Pennsylvania against the Constitution and the laws of the United States "would yield to time and reflection, I thought it sufficient, in the first instance, rather to take

measures for calling for the militia, than immediately to embody them; but the moment is now come, when the overtures of forgiveness, with no other condition, than a submission to Law, have been only partially accepted—when every form of conciliation not inconsistent with the being of Government, has been adopted without effect . . . when, therefore, Government is set at defiance, the contest being whether a small portion of the United States shall dictate to the whole union, and at the expence of those, who desire peace, indulge a desperate ambition; Now therefore I . . . in obedience to that high and irresistible duty, consigned to me by the Constitution, 'to take care that the laws be faithfully executed;' deploring that the American name should be sullied by the outrages of citizens on their own Government; . . . but resolved . . . to reduce the refractory to a due subordination to the law; Do Hereby declare and make known, that with a satisfaction, which can be equalled only by the merits of the Militia summoned into service from the States of New-Jersey, Pennsylvania, Maryland, and Virginia, I have received intelligence of their patriotic alacrity, in obeying the call of the present, tho' painful, yet commanding necessity; . . . And I do, moreover, exhort all individuals, officers, and bodies of men, to contemplate with abhorrence the measures leading directly or indirectly to those crimes, which produce this resort to military coercion. . . . And lastly, I again warn all persons, whomsoever and wheresoever, not to abet, aid, or comfort the Insurgents aforesaid, as they will answer the contrary at their peril."

Even those who strongly opposed the administration's fiscal policy viewed the insurrection, said Washington, "with universal indignation; and abhorrence; except by those who have never missed an opportunity by side blows, or otherwise, to aim their shafts at the General Government." Washington resolved to travel from Philadelphia to meet the troops in the field at the rendezvous at Carlisle, Pennsylvania, gathering information about the insurrection from inhabitants along his way. His journey is described in his diary entries for 30 September to 20 October 1794. The insurgents, identified as "only small vagrant parties," dispersed in the face of so large a show of force, and Washington returned to Philadelphia by the end of October. His "earnest wish," he wrote, had been to bring the inhabitants on the frontier "to a sense of their duty, by mild, & lenient means," but failing that, measures had been taken "to convince them that the government could, & would enforce obedience to the laws—not suffering them to be insulted with impunity."

Related entries: Distillery; Hamilton, Alexander; Madison, James; Mifflin, Thomas; Presidency; Spirituous Liquors; Wayne, Anthony

Suggestions for further reading:
Diaries, vol. 6.
"To Thomas Jefferson," 15 September 1792 (*Pres. Ser.,* vol. 11).
"To Alexander Hamilton," 31 October 1794 (Syrett, *Hamilton Papers,* vol. 17).
"To Alexander Hamilton," 5 November 1794 (Syrett, *Hamilton Papers,* vol. 17).
Baldwin, Leland. 1939. *Whiskey Rebels: The Story of a Frontier Uprising.* Pittsburgh.
Slaughter, Thomas P. 1986. *The Whiskey Rebellion: Frontier Epilogue to the American Revolution.* New York.

"Whistling Bullets"

Washington's famous description of his first encounter with the dangers and thrills of enemy gunfire was added as an afterthought to his account of the defeat by his Virginia troops of the French at Great Meadows in May 1754, written to his younger brother John Augustine Washington: "I fortunately escaped without a wound, tho' the right Wing where I stood was exposed to & received all the Enemy's fire and was the part where the man was killed & the rest wounded. I

can with truth assure you, I heard Bullets whistle and believe me there was something charming in the sound." Of this latter remark George II is reputed to have said, "He would not say so, if he had been used to hear many." Horace Walpole, perhaps with more accuracy than charity, called Washington a "brave braggart." Washington apparently came to share the king's judgment, for many years later, when someone asked him if it were true that he had ever expressed such a sentiment, Washington replied, "If I said so, it was when I was young." The future general was, after all, as Washington Irving reminded his readers, but 22 years old, flushed with the success of his first battle, and writing to a brother. Without a doubt Washington found the excitement and peril of battle exhilarating; and his daring showed that Washington was, in the words of another nineteenth-century writer, "courageous, even to rashness." The incident first revealed the fearlessness and poise that came to characterize Washington's demeanor during the battles of the Revolutionary War.

Related entries: Fort Necessity Campaign; Indian Prophecy, The; Washington, John Augustine

Suggestion for further reading:
"To John Augustine Washington," 31 May 1754 (*Col. Ser.,* vol. 1).

White Plains, Battle of

By mid-October 1776 it became clear to Washington that British general William Howe was "pursuing with great Industry" a plan to outflank the Continental army and trap it on Manhattan Island or in lower Westchester County by penetrating the New York countryside from Long Island Sound. When a 4,000-man force sailed from the sound through Hell Gate on 12 October in the first attempt to effect that plan, it failed only because two dozen well-placed Pennsylvania sharpshooters were able to keep the British troops from crossing the East River on a narrow bridge at Throg's Neck. Six days later Howe's troops successfully crossed three miles up-river at Pell's Point, forcing Washington to redeploy most of his troops from Harlem Heights to White Plains, leaving only 2,800 on Manhattan Island to guard Fort Washington. Ten days later Howe moved 13,000 troops toward the new Continental army encampment at White Plains. Washington was headquartered at the house of Jacob Purdy, about a half mile from the intersection of the principal roads running through the village. On the day of the battle, 28 October, Washington moved his headquarters about a mile and a half to the north to the small frame farmhouse of Ann Fisher Miller (c.1727–1819), recently widowed when her husband, Elijah (1728–1776), a militia officer, had fallen in a skirmish near Hell Gate.

Across the Bronx River to the southwest of the American encampment lay Chatterton Hill, a 180-foot-high, steep, mile-long ridge flanked on two sides by the Bronx. The Americans had posted a few regiments of militia levies on Chatterton Hill but made no attempts to construct fortifications. In fact, Chatterton Hill had been neglected altogether until shortly before Howe's arrival at White Plains, when Washington and several of his generals rode over to reconnoiter the hill. They considered Chatterton Hill a "very commanding height, worthy of attention," but no more so than other grounds to the north, where they intended to reconnoiter next. The news that the British army had broken camp and was marching in their direction halted the generals' reconnaissance, however.

Howe's forces marched in two columns, commanded by British general Henry Clinton and Hessian general Leopold Philipp, Freiherr von Heister (d. 1777). About two miles outside the American lines they began to encounter steady resistance from American sharpshooters concealed behind fences and walls, delaying their march for about an hour. By noon the riflemen had been driven back to their own lines, however, and Howe had arrived at White Plains. Howe recognized Chatterton Hill as critical terrain and immediately ordered eight regiments and a dozen artillery to cross the rain-swollen Bronx and ascend the heavily wooded southeastern slope of the hill. By then Washington had ordered 2,000 reinforcements to the hill to assist the militia levies. The American troops put up a stubborn resistance for several hours before being forced to make a "confused and precipitate retreat" by the overwhelming superiority of enemy troops, assisted by "a heavy cannonade from a great number of field-pieces advantageously disposed on several rising grounds."

Although the Battle of White Plains was a defeat for Washington, his troops had fought bravely, and the enemy had suffered twice as many casualties—the Americans lost about 150 killed or wounded compared with the British and Hessian totals of 336 men killed, wounded, or missing. After the battle Howe entrenched his forces on Chatterton Hill, and Washington moved the Continental army a mile and a half north of White Plains to the hill he had wanted to reconnoiter with his generals the morning of the battle, "& by degrees got Strongly posted on advantageous Grounds" that the enemy considered "an Exceeding Strong Position." The American redeployment effectively ended the British efforts to outflank and trap Washington's army, and Howe evacuated White Plains on 4 November.

Related entries: Clinton, Henry; Fort Washington; Harlem Heights, Battle of; Kip's Bay, New York

Suggestions for further reading:
"General Orders," 21 October 1776 (*War Ser.,* vol. 7).
"Robert Hanson Harrison to John Hancock," 29 October 1776 (*War Ser.,* vol. 7).

"To John Augustine Washington," 6–19
November 1776 (*War Ser.,* vol. 7).
Wilson, Rufus R., ed. 1798. *Heath's Memoirs of the American War.* Reprint, 1904. New York.

Whitting, Anthony (d. 1793)

Anthony Whitting first served as Washington's overseer at his Ferry and French's farms. The Englishman came with letters of recommendation from Gen. James Dickinson and U.S. congressman Lambert Cadwalader in 1790. Whitting formerly had managed the estate of Cadwalader's deceased brother but at this time was residing at Alexandria. Washington enquired into Whitting's background and gave him the gist of Cadwalader's evaluation of him. "He thinks you have a competent knowledge in the business of agriculture, and understand the economy of a farm—That he believes you to be industrious, and has no distrust of your honesty.["] Cadwalader was obliged to add, Washington also informed Whitting, that "you are too much given to your pleasures—however of the impropriety of this he hoped and believed you were convinced, and of course would reform." Washington did offer Whitting the position of farm manager in mid-April 1790, and they signed an agreement about a month later.

Whitting gradually assumed George Augustine Washington's duties as farm manager at Mount Vernon during the summer of 1792, and when Washington's nephew died the following February, Whitting took over complete management of the estate for a few months before his own death that June. Whitting received long letters of detailed instructions from Washington, who was in Philadelphia during most of this time. "I shall now briefly say," he wrote in one of them, "that the trust I have reposed in you is great, & my confidence that you will faithfully discharge it, is commensurate thereto. I am persuaded of your abilities, industry & integrity; cautioning you only, against undertaking more than you can execute *well,* under almost any circumstances; and against (but this I have no cause to suspect) being absent from your business; as example, be it good or bad, will be followed by all those who look up to you."

When writing to Washington about the health of his tubercular nephew George Augustine in August 1791, Dr. James Craik observed that he had also examined Whitting, who "tho to appearance a Stout able, well made mans I am affraid is not free from the same danger. altho he complains of no pain at present, yet he has had repeated discharges of Blood from his Lungs lately, which recur on any fit of Anger, or extraordinary exertions of the Lungs, which I am affraid may for[m] an ulcer at last." Washington expressed great concern for Whitting after learning of his illness, repeatedly urging him not to overexert and to make use of any of the household goods usually reserved for Mount Vernon's guests. Whitting's condition declined, however, and he died in June 1793. When seeking another farm manager after his death, Washington wrote that, if he could find "a man as well qualified for my purposes as the late Mr. Whitting . . . I should esteem myself very fortunate." Six months later, however, Washington had learned otherwise of Whitting. He wrote the new overseer, William Pearce, about the importance of setting a proper example for the overseers, which "unhapply this was not set (from what I have learnt lately) by Mr. Whitting, who, it is said, drank freely, kept bad company at my house and in Alexandria, and was a very debauched person."

Related entry: Mount Vernon

Suggestions for further reading:
"From George Augustine Washington," 26 March 1790 (*Pres. Ser.,* vol. 5).
"To Anthony Whitting," 14 April 1790 (*Pres. Ser.,* vol. 5).
"To William Tilghman," 21 July 1793 (*Writings,* vol. 33).

"To William Pearce," 18 December 1793
(*Writings*, vol. 33).

Wills Creek

The area around the confluence of Wills Creek, which flows through Pennsylvania and Maryland, and the Potomac River, at present-day Cumberland, Maryland, became the strategic gateway to the west when the Ohio Company established its frontier headquarters there in 1750. Across from the mouth of the creek the company built its so-called "New Store," a storehouse from which the company's operatives made surveys and located sites for future settlement. A road from Wills Creek to the Monongahela River, the first across the Allegheny Mountains fit for wheel-carriages, was begun in 1752 and completed by General Braddock's army in 1755.

Washington first camped at Wills Creek in November 1753 while on his journey to the French commandant at the Forks of the Ohio, and the following April he camped there again while making plans for the expedition ordered by Virginia governor Robert Dinwiddie to construct a fort at the Forks of the Ohio. After the battle at Great Meadows and the capitulation of Fort Necessity in July 1754, Washington marched the survivors back to Wills Creek to count their losses and tend their wounds. An exceedingly "small Stoccado Fort" subsequently was built at Wills Creek, named Camp Mount Pleasant, but a more substantial stockade was erected across from the New Store, on the western riverbank of Wills Creek, by Virginia and Maryland provincial troops in the fall of 1754. The new fort, named in honor of William Augustus, duke of Cumberland, became the "advanced staging area" for Braddock's march to Fort Duquesne in April 1755.

A detail of an eighteenth-century painting of George Washington reviewing the western troops at Fort Cumberland, Maryland (Library of Congress)

Fort Cumberland, as described by Washington, was a crude log fort on a ridge overlooking the confluence of Wills Creek and the Potomac but rendered useless by its being surrounded by several higher hills, all within cannon shot. The fort was about forty square yards, with walls ranging from nine to twelve feet high. Its bastions were equipped with nine or ten four-pounders, hardly sufficient for defense. Inside the fort stood the commander's house, two guard rooms, four storehouses, and a powder magazine. The soldiers' barracks, "ill-built" and susceptible to fire, lay outside the fort. "No person can move about the place without being seen," wrote Washington, and "any number of men can come under the banks of potomac and Will's Creek, within pistol-shot of the Barracks, and fort itself; without being exposed to a shot from cannon or small arms." Moreover, because of its remoteness, Fort Cumberland could not contribute to the protection of the inhabitants of the frontier settlements.

After Braddock's defeat in 1755 Washington became persuaded that the Virginia troops should be withdrawn from Wills Creek. Fort Cumberland, "a place very useless in itself," answered no particular purpose for Virginia other than "employing 170 men, who might be of other service elsewhere," to guard the Potomac River. In the context of Pennsylvania, Maryland, and Virginia in general, however, the fort "is of the first importance, and might answer great purposes, were it on a good spot of ground made cannon-proof, & well garrisoned." The degree of intercolonial cooperation necessary to properly fortify and sustain the area did not exist, however, and Washington eventually succeeded in turning over control of Fort Cumberland to Maryland, which in turn abandoned it in 1765.

Washington traveled to Wills Creek two other times. The first was while on the trip to his western landholdings in September 1784, accompanied by his old friend Dr. James Craik and Craik's son William, and by Washington's nephew Bushrod Washington. In his diary Washington noted little besides the effect the weather and the roads had on their travel. The following year a town was laid out near the site of the abandoned fort, officially incorporated as Cumberland in 1787. The last time Washington passed through Wills Creek was more memorable, however, for it was during his presidency, while traveling from Philadelphia to western Pennsylvania in October 1794 with the militia called to suppress the insurgents taking part in the so-called Whiskey Insurrection. Washington arrived at Cumberland before noon on 16 October, when he was met three miles outside town by three troops of light dragoons and an artillery announcement. Washington remained at Cumberland on 17 and 18 October to ascertain the strength of the troops and the adequateness of their provisions before proceeding to Bedford, where he remained for several days before returning to Philadelphia, apparently by way of Chambersburg rather than Wills Creek.

Related entries: Cresap, Thomas; Forbes Campaign; Fort Necessity Campaign; Gist, Christopher

Suggestions for further reading:
Diaries, vols. 1, 4, 6.
"To Thomas Cresap," 18 April 1754 (*Col. Ser.,* vol. 1).
"Account of the Capitulation of Fort Necessity," 1756 (*Col. Ser.,* vol. 1).
"Council of War," 30 October 1756 (*Col. Ser.,* vol. 3).

Wooden Teeth

See False Teeth.

Portrayal of the surrender of British forces by Maj. Gen. Charles O'Hara at Yorktown (Library of Congress)

Yorktown, Battle of

Lord Cornwallis's equivocal victory over Continental army and militia troops at Guilford Courthouse, North Carolina, in March 1781 resulted not in the subjection of North Carolina, as he had planned, but in a fateful decision to abandon the state for its northern neighbor, Virginia. A fruitless campaign in the spring and early summer convinced Cornwallis that the decisive event he was looking for was not to be found in central Virginia, and he began planning a major operation in the Chesapeake area, requesting reinforcements from British general Henry Clinton in New York. Cornwallis established his base at the small village of Yorktown, a thriving tobacco port on the York River thirteen miles east of the state's colonial capital, Williamsburg. Meanwhile, Washington, contemplating an attack on the British at New York City, was kept abreast of the "distressed" affairs in his home state by letters from Lafayette, who was in command of the military in the state, and Virginia governor Thomas Jefferson.

Discussions with French general Rochambeau in mid-August convinced Washington that a joint French-American operation against Cornwallis would offer the best chance for a major victory over the British. Leaving diversionary forces in New York, the two generals accordingly marched south by way of Princeton, Philadelphia, and Mount Vernon, reaching the Yorktown Peninsula in mid-September with 2,500 Continental and 4,000 French troops. French admiral François Joseph Paul, comte de Grasse (1722–1788), meanwhile, arrived in the Chesapeake Bay from the West Indies in late August with twenty-nine warships and, after wresting control from the British fleet in the bay, blocked the mouth of the York River, effectively cutting off any assistance for Cornwallis from the British fleet. With 3,000 men from the French fleet, Lafayette's force, and militia and other reinforcements, the combined allied force totaled nearly 20,000 troops (11,133 Americans and 8,800 French), more than enough to surround Yorktown and Cornwallis's entire force, numbering nearly 10,400 (8,885 land forces and approximately 1,500 seamen). Before the end of September, the allies had moved to within one mile of Cornwallis's defenses, and on 9 October they began a steady bombardment, eventually employing more than 100 pieces of artillery. British redoubts numbers 9 and 10 were simultaneously taken five days later. A gallant but futile British sortie on 16 October, led by Lt. Col. Robert Abercromby, resulted in the ineffectual spiking of a half dozen of the allies' artillery. That same night Cornwallis tried to ferry his troops across the York River in a desperate effort to escape

357

the siege, but a storm frustrated the attempt. The next day Cornwallis asked for terms, and negotiations took place on 18 October.

The surrender took place on 19 October at two o'clock in the afternoon. Brig. Gen. Charles O'Hara (d. 1802), Cornwallis's second in command, stood in for his commander, who pleaded illness. When O'Hara attempted to surrender his sword to Washington, the latter steered him to Maj. Gen. Benjamin Lincoln. The defeated British troops slowly marched through the victorious American and French armies accompanied by the "sound of music, not military marches, but of certain airs, which had in them so peculiar a strain of melancholy." Forbidden to play American tunes, the British reputedly played the tune "When the King Enjoys His Own Again," to which had been adapted "The World Turn'd Upside Down." When the surrender was over, Washington sent his aide-de-camp Tench Tilghman to Philadelphia to personally deliver the articles of capitulation to the Continental Congress. The following day, "in order to diffuse the general Joy through every Breast," Washington issued pardons to every soldier of the American army then held in confinement.

When both sides tallied up their losses, they were relatively light. The British and Hessian casualties totaled 552, including 156 killed, 326 wounded, and 70 missing; French casualties of 253 included 60 killed; and American casualties were 23 killed and 56 wounded. Although scattered fighting continued, the Battle of Yorktown was the last major battle of the Revolutionary War. Immediately after the surrender, Lord North, the British prime minister, resigned, and his successors decided that it was in Britain's best interest to end the war.

Today Yorktown Battlefield lies in and around the colonial town of Yorktown. The park contains the restored fortifications and gun emplacements of the opposing armies as well as a museum, the Yorktown Victory Center. Nine eighteenth-century buildings have survived in the town, including Cornwallis's headquarters at the house of Thomas Nelson, a signer of the Declaration of Independence, and one mile away is the restored house of Augustine Moore, where the articles of capitulation for Cornwallis's army were drafted.

Related entries: Clinton, Henry; Cornwallis, Charles, Second Earl Cornwallis; Lafayette

Suggestions for further reading:
Diaries, vol. 6.
"To Thomas McKean," 1, 12, 16, 19, 27–29 October 1781 (*Writings,* vol. 23).
"General Orders," 6, 15, 20 October 1781 (*Writings,* vol. 23).
"To Cornwallis," 17, 18 October 1781 (*Writings,* vol. 23).
"To Noah Webster," 31 July 1788 (*Con. Ser.,* vol. 6).
"Naval Operations off the Virginia Capes, Sept. 5–11, 1781" (vol. 5, appendix 4). Douglas Southall Freeman. 1948–1957. 7 vols. *George Washington: A Biography.* New York.
"The Aftermath of Yorktown" (vol. 5, appendix 5). Douglas Southall Freeman. 1948–1957. 7 vols. *George Washington: A Biography.* New York.
Johnston, Henry P. 1881. *The Yorktown Campaign and the Surrender of Cornwallis, 1781.* New York.

Young, Arthur (1741–1820)

About 1785 Washington began a correspondence with Arthur Young, the English agriculturalist and author and editor of a periodical called the *Annals of Agriculture.* Already convinced of the superiority of the English system of husbandry, the correspondence and the *Annals* gave Washington ideas for his ongoing agricultural pursuits at Mount Vernon, including experimenting with crop rotation, introducing new crops, and erecting new barns. In addition to offering Washington advice on farming matters,

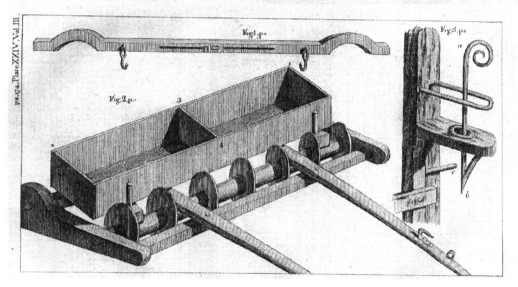

Plates from Arthur Young's **Farmer's Tour through the East of England,** *London, 1771 (University of Virginia)*

Young sent Washington seeds for plants unknown in America, a plow, and a plan for a rectangular brick barn and stable complex, which Washington erected at Mount Vernon, with some modifications, between 1788 and 1791. The barn, said Washington, was "equal, perhaps, to any in America, and for conveniences of all sorts, particularly for sheltering and feeding horses, cattle, &c. scarcely to be exceeded any where." The plan for Washington's brick barn and barnyard was in fact engraved in the *Annals.* Young published some of his correspondence with Washington shortly after Washington's death.

Related entries: The Two James Andersons; Mount Vernon

Suggestion for further reading:
Diaries, vols. 1, 4, 5.

The following selections from Washington's writings, arranged in chronological order, represent a tiny fraction of the approximately 135,000 documents that comprise his papers. The location and date under each title indicate where and when Washington wrote the document, if known.

Rules of Civility and Decent Behaviour in Company and Conversation
c.1642

The origin of these maxims, found in Washington's school exercises and long identified with him because they were so fully exemplified in his life, has been traced all the way back to Reformation Europe. Washington's version of the rules apparently was based on a seventeenth-century English-language edition of the rules that had been translated from an even earlier French version by Francis Hawkins of London.

Rules of Civility & Decent Behaviour In Company and Conversation

1st Every Action done in Company, ought to be with Some Sign of Respect, to those that are Present.

2d When in Company, put not your Hands to any Part of the Body, not usualy Discovered.

3d Shew Nothing to your Freind that may affright him.

4 In the Presence of Others Sing not to yourself with a humming Noise, nor Drum with your Fingers or Feet.

5th If You Cough, Sneeze, Sigh, or Yawn, do it not Loud but Privately; and Speak not in your Yawning, but put Your handkerchief or Hand before your face and turn aside.

6th Sleep not when others Speak, Sit not when others stand, Speak not when you Should hold your Peace, walk not on when others Stop.

7th Put not off your Cloths in the presence of Others, nor go out your Chamber half Drest

8th At Play and at Fire its Good manners to Give Place to the last Commer, and affect not to Speak Louder than Ordinary.

9th Spit not in the Fire, nor Stoop low before it neither Put your Hands into the Flames to warm them, nor Set your Feet upon the Fire especially if there be meat before it.

10th When you Sit down, Keep your Feet firm and Even, without putting one on the other or Crossing them.

11th Shift not yourself in the Sight of others nor Gnaw your nails.

12th Shake not the head, Feet, or Legs rowl not the Eys lift not one eyebrow higher than the other wry not the mouth, and bedew no mans face with your Spittle, by approaching too near him when you Speak.

13th Kill no Vermin as Fleas, lice ticks &c in the Sight of Others, if you See any filth or thick Spittle put your foot Dexteriously upon it if it be upon the Cloths of your Companions, Put it off privately, and if it be upon your own Cloths return Thanks to him who puts it off.

14th Turn not your Back to others especially in Speaking, Jog not the Table or Desk on which Another reads or writes, lean not upon any one.

15th Keep your Nails clean and Short, also your Hands and Teeth Clean yet without Shewing any great Concern for them.

16th Do not Puff up the Cheeks, Loll not out the tongue rub the Hands, or beard, thrust out the lips, or bite them or keep the Lips too open or too Close.

17th Be no Flatterer, neither Play with any that delights not to be Play'd Withal.

18th Read no Letters, Books, or Papers in Company but when there is a Necessity for the doing of it you must ask leave: come not near the Books or Writings of Another so as to read them unless desired or give your opinion of them unask'd also look not nigh when another is writing a Letter.

19th Let your Countenance be pleasant but in Serious Matters Somewhat grave.

20th The Gestures of the Body must be Suited to the discourse you are upon.

21st Reproach none for the Infirmaties of Nature, nor Delight to Put them that have in mind thereof.

22d Shew not yourself glad at the Misfortune of another though he were your enemy.

23d When you see a Crime punished, you may be inwardly Pleased; but always shew Pity to the Suffering Offender.

24th Do not laugh too loud or too much at any Publick Spectacle.

25th Superfluous Complements and all Affectation of Ceremonie are to be avoided, yet where due they are not to be Neglected.

26th In Pulling off your Hat to Persons of Distinction, as Noblemen, Justices, Churchmen &c make a Reverence, bowing more or less according to the Custom of the Better Bred, and Quality of the Person. Amongst your equals expect not always that they Should begin with you first, but to Pull off the Hat when there is no need is Affectation, in the Manner of Saluting and resaluting in words keep to the most usual Custom.

27th Tis ill manners to bid one more eminent than yourself be covered as well as not to do it to whom it's due Likewise he that makes too much haste to Put on his hat does not well, yet he ought to Put it on at the first, or at most the Second time of being ask'd; now what is herein Spoken, of Qualification in behaviour in Saluting, ought also to be observed in taking of Place, and Sitting down for ceremonies without Bounds is troublesome.

28th If any one come to Speak to you while you are are Sitting Stand up tho he be your Inferiour, and when you Present Seats let it be to every one according to his Degree.

29th When you meet with one of Greater Quality than yourself, Stop, and retire especially if it be at a Door or any Straight place to give way for him to Pass.

30th In walking the highest Place in most Countrys Seems to be on the right hand therefore Place yourself on the left of him whom you desire to Honour: but if three walk together the middest Place is the most Honourable the wall is usually given to the most worthy if two walk together.

31st If any one far Surpasses others, either in age, Estate, or Merit yet would give Place to a meaner than himself in his own lodging or elsewhere the one ought not to except it, So he on the other part should not use much earnestness nor offer it above once or twice.

32d To one that is your equal, or not much inferior you are to give the cheif Place in your Lodging and he to who 'tis offered ought at the first to refuse it but at the Second to accept though not without acknowledging his own unworthiness.

33d They that are in Dignity or in office have in all places Preceedency but whilst they are Young they ought to respect those that are their equals in Birth or other Qualitys, though they have no Publick charge.

34th It is good Manners to prefer them to whom we Speak before ourselves especially if they be above us with whom in no Sort we ought to begin.

35th Let your Discourse with Men of Business be Short and Comprehensive.

36th Artificers & Persons of low Degree ought not to use many ceremonies to Lords, or Others of high Degree but Respect and highly Honour them, and those of high Degree ought to treat them with affibility & Courtesie, without Arrogancy.

37th In Speaking to men of Quality do not lean nor Look them full in the Face, nor approach too near them at lest Keep a full Pace from them.

38th In visiting the Sick, do not Presently play the Physicion if you be not Knowing therein.

39th In writing or Speaking, give to every Person his due Title According to his Degree & the Custom of the Place.

40th Strive not with your Superiers in argument, but always Submit your Judgment to others with Modesty.

41st Undertake not to Teach your equal in the art himself Proffesses; it Savours of arrogancy.

42d Let thy ceremonies in Courtesie be proper to the Dignity of his place with whom thou conversest for it is absurd to act the same with a Clown and a Prince.

43d Do not express Joy before one sick or in pain for that contrary Passion will aggravate his Misery.

44th When a man does all he can though it Succeeds not well blame not him that did it.

45th Being to advise or reprehend any one, consider whether it ought to be in publick or in Private; presently, or at Some other time in what terms to do it & in reproving Shew no Sign of Cholar but do it with all Sweetness and Mildness.

46th Take all Admonitions thankfully in what Time or Place Soever given but afterwards not being culpable take a Time & Place convenient to let him him know it that gave them.

47th Mock not nor Jest at any thing of Importance break no Jest that are Sharp Biting and if you Deliver any thing witty and Pleasent abstain from Laughing thereat yourself.

48th Wherein you reprove Another be unblameable yourself; for example is more prevalent than Precepts.

49 Use no Reproachfull Language against any one neither Curse nor Revile.

50th Be not hasty to beleive flying Reports to the Disparagement of any.

51st Wear not your Cloths, foul, unript or Dusty but See they be Brush'd once every day at least and take heed that you approach not to any uncleaness.

52d In your Apparel be Modest and endeavour to accomodate Nature, rather than to procure Admiration keep to the Fashion of your equals Such as are Civil and orderly with respect to Times and Places.

53d Run not in the Streets, neither go too slowly nor with Mouth open go not Shaking yr Arms kick not the earth with yr feet, go not upon the Toes, nor in a Dancing fashion.

54th Play not the Peacock, looking every where about you, to See if you be well Deck't, if your Shoes fit well if your Stokings Sit neatly, and Cloths handsomely.

55th Eat not in the Streets, nor in the House, out of Season.

56th Associate yourself with Men of good Quality if you Esteem your own Reputation; for 'tis better to be alone than in bad Company.

57th In walking up and Down in a House, only with One in Company if he be Greater than yourself, at the first give him the Right hand and Stop not till he does and be not the first that turns, and when you do turn let it be with your face towards him, if he be a Man of Great Quality, walk not with him Cheek by Joul but Somewhat behind him; but yet in Such a Manner that he may easily Speak to you.

58th Let your Conversation be without Malice or Envy, for 'tis a Sign of a Tractable and Commendable Nature: And in all Causes of Passion admit Reason to Govern.

59th Never express anything unbecoming, nor Act agst the Rules Moral before your inferiours.

60th Be not immodest in urging your Freinds to Discover a Secret.

61st Utter not base and frivilous things amongst grave and Learn'd Men nor very Difficult Questians or Subjects, among the Ignorant or things hard to be believed, Stuff not your Discourse with Sentences amongst your Betters nor Equals.

62d Speak not of doleful Things in a Time of Mirth or at the Table; Speak not of Melancholy Things as Death and Wounds, and if others Mention them Change if you can the Discourse tell not your Dreams, but to your intimate Friend.

63d A Man ought not to value himself of his Atchievements, or rare Qualities of wit; much less of his riches Virtue or Kindred.

64th Break not a Jest where none take pleasure in mirth Laugh not aloud, nor at all without Occasion, deride no mans Misfortune, tho' there seem to be Some cause.

65th Speak not injurious Words neither in Jest nor Earnest Scoff at none although they give Occasion.

66th Be not forward but friendly and Courteous; the first to Salute hear and answer & be not Pensive when it's a time to Converse.

67th Detract not from others neither be excessive in Commanding.

68th Go not thither, where you know not, whether you Shall be Welcome or not. Give not Advice whth being Ask'd & when desired do it briefly.

69 If two contend together take not the part of either unconstrained; and be not obstinate in your own Opinion, in Things indiferent be of the Major Side.

70th Reprehend not the imperfections of others for that belongs to Parents Masters and Superiours.

71st Gaze not on the marks or blemishes of Others and ask not how they came. What you may Speak in Secret to your Friend deliver not before others.

72d Speak not in an unknown Tongue in Company but in your own Language and that as those of Quality do and not as the Vulgar; Sublime matters treat Seriously.

73d Think before you Speak pronounce not imperfectly nor bring out your Words too hastily but orderly & distinctly.

74th When Another Speaks be attentive your Self and disturb not the Audience if any hesitate in his Words help him not nor Prompt him without desired, Interrupt him not, nor Answer him till his Speech be ended.

75th In the midst of Discourse ask not of what one treateth but if you Perceive any Stop because of your coming you may well intreat him gently to Proceed: If a Person of Quality comes in while your Conversing it's handsome to Repeat what was said before.

76th While you are talking, Point not with your Finger at him of Whom you Discourse nor Approach too near him to whom you talk especially to his face.

77th Treat with men at fit Times about Business & Whisper not in the Company of Others.

78th Make no Comparisons and if any of the Company be Commended for any brave act of Vertue, commend not another for the Same.

79th Be not apt to relate News if you know not the truth thereof. In Discoursing of things you Have heard Name not your Author always A Secret Discover not.

80th Be not Tedious in Discourse or in reading unless you find the Company pleased therewith.

81st Be not Curious to Know the Affairs of Others neither approach those that Speak in Private.

82d Undertake not what you cannot Perform but be Carefull to keep your Promise.

83d When you deliver a matter do it without Passion & with Discretion, however mean the Person be you do it too.

84th When your Superiours talk to any Body hearken not neither Speak nor Laugh.

85th In Company of these of Higher Quality than yourself Speak not till you are ask'd a Question then Stand upright put of your Hat & Answer in few words.

86 In Disputes, be not So Desireous to Overcome as not to give Liberty to each one to deliver his Opinion and Submit to the Judgment of the Major Part especially if they are Judges of the Dispute.

87th Let thy carriage be such as becomes a Man Grave Settled and attentive to that which is spoken. Contradict not at every turn what others Say.

88th Be not tedious in Discourse, make not many Digressions, nor repeat often the Same manner of Discourse.

89th Speak not Evil of the absent for it is unjust.

90 Being Set at meat Scratch not neither Spit Cough or blow your Nose except there's a Necessity for it.

91st Make no Shew of taking great Delight in your Victuals, Feed not with Greediness; cut your Bread with a Knife, lean not on the Table neither find fault with what you Eat.

92d Take no Salt or cut Bread with your Knife Greasy.

93 Entertaining any one at table it is decent to present him wt. meat, Undertake not to help others undesired by the Master.

94th If you Soak bread in the Sauce let it be no more than what you put in your Mouth at a time and blow not your broth at Table but Stay till Cools of it Self.

95th Put not your meat to your Mouth with your Knife in your hand neither Spit forth the Stones of any fruit Pye upon a Dish nor Cast anything under the table.

96 It's unbecoming to Stoop much to ones Meat Keep your Fingers clean & when foul wipe them on a Corner of your Table Napkin.

97th Put not another bit into your Mouth til the former be Swallowed let not your Morsels be too big for the Gowls.

98th Drink not nor talk with your mouth full neither Gaze about you while you are Drinking.

99th Drink not too leisurely nor yet too hastily. Before and after Drinking wipe your Lips breath not then or Ever with too Great a Noise, for its uncivil.

100 Cleanse not your teeth with the Table Cloth Napkin Fork or Knife but if Others do it let it be done wt. a Pick Tooth.

101st Rince not your Mouth in the Presence of Others.

102d It is out of use to call upon the Company often to Eat nor need you Drink to others every Time you Drink.

103d In Company of your Betters be not longer in eating than they are lay not your Arm but only your hand upon the table.

104th It belongs to the Chiefest in Company to unfold his Napkin and fall to Meat first, But he ought then to Begin in time & to Dispatch with Dexterity that the Slowest may have time allowed him.

105th Be not Angry at Table whatever happens & if you have reason to be so, Shew it not but on a Chearfull Countenance especially if there be Strangers for Good Humour makes one Dish of Meat a Feast.

106th Set not yourself at the upper of the Table but if it be your Due or that the Master of the house will have it So, Contend not, least you Should Trouble the Company.

107th If others talk at Table be attentive but talk not with Meat in your Mouth.

108th When you Speak of God or his Atributes, let it be Seriously & with Reverence. Honour & Obey your Natural Parents altho they be Poor.

109th Let your Recreations be Manfull not Sinfull.

110th Labour to keep alive in your Breast that Little Spark of Celestial fire Called Conscience.

Finis

To Lawrence Washington
5 May 1749

This is the earliest of Washington's letters known to have survived. It concerns his half brother Lawrence's decision to sail for England in search of medical advice about his deteriorating health, brought on by tuberculosis, his mother's imminent removal from Westmoreland County to King George County, and the possible effects of a proposed change in the ferry service across the Rappahannock River at Ferry Farm, Washington's boyhood home near Fredericksburg, Virginia.

Dear Brother

I hope your Cough is much mended Since I saw you last, if so likewise hope you have given over the thoughts of leaving Virginia.

As there is not an absolute occasion of my coming down, hope you'l get the Deeds acknowledged without Me; my Horse is in very poor order to undertake such a journey, and is in no likelihood of mending for want of Corn sufficient to support him; tho' if there be any certainty in the Assembly's not rising untill the latter end of May, will if I can be down by that; As my Mothers term of Years is out at that Place at Bridge Creek, she designs to Settle a Quarter on that Peice at Deep Run, but seems backward of doing it untill the Right is made good, for fear of accidents.

It's Reported here that Mr Spotswood intends to put down the Ferry that is kept at the Wharf where he now Lives, and that Major

Frans Talliaferro intends to petition the Assembly for an Act to have it kept from his House over against my Mothers Quarter, and right through the very Heart and best of the Land; whereas he can have no other view in it but for the Conveniencey of a small Mill he has on the Water side, that will not Grind above three Months in the twelve, and the great inconveniency and prejudice it will be to us, hope it will not be granted; besides, I do not see where he can Possibly have a Landing Place on his side that will ever be Sufficient for a Lawful Landing (by reason of the steepness of the Banks;) I think we suffer enough with the Free Ferry, without being troubled with such an unjust and iniquitious Petition as that, but hope as its only a flying report he will consider better of it and drop his pretentions. I should be glad (if its not too much trouble) to hear from you in the mean while remain with my Love to my Sister Dear sir Your Affectionate Brother

George Washington

To Robin
c. 1749–1750

This early letter is one of three in which Washington refers to being cheered as well as distracted from the painful memory of an unnamed "Low Land Beauty" by Mary Cary (1733–1781), the sister of Sarah Cary Fairfax (c. 1730–1811), the wife of his close friend George William Fairfax (1724–1787). Robin may be Washington's cousin Robert Washington (b. 1730) of Chotank in Stafford County, Virginia, whom Washington remembered in his will with Robert's brother Lawrence as "the acquaintances and friends of my Juvenile years."

Dear Friend Robin

As its the greatest mark of friendship and esteem absent Friends can shew each other in Writing and often communicating their thoughts to his fellow companions makes me endeavour to signalize myself in acquainting you from time to time and at all times my situation and employments of Life and could Wish you would take half the Pains of contriving me a Letter by any oppertunity as you may be well assured of its meeting with a very welcome reception my Place of Residence is at present at his Lordships where I might was my heart disengag'd pass my time very pleasantly as theres a very agreeable Young Lady Lives in the same house (Colo. George Fairfax's Wife's sister) but as thats only adding Fuel to fire it makes me the more uneasy for by often and unavoidably being in Company with her revives my former Passion for your Low Land Beauty whereas was I to live more retired from yound Women I might in some measure eliviate my sorrows by burying that chast and troublesome Passion in the grave of oblivion or etarnall forgetfulness for as I am very well assured that's the only antidote or remedy that I ever shall be releivd by or only recess than can administer any cure or help to me as I am well convinced was I ever to attempt any thing I should only get a denial which would be only adding grief to uneasiness.

Memorandum
c. 1749–1750
Washington wrote this undated memorandum in the notebook that contains his diary entries for the surveying trip that he made for Lord Fairfax beginning in 1749.

Memorandom to have my Coat made by the following Directions to be made a Frock with a Lapel Breast the Lapel to Contain on each side six Button Holes and to be about 5 or 6 Inches wide all the way equal and to turn as the Breast on the Coat does to have it made very Long Waisted and in Length to come down to or below the Bent of the knee the Waist from the armpit to the Fold to be exactly as long or Longer than from thence to the Bottom not to have more than one fold in the Skirt and the top to be made just to turn in and three Button Holes the Lapel at the top to turn as the Cape of the Coat and Bottom to Come Parrallel with the Button Holes the Last Button hole in the Breast to be right opposite to the Button on the Hip.

To Richard Corbin
c. February–March 1754
Washington apparently wrote this letter after receiving his commission as major of the regiment formed for an expedition to the Ohio Country, which Corbin, a member of the governor's council, apparently had forwarded to him in late February 1754. Virginia governor Robert Dinwiddie sent Washington a lieutenant colonel's commission in mid-March 1754.

Dear Sir:

In a conversation at Green Spring you gave me some room to hope for a commission above that of a Major, and to be ranked among the chief officers of this expedition. The command of the whole forces is what I neither look for, expect, nor desire; for I must be impartial enough to confess, it is a charge too great for my youth and inexperience to be intrusted with. Knowing this, I have too sincere a love for my country, to undertake that which may tend to the prejudice of it. But if I could entertain hopes that you thought me worthy of the post of Lieutenant-colonel, and would favour me so far as to mention it at the appointment of officers, I could not but entertain a true sense of the kindness.

I flatter myself that under a skilful commander, or man of sense, (which I most sincerely wish to serve under,) with my own application and diligent study of my duty, I shall be able to conduct my steps without censure, and in time, render myself worthy of the promotion that I shall be favoured with now.

To Robert Dinwiddie
Great Meadows, Pennsylvania, 29 May 1754
Washington opens this letter with a lengthy discussion of his grievances concerning his pay as an officer in the Virginia Regiment. He then gives accounts of his meeting with the Seneca chief Half-King and of the Virginia Regiment's recent engagement with the French, in which Joseph Coulon de Villiers, sieur de Jumonville, was killed.

Honble Sir

To answer your Honour's Letter of the 25th by Mr Birney—I shall begin with assuring you, that nothing was farther from my intention than to recede, thô I then pressd and still desire that my Services may be voluntary rather than on the present Pay—I am much concernd that your Honour should seem to charge me with ingratitude for your generous, and my undeserved favours, for I assure you Honble Sir, nothing is a greater stranger to my Breast, or a Sin that my Soul more abhor's than that black and detestable one Ingratitude. I retain a true Sense of your kindness, and want nothing but oppertunity to give testimony of my willingness to oblige as far as my Life or fortune will extend.

I cou'd not object to the Pay before I knew it. I dare say your Honour remembers the first Estimation allowed a Lieutt Colo. 15/ and Majr 12/6 which I then complained very much off; till your Honour assurd me that we were to be furnish'd with proper necessary's and offerd that as a reason why the pay was Less than British: after this when you were so kind to preferr me to the Comn I now have, and at the same time acquainted me that I was to have but 12/6— This, with some other Reason's induced me to acquaint Colo. Fairfax with my intention of Resigning, which he must well remember as it happd at Belhaven; and was there that he disswaded me from it and promised to represent the trifling pay to your Honour, who would endeavour (as I at the same time told him that the Speaker thought the Officr's pay too small) to have it enlarg'd.

As to the Number's that applied for Commission's and to whom we were preffer'd; I believe, had those Gentlemen been as knowing of this Country, and as Sensible of the difficulties that would attend a Campaign here as I then was—I concive your Honour wd not have been so troublesomly sollicited as you were; yet, I do not offer this as a reason for quitting the Service. for my own part I can answer, I have a Constitution hardy enough to encounter and undergo the most severe tryals, and I flatter myself resolution to Face what any Man durst, as shall be prov'd when it comes to the Test, which I believe we are upon the Border's off.

There is nothing Sir (I believe) more certain than that the Officer's on the Canada Expedition had British pay allowd, whilst they were in the Service, Lieutt Wag[gene]r Captn Trent, and several other's whom I have conversed with on tht Head, and were engagd in it, affirm it for truth: therefore Honble Sir, as this can't be allow'd; suffer me to serve a Volunteer which I assure you will be the next reward to British pay, for As my Services, so far as I have knowledge will equal those of the best Officer, I make it a point of Honr to serve for less and accept a medium.

Nevertheless, I have communicated your Honour's Sentiments to them; and as far as I could put on the Hipocrite, set forth the advantages that may accrue, and advis'd them to accept the Terms, as a refusal might reflect dishonour upon their Character; leaving it to the World to assign what reason's they please for quitting the Service—I am very sensible of the pernicious consequence that will attend their resigning, as they have by this gain'd some experience of the Military Art, have a tolerable knowledge of the Country, being sent most of them out at different times with partys: and now are accustom'd to the hardships and fatiegue of Living as we do, which I believe were it truely stated, wd prevent your Honour from many troublesome Sollicitations from others for Comns[.] This last motive, has, and will induce me to do what I can to reconcile matter's; thô I really believe there is some tht will not remain long witht an alteration.

They have promis'd to consider of it, and give your Honour an answer. I was not ignorant of the allowe which Colo. Fry has for his Table, but being a dependt there myself deprives me of the pleasure of inviting an Officer or Friend, which to me wd be more agreeable than the Nick Nacks I shall meet with there.

And here I cannot forbear answering one thing more in your Honrs Letter on this head; which (too) is more fully express'd in a paragraph of Colo. Fairfax's to me as follows "If on the British Establishment Officer's are allowd more Pay, the Regimentals they are oblig'd annually to furnish, their necessary Table and other Incidents being considerd, little or no savings will be their Portion"—I believe it is well known we have been at the expence of the Regimentals (and it is still better known,[)] that Regimentals, and every other necessary that we were under an indispensable necessity of purchasing or this Expedition, were not to be bought for less Virga curr[enc]y, than British Officer's cd get for sterling money; which they ought to have been, to put us upon a parity in this respect, then Colo. Fairfax observes that their Table and other Incident charges prevents them frm saving much: if they dont save much, they have the enjoyment of their Pay which we neither have in one sense nor the other: We are debarr'd the pleasure of good Living, which Sir (I dare say with me you will concur) to one who has always been used to it; must go somewhat hard to be confin'd to a little salt provision and Water: and do duty, hard, laborious duty that is almost inconsistent with that of a Soldier, and yet have the same Reductions as if we were allowd luxuriously: My Pay accordg to the British

Establisht & common exchange is near 22/ pr Day, in the R[oo]m of that the Committee (for I can't in the least imagine yr Hr had any h[an]d in it) has provided 12/6 so long as the Service requires me, whereas, one half of the other is ascertain'd to the British Officer's forever: now if we shd be fortunate enough to drive the French from Ohio—as far as your Honour wd please have them sent to—in any short time, our Pay will not be sufficient to discharge our first expences.

I would not have your Honour imagine from this, that I have said all these things to have the Pay encreas'd—but to justify myself, and shew your Honour that our complaints are not frivolous, but are founded upon strict Reason: for my own part, it is a matter almost indefferent whether I serve for full pay, or as a generous Volunteer; indeed, did my circumstances corrispond with my Inclination, I shd not hesitate a moment to prefer the Latter: for the motives that lead me here were pure and Noble I had no view of acquisition but that of Honour, by serving faithfully my King and Country.

As your Honour has recommended Mr Willis you may depend I shall with pleasure do all that I can for him.

But above all Sir, you may depend I shall take all possible means of procureing intelligence, and guarding against surprises, and be assur'd nothing but very unequal number's shall engage me to submit or Retreat.

Now Sir, as I have answer'd your Honour's Letters I shall beg leave to acqt you with what has happen'd since I wrote by Mr Gist; I then acquainted you that I had detach'd a party of 75 Men to meet with 50 of the French who we had Intelligence were upon their March towards us to Reconnoitre &ca[.] Abt 9 Oclock the same Night, I receivd an express from the Half King who was Incampd with several of His People abt 6 Miles of, that he had seen the Tract of two French Men xing the Road and believ'd the whole body were lying not far off, as he had an acct of that number passing Mr Gist—I set out with 40 Men before 10, and was from that time till near Sun rise before we reach'd the Indian's Camp, havg Marched in small path, & heavy Rain, and a Night as Dark as it is possible to concieve—we were frequently tumbling one over another, and often so lost that 15 or 20 Minutes search would not find the path again.

When we came to the Half King I council'd with him, and got his assent to go hand in hand and strike the French. accordingly, himself, Monacatoocha, and a few other Indians set out with us, and when we came to the place where the Tracts were, cover their lodgment which they did abt half a mile from the Road in a very obscure place surrounded with Rocks. I thereupon in conjuction with Half King & Monacatoocha, formd a disposion to attack them on all sides, which we accordingly did and after an Engagement of abt 15 Minutes we killd 10, wounded one and took 21 Prisoner's, amongst those that were killd was Monsieur De Jumonville the Commander, Principl Officers taken is Monsieur Druillong and Monsr Laforc, who your Honour has often heard me speak of as a bold Enterprising Man, and a person of gt subtilty and cunning with these are two Cadets—These Officers pretend they were coming on an Embassy, but the absurdity of this pretext is too glaring as your Honour will see by the Instructions and summons inclos'd: There Instructions wre to reconnoitre the Country, Roads, Creeks &ca to Potomac; which they were abt to do, These Enterpriseing Men were purposely choose out to get intelligence, which they were to send Back by some brisk dispatches with mention of the Day that they were to serve the Summon's; which could be through no other view, than to get sufficient Reinforcements to fall upon us imediately after. This with several other Reasons induc'd all the Officers to beleive firmly that they were sent as spys rather than any thing else, and has occasiond my sending them as prisoners, tho they expected (or at least had some faint hope of being continued as ambassadors) They finding where we were Incamp'd, instead of coming up in a Publick manner sought out one of the most secret Retirements; fitter for a Deserter than an Ambassador to incamp in—s[t]ayd there two or 3 days sent Spies to Reconnoitre our Camp as we are told, tho they deny it—Their whole Body movd back near 2 Miles, sent off two runnors to acquaint Contracoeur with our strength, and where we were Incamp'd &ca now 36 Men wd almost have been a Retinue for a Princely Ambassador, instead of Petit, why did they, if there design's were open stay so long within 5 Miles of us witht delivering his Ambassy, or acquainting me with it; his waiting cd be with no other design than to get Detachts to enforce the Summons as soon as it was given, they had no occasion to send out Spy's; for the Name of Ambassador is Sacred among all Nations; but it was by the Tract of these Spy's they were discoverd, and we got Intilligence of them—They wd not have retird two Miles back witht delivering the Summons and sought a sculking place (which to do them justice was done with gt Judgment) but for some especial reason: Besides The Summon's is so insolent, & savour's so much of Gascoigny that if two Men only had come openly to deliver it. It was too great Indulgence to have sent them back.

The Sense of the Half King on this Subject is, that they have bad Hearts, and that this is a mere pretence, they never designd to have come to us but in a hostile manner, and if we were so foolish as to let them go again, he never would assist us in taking another of them[.] Besides, looseing La Force I really think wd tend more to our disservice than 50 other Men, as he is a person whose active Spirit, leads him into all parlys, and brought him acquainted with all parts, add to this a perfect use of the Indian Tongue, and gt influence with the Indian He Ingenuously enough confessed that as soon as he saw the commission & Instructions that he believd and then said he expected some such tendency tho he pretends to say he does not believe the Commander had any other but a good design.

In this Engagement we had only one Man killd, and two or three wounded, among which was Lieut Waggener slightly—a most miraculous escape, as Our Right Wing was much exposd to their Fire and receivd it all.

The Half King receiv'd your Honour's speech very kind: but desird me to inform you that he could not leave his People at this time, thinking them in great Danger—He is now gone to the xing for their Familys to bring to our Camp & desird I wd send some Men and Horses to assist them up; which I have accordingly done—sent 30 Men & upwards of 20 Horses. He say's if your Honr has any thing to say you may communicate by me &ca; and that if you have a present for them it may be kept to another occasion, after sending up some things for their imediate use, He has declar'd to send these Frenchmens Scalps with a Hatchet to all the Nations of Indian's in union with them, and did that very day give a Hatchet and a large Belt of Wampum to a Delaware Man to carry to Shingiss: he promis'd me to send down the River for all the Mingo's & Shawnesse to our camp, where I expect him to Morrow with 30 or 40 Men with their wives & Children, to confirm what he has said here, he has sent your Honour a String of Wampum.

As these Runnors went of to the Fort on Sunday last, I shall expect every hour to be attackd and by unequal number's, which I must withstand if there is 5 to 1 or else I fear the Consequence will be we shall loose the Indians if we suffer ourselves to be drove Back, I dispatchd an express imediately to Colo. Fry with this Intelligence desiring him to send me Reinforcements with all imaginable dispatch.

Your Honour may depend I will not be surprizd, let them come what hour they will—and this is as much as I can promise—but my best endeavour's shall not be wanting to deserve more, I doubt not but if you hear I am beaten, but you will at the same hear that we have done our duty in fighting as long there was a possibility of hope.

I have sent Lieutt West accompanied with Mr Sprilldorph & a Guard of 20 Men to conduct the Prisoners in, and I believe the Officer's have acquainted him what answer to return yr Honour.

Monsiur La-Force, and Monsieur Druillong beg to be recommend to your Honour's Notice, and I have promis'd they will meet with all the favours that's due to Imprison'd Officer's: I have shew'd all the respect I cou'd to them here, and have given some necessary cloathing by which I have disfurnish'd myself, for having brought no more than two or three Shirts from Wills Ck that we might be light I was ill provided to furnish them I am Yr Honour's most Obt Hble Servt

Go: Washington

NB I have neither seen nor heard any particular acct of the Twigtwees since I came on these Water's, we have already began a Palisadod Fort and hope to have it up tomorrow I must beg leave to acqt yr honor tht Captn Vanbraam & Monsr Peyrouney has behav'd extreamely well since they came out—& I hope will meet with yr Honrs favr.

Account of the Capitulation of Fort Necessity

Williamsburg, Virginia, 19 July 1754

This account of the defeat of the Virginia Regiment at Great Meadows, Pennsylvania, by the French force under the command of Louis Coulon de Villiers on 9 July 1754 appeared in the Williamsburg Virginia Gazette ten days later and is preceded by the following sentence: "On Wednesday last arrived in Town, Colonel George Washington and Captain James Maccay, who gave the following Account to his Honour the Governor, of the late Action between them and the French, at the Great Meadows in the Western Parts of this Dominion." James Mackay (d. 1785), captain of a South Carolina independent company serving in the British army, had joined Washington at Great Meadows in June.

The third of this Instant July, about 9 o'-Clock, we received Intelligence that the French, having been reinforced with 700 Recruits, had left Monongehela, and were in full March with 900 Men to attack us. Upon this, as our Numbers were so unequal, (our whole Force not exceeding 300) we prepared for our Defence in the best Manner we could, by throwing up a small Intrenchment, which we had not Time to perfect, before our Centinel gave Notice, about Eleven o'Clock, of their Approach, by firing his Piece, which he did at the Enemy, and as we learned afterwards killed three of their Men, on which they began to fire upon us, at about 600 Yards Distance, but without any Effect: We immediately called our Men to their Arms, and drew up in Order before our Trenches; but as we looked upon this distant Fire of the Enemy only as an Artifice to intimidate, or draw our Fire from us, we waited their nearer Approach before we returned their Salute. They then advanced in a very irregular Manner to another Point of Woods, about 60 Yards off, and from thence made a second Discharge; upon which, finding they had no Intention of attacking us in the open Field, we retired into our Trenches, and still reserved our Fire; as we expected from their great Superiority of Numbers, that they would endeavour to force our Trenches; but finding they did not seem to intend this neither, the Colonel gave orders to fire, which was done with great Alacrity and Undauntedness. We continued this unequal Fight, with an Enemy sheltered behind the Trees, ourselves without Shelter, in Trenches full of Water, in a settled Rain, and the Enemy galling us on all Sides incessantly from the Woods, till 8 o'Clock at Night, when the French called to Parley: From the great Improbability that such a vastly superior Force, and possessed of such an Advantage, would offer a Parley first, we suspected a Deceit, and therefore refused to consent that they should come among us; on which they desired us to send an Officer to them, and engaged their Parole for his Safety; we then sent Capt. Van Braam, and Mr. Peyronee, to receive their Proposals, which they did, and about Midnight we agreed that each Side should retire without Molestation, they back to their Fort at Monongehela, and we to Wills's Creek: That we should march away with all the Honours of War, and with all our Stores, Effects and Baggage. Accordingly the next Morning, with our Drums beating and our Colours flying, we began our March in good Order, with our Stores, &c. in Convoy; but we were interrupted by the Arrival of a Reinforcement of 100 Indians among the French, who were hardly restrained from attacking us, and did us considerable Damage by pilfering our Baggage. We then proceeded, but soon found it necessary to leave our Baggage and Stores; the great Scarcity of our Provisions obliged us to use the utmost Expedition, and having neither Waggons nor Horses to transport them. The Enemy had deprived us of all our Creatures; by killing, in the Beginning of the Engagement, our Horses, Cattle, and every living Thing they could, even to the very Dogs. The Number of the Killed on our Side was thirty, and seventy wounded; among the former was Lieutenant Mercier, of Captain Maccay's independent Company; a Gentleman of true military Worth, and whose Bravery would not permit him to retire, though dangerously wounded, till a second Shot disabled him, and a third put an End to his Life, as he was carrying to the Surgeon. Our Men behaved with singular Intrepidity, and we determined not to ask for Quarter, but with out Bayonets screw'd, to sell our Lives as dearly as possibly we could. From the Numbers of the Enemy, and our Situation, we could not hope for Victory; and from the Character of those we had to encounter, we expected no Mercy, but on Terms that we positively resolved not to submit to.

The Number killed and wounded of the Enemy is uncertain, but by the Information given by some Dutch in their Service to their Countrymen in ours, we learn that it amounted to above three hundred; and we are induced to believe it must be very considerable, by their being busy all Night in burying their Dead, and yet many remained the next Day; and their Wounded we know was considerable, by one of our Men, who had been made Prisoner by them after signing the Articles, and who, on his Return told us, that he saw great Numbers much wounded and carried off upon Litters.

We were also told by some of their Indians after the Action, that the French had an Officer of distinguishable Rank killed. Some considerable Blow they must have received, to induce them to call first for a Parley, knowing, as they perfectly did, the Circumstances we were in.

Notes on the Navigation of the Potomac River above the Great Falls
July–August 1754

Washington made the canoe trip discussed in this selection shortly after reporting to Williamsburg, Virginia, following the Virginia Regiment's defeat by the French at Great Meadows in western Pennsylvania. The seventy-six-foot drop of the Great Falls of the Potomac River impeded navigation of the river until February 1802, when the Potomac Company opened a series of locks and canals enabling vessels to bypass it. Washington describes in his diaries a similar trip that he made along the same route in August 1785 while serving as the first president of the Potomac Company.

Reference Above the Mouth of Shan[andoa]h there is but one fall and that is smooth and shallow which prevents Craft from passing at all times—Abt ½ Mile below is the place Esteem'd the most difficult It runs exceeding swift for wch reason it is call'd the spout and the bottom being very Rocky occasions rough water which will prevent small Canoes ever passing as our's that was large had like to have fill'd—There continues for near three Miles Rocky & uneven—Water in which dist[anc]e and towards the latter end there is two other Falls one swift & ugly but when the River is higher than ordinary a passage may be had r[oun]d a small Island—which passage may be greatly improved –There is also a passage at the spout which vessels may, and have been hald up by

near the shoar, and this may yet be improved— Abt 12 Miles below this is another Fall but very easy and passable and abt 2 Miles from that is a cluster of small Islands with many Rocks and swift water which render's the passage somewhat precarious: from this to the Seneca Fall is a fine smooth even Water as can be desir'd The Seneca Fall is easily pass'd in two places and Canoes may continue within two Miles of the Great Falls but further it is not possible therefore the expence and trouble of going up Seneca Falls will not answer the Charges as all Carriages are oblig'd to pass difficult Bridge from whence it is but 8 Miles to the Landing place at Mr Barnes Quarter at the Sugerlands and is 5 Miles to any Landing below the aforesd Falls of Seneca.

To Robert Hunter Morris
Winchester, Virginia, 9 April 1756

This letter reports of an engagement near the North River in Hampshire County, between the Virginia Regiment and a party of French, in which the French commander, French Canadian Alexandre d'Agneau Douville, was killed. Robert Hunter Morris (c.1700–1764), a native of New York who had been councillor and chief justice of the colony of New Jersey in the 1740s, was then serving as resident governor of Pennsylvania.

Dear Sir

I had scarce reachd Williamsburg, before an express was after me with news of the French & Indians advancing within our Settlements, and doing incredible mischief to the Inhabitants which obligd me to postpone my business there, and hurry to their assistance with all expedition: when I came to this place I found everythings in deep confusion: and the poor distressd Inhabitants under a general consternation. I therefore collected such force as I coud immediately raise, and sent them in such parties, and to such places as twas judged most likely to meet with the Enemy: one of which, under the command of Mr Paris, luckily fell in with a small body of them as they were surrounding a small Fort on the No. River of Cacapehon; whom they engaged, and (after half an hour's close firing) put to flight with the loss of their commander Monsr Donville (killd) & three or four more mortally wounded. The accident that has determined the fate of Monsieur; has, I believe, dispers'd his Party: for I dont hear of any mischief done in this Colony since, thô we are not without numbers who are makeing hourly discoverys.

I have sent you a copy of the Instructions that were found about this Officer: that you may see how bold and enterprising the Enemy have grown, how unconfind are thes ambitious design's of the French: and how much it will be in their power, (if the Colonys continue in their fatal Lethargy) to give a final stab to liberty, & Property.

Nothing I more sincerely wish than a union to the Colonys in this time of Eminent danger: and that you may find your assembly in a temper of mind to act consistently with their preservation. What Maryland has, or will do I know not: but this I am certain off, that Virginia will do every thing that can be expected to promote the publick good.

I went to Williamsburg fully resolved to resign my Commission, but was disswaded from it, at least for a time. If the hurry of business in which I know your honour is genlly engagd: will admit of an oppertunity to murder a little time in writing to me. I shoud receive the favour as a mark of that esteem, which I coud wish to merit, by shewing at all times when its in my power, how much I am Dear Sir Yr honours most Obt & most Hble Servt

Go: Washington

P.S. A Letter this instant arriving from Williamsburg, informs, that our Assembly have voted 20,000£s more and that their Forces shd be increas'd to 2000 Men. a laudable example this, and I hope not a singular one.

The inclosed to Colo. Gage I beg the favr of you to forward.

To Robert Dinwiddie
Winchester, Virginia, 27 April 1756

In this letter Washington reiterates his concern for the settlers on the frontier and renews his requests for militia reinforcements and for the erection of a fort at Winchester. The Virginia House of Burgesses approved expenditures for the building of a small fort at Winchester after Governor Dinwiddie sent this letter to the House.

Honorable Sir,

I sent an Express to Fort Cumberland on Tuesday last, who is just returned with the enclosed Letters; which I send, to prevent the trouble of extracting a part.

In my letter to Colonel Stephen, I did, among other things, inform him of the accusations laid to his charge; and that he must expect to have the matter enquired into: your Honor will see what he says upon the subject.

Desolation and murder still increase; and no prospects of Relief. The Blue-Ridge is now our Frontier; no men being left in this County, except a few that keep close with a number of women and children, in Forts which they have erected for that purpose. There are now no Militia in this County; when there were, they could not be brought into action. If the Inhabitants of the adjacent Counties pursue the same system of Disobedience, the whole must fall an inevitable sacrifice: and there is room to fear they have caught the infection; since I have sent (besides divers Letters to Lord Fairfax) express after express, to hurry them on; and yet have no tidings of their march. We have the greatest reason in life to believe, that the number of the Enemy is very considerable; as they are spread all over this part of the Country: and that their Success, and the Spoils with which they have enriched themselves, dished up with a good deal of french policy—will encourage the Indians of distant nations to fall upon our Inhabitants in greater numbers, and, if possible, with greater rapidity—They enjoy the sweets of a profitable War, and will no doubt improve the Success, which ever must attend their arms— without we have Indians to oppose theirs. I would therefore advise, as I often have done, that there should be neither trouble nor expence omitted to bring the few, who are still inclined, into our Service; and that too with the greatest care and expedition—A small number, just to point out the wiles and tracts of the Enemy, is better than none: for which reason I must earnestly recommend, that those who accompanied Major Lewis, should be immediately sent up: and such of the Catawba's as can be engaged in our Interest; if such another torrent as this has been (or may be ere it is done) should press upon our Settlements, there will not be a living creature left in Frederick-County: and how soon Fairfax and Prince William may share its fate, is easily conceived, if we only consider a cruel blood-thirsty Enemy, Conquerors! already possessed of the finest part of Virginia; plenteously filled with all kinds of Provision: pursuing a people filled with fear and consternation, at the inhuman murders of these barbarous Savages!

I have exerted every means that I could think of to quiet the minds of these unhappy people: but, for a man to have inclination, and not power, he may as well be without either, for the assistance he can give.

The Inhabitants of the County who are now in Forts are greatly distressed for want of ammunition and Provision; and are incessantly importuning me for both; neither of which have I at this place, to spare. and if I had, I should be much embarrassed how to act—I could not be safe in delivering either, without our orders. and to hear the cries of the hungry, who have fled for refuge to these places, with nothing more than they carried on their backs, is exceedingly moving. Therefore I hope your Honor will give directions concerning this matter.

I have wrote to the Assembly, setting forth the great and absolute necessity there is of erecting a large and strong Fort at this place, to serve as a Receptacle for all our Stores, &c. and a place of Refuge for the women and Children in times of danger. Was this necessary work compleated, the men would upon any alarm (as they say themselves) immediately lodge their families here, and turn out against the Enemy: But without some such place of Defence, they must always fly in the manner they have, in order to secure their wives and Children!

This is the place generally fixed upon, as it has a free and open communication with all the Country, from its centrical situation; it also secures the communication with the neighbouring colonies as well as the Trade, to the Rivers of Rappahannock, Potomack, &c. and, though trifling in itself, a place of the utmost importance to the Country in general; being contiguous to that part of our Frontiers (but alas! this is the utmost Frontiers at present) which ever must, if any, sustain the attack of numbers, as it is the nearest to Fort Duquisne, to which place we have opened a free communication. It is also contiguous to their Indian Allies; who are at present higher up the Ohio than themselves: It is also conveniently situated for procuring the earliest intelligence when the Enemy is about; and to obtain relief from the Militia below—In short, it would be needless to urge

all the cogent reasons that plead in its behalf, and shew how conveniently situated it is for the commanding Officer to reside at. But one I shall add, which alone would be sufficient; and that is what I have before observed: vizt The procuring Intelligence. This I now am truly sensible of, from the experience I have had since I came to this place. Since the first murders were committed by the Indians, I have never missed of receiving intelligence of their motions: while Colonel Stephen has, in a manner, lived in total ignorance thereof: the reason is very obvious; for Fort Cumberland being detached so far without the Inhabitants, no person thinks of alarming them; but immediately, upon the first fright, retire into the Inhabitants. And Secondly; it is absolutely necessary to have one large Magazine, to supply the different Forts with Stores, &c. which Magazine should be rather within the Inhabitants, for the greater Security in receiving and delivering them out again; and furnishing any reinforcements that may arrive from below, with Provision, ammunition, &c. which will always facilitate their march—There should also be ammunition lodged here for supplying the country-people, when found useful.

Your Honor will observe some parts of Colonel Stephens Letters; as about reinforcements from the second Division, and the number of men, &c. which were only finesse's in case the letters had fallen into the Enemys hand. The letters that conveyed the true accounts, were put into the pummel of the Saddle; as were mine to him.

I have been formerly, and am at present pretty full in offering my opinion and counsel upon matters which regard the public Safety and Interest; and that has been solely the view of all my thoughts, words and actions. And, in order to avoid censure in every part of my conduct; I make it a Rule to obey the Dictates of your Honor, the Assembly, and a good conscience!

I shall not hereafter trouble you further on these Topics; as I can add nothing to what I have said. I am your Honors' &c.

G:W.

To Thomas Knox
Mount Vernon, 26 December 1756
This letter concerns Washington's order from a merchant in Bristol, England, for articles needed for his planta-

tion. Another order placed to the same merchant, written four days later, was for personal items. Washington paid for the orders with proceeds from the sale of tobacco.

Sir,

Your favour of the 28th September came to hand the 20th Instt. My Goods, that is such part as you have sent me I am told will be round from Rappahannock River shortly—I can't help expressing great concern, and some Surprize at your not sending the following Articles, which were Included in an Invoice sent the 18th Jany last, the Receipt of which you acknowledge (viz.)

4 dozn plaid Hose
½ dozn Scythes & Stones
4 Curry Combs & Brushes
1 Dozn Weeding Hoes
1 dozn narrow & ½ dozn Grubg Do
20M 8d. Nails
20M 10d. Ditto—10M 20d.
20M 4d. Ditto 5M 6d. and
1 Dozn Logwood Axes.

These Articles Sir, I greatly wanted, and must now be obligd to buy in the Country for this years use at exorbitant prices and that perhaps after sending over good part of the Country before they can be procurd.

On board the Nugent Only I have 14 Hogsheads Tobo of the best Mountn Sweets-cented—your best endeavours in the Sales will be exerted I hope in my favour—Tobo of the like kind, sent by my acquaintances to the London Market commands great prices, and this of mine made upon the same sort of Land as theirs is and handled equally as Neat will, I flatter myself, sell full as high in that of Bristol.

The nett proceeds of this Latter, and Balle of the former Tobo please to pay to Mr Richd Washington of London, who is directed to draw upon you to the amount. Please also to Insure one hundd pounds on the 14 Hogsheads, a Sum much less than the value of the Tobacco but I choose to risk part—I doubt not of hearing from you soon & receiving Accounts of Sales, & Acct Currt. I am Sir Yr Most Obedt Hble Servt

Go: Washington

Recipe for Small Beer
c. November 1757
Washington included the following recipe for small beer in the paper book of notes and memorandums that he made between June and November 1757.

To make Small Beer

Take a large Siffer full of Bran Hops to your Taste. Boil these 3 hours. then strain out 30 Gallns into a Cooler put in 3 Gallns Molasses while the Beer is Scalding hot or rather draw the Molasses into the Cooler & Strain the Beer on it while boiling Hot[.] let this stand till it is little more than Blood warm then put in a quart of Yest if the weather is very Cold cover it over with a Blanket & let it work in the Cooler 24 hours then put it into the Cask—leave the Bung open till it is almost done working—Bottle it that day week it was Brewed.

To Thomas Knox
Mount Vernon, 30 December 1757
Sir,

Since writing the forgoing Letter I find myself in want of the following Articles, besides those contain therein please to send the whole to me therefore by the first Vessel to Potomack or Rappahannock.

100 Wt of dble and 150 of Single refind Sugar.
1 Cask bottled Beer.
1 ps. Irish Linnen @ 4/
1 ps. Ditto @ 1/3
1 ps. Ditto @1/
½ ps. finest Cambrick, ½ ps. Ditto of midling Do
1 Gross Shirt buttons—thrd to suit the above Linn & Cambrick
2 pr fine workd Ruffles @ 21/ each pair
2 Setts compleat Shoe Brushes
½ dozn pair thrd hose at 5/
40 Shillings worth of Spices sorted.
10 lb. Coffee—20 lb. Chocolate
6 lb. best Hyson Tea—6 lb. best Green Ditto.
50 Wt dble Gloster Cheese—12 lb. Durham Mustard
50 lb. Soap
6 Grind Stones
1 Compleat Saddle, bridle, &ca for furniture
1 Sett Holster Caps & Housing of fine blew Cloth with a small edging of Silver Embroidery round them. Yr Most Obedt

Go: Washington

To the Officers of the Virginia Regiment
New Kent County, Virginia, 10 January 1759
Washington wrote this letter after receiving an address signed by twenty-seven officers of the Virginia Regi-

ment, written on the last day of 1758, expressing their regret about Washington's decision to resign his commission. "Judge then," the address says in part, "how sensibly we must be Affected with the loss of such an excellent Commander, such a sincere Friend, and so affable a Companion. How rare is it to find those amiable Qualifications blended together in one Man? How great the Loss of such a Man? Adieu to that Superiority, which the Enemy have granted us over other Troops, and which even the Regulars and Provincials have done us the Honor publicly to acknowledge! Adieu to that strict Discipline and order, which you have always maintan'd! Adieu to that happy Union and Harmony, which has been our principal Cement!

"It gives us an additional Sorrow, when we reflect, to find, our unhappy Country will receive a loss, no less irreparable, than ourselves. Where will it meet a Man so experienc'd in military Affairs? One so renown'd for Patriotism, Courage and Conduct? Who has so great knowledge of the Enemy we have to deal with? Who so well acquainted with their Situation & Strength? Who so much respected by the Soldiery? Who in short so able to support the military Character of Virginia?" Washington addressed his reply to "Captain Robert Steward and Gentlemen Officers of the Virginia Regiment."

My dear Gentlemen.

If I had words that could express the deep sense I entertain of your most obliging & affectionate address to me, I should endeavour to shew you that *gratitude* is not the smallest engredient of a character you have been pleased to celebrate; rather, give me leave to add, as the effect of your partiality & politeness, than of my deserving.

That I have for some years (under uncommon difficulties, which few were thoroughly acquainted with) been able to conduct myself so much to your satisfaction, affords me the greatest pleasure I am capable of feeling; as I almost despared of attaining that end—so hard a matter is it to please, when one is acting under disagreeable restraints! But your having, nevertheless, so fully, so affectionately & so publicly declared your approbation of my conduct, during my command of the Virginia Troops, I must esteem an honor that will constitute the greatest happiness of my life, and afford in my latest hours the most pleasing reflections. I had nothing to boast, but a steady honesty—this I made

the invariable rule of my actions; and I find my reward in it.

I am bound, Gentlemen, in honor, by inclination & by every affectionate tye, to promote the reputation & interest of a Corps I was once a member of; though the Fates have disjoined me from it now, I beseech you to command, with equal confidence & a greater degree of freedom than ever, my best services. Your Address is in the hands of the Governor, and will be presented by him to the Council. I hope (but cannot ascertain it) that matters may be settled agreeable to your wishes. On me, depend for my best endeavours to accomplish this end.

I should dwell longer on this subject, and be more particular in my answer, did your address lye before me. Permit me then to conclude with the following acknowledgments: first, that I always thought it, as it really was, the greatest honor of my life to command Gentlemen, who made me happy in their company & easy by their conduct: secondly, that had every thing contributed as fully as your obliging endeavours did to render me satisfied, I never should have been otherwise, or have had cause to know the pangs I have felt at parting with a Regiment, that has shared my toils, and experienced every hardship & danger, which I have encountered. But this brings on *reflections* that fill me with grief & I must strive to forget them; in thanking you, Gentlemen, with uncommon sincerity & true affection for the honor you have done me—for if I have acquired any reputation, it is from you I derive it. I thank you also for the love & regard you have all along shewn me. It is in this, I am rewarded. It is herein I glory. And lastly I must thank you for your kind wishes. To assure you, that I feel every generous return of mutual regard—that I wish you every honor as a collective Body & every felicity in your private Characters, is, Gentlemen, I hope unnecessary—Shew me how I can demonstrate it, and you never shall find me otherwise than your Most obedient, most obliged and most affectionate

Go. Washington

To Robert Cary & Co.
Williamsburg, Virginia, 1 May 1759
This is Washington's first letter to the large London merchant firm that had long handled the business af-

Gentn

The Inclosd is the Ministers Certificate of my Marriage with Mrs Martha Custis—properly as I am told—Authenticated, you will therefore for the future please to address all your Letters which relate to the Affairs of the late Danl Parke Custis Esqr. to me. as by Marriage I am entitled to a third part of that Estate, and Invested likewise with the care of the other two thirds by a Decree of our Genl Court which I obtain in order to Strengthen the Power I before had in consequence of my Wifes Administration.

I have many Letters of yours in my possession unanswerd, but at present this serves only to advise you of the above Change and at the sametime to acquaint you that I shall continue to make you the same Consignments of Tobo as usual, and will endeavour to encrease it in proportion as I find myself and the Estate benefitted thereby.

The Scarcity of the last Years Crop; and the high prices of Tobo consequent thereupon woud in any other Case, have inducd me to sell the Estates Crop (which indeed is only 16 Hhds) in the Country but for a present, & I hope small advantage only I did not care to break the Chain of Corrispondance that has so long Subsisted, and therefore have, according to your desire, given Capt Talman an offer of the whole.

On the other side is an Invoice of some Goods which I beg of you to send me by the first Ship bound either to Potomack or Rappahannock, as I am in immediate want of them, Let them be Insurd, and in case of accidents re-shipd witht Delay. Direct for me at Mount Vernon Potomack River Virginia; the former is the name of my Seat the other the River on which 'tis Situated. I am Gentn Yr Most Obedt Hble Servt

Go: Washington

Invoice of Sundry Goods to be Shipd by Robt Cary Esq. and Company for the use of George Washington—viz.

1 Tester Bedstead 7½ feet pitch, with fashionable blew or blew and white Curtains to suit a Room lind wt. the Incld paper Window Cur-

tains of the same for two Windows; with either Papier Maché Cornish to them, or Cornish coverd with the Cloth 1 fine Bed Coverlid to match the Curtains 4 Chair bottoms of the same; that is, as much Covering suited to the above furniture as will go over the Seats of 4 Chairs (which I have by me) in order to make the whole furniture of this Room uniformly handsome and genteel.

1 Fashionable Sett of Desert Glasses, and Stands for Sweet Meats Jellys &ca together with Wash Glasses and a proper stand for these also 2 Setts of Chamber, or Bed Carpets—Wilton 4 fashionable China Branches, & Stands, for Candles 2 neat fire Screens 50 lb. Spirma Citi Candles 6 Carving knives and Forks—handles of Staind Ivory and bound with Silver A pretty large Assortment of Grass Seeds—among which let there be a good deal of Lucerne & St Foin, especially the former—also a good deal of English, or blew Grass[.] Clover Seed I have 1 Large, neat, and easy Couch for a Passage 50 Yards of best Floor Matting.

2 pair of fashionable mixd, or Marble Col[ore]d Silk Hose 6 pair of finest Cotton Ditto 6 pr of finest thread Ditto 6 pr of midling Do to cost abt 5/ 6 pr of Worsted Do of the best sorted—2 pr of wch to be White N.B. all the above Stockings to be long, and tolerably large 1 piece of finest and most fashionable Stock Tape 1 Suit of Cloaths of the finest Cloth & fashionable Colour made by the Inclosd measure.

The newest, and most approvd Treatise of Agriculture—besides this, send me a small piece in Octavo—calld a new System of Agriculture, or a Speedy way to grow Rich Langleys Book of Gardening Gibson, upon Horses the latest Edition in Quarto.

Half a dozn pair of Men's neatest Shoes and Pumps, to be made by one Didsbury on Colo. Baylors Last—but a little larger than his—& to have high Heels 6 pr Mens riding Gloves rather larger than the middle size One neat Pocket Book, capable of receiving Memorandoms & small Cash Accts to be made of Ivory, or any thing else that will admit of cleaning Fine soft Calf Skin for a pair of Boots—Ben. leathr for Soles.

Six Bottles of Greenhows Tincture.

Order from the best House in Madeira a Pipe of the best old Wine, and let it be Securd from Pilferers.

Go: Washington

To George Muse
Mount Vernon, 29 January 1774

This letter concerns the patent of bounty lands in the Ohio Country given to the officers of the first Virginia Regiment under the provisions of Virginia governor Robert Dinwiddie's Proclamation of 1754. The lieutenant colonel of the regiment, George Muse, second in command after Washington, had been accused by his fellow officers of acting cowardly during the regiment's engagement with the French and Indian forces at Fort Necessity in July 1754. Although Muse resigned his commission soon afterward, the Virginia council nevertheless determined that he was still entitled to receive his share of the bounty—totaling 15,000 acres. When after the passage of nearly twenty years the acreage was finally apportioned, Muse apparently concluded that he had been shortchanged and somehow cast the blame on his former commander. An indiscreet letter on the subject written while intoxicated roused Washington's ire and elicited one of the most blatant displays of his notorious temper.

Sir,

Your impertinent Letter of the 24th ulto, was delivered to me yesterday by Mr [Charles] Smith—As I am not accustomed to receive such from any Man, nor would have taken the same language from you personally, without letting you feel some marks of my resentment; I would advise you to be cautious in writing me a second of the same tenour; for though I understand you were drunk when you did it, yet give me leave to tell you, that drunkenness is no excuse for rudeness; & that, but for your stupidity & sottishness you might have known, by attending to the public Gazettes, (particularly Rinds of the 14th of January last) that you had your full quantity of ten thousand acres of Land allow'd you; that is, 9073 acres in the great Tract of 51,302 acres, & the remainder in the small tract of 927 acres; whilst I wanted near 500 acres of my quantity, Doctr [James] Craik 300 of his, and almost every other claimant little or much of theirs. But suppose you had really fallen short 73 acres of your

10,000, do you think your superlative merit entitles you to greater indulgences than others? or that I was to make it good to you, if it did? when it was at the option of the Governor & Council to have allowed you but 500 acres in the whole, if they had been inclin'd so to do. If either of these should happen to be your opinion, I am very well convinced you will stand singular in it; & all my concerns is, that I ever engag'd in behalf of so ungrateful & dirty a fellow as you are. But you may still stand in need of my assistance, as I can inform you that your affairs, in respect to these Lands, do not stand upon so solid a basis as you may imagine, & this you may take by way of hint; as your coming in for *any*, much less a *full share* may still be a disputed point, by a Gentleman [George Mercer] who is not in this Country at this time, & who is exceedingly dissatisfyed therewith. I wrote to you a few days ago concerning the other distribution, proposing an easy method of dividing our Lands; but since I find in what temper you are, I am sorry I took the trouble of mentioning the Land, or your name in a Letter, as I do not think you merit the least assistance from

G: Washington

Address to the Continental Congress
Philadelphia, 16 June 1775

This short address was Washington's reply to Congress's official communication that it had appointed him commander in chief of the Continental army. The document is in Edmund Pendleton's writing, except for a brief interlineation subsequently made by Washington, and is prefaced with an introductory paragraph: "The President [John Hancock] informed Colo. Washington that the Congress had yesterday, Unanimously made choice of him to be General & Commander in Chief of the American Forces, and requested he would accept of that Appointment; whereupon Colo. Washington, standing in his place, Spake as follows."

Mr President, Tho' I am truly sensible of that high Honour done me in this Appointment, yet I feel great distress, from a consciousness that my abilities & Military experience may not be equal to the extensive & important Trust: However, as the Congress desire it I will enter upon the momentous duty, & exert every power I

Possess In their service & for the Support of the glorious Cause: I beg they will accept my most cordial thanks for this distinguished testimony of their Approbation.

But lest some unlucky event should happen unfavourable to my reputation, I beg it may be rememberd by every Gentn in the room, that I this day declare with the utmost sincerity, I do not think my self equal to the Command I am honoured with.

As to pay, Sir, I beg leave to Assure the Congress that as no pecuniary consideration could have tempted me to have accepted this Arduous emploiment at the expence of my domestk ease & happiness I do not wish to make any proffit from it: I will keep an exact Account of my expences; those I doubt not they will discharge & that is all I desire.

General Orders on Profanity
New York, 3 August 1776
The following General Orders on profanity was issued to the Continental army at New York about three weeks before the Battle of Long Island.

Parole Uxbridge
Countersign Virginia

That the Troops may have an opportunity of attending public worship, as well as take some rest after the great fatigue they have gone through; The General in future excuses them from fatigue duty on Sundays (except at the Ship Yards, or special occasions) until further orders. The General is sorry to be informed that the foolish, and wicked practice, of profane cursing and swearing (a Vice heretofore little known in an American Army) is growing into fashion; he hopes the officers will, by example, as well as influence, endeavour to check it, and that both they, and the men will reflect, that we can have little hopes of the blessing of Heaven on our Arms, if we insult it by our impiety, and folly; added to this, it is a vice so mean and low, without any temptation, that every man of sense, and character, detests and despises it.

[Privates] Clarkson and Chase under confinement for Desertion, and reinlistment into the Artillery, from another Corps, to return to Capt. [Sebastian] Bauman's Company until Col. [Samuel] Ellmores Regiment, wh. claims them, comes into camp.

To the Officers of the Army
Newburgh, New York, 15 March 1783
This impassioned letter was written to the officers of the Continental army as part of Washington's attempt to quash the Newburgh Conspiracy near the end of the Revolutionary War.

Gentlemen: By an anonymous summons, an attempt has been made to convene you together; how inconsistent with the rules of propriety! how unmilitary! and how subversive of all order and discipline, let the good sense of the Army decide.

In the moment of this Summons, another anonymous production was sent into circulation, addressed more to the feelings and passions, than to the reason and judgment of the Army. The author of the piece, is entitled to much credit for the goodness of his Pen and I could wish he had as much credit for the rectitude of his Heart, for, as Men see thro' different Optics, and are induced by the reflecting faculties of the Mind, to use different means, to attain the same end, the Author of the Address, should have had more charity, than to mark for Suspicion, the Man who should recommend moderation and longer forbearance, or, in other words, who should not think as he thinks, and act as he advises. But he had another plan in view, in which candor and liberality of Sentiment, regard to justice, and love of Country, have no part; and he was right, to insinuate the darkest suspicion, to effect the blackest designs.

That the Address is drawn with great Art, and is designed to answer the most insidious purposes. That it is calculated to impress the Mind, with an idea of premeditated injustice in the Sovereign power of the United States, and rouse all those resentments which must unavoidably flow from such a belief. That the secret mover of this Scheme (whoever he may be) intended to take advantage of the passions, while they were warmed by the recollection of past distresses, without giving time for cool, deliberative thinking, and that composure of Mind which is so necessary to give dignity and stability to measures is rendered too obvious, by the mode of conducting the business, to need other proof than a reference to the proceeding.

Thus much, Gentlemen, I have thought it incumbent on me to observe to you, to shew upon what principles I opposed the irregular and hasty meeting which was proposed to have been held on Tuesday last: and not because I wanted a disposition to give you every oppertunity consistent with your own honor, and the dignity of the Army, to make known your grievances. If my conduct heretofore, has not evinced to you, that I have been a faithful friend to the Army, my declaration of it at this time wd. be equally unavailing and improper. But as I was among the first who embarked in the cause of our common Country. As I have never left your side one moment, but when called from you on public duty. As I have been the constant companion and witness of your Distresses, and not among the last to feel, and acknowledge your Merits. As I have ever considered my own Military reputation as inseperably connected with that of the Army. As my Heart has ever expanded with joy, when I have heard its praises, and my indignation has arisen, when the mouth of detraction has been opened against it, it can *scarcely be supposed,* at this late stage of the War, that I am indifferent to its interests. But, how are they to be promoted? The way is plain, says the anonymous Addresser. If War continues, remove into the unsettled Country; there establish yourselves, and leave an ungrateful Country to defend itself. But who are they to defend? our Wives, our Children, our Farms, and other property which we leave behind us. or, in this state of hostile seperation, are we to take the two first (the latter cannot be removed), to perish in a Wilderness, with hunger, cold and nakedness? If Peace takes place, never sheath your Swords Says he untill you have obtained full and ample justice; this dreadful alternative, of either deserting our Country in the extremest hour of her distress, or turning our Arms against it, (which is the apparent object, unless Congress can be compelled into instant compliance) has something so shocking in it, that humanity revolts at the idea. My God! what can this writer have in view, by recommending such measures? Can he be a friend to the Army? Can he be a friend to this Country? Rather, is he not an insidious Foe? Some Emissary, perhaps, from New York, plotting the ruin of both, by sowing the seeds of discord and seperation between the Civil and Military powers of the Continent? And what a Compliment does he pay to our Understandings, when he recommends measures in either alternative, impracticable in their Nature?

But here, Gentlemen, I will drop the curtain, because it wd. be as imprudent in me to assign my reasons for this opinion, as it would be insulting to your conception, to suppose you stood in need of them. A moment's reflection will convince every dispassionate Mind of the physical impossibility of carrying either proposal into execution.

There might, Gentlemen, be an impropriety in my taking notice, in this Address to you, of an anonymous production, but the manner in which that performance has been introduced to the Army, the effect it was intended to have, together with some other circumstances, will amply justify my observations on the tendency of that Writing. With respect to the advice given by the Author, to suspect the Man, who shall recommend moderate measures and longer forbearance, I spurn it, as every Man, who regards that liberty, and reveres that justice for which we contend, undoubtedly must; for if Men are to be precluded from offering their Sentiments on a matter, which may involve the most serious and alarming consequences, that can invite the consideration of Mankind, reason is of no use to us; the freedom of Speech may be taken away, and, dumb and silent we may be led, like sheep, to the Slaughter.

I cannot, in justice to my own belief, and what I have great reason to conceive is the intention of Congress, conclude this Address, without giving it as my decided opinion, that that Honble Body, entertain exalted sentiments of the Services of the Army; and, from a full conviction of its merits and sufferings, will do it compleat justice. That their endeavors, to discover and establish funds for this purpose, have been unwearied, and will not cease, till they have succeeded, I have not a doubt. But, like all other large Bodies, where there is a variety of different Interests to reconcile, their deliberations are slow. Why then should we distrust them? and, in consequence of that distrust, adopt measures, which may cast a shade over that glory which, has been so justly acquired; and tarnish the reputation of an Army which is celebrated thro' all Europe, for its fortitude and Patriotism? and for what is this done? to bring the object we seek nearer? No! most certainly, in my opinion, it will cast it at a greater distance.

For myself (and I take no merit in giving the assurance, being induced to it from principles of gratitude, veracity and justice), a grateful sence of the confidence you have ever placed in me, a recollection of the chearful assistance, and prompt obedience I have experienced from you, under every vicissitude of Fortune, and the sincere affection I feel for an Army, I have so long had the honor to Command, will oblige me to declare, in this public and solemn manner, that, in the gratification of every wish, so far as may be done consistently with the great duty I owe my Country, and those powers we are bound to respect, you may freely command my Services to the utmost of my abilities.

While I give you these assurances, and pledge myself in the most unequivocal manner, to exert whatever ability I am possessed of, in your favor, let me entreat you, Gentlemen, on your part, not to take any measures, which, viewed in the calm light of reason, will lessen the dignity, and sully the glory you have hitherto maintained; let me request you to rely on the plighted faith of your Country, and place a full confidence in the purity of the intentions of Congress; that, previous to your dissolution as an Army they will cause all your Accts. to be fairly liquidated, as directed in their resolutions, which were published to you two days ago, and that they will adopt the most effectual measures in their power, to render ample justice to you, for your faithful and meritorious Services. And let me conjure you, in the name of our common Country, as you value your own sacred honor, as you respect the rights of humanity, and as you regard the Military and National character of America, to express your utmost horror and detestation of the Man who wishes, under any specious pretences, to overturn the liberties of our Country, and who wickedly attempts to open the flood Gates of Civil discord, and deluge our rising Empire in Blood. By thus determining, and thus acting, you will pursue the plain and direct road to the attainment of your wishes. You will defeat the insidious designs of our Enemies, who are compelled to resort from open force to secret Artifice. You will give one more distinguished proof of unexampled patriotism and patient virtue, rising superior to the pressure of the most complicated sufferings; And you will, by the dignity of your Conduct, afford occasion for Posterity to say, when speaking of the glorious example you have exhibited to Mankind, "had this day been

wanting, the World had never seen the last stage of perfection to which human nature is capable of attaining."

Farewell Address to the Army
Rocky Hill, New Jersey, 2 November 1783
A docket on the manuscript reads: "Rocky Hill 2d Novr 1783 Genl Washington's Farewell Orders to the Armies of the United States."

Genll Washington's Farewell Orders issued to the Armies of the United States of America the 2d day of Novr 1783—Rocky Hill, near Princeton,

The United States in Congress assembled, after giving the most honorable testimony to the Merits of the Federal Armies, and presenting them with the thanks of their Country for their long, eminent and faithful Services, having thought proper, by their Proclamation bearing date the 18th day of October last, to discharge such part of the Troops as were engaged for the War, and to permit the Officers on Furlough to retire from Service from and after tomorrow, which Proclamation having been communicated in the public papers for the information and government of all concerned. it only remains for the Commander in Chief to address himself once more, and that for the last time, to the Armies of the United States (however widely dispersed the Individuals who composed them may be) and to bid them an affectionate—a long farewell.

But before the Commander in Chief takes his final leave of those he holds most dear, he wishes to indulge himself a few moments in calling to mind a slight review of the past, He will then take the liberty of exploring with his Military friends their future prospects, of advising the general line of conduct which in his opinion ought to be persued, and he will conclude the Address, by expressing the obligations he feels himself under for the spirited and able assistance he has experienced from them, in the performance of an arduous Office.

A contemplation of the compleat attainment (at a period earlier than could have been expected) of the object for which we contended, against so formidable a power, cannot but inspire us with astonishment and gratitude—The disadvantageous circumstances on our part, under which the War was undertaken, can never be forgotten—The singular interpositions of

Providence in our feeble condition were such, as could scarcely escape the attention of the most unobserving—where the unparalleled perseverence of the Armies of the United States, through almost every possible suffering and discouragement, for the space of eight long years was little short of a standing Miracle.

It is not the meaning nor within the compass of this Address, to detail the hardships peculiarly incident to our Service, or to discribe the distresses which in several instances have resulted from the extremes of hunger and nakedness, combined with the rigors of an inclement season. Nor is it necessary to dwell on the dark side of our past affairs. Every American Officer and Soldier must now console himself for any unpleasant circumstances which may have occurred, by a recollection of the uncommon scenes in which he has been called to act, no inglorious part; and the astonishing Events of which he has been a witness—Events which have seldom, if ever before, taken place on the stage of human action, nor can they probably ever happen again. For who has before seen a disciplined Army formed at once from such raw Materials? Who that was not a witness could imagine, that the most violent local prejudices would cease so soon, and that Men who came from the different parts of the Continent, strongly disposed by the habits of education, to dispise and quarrel with each other, would instantly become but one patriotic band of Brothers? Or who that was not on the spot can trace the steps by which such a wonderful Revolution has been effected, and such a glorious period put to all our Warlike toils?

It is universally acknowledged that the enlarged prospect of happiness, opened by the confirmation of our Independence and Sovereignty, almost exceeds the power of description. And shall not the brave Men who have contributed so essentially to these inestimable acquisitions, retiring victorious from the Field of War, to the Field of Agriculture, participate in all the blessings which have been obtained? In such a Republic, who will exclude them from the rights of Citizens and the fruits of their labours? In such a Country so happily circumstanced the persuits of Commerce and the cultivation of the Soil, will unfold to industry the certain road to competence. To those hardy Soldiers, who are actuated by the spirit of adventure, the Fisheries will afford ample and profitable employment, and the extensive and fertile Regions of the West will yield a most happy Asylum to those, who, fond of domestic enjoyment are seeking for personal independence. Nor is it possible to conceive that any one of the United States will prefer a National Bankrupcy and a dissolution of the Union, to a compliance with the requisitions of Congress and the payment of its just debts—so that the Officers and Soldiers may expect considerable assistance in recommencing their civil occupations from the sums due to them from the Public, which must and will most inevitably be paid.

In order to effect this desirable purpose, and to remove the prejudices which may have taken possession of the Minds of any of the good People of the States, it is earnestly recommended to all the Troops that with strong attachments to the Union, they should carry with them into civil Society the most conciliating dispositions; and that they should prove themselves not less virtuous and usefull as Citizens, than they have been persevering and victorious as Soldiers. What tho' there should be some envious Individuals who are unwilling to pay the Debt the public has contracted, or to yield the tribute due to Merit, yet let such unworthy treatment produce no invective, or any instance of intemperate conduct, let it be remembered that the unbiased voice of the Free Citizens of the United States has promised the just reward, and given the merited applause, let it be known and remembered that the reputation of the Federal Armies is established beyond the reach of Malevolence, and let a conciousness of their atchievements and fame, still incite the Men who composed them to honorable Actions; under the persuasion that the private virtues of economy, prudence and industry, will not be less amiable in civil life, than the more splendid qualities of valour, perseverence and enterprise, were in the Field: Every one may rest assured that much, very much of the future happiness of the Officers and Men, will depend upon the wise and manly conduct which shall be adopted by them, when they are mingled with the great body of the Community. And altho', the General has so frequently given it as his opinion in the most public and explicit manner, that unless the principles of the Federal Government were properly supported, and the Powers of the Union encreased, the honor, dignity and justice of the Nation would be lost for ever; yet he cannot help repeating on this occasion, so interesting a sentiment, and leaving it as his last injunction to every Officer and every Soldier, who may view the subject in the same serious point of light, to add his best endeavours to those of his worthy fellow Citizens towards effecting these great and valuable purposes, on which our very existence as a Nation so materially depends.

The Commander in Chief conceives little is now waiting to enable the Soldier to change the Military character into that of the Citizen, but that steady and decent tenor of behaivour which has generally distinguished, not only the Army under his immediate Command, but the different Detachments and seperate Armies, through the course of the War; from their good sense and prudence he anticipates the happiest consequences; And while he congratulates them on the glorious occasion which renders their Services in the Field no longer necessary, he wishes to express the strong obligations he feels himself under, for the assistance he has received from every Class—and in every instance. He presents his thanks in the most serious and affectionate manner to the General Officers, as well for their Counsel on many interesting occasions, as for their ardor in promoting the success of the plans he had adopted—To the Commandants of Regiments and Corps, and to the other Officers for their great Zeal and attention in carrying his orders promptly into execution—To the Staff for their alacrity and exactness in performing the duties of their several Departments—And to the Non-commissioned officers and private Soldiers, for their extraordinary patience in suffering, as well as their invincible fortitude in Action—To the various branches of the Army, the General takes this last and solemn oppertunity of professing his inviolable attachment & friendship—He wishes more than bare professions were in his power, that he was really able to be usefull to them all in future life; He flatters himself however, they will do him the justice to believe, that whatever could with propriety be attempted by him, has been done. And being now to conclude these his last public Orders, to take his ultimate leave, in a short time, of the Military Character, and to bid a final adieu to the Armies he has so long had

the honor to Command—he can only again offer in their behalf his recommendations to their grateful Country, and his prayers to the God of Armies. May ample justice be done them here, and may the choicest of Heaven's favors both here and hereafter attend those, who under the divine auspices have secured innumerable blessings for others: With these Wishes, and this benediction, the Commander in Chief is about to retire from service—The Curtain of seperation will soon be drawn—and the Military Scene to him will be closed for ever.

Resignation Address to the Continental Congress
Annapolis, Maryland, 23 December 1783
On Saturday, 20 December 1783, Washington wrote to the Continental Congress, notifying it of his arrival in Annapolis, Maryland, with the intention of "asking leave to resign the commission he has the honor of holding in their service, and desiring to know their pleasure in what manner it will be most proper to offer his resignation; whether in writing or at an audience." Upon reading the letter, Congress resolved that Washington "be admitted to a public audience, on Tuesday next, at twelve o'clock." On the following Tuesday, 23 December 1783, Washington, "according to order . . . was admitted to a public audience, and being seated, the President, after a pause, informed him, that the United States in Congress assembled, were prepared to receive his communications." Washington then arose and delivered the following address.

Mr President
The great events on which my resignation depended having at length taken place; I have now the honor of offering my sincere Congratulations to Congress & of presenting myself before them to surrender into their hands the trust committed to me, and to claim the indulgence of retiring from the Service of my Country.

Happy in the confirmation of our Independence and Sovereignty, and pleased with the oppertunity afforded the United States of becoming a respectable Nation, I resign with satisfaction the Appointment I accepted with diffidence—A diffidence in my abilities to accomplish so arduous a task, which however was superseded by a confidence in the rectitude of our Cause, the support of the Supreme Power of the Union, and the patronage of Heaven.

The Successful termination of the War has verified the more sanguine expectations—and my gratitude for the interposition of Providence, and the assistance I have received from my Countrymen encreases with every review of the momentous Contest.

While I repeat my obligations to the Army in general, I should do injustice to my own feelings not to acknowledge in this place the peculiar Services and distinguished merits of the Gentlemen who have been attached to my person during the War. It was impossible the choice of confidential Officers to compose my family should have been more fortunate. Permit me Sir, to recommend in particular those, who have continued in Service to the present moment, as worthy of the favorable notice & patronage of Congress.

I consider it an indispensable duty to close this last solemn act of my Official life, by commanding the Interests of our dearest Country to the protection of Almighty God, and those Who have the superintendence of them, to his holy keeping.

Having now finished the work assigned me, I retire from the great theatre of Action—and bidding an Affectionate farewell to this August body under whose orders I have so long acted, I here offer my Commission, and take my leave of all the employments of public life.

To James Craik
Mount Vernon, 25 March 1784
In this interesting letter to his lifelong close friend, Washington candidly discusses the subject of how historians might treat his life.

Dear Sir,

In answer to Mr [John] Bowie's request to you, permit me to assure that Gentleman, that I shall at all times be glad to see him at this retreat—That whenever he is here, I will give him the perusal of any public papers antecedent to my appointment to the command of the American army—that he may be laying up materials for his work. And whenever Congress shall have opened *their* Archives to any Historian for information, that he shall have the examination of all others in my possession which are subsequent thereto, but that 'till this epoch, I do not think myself at liberty to unfold papers which contain all the occurrences & transactions of my *late* command; first, because I conceive it to be re-

spectful to the sovereign power to let them take the lead in this business—& next, because I have, upon this principle, refused Doctr [William] Gordon & others who are about to write the History of the revolution this priviledge.

I will frankly declare to you, My Dr Doctor that any memoirs of my life, distinct & unconnected with the general history of the war, would rather hurt my feelings than tickle my pride whilst I lived. I had rather glide gently down the stream of life, leaving it to posterity to think & say what they please of me, than by an act of mine to have vanity or ostentation imputed to me—And I will furthermore confess that I was rather surprized into a consent, when Doctr [John] Witherspoon (very unexpectedly) made the application, than considered the tendency of that consent. It did not occur to me at that moment, from the manner in which the question was propounded—that no history of my life, without a very great deal of trouble indeed, could be written with the least degree of accuracy—unless recourse was had to me, or to my papers for information—that it would not derive sufficient authenticity without a promulgation of this fact—& that such a promulgation would subject me to the imputation I have just mentioned—which would hurt me the more, as I do not think vanity is a trait of my character.

It is for this reason, & candour obliges me to be explicit, that I shall stipulate against the publication of the memoirs Mr Bowie has in contemplation to give the world, 'till I shou'd see more probability of avoiding the darts which *I think* would be pointed at me on such an occasion; and how far, under these circumstances, it wou'd be worth Mr Bowie's while to spend time which might be more usefully employed in other matters, is with him to consider; as the practicability of doing it efficiently, without having free access to the documents of this War, which must fill the most important pages of the Memoir, & which for the reasons already assigned cannot be admitted at present, also is. If nothing happens more than I at present foresee, I shall be in Philadelphia on or before the first of May; where 'tis probable I may see Mr Bowie & converse further with him on this subject—in the mean while I will thank you for communicating these Sentiments. I am very truly Your affectionate friend & Servt

G: Washington

Advertisement for Royal Gift
Alexandria, Virginia, 2 March 1786
ROYAL GIFT.

A JACK-ASS of the first race in the kingdom of Spain, will cover mares and Jonnies (she asses) at Mount Vernon the ensuing spring.—The first for Ten, the latter for Fifteen Pounds the season.— Royal Gift is four years old, is between 14½ and 15 hands high, and will grow, it is said, till he is 20 or 25 years of age.—He is very boney and stout made, of a dark colour, with light belly and legs.—The advantages, which are many, to be derived from the propagation of asses from this animal (the first of the kind that ever was in North America) and the usefulness of mules, bred from a Jack of his size, either for the road or team, are well known to those who are acquainted with this mongrel race.—For the information of those who are not, it may be enough to add, that their great strength, longevity, hardiness, and cheap support, give them a preference of horses that is scarcely to be imagined. As the Jack is young, and the General has many mares of his own to put to him, a limited number only will be received from others, and these entered in the order they are offered.—Letters directed to Subscriber, by the post or otherwise, under cover to the General, will be entered on the day they are received, till the number is completed, of which the writers shall be informed, to prevent trouble or expence to them.

The Virginia Journal and Alexandria Advertiser.

To Annis Boudinot Stockton
Mount Vernon, 31 August 1788

Washington's correspondence with the recipient of this letter, where it has survived, is always delightful, but none so much so as the letter that follows. Annis Boudinot Stockton (1736–1801), an ardent admirer of Washington's who sometimes composed poetry in his honor, was the sister of Elias Boudinot (1740–1821), the mother-in-law of Benjamin Rush (1746–1813), and the widow of Richard Stockton (1730–1781), a signer of the Declaration of Independence. Washington stopped briefly at Morven, the estate and elegant mansion in Princeton, New Jersey, where she and her husband had settled in the 1750s, on his way to Yorktown, Virginia, in August 1781.

I have received and thank you very sincerely, my dear Madam, for your kind letter of the 3d instant. It would be in vain for me to think of acknowledging in adequate terms the delicate compliments, which, though expressed in plain prose, are evidently inspired by the Muse of Morven. I know not by what fatality it happens that even Philosophical sentiments come so much more gracefully (forcibly I might add) from your Sex, than my own. Otherwise I should be strongly disposed to dispute your Epicurean position concerning the œconomy of pleasures. Perhaps, indeed, upon a self-interested principle—because I should be conscious of becoming a gainer by a different practice. For, to tell you the truth, I find myself altogether interested in establishing in theory, what I feel in effect, that we can never be cloyed with the pleasing compositions of our female friends.

You see how selfish I am, and that I am too much delighted with the result to perplex my head much in seeking for the cause. But with Cicero in speaking respecting his belief of the immortality of the Soul, I will say, if I am in a grateful delusion, it is an innocent one, and I am willing to remain under its influence. Let me only annex one hint to this part of the subject, while you may be in danger of appreciating the qualities of your friend too highly, you will run no hazard in calculating upon his sincerity or in counting implicitly on the reciprocal esteem and friendship which he entertains for yourself.

The felicitations you offer on the present prospect of our public affairs are highly acceptable to me, and I entreat you to receive a reciprocation from my part. I can never trace the concatenation of causes, which led to these events, without acknowledging the mystery and admiring the goodness of Providence. To that superintending Power alone is our retraction from the brink of ruin to be attributed. A spirit of accomodation was happily infused into the leading characters of the Continent, and the minds of men were gradually prepared by disappointment, for the reception of a good government. Nor would I rob the fairer Sex of their share in the glory of a revolution so honorable to human nature, for, indeed, I think you Ladies are in the number of the best Patriots America can boast.

And now that I am speaking of your Sex, I will ask whether they are not capable of doing something towards introducing fœderal fashions and national manners? A good general government, without good morals and good habits, will not make us a happy People; and we shall deceive our selves if we think it will. A good government will, unquestionably, tend to foster and confirm those qualities, on which public happiness must be engrafted. Is it not shameful that we should be the sport of European whims and caprices? Should we not blush to discourage our own industry & ingenuity by purchasing foreign superfluities & adopting fantastic fashions, which are, at best, ill suited to our stage of Society? But I will preach no longer on so unpleasant a subject; because I am persuaded that you & I are both of a Sentiment, and because I fear the promulgation of it would work no reformation.

You know me well enough, my dear Madam, to believe me sufficiently happy at home, to be intent upon spending the residue of my days there. I hope that you and yours may have the enjoyment of your health, as well as Mrs Washington & myself: that enjoyment, by the divine benediction, adds much to our temporal felicity. She joins with me in desiring our compliments may be made acceptable to yourself & Children. It is with the purest sentiment of regard & esteem I have always the pleasure to subscribe myself, Dear Madam, Your sincere friend and Obedt Humble Servt

Go: Washington

Washington's Thanksgiving Proclamation
New York, 3 October 1789

At the urging of Congress Washington proclaimed a national day of Thanksgiving for the day of 26 November 1789. Anti-Federalist newspapers attacked the idea on the grounds that the president should not have addressed the people directly but rather recommended to the supreme executives of the states that they might appoint a day of thanksgiving. Washington followed his own counsel, however, and he attended one of the church services that took place in New York City on the day.

By the President of the United States of America. a Proclamation.

Whereas it is the duty of all Nations to acknowledge the providence of Almighty God, to obey his will, to be grateful for his benefits, and humbly to implore his protection and favor— and whereas both Houses of Congress have by their joint Committee requested me "to recommend to the People of the United States a day of public thanksgiving and prayer to be observed by acknowledging with grateful hearts the many signal favors of Almighty God especially by affording them an opportunity peaceably to establish a form of government for their safety and happiness."

Now therefore I do recommend and assign Thursday the 26th day of November next to be devoted by the People of these States to the service of that great and glorious Being, who is the beneficent Author of all the good that was, that is, or that will be—That we may then all unite in rendering unto him our sincere and humble thanks—for his kind care and protection of the People of this Country previous to their becoming a Nation—for the signal and manifold mercies, and the favorable interpositions of his Providence which we experienced in the tranquillity, union, and plenty, which we have since enjoyed—for the peaceable and rational manner, in which we have been enabled to establish constitutions of government for our safety and happiness, and particularly the national One now lately instituted—for the civil and religious liberty with which we are blessed; and the means we have of acquiring and diffusing useful knowledge; and in general for all the great and various favors which he hath been pleased to confer upon us.

and also that we may then unite in most humbly offering our prayers and supplications to the great Lord and Ruler of Nations and beseech him to pardon our national and other transgressions—to enable us all, whether in public or private stations, to perform our several and relative duties properly and punctually—to render our national government a blessing to all the people, by constantly being a Government of wise, just, and constitutional laws, discreetly and faithfully executed and obeyed—to protect and guide all Sovereigns and Nations (especially such as have shewn kindness onto us) and to bless them with good government, peace, and concord—To promote the knowledge and practice of true religion and virtue, and the encrease of science among them and us—and generally to grant unto all Mankind such a degree of temporal prosperity as he alone knows to be best.

Given under my hand at the City of New-York the third day of October in the year of our Lord 1789.

Go: Washington

Advertisement for Royal Gift and the Knight of Malta

Alexandria, Virginia, 22 April 1790

Royal Gift AND THE *Knight of Malta* Will cover MARES and JENNETS, at Mount-Vernon, the ensuing Season—Thereafter one of them will be removed from thence.—The Price for Mares will be *Ten Dollars, Half a Dollar* per Week for Pasturage, and *Two and Six Pence* to the Groom; and for Jennets *Three Guineas,* and *Two and Six Pence.* No Charge will be made for Pasturage of the latter, provided they are taken away by the first of August; but if longer continued the above Price will be demanded thenceforward per Week. The Pasture and Fences are good, but no Warranty will be given against Escapes or Accidents.

The Qualities and Sizes of these two Animals have been often described; it is only necessary, therefore, to add, that they have increased in Size since last Year.

JOHN FAIRFAX,
March 1, 1790
Manager.
The Virginia Journal and Alexandria Advertiser.

Address to the Hebrew Congregation of Newport, Rhode Island

Newport, Rhode Island, 18 August 1790

The most succinct statement by Washington about his views on freedom of conscience and religious toleration was given in response to the welcome address that he received from the Hebrew Congregation of Newport, Rhode Island, while visiting the city during his first term as president. The body of the letter, in the writing of his secretary, Tobias Lear, incorporates the language of the congregation's address.

Gentlemen.

While I receive, with much satisfaction, your Address replete with expressions of affection and esteem; I rejoice in the opportunity of assuring you, that I shall always retain a grateful remembrance of the cordial welcome I experienced in my visit to Newport, from all classes of Citizens.

The reflection on the days of difficulty and danger which are past is rendered the more sweet, from a consciousness that they are succeeded by days of uncommon prosperity and security. If we have wisdom to make the best use of the advantages with which we are now

favored, we cannot fail, under the just administration of a good Government, to become a great and a happy people.

The Citizens of the United States of America have a right to applaud themselves for having given to mankind examples of an enlarged and liberal policy: a policy worthy of imitation. All possess alike liberty of conscience and immunities of citizenship[.] It is now no more that toleration is spoken of, as if it was by the indulgence of one class of people, that another enjoyed the exercise of their inherent natural rights. For happily the Government of the United States, which gives to bigotry no sanction, to persecution no assistance requires only that they who live under its protection should demean themselves as good citizens, in giving it on all occasions their effectual support.

It would be inconsistent with the frankness of my character not to avow that I am pleased with your favorable opinion of my Administration, and fervent wishes for my felicity. May the Children of the Stock of Abraham, who dwell in this land, continue to merit and enjoy the good will of the other Inhabitants; while every one shall sit in safety under his own vine and figtree, and there shall be none to make him afraid. May the father of all mercies scatter light and not darkness in our paths, and make us all in our several vocations useful here, and in his own due time and way everlastingly happy.

Go: Washington

Opinion of the General Officers

Philadelphia, March 9, 1792.

This memorandum contains Washington's opinions of the general officers from the Revolutionary War that were to be considered as candidates for the commander in chief of the U.S. Army. It was considered at a cabinet meeting on 9 March 1792 attended by Thomas Jefferson, Alexander Hamilton, and Henry Knox.

The following list contain the names of all the General Officers now living, and in this Country, as low as *actual* Brigadiers inclusively. Except those who it is conjectured would not, from age, want of health, and other circumstances come forward by any inducements that could be offered to them, and such as ought not to be named for the important trust of Commander in Chief.

Major General [Benjamin] Lincoln. Sober, honest, brave and sensible, but infirm; past the vigor of life, and reluctantly (if offered to him) would accept the appointment.

Majr. Genl. [Frederick] Baron de Steuben. Sensible, Sober and brave; well acquainted with Tactics and with the arrangement and discipline of an Army. High in his ideas of Subordination; impetuous in his temper; ambitious, and a foreigner.

Majr. Genl. [William] Moultree. Brave, and it is believed accommodating in his temper. Served the whole of last War; and has been an Officer in the proceeding one, at least had been engaged in an Expedition against the Cherokees; having defeated them in one or two considerable actions. What the resources, or powers of his mind are; how active he may be; and whether temperate or not, are points I cannot speak to with decision because I have had little or no opportunities to form an opinion of him.

Brigadier (but by Brevet Majr General) [Lachlan] McIntosh. Is old and inactive; supposed to be honest and brave. Not much known in the Union, and therefore would not obtain much confidence, or command much respect; either in the Community or the Army.

Majr. General (by Brevet) [Anthony] Wayne. More active and enterprising than Judicious and cautious. No œconomist it is feared. Open to flattery; vain; easily imposed upon; and liable to be drawn into scrapes. Too indulgent (the effect perhaps of some of the causes just mentioned) to his Officers and men. Whether sober, or a little addicted to the bottle, I know not.

Majr. Genl. (by Brevet) [George] Weedon. Not supposed to be an Officer of much resource though not deficient in a competent share of understanding; rather addicted to ease and pleasure; and no enemy it is said to the bottle; never has had his name brot. forward on this acct.

Majr. Genl. (by Brevet) [Edward] Hand. A sensible and judicious man; his integrity unimpeached; and was esteemed a pretty good Officer. But, if I recollect rightly, not a very active one. He has never been charged with intemperance to my knowledge; His name has rarely been mentioned under the present difficulty of chusing an Officer to comm'd, but this may, in a great measure, be owing to his being at a distance.

Majr. Genl (by Brevet) [Charles] Scott. Brave and means well; but is an officer of inadequate

abilities for extensive command; and, by report, is addicted to drinking.

Majr. Genl (by Brevet) [Jedidiah] Huntington. Sober, sensible and very discreet. Has never discover'd much enterprise; yet, no doubt has ever been entertained [sic] of his want of spirit, or firmness.

Brigadier General [James] Wilkenson. Is, by brevet Senr to those whose names follow; but the appointment to this rank was merely honorary. and as he was but a short time in Service, little can be said of his abilities as an Officer. He is lively, sensible, pompous and ambitious; but whether sober, or not, is unknown to me.

Brigadier General [Mordecai] Gist. Little has been said of his qualifications as a General Officer. His activity, and attention to duty is somewhat doubtful; tho' his spirit, I believe, is unimpeached.

Brigadier General [William] Irvine. Is sober, tolerably sensible and prudent. It is said he is an œconomist; and supported his authority whilst he was entrusted with a seperate command; but I have no recollection of any circumstance that marks him as a decidedly good, or indifferent Officer.

Brigadier General [Daniel] Morgan. Has been fortunate, and has met with eclat. Yet there are different opinions with respect to his abilities as an Officer. He is accused of using improper means to obtain certificates from the Soldiers. It is said he has been (if the case is not so now) intemperate: that he is troubled with a palpitation which often lays him up; and it is not denied that he is illiterate.

Brigadier General [Otho Holland] Williams. Is a sensible man, but not without vanity. No doubt, I believe, is entertained of his firmness: and it is thought he does not want activity; but it is not easy, where there is nothing conspicuous in a character, to pronounce decidedly upon a Military man who has always acted under the immediate orders of a superior Officer; unless he has been seen frequently in Action. The discipline, interior œconomy and police of his Corps is the best evidence one can have of his talents in this line and of this, in the case of Genl. Williams I can say nothing; as he was appointed a Brigadier after he left the Northern to join the Southern army. But a material objection to him is delicate health (if there has been no change in his Constitution), for he has gone to the Sweet Springs two or three years successively in such bad health as to afford little hope of his ever returning from them.

Brigadier General Rufus Putnam. Possesses a strong mind, and is a discreet man. No question has ever been made (that has come to my knowledge) of his want of firmness. In short, there is nothing conspicuous in his character. And he is but little known out of his own State, and a narrow circle.

Brigadier Genl (by Brevet) [Charles Cotesworth] Pinckney. A Colonel since Septr. 16th. 1776; but appointed a Brigadr. by brevet at the close of the War, *only*. In this gentleman many valuable qualities are to be found. He is of unquestionable bravery. Is a man of strict honor, erudition and good sense: and it is said has made Tactics a study. But what his spirit for enterprise is, whether active or indolent; or fitted for arrangement, I am unable to say, never having had any opportunity to form a judgment of his talents as a Military character. The capture of Charleston put an end to his Military Services: but his junr. Rank, and being little known in this part of the Union, are the two considerations most opposed to him; particularly the latter, as it is more than probable his being a prisoner prevented his promotion: which ought not to be any bar to his ranking as a Brigadier from the time that others of his standing as a Colonel, were promoted.

The above and foregoing closes the list of *all the General Officers* who as has been observed from age, want of health, disinclination, or peculiar circumstances, can be brought into view; from whom to chuse an Officer to command the Troops of the U.S.

If from either of the three Major Generals, which have been mentioned; or from those made so by *brevet,* the Commander of the Troops should be taken, no junior Officer can decline serving on the score of Rank; although he may desire, and have had expectations of being, first in command, himself.

Under this idea, and upon the principle of distribution, the arrangement of the Commanding Officer, and those next in grade to him, may be placed in the following points of view.

Commander. Lincoln or . . . Moultrie.

Under either of these Major Generals might serve as Brigadiers:

Wayne unless by being a Majr. Genl. by brevet, and seeking the command himself he should recoil at it.

Morgan for one of the above reasons would also revolt viz. command or Williams or [William] Darke.

Wilkinson. [Andrew] Pickens. [John] Brooks.

If Lincoln commands, Brooks cannot be appointed and if Moultree commands, the same will happen to Pickens.

If Pennsylvania gives the Commanding Officer, and he is of the Rank (by brevet) of Majr. Generl; the above arrangement is equally applicable on the principle of distribution, and as unexceptionable on the score of rank. But if, in the first case, Wayne, Morgan and Williams refuse to serve, and in the Second, the two last do it unless it be as Commander; then some others, junr. in dates of Commission, or of inferior rank, must be resorted to.

If upon a full view of characters, and circumstances, General Pinckney should be deemed the most eligible for the command; it would be a fruitless attempt, and a waste of time to propose to those Officers who have been his Seniors, to engage again subordinately; especially if they have been his seniors in the line of *Colonels:* and here I would draw a line which I think is a just one, and that is, that his Colonels and not his Brigadrs. Commission, ought to decide his Rank as a General Officer, because it would be hard upon him to suffer in it, on acct. of his captivity; when motives of policy and not demerit, suspended (as may fairly be presumed) his promotion during that period: but why, when it did take place, Rank was not (to a certain antecedent date) restord I am unable to conceive.

If this be fair reasoning (and I really think it is) neither Morgan nor Williams would have ground to object against serving under Pinckney; but as it is more than probable they will look to what is, rather than to what ought to be; a difficulty would be made on the subject of Rank; especially if there is any dereliction in them to the Service in any other character than that of Commanding it, and therefore it would be expedient perhaps to look for Officers of junr. Rank, and in that case may come in as Brigadiers. Wilkenson, whose rank is very questionable. Darke,—or [John Eager] Howard. [Marinus] Willet,—or [William Stephens] Smith. [John] Brooks.

If Governor Lee should be prefered to the Command, then Officers of lower grades than any that have been mentioned, in the preceding pages, must be sought after, as all of those are greatly his Seniors, and there being, in my opinion but little ground to hope, that either the Military talents which he has displayed in the course of the War, or his present dignified Station, would reconcile any of them to act a Subordinate part; except it be Wilkenson; who, as has been observed before, from having been but a short time in Service, and quitting it at an early period of the War, would have but little or no cause to complain. As also Pickins, who has never been in the Continental line. The arrangemt. wd then be, in this case.

Govr. Lee . . . Commander. Brigadrs.— Wilkenson, Pickens.

Farewell Address
United States 19 September 1796

Washington's Farewell Address was drafted with the help of James Madison and Alexander Hamilton and published in newspapers. The standard sources are Horace Binney, An Inquiry into the Formation of Washington's Farewell Address *(Philadelphia, 1859); Victor Hugo Paltsits,* Washington's Farewell Address in Facsimile, with Transliterations of all the Drafts of Washington, Madison, & Hamilton, Together with Their Correspondence and Other Supporting Documents *(New York, 1935); and Matthew Spalding and Patrick J. Garrity,* A Sacred Union of Citizens: George Washington's Farewell Address and the American Character *(Lanham, Maryland, 1996).*

Friends, & Fellow—Citizens.

The period for a new election of a Citizen, to Administer the Executive government of the United States, being not far distant, and the time actually arrived, when your thoughts must be employed in designating the person, who is to be cloathed with that important trust, it appears to me proper, especially as it may conduce to a more distinct expression of the public voice, that I should now apprise you of the resolution I have formed, to decline being considered among the number of those, out of whom a choice is to be made.

I beg you, at the sametime, to do me the justice to be assured, that this resolution has not been taken, without a strict regard to all the considerations appertaining to the relation, which binds a dutiful Citizen to his country— and that, in withdrawing the tender of service which silence in my Situation might imply, I am influenced by no diminution of zeal for your future interest, no deficiency of grateful respect for your past kindness; but am supported by a full conviction that the step is compatible with both.

The acceptance of, & continuance hitherto in, the Office to which your Suffrages have twice called me, have been a uniform sacrifice of inclination to the opinion of duty, and to a deference for what appeared to be your desire. I constantly hoped, that it would have been much earlier in my power, consistently with motives, which I was not at liberty to disregard, to return to that retirement, from which I had been reluctantly drawn. The strength of my inclination to do this, previous to the last Election, had even led to the preparation of an address to declare it to you; but mature reflection on the then perplexed & critical posture of our Affairs with foreign nations, and the unanimous advice of persons entitled to my confidence, impelled me to abandon the idea.

I rejoice, that the state of your concerns, external as well as internal, no longer renders the pursuit of inclination incompatible with the sentiment of duty, or propriety; & am persuaded whatever partiality may be retained for my services, that in the present circumstances of our country, you will not disapprove my determination to retire.

The impressions, with which, I first undertook the arduous trust, were explained on the proper occasion. In the discharge of this trust, I will only say, that I have, with good intentions, contributed towards the Organization and Administration of the government, the best exertions of which a very fallible judgment was capable. Not unconscious, in the outset, of the inferiority of my qualifications, experience in my own eyes, perhaps still more in the eyes of others, has strengthned the motives to diffidence of myself; and every day the encreasing weight of years admonishes me more and more, that the shade of retirement is as necessary to me as it will be welcome. Satisfied that if any circumstances have given peculiar value to my services, they were temporary, I have the consolation to believe, that while choice and prudence invite me to quit the political scene, patriotizm does not forbid it.

In looking forward to the moment, which is intended to terminate the career of my public life, my feelings do not permit me to suspend the deep acknowledgment of that debt of gratitude wch I owe to my beloved country, for the many honors it has conferred upon me; still more for the stedfast confidence with which it has supported me; and for the opportunities I have thence enjoyed of manifesting my inviolable attachment, by services faithful & persevering, though in usefulness unequal to my zeal. If benefits have resulted to our country from these services, let it always be remembered to your praise, and as an instructive example in our annals, that, under circumstances in which the Passions agitated in every direction were liable to mislead, amidst appearances sometimes dubious, viscissitudes of fortune often discouraging, in situations in which not unfrequently want of Success has countenanced the spirit of criticism, the constancy of your support was the essential prop of the efforts, and a guarantee of the plans by which they were effected. Profoundly penetrated with this idea, I shall carry it with me to my grave, as a strong incitement to unceasing vows that Heaven may continue to you the choicest tokens of its beneficence—that your Union & brotherly affection may be perpetual—that the free constitution, which is the work of your hands, may be sacredly maintained—that its Administration in every department may be stamped with wisdom and Virtue—that, in fine, the happiness of the people of these States, under the auspices of liberty, may be made complete, by so careful a preservation and so prudent a use of this blessing as will acquire to them the glory of recommending it to the applause, the affection—and adoption of every nation which is yet a stranger to it.

Here, perhaps, I ought to stop. But a solicitude for your welfare, which cannot end but with my life, and the apprehension of danger, natural to that solicitude, urge me on an occasion like the present, to offer to your solemn contemplation, and to recommend to your frequent review, some sentiments; which are the result of much reflection, of no inconsiderable observation, and which appear to me all important to the permanency of your felicity as a People. These will be offered to you with the more freedom as you can only see in them the disinterested warnings of a parting friend, who can possibly have no personal motive to biass his counsel. Nor can I forget, as an encouragement to it, your endulgent reception of my sentiments on a former and not dissimilar occasion.

Interwoven as is the love of liberty with every ligament of your hearts, no recommendation of mine is necessary to fortify or confirm the Attachment.

The Unity of Government which constitutes you one people is also now dear to you. It is justly so; for it is a main Pillar in the Edifice of your real independence, the support of your tranquility at home; your peace abroad; of your safety; of your prosperity; of that very Liberty which you so highly prize. But as it is easy to foresee, that from different causes & from different quarters, much pains will be taken, many artifices employed, to weaken in your minds the conviction of this truth; as this is the point in your political fortress against which the batteries of internal & external enemies will be most constantly and actively (though often covertly & insidiously) directed, it is of infinite moment, that you should properly estimate the immense value of your national Union to your collective & individual happiness; that you should cherish a cordial, habitual & immoveable attachment to it; accustoming yourselves to think and speak of it as of the Palladium of your political safety and prosperity; watching for its preservation with jealous anxiety; discountenancing whatever may suggest even a suspicion that it can in any event be abandoned, and indignantly frowning upon the first dawning of every attempt to alienate any portion of our Country from the rest, or to enfeeble the sacred ties which now link together the various parts.

For this you have every inducement of sympathy and interest. Citizens by birth or choice, of a common country, that country has a right to concentrate your affections. The name of American, which belongs to you, in your national capacity, must always exalt the just pride of Patriotism, more than any appellation derived from local discriminations. With slight shades of difference, you have the same Religeon, Manners, Habits & political Principles. You have in a common cause fought & triumphed together—The independence & liberty you possess are the work of joint councils, and joint efforts—of common dangers, sufferings and successes.

But these considerations, however powerfully they address themselves to your sensibility are greatly outweighed by those which apply more immediately to your Interest. Here every portion of our country finds the most commanding motives for carefully guarding & preserving the Union of the whole.

The North, in an unrestrained intercourse with the South, protected by the equal Laws of a common government, finds in the productions of the latter, great additional resources of Maratime & commercial enterprise and—precious materials of manufacturing industry. The South in the same Intercourse, benefitting by the Agency of the North, sees its agriculture grow & its commerce expand. Turning partly into its own channels the seamen of the North, it finds its particular navigation envigorated; and while it contributes, in different ways, to nourish & increase the general mass of the National navigation, it looks forward to the protection of a Maratime strength, to which itself is unequally adapted. The East, in a like intercourse with the West, already finds, and in the progressive improvement of interior communications, by land & water, will more & more find a valuable vent for the commodities which it brings from abroad, or manufactures at home. The West derives from the East supplies requisite to its growth & comfort—and what is perhaps of still greater consequence, it must of necessity owe the Secure enjoyment of indispensable outlets for its own productions to the weight, influence, and the future maritime strength of the Atlantic side of the Union, directed by an indissoluble community of Interest as one Nation. Any other tenure by which the West can hold this essential advantage, whether derived from its own seperate strength, or from an apostate & unnatural connection with any foreign Power, must be intrinsically precarious.

While then every part of our country thus feels an immediate & particular Interest in Union, all the parts combined cannot fail to find in the united mass of means & efforts greater strength, greater resource, proportionably greater security from external danger, a less frequent interruption of their Peace by foreign Nations; and, what is of inestimable value! they must derive from Union an exemption from those broils and Wars between themselves, which so frequently afflict neighbouring countries, not tied together by the same government; which their own rivalships alone would be sufficient to produce, but which opposite foreign alliances, attachments & intriegues would stimulate & imbitter. Hence likewise they will avoid the necessity of those overgrown Military establishments, which under any form of Government are inauspicious to liberty, and which are to be regarded as particularly hostile to Republican Liberty: In this sense it is, that your union ought to be considered as a main prop of your liberty, and that the love of the one ought to endear to you the preservation of the other.

These considerations speak a persuasive language to every reflecting & virtuous mind, and exhibit the continuance of the Union as a primary object of Patriotic desire. Is there a doubt, whether a common government can embrace so large a sphere? Let experience solve it. To listen to mere speculation in such a case were criminal. We are authorized to hope that a proper organization of the whole, with the auxiliary agency of governments for the respective Subdivisions, will afford a happy issue to the experiment. 'Tis well worth a fair and full experiment. With such powerful and obvious motives to Union, affecting all parts of our country, while experience shall not have demonstrated its impracticability, there will always be reason, to distrust the patriotism of those, who in any quarter may endeavor to weaken its bands.

In contemplating the causes wch may disturb our Union, it occurs as matter of serious concern, that any ground should have been furnished for characterizing parties by Geographical discriminations—Northern and Southern—Atlantic and Western; whence designing men may endeavour to excite a belief that there is a real difference of local interests and views. One of the expedients of Party to acquire influence, within particular districts, is to misrepresent the opinions & aims of other Districts. You cannot shield yourselves too much against the jealousies & heart burnings which spring from these misrepresentations. They tend to render Alien to each other those who ought to be bound together by fraternal Affection. The Inhabitants of our Western country have lately had a useful lesson on this head. They have Seen, in the Negociation by the Executive, and in the unanimous ratification by the Senate, of the Treaty with Spain, and in the universal satisfaction at that event, throughout the United States, a decisive proof how unfounded were the suspicions propagated among them of a policy in the General Government and in the Atlantic States unfriendly to their Interests in regard to the Mississippi. They have been witnesses to the formation of two Treaties, that with G: Britain and that with Spain, which secure to them every thing they could desire, in respect to our Foreign relations, towards confirming their prosperity. Will it not be their wisdom to rely for the preservation of these advantages on the Union by wch they were procured? Will they not henceforth be deaf to those Advisers, if such there are, who would sever them from their Brethren and connect them with Aliens?

To the efficacy and permanency of Your Union, a Government for the whole is indispensable. No Alliances however strict between the parts can be an adequate substitute. They must inevitably experience the infractions & interruptions which all Alliances in all times have experienced. Sensible of this momentous truth, you have improved upon your first essay, by the adoption of a Constitution of Government, better calculated than your former for an intimate Union, and for the efficacious management of your common concerns. This government, the offspring of our own choice uninfluenced and unawed, adopted upon full investigation & mature deliberation, completely free in its principles, in the distribution of its powers, uniting security with energy, and containing within itself a provision for its own amendment, has a just claim to your confidence and your support. Respect for its authority, compliance with its Laws, acquiescence in its measures, are duties enjoined by the fundamental maxims of true Liberty. The basis of our political Systems is the right of the people to make and to alter their Constitutions of Government. But the Constitution which at any time exists, 'till changed by an explicit and authentic act of the whole People, is sacredly obligatory upon all. The very idea of the power and the right of the People to establish Government presupposes the duty of every Individual to obey the established Government.

All obstructions to the execution of the Laws, all combinations and Associations, under whatever plausible character, with the real design to direct, controul counteract, or awe the regular deliberation and action of the Constituted authorities are distructive of this fundamental principle and of fatal tendency. They serve to Organize faction, to give it an artificial and extraordinary force—to put in the place of the delegated will of the Nation, the will of a party; often a small but artful and enterprizing minority of the Community; and, according to the alternate triumphs of different parties, to make the public Administration the Mirror of the ill concerted and incongruous projects of faction, rather than the Organ of consistent and wholesome plans digested by common councils and modefied by mutual interests. However combinations or Associations of the above description may now & then answer popular ends, they are likely, in the course of time and things, to become potent engines, by which cunning, ambitious and unprincipled men will be enabled to subvert the Power of the People, & to usurp for themselves the reins of Government; destroying afterwards the very engines which have lifted them to unjust dominion.

Towards the preservation of your Government and the permanency of your present happy state, it is requisite, not only that you steadily discountenance irregular oppositions to its acknowledged authority, but also that you resist with care the spirit of innovation upon its principles however specious the pretexts. One method of assault may be to effect, in the forms of the Constitution, alterations which will impair the energy of the system, and thus to undermine what cannot be directly overthrown. In all the changes to which you may be invited, remember that time and habit are at least as necessary to fix the true character of Governments, as of other human institutions—that experience is the surest standard, by which to test the real tendency of the existing Constitution of a Country—that facility in changes upon the credit of mere hypotheses & opinion exposes to perpetual change, from the endless variety of hypotheses and opinion: and remember, especially, that for the efficient management of your common interests, in a country so extensive as ours, a Government of as much vigour as is consistent with the perfect security of Liberty is indispensable—Liberty itself will find in such a Government, with powers properly distributed and adjusted, its surest Guardian. It is indeed little else than a name, where the Government is too feeble to withstand the enterprises of faction, to confine each member of the Society within the limits prescribed by the laws & to maintain all in the secure & tranquil enjoyment of the rights of person & property.

I have already intimated to you the danger of Parties in the State, with particular reference to the founding of them on Geographical discriminations. Let me now take a more comprehensive view, & warn you in the most solemn manner against the baneful effects of the Spirit of Party, generally.

This Spirit, unfortunately, is inseperable from our nature, having its root in the strongest passions of the human Mind. It exists under different shapes in all Governments, more or less stifled, controuled, or repressed; but in those of the popular form it is seen in its greatest rankness and is truly their worst enemy.

The alternate domination of one faction over another, sharpened by the spirit of revenge natural to party dissention, which in different ages & countries has perpetrated the most horrid enormities, is itself a frightful despotism. But this leads at length to a more formal and permanent despotism. The disorders & miseries, which result, gradually incline the minds of men to seek security & repose in the absolute power of an Individual: and sooner or later the chief of some prevailing faction more able or more fortunate than his competitors, turns this disposition to the purposes of his own elevation, on the ruins of Public Liberty.

Without looking forward to an extremity of this kind (which nevertheless ought not to be entirely out of sight) the common & continual mischiefs of the spirit of Party are sufficient to make it the interest and the duty of a wise People to discourage and restrain it.

It serves always to distract the Public Councils and enfeeble the Public Administration. It agitates the Community with ill founded Jealousies and false alarms, kindles the animosity of one part against another, foments occasionally riot & insurrection. It opens the door to foreign influence & corruption, which find a facilitated access to the government itself through the channels of party passions. Thus the policy and the will of one country, are subjected to the policy and will of another.

There is an opinion that parties in free countries are useful checks upon the Administration

of the Government and serve to keep alive the spirit of Liberty. This within certain limits is probably true—and in Governments of a Monarchical cast Patriotism may look with endulgence, if not with favour, upon the spirit of party. But in those of the popular character, in Governments purely elective, it is a spirit not to be encouraged. From their natural tendency, it is certain there will always be enough of that spirit for every salutary purpose. And there being constant danger of excess, the effort ought to be, by force of public opinion, to mitigate & assuage it. A fire not to be quenched; it demands a uniform vigilance to prevent its bursting into a flame, lest instead of warming it should consume.

It is important, likewise, that the habits of thinking in a free Country should inspire caution in those entrusted with its Administration, to confine themselves within their respective Constitutional Spheres; avoiding in the exercise of the Powers of one department to encroach upon another. The spirit of encroachment tends to consolidate the powers of all the departments in one, and thus to create whatever the form of government, a real despotism. A just estimate of that love of power, and proneness to abuse it, which predominates in the human heart, is sufficient to satisfy us of the truth of this position. The necessity of reciprocal checks in the exercise of political power; by dividing and distributing it into different depositories, & constituting each the Guardian of the Public Weal against invasions by the others, has been evinced by experiments ancient & modern; some of them in our country & under our own eyes. To preserve them must be as necessary as to institute them. If in the opinion of the People, the distribution or modification of the Constitutional powers be in any particular wrong, let it be corrected by an amendment in the way which the Constitution designates. But let there be no change by usurpation; for though this, in one instance, may be the instrument of good, it is the customary weapon by which free governments are destroyed. The precedent must always greatly overbalance in permanent evil any partial or transient benefit which the use can at any time yield.

Of all the dispositions and habits which lead to political prosperity, Religion and morality are indispensable supports. In vain would that man claim the tribute of Patriotism, who should labour to subvert these great Pillars of human happiness, these firmest props of the duties of Men & citizens. The mere Politican, equally with the pious man ought to respect & to cherish them. A volume could not trace all their connections with private & public felicity. Let it simply be asked where is the security for property, for reputation, for life, if the sense of religious obligation desert the Oaths, which are the instruments of investigation in Courts of Justice? And let us with caution indulge the supposition, that morality can be maintained without religion. Whatever may be conceded to the influence of refined education on minds of peculiar structure—reason & experience both forbid us to expect that National morality can prevail in exclusion of religious principle.

'Tis substantially true, that virtue or morality is a necessary spring of popular government. The rule indeed extends with more or less force to every species of Free Government. Who that is a sincere friend to it, can look with indifference upon attempts to shake the foundation of the fabric.

Promote then as an object of primary importance, Institutions for the general diffusion of knowledge. In proportion as the structure of a government gives force to public opinion, it is essential that public opinion should be enlightened.

As a very important source of strength & security, cherish public credit. One method of preserving it is to use it as sparingly as possible: avoiding occasions of expence by cultivating peace, but remembering also that timely disbursements to prepare for danger frequently prevent much greater disbursements to repel it—avoiding likewise the accumulation of debt, not only by shunning occasions of expence, but by vigorous exertions in time of Peace to discharge the Debts which unavoidable wars may have occasioned, not ungenerously throwing upon posterity the burthen which we ourselves ought to bear. The execution of these maxims belongs to your Representatives, but it is necessary that public opinion should cooperate. To facilitate to them the performance of their duty, it is essential that you should practically bear in mind, that towards the payment of debts there must be Revenue—that to have Revenue there must be taxes—that no taxes can be devised which are not more or less inconvenient & unpleasant—that the intrinsic embarrassment inseperable from the Selection of the proper objects (which is always a choice of difficulties) ought to be a decisive motive for a candid construction of the Conduct of the Government in making it, and for a spirit of acquiescence in the measures for obtaining Revenue which the public exigencies may at any time dictate.

Observe good faith & justice towds all Nations. Cultivate peace & harmony with all—Religion & morality enjoin this conduct; and can it be that good policy does not equally enjoin it? It will be worthy of a free, enlightened, and, at no distant period, a great Nation, to give to mankind the magnanimous and too novel example of a People always guided by an exalted justice & benevolence. Who can doubt that in the course of time and things the fruits of such a plan would richly repay any temporary advantages wch might be lost by a steady adherence to it? Can it be, that Providence has not connected the permanent felicity of a Nation with its virtue? The experiment, at least, is recommended by every sentiment which ennobles human Nature. Alas! is it rendered impossible by its vices?

In the execution of such a plan nothing is more essential than that permanent inveterate antipathies against particular Nations and passionate attachments for others should be excluded; and that in place of them just & amicable feelings towards all should be cultivated. The Nation, which indulges towards another an habitual hatred, or an habitual fondness, is in some degree a slave. It is a slave to its animosity or to its affection, either of which is sufficient to lead it astray from its duty and its interest. Antipathy in one Nation against another—disposes each more readily to offer insult and injury, to lay hold of slight causes of umbrage, and to be haughty and intractable, when accidental or trifling occasions of dispute occur. Hence frequent collisions, obstinate envenomed and bloody contests. The Nation, prompted by ill will & resentment sometimes impels to War the Government, contrary to the best calculations of policy. The Government sometimes participates in the national propensity, and adopts through passion what reason would reject; at other times, it makes the animosity of the Nation subservient to projects of hostility instigated by pride, ambition and other sinister & pernicious motives. The peace often, sometimes perhaps the Liberty, of Nations has been the victim.

So likewise, a passionate attachment of one Nation for another produces a variety of evils. Sympathy for the favourite nation, facilitating the illusion of an imaginary common interest, in cases where no real common interest exists, and infusing into one the enmities of the other, betrays the former into a participation in the quarrels & Wars of the latter, without adequate inducement or justification: It leads also to concessions to the favourite Nation of priviledges denied to others, which is apt doubly to injure the Nation making the concessions—by unnecessarily parting with what ought to have been retained—& by exciting jealousy, ill will, and a disposition to retaliate, in the parties from whom eql priviledges are withheld: And it gives to ambitious, corrupted, or deluded citizens (who devote themselves to the favourite Nation) facility to betray, or sacrifice the interests of their own country, without odium, sometimes even with popularity; gilding with the appearances of a virtuous sense of obligation a commendable deference for public opinion, or a laudable zeal for public good, the base or foolish compliances of ambition corruption or infatuation.

As avenues to foreign influence in innumerable ways, such attachments are particularly alarming to the truly enlightened and independent Patriot. How many opportunities do they afford to tamper with domestic factions, to practice the arts of seduction, to mislead public opinion, to influence or awe the public Councils! Such an attachment of a small or weak, towards a great & powerful Nation, dooms the former to be the satellite of the latter.

Against the insidious wiles of foreign influence, (I conjure you to believe me fellow citizens,) the jealousy of a free people ought to be constantly awake; since history and experience prove that foreign influence is one of the most baneful foes of Republican Government. But that jealousy to be useful must be impartial; else it becomes the instrument of the very influence to be avoided, instead of a defence against it. Excessive partiality for one foreign nation and excessive dislike of another, cause those whom they actuate to see danger only on one side, and serve to veil and even second the arts of influence on the other. Real Patriots, who may resist the intriegues of the favourite, are liable to become suspected and odious; while its tools and dupes usurp the applause & confidence of the people, to surrender their interests.

The Great rule of conduct for us, in regard to foreign Nations is in extending our comercial relations to have with them as little political connection as possible. So far as we have already formed engagements let them be fulfilled, with perfect good faith. Here let us stop.

Europe has a set of primary interests, which to us have none, or a very remote relation. Hence she must be engaged in frequent controversies, the causes of which are essentially foreign to our concerns. Hence therefore it must be unwise in us to implicate ourselves, by artificial ties, in the ordinary vicissitudes of her politics, or the ordinary combinations & collisions of her friendships, or enmities.

Our detached & distant situation invites and enables us to pursue a different course. If we remain one People, under an efficient government, the period is not far off, when we may defy material injury from external annoyance; when we may take such an attitude as will cause the neutrality we may at any time resolve upon to be scrupulously respected; when belligerent nations, under the impossibility of making acquisitions upon us, will not lightly hazard the giving us provocation; when we may choose peace or War, as our interest guided by justice shall Counsel.

Why forego the advantages of so peculiar a situation? Why quit our own to stand upon foreign ground? Why, by interweaving our destiny with that of any part of Europe, entangle our peace and prosperity in the toils of European Ambition, Rivalship, Interest, Humour or Caprice?

'Tis our true policy to steer clear of permanent Alliances, with any portion of the foreign World—So far, I mean, as we are now at liberty to do it—for let me not be understood as capable of patronising infidility to existing engagements, (I hold the maxim no less applicable to public than to private affairs, that honesty is always the best policy)—I repeat it therefore, Let those engagements be observed in their genuine sense. But in my opinion, it is unnecessary and would be unwise to extend them.

Taking care always to keep ourselves, by suitable establishments, on a respectably defensive posture, we may safely trust to temporary alliances for extraordinary emergencies.

Harmony, liberal intercourse with all Nations, are recommended by policy, humanity and interest. But even our Commercial policy should hold an equal and impartial hand: neither seeking nor granting exclusive favours or preferences; consulting the natural course of things; diffusing & deversifying by gentle means the streams of Commerce, but forcing nothing; establishing with Powers so disposed—in order to give to trade a stable course, to define the rights of our Merchants, and to enable the Government to support them—conventional rules of intercourse; the best that present circumstances and mutual opinion will permit, but temporary, & liable to be from time to time abandoned or varied, as experience and circumstances shall dictate; constantly keeping in view, that 'tis folly in one Nation to look for disinterested favors from another—that it must pay with a portion of its Independence for whatever it may accept under that character—that by such acceptance, it may place itself in the condition of having given equivalents for nominal favours and yet of being reproached with ingratitude for not giving more. There can be no greater error than to expect, or calculate upon real favours from Nation to Nation. 'Tis an illusion which experience must cure, which a just pride ought to discard.

In offering to you, my Countrymen, these counsels of an old and affectionate friend, I dare not hope they will make the strong and lasting impression, I could wish—that they will controul the usual current of the passions, or prevent our Nation from running the course which has hitherto marked the Destiny of Nations: But if I may even flatter myself, that they may be productive of some partial benefit, some occasional good; that they may now & then recur to moderate the fury of party spirit, to warn against the mischiefs of foreign Intriegue, to guard against the Impostures of pretended patriotism—this hope will be a full recompence for the solicitude for your welfare, by which they have been dictated.

How far in the discharge of my Official duties, I have been guided by the principles which have been delineated, the public Records and other evidences of my conduct must witness to You and to the world. To myself, the assurance of my own conscience is, that I have at least believed myself to be guided by them.

In relation to the still subsisting War in Europe, my Proclamation of the 22d of April 1793 is the index to my Plan. Sanctioned by your approving voice and by that of Your Representatives in both Houses of Congress, the spirit of that measure has continually governed me; uninfluenced by any attempts to deter or divert me from it.

After deliberate examination with the aid of the best lights I could obtain I was well satisfied that our Country, under all the circumstances of the case, had a right to take, and was bound in duty and interest, to take a Neutral position. Having taken it, I determined, as far as should depend upon me, to maintain it, with moderation, perseverence & firmness.

The considerations, which respect the right to hold this conduct, it is not necessary on this occasion to detail. I will only observe, that according to my understanding of the matter, that right, so far from being denied by any of the Belligerent Powers has been virtually admitted by all.

The duty of holding a neutral conduct may be inferred, without any thing more, from the obligation which justice and humanity impose on every Nation, in cases in which it is free to act, to maintain inviolate the relations of Peace and amity towards other Nations.

The inducements of interest for observing that conduct will best be referred to your own reflections & experience. With me, a predominant motive has been to endeavour to gain time to our country to settle & mature its yet recent institutions, and to progress without interruption, to that degree of strength & consistency, which is necessary to give it, humanly speaking, the command of its own fortunes.

Though in reviewing the incidents of my Administration, I am unconscious of intentional error—I am nevertheless too sensible of my defects not to think it probable that I may have committed many errors. Whatever they may be I fervently beseech the Almighty to avert or mitigate the evils to which they may tend. I shall also carry with me the hope that my Country will never cease to view them with indulgence; and that after forty five years of my life dedicated to its Service, with an upright zeal, the faults of incompetent abilities will be consigned to oblivion, as myself must soon be to the Mansions of rest.

Relying on its kindness in this as in other things, and actuated by that fervent love towards it, which is so natural to a Man, who views in it the native soil of himself and his progenitors for several Generations; I anticipate with pleasing expectation that retreat, in which I promise myself to realize, without alloy, the sweet enjoyment of partaking, in the midst of my fellow Citizens, the benign influence of good Laws under a free Government—the ever favourite object of my heart, and the happy reward, as I trust, of our mutual cares, labours and dangers.

Go: Washington

CHRONOLOGY

1731/32   Born to Augustine and Mary Ball Washington at Popes Creek in Westmoreland County, Virginia, near the banks of the Potomac River.

Note: Washington's birth occurred in 1731 by the Old Style calendar (Julian), and 1732 by the New Style calendar (Gregorian). The New Style calendar, which added eleven days and began the new year in January rather than March, was not adopted by Great Britain and the colonies until 1752, however.

1743   Death of Augustine Washington, Washington's father.

Hunting Creek estate renamed Mount Vernon by Lawrence Washington, and construction of mansion house begun.

1745   Returns to live with his mother at Fredericksburg.

Attends school.

1746   Considers entering British navy but abandons idea at his mother's request.

1747   Leaves school to live at Mount Vernon with his half brother Lawrence Washington.

1748   Takes surveying trip to Shenandoah Valley of Virginia with James Genn, surveyor for Prince William County, and George William Fairfax.

1749   Appointed public surveyor.

1751   Sails for West Indies with ailing half brother Lawrence Washington.

1752   Becomes residuary heir to Mount Vernon after the death of Lawrence Washington from tuberculosis.

1753   Sent by Virginia governor Robert Dinwiddie to the Ohio Country to challenge the French claims to the Allegheny River Valley.

Journal of the expedition is published.

1754   Appointed lieutenant colonel of a Virginia regiment.

Dinwiddie's Proclamation concerning bounty lands for French and Indian War service.

Defeats French and Indians at Great Meadows.

Attacks Jumonville, and surrenders at Fort Necessity.

Ill health.

Sojourns at Mount Vernon.

Resigns commission.

1755   Serves as aide-de-camp to General Braddock on disastrous campaign against the French on the Monongahela River.

Becomes commander in chief of the Virginia forces.

1756   Commands Virginia provincial troops.

Takes military mission to New York and Boston.

1758   Suffers again from ill health.

Courtship with Martha Dandridge Custis.

Marches to the Ohio as part of Gen. John Forbes's expedition to Fort Duquesne.

Resigns commission and is elected to the Virginia House of Burgesses.

1759	Marries Martha Custis at White House, Virginia.
	Takes seat in Virginia House of Burgesses.
1763	Dinwiddie's Proclamation concerning bounty lands for French and Indian War service.
1765	Serves as commissioner for settling the military accounts of the colony.
1769	Disapproves of Stamp Acts.
1770	Journey to the Ohio and Kanawha Rivers.
1773	Stepdaughter Martha Parke "Patsy" Custis dies.
	Approves Committee of Correspondence.
1774	Attends meeting at the Raleigh tavern after prorogation by Governor Dunmore.
	Appointed by Virginia Convention as a delegate to the first Continental Congress.
	Presides over Fairfax County meeting that draws up the Fairfax Resolves.
1775	Elected to second Continental Congress.
	Chosen commander in chief of the Continental army.
	Takes command of the army at Cambridge, Massachusetts.
	Siege of Boston.
1776	Occupies Dorchester Heights and sees British evacuate Boston.
	Leaves Boston for New York.
	Battle of Long Island and Washington's retreat.
	Affair at Kip's Bay and Battle of Harlem Heights, New York.
	Battle of White Plains, New York.
	Loss of Forts Lee and Washington and retreat through New Jersey.

	Battle of Trenton, New Jersey.
	Congress invests with dictatorial powers.
	Receives honorary LL.D. from Harvard College.
1777	Battle of Princeton, New Jersey.
	Winter quarters at Morristown, New Jersey.
	Moves toward Philadelphia to meet British general William Howe.
	Battle of Brandywine, Pennsylvania.
	Battle of Germantown, Pennsylvania.
	Winters at Valley Forge, Pennsylvania.
1778	Conway Cabal.
	British evacuate Philadelphia.
	Battle of Monmouth Courthouse, New Jersey.
	Arrival of D'Estaing's fleet.
	Rhode Island campaign fails.
	In winter quarters at Middlebrook, New Jersey.
1779	Captures Stony Point.
	Sullivan sent to Indian country.
	Winters at Morristown, New Jersey.
1780	Rochambeau arrives at Newport.
	Gates defeated at Camden.
	Arnold's Conspiracy.
	In winter quarters at Tappen (Totowa), New York.
1781	Pennsylvania troops mutiny.
	Meets Rochambeau at Wethersfield, Connecticut.
	With army before New York.
	Marches with the French for Virginia.
	Stepson John Parke Custis dies.
	Defeats Cornwallis at Yorktown, Virginia.

1782	At Newburgh, New York.	1793	Proclamation of neutrality.

1782   At Newburgh, New York.

Urged to become king.

Provisional treaty of peace.

1783   Newburgh Conspiracy.

Cessation of hostilities.

Circular letter to states.

Definitive treaty of peace signed.

Takes leave of army.

Last meeting with his officers.

Resigns commission, and retires to Mount Vernon.

1784   Engaged in canal projects to connect the Ohio with the Virginia tidewater.

Working for union.

1786   Annapolis Convention.

1787   Presides over Constitutional Convention.

Signs new Constitution.

1788   Efforts to secure adoption of Constitution by the states.

1789   Declared president of the United States, and inaugurated 30 April.

Makes a tour of northeastern states.

Death of mother, Mary Ball Washington.

1790   Federal City to be on the Potomac.

Assumption of Revolutionary War debts.

Cabinet differences.

1791   Makes a tour of southern states.

Gen. Arthur St. Clair's defeat by Indians near Wabash River.

1792   Elected to second term as president.

1793   Proclamation of neutrality.

Recall of Genêt.

Jefferson and Hamilton resign from cabinet.

Edmund Randolph appointed secretary of state.

1794   Monroe sent to France.

Randolph resigns, and Timothy Pickering takes his place.

Jay's Treaty, forcing British to evacuate western forts as stipulated in Treaty of Paris.

Whiskey Rebellion in Pennsylvania.

Gen. Anthony Wayne defeats Indians at Fallen Timbers in the Northwest Territory (now Toledo, Ohio).

1795   Signs Treaty of San Lorenzo with Spain, opening Mississippi River to American navigation and setting southern boundary of the United States.

Treaty of Greenville, by which Indian nations cede lands of present-day Ohio, Indiana, and Michigan.

Jay's Treaty ratified.

1796   Pinckney appointed minister to France.

Issues Farewell Address.

1797   Retires from presidency and returns home to Mount Vernon.

XYZ mission to France.

Preparations for war with France.

1798   Alien and sedition laws.

Virginia and Kentucky Resolutions.

Commander in chief of the armies of the United States of America.

1799   Last illness, death, and burial at Mount Vernon.

Familial Relationships

Note: The familial relationship of the following individuals to George Washington appears following their names and, when known, birth and death dates. Spouses of uncles are listed as aunts, spouses of nephews are listed as nieces, spouses of grandnephews are listed as grandnieces, etc. Surnames of females appear in bold type.

Allerton, Willoughby (d. 1759): first husband of Anne **Steptoe** Allerton Washington

Ashton, Ann **Washington** (1752–1777): niece, daughter of half brother Augustine Washington

Ashton, Ann: grandniece, daughter of Ann **Washington** Ashton

Ashton, Burdett (1747–1814): nephew, husband of Ann **Washington** Ashton

Ashton, Burdett (1773–1812): grandnephew, son of Ann **Washington** Ashton

Ashton, Charles Augustine (1770–1800): grandnephew, son of Ann **Washington** Ashton

Aylett, John (1748–1777): brother-in-law, first husband of Elizabeth **Dandridge** Aylett

Ball, Burgess (1749–1800): nephew, first husband of Frances **Washington** Ball Peyton

Ball, Burgess (1773–1793): grandnephew, son of Frances **Washington** Ball Peyton

Ball, Hannah **Atherold** (d. 1694): great-grandmother, grandmother of Mary **Ball** Washington

Ball, Joseph (c.1649–c.1711): grandfather, father of Mary **Ball** Washington and husband of Mary Johnson Ball Hewes

Ball, Joseph (d. 1760): uncle, brother of Mary **Ball** Washington

Ball, William: great-great-grandfather, great-grandfather of Mary **Ball** Washington

Ball, William (c.1615–1680): great-grandfather, grandfather of Mary **Ball** Washington

Bassett, Anna Maria **Dandridge** (1739–1777): sister-in-law, sister of Martha **Dandridge** Custis Washington

Bassett, Anna Maria (1760–c.1763): niece, niece of Martha **Dandridge** Custis Washington

Bassett, Anna Maria ("Nancy"; 1763–1773): niece, niece of Martha **Dandridge** Custis Washington

Bassett, Burwell, Sr. (1734–1793): brother-in-law, husband of Anne **Dandridge** Bassett

Bassett, Burwell, Jr. (1764–1841): nephew, nephew of Martha **Dandridge** Custis Washington

Bassett, Elizabeth ("Betcy"; 1758–1773): niece, niece of Martha **Dandridge** Custis Washington

Bassett, Elizabeth Carter **Browne**: niece, wife of John Bassett

Bassett, Elizabeth **McCarty**: niece, first wife of Burwell Bassett, Jr.

Bassett, John (1765–1826): nephew, nephew of Martha **Dandridge** Custis Washington

Bassett, Virginia (b. 1787): grandniece, daughter of John Bassett

Bassett, William ("Billy"; 1760–1775): nephew, nephew of Martha **Dandridge** Custis Washington

Brooks, Christopher: godfather

Bushrod, John (d. 1760): second husband of Mildred **Washington** Bushrod

Bushrod, Mildred **Washington** (c.1720–1785): cousin

Butler, Edward George Washington (1800–1888): step-great grandson-in-law and step-grandnephew, husband of Frances Parke **Lewis** Butler

Butler, Frances Parke **Lewis** (1799–1875): step-great-granddaughter and step-grandniece, daughter of Eleanor Parke **Custis** Lewis and Lawrence Lewis

Butler, William: great-great-great-grandfather, father of Margaret **Butler** Washington

Carter, Betty **Lewis** (1765–1830): niece, daughter of Betty **Washington** Lewis

Carter, Charles, Jr. (1765–1829): nephew, husband of Betty **Lewis** Carter

Chichester, Ann **Gordon** (1743–1765): first wife of Richard Chichester, Jr.

Chichester, Ellen **Ball**: cousin

Chichester, Richard, Sr. (d. 1743): husband of Ellen **Ball** Chichester

Chichester, Richard, Jr. (1736–1796): cousin

Chichester, Sarah **McCarty** (d. 1826): second wife of Richard Chichester, Jr.

Claiborne, Anne **Dandridge**: niece, niece of Martha **Dandridge** Custis Washington

Claiborne, William Dandridge (d. 1811): nephew, husband of Anne **Dandridge** Claiborne

Conrad, Charles Magill Conrad (1804–1878): step-great-grandson-in-law and step-grand-nephew, husband of Mary Eliza Angela **Lewis** Conrad

Conrad, Mary Eliza Angela **Lewis** ("Ped," "Tiffin"; 1813–1839): step-great-granddaughter and step-grandniece, daughter of Eleanor Parke **Custis** Lewis and Lawrence Lewis

Custis, Daniel Parke (1711–1757): first husband of Martha **Dandridge** Custis Washington

Custis, Daniel Parke (1751–1754): son of Martha **Dandridge** Custis Washington and her first husband, Daniel Parke Custis

Custis, Frances Parke (1753–1756): daughter of Martha **Dandridge** Custis Washington and her first husband, Daniel Parke Custis

Custis, George Washington Parke ("Tub," "Wash," "Boy"; 1781–1857): step-grandson, son of John Parke Custis

Custis, John (1678–1749): first father-in-law of Martha **Dandridge** Custis Washington

Custis, John Parke ("Jacky"; 1754–1781): stepson, son of Martha **Dandridge** Custis Washington and her first husband, Daniel Parke Custis

Custis, Martha Parke ("Patsy"; c.1756–1773): stepdaughter, daughter of Martha **Dandridge** Custis Washington and her first husband Daniel Parke Custis

Custis, Mary Lee **Fitzhugh** (1788–1853): step-granddaughter-in-law, wife of George Washington Parke Custis

Dandridge, Bartholomew, Sr. (1737–1785): brother-in-law, brother of Martha **Dandridge** Custis Washington

Dandridge, Bartholomew, Jr. ("Bat," "Bart"; c.1772–1802): nephew, nephew of Martha **Dandridge** Custis Washington

Dandridge, Bartholomew (b. 1691): uncle, uncle of Martha **Dandridge** Custis Washington

Dandridge, Frances Jones (1710–1785): mother-in-law, mother of Martha **Dandridge** Custis Washington

Dandridge, Frances Lucy: niece, niece of Martha **Dandridge** Custis Washington

Dandridge, Francis (b. 1697): uncle, uncle of Martha **Dandridge** Custis Washington

Dandridge, Francis (1744–1758): brother-in-law, brother of Martha **Dandridge** Custis Washington

Dandridge, John (1700–1756): father-in-law, father of Martha **Dandridge** Custis Washington

Dandridge, John (1733–1749): brother-in-law, brother of Martha **Dandridge** Custis Washington

Dandridge, John (d. 1799): nephew, nephew of Martha **Dandridge** Custis Washington

Dandridge, Judith Burbidge: niece, niece of Martha **Dandridge** Custis Washington

Dandridge, Julius Burbidge: nephew, nephew of Martha **Dandridge** Custis Washington

Dandridge, Mary (b. 1693): aunt, aunt of Martha **Dandridge** Custis Washington

Dandridge, Mary **Burbidge** (d. 1809): sister-in-law, wife of Bartholomew Dandridge, Sr.

Dandridge, Mary Burbidge: niece, niece of Martha **Dandridge** Custis Washington

Dandridge, Rebecca Jones **Minge**: niece, wife of nephew John Dandridge

Dandridge, William (1689–1743): uncle, uncle of Martha **Dandridge** Custis Washington

Dandridge, William (1734–1776): brother-in-law, brother of Martha **Dandridge** Custis Washington

Dandridge, William: nephew, nephew of Martha **Dandridge** Custis Washington

Dawson, Elizabeth **Churchill** Bassett (1709–1779): mother-in-law of Martha Dandridge Custis Washington's sister, Anna Maria **Dandridge** Bassett

Fairfax, Elizabeth Blair **Cary**: wife of Ferdinando Fairfax

Fairfax, Ferdinando (1769–1820) godson, son of Bryan Fairfax

Fitzhugh, Nicholas: grandnephew, husband of Sarah **Ashton** Fitzhugh

Fitzhugh, Sarah **Ashton** (b. c.1775): grandniece, daughter of Ann Washington **Ashton** Fitzhugh

Gayle, George (d. 1712): step-grandfather, second husband of Mildred **Warner** Washington

Gayle, Mildred (d. 1696): aunt, daughter of Mildred **Warner** Washington Gayle

Gayle, Mildred (c.1697–1747): aunt, daughter of Mildred **Warner** Washington Gayle

Gayle, Mildred **Warner** Washington (c.1671–1701): grandmother, wife of grandfather Lawrence Washington, and second wife of George Gayle

Gregory, Roger (d. c.1731): second husband of Mildred **Washington** Lewis Gregory Willis

Halyburton, Martha **Dandridge** ("Patty"): niece, niece of Martha **Dandridge** Custis Washington

Halyburton, William: nephew, husband of Martha **Dandridge** Halyburton

Hammond, Mildred **Washington** (d. 1804): niece, daughter of Charles Washington

Hammond, Thomas: nephew, husband of Mildred **Washington** Hammond

Harper, Robert (d. c.1782): husband of Sarah **Washington** Harper

Harper, Sarah **Washington**: cousin, daughter of John Washington of Leedstown

Haynie, Elizabeth **Johnson** (d. 1796): cousin, niece of Mary **Ball** Washington

Haynie, Sally Ball (b. c.1779): cousin, grandniece of Mary **Ball** Washington

Henley, Bartholomew H. (b. 1788): nephew, nephew of Martha **Dandridge** Custis Washington

Henley, Elizabeth **Dandridge** Aylett ("Betsy"; 1749–c.1800): sister-in-law, sister of Martha **Dandridge** Custis Washington

Henley, John Dandridge (1781–1835): nephew, nephew of Martha **Dandridge** Custis Washington

Henley, Leonard (d. 1798): brother-in-law, second husband of Elizabeth **Dandridge** Aylett

Henley, Robert (1782–1827): nephew, nephew of Martha **Dandridge** Custis Washington

Hewes, Mary Johnson Ball (d. 1721): grandmother, mother of Mary **Ball** Washington

Hewes, Richard (d. c.1713): step-grandfather, husband of Mary Johnson Ball Hewes

Johnson, Elizabeth: aunt, half sister of Mary **Ball** Washington

Jones, Orlando (1681–1719): grandfather-in-law, grandfather of Martha **Dandridge** Custis Washington

Jones, Martha **Macon** Jones (d. 1716): grandmother-in-law, grandmother of Martha **Dandridge** Custis Washington

Jones, Roland ("Rowland"; 1644–1688): great-grandfather-in-law, great-grandfather of Martha **Dandridge** Custis Washington

Kennon, Britannia Wellington **Peter** ("Brit"; 1815–1911): step-great-granddaughter, daughter of Martha Parke **Custis** Peter

Law, Elizabeth Parke **Custis** ("Eliza," "Betsey"; 1776–1832): step-granddaughter, daughter of John Parke Custis

Law, Thomas (1756–1834): step-grandson-in-law, husband of Elizabeth Parke **Custis** Law

Lear, Benjamin Lincoln (1791–1832): son of Tobias Lear and his first wife, Mary **Long** Lear

Lear, Frances **Bassett** Washington ("Fanny"; 1767–1796): niece, niece of Martha **Dandridge** Custis Washington, wife of George Augustine Washington and second wife of Tobias Lear

Lear, Frances Dandridge **Henley** ("Fanny"; 1779–1856): niece, niece of Martha **Dandridge** Custis Washington and third wife of Tobias Lear

Lear, Mary **Long** ("Polly"; d. 1793): first wife of Tobias Lear

Lear, Mary **Stilson**: mother of Tobias Lear

Lear, Tobias (1762–1816): nephew, second husband of Frances **Bassett** Washington Lear and first husband of Frances Dandridge **Henley** Lear

Lee, George (1714–1761): second husband of Ann **Fairfax** Washington

Lee, Mary Anna Randolph **Custis** (1808–1873): step-great-granddaughter, daughter of George Washington Parke Custis

Lee, Mildred **Washington** ("Milly"; b. 1760): niece, daughter of John Augustine Washington

Lee, Robert E. (1807–1870): step-great-grandson-in-law, husband of Mary Anna Randolph **Custis** Lee

Lee, Thomas (1758–1805): nephew, husband of Mildred **Washington** Lee

Lewis, Ann **Alexander** ("Nancy"; b. 1756): niece, wife of Fielding Lewis, Jr.

Lewis, Augustine (1752–1755): nephew, son of Betty **Washington** Lewis

Lewis, Betty **Washington** (1733–1797): sister

Lewis, Catherine **Daingerfield** (1764–1820): niece, wife of George Lewis

Lewis, Catherine **Washington** (1724–1750): cousin, daughter of uncle John Washington and first wife of Fielding Lewis, Sr.

Lewis, Charles (1760–1775): nephew, son of Betty **Washington** Lewis

Lewis, Eleanor Agnes Freire (1805–1820): step-great-granddaughter and step-grandniece, daughter of Eleanor Parke **Custis** Lewis and Lawrence Lewis

Lewis, Eleanor Parke **Custis** ("Nelly"; 1779–1852): step-granddaughter, daughter of

John Parke Custis and second wife of Lawrence Lewis

Lewis, Ellen Hackley **Pollard** (1776–1859): niece, wife of Howell Lewis

Lewis, Esther Maria **Coxe** (1804–1885): step-great-granddaughter-in-law, wife of Lorenzo Lewis

Lewis, Fielding, Sr. (1725–1782): brother-in-law, husband of Catherine **Washington** Lewis and husband of Betty **Washington** Lewis

Lewis, Fielding, Jr. (1751–1803): nephew, son of Betty **Washington** Lewis

Lewis, Fielding Augustine (1807–1809): step-great-grandson and step-grandnephew, son of Eleanor Parke **Custis** Lewis and Lawrence Lewis

Lewis, George (1757–1821): nephew, son of Betty **Washington** Lewis

Lewis, George Washington Custis (1810–1811): step-great-grandson and step-grandnephew, son of Eleanor Parke **Custis** Lewis and Lawrence Lewis

Lewis, Howell (1771–1822): nephew, son of Betty **Washington** Lewis

Lewis, John (1747–1825): step-nephew, stepson of Betty **Washington** Lewis

Lewis, Judith Carter **Browne** (1773–1830): niece, wife of Robert Lewis

Lewis, Lawrence (1767–1839): nephew, son of Betty **Washington** Lewis and husband of Eleanor Parke **Custis** Lewis

Lewis, Lawrence Fielding (d. 1802): step-great-grandson and step-grandnephew, son of Eleanor Parke **Custis** Lewis and Lawrence Lewis

Lewis, Lorenzo (1803–1847): step-great-grandson and step-grandnephew, son of Eleanor Parke **Custis** Lewis and Lawrence Lewis

Lewis, Martha Betty (1801–1802): step-great-granddaughter and step-grandniece, daughter of Eleanor Parke **Custis** Lewis and Lawrence Lewis

Lewis, Mary (b. and d. 1759): niece, daughter of Betty **Washington** Lewis

Lewis, Nancy (b. 1790): grandniece, daughter of Fielding Lewis, Jr.

Lewis, Robert ("Bob"; 1769–1829): nephew, son of Betty **Washington** Lewis

Lewis, Samuel (1763–1774): nephew, son of Betty **Washington** Lewis

Lewis, Susannah **Edmundson** (d. 1790): niece, first wife of Lawrence Lewis

Lewis, Warner (b. 1720): cousin

Lewis, Warner (1755–1756): nephew, son of Betty **Washington** Lewis

Lyons, Judith **Bassett**: niece, niece of Martha **Dandridge** Custis Washington

Macon, Gideon (1650–1703): great-grandfather-in-law, great-grandfather of Martha **Dandridge** Custis Washington

Parks, Andrew: nephew, husband of Harriot **Washington** Parks

Parks, Harriot **Washington** (1776–1822): niece, daughter of brother Samuel Washington

Peter, Columbia Washington (1797–1820): step-great-granddaughter, daughter of Martha Parke **Custis** Peter

Peter, John Parke Custis (1799–1848): step-great-grandson, son of Martha Parke **Custis** Peter

Peter, Martha Eliza Eleanor (1796–1800): step-great-granddaughter, daughter of Martha Parke **Custis** Peter

Peter, Martha Parke **Custis** ("Patty," "Patsy"; 1777–1854): step-granddaughter, daughter of John Parke Custis

Peter, Thomas (1769–1834): step-grandson-in-law, husband of Martha Parke **Custis** Peter

Peyton, Frances **Washington** Ball (d. 1815): niece, daughter of Charles Washington

Peyton, Francis (d. 1808): nephew, husband of Frances **Washington** Ball Peyton

Rogers, Eliza **Law** ("Rosebud"; 1797–1822): step-great-granddaughter, daughter of Elizabeth Parke **Custis** Law

Rogers, Lloyd Nicholas (c.1787–1860): step-great-grandson-in-law, husband of Eliza **Law** Rogers

Snickers, Frances **Washington** (b. 1775): cousin, daughter of Warner Washington, Jr.

Snickers, William (b. 1759): husband of Frances **Washington** Snickers

Spotswood, Alexander (1751–1818): nephew, husband of Elizabeth **Washington** Spotswood

Spotswood, Elizabeth **Washington** (1750–1814): niece, daughter of half brother Augustine Washington

Stuart, David (1753–c.1814): second husband of Eleanor **Calvert** Custis Stuart

Stuart, Eleanor **Calvert** Custis ("Nelly"; c.1757–1811): stepdaughter-in-law, wife of John Parke Custis and wife of David Stuart

Thornton, Anna Maria **Washington** (1788–1814): grandniece, daughter of George Augustine Washington and Frances **Bassett** Washington Lear

Thornton, Frances **Gregory** (b. c.1716): cousin, wife of Francis Thornton and mother-in-law of Charles Washington

Thornton, Francis (1714–1749): father of Mildred **Thornton** Washington and father-in-law of Charles Washington

Thornton, Jane **Washington** (1756–1833): niece, daughter of half brother Augustine Washington

Thornton, John: nephew, husband of Jane **Washington** Thornton

Thornton, John (d. 1777): husband of Mildred **Gregory** Thornton, father of Mildred **Thornton** Washington and second father-in-law of brother Samuel Washington

Thornton, Mildred **Gregory**: cousin, wife of John Thornton and second mother-in-law of brother Samuel Washington

Thornton, Reuben: first husband of Elizabeth **Gregory** Thornton Walker

Thornton, Reuben (1781–1835): grandnephew, husband of Anna Maria **Washington** Thornton

Throckmorton, Albion (d. c.1795): husband of Mildred **Washington** Throckmorton

Throckmorton, Mildred **Washington** (c.1766–1804): cousin, daughter of Warner Washington, Sr.

Twigden, Amphillis (d. 1655): great-great-grandmother, wife of great-great-grandfather Lawrence Washington

Walker, Elizabeth **Gregory** Thornton (b. c.1718): cousin, wife of Reuben Thornton and second wife of Thomas Walker

Walker, Mildred **Thornton** Meriwether (d. 1778): wife of Thomas Walker and sister of Francis, John, and Reuben Thornton

Walker, Thomas (1715–1794): husband of Mildred **Thornton** Meriwether Walker and second husband of Elizabeth **Gregory** Thornton Walker

Washington, Ann: cousin, daughter of Henry Washington of Middlesex

Washington, Ann **Fairfax** (d. 1761): sister-in-law, wife of half brother Lawrence Washington

Washington, Anne **Aylett** (d. c.1773): sister-in-law, wife of half brother Augustine Washington

Washington, Anne Aylett (1783–1804): grandniece, daughter of William Augustine Washington

Washington, Anne **Gerrard** Broadhurst Brett (d. c.1675): step-great-grandmother, second wife of great-grandfather John Washington

Washington, Anne of Sulgrave Manor (b. and d. 16th century): great-great-great-great-great-grandmother, wife of great-great-great-great-great-grandfather Lawrence Washington

Washington, Anne **Pope** (d. 1668): great-grandmother, first wife of great-grandfather John Washington

Washington, Anne **Steptoe** Allerton (1739–1777): sister-in-law, fourth wife of brother Samuel Washington

Washington, Augustine (1694–1743): father

Washington, Augustine ("Austin"; 1720–1762): half brother

Washington, Augustine (1767–1784): nephew, son of John Augustine Washington

Washington, Augustine (1780–1797): grandnephew, son of William Augustine Washington

Washington, Bushrod (1762–1829): nephew, son of John Augustine Washington

Washington, Bushrod, Jr. (1785–1830): grandnephew, son of William Augustine Washington

Washington, Catherine: cousin, daughter of Henry Washington of Middlesex

Washington, Catherine **Whiting** (1694–1743): wife of uncle John Washington

Washington, Charles (1738–1799): brother

Washington, Charles Augustine (b. c.1790): grandnephew, son of George Augustine Washington and Frances **Bassett** Washington Lear

Washington, Corbin (1765–c.1799): nephew, son of John Augustine Washington

Washington, Elizabeth: cousin, daughter of uncle John Washington

Washington, Elizabeth ("Betcy"): cousin, daughter of Henry Washington of Middlesex

Washington, Elizabeth **Foote** (d. c.1812): wife of Lund Washington

Washington, Elizabeth **Lund**: wife of Townshend Washington, Sr. and mother of Lund Washington

Washington, Elizabeth **Macon**: first wife of Warner Washington, Sr.

Washington, Ferdinand (1767–1788): son of brother Samuel Washington

Washington, Frances **Gerrard**: step-great-grandmother, third wife of great-grandfather John Washington

Washington, Frances **Townshend** (b. 1767): niece, second wife of Thornton Washington

Washington, George (b. c.1758): nephew, son of half brother Augustine Washington

Washington, George Augustine (c.1758–1793): nephew, son of Charles Washington and husband of Frances **Bassett** Washington Lear

Washington, George Corbin (1789–1854): grandnephew, son of William Augustine Washington

Washington, George Fayette (b. and d. 1787): grandnephew, son of George Augustine and Frances **Bassett** Washington Lear

Washington, George Fayette (1790–1867): grandnephew, son of George Augustine and Frances **Bassett** Washington Lear

Washington, George Steptoe (c.1773–1808): nephew, son of brother Samuel Washington

Washington, Hannah **Bushrod** (c.1738–c.1801): sister-in-law, wife of John Augustine Washington

Washington, Hannah Bushrod (1778–1797): grandniece, daughter of William Augustine Washington

Washington, Hannah **Fairfax** (1742–1804): second wife of Warner Washington, Sr.

Washington, Hannah **Lee** (1765–1801): niece, wife of Corbin Washington

Washington, Henry ("Harry"): cousin, son of uncle John Washington

Washington, Henry (1765–1812): cousin, son of cousins Lawrence and Susannah Washington

Washington, Henry of Hylton (1694–1747): cousin

Washington, Henry of Middlesex (c.1718–1763): cousin

Washington, Jane **Butler** (1699–1729): first wife of father Augustine Washington

Washington, Jane Champe: sister-in-law, first wife of brother Samuel Washington

Washington, Jane **Washington** ("Jenny"; 1759–1791): niece, daughter of John Augustine Washington and wife of William Augustine Washington

Washington, John (1632–1677): great-grandfather

Washington, John (c.1663–1697): granduncle

Washington, John (1692–1746): uncle

Washington, John (d. 1742): cousin, son of John Washington of Chotank and father of Lawrence Washington of Chotank

Washington, John Augustine ("Jack"; 1736–1787): brother

Washington, John of Chotank: cousin, cousin of grandfather Lawrence Washington

Washington, John of Leedstown ("Lame"; d. 1787): cousin, son of cousin Robert Washington of Westmoreland

Washington, John of Hylton (1730–1782): cousin, son of Henry Washington of Hylton

Washington, John of Suffolk (1740–1777): cousin, great-grandson of great-granduncle Lawrence Washington

Washington, John Thornton Augustine (1783–1841): grandnephew, son of Thornton Washington

Washington, Julia Ann **Blackburn** ("Nancy"; 1768–1829): niece, wife of Bushrod Washington

Washington, Lawrence (c.1568–1616): great-great-great-grandfather

Washington, Lawrence (1602–1652): great-great-grandfather

Washington, Lawrence (1635–1677): great-granduncle

Washington, Lawrence (1660–1698): grandfather

Washington, Lawrence (c.1718–1752): half brother

Washington, Lawrence (1749–c.1774): cousin, husband of Susannah Washington

Washington, Lawrence, Jr. (d. 1809): cousin, son of Lawrence Washington of Chotank

Washington, Lawrence Augustine (1775–1824): nephew, son of brother Samuel Washington

Washington, Lawrence of Chotank (1728–c.1813): cousin

Washington, Lawrence of Belmont (1740–1799): cousin, great-grandson of great-granduncle Lawrence Washington

Washington, Lawrence of Sulgrave Manor (c.1500–1584): great-great-great-great-great-grandfather

Washington, Lund (1737–1796): cousin, great-grandson of great-granduncle Lawrence Washington

Washington, Margaret **Butler** (d. 1651): great-great-great-grandmother, wife of great-great-great-grandfather Lawrence Washington

Washington, Maria **Traner**: grandniece, wife of George Fayette Washington

Washington, Martha **Dandridge** Custis (1731–1802): wife

Washington, Mary **Ball** (c.1708–1789): mother

Washington, Mary Dorcas **Wood** (d. 1835): niece, wife of Lawrence Augustine Washington

Washington, Mary **Lee** (b. 1764): niece, second wife of William Augustine Washington

Washington, Mary **Massey**: wife of cousin John Washington of Chotank

Washington, Mildred (1739–1740): sister

Washington, Mildred **Berry**: niece, first wife of Thornton Washington

Washington, Mildred **Thornton** (b. c.1739): cousin and sister-in-law, wife of Charles Washington and daughter of Francis Thornton

Washington, Mildred **Thornton** (c.1741–c.1762): cousin and sister-in-law, second wife of brother Samuel Washington and daughter of Mildred **Gregory** Thornton

Washington, Robert of Chotank ("Robin"; b. 1730): cousin, brother of Lund Washington

Washington, Robert of Sulgrave Manor (1540–1619): great-great-great-great-grandfather

Washington, Robert of Westmoreland (d. 1765): cousin

Washington, Samuel (1734–1781): brother

Washington, Samuel (c.1765–1832): nephew, son of Charles Washington

Washington, Samuel (1786–1867): grandnephew, son of Thornton Washington

Washington, Sarah **Tayloe**: niece, third wife of William Augustine Washington

Washington, Susannah **Washington** (b. c.1742): cousin, wife of cousin Lawrence Washington

Washington, Thacker: cousin, son of Henry Washington of Middlesex

Washington, Thomas Berry (1780–1794): grandnephew, son of Thornton Washington

Washington, Thornton (1760–1787): nephew, son of brother Samuel Washington and cousin Mildred **Thornton** Washington

Washington, Townshend, Sr. (1705–c.1744): cousin, grandson of great-granduncle Lawrence Washington

Washington, Townshend, Jr. (b. 1736): cousin, great-grandson of great-granduncle Lawrence Washington

Washington, Warner, Jr. (1751–1829): cousin, son of Warner Washington, Sr., and father of Frances **Washington** Snickers

Washington, Warner, Sr. (1722–1790): cousin, son of uncle John Washington and father of Mildred **Washington** Throckmorton

Washington, William (1752–1810): cousin

Washington, William (1785–1830): cousin, son of William Washington

Washington, William Augustine (1747–1810): nephew, son of half brother Augustine Washington and husband of Jane **Washington** Washington

Whiting, Beverley: godfather

Whiting, Hannah **Washington** (b. 1735): cousin, daughter of uncle John Washington

Whiting, Matthew (1730–1810): husband of Hannah **Washington** Whiting

Whiting, Matthew (b. c.1755): cousin, son of Hannah **Washington** Whiting

Williams, America Pinckney **Peter** ("Mec"; 1803–1842): step-great-granddaughter, daughter of Martha Parke **Custis** Peter

Williams, William George (1801–1846): step-great-grandson-in-law, husband of America Pinckney **Peter** Williams

Willis, Henry (1691–1740): uncle, third husband of Mildred **Washington** Lewis Gregory Willis

Willis, Lewis (1734–1813): cousin

Willis, Mildred **Washington** Lewis Gregory (1696–c.1745): aunt and godmother

Willison, John: nephew, husband of Mary **Dandridge** Willison

Willison, Mary **Dandridge** ("Polly"): niece, niece of Martha Dandridge Custis Washington

Wright, Ann **Washington** (c.1662–c.1697): grandaunt, daughter of great-grandfather John Washington

Wright, Francis (d. 1713): granduncle, husband of Ann **Washington** Wright

Revolutionary War Military Family

Hodijah Baylies (1756–1842), Massachusetts
Extra aide-de-camp, May 1782–December 1783

George Baylor (1752–1784), Virginia
Aide-de-camp, August 1775–January 1777

Richard Cary (c.1746–1806), Massachusetts
Aide-de-camp, June–December 1776

David Cobb, Jr. (1748–1830), Massachusetts
Aide-de-camp, June 1781–January 1783, and June–December 1783

John Fitzgerald (d. 1799), Virginia
Aide-de-camp, October 1776–July 1778

Peregrine Fitzhugh (1759–1811), Maryland
Extra aide-de-camp, July–October 1781

Caleb Gibbs (1748–1818), Rhode Island
Supplemental aide-de-camp, May 1776–January 1781

William Grayson (c.1736–1790), Virginia
Assistant secretary, June–August 1776
Aide-de-camp, August 1776–January 1777

Alexander Hamilton (1757–1804), New York
Aide-de-camp, March 1777–April 1781

Alexander Contee Hanson (1749–1806), Maryland
Assistant secretary, June–September 1776

Robert Hanson Harrison (1745–1790), Maryland
Aide-de-camp, November 1775–May 1776
Secretary, May 1776–March 1781

David Humphreys (1752–1818), Connecticut
Aide-de-camp, June 1780–December 1783

George Johnston, Jr. (1750–1777), Virginia
Aide-de-camp, January–October 1777

John Laurens (1754–1782), South Carolina
Extra aide-de-camp, September–October 1777
Aide-de-camp, October 1777–March 1779, and September–November 1781

George Lewis (1757–1821), Virginia
Supplemental aide-de-camp, May 1776–February 1779

James McHenry (1753–1816), Maryland
Assistant secretary, May 1778–August 1780

Richard Kidder Meade (1746–1805), Virginia
Aide-de-camp, March 1777–October 1780

Thomas Mifflin (1744–1800), Pennsylvania
Aide-de-camp, July 1775–August 1775

Stephen Moylan (1737–1811), Pennsylvania
Aide-de-camp, March–June 1776
Volunteer aide-de-camp, October 1776–January 1777

William Palfrey (1741–1780), Massachusetts
Aide-de-camp, March–April 1776

Pierre Penet (d. 1812), France
Brevet aide-de-camp, October 1776–January 1783

Edmund Randolph (1753–1813), Virginia
Aide-de-camp, August–November 1775

Joseph Reed (1741–1785), New Jersey
Secretary, July–October 1775

William Stephens Smith (1755–1816), New York
Aide-de-camp, July 1781–May 1782

Peter Presly Thornton (1750–c.1780), Virginia
Extra aide-de-camp, August–September 1777

Tench Tilghman (1744–1786), Maryland
Volunteer aide-de-camp, August 1776–June 1780
Aide-de-camp, June 1780–December 1782

John Trumbull (1756–1843), Connecticut
Aide-de-camp, July–August 1775

Jonathan Trumbull, Jr. (1740–1809), Connecticut
Secretary, June 1781–August 1783

Richard Varick (1753–1831), New Jersey
Record secretary, May 1781–November 1783

Benjamin Walker (1753–1818), New York
Aide-de-camp, January 1782–December 1783

John Walker (1744–1809), Virginia
February–March 1777

George Augustine Washington (c.1758–1793), Virginia
Volunteer aide-de-camp, September 1779–May 1781, and December 1781–May 1782

Samuel Blachley Webb (1753–1807), Connecticut
Aide-de-camp, June 1776–January 1777

Principal Executive Officers during Washington's Administrations

Note: Some officeholders held office beyond the terms of Washington's presidency.

President
George Washington (1732–1799; Virginia), 30 April 1789–3 March 1797

Vice President
John Adams (1735–1826; Massachusetts), 30 April 1789–3 March 1797

Secretary of State
John Jay (1745–1829; New York), acting ad interim, 26 September 1789–22 March 1790
Thomas Jefferson (1743–1826; Virginia), 22 March 1790–31 December 1793 (commissioned Secretary of State 26 September 1789; assumed office 22 March 1790)
Edmund Randolph (1753–1813; Virginia), 2 January 1794–20 August 1795
Timothy Pickering (1745–1829; Massachusetts), 20 August 1795–12 May 1800 (acting Secretary of State from 20 August until commissioned, 10 December 1795)

Secretary of the Treasury
Alexander Hamilton (1757–1804; New York), 11 September 1789–31 January 1795
Oliver Wolcott, Jr. (1760–1833; Connecticut), 2 February 1795–31 December 1800

Secretary of War
Henry Knox (1750–1806; Massachusetts), 12 September 1789–31 December 1794
Timothy Pickering, 2 January 1795–5 February 1796
James McHenry (1753–1816; Maryland), 6 February 1796–31 May 1800 (commissioned Secretary of War 27 January 1796; assumed office 6 February)

Attorney General
Edmund Randolph, (1753–1813; Virginia) 2 February 1790–2 January 1794 (commissioned 26 September 1789; assumed office 2 February 1790)
William Bradford (1755–1795; Pennsylvania), 27 January 1794–23 August 1795
Charles Lee (1758–1815; Virginia), 10 December 1795–3 March 1801
No incumbent from death of Bradford to appointment of Lee

Postmaster General
Samuel Osgood (1748–1813; Massachusetts), 26 September 1789–19 August 1791
Timothy Pickering, 19 August 1791–2 January 1795 (commissioned 12 August 1791; assumed office 19 August)
Joseph Habersham (1751–1815; Georgia), 25 February 1795–2 November 1801

BIBLIOGRAPHY

Abbot, W. W. 1989. "An Uncommon Awareness of Self: The Papers of George Washington" (*Prologue: Quarterly of the National Archives,* vol. 21).

Abbot, W. W., Dorothy Twohig, Philander D. Chase, et al., eds. 1983–. 5 ser. 47 vols. to date. *The Papers of George Washington.* Charlottesville, VA.

Alden, John R. 1951. *Charles Lee, Traitor or Patriot?* Baton Rouge, LA.

———. 1948. *General Gage in America.* Baton Rouge, LA.

———. 1974. *Robert Dinwiddie: Servant of the Crown.* Charlottesville, VA.

Allen, W. B., ed. 1983. 2 vols. *Works of Fisher Ames.* Indianapolis.

André, John. 1904. *Major André's Journal: Operations of the British Army . . . June, 1777, to November 1778 . . .* Tarrytown, NY.

Arnebeck, Bob. 1991. *Through a Fiery Trial: Building Washington, 1790–1800.* Lanham, MD.

Bacon-Foster, Corra. 1912. *Early Chapters in the Development of the Patomac Route to the West.* Washington, DC.

Baker, William S. 1880. *The Engraved Portraits of Washington, with Notices of the Originals and Brief Biographical Sketches of the Painters.* Philadelphia.

Baldwin, Leland. 1939. *Whiskey Rebels: The Story of a Frontier Uprising.* Pittsburgh.

Batchelder, Samuel F. 1925. *The Washington Elm Tradition: "Under This Tree Washington First Took Command of the American Army?"* Cambridge, MA.

Beltzhoover, George M., Jr. 1900. *James Rumsey, the Inventor of the Steamboat.* Charleston, WV.

Bemis, Samuel F. 1923. *Jay's Treaty.* New York.

Billias, George Athan, ed. 1964. *George Washington's Generals.* New York.

Binney, Horace. 1859. *An Inquiry into the Formation of Washington's Farewell Address.* Philadelphia.

Bliven, Bruce, Jr. 1955–1956. *Battle for Manhattan.* New York.

Boatner, Mark Mayo, III. 1966. *Encyclopedia of the American Revolution.* New York.

Bodle, Wayne K., and Jacqueline Thibaut. 1980. 3 vols. *Valley Forge Historical Research Report.* Valley Forge, PA.

Boller, Paul F. 1963. *George Washington and Religion.* Dallas.

Boucher, Jonathan. 1797. *A View of the Causes and Consequences of the American Revolution in Thirteen Discourses. Preached in North America between the Years 1763 and 1775.* London.

Bourne, Miriam Anne. 1982. *First Family: George Washington and His Intimate Relations.* New York.

Boyd, Thomas. 1929. *Mad Anthony Wayne.* New York.

Brady, Patricia, ed. 1991. *George Washington's Beautiful Nelly: The Letters of Eleanor Parke Custis Lewis to Elizabeth Bordley Gibson, 1794–1851.* Columbia, SC.

Brandt, Clare. 1994. *The Man in the Mirror: A Life of Benedict Arnold.* New York.

Brant, Irving. 1941–1961. 6 vols. *James Madison.* New York.

Brigham, David R. 1995. *Public Culture in the Early Republic: Peale's Museum and Its Audience.* Washington, DC.

Brockett, F. L. 1899. *The Lodge of Washington. A History of the Alexandria Washington Lodge, No. 22, A. F. and A. M. of Alexandria, Va., 1783–1876.* Alexandria, VA.

Brookhiser, Richard. 1996. *Founding Father: Rediscovering George Washington.* New York.

Brooks, Noah. 1900. *Henry Knox: A Soldier of the Revolution.* New York.

Buel, Richard, Jr. 1980. *Dear Liberty: Connecticut's Mobilization for the Revolutionary War.* Middletown, CT.

Butterfield, L. H., et al., eds. 1961. 4 vols. *Diary and Autobiography of John Adams.* Cambridge, MA.

Butterfield, L. H., ed. 1951. 2 vols. *Letters of Benjamin Rush.* Princeton, NJ.

Callahan, Charles H. 1913. *Washington: The Man and the Mason.* Washington, DC.

Callahan, North. 1958. *Henry Knox: General Washington's General*. New York.

Carter, Clarence Edwin. 1910–1911. "Documents Relating to the Mississippi Land Company, 1763–1769" (*American Historical Review*, vol. 16).

Champagne, Roger J. 1975. *Alexander McDougall and the American Revolution in New York*. Schenectady, NY.

Chinard, Gilbert. 1929. *The Letters of Lafayette and Jefferson*. Baltimore.

Clarfield, Gerard H. 1980. *Timothy Pickering and the American Republic*. Pittsburgh.

Coleman, Mary Haldane. 1938. *St. George Tucker, Citizen of No Mean City*. Richmond, VA.

Craik, James. 1938. "Boyhood Memories of Dr. James Craik, D. D., L.L.D." (*Virginia Magazine of History and Biography*, vol. 46).

Cullen, Charles. 1987. *St. George Tucker and Law in Virginia 1772–1804*. New York.

Cunliffe, Marcus. 1958. *George Washington: Man and Monument*. Reprint, 1998. Mount Vernon, VA.

———, ed. 1962. *The Life of Washington*. Cambridge, MA.

Custis, George Washington Parke. 1828. *The Indian Prophecy: A National Drama in Two Acts, Founded upon a Most Interesting and Romantic Occurence in the Life of General Washington, to Which is Prefixed a Memoir of the Indian Prophecy*. Georgetown, DC.

———. 1860. *Recollections and Private Memoirs of Washington*. New York.

Dalzell, Robert F., Jr., and Lee Baldwin Dalzell. 1998. *George Washington's Mount Vernon: At Home in Revolutionary America*. New York.

Darlington, William M., ed. 1893. *Christopher Gist's Journals with Historical, Geographical, and Ethnological Notes and Biographies of His Contemporaries*. Cleveland.

Davenport, Beatrix Cary, ed. 1939. 2 vols. *A Diary of the French Revolution by Gouverneur Morris*. Boston.

De Conde, Alexander. 1958. *Entangling Alliance: Politics and Diplomacy Under George Washington*. Durham, NC.

Decatur, Stephen, Jr. 1933. *Private Affairs of George Washington from the Records and Accounts of Tobias Lear, Esquire, His Secretary*. Boston.

Drake, Francis S. 1873. *Life and Correspondence of Henry Knox*. Boston.

Felder, Paula S. 1998. *Fielding Lewis and the Washington Family: A Chronicle of 18th Century Fredericksburg*. Fredericksburg, VA.

Fields, Joseph E., ed. 1994. *"Worthy Partner": The Papers of Martha Washington*. Westport, CT.

Fitzpatrick, John C. 1929. *The George Washington Scandals*. Alexandria, VA.

———, ed. 1931–1944. 39 vols. *The Writings of George Washington*. Washington, DC.

Ford, Worthington Chauncey. 1889. *The Spurious Letters Attributed to Washington*. New York.

———. 1893–1894. 3 vols. *Webb Correspondence and Journals*. New York.

———, ed. 1889–1893. 14 vols. *The Writings of George Washington*. New York.

Freeman, Douglas Southall. 1948–1957. 7 vols. *George Washington: A Biography*. New York.

Gardiner, Asa Bird. 1905. *The Order of the Cincinnati in France, Its Organization and History: With the Military or Naval Records of the French Members Who Became Such by Reason of Qualifying Service in the Army or Navy of France or of the United States in the War of the Revolution for American Independence*. Providence, RI.

Gerlach, Don R. 1964. *Philip Schuyler and the American Revolution in New York*. Lincoln, NE.

Godfrey, Carlos E. 1904. *The Commander-in-Chief's Guard*. Washington, DC.

Gottschalk, Louis R., ed. 1935–1950. 4 vols. *Lafayette Comes to America*. Chicago.

Greene, George W. 1867–1871. 3 vols. *Life of Nathanael Greene*. New York.

Griswold, Mac K. 1999. *Washington's Gardens at Mount Vernon: Landscape of the Inner Man*. New York.

Hamer, Philip M., George C. Rogers, Jr., David R. Chesnutt, et al., eds. 1968—. 15 vols. to date. *The Papers of Henry Laurens*. Columbia, SC.

Hamilton, Charles, ed. 1959. *Braddock's Defeat*. Norman, OK.

Hammond, Otis G., ed. 1930–1939. 3 vols. *Letters and Papers of Major-General John Sullivan, Continental Army*. Collections of the New Hampshire Historical Society.

Hannah, Charles A. 1911. 2 vols. *The Wilderness Trail, or The Ventures and Adventures of the Pennsylvania Traders on the Allegheny Path*. New York.

Harrington, J. C. 1954–1955. "Metamorphosis of Fort Necessity" (*Western Pennsylvania Historical Magazine*, vol. 37).

Harris, C. M., ed. 1995. *Papers of William Thornton, 1781–1802.* Charlottesville, VA.

Hart, Charles Henry, and Edward Biddle. 1911. *Memoirs of the Life and Works of Jean Antoine Houdon, the Sculptor of Voltaire and of Washington.* Philadelphia.

Hastings, Hugh, and J. A. Holden, eds. 1899–1914. 10 vols. *The Public Papers of George Clinton.* Reprint, 1973. New York.

Hatch, Charles E., Jr. 1979. *Popes Creek Plantation: Birthplace of George Washington.* Washington's Birthplace, VA.

Haworth, Paul Leland. 1915. *George Washington: Farmer, Being an Account of His Home Life and Agricultural Activities.* Indianapolis.

Helderman, Leonard C. 1932. *George Washington: Patron of Learning.* New York.

Henderson, Archibald. 1923. *Washington's Southern Tour, 1791.* Boston and New York.

Henriques, Peter R. 2000. *The Death of George Washington: He Died as He Lived.* Mount Vernon, VA.

———. 1979. "George Washington: The Amiable Side" (*Northern Virginia Heritage,* vol. 1).

———. "Major Lawrence Washington Versus the Reverend Charles Green: A Case Study of the Squire vs. the Parson" (*Virginia Magazine of History and Biography,* vol. 100).

Hirschfeld, Fritz. 1997. *George Washington and Slavery: A Documentary Portrayal.* Columbia, MO.

Hofstra, Warren R., ed. 1998. *George Washington and the Virginia Backcountry.* Madison, WI.

Hoppin, Charles Arthur. 1926. "The House in Which George Washington Was Born" (*Tyler's Quarterly Historical and Genealogical Magazine,* vol. 8).

Hughes, Sarah S. 1979. *Surveyors and Statesmen: Land Measuring in Colonial Virginia.* Richmond, VA.

Hume, Edgar Erskine. 1941. *General Washington's Correspondence Concerning the Society of the Cincinnati.* Baltimore.

Humphreys, David. 1788. *An Essay on the Life of the Honourable Major-General Israel Putnam.* Hartford, Conn.

———. 1804. *The Miscellaneous Works of David Humphreys.* Reprint, 1968. Gainesville, FL.

Hutchinson, William, William Rachal, Robert Rutland, J. C. A. Stagg, et al., eds. 1962–. 3 sers. 25 vols. to date. *The Papers of James Madison.* Chicago and Charlottesville, VA.

Hutson, J. H. 1980. *John Adams and the Diplomacy of the American Revolution.* Lexington, KY.

Idzerda, Stanley J., and Robert R. Crout, et al., eds. 1977–. 5 vols. to date. *Lafayette in the Age of the American Revolution: Selected Letters and Papers, 1776–1790.* Ithaca, NY.

Jackson, Donald, and Dorothy Twohig, eds. 1976–1979. 6 vols. *The Diaries of George Washington.* Charlottesville, VA.

Johnson, Patricia Givens. 1980. *General Andrew Lewis of Roanoke and Greenbrier.* Christiansburg, VA.

Johnston, Henry P. 1897. *The Battle of Harlem Heights, September 16, 1776; with a Review of the Events of the Campaign.* Reprint, 1970. New York.

———. 4 vols. *The Correspondence and Public Papers of John Jay, 1763–1781.* New York.

———. 1881. *The Yorktown Campaign and the Surrender of Cornwallis, 1781.* New York.

Kahler, Gerald Edward. 1997. "Gentlemen of the Family: General George Washington's Aides-de-Camp and Military Secretaries" (M.A. thesis, University of Richmond). Richmond, VA.

Kaminski, John P. 1993. *George Clinton: Yeoman Politician of the New Republic.* Madison, WI.

King, George H. S. 1937. "Washington's Boyhood Home" (*William and Mary Quarterly,* 2d ser., vol. 17).

Kite, Elizabeth S. 1929. *L'Enfant and Washington, 1791–1792.* Baltimore.

Klapthor, Margaret Brown, and Howard Alexander Morrison. 1982. *George Washington: A Figure upon the Stage.* Washington, DC.

Knollenberg, Bernhard. 1940. *Washington and the Revolution.* New York.

Knopf, Richard C. 1960. *Anthony Wayne, a Name in Arms: Soldier, Diplomat, Defender of Expansion Westward of a Nation.* Pittsburgh.

Lawrence, Alexander A. 1951. *Storm over Savannah.* Athens, GA.

Lear, Tobias. 1906. *Letters and Recollections of George Washington: Being Letters to Tobias Lear and Others between 1790 and 1799.* New York.

Leduc, Gilbert. F. 1943. *Washington and "The Murder of Jumonville."* Boston.

Lee Papers. 1872–1875. 4 vols. New-York Historical Society Collections.

Leibiger, Stuart. 1999. *Founding Friendship: George Washington, James Madison, and the Cre-*

ation of the American Republic. Charlottesville, VA.

Longmore, Paul K. 1988. *The Invention of George Washington.* Reprint, 1999. Charlottesville, VA.

Lossing, Benson J. 1872–1873. 2 vols. *Life and Times of Philip Schuyler.* New York.

———. 1886. *Mary and Martha, the Mother and the Wife of George Washington.* New York.

Malone, Dumas. 1948–1982. 6 vols. *Jefferson and His Time.* Boston.

Manders, Eric I. 1978. *The Battle of Long Island.* Monmouth Beach, NJ.

Marshall, John. 1805–1807. *The Life of George Washington.* Philadelphia.

Martin, James Kirby. 1997. *Benedict Arnold: Revolutionary Hero, an American Warrior Reconsidered.* New York.

Marx, Rudolph. 1955. "A Medical Profile of George Washington" (*American Heritage,* vol. 6).

Mattern, David B. 1995. *Benjamin Lincoln and the American Revolution.* Columbia, SC.

Mayo, Katherine. 1938. *General Washington's Dilemma.* New York.

McDowell, William, Jr., ed. 1970. "Affidavit of John Shaw" (*Colonial Records of South Carolina: Documents Relating to Indian Affairs, 1754–1757,* 2d ser., vol. 2).

McGuire, Thomas J. 1994. *The Surprise of Germantown, or, The Battle of Cliveden, October 4th 1777.* Philadelphia.

Miller, Lillian, ed. 1983–1996. 4 vols. *The Selected Papers of Charles Willson Peale and His Family.* New Haven, CT.

Minutes of the Vestry: Truro Parish Virginia, 1732–1785. 1974. Lorton, VA.

Mitchell, Broadus. 1957. 2 vols. *Alexander Hamilton.* New York.

Moore, Charles, ed. 1931. *George Washington's Rules of Civility and Decent Behaviour in Company and Conversation.* New York.

Morgan, Edmund S. 1980. *The Genius of George Washington.* Washington, DC.

Munson, James D. 1986. *Colo. John Carlyle, Gent.: A True and Just Account of the Man and His House, 1720–1780.* Fairfax Station, VA.

Myers, Minor, Jr. 1983. *Liberty without Anarchy: A History of the Society of the Cincinnati.* Charlottesville, VA.

Nelson, Paul David. 1976. *General Horatio Gates: A Biography.* Baton Rouge, LA.

———. 1987. *William Alexander, Lord Stirling.* University, AL.

Onuf, Peter S., ed. 1996. *The Life of Washington by Mason Locke Weems: A New Edition with Primary Documents and Introduction.* Armonk, NY.

Paltsits, Victor Hugo. 1935. *Washington's Farewell Address in Facsimile, with Transliterations of all the Drafts of Washington, Madison, & Hamilton, Together with Their Correspondence and Other Supporting Documents.* New York.

Peterson, Merrill D. 1970. *Thomas Jefferson and the New Nation: A Biography.* New York.

Potter, Eliphalet Nott. 1895. *Washington: A Model in His Library and Life.* New York.

Prince, Carl E., et al., eds. 1979–1988. 5 vols. *The Papers of William Livingston.* New Brunswick, NJ.

Prince, William S., ed. 1977. *The Poems of St. George Tucker of Williamsburg, Virginia 1752–1827.* New York.

Prussing, Eugene E. 1927. *The Estate of George Washington, Deceased.* Boston.

Ramsay, David. 1789. 2 vols. *History of the American Revolution.* Philadelphia.

———. 1785. 2 vols. *History of the Revolution of South Carolina.* Trenton, NJ.

———. 1807. *Life of Washington.* New York.

———. 1816–1817. 3 vols. *The History of the United States.* Philadelphia.

Reed, William Bradford. 1847. 2 vols. *Life and Correspondence of Joseph Reed.* Philadelphia.

Renfro, Herbert G. 1916. *Life and Works of Phillis Wheatley.* Washington, DC.

Rhodehamel, John. 1998. *The Great Experiment: George Washington and the American Republic.* San Marino, CA.

Ribblett, David L. 1993. *Nelly Custis: Child of Mount Vernon.* Mount Vernon, VA.

Rice, Howard C., Jr., and Anne S. K. Brown. 1972. *The American Campaigns of Rochambeau's Army, 1780, 1781, 1782, 1783.* Princeton, NJ, and Providence, RI.

Riley, Edward M., ed. 1948. "St. George Tucker Journal of the Siege of Yorktown, 1781" (*William and Mary Quarterly,* 3d ser., vol. 5).

Roberts, Kenneth, ed. 1947. *March to Quebec, Journals of the Members of Arnold's Expedition.* New York.

Roche, John F. 1957. *Joseph Reed: A Moderate in the American Revolution.* New York.

Rorabaugh, W. J. 1979. *The Alcoholic Republic: An American Tradition.* New York.

Rossiter, Clinton. 1966. *1787: The Grand Convention*. New York.

Royster, Charles. 1999. *The Fabulous History of the Dismal Swamp Company: A Story of George Washington's Times*. New York.

———. 1981. *Light-Horse Harry Lee and the Legacy of the American Revolution*. New York.

Rutland, Robert A., ed. 1970. 3 vols. *The Papers of George Mason, 1725–1792*. Chapel Hill, NC.

Sachse, Julius F. 1915. *Masonic Correspondence of Washington as Found among the Washington Papers in the Library of Congress*. Philadelphia.

Schroeder, John Frederick. 1854–1855. *Maxims of Washington: Political, Social, Moral, and Religious*. New York.

Schwartz, Barry. 1987. *George Washington: The Making of an American Symbol*. Ithaca, NY.

Scott, Pamela. 1995. *Temple of Liberty: Building the Capitol for a New Nation*. New York.

Scribner, Robert L., and Brent Tarter, eds. 1977. *Revolutionary Virginia: The Road to Independence* (vol. 3). Charlottesville, VA.

Sellers, Charles Coleman. 1969. *Charles Willson Peale*. New York.

Shaffer, Arthur H. 1991. *To Be an American: David Ramsay and the Making of the American Consciousness*. Columbia, SC.

Showman, Richard K., et al., eds. 1976–. 12 vols. *The Papers of General Nathanael Greene*. Chapel Hill, NC.

Simms, William Gilmore, ed. 1867. *The Army Correspondence of John Laurens in the Years 1777–78*. New York.

Sizer, Theodore, ed. 1953. *The Autobiography of Colonel John Trumbull*. Reprint, 1970. New York.

Slaughter, Philip. 1908. *The History of Truro Parish in Virginia*. Philadelphia.

Slaughter, Thomas P. 1986. *The Whiskey Rebellion: Frontier Epilogue to the American Revolution*. New York.

Smith, Paul H., et al., eds. 1976–1998. 26 vols. *Letters of Delegates to Congress, 1774–1789*. Washington, DC.

Smith, Richard Norton. 1993. *Patriarch: George Washington and the New American Nation*. New York.

Smith, Samuel S. 1976. *The Battle of Brandywine*. Monmouth Beach, NJ.

———. 1967. *The Battle of Princeton*. Monmouth Beach, NJ.

———. 1965. *The Battle of Trenton*. Monmouth Beach, NJ.

Smith, William Henry, ed. 1882. 2 vols. *The St. Clair Papers*. Cincinnati.

Smith, William Raymond. 1966. *History as Argument: Three Patriot Historians of the American Revolution*. The Hague, the Netherlands.

Snowden, William H. 1894. *Some Old Historic Landmarks of Virginia and Maryland Described in a Hand-book for the Tourist . . .* Philadelphia.

Sognnaes, Reidar F. 1973. "America's Most Famous Teeth" (*Smithsonian,* vol. 3).

Spalding, Matthew, and Patrick J. Garrity. 1996. *A Sacred Union of Citizens: George Washington's Farewell Address and the American Character*. Lanham, MD.

Sparks, Jared, ed. 1834–1837. 12 vols. *The Writings of George Washington: Being His Correspondence, Addresses, Messages, and Other Papers . . .* Boston.

Stegeman, John F. 1984. "Lady of Belvoir: This Matter of Sally Fairfax" (*Virginia Cavalcade,* vol. 34).

Steiner, Bernard C. 1907. *The Life and Correspondence of James McHenry*. Cleveland.

Stillé, Charles J. 1893. *Major-General Anthony Wayne and the Pennsylvania Line in the Continental Army*. Philadelphia.

Stryker, William S. 1898. *The Battles of Trenton and Princeton*. Reprint, 1967. Spartanburg, SC.

Syrett, Harold C. et al., eds. 1961–1987. 27 vols. *Papers of Alexander Hamilton*. New York.

Tatsch, J. Hugo. 1931. *The Facts About George Washington as a Freemason*. New York.

Thayer, Theodore. 1960. *Nathanael Greene: Strategist of the Revolution*. New York.

Tilghman, Tench. 1876. *Memoir of Lieut. Col. Tench Tilghman, Secretary and Aid to Washington. . . .* Reprint, 1971. New York.

Tompkins, E. P., and J. Lee Davis. 1939. *The Natural Bridge and Its Historical Surroundings*. Natural Bridge, VA.

The Trumbull Papers. 1902. 3 vols. Collections of the Massachusetts Historical Society (5th ser.). Boston.

Turner, Ella May. 1930. *James Rumsey, Pioneer in Steam Navigation*. Scottdale, PA.

Uhlendorf, Bernhard A., ed. 1938. *Siege of Charleston*. Ann Arbor, MI.

Valentine, Alan. 1969. *Lord Stirling*. New York.

Van Doren, Carl. 1948. *The Great Rehearsal: The Story of the Making and Ratifying of the Constitution of the United States.* New York.

———. 1941. *Secret History of the American Revolution.* Garden City, NJ.

Volwiler, Albert T. 1926. *George Croghan and the Westward Movement, 1741–1782.* Cleveland.

Wainwright, Nicholas B. 1959. *George Croghan: Wilderness Diplomat.* Chapel Hill, NC.

Wallace, Willard M. 1954 *Traitorous Hero: The Life and Fortunes of Benedict Arnold.* New York.

Ward, Harry M. 1989. *Major General Adam Stephen and the Cause of American Liberty.* Charlottesville, VA.

Warren, Jack D., Jr. 2000. *The Presidency of George Washington.* Mount Vernon, VA.

Waterman, Thomas Tileston. 1946. *The Mansions of Virginia, 1706–1776.* Chapel Hill, NC.

Weedon, George. 1902. *Valley Forge Orderly Book of General George Weedon of the Continental Army under Command of Genl. George Washington, in the Campaign of 1777–8.* New York.

Weems, Mason Locke. 1809. 9th ed. *The Life of George Washington; With Curious Anecdotes, Equally Honourable to Himself and Exemplary to His Young Countrymen.* Philadelphia.

Wehmann, Howard H. 1972. "To Major Gibbs with Much Esteem" *(Prologue,* vol. 4).

Wells, Walter A. 1927. "Last Illness and Death of Washington" (*Virginia Medical Monthly,* vol. 53).

Whittemore, Charles P. 1961. *A General of the Revolution: John Sullivan of New Hampshire.* New York.

Wick, Wendy C. 1982. *George Washington, An American Icon: The Eighteenth-Century Graphic Portraits.* Charlottesville, VA.

Wickwire, Franklin, and Mary Wickwire. 1970. *Cornwallis: The American Adventure.* Boston.

Willcox, William B., ed. 1954. *The American Rebellion: Sir Henry Clinton's Narrative of His Campaigns, 1775–1782, with an Appendix of Original Documents.* New Haven, CT.

———. 1964. *Portrait of a General: Sir Henry Clinton.* New York.

Wills, Gary. 1984. *Cincinnatus: George Washington and the Enlightenment.* Garden City, NY.

Wilson, Rufus R., ed. 1798. *Heath's Memoirs of the American War.* Reprint, 1904. New York.

Zagarri, Rosemarie. 1991. *David Humphreys' "Life of General Washington" with George Washington's "Remarks."* Athens, GA.

Zall, P. M. 1989. *George Washington Laughing: Humorous Anecdotes by and about Our First President from Original Sources.* Hamden, CT.

INDEX

Fitzhugh, Peregrine, 411
Fitzhugh, William, 109, 153
Fitzpatrick, John C.
    Diaries of Washington, 243
    Writings of Washington, 243
Florida, 265. *See also* East Florida;
    West Florida
Flowing Springs Run, 328
Foote, William H., 180
Forbes, Eleanor, 76, 266
Forbes, John, 125
    Campaign, 64, **113–114,** 115,
    157, 190, 213, 215, 251, 399
Ford, Jacob, 227
Ford, Worthington Chauncey,
    Writings of Washington, 243
Forks of the Ohio, 64, 113–116,
    213, 251, 354
    fort at, 143, 354
Fort Cumberland, 35, 63, 73, 114,
    127, 152, 215, 252, 294,
    298, 355, 372, 373
    illus., 354
Fort Dinwiddie, 190
Fort Duquesne, 34, 113, 114–117,
    157, 183, 190, 213, 215,
    242, 321, 354, 373, 399
Fort Hill, 115
Fort Independence, 201
Fort Le Boeuf, 86, 132, 173
Fort Lee, 58, 296
Fort Ligonier, 279
Fort Loudoun, 98, **114–115**
Fort McHenry, 209
Fort Montgomery, 48, 50
Fort Necessity
    campaign and capitulation, 34,
    60, 63, 86, **115–119,** 132,
    143, 173, 190, 213, 230,
    298, 320–321, 370–371,
    377, 399
    Washington's "Account of the
    Capitulation," **370–371**
Fort Necessity National
    Battlefield, 118
Fort Niagara, 183
Fort Pitt, 62, 63, 64, 136, 159, 191,
    219, 339
Fort Stanwix, 190
Fort Ticondero, GA. *See*
    Ticonderoga, NY
Fort Washington (New York), 58,
    119–120, 209, 308, 352
Fort Washington (Ohio River),
    279
Fort William and Mary, 235

Fort William Henry, 14
Fortune (brigantine), 13
Four Mile Run, 67
Fowey (British warship), 90
France, 7, 15, 21–22, 56, 57, 66,
    99, 115, 133, 143, 150, 164,
    174, 176, 179, 181, 188,
    221, 225, 226, 257, 273,
    289, 293, 321
    fleet from, 50
    Quasi-War, 2, 66, 131, 145,
    171, 182, 209, 243, 248,
    263–264, 401
    See also French and Indian
    War
Franklin, Benjamin, 1, 40, 54, 96,
    150, 161, 164, 175, 179,
    181, 203, 269, 278, 310
    wills cane to Washington, 330
Franklin, William, published
    writings, 203
Franklin, PA, 173
Franklin County, PA, 215
Franks, David Solebury, 16
Fraunces, Andrew G., 121
Fraunces, Samuel, **120–121**
    tavern of, 104, 120–121
Frederick County, VA, 61, 141,
    200, 214, 217, 298, 372
Fredericksburg, VA, 32, 84,
    109–110, 122, 187, 190,
    191–192, 195, 196, 199,
    200, 215, 216, 320, 327,
    329, 332, 335, 337, 346, 365,
    399
Freeman, Douglas Southall, xv, 1,
    8, 24, 61, 69, 81, 90, 93, 95,
    119, 132, 143, 151, 190,
    300, 308
Freeman's Farm, Battle of, 15
Freemasonry, **121–124**
    illus., 121
French, Daniel, 249
French and Indian War, xiv, xvi,
    14, 34, 35, 39, 43, 48,
    59–60, 61, 62, 63–64, 67,
    70, 90, 95, 113, 114–118,
    119, 124, 125, 147,
    157–158, 173, 179,
    189–190, 207, 213, 215,
    216, 218–220, 241, 243,
    244, 261, 270, 271, 279,
    280, 295, 298, 300, 323,
    325, 331, 346, 366–373,
    375, 377, 399, 400. *See also*
    France

Fry, Joshua, 116, 117, 213, 367, 369
    Fry-Jefferson map, 115

Gage, Thomas, **125–126,** 158, 372
Gaine, Hugh, Loyalist newspaper,
    203
Gayle, George, 326
Gayle, Mildred, 326
Gayle, Mildred Warner
    Washington, 326
Galloway, Scotland, 60
Gates, Elizabeth Phillips, 128
Gates, Horatio, 1, 11, 15, 36, 56,
    57, 58, **126–129,** 139, 160,
    175, 202, 281, 301–302,
    310, 313, 400
    illus., 127
Gates, Mary Vallance, 128
Gates, Robert, 128
Gauley River, 135
Gazette of the United States, 30
Genet, Edmund, 257
Geneva, Switzerland, 8, 57, 180
Gentleman's Magazine, 94
George III, King of England, 58,
    77, 83, 90, 98, 107, 117,
    126, 221–222, 234, 252,
    310, 368
    remarks about Washington, 351
George Washington Birthplace
    National Monument, 250
George Washington's
    Fredericksburg Foundation,
    110, 196
Georgetown, MD, 189
Georgia, 40, 111, 139–140, 180,
    256, 285, 290, 300, 321,
    344, 412
    Washington's trip to, 141, 290
Germain, George, Lord Sackville.
    See Sackville, Lord George
    Germain, first viscount
German Reformed Church (York,
    PA), 153
Germantown, Battle of, 56, 58, 62,
    129–130, 139, 157, 170,
    181, 208, 245, 247, 295,
    299, 302, 343, 346, 400
Germantown Road, 129
Germany, 50
    immigrants from, 7, 87, 292,
    305
    troops from, 37, 79, 120, 129,
    148, 204, 224, 279, 302,
    309, 346, 352, 358
Gerry, Elbridge, 12

ABOUT THE AUTHOR

Frank E. Grizzard, Jr., is Director of the Lee Family Digital Archive, an online repository of the papers of the historical Lee family of Virginia. He formerly was Senior Associate Editor at the Papers of George Washington editorial project at the University of Virginia. A frequent lecturer on historical topics, his other publications on America's First President include several volumes of edited correspondence and *The Ways of Providence: Religion and George Washington.* He is the author of *"The Hobby of My Old Age": Thomas Jefferson and the Construction of the University of Virginia,* and co author, with D. Boyd Smith, of *The Jamestown Colony: An Encyclopedia.* Mr. Grizzard is a native of Virginia and currently resides in Charlottesville with his wife and six children.

Printed in the United States
210582BV00003B/1-24/A

9 780976 823803